Dear Subscriber:

Customer service is something every successful company likes to think it has. We work hard to make our service the best.

It begins with acquisition of rights to the finest authors and titles in the marketplace and ends with delivery to you of a first-class piece of work that is wrapped with an absolutely iron-clad guarantee.

Our guarantee is that you must be pleased and satisfied with all aspects of our service, from accuracy of catalog description to enjoyment of the reading. Nothing less will do.

But it doesn't stop there. We bring you great readers with national followings, like Dick Estell, the "radio reader" for National Public Radio. And information about related services, like Home Film Festival and Traveller's Bookstore. And suggestions for print copies of books we think you will enjoy. Plus lists of B-O-T™ best sellers... and personal responses to your inquiries... and printouts of your book history whenever we exchange correspondence with customers.

So for 1988, our twelfth year, we send greetings and thanks to our 60,000 subscribers... not only for the books you order from us, but for the friends and associates you refer... in 1987, as in all years before, our single most important source of growth.

Yours sincerely,

Duvall Y. Hecht
President

Table of Contents

Rental Selections

Rental Selections are on a 30-day rental.

Sale Selections

Allow 4-6 weeks delivery on all sales items.

It's easy for you to enjoy our Books on Tape™ service!

- Easy Visa and MasterCard ordering by simply calling **1-800-626-3333**
- Easy to return, postage-paid shipping cartons
- **FREE** Rentals
- Discounts on multiple rentals
- Interval Delivery
- Gift Certificates

There are many ways to utilize the service offered by Books on Tape™. Can you think of times when a best seller from Books on Tape™ would make your day more enjoyable?

B-O-T™ Discount Plan

1. Anytime you place a rental order for 3 books, you get a 10% discount.
2. Anytime you place a rental order for 10 books you get a 10% discount plus a free rental selection—a 20% discount.
3. With either of our discount plans comes interval delivery. You specify when you want your rental selections to arrive.

Special $5 *Gift Offer*
Introduce a Friend to Books on Tape™ Service

Choosing gifts is often difficult, time-consuming and expensive. But here is an unbeatable offer.

Introduce a friend not already a Books on Tape™ customer to our unique service for only $5.00. We'll send them your choice of any rental title (or Part I of any multi-part book) with your compliments. This price also includes pre-paid postage and a copy of our current catalog.

Great deal . . . but it gets better! When your friend places an initial order with us, it will be at our regular price and we will credit you with a **FREE** rental to thank you for your referral. Please call 1-800-626-3333 to place your gift order.

FREE
Rental from
Books on Tape™

You'll get a FREE rental book by sharing the Books on Tape™ service with a friend. All you do is give us your friend's name and address. Then, when your friend becomes a regular customer of Books on Tape™ and mentions your name, we'll send *you* a FREE rental book of your choice.

OR

Just order 10 or more rental selections at one time and get your choice of a bonus rental book, absolutely free. (Plus, you'll automatically qualify for a 10% discount.)

Your 100% money-back guarantee

You must be completely satisfied with all aspects of our service. If for any reason you aren't, you may return your tapes for a full refund of the rental or sale price for Books on Tape™ produced titles.

Want a copy of your very own?

Rental selections from Books on Tape™ are available for purchase. We sell copies of our full-length readings to libraries and individual collectors.

All purchased Books on Tape™ titles now come in our attractive and sturdy vinyl cases. Initially developed for our library customers, these beautifully crafted blue cases come complete with the title, author and narrator displayed on the front cover as well as the spine.

As another special touch, we'll also personalize the book with your name or the name of the recipient.

At $8.00 per cassette, the sale price is listed with each rental title offered for sale in this catalog.

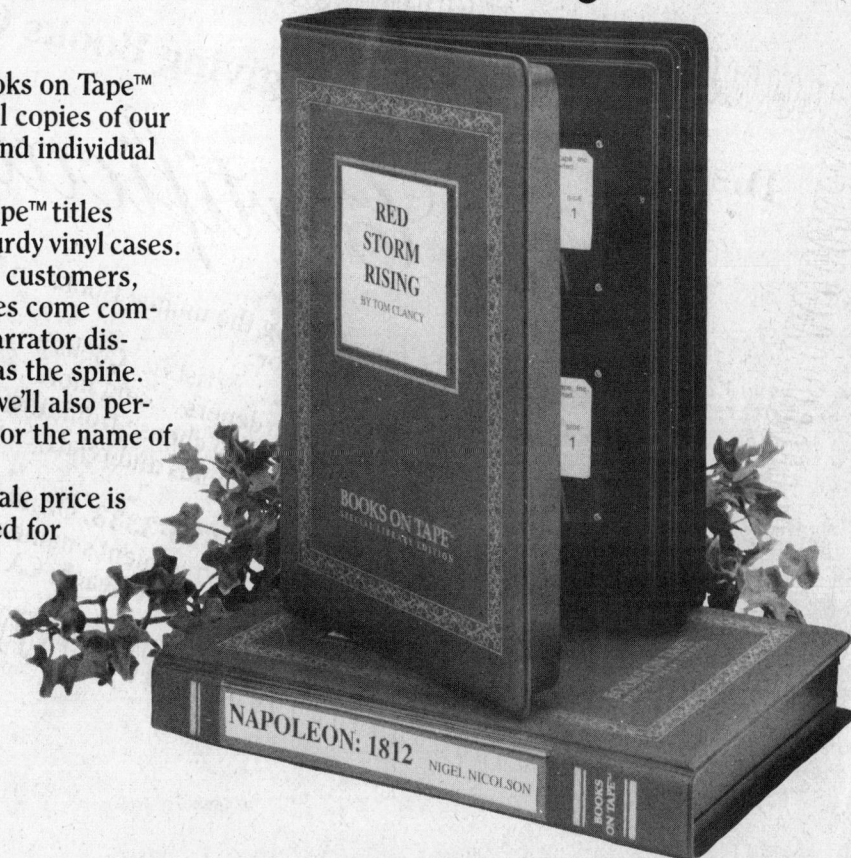

How to find books you enjoy

When you have particularly enjoyed listening to a book, chances are that you will enjoy other books by the same author.

To find, consult our index located at the back of this catalog. Not only are all titles listed, but so is each author's name, complete with other titles by that author available on cassette from Books on Tape.™

FREE replacements for broken cassettes

If your cassette breaks, just call **1-800-626-3333** and a replacement will be sent immediately by first class mail.

Books on Tape™ regrets that it cannot be responsible for lost or stolen cassettes. Customers will be billed $8.00 per cassette minus the rental price. We are not responsible for equipment failure. As with all cassettes, protect from moisture, sunlight and heat.

Discover the pleasure of giving Books On Tape™

Gift Certificates

Experience the fun of giving the unique Books on Tape™ gift certificate. It's a thoughtful gift for:

Commuters...Artists...Cooks
Joggers...Gardeners...and more!

In fact with 2500 selections to choose from, the B-O-T™ gift certificate will be appreciated by friends and relatives who enjoy books as much as you do.

To order, simply call **1-800-626-3333**. Or mail a check for any amount over $15.00 along with the recipient's name and address to:

Books on Tape,™ P.O. Box 7900, Newport Beach, CA 92658.

ABROAD

By Paul Fussell
(1673) 10-1 hour cassettes
Rental—$15.50 Purchase—$80.00
Read by Christopher Hurt

Distinguishing between yesterday's "travel" and today's "tourism"—roughly comparable to the difference between the *Ile de France* and a Boeing 747—Paul Fussell contends that genuine travel is a lost art. Lost it may be, but in *Abroad* we experience it vicariously.

Abroad celebrates that last age of travel, the period between the two world wars, memorialized in their journals by a corp of British writers: D.H. Lawrence, Graham Greene, Evelyn Waugh, Norman Douglas and Robert Byron.

A celebrated author in his own right, Fussell takes us on a tour of the great ships and hotels, of adventures in exotic places, and suggests "what it felt like to be young and clever and literate in the final age of travel."

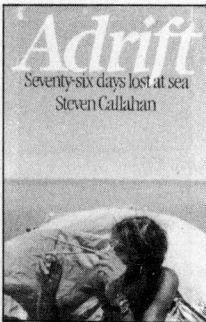

ADRIFT

By Steven Callahan
(2015) 6-1½ hour cassettes
Rental—$16.50 Purchase—$48.00
Read by Dick Estell
A Christopher Enterprises Recording

When Steven Callahan's small sloop sank west of the Canary Islands, he found himself adrift in the Atlantic in a five-foot inflatable raft, with only enough food and water to survive 18 days.

Finally, out of flares and out of the shipping lanes, his only hope was to try to float to the Caribbean.

On the 75th day he spotted land. In 76 days he had drifted 1800 miles, the only man in history to have survived more than a month alone at sea in an inflatable raft.

"There are many tales of survival, but *Adrift* is twenty thousand leagues over the rest." *(Kirkus Reviews)*
Slightly edited for radio presentation.

ADMIRAL HORNBLOWER IN THE WEST INDIES

By C.S. Forester
(1347-C) 8-1 hour cassettes
Rental—$14.50 Purchase—$64.00
Read by Richard Green

Napoleon is finally defeated, but the world, far from falling into an easy rhythm of peace, seethes. France's empire is ripe for plucking, her citizens for *revanche*. Out of retirement and into this maelstrom comes Hornblower, assigned military and diplomatic chores for which only he is suited. The reader's anticipation is not disappointed, for where Hornblower sails, the law prevails—and in this final voyage with the Admiral, he has never been more engaging or in greater command.

AFRICAN HUNTER

By James Mellon
(1085) 7-1½ hour cassettes
Rental—$15.50 Purchase—$56.00
Read by Michael Prichard

The author takes us on a tour of Africa as he pursues obscure exotica in chapters such as "The Elements of Danger" and "My First Lion Mauling." Hunting big game is a perfect transposition of life in the corporate jungle, and who better to treat the subject than James Mellon, scion of the banking family. Planning, logistics, target, kill and trophy are all developed in rich narrative detail by experts in their respective fields.

THE AGE OF MOUNTAINEERING

By James Ramsey Ullman
(1364) 9-1½ hour cassettes
Rental—$16.50 Purchase—$72.00
Read by Bob Erickson

Since the conquest of Everest in 1953, mountaineering has attracted increasing numbers of followers. Its growth is second only to white water rafting in participation sports.

Improvements in technique and equipment have helped men and women achieve goals that would have been unattainable in an earlier day.

James Ramsey Ullman, a fine climber himself, celebrated mountaineering as a physical and spiritual adventure. He sees in nature the antidote to civilized stress and believes we grow best out-of-doors.

Other Ullman titles recorded by B-O-T appear in our Index.

For Visa and MasterCard order line 1-800-626-3333

AIRBORNE

By William F. Buckley, Jr.
(1323) 8-1 hour cassettes
Rental—$14.50 Purchase—$64.00
Read by Dan Lazar

Airborne is William F. Buckley, Jr.'s description of his sail across the wide Atlantic with his son and five friends. The trip, for fifteen years a dream, for fifteen months a planned operation, was always a risk: one doesn't set out haphazardly in a small sailboat across 4,400 miles of ocean. Buckley's account of perils is, as one might expect, instructive, nonchalant and terrifying.

ALL SAIL SET

By Armstrong Sperry
(1957) 5-1 hour cassettes
Rental—$11.50 Purchase—$40.00
Read by Michael Prichard

Who can love the sea and its ships and remain unmoved by the tale of its taming? *Great Republic, Sovereign of the Seas, Lightning, Star of Empire* and *Westward Ho*—these names ring from an era when windships were queen and sail was king. But the most famous, the one that captured the heart of the nation, was *Flying Cloud*.

All Sail Set won the Newberry Prize for young readers in 1936. It carries its years well and is as vigorous and compelling today as when it was written 50 years ago.

ALONE

By Admiral Richard E. Byrd
(2034) 9-1 hour cassettes
Rental—$15.50 Purchase—$72.00
Read by Wolfram Kandinsky

At the beginning of this century only the Poles remained unexplored. They were magnets for great adventuring and scientific spirits, men like Richard Byrd.

By 1934 Byrd was already famous. he had commanded the first Arctic transpolar flight and led several expeditions to Antarctica. His next project was to set up a weather station close to the South Pole and, with a staff of three, remain there through the six-month winter.

In the event, Byrd elected a solo mission. The story of the half year he spent in frozen and black isolation is a remarkable testament to his courage, his resilience and tenacity.

ALONE ACROSS THE ATLANTIC

By Sir Francis Chichester
(2054) 7-1 hour cassettes
Rental—$13.50   Purchase—$56.00
Read by Peter McDonald

A brave man in a small boat alone on a big sea. Vintage Chichester, written after the 1960 Singlehanded Transatlantic Race, before Sir Francis made his epic, solo voyage around the world.

Chichester was a courageous explorer and gifted navigator. In this book he shares his fears and moments of exhilaration on the Atlantic. The result is both a practical tale about *Gipsy Moth III's* sailing victory, and a day-by-day sharing of adventure by her skipper.

Gipsy Moth Circles the World also by Sir Francis is available on cassette from Books on Tape.

ANGLESEY AND LLEYN SHIPWRECKS and LIFEBOAT VC

By Ian Skidmore
(1717) 8-1 hour cassettes
Rental—$14.50   Purchase—$64.00
Read by Ralph Cosham

Few areas of the British coastline pose more danger to shipping than the stretch between the Lleyn Peninsula and Liverpool Bay. In *Anglesey and Lleyn Shipwrecks,* Ian Skidmore brings to life stories of shipwreck that range from heroism and gallantry to looting and murder. They date back to Roman times.

In Lifeboat VC, the second book in this recording, Skidmore writes of the exploits of Dick Evans, one of the most famous of a gallant group of men who risk their lives to save others in peril on the sea—the British lifeboatmen.

AT HOME IN THE WOODS

By Vena and Bradford Angier
(1197) 8-1 hour cassettes
Rental—$14.50   Purchase—$64.00
Read by Dan Lazar

Vena and Bradford Angier were disillusioned with city life. Brad was a journalist, and Vena, a dance director. One day they packed up all their belongings and set off for a remote spot in the woods of British Columbia. This is the story of their first year "living the life of Thoreau today"—simply, happily and successfully.

AWAY FROM IT ALL

By Sloan Wilson
(2075) 7-1½ hour cassettes
Rental—$15.50   Purchase—$56.00
Read by Ron Shoop

Away From It All is Sloan Wilson, first person singular. He tells what happens when he abandons writing and pursues a life-long dream.

The dream is a boat. But to live it he has to include his second wife and their two-year-old daughter. Wilson takes the chance.

"At one level the story of a cruise to the Bahamas, at another the tale of a man approaching middle age who faces up to his boredom and has the courage to change." *(Editorial Review Services)*

Other Wilson titles available from B-O-T include *All the Best People, The Man in the Gray Flannel Suit* and *A Summer Place.*

BEAT TO QUARTERS

By C.S. Forester
(1615) 7-1½ hour cassettes
Rental—$15.50   Purchase—$56.00
Read by Stuart Courtney

Another exciting addition to our growing collection of sea stories, *Beat to Quarters* is a favorite among devotees of Horatio Hornblower, England's most durable sailor.

The creation of C.S. Forester *(African Queen; The Good Shepherd),* Hornblower is known and admired throughout the Western world. Winston Churchill was a notable enthusiast; he mentioned Hornblower in his WW II memoirs.

In *Beat to Quarters,* a still young Hornblower is captain of the 36-gun frigate *Lydia.* He sets his course for Spain and Nicaragua in his ongoing quest to cut Napoleon's lines wherever he crosses them.

BIPLANE

By Richard Bach
(1162) 6-1 hour cassettes
Rental—$12.50   Purchase—$48.00
Read by Michael Prichard

Richard Bach purchased a 1929 "aviation antique." He set out to fly it from North Carolina to Los Angeles, a 2700-mile sentimental journey. It became a trip into the past, of flight at treetop height, of take-offs and landings in fields and meadows, of open cockpits and freezing temperatures in the cold empty passes of western mountains. *Biplane* is Bach's journal of this adventure, a lyric account of one man's unique move backward through time.

BLUE HIGHWAYS: A JOURNEY INTO AMERICA

By William Least Heat Moon
(1906) 5-1 hour cassettes
Rental—$11.50   Purchase—$40.00
Read by Karl Schmidt

Robert Penn Warren writes, "When least Heat Moon (the translation of the tribal name in his mixed blood) lost his job, he got a half-ton Ford van, packed a few necessities, and set out to follow the track of various ancestors and write a book about America . . . it is a masterpiece."

"Everywhere, Moon drew people into conversation—in bars and in communities of Trappists. He has a genius for finding people who have not even found themselves, exploring their lives, capturing their language. In short, he makes America seem new, in a very special way, and its people new. *Blue Highways* is a magnificent and unique tour, with the price of gasoline no object."

Note: This book was originally recorded for radio and is slightly abridged.

THE BLUE NILE

By Alan Moorehead
(1021) 8-1½ hour cassettes
Rental—$15.50   Purchase—$64.00
Read by Ian Whitcomb

The Blue Nile is Moorehead's study of the history of the Nile in the 19th century. The river is used as a framework to recount four thrilling expeditions: the expedition of James Bruce, the Scotsman who fixed the source of the Nile in 1770; Napoleon's invasion of Egypt in 1798; Mohammed Ali's campaigns in the Sudan in the early 1820's and Napier's thrust against the Ethiopian Emperor Theodore at Magdala in 1868. It's a bizarre, exciting tale, superbly told.

BLUE WATER COASTER

By Francis E. Bowker
(1047) 8-1 hour cassettes
Rental—$14.50   Purchase—$64.00
Read by Jonathan Reese

Captain "Biff" Bowker's book is the true story of two voyages undertaken in sailing schooners during the late 1930's. How it was 50 years ago in the closing days of sail is vividly recalled by Bowker in this year of a youth's adventures at sea. *Blue Water Coaster* is a shining testimony to the ability of man and ship to accomplish so much with so very little.

**FREE rental from
Books on Tape™
See page 3**

FROM HEAVEN LAKE

By Vikram Seth
(1273) 5-1½ hour cassettes
Rental—$13.50   Purchase—$40.00
Read by Michael Prichard

In the summer of 1981 Vikram Seth, an Indian postgraduate student at Nanjing University, decided on a politically difficult and geographically hazardous journey: he would hitchhike home to Delhi by way of Tibet.

Seth is equal to the challenge, and moreover proves to be an observant and resourceful traveller. He endures bureaucratic delay, climatic extremes and the protracted discomforts of long-distance lorries with equal aplomb. In the event, he makes his way from the arid wastes of China's far west to the Potala Palace in Lhasa.

"Seth is a stimulating and evocative companion. *From Heaven Lake* is a travel book to put alongside those of Bruce Chatwin and Paul Theroux." *(Editorial Review Service)*

GALE FORCE

By Elleston Trevor
(1566) 6-1½ hour cassettes
Rental—$14.50   Purchase—$48.00
Read by Rupert Keenlyside

"When Captain Carlsen was finally rescued from the *Flying Enterprise* after days alone aboard his doomed ship, many people must have thought: 'What a tale Conrad would have made of this.' Elleston Trevor has done it. Gale Force transforms an epic of our own time into a novel of the sea with a dramatic grip and haunting descriptive power which irresistibly reminds the reader of *Typhoon* . . . This book will move and enthrall all who feel the fascination of the cruel and mighty sea."—Joseph Taggart, writing in the *Star*

GOOD BOATS

By Roger C. Taylor
(1498) 7-1 hour cassettes
Rental—$13.50   Purchase—$56.00
Read by Bob Erickson

In *Good Boats* Taylor shares his favorite designs with fellow boat lovers. We learn how to interpret boat plans, and we also pick up some basic seamanship.

Taylor studied maritime history at Harvard under Samuel Eliot Morison and is retired from the Naval Reserve as a Commander. He was editorial director of the U.S. Naval Institute until 1969 when he established the International Marine Publishing Company.

THE GOOD SHEPHERD and THE LAST NINE DAYS OF THE BISMARCK

By C.S. Forester
(1348) 7-1½ hour cassettes
Rental—$15.50   Purchase—$56.00
Read by Richard Green

C.S. Forester's name on a novel gives promise of excellent entertainment, but always something more—the development of character, the flow of history, the stress of events. *The Good Shepherd* is in this genre.

A convoy is ploughing through icy, submarine-infested North Atlantic seas during the most critical days of WW II. In charge is Commander George Krause, an untested veteran of the U.S. Navy. He faces 48 hours of desperate peril.

The Last Nine Days of the Bismarck is one of the most dramatic sea stories of all time: the death of Hitler's proudest, deadliest battleship, at the moment when it might have turned the course of history.

GOODBYE TO A RIVER

NEW

By John Graves
(2055) 7-1½ hour cassettes
Rental—$15.50   Purchase—$56.00
Read by Wolfram Kandinsky

October is the best month on the Brazos . . . especially the part near Fort Worth, where John Graves grew up. As a boy he hunted, fished and camped by the river. He cherished its stories . . . pillage and murder, friendship and foolery, that gave names to the bends and crossings. Thus the Brazos took on special meaning for him.

In 1957 he learned the river would be dammed, drowning much he remembered. So he took a belated canoe trip on it, alone, to bid it farewell. This is the narrative of that trip—three rain-soaked, wind-driven autumn weeks, bucking rapids, scraping sudden rocks, making and breaking camp.

"Every rare gift of blue-golden weather, every bird, every tale of violence and pride, is remembered with the keenness of the last goodbye." *(Reports for Readers)*

For quick ordering
1-800-626-3333

The Great LOBSTER Chase

THE REAL STORY OF MAINE LOBSTERS AND THE MEN WHO CATCH THEM

Mike Brown

NEW

THE GREAT LOBSTER CHASE

By Mike Brown
(2123) 7-1½ hour cassettes
Rental—$15.50   Purchase—$56.00
Read by Richard Wulf

This book is wrenched from the cold blue and green and steel gray of Maine's coastal waters. It is distilled from fish houses hung with pot buoys, from traps stacked on shore and from that moment when the incoming trap breaks the ocean's surface and the lobster is there or not. The cast of characters is varied, some of them are barely fictional, most of them entirely real.

"*The Great Lobster Chase* is anecdotal, uproarious, sober, and through it you will begin to understand what happens in the pierside shacks, the sardine packing plants, the co-ops . . . and most important, in the boats and on the ocean bottom." *(Publisher's Source)*

Mike Brown is a fisherman, writer, newspaper editor and lifelong resident of coastal Maine. A book of related interest is *Charlie York: Main Coast Fisherman* by Harold B. Clifford, also available from Books on Tape.

THE GREAT RAILWAY BAZAAR

By Paul Theroux
(1867) 10-1½ hour cassettes
Rental—$16.50   Purchase—$80.00
Read by Michael Prichard

In this unique and entertaining odyssey, Paul Theroux captures the telling details of landscape and character that consistently distinguish his novels. *The Great Railway Bazaar* records this solitary traveler's reflections as he traverses two continents—through the deserts of Iran, the war zone of Vietnam, the snowfields of Japan and Siberia—on the trains with the wonderful names.

Paul Theroux was born in Medford, Massachusetts, in 1941, and has lived and taught in Africa and Singapore. *The Great Railway Bazaar* was selected by the editors of The New York Times Book Review as one of the outstanding books of the year.

GYPSY MOTH CIRCLES THE WORLD

By Sir Francis Chichester
(1905) 7-1½ hour cassettes
Rental—$15.50   Purchase—$56.00
Read by Rodney Lay

Francis Chichester was an English Charles Lindbergh. In the early decades of this century he mapped new air routes, flew uncharted skies, pioneered solo in his lovely plane.

Chichester's body aged but not his spirit. In his 60s he set himself the ultimate sailing challenge . . . to circle the world alone. This indomitable man tells how he turned his dream into a remarkable triumph. For on his completion of the 29,630 mille circumnavigation, Queen Elizabeth II knighted him with the very sword that her namesake gave to Sir Francis Drake four centuries ago.

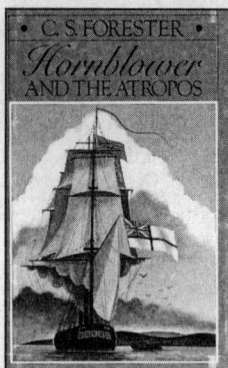

HORNBLOWER AND THE ATROPOS

By C.S. Forester
(1614) 8-1½ hour cassettes
Rental—$15.50   Purchase—$64.00
Read by Stuart Courtney

Hornblower, newly appointed to rank and responsibility, has more than his share of concern when his ship *H.M.S. Atropos* springs a sizable leak during ceremonies honoring the passing of Lord Nelson. Hornblower has no need for the humiliation that would visit him should he deliver the venerated Admiral's body to the muddy depths of the River Thames!

But Hornblower skirts this disaster and sails once more for foreign shores. The Atropos seeks a sunken treasure in Turkish waters . . . a task made all the more harrowing when Hornblower drives his outgunned sloop directly into battle with a great Spanish frigate.

HORNBLOWER AND THE HOTSPUR

By C.S. Forester
(1613) 10-1½ hour cassettes
Rental—$16.50   Purchase—$80.00
Read by Stuart Courtney

The problem with Hornblower books is that they are addictive . . . not just to youngsters, but to adults as well. Winston Churchill, for instance, read them en route to naval rendezvous during WW II.

Hornblower and the Hotspur is the tenth volume in C.S. Forester's saga of the legendary commander. It sees him embarked on a marriage and a new command, adventures that require equal resolution and stamina.

I LIKE IT HERE

By Kingsley Amis
(2074) 7-1 hour cassettes
Rental—$13.50   Purchase—$56.00
Read by Barry Philips

Garnet Bowen is a literary gent from Wales, author of one obscure book, disconsolate husband, father and son-in-law. When he gets an offer that requires travel to Portugal, he figures it can't be worse than London. But it is.

"Kingsley Amis strikes again. Not only is he funny—and he is very funny, as anyone who has read *Lucky Jim* knows—his very absurdities are profound." *(E.R.S. Reviews)*

Stanley and the Women, Lucky Jim and *The Alteration* are all Kingsley Amis titles available from B-O-T.

ICEBOUND

By Leonard F. Guttridge
(1718) 8-1½ hour cassettes
Rental—$15.50   Purchase—$64.00
Read by John MacDonald

A century ago the poles were as remote as Mars and their quest as formidable. So when the *Jeannette* left San Francisco to claim the Northern prize, all eyes were on her. Then she vanished, or nearly.

Trapped in the ice for two winters, *Jeannette* eventually buckled and sank. Her crew escaped drowning but nearly died of exposure. They hauled three boats hundreds of miles to open water. When launched, only two make landfall . . . Siberia, nearly as remote and inhospitable as the ice pack they had left.

"*Icebound* puts modern exploration in perspective by reminding us of the isolation and hardships experienced by explorers before the age of modern technology." —George Van B. Cochran, M.D., The Explorers Club

**For faster credit card
ordering call 1-800-626-3333**

MasterCard   VISA

THE INNOCENT AMBASSADORS

By Philip Wylie
(1521) 10-1½ hour cassettes
Rental—$16.50   Purchase—$80.00
Read by Charles Garst

What begins as a flight to Hawaii in 1956 to see their first grandchild expands to nearly a three-month trip around the world for Wylie and his wife. Among the places they visit are China, Japan, India, Turkey and the Middle East.

Wylie described the trip as "astounding—a journey that informed and appalled me, even in the areas where I thought myself both better informed and more appalled than most of my fellow Americans."

"An intellectually stimulating tour with one of the most persuasive traveling companions you could hope to find." *(San Francisco Chronicle)*

KINGDOM BY THE SEA

By Paul Theroux
(1943) 10-1½ hour cassettes
Rental—$16.50   Purchase—$80.00
Read by Michael Prichard

In the best tradition of *The Great Railway Bazaar* and *The Old Patagonian Express*, Paul Theroux's latest journey rolls along the coast of England. Because, as Theroux notes, "Britain is her coast," he decided such a tour would offer the truest picture of the state of the kingdom.

"Theroux presents a vivid picture of a complex country and her people with tart irony, humor, sympathy and insight . . . almost as good as taking the trip with the author alongside." *(Editorial Review Service)*

AN L. FRANCIS HERRESHOFF READER

By L. Francis Herreshoff
(1497) 7-1½ hour cassettes
Rental—$15.50   Purchase—$56.00
Read by Grover Gardner

Herreshoff was a designer of boats whose sense of beauty and proportion survives to this day in some of his memorable creations. He was also a sailor of rare perception, and his comments about boats and boating are entertaining and valuable.

The author treats us to a discourse on the history of yachting and spins a number of entertaining yarns about life on the sea.

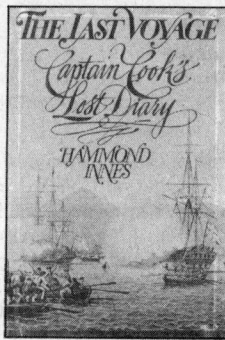

THE LAST VOYAGE: CAPTAIN COOK'S LOST DIARY

By Hammond Innes
(1812) 8-1 hour cassettes
Rental—$14.50   Purchase—$64.00
Read by Paul Shay

In *The Last Voyage*, Hammond Innes imagines the private journal that Captain James Cook might have kept on the voyage that ended in his death in 1779.

While trying to find a Northwest passage connecting the Atlantic and Pacific Oceans, Cook's ship, the *Resolution*, was blocked by a massive ice wall along the Bering Strait. Cook successfully freed his ship, and planned another attempt for the following summer. Cook then returned to Hawaii, where he was killed by the islanders in a skirmish over a stolen boat.

"An account to be prized by the armchair salt who likes to hear the winds moan and the timbers creak—but only as the logs in the fireplace split." *(The Saturday Review)*

LIEUTENANT HORNBLOWER

By C.S. Forester
(1612) 8-1 hour cassettes
Rental—$14.50   Purchase—$64.00
Read by Bill Kelsey

This is the seventh novel in the Horatio Hornblower saga. In it, Hornblower emerges from his apprenticeship as midshipman to assume the responsibilities that await him as a lieutenant.

Chronologically this novel falls between *Mr. Midshipman Hornblower* and *Captain Horatio Hornblower*. It works us alongside this lanky and laconic young man who distinguishes himself in his first independent command.

"The young Hornblower is all one can wish of a naval hero at the start of his meteoric career." *(Library Journal)*

LORD HORNBLOWER

By C.S. Forester
(1347-B) 8-1 hour cassettes
Rental—$14.50   Purchase—$64.00
Read by Richard Green

This book concludes Hornblower's private war with Napoleon.

Mutiny is the subject, but not by Hornblower's men. Before the problem is solved the audacious Admiral broadens the action and, immeasurably aided by his faithful Captain Bush, secures a breach in Napoleon's defenses.

"No other contemporary writer can equal Forester at this kind of storytelling. It is not the action so much as the character of Hornblower that lifts the story up." *(The Chicago Tribune)*

THE MAN WHO WALKED THROUGH TIME

By Colin Fletcher
(1052) 7-1 hour cassettes
Rental—$13.50   Purchase—$56.00
Read by Scott Forbes

Colin Fletcher is one of our great outdoor authors and he is at his best in this book. Equipped with a backpack, purpose and stamina, he takes on the Grand canyon of the Colorado and conquers it singlehandedly.

"His descriptions of the grandeur, wildlife, anthropological findings, and especially the geology of the Canyon are sure to afford pleasure . . . [We learn] how to appreciate the 'real' message of the wilderness." *(Book Review Service)*

**Special 10% discount
See page 2**

MASTER OF THIS VESSEL

By Gwyn Griffin
(1238) 12-1½ hour cassettes
Rental—$17.50   Purchase—$96.00
Read by Wolfram Kandinsky

This powerful book, written by a modern Conrad, is a tale of conflict and adventure at sea. It is the story of Serafino Ciccolanti, a young professional sailor who becomes Chief Officer on a small ship bound for Australia. When the Captain dies en route, Ciccolanti reluctantly takes command. A simmering brew of personal rivalries robs Ciccolanti of his effectiveness, and when the ship is beset by storm, the crew mutinies.

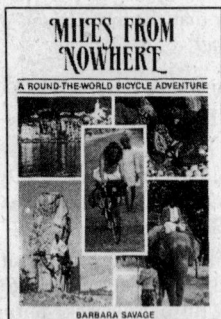

MILES FROM NOWHERE

By Barbara Savage
(2013) 11-1½ hour cassettes
Rental—$19.50   Purchase—$88.00
Read by Dick Estell
A Christopher Enterprises Recording

This is the delightful and often humorous story of an around-the-world bicycle trip taken by two young people, Barbara and Larry Savage.

It took them two years and 25 countries. Along the way, these neophyte cyclists encountered warm-hearted strangers, bicycle-hating drivers, rock-throwing Egyptians, over-protective Thai policemen, and great personal joys.

They returned to a new life in Santa Barbara, one Barbara never lived to savor. She was killed in a street accident, Barbara and her bicycle vs. a truck. We are lucky to have this memoir, throughout which her vitality, warmth and compassion glow.
Slightly edited for radio presentation.

MONSARRAT AT SEA

By Nicholas Monsarrat
(1127) 10-1½ hour cassettes
Rental—$16.50   Purchase—$80.00
Read by Richard Green

Monsarrat at Sea is a stirring anthology which brings together, with one exception, all the author's short stories of the sea. Much of the material derives from his service in the Atlantic during World War II. This collection includes "The Longest Love, The Longest Hate"; "Three Corvettes: H.M. Corvette, East Coast Corvette, Corvette Command"; "I Was There"; "A Ship to Remember"; "It Was Cruel"; "The Ship That Died of Shame" and "'H.M.S. Marlborough Will Enter Harbour'" which Monsarrat called "the best . . . I ever wrote."

MORE GOOD BOATS

By Roger C. Taylor
(1499) 8-1 hour cassettes
Rental—$14.50   Purchase—$64.00
Read by Bob Erickson

In *More Good Boats*, the author brings us 36 new articles on fine traditional boat designs. This collection encompasses a wide range of types and sizes, all fitting Taylor's definition: "A good boat is handsome, able and seakindly."

MOXIE

By Philip S. Weld
(1584) 8-1 hour cassettes
Rental—$14.50   Purchase—$64.00
Read by Christopher Hurt

Moxie is the account of Philip Weld's great sailing victory in the 1980 *Observer* Singlehanded Transatlantic Race (OSTAR). On a course which spanned 2,810 miles from Plymouth, England to Newport, Rhode Island, Weld won in the record-breaking time of seventeen days, twenty-three hours and twelve minutes. Not only did this make Weld the first American to win but, at a lean sixty-five years, the oldest as well.

More than a gripping narrative of the 1980 contest, *Moxie* is also an adventure—told in flashback and anecdote—about Philip Weld's life; a tale fully as extraordinary as his heroic OSTAR triumph.

MR. MIDSHIPMAN HORNBLOWER

By C.S. Forester
(1611) 8-1 hour cassettes
Rental—$14.50   Purchase—$64.00
Read by Bill Kelsey

Horatio Hornblower was born in C.S. Forester's fertile imagination and became arguably more famous, certainly more personal, than Nelson, Cook and Drake combined. He fought in a dozen major campaigns during the Napoleonic wars, and it was in these pages that we first got a glimmer of just how much Bonaparte was hated, and why.

Forester's genius was not tidy, and so this story, which sets Hornblower on course at age 17, is Forester's sixth book about him, though it should have been the first. Lieutenant Hornblower, which follows it, carries the intrepid young man another step forward in his career.

MUSIC IN EVERY ROOM: AROUND THE WORLD IN A BAD MOOD

NEW

By John Krich
(2088) 8-1½ hour cassettes
Rental—$15.50   Purchase—$64.00
Read by Richard Brown

Music in Every Room charts the third world journey of John Krich, dreamer but doer, and his traveling partner, Iris, once a happy college cheerleader, now feminist and hopeful mystic.

No matter their differing personalities, their offbeat style and stereopticon vision work. They report Macao, Bali, Thailand, Katmandu, Calcutta, The Himalayas, Afghanistan, Iran and Turkey as few have ever seen them.

"Krich's literate, frequently caustic tale is a triumph. *Music in Every Room* is a new age adventure, a humorous spoof by an award-winning novelist on the disappointments and corruptions of modern travel." *(E.R.S. Reviews)*

NO ROOM IN THE ARK

By Alan Moorehead
(1244) 8-1 hour cassettes
Rental—$14.50   Purchase—$64.00
Read by Victor Rumbellow

Alan Moorehead, a widely respected reporter, earned his reputation as a war correspondent during WW II. Like his earlier *Blue Nile,* this book is a story of African exploration.

No Room in the Ark describes Moorehead's journey from Johannesburg to Uganda, the Belgian Congo and Kenya. The main theme is the impact of civilization on the wild animals of Southern and Eastern Africa. The prognosis: not good.

NORTHWEST PASSAGE

By Willy de Roos
(1838) 8-1 hour cassettes
Rental—$14.50   Purchase—$64.00
Read by John MacDonald

The search for a passage from Europe to the Far East via the ice-blocked waters of arctic Canada has beckoned explorers for centuries. Countless men have risked their lives in these polar seas. Only in 1906 was the feat accomplished by Roald Amundsen in his 50-ton cutter *Gjoa.*

Northwest Passage is the story of Willy de Roos and his successful attempt in 1977 in a 13-metre steel ketch, the smallest boat ever to complete the passage and the first sailing boat since the *Gjoa.* Even with all the information gathered by previous explorers, de Roos found conditions scarcely less awesome.

OIL AND WATER

By Edward Cowan
(1004) 10-1 hour cassettes
Rental—$15.50   Purchase—$80.00
Read by Greg Shannon

Meet the *Torrey Canyon,* a globe-circling supertanker which made herself famous by driving fatally onto the Seven Stones Reef, just twenty miles from the Cornish coast. It was the first major oil spill, and its reverberations still echo. Edward Cowan traces the voyage and its aftermath and tells a thoughtful story of petronomics in this interdependent age through which we are now voyaging.

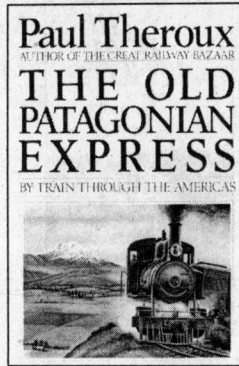

THE OLD PATAGONIAN EXPRESS

By Paul Theroux
(1871) 12-1½ hour cassettes
Rental—$17.50   Purchase—$96.00
Read by Michael Prichard

In *The Old Patagonian Express,* Theroux rides the more or less continuous track from his home in Boston to the Great Plain of Patagonia in southern Argentina. His writer's eye misses no detail, and he serves up delights such as the brawling soccer fans of El Salvador, a bogus priest in Cali, and a desperate American woman searching for her lover in Veracruz. To this he adds an extraordinary account of his meeting with author Jorge Luis Borges in Argentina.

"Wonderful . . . a journey of discovery and encounter . . . an exotic amalgam of fact and fantasy that reads like fiction." *(Philadelphia Inquirer)*

OUT IN THE MIDDAY SUN   NEW

By Elspeth Huxley
(2051) 8-1½ hour cassettes
Rental—$15.50   Purchase—$64.00
Read by Donada Peters

With the same charm that made *The Flame Trees of Thika* so memorable, Elspeth Huxley evokes the Africa of her adult life, in particular the legendary personalities of Kenya between the wars, the men and women who gave the country its character and helped shape its destiny.

"A memorable portrait of Kenya in change. Only a writer with her skill, her deep-rooted love of the country, and her intimate knowledge of its people could bring out so clearly both the romance and the realities of African life." *(E.R.S. Reviews)*

OVERBOARD

By Hank Searls
(1625) 7-1½ hour cassettes
Rental—$15.50   Purchase—$56.00
Read by Michael Prichard

Mitch Gordon, lawyer and yachtsman, awakens 70 miles from Tahiti to find himself alone in his 40-foot ketch. Sometime in the last dark hours his wife Lindy has been swept overboard into the giant Pacific swells. For thirty-six hours he clings aloft in the tropical sun, tracing and retracing the vessel's course. Lindy, buoyed by a flimsy life-jacket, struggles to survive until he can find her.

In his fiction, Hank Searls has always drawn on personal experience. He is the author of *The Big X, The Crowded Sky, Heroship* and *Lost Prince.* He lives with his wife aboard their ketch in the South Pacific.

POSTED MISSING

By Alan Villiers
(1161) 8-1½ hour cassettes
Rental—$15.50   Purchase—$64.00
Read by Dan Lazar

"On the face of it, it would seem difficult to mislay a battleship . . . and yet a 20,000 ton battleship is missing in the North Atlantic, gone without a vestige remaining, sunk in the sea somewhere off the Azores with not even a floating lifebuoy left as a temporary mark above the watery grave." Thus the *Sao Paulo* joined the list of ships "posted missing" by Lloyds of London during the first half of the 20th century.

Lloyds conducted official inquiries into these disappearances. Alan Villiers attended these hearings and presents his findings in this fascinating study.

QUEST FOR THE LOST CITY

By Dana Lamb
(1586) 10-1½ hour cassettes
Rental—$16.50   Purchase—$80.00
Read by Jeanne Hobson

His appetite for adventure whetted by an earlier voyage to the south in a homemade sailing canoe, Dana Lamb decided to investigate the mysterious city of ancient palaces rumored to exist in the jungled interior.

Lamb and his wife plunged into the search with the enthusiasm and energy that brought them through their earlier experience. But this time there were no friendly beaches, no sparkling water, no open sea. This time they plowed through canopied forests, malarial swamps and a hostile environment that nearly drained them of their resolve.

"A fantastic trip filled with unbelievable hardships. Makes one marvel at their audacity." *(Editorial Review Service)*

RETURN TO TIBET

By Heinrich Harrer
(2064) 7-1 hour cassettes
Rental—$13.50   Purchase—$56.00
Read by Grover Gardner

In *Seven Years in Tibet,* Heinrich Harrer related his escape from British internment in India, his epic hike to Tibet, and his seven idyllic years there. Thirty years later, in 1982, he went back. Three decades are small in the flow of time, but the changes were profound.

In *Return to Tibet,* Harrer shows us the present-day regime under Chinese rule and compares it with the freedom of the past, when religion and faith were central to life. He proposes solutions to the country's problems and with the Dalai Lama discusses ways of preserving the Tibetans national character and homeland.

Seven Years in Tibet by Harrer is also available on cassette from Books on Tape.

THE RIDDLE OF THE SANDS

By Erskine Childers
(9049) 8-1½ hour cassettes
Rental—$16.50   Purchase—$64.00
Read by Walter Zimmerman and
Jim Roberts
A Jimcin Recording

The Riddle of the Sands, written in 1902, reflects the tensions and the sense of imminent danger that grew ever stronger as Europe moved toward WWI. In this tale, two Englishmen cruising among the Frisian Islands near the German coast uncover a carefully laid plan for the invasion of England. The thread of romance that runs through this mystery and the spirit of daring that animates the two English adventurers unite with the international problem to make *The Riddle of the Sands* an unusually absorbing story.

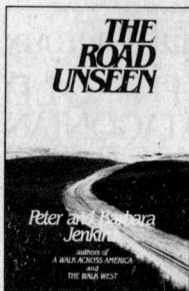

THE ROAD UNSEEN

By Peter and Barbara Jenkins
(2072) 6-1½ hour cassettes
Rental—$14.50
Read by Paul Shay and Jeanne Hopson

Peter Jenkins began his walk, recounted in *A Walk Across America,* in 1973. Three years later, he met and married Barbara Pennell, and together they walked from New Orleans to the Oregon coast. This trek became the subject of *The Walk West.*

In *The Road Unseen,* the Jenkins tell of their spiritual journey. Their walk across America, although an exhilarating adventure, was also an exhausting test of their physical and spiritual endurance. It became a crucible for their Christian faith.

"Finally, my friends Peter and Barbara tell the stories that reveal their spiritual pilgrimage . . . the book I've been waiting for!" —James C. Dobson, Ph.D.

ROUND THE WORLD ON A WHEEL

By John Foster Fraser
(1769) 10-1½ hour cassettes
Rental—$16.50   Purchase—$80.00
Read by Michael Prichard

John Foster Fraser was a professional journalist whose brilliant travel articles and books were famous at the end of the last century and for more than two decades of this one. In July 1896 he set out on the remarkable journey recorded in this book, accompanied by two friends.

They cycled for 19,237 miles, through seventeen countries and across three continents, returning to London after two years and two months of adventurous travel.

Fraser's book is a vivid, exciting and absorbing account of that truly amazing global journey, undertaken at a time when very few of the inhabitants of eastern Europe and Asia had ever seen a bicycle.

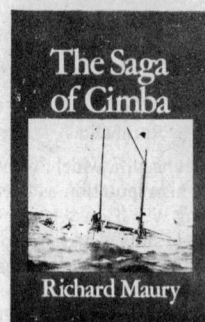

THE SAGA OF CIMBA

By Richard Maury
(2057) 6-1 hour cassettes
Rental—$12.50   Purchase—$48.00
Read by Christopher Hurt

This journey by a young American through big seas in a small ship has become a classic of adventure.

Richard Maury went to sea because he loved being there; in a sense it was his destination. His cruise over thousands of miles of deep water is the story of a boat rather then of her skipper. You know every inch of *Cimba* by the time you have seen her to the Fijis.

"When first published, *Cimba* was the best book in years about deep sea cruising in a small yacht. Since then, it has become a classic." *(Rudder Magazine)*

SAILING ALONE AROUND THE WORLD

By Joshua Slocum
(1012) 7-1 hour cassettes
Rental—$13.50   Purchase—$56.00
Read by Jonathan Reese

Written before the turn of the century, *Sailing Alone Around the World* is a classic tale of the sea. Slocum was 51 when he circled the globe in a 36-foot craft of his own construction. This book is a "must" for those who have never read it, also for armchair sailors who navigated its pages long ago and now wish to relive the story in its recorded form. Guaranteed to interest any young person in those twin delights, the sea and good literature.

SCHOONERMAN

By Captain Richard England
(1791) 9-1½ hour cassettes
Rental—$16.50   Purchase—$72.00
Read by Stuart Courtney

The great schooner fleets of the British Home Trade are no more. Unable to compete for cargoes with steam-powered vessels, they were driven to extinction between the world wars.

Schoonerman is a tribute to those tough individualists, the masters and crews, who spent their lives under sail. Yet it is more—it is a beautifully written first-hand account of the schoonerman's life by one of their last survivors.

Captain England went to sea as a ship's boy in the 1920's when the schooners were in final flower. A gifted and observant writer, England evokes the men, the dangers and deep satisfactions of this trade.

SEA AND ISLANDS

By Hammond Innes
(2149) 8-1½ hour cassettes
Rental—$15.50   Purchase—$64.00
Read by Larry McKeever

Hammond Innes not only writes about the sea; he knows it from first hand experience. His ocean-going yacht, *Mary Deare,* was built to his specifications; in it he and his wife have covered many thousands of miles exploring the coasts and islands of Europe from Scandinavia to Turkey.

The first part of *Sea and Islands* is a record of these journeys . . . sailing among the coves of Ithaca to pinpoint the site of Oydsseus's palace or looking at Troy as the Greeks first saw it . . . from the sea.

The second part is a record of other travels ranging from the Western Isles to remote Addu Atoll in the Indian Ocean.

"Innes's knowledge of the sea and sailing of small ships is unmatched by any novelist today." —Francis Chichester. (Of related interest: *Ulysses Found* by Ernle Bradford.)

**Books on Tape™'s service
is 100% guaranteed**

A SENTIMENTAL SAFARI

By Kermit Roosevelt
(1798) 7-1½ hour cassettes
Rental—$15.50   Purchase—$56.00
Read by Bob Erickson

A Sentimental Safari is more than a story of a hunt for Africa's big game. It is also the story of how three contemporary Roosevelts rediscovered their respective grandfathers.

Kermit Roosevelt, grandson of Theodore, wanted to retrace the trails of the great African hunt taken by his father and grandfather in 1910. When his professional commitments allowed him time, he studied *African Game Trails,* T.R.'s famous account of that earlier safari, and with his sons set out to retrace its tracks.

SEVEN YEARS IN TIBET

By Heinrich Harrer
(2045) 8-1½ hour cassettes
Rental—$15.50   Purchase—$64.00
Read by Richard Wulf

In 1943, Heinrich Harrer, a youthful Austrian adventurer, noted mountain climber, and skier, made a successful escape from an internment camp in India through the rugged Himalayan passes to the Forbidden City of Lhasa in Tibet.

From destitute vagabond, he rose to the position of tutor and confidant to the fourteen-year-old Dalai Lama until their parting in 1950, when the Chinese Communists overran the country. His classic work of travel, adventure, and brilliant observation has been updated to include post-1950 events.

"First there is the incredibly adventurous twenty-one-month trek across rugged mountain and desolate plain to the mysterious heartland of Tibet; then the fascinating picture, rich in amazing detail, of life in Lhasa." *(Atlantic Monthly)*

THE SHIP

By C.S. Forester
(1620) 9-1 hour cassettes
Rental—$15.50   Purchase—$72.00
Read by Stuart Courtney

The Ship is the British light cruiser *Artemis,* the time is half way through WW II, the location is the Mediterranean, where the *Artemis* is enroute to Malta. An uneventful afternoon turns into a lethal night action when a major strike force of the Italian fleet moves in to attack.

The book is an excellent description of a fighting ship and of the complex mechanism, trained manpower, and careful organization necessary in combat. The graphically detailed account leads to a dramatic climax." *(Booklist)*

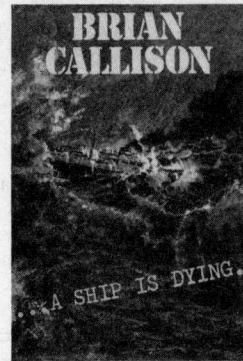

A SHIP IS DYING

By Brian Callison
(1248) 7-1 hour cassettes
Rental—$13.50   Purchase—$56.00
Read by Dan Lazar

Three minutes before collision, the second mate glimpses a foam-shrouded shape half a mile ahead. Seventeen minutes later the ship plunges beneath the icy waters of the North Sea.

The author, exercising great skill, authority and imagination, portrays these seventeen catastrophic minutes so vividly that the listener feels every shudder as the ship is torn to pieces.

SHIP OF THE LINE

By C.S. Forester
(2146) 6-1½ hour cassettes
Rental—$14.50   Purchase—$48.00
Read by Bill Kelsey

This sixth installment in C.S. Forester's eleven-volume chronicle of Horatio Hornblower places the captain in the gravest danger yet.

The time is May, 1810, deep into the Napoleonic Wars. Hornblower, newly in command of his first ship of the line is on his way to Spain with a ragtag, brutish crew. All their seamanship and all of Hornblower's ingenuity are demanded when the *Sutherland* takes on four French men-of-war.

THE SHIP THAT DIED OF SHAME AND OTHER STORIES

By Nicholas Monsarrat
(1217) 8-1 hour cassettes
Rental—$14.50   Purchase—$64.00
Read by Victor Rumbellow

This collection of 11 short stories ranges from South Africa to England to Canada. The title story takes us on board a small gunboat with a distinguished WW II record; the shame is that it is being used as a smuggler.

Other stories include "Oh to be in England," "The Reconciliation," "The List," "The Thousand Islands Snatch," "Up the Garden Path," "The Man Who Wanted a Mark IX," "I Was There," "The Dinner Party," "Licensed to Kill" and "Postscript."

SQUARE RIGGER ROUND THE HORN

By C. Ray Wilmore
(1020) 8-1 hour cassettes
Rental—$14.50   Purchase—$64.00
Read by Jonathan Reese

What was it like to grow up in the last few years of sail, to dream boyhood dreams of the sea and then, while still a young man, to realize them? Ray Wilmore did just that and now, after a half century, shares his great adventure with us. Because it begins with a young man kicking over a conventional business career, we offer it to our sober and industrious listeners with regret because the square riggers, alas, are no longer there as a runaway's destination.

STEAMING TO BAMBOOLA

By Christopher Buckley
(1686) 6-1½ hour cassettes
Rental—$14.50   Purchase—$48.00
Read by Justin Hecht

Steaming to Bamboola is a story of the author's time at sea. He tells first-hand about typhoons, cargoes, smuggling, mid-ocean burials, rescues, stowaways, hard places, hard drinking and hard romance. It is the tale of a ship and her crew, men fated to wander for a living—always steaming to, but never quite reaching, Bamboola.

Christopher Buckley, formerly the managing editor and roving editor of *Esquire,* has written for the *New York Times,* the *American Spectator, New York Magazine* and the *London Evening Standard.*

STRANGER TO THE GROUND

By Richard Bach
(1036) 6-1 hour cassettes
Rental—$12.50   Purchase—$48.00
Read by Duane Young

"Sentiment," says the author, "is the curse of those who write about the sky." With a display of artistic restraint that matches his aerial virtuosity, Richard Bach relates a breathtaking experience in the skies over Europe. This book, not the more famous *Jonathan Livingston Seagull,* placed Bach in the company of Charles Lindbergh and Antoine St. Exupery as translators to the earthbound of the sky and the men who roam its wilderness.

THE STRONG BROWN GOD

By Sanche DeGramont
(1607) 9-1½ hour cassettes
Rental—$16.50   Purchase—$72.00
Read by Christopher Hurt

It is surprising to learn how little was known about Africa, particularly the third of it that lies below the Sahara Desert, until about a century ago.

This part of Africa has always been the most populous. It was home to native African cultures back to antiquity.

The Strong Brown God is the story of the European explorers who tried, first, to find the source of the fabled river. It is also the story of an imperialist march that was frustrated as much by mosquitoes as by Africans. The book reminds us that England and France almost went to war over the possession of a few mudwalled outposts along the Niger.

SUPERSHIP

By Noel Mostert
(1022) 10-1½ hour cassettes
Rental—$16.50   Purchase—$80.00
Read by Jonathan Reese

Subscribers to *The New Yorker* will remember this epic from its serialized appearance there. Written in the aftermath of the Arab oil embargo, *Supership* vividly recounts life at sea on a modern supertanker. A beautiful story of today's nomads of the sea and the schizophrenic lives they lead.

SURVIVE THE SAVAGE SEA

By Dougal Robertson
(2043) 8-1 hour cassettes
Rental—$14.50   Purchase—$64.00
Read by Paul Shay

On June 15, 1972, the 43-foot schooner *Lucette,* sailed by a Scottish ex-farmer and his family, was attacked by killer whales in the Pacific and sank in 60 seconds.

Set adrift in an inflatable rubber raft with a fiberglass dinghy to tow it, Dougal Robertson and his crew of five—his wife, eighteen-year-old son, twelve-year-old twin boys, and a student friend—struggled to survive. Equipped with food and water for three days, six people alone in the vast reaches of the Pacific refused to admit defeat.

"One of the most astounding survival stories ever told, *Survive the Savage Sea* is an enthralling book that should take its place among the classics of heroic literature." *(Publishers Source)*

TALES OF THE FISH PATROL

By Jack London
(9519) 3-1 hour cassettes
Rental—$9.50   Purchase—$24.00
Read by Jim Roberts
A Jimcin Recording

Originally published in periodicals and then collected and issued as a book in 1905, these seven stories are based on London's own youthful adventures as an oyster pirate. At sixteen his common sense, to which he listened but rarely, suggested he change sides. Thus he joined the Fish Patrol.

In the early 1900's, San Francisco Bay was plagued by oyster pirates who plundered in broad daylight. Catching these rascals satisfied even London's appetite for adventure, but more important gave us a record of these outlaw times captured by one of the world's greatest storytellers.

FREE rental from Books on Tape™
See page 3

THE THOUSAND-MILE SUMMER

By Colin Fletcher
(2164) 7-1 hour cassettes
Rental—$13.50   Purchase—$56.00
Read by Chris Hunt

NEW

At three o'clock one sleepless night, Colin Fletcher decided that what he must do was walk the length of California. He could only fumble with the supporting reasons, but he knew it was a hike he had to make.

Fletcher followed lonely stretches of the Colorado, crossed the Mojave, walked the trough of Death Valley and wandered through the High Sierras. Along the way he stumbled across an unspoiled ghost town and visited frontiers unseen by most Californians.

William Hogan with *The San Francisco Chronicle* writes that *The Thousand-Mile Summer* "is one of the most remarkable outdoor journals I have ever read and I recommend it unreservedly, as a rare treat."

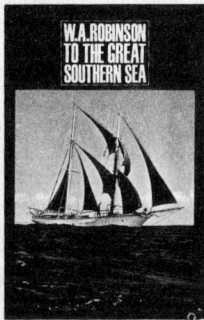

TO THE GREAT SOUTHERN SEA

By William Albert Robinson
(2147) 8-1 hour cassettes
Rental—$14.50   Purchase—$64.00
Read by Paul Shay

NEW

This compelling story invites us the the mighty ocean seas and the faraway places that lie beyond them.

To the Great Southern Sea is W.A. Robinson's tale of his 11-month, 15,000-mile voyage in his 70-foot brigantine *Varua*. Departing from Tahiti, *Varua* crossed the Great Southern Sea on the track of the now-vanished square-riggers running their easting down to the Horn.

"An epic fight with a deadly storm, the enchantment of sun-sparkled seas, new vistas and fascinating landfalls . . . Robinson's story is the timeless one of man against the elements, his celebration in victory." *(Editorial Review Services)*

TRAVELLERS IN EUROPE

By J.G. Links
(1660) 7-1½ hour cassettes
Rental—$15.50   Purchase—$56.00
Read by Jill Masters

Horace traveling with his friends Virgil and Maecenas from Rome to Brindisi; the Venetian ambassador Andrea Trevisano on his way to the court of Henry VII in London; Albrecht Durer in route to the Netherlands; Montaigne searching for health in Italy; Bulstrode Whitelocke, a confidant of Cromwell, hurrying to Queen Christina of Sweden—what do they have in common? They all made their journeys in the days before travel and travel-writing became industries—and they were all keenly observant diarists.

J.G. Links presents twenty-two European travelers, famous in their time, and lets them speak in their own words.

TWO YEARS BEFORE THE MAST

By Richard Henry Dana, Jr.
(1107) 10-1½ hour cassettes
Rental—$16.50   Purchase—$80.00
Read by Dan Lazar

This book has probably infected more young men with sea fever than any other volume ever written. In the years after its publication in 1840, however, the novel had a less romantic influence: its realistic portrayal of the common sailor's dismal treatment at sea awakened contemporary social conscience and led to maritime reform.

Richard Henry Dana (for whom Dana Point in California is named) shipped from Boston as an ordinary seaman on the vessel *Pilgrim* in 1834. He sailed 'round the Horn to California where he remained for a year, most of the time collecting hides from seaside ranches.

ULTIMATE NORTH

By Robert Douglas Mead
(1010) 7-1½ hour cassettes
Rental—$15.50   Purchase—$56.00
Read by Michael Prichard

Few places have ever captured the American imagination like the North and few projects could be more exciting than canoeing the McKenzie River from Lake Athabaska to the Bering Sea, particularly with one's own son. Yet Robert Mead, a scholar and author, brought it off.

Michael Prichard's reading is perfectly tuned for winter nights before a fire-warmed hearth or while cruising through twilight traffic, homewardbound in the commuter stream.

ULYSSES FOUND

By Ernle Bradford
(1727) 8-1 hour cassettes
Rental—$14.50   Purchase—$64.00
Read by Walter Zimmerman

Was Homer's *Odyssey* based on fact, or was it merely a romantic tale of early wanderlust?

Ernle Bradford spent seven years in the Mediterranean in his own small sailing yacht, tracking Ulysses on the basis of clues contained in *The Odyssey*.

"If you are either a sailor or a lover of classical antiquity you will want this book. If you are both, you will revel in it. Bradford's adventures on the trail of Ulysses wove a spell for him. His narrative envelopes us within it too. He is a good chap to meet, if only in his book. For our part, we would like to sail with him." (Edmund Fuller, writing in *The Wall Street Journal*)

VANISHED FLEETS

By Alan Villiers
(1193) 7-1½ hour cassettes
Rental—$15.50   Purchase—$56.00
Read by by Dan Lazar

In the late 19th century, with airplanes and automobiles just around the corner, whaling filled an important place in the world economy. The ports that served the whaling fleet were prosperous and secure, none more so than those in Tasmania. *Vanished Fleets* tells the story of those times and places.

Villiers wrote this book while serving as foremast hand in a Cape Horn "windship." He brings to his work an authentic taste of the sea.

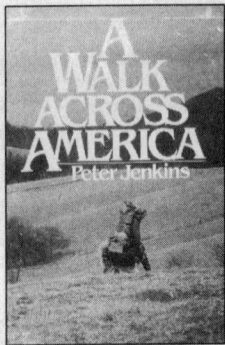

A WALK ACROSS AMERICA

By Peter Jenkins
(1734) 7-1½ hour cassettes
Rental—$15.50
Read by Paul Shay

On the morning of October 15, 1973, a young man set out on an extraordinary journey. Peter Jenkins and his dog Cooper began their long walk that ended early for Cooper, but carried Jenkins across the continent.

"I was so discouraged by what I'd been hearing about this country that I decided I'd go and find out for myself . . . Well, it's been more than five years and I'm still walking. I found it wasn't enough to walk through America. I had to stop and work and live with the people. And there I found it—the real America I'd been looking for—at home among the people."

In this book Jenkins records the first half of his journey, from Alfred, New York, to the Gulf of Mexico, where he met and fell in love with a young seminarian, Barbara Pennell.

THE WALK WEST

By Peter and Barbara Jenkins
(2006) 12-1½ hour cassettes
Rental—$17.50
Read by Paul Shay and Jeanne Hopson

In 1973 a young man began a journey spanning the continental United States. Peter Jenkins wrote about the first half of that journey in *A Walk Across America*.

The Walk West begins in New Orleans, when Peter and Barbara, now married, set out to discover the rest of America together—through Louisiana, Texas, New Mexico to the edge of the Pacific.

"As Peter and Barbara walk through storm, tornado and blazing sun, across golden prairies and snow-capped mountains, they celebrate this country in one of the most exultant voyages of our time. America took *A Walk Across America* to heart; *The Walk West* completes the journey, singing with love of a great land and a great people." *(Publisher's Source)*

WHEN THE GOING WAS GOOD

By Evelyn Waugh
(2076) 9-1½ hour cassettes
Rental—$16.50   Purchase—$72.00
Read by Octavius Black

Between 1928 and 1935 Evelyn Waugh wrote four travel books: *Labels, Remote People, Ninety-Two Days* and *Waugh in Abyssinia,* about journeys he made in Africa, South America and the Middle East.

In 1945 he excerpted five long pieces from these books and published them as *When the Going Was Good,* which has become, in itself, a classic of the genre. In it Waugh comes of age as the world approaches war. He reports an era that is completely gone and almost forgotten.

"A splendid companion to Waugh's popular fiction, this volume displays all the wit, intelligence, candor and artistry that make him one of the finest writers of English prose in this century." *(Publisher's Source)*

WHITE JACKET or THE WORLD IN A MAN-OF-WAR

By Herman Melville
(9525) 13-1½ hour cassettes
Rental—$19.50   Purchase—$104.00
Read by Walter Zimmerman
A Jimcin Recording

Melville's art mirrors his young life. He was a vigorous man who lived 72 years (1819-91) but who found his inspiration when he went to sea at 18. Melville's stories ring with authenticity, and *White Jacket,* which was written at the height of his powers, drips salt, sweat and spray. It is the story of life on a U.S. Navy ship of the line in the 1840's and one scene, a flogging, was so vivid and powerful that it influenced Congress to write legislation abolishing the practice.

Listeners who enjoy *White Jacket* will want to hear other Melville stories [particularly "Bartleby the Scrivener" from *Melville: Six Short Novels* and may enjoy C.S. Forester's admirable Horatio Hornblower series. B-O-T has also recorded *Moby Dick.*

THE WHITE NILE

By Alan Moorehead
(1043) 7-1½ hour cassettes
Rental—$15.50   Purchase—$56.00
Read by Chris Winfield

Before writing his widely acclaimed *The Blue Nile,* Alan Moorehead worked as a journalist and war correspondent for newspapers in Australia and England. His stories stepped right out of the print.

The same presence is at hand in these pages. Explorers feverish with malaria and ambition play their desperate parts and make this tale of the other Nile a living study in colonial and African history. Highly recommended.

WILDERNESS SURVIVAL

By Berndt Berglund
(1290) 7-1 hour cassettes
Rental—$13.50   Purchase—$56.00
Read by Michael Prichard

Everyone going camping or just out for an afternoon hike should know the basic techniques of survival; at least how to overcome cold, hunger and panic, to construct shelters, make fires and signals, build traps and snares. *Wilderness Survival* explains these techniques in detail.

In addition, this book covers how to collect edible plants, butcher game, and make camp implements. Chapters also include survival psychology, first aid, using maps and compasses, and understanding nature.

WIND SONG

By Patrick and June Ellam
(1206) 8-1 hour cassettes
Rental—$14.50   Purchase—$64.00
Read by Dan Lazar

Patrick and June Ellam dreamed of running away to sea—and decided to make a go of it by starting their own yacht delivery business. They set off on a series of adventures that took them from their New York headquarters to Venezuela, Cuba, New Brunswick, London, Paris and all the places in between. Not only a narrative of fascinating experiences, *Wind Song* is a practical guide for achieving independence with a maritime enterprise.

NOTE: For additional recordings of classics of adventure, travel and the sea please refer to our Classics and Family section.

**For quick ordering
1-800-626-3333**

ADMIRAL OF THE OCEAN SEA: A LIFE OF CHRISTOPHER COLUMBUS

By Samuel Eliot Morison
(1954-A) 9-1½ hour cassettes
Rental—$16.50   Purchase—$72.00
(1954-B) 7-1½ hour cassettes
Rental—$15.50   Purchase—$56.00
Read by John McDonald

Like Columbus, Morison was a venturesome sailor. In his search for new material, he cruised the Caribbean, traced Columbus's travels along the coast of Santo Domingo, crossed the Atlantic from Portugal, and combed the coasts of Cuba and the Bahamas in a ketch.

"This is a sailor's life of the greatest sailor of them all. There has never been a biography of Columbus like it. The reader will feel that he knows Columbus—who and what he was, what he did and how he did it—better than the men who sailed with him." *(Publisher's Source)*

THE AGONY AND THE ECSTASY

By Irving Stone
(1061-A) 10-1½ hour cassettes
Rental—$16.50   Purchase—$80.00
(1061-B) 11-1½ hour cassettes
Rental—$17.50   Purchase—$88.00
Read by Daniel Grace

Michelangelo Buonarroti was born in Florence in 1475 and died 89 years later in Rome. We meet his contemporaries, his benefactors, and the important personages of Renaissance art and politics. Michelangelo emerges in his field of the visual arts as Beethoven emerged in music: the universal commanding genius for all time.

"Coloring his narrative with bold, free strokes, Stone has written an important and thoroughly enjoyable novel." *(Saturday Review)*

ALEXANDER OF RUSSIA

By Henri Troyat
(1617) 10-1½ hour cassettes
Rental—$16.50   Purchase—$80.00
Read by John MacDonald

In Paris and London, crowds hailed Alexander as the man who had conquered Napoleon, as the liberator of Europe, and as a benevolent, enlightened monarch. But in his own country, where serfs were still traded as chattel, it was a different story.

Alexander had been raised by his grandmother, Catherine the Great. She imported a Swiss tutor who schooled him in democracy and agnosticism. Thus Alexander labored to square his liberal hopes with the difficult realities of Russia.

ALEXANDER THE GREAT: KING, COMMANDER AND STATESMAN

By N.G.L. Hammond
(1770) 10-1½ hour cassettes
Rental—$16.50   Purchase—$80.00
Read by Michael Prichard

By any measure Alexander was a remarkable individual. Each age produces its own interpretations of him. In our day his great popularizer has been Mary Renault whose books are listed in our Index.

That said, Alexander remains a fascinating subject for specialists, and this study is very able. The author is a historian of note, an Honorary Fellow of Cambridge University, and a lifelong student of his subject.

"This book has been eagerly awaited. It presents Alexander as he functioned. The hero-worship came later." *(Book Review Service)*

ALICE: THE LIFE AND TIMES OF ALICE ROOSEVELT LONGWORTH

By Howard Teichmann
(1774) 7-1 hour cassettes
Rental—$13.50   Purchase—$56.00
Read by Jay Fitts

Alice Roosevelt Longworth was the daughter of Theodore Roosevelt, America's 26th president.

Possessed of a sharp wit and a stunning, non-conforming perception, her opinions and views were sought by our nation's politicians and journalists. Usually keeping removed from national attention, her life became something of an enigma in American letters.

Teichmann illuminates Alice and with his talents as a dramatist lights up her character with a unique three-dimensional quality. She becomes an American "woman for all seasons."

"This is biography that is delightful, discerning and disarming—can we really ask for more?" *(Christian Science Monitor)*

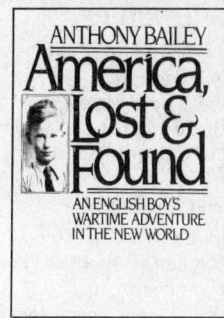

ANTHONY BAILEY
America, Lost & Found
AN ENGLISH BOY'S WARTIME ADVENTURE IN THE NEW WORLD

AMERICA, LOST & FOUND — NEW

By Anthony Bailey
(2114) 5-1 hour cassettes
Rental—$11.50   Purchase—$40.00
Read by Grover Gardner

America, Lost & Found is a memoir and an adventure. Anthony Bailey was seven in 1940 when he was evacuated to the United States—one of 16,000 children sent overseas at a time when a Nazi invasion of England seemed likely.

Bailey, the son of a bank manager who lived on an unpaved road near Southhampton, was transported to a mansion in Dayton, Ohio. For four years the Spaeths were his family, while the memories of his parents and younger sister grew faint.

"This is an account of a double childhood—of a small boy who became American while never ceasing to be British. It evokes, lovingly, a detailed picture of America during the war, and presents a view of this country that perhaps only someone with one English and one American eye could create." *(E.R.S. Reviews)*

AMERICAN CAESAR: DOUGLAS MacARTHUR 1880-1964

By William Manchester
(1681-A) 12-1½ hour cassettes
Rental—$17.50   Purchase—$96.00
(1681-B) 13-1½ hour cassettes
Rental—$18.50   Purchase—$104.00
Read by Wolfram Kandinsky

Like Patton, MacArthur was always controversial. He was either loved or hated. Manchester helps us understand why.

MacArthur was not only a lean, chiseled military genius and master of strategy; he also suffered unexplained lapses. For example, he knew of the Pearl Harbor attack but neglected to deploy his Philippine air force, a failure which resulted in its total destruction. And the success of his Inchon invasion was all but undone by the Chinese hordes that later swarmed across the Yalu—a response easily predicted, disastrously ignored.

"*American Caesar* is gracefully written, impeccably researched and scrupulous in every way . . . a thrilling and profoundly ponderable piece of work." *(Newsweek)*

THE ARMS OF KRUPP 1587-1968

By William Manchester
(1679-A) 15-1½ hour cassettes
Rental—$18.50   Purchase—$120.00
(1679-B) 15-1½ hour cassettes
Rental—$18.50   Purchase—$120.00
Read by Peter MacDonald

This skillfully written and carefully documented study might be subtitled "Power and Its Corruption." For in their dedication to German military supremacy the Krupps moved from traditional industrialism to acquisition, monopoly, finance and politics. At its peak, the Krupp network was ubiquitous in Germany.

The Krupps not only armed Germany but helped finance three major wars. They misjudged Hitler, believing they could control him. For his part in Hitler's rise and Germany's aggressions, Alfred Krupp was tried at Nuremburg. Depending on the point of view, he was appropriately or shamefully acquitted.

THE AUTOBIOGRAPHY OF BENJAMIN FRANKLIN

By Benjamin Franklin
(9038) 6-1 hour cassettes
Rental—$12.50   Purchase—$48.00
Read by Walter Covell
A Jimcin Recording

Benjamin Franklin's wide range of activities and interests opened the doors of the world to him. Printer, inventor, philosopher, champion of liberty, his influence has been felt by every American generation.

At one time he was appointed postmaster of Philadelphia and succeeded in making a profit out of it. He organized the citizenry to pave and light the streets, started a fire brigade and a fire insurance company, founded a lending library, helped build a hospital and got underway an academy which later became the University of Pennsylvania.

To everything he touched, including his autobiography, he brought originality and wit.

BREAKING IN, BREAKING OUT

By Nicholas Monsarrat
(1089) 12-1½ hour cassettes
Rental—$17.50   Purchase—$96.00
Read by Chris Winfield

Nicholas Monsarrat was a noted English novelist, best known for *The Cruel Sea. Breaking In, Breaking Out* is an engaging and candid autobiography in which we follow Monsarrat to Cambridge, the Royal Navy, South Africa and Canada. We learn much about him, much more about the world through which he traveled. Monsarrat resists sentimentality while clearly expressing his hopes and frustrations as a writer and man.

BUYING THE NIGHT FLIGHT

By Georgie Anne Geyer
(1839) 8-1½ hour cassettes
Rental—$15.50   Purchase—$64.00
Read by Mary Woods

Once a cub reporter for the *Chicago Daily News,* Georgie Anne Geyer made her career as a foreign correspondent. She met the men and women who changed the world, often to our discomfort: Fidel Castro, Yassar Arafat, the Ayatollah Khomeini and Muammar Qaddafi.

Buying the Night Flight is Geyer's autobiographical story. In it she shares the experience of covering revolutions and reporting the hopes and tragedies they represent. She also reports another revolution, one that took place in her heart and soul—the "inner revolution of a whole watershed generation of women."

"A highly readable and revealing personal narrative, including fascinating encounters and incisive international reporting, that matches genuine scoops with serious analysis." —Zbigniew Brzezinski, Former National Security Advisor

CAPTAIN JAMES COOK

By Alan Villiers
(1336) 8-1½ hour cassettes
Rental—$15.50   Purchase—$64.00
Read by Richard Green

Captain Cook was history's greatest explorer. Alan Villiers helps us come to grips with the scope of Cook's accomplishments. As a deep-water sailor himself, Villiers puts into perspective not only the technical problems and accomplishments but those of body and spirit as well.

"His use of seafaring terms gives his story an Elizabethan richness of language, while the feel of the open sea, of the various weathers and the challenge of the ships can be felt on every page. It must have been hell to sail on those cockleshells, but it makes the blood tingle to read about them." *(The New York Times)*

**Special 10% discount
See page 2**

CATHERINE THE GREAT

By Henri Troyat
(1427-A) 7-1½ hour cassettes
Rental—$15.50   Purchase—$56.00
(1427-B) 8-1½ hour cassettes
Rental—$15.50   Purchase—$64.00
Read by Jill Masters

She was born Sophie Augusta Fredericka on April 21, 1729 to obscure German nobility. She became Catherine II of Russia—Catherine the Great.

At fourteen, a bride in an arranged marriage, she was introduced to a court generally considered to be the most licentious in the world. But the court looked tame next to her husband and in-laws!

She triumphed to become the most powerful woman in the world. But she was also the loneliest, in spite of her legions of lovers, one of whom was Potemkin. Catherine had it in her power to make him a prince, and believed that together they could make Russia great again.

"The story of Russia's passionate empress . . . brilliantly captures one of the most colorful figures of all times!" *(Doubleday Book Club News)*

CHARLES CHAPLIN: MY AUTOBIOGRAPHY

By Charles Chaplin
(1983) 12-1½ hour cassettes
Rental—$17.50   Purchase—$96.00
Read by Grover Gardner

Charles Chaplin was born in London in 1889 to actor parents. His career in films started in 1914 with a string of single-reelers for Keystone Comedy Film Company. Success was immediate, and nine years later, to get better terms, he helped form United Artists.

Chaplin's life was full of controversy, from his memorable arguments with the government about taxes to his marriage late in life to Oona O'Neill, daughter of playwright Eugene and two generations his junior. By her he sired an extensive brood. She in turn cared for him devotedly through the remainder of his long life (he died on Christmas Day, 1977).

"From a destitute childhood in Victorian London to fame without frontiers . . . one of the success extravaganzas of the century." *(Publisher's Source)*

CHRISTOPHER COLUMBUS, MARINER

By Samuel Eliot Morison
(1779) 7-1 hour cassettes
Rental—$13.50   Purchase—$56.00
Read by John MacDonald

This is the story of Columbus the seaman, told by a skilled historian, noted witer, and accomplished navigator who actually followed Columbus's original courses under sail. The result was the definitive biography, *Admiral of the Ocean Sea*, which was awarded a Pulitzer Prize.

In *Christopher Columbus, Mariner,* Admiral Morison rewrites the entire story of the discoverer's life and voyages in a straightforward narrative, giving his own conclusions to the numerous controversial points in Columbus's career.

Admiral of the Ocean Sea is also available on cassette from Books on Tape.

THE CHURCHILLS

By A.L. Rowse
(1080-A) 8-1½ hour cassettes
Rental—$15.50   Purchase—$64.00
(1080-B) 7-1½ hour cassettes
Rental—$15.50   Purchase—$56.00
Read by Richard Green

A.L. Rowse is an English historian best known for his studies of the Elizabethan age. He spent years researching this book and tells the story of one of England's first families vividly and in great detail.

Rowse highlights the family's most distinguished member, Sir Winston. Young Churchill fought in the Boer War, attained (then lost) political eminence in WW I. Always articulate and straightforward, Churchill never ducked an issue. His life teaches us the importance of maintaining one's own beliefs rather than tacking to every change in the wind.

For other excellent Rowse titles, please refer to our Index.

Rental Section At-a-Glance

A CORNISH CHILDHOOD

By A.L. Rowse
(1616) 10-1½ hour cassettes
Rental—$16.50   Purchase—$80.00
Read by Stuart Courtney

A Cornish Childhood is the first book in a three-part autobiography of an extraordinary man. Rich in descriptions of the author's beloved Cornwall, it is an affectionate memoir that recalls the sights and sounds and special moments of childhood in a bygone era.

It is also frank in its recollection of loneliness, of the disquieting sense of war looming on the horizon, of the anguish of insecurity in the quest for sponsors and scholarships. For Rowse was born into a working family in a very class-conscious England.

The end of *A Cornish Childhood* marks the beginning of a long and fascinating life in the world of letters. Rowse went to Oxford as a scholar in English Literature at Christ Church, and became a Fellow of All Souls at the age of 21. He is regarded today as the world's leading Elizabethan scholar.

"A.L. Rowse titles available through B-O-T include *The Churchills, The Elizabethans and America, The England of Elizabeth* and *The Expansion of Elizabethan England.*

A CORNISHMAN ABROAD

By A.L. Rowse
(1875) 10-1½ hour cassettes
Rental—$16.50   Purchase—$80.00
Read by Stuart Courtney

A Cornishman Abroad is the third volume in the autobiography of A.L. Rowse, distinguished Elizabethan historian, poet and man of letters. It is the story of Rowse's pilgrimage to France and Weimar Germany where he sought the culture unavailable to him in the working class home of his youth.

"This autobiography reveals itself as the portrait not only of one of the most individual writers in our time—but of his generation and the social revolution of the century. *(E.R.S. Reviews)*

A CORNISHMAN AT OXFORD

By A.L. Rowse
(1982) 8-1½ hour cassettes
Rental—$15.50   Purchase—$64.00
Read by Stuart Courtney

A Cornishman at Oxford is the second part of A.L. Rowse's trilogy which began with *A Cornish Childhood.*

This volume deals with Rowse's nervous arrival at Oxford on scholarship. He is persuaded to switch from literature to history—a momentous decision for Rowse and his readers.

Rowse writes of the loss he felt on leaving his native Cornwall, of his First Class Honours and subsequent election to a prestigious Fellowship at All Souls College. Never one for politics, Rowse skewers the pretentious and overrated, those institutional sacred cows he consistently refuses to worship.

CROMWELL

By Antonia Fraser
(1827-A) 8-1½ hour cassettes
Rental—$15.50   Purchase—$64.00
(1827-B) 8-1½ hour cassettes
Rental—$15.50   Purchase—$64.00
(1827-C) 9-1½ hour cassettes
Rental—$16.50   Purchase—$72.00
Read by Donada Peters

No Englishman ever had a greater impact on the history of his nation. None has been more consistently misunderstood, misrepresented or maligned. He called himself "Oliver Protector," others called him traitor, usurper, seditionist . . . but no one disputed his greatness.

Antonia Fraser offers us a magnificent biography of this complex and enigmatic man. She shows him whole: the young radical agitator, the confident and victorious general, the nonpareil soldier, the nervous politician, the ruthless statesman.

"With her historian's understanding of Cromwell's times, with her biographer's insight into the flow of his thought and personality, Fraser brings us into the presence of this military and political genius who believed he was God's chosen instrument." *(E.R.S Services)*

DARWIN AND THE BEAGLE

By Alan Moorehead
(1599) 6-1 hour cassettes
Rental—$12.50   Purchase—$48.00
Read by Michael Prichard

When the *H.M.S. Beagle* sailed in 1831, she carried a young naturalist, Charles Darwin, at age 22 still unknown. Destined for the church, Darwin was cozily at ease with creation as explained in Genesis.

But everything he encountered on the voyage—from the primitive people of Tierra del Fuego to the finches of the Galapagos Islands, from earthquakes and eruptions to fossil seashells gathered at 12,000 feet in the Andes—challenged biblical assumptions and led finally to *The Origin of Species.*

"Mr. Moorehead's admirable prose style, his entrancing narrative . . . are beyond praise." *(The London Times Literary Supplement)*

DEVIL WATER

By Anya Seton
(1221-A) 8-1½ hour cassettes
Rental—$15.50   Purchase—$64.00
(1221-B) 10-1½ hour cassettes
Rental—$16.50   Purchase—$80.00
Read by Penelope Dellaporta

Devil Water is the true story of Charles Radcliffe, who escaped from Newgate prison in 1715 after his brother's execution, and of his daughter Jenny. Jenny was the child of a secret marriage; father and daughter share a strong and abiding affection.

When Jenny immigrates to America, she and her father suffer years of separation. The themes of this book are loyalty and courage. Like all Seton's books, this one combines thoroughly documented history with superb storytelling.

Her biography of Aaron Burr's daughter, *My Theodosia;* the intriguing love story *Green Darkness;* and *The Winthrop Woman* are also available from B-O-T.

DISRAELI

By Andre Maurois
(1618) 6-1½ hour cassettes
Rental—$14.50   Purchase—$80.00
Read by Bill Kelsey

1874 was a climactic year for Benjamin Disraeli. A dandy, an occasional novelist, a brilliant orator and shrewd parliamentary tactician, he acted as though he always knew he would be Prime Minister . . . and now he was.

He traveled a singular road. Dizzy's grandfather was an Italian-Jewish emigre who got rich on speculation. His father, a studious man of strong convictions, lived on the inheritance. He broke with the Synagogue and had his son baptized in the Church of England.

"Maurois' book is wholly a work of art, staged and lighted with wit, style, finesse and humor." *(The Yale Review)*

DISTURBER OF THE PEACE
The Life and Riotous Times of H.L. Mencken

By William Manchester
(1676) 9-1½ hour cassettes
Rental—$16.50   Purchase—$72.00
Read by John MacDonald

Once, when asked why, if he found so much to complain about in America, he bothered to live there, H.L. Mencken immediately quipped: "Why do men go to zoos?"

Mencken was co-founder and editor of two legendary magazines, *The Smart Set* and *The American Mercury.* He has been called "the most powerful personal influence on a whole generation of American people."

"Now it has been done. A book has been written about H.L. Mencken which is worthy of the man and of his influence on American letters." *(New York Herald Tribune)*

EDGAR CAYCE:
THE SLEEPING PROPHET

By Jess Stearn
(1187) 8-1½ hour cassettes
Rental—$15.50   Purchase—$64.00
Read by Dan Lazar

Journalist Jess Stearn has written a startling biography of America's most famous mystic, Edgar Cayce. By examining files maintained by the Cayce Foundation, by meeting Cayce's friends and devotees and consulting scientists and doctors, Stearn verifies Cayce's psychic abilities. Stearn concludes, "His batting average on predictions was incredibly high, close to 100 . . . so much of what he said has come so miraculously true."

ELEANOR ROOSEVELT:
A PERSONAL AND PUBLIC LIFE

By William T. Youngs
(1716) 7-1½ hour cassettes
Rental—$15.50   Purchase—$56.00
Read by Donada Peters

This engaging biography traces Eleanor Roosevelt's life from childhood to her years as the wife of a president and mother of five.

Youngs is an excellent guide. His book revivifies one of the truly singular women of this century. Frank Freidel describes Youngs' work as " . . . beautifully written, fresh and thoughtful . . . the reader leaves it with a new understanding and appreciation of Eleanor Roosevelt and what a remarkable person she was."

But Mrs. Roosevelt had her own words: "I feel it in me sometimes that I can do much more than I am doing, and I mean to try until I do succeed."

EMINENT VICTORIANS

By Lytton Strachey
(1815) 9-1½ hour cassettes
Rental—$16.50   Purchase—$72.00
Read by Jill Masters

When it was published in 1918, *Eminent Victorians* became one of the first books to take apart the heroes of an earlier era. Its irreverent essays on Cardinal Manning, Florence Nightingale, Dr. Arnold and General Gordon found an eager audience in the post-WW I generation.

Strachey debunks the myths surrounding these Victorian personalities. His estimates now require considerable revision, but retain authority.

**TOLL FREE credit card
order line 1-800-626-3333**

MasterCard   VISA

ENGLAND, FIRST & LAST

By Anthony Bailey
(2153) 7-1 hour cassettes
Rental—$13.50   Purchase—$56.00
Read by Grover Gardner

This engaging memoir is a successor volume to Anthony Bailey's *America, Lost & Found,* an account of his experiences when, as a child, he was evacuated to the United States during WW II. In *England, First & Last*, Bailey tells us what happened when he left his comfortable war-time home in Dayton, Ohio, as a boy of eleven and returned to his native England.

England, First & Last is about coming of age in an exhausted, impoverished yet still proud country. It is also about readjusting to one's family and world when one feels a stranger. And it recalls with affection the special pangs of boyhood.

America, Lost & Found is also recorded on cassette by Books on Tape.

FIRE FROM HEAVEN

By Mary Renault
(1067) 11-1½ hour cassettes
Rental—$17.50   Purchase—$88.00
Read by Ian Whitcomb

Fire from Heaven is the story of Alexander the Great's childhood and youth. As a king's son, Alexander had Aristotle as his private tutor, and he grew up knowing the great men of his day. Alexander steps forth from these pages as a young man with a shining sense of purpose and an immaculate concept of personal honor.

"An authentic work of scholarship and imagination, a great pageant, an artistic triumph, the whole novel is rich and expertly controlled." *(Best Sellers)*

FIRST LADY FROM PLAINS
Rosalynn Carter

FIRST LADY FROM PLAINS

By Rosalynn Carter
(1772) 9-1½ hour cassettes
Rental—$16.50   Purchase—$72.00
Read by Mary Woods

This is the story of a small-town girl from Georgia who commanded the world's attention when she traveled the globe as a special presidential envoy. And it is also the story of a love affair that carried two childhood sweethearts through years of hard work, family campaigning and ambitious preparation, into the White House.

"Behind the scenes at the White House, from the festivities of State Dinners and world travel as special presidential ambassador to a very personal tour of the mansion and its many treasures." *(Studio Reviews)*

THE FLAME TREES OF THIKA
Memories of an African Childhood

By Elspeth Huxley
(1783) 8-1½ hour cassettes
Rental—$15.50   Purchase—$64.00
Read by Wanda McCaddon

Elspeth Huxley, who spent her early years on a small farm in Kenya in the early 1900's, recreates for us a vanished Africa, and shows it to us from the magical and arresting viewpoint of a perceptive child. It is an Africa of plentiful big game, rich tribal culture, and white settlers striving to wrest fortunes from the unforgiving bush.

The book ends with the start of WW I and the breakup of this relatively untroubled phase of colonial life. Happily there is a sequel,*The Mottled Lizard,* also available from B-O-T.

"A vivid evocation of the ways and landscape of antique Africa . . . Can well stand in comparison with Isak Dinesen's *Out of Africa.*" *(Atlantic Monthly)*

GEORGE ORWELL: A LIFE

By Bernard Crick
(1596-A) 9-1½ hour cassettes
Rental—$16.50   Purchase—$72.00
(1596-B) 8-1½ hour cassettes
Rental—$15.50   Purchase—$64.00
Read by Rupert Keenlyside

Even though 1984 is now behind us, Orwell continues to influence our lives and thoughts.

Bernard Crick's biography puts the many forces that shaped Orwell into perspective. More than anything else Orwell feared the state. As an outgrowth of this fear, Orwell disected propaganda and exposed the many ways in which language can be made a tool of tyranny.

While he is known mainly for 1984 and *Animal Farm,* Orwell was far ahead of his time as a critic of literature and popular culture. He was one of the finest English essayists of the century.

GOODBYE, DARKNESS

By William Manchester
(1682) 11-1½ hour cassettes
Rental—$17.50   Purchase—$88.00
Read by Christopher Hurt

The nightmares began for William Manchester 23 years after WW II. In his dreams he lived with the recurring image of a battle-weary youth (himself), "angrily demanding to know what had happened to the three decades since he had laid down his arms."

To find out, Manchester visited those places in the Pacific where as a young Marine he fought the Japanese, and in this book examines his experiences in the line with his fellow soldiers (his "brothers"). He gives us an honest and unabashedly emotional account of his part in the war in the Pacific.

"The most moving memoir of combat on WW II that I have ever read. A testimony to the fortitude of man . . . a gripping, haunting, book." —William L. Shirer

GOODBYE TO ALL THAT

By Robert Graves
(1439) 8-1½ hour cassettes
Rental—$15.50   Purchase—$64.00
Read by Richard Green

Goodbye to All That is the author's autobiographical statement about WW I and the disillusionment that set in afterward. Graves went to Oxford, knew T.E. Lawrence and the Bloomsbury set, lived at the artistic center as one of the reigning spirits. But in 1929 he abdicated and went to Majorca, there to live at his own pace and to produce works of his own design and construction.

"Argument about which is the finest set of British memoirs of WW I stops here. If there are standard works of autobiography, this is one." *(The List of Books)*

One of the finest modern British authors, Robert Graves is perhaps best known for his historical novels, *I Claudius and Claudius the God.*

GREAT CAPTAINS UNVEILED

By B.H. Liddell Hart
(1452) 8-1½ hour cassettes
Rental—$15.50   Purchase—$64.00
Read by Stuart Courtney

Great Captains Unveiled analyzes the careers of six of the greatest military leaders in history. These include Jenghiz Khan, founder of the Mongol Empire, and Subutai, his chief general—who between them nearly conquered the whole medieval world; Marshall Saxe, 18th century French military prophet; Gustavus Adolphus, founder of modern war; Wallenstein, the German enigma; and General Wolfe, whom Hart terms "grandsire of the United States."

After he was gassed in WW I, Liddell Hart became chief historian and strategist for the English army. He developed the concept of blitzkrieg: rejected in his own country, it was adopted by the Germans. He survived this irony and turned increasingly to writing as a means of publicizing his views.

THE GREEK TREASURE

By Irving Stone
(1154) 15-1½ hour cassettes
Rental—$18.50   Purchase—$120.00
Read by Penelope Dellaporta

Heinrich Schliemann was the discoverer of Troy, and *The Greek Treasure* is the story of that early archaeological adventure. But Schliemann went to Asia Minor for more than artifacts; he came to find a woman who would be "the hand of God" on his shoulder and when, at age 47, he met the 17-year-old Sophia Engastromeno, he took her as his companion for the remainder of his life.

Irving Stone's vivid prose paints a story that is stranger than any fiction. It carries the reader back one hundred years to a frontier that was wild and exciting, and sets him on a journey of discovery that only a man of incredible vision could have lived.

GROWING UP

By Russell Baker
(1853) 7-1½ hour cassettes
Rental—$15.50   Purchase—$56.00
Read by Michael Prichard

Russell Baker is the 1979 Pulitzer Prize winner for Distinguished Commentary and a columnist for *The New York Times.* This book traces his youth in the mountains of rural Virginia.

When Baker was only five, his father died. His mother, strong-willed and matriarchal, never looked back. After all, she had three children to raise.

These were depression years, and Mrs. Baker moved her fledgling family to Baltimore. Baker's mother was determined her children would succeed, and we know her regimen worked for Russell. He did everything from delivering papers to hustling subscriptions for the Saturday Evening Post. As is often the case, early hardships made the man.

Rental Section At-a-Glance

HAPPY DAYS

By H.L. Mencken
(1002) 8-1 hour cassettes
Rental—$14.50   Purchase—$64.00
Read by Daniel Grace

H.L. Mencken spent most of his life as a reporter, editor, and columnist for the *Baltimore Sun.* As a gifted critic of American life and institutions, Mencken exercised a wide influence. In *Happy Days* Mencken recalls his boyhood in Baltimore just prior to the turn of the century. The stories are very funny; moreover, they reveal a personal warmth that in his journalism Mencken took pains to hide.

HEATHEN DAYS

By H.L. Mencken
(1044) 8-1 hour cassettes
Rental—$14.50   Purchase—$64.00
Read by Daniel Grace

H.L. Mencken was crusty, forthright and cynical, yet sensitive to the unchanging ironies of life. This sensitivity gives all Mencken's work great freshness and spice. *Heathen Days* covers the years from 1890 to 1936 and puts the lash to a number of memorable politicians. As with many waspish public personalities, Mencken was gentle enough once you got him in the parlor!

HERE AT THE NEW YORKER

By Brendan Gill
(1123) 10-1½ hour cassettes
Rental—$16.50   Purchase—$80.00
Read by Wolfram Kandinsky

For more than 50 years *The New Yorker* has boldly recorded the contemporary scene in succinct prose veined with urbane wit. Brendan Gill worked for this prestigious magazine for 40 years and in *Here at the New Yorker* celebrates two anniversaries; the 50th of the magazine, and the 40th of the author's employment there. Told with candor and enthusiasm, *Here at the New Yorker* offers a marvelous view of the literary notables of the last half-century.

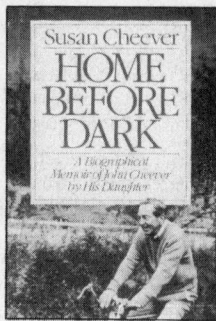

HOME BEFORE DARK

By Susan Cheever
(1560) 8-1½ hour cassettes
Rental—$15.50   Purchase—$64.00
Read by Penelope Dellaporta

"I have been a storyteller since the beginning of my life, rearranging facts in order to make them more interesting and sometimes more significant," John Cheever wrote in his private journal in 1961. "I have turned my eccentric old mother into a woman of wealth and position and made my father a captain at sea. I have improvised a background for myself—genteel, traditional—and it is generally accepted."

Susan Cheever gives us a moving chronicle of her father's successes and failures, his fight with alcoholism, his literary triumphs of the 1970's, the doubts and fears of his last years and finally the struggle with cancer that was his last.

IMMORTAL WIFE

By Irving Stone
(1633-A) 10-1½ hour cassettes
Rental—$16.50   Purchase—$80.00
(1633-B) 7-1½ hour cassettes
Rental—$15.50   Purchase—$56.00
Read by Penelope Dellaporta

Jessie Benton was the spirited daughter of a powerful senator, Thomas Hart Benton of Missouri. Jessie was determined to marry a man whose career she could share and strengthen. At 16, she met her match—John C. Fremont, then a lieutenant in the U.S. Topographical Corps.

Jessie was prepared for the mental and physical challenges of her marriage. Her loyalty and strong will sustained Fremont through his court-martial; she helped him become the first senator from California and a candidate for the U.S. presidency.

"Besides plenty of good, sound facts, the book has romance, adventure and a lively style." *(The New Yorker)*

IN MEMORY YET GREEN

By Isaac Asimov
(1300-A) 10-1½ hour cassettes
Rental—$16.50   Purchase—$80.00
(1300-B) 10-1½ hour cassettes
Rental—$16.50   Purchase—$80.00
Read by Dan Lazar

Isaac Asimov is the original quidnunc. He was born curious and expository. He works ten hours a day, seven days a week, and the result is a cornucopia of essays, novels, science fiction, biographies and discourses on events ranging from metaphysics to metacarpals. One of the most versatile men of letters of our day, Asimov tells how he got it all together in this first part of his evergreen biography.

IVAN THE TERRIBLE

By Henri Troyat
(1986) 6-1½ hour cassettes
Rental—$14.50   Purchase—$48.00
Read by John MacDonald

Ivan the Terrible was one of history's most frightening rulers. Raised without a mother or father, he grew up among those who wished him dead, a wish he most heartily reciprocated. He learned the lessons of survival in a court without conscience.

By the time of his coronation at age 17, his hunger for blood was matched only by his other sensual appetites. Ivan was the first Russian ruler to call himself Czar, to gain for himself the power of an autocrat, and to leave behind a record that would make Stalin blush.

"No biographer has painted the tumult and suffering of Russia's past more vividly . . . a master of the anecdote that helps explain motive and madness . . . this graphic accounts of imperial butchery are damaging: Ivan as a beast that only a Mother Russia could love." *(Time)*

Henri Troyat's bestselling *Catherine the Great* and *Alexander of Russia* are available on cassette from Books on Tape.

JACK LONDON: SAILOR ON HORSEBACK

By Irving Stone
(1084) 9-1½ hour cassettes
Rental—$16.50   Purchase—$72.00
Read by Wolfram Kandinsky

Jack London was one of the most turbulent figures ever to appear on the American literary scene. Compelled, driven, uncontrollably urged, London's genius emerges from this story—from a life fraught with adventure, inner struggle, and suffering at the hands of his critics. Irving Stone's narrative gives us an insight into the development of the forces integral to London's life and career.

JEB STUART: THE LAST CAVALIER

By Burke Davis
(2126) 11-1½ hour cassettes
Rental—$19.50   Purchase—$88.00
Read by Dick Estell
A Christopher Enterprises Recording

General James Ewell Brown Stuart was a dashing and enigmatic hero of the Confederate Army and his biography is a life-size portrait that captures his boyhood and training at West Point, his years on the Western Frontier, his decision to stand by Virginia and his exploits during the momentous war years.

The battle scenes come to life as Stuart, his cape and black-plumed hat flying, leads the raid on Chambersburg, fights at First and Second Manassas, commands fatally wounded Jackson's troops at Chancellorsville, heads the bold maneuver around McClellan's forces on The Peninsula near Richmond, and battles at Gettysburg and at Yellow Tavern . . . the battle that was to be his last.

"Stuart was a hero, but a flawed one. This book puts his greatness and his failures in perspective." *(Publisher's Source)*
Slightly edited for radio presentation.

JONATHAN SWIFT

By A.L. Rowse
(1182) 8-1 hour cassettes
Rental—$14.50   Purchase—$64.00
Read by Erik Bauersfeld

Jonathan Swift, one of England's greatest satirists, is best known for *Gulliver's Travels*. But to A.L. Rowse, Swift is a tragic hero—vacillating between instinct and reason, between success and failure. Swift was a genius who comes to life in the pages of this excellent biography.

THE LARDNERS: MY FAMILY REMEMBERED

By Ring Lardner, Jr.
(1056) 8-1½ hour cassettes
Rental—$15.50   Purchase—$64.00
Read by Daniel Grace

Ring Lardner, Jr. is the son of a famous man and grew up happily in his company. He examines the sources of his father's talent and gives us a picture of life with a celebrity in the 1920's and 1930's. Young Lardner himself became a writer and suffered blacklisting in the McCarthy era. His message: talent not only pays—it costs.

FREE rental from Books on Tape™
See page 3

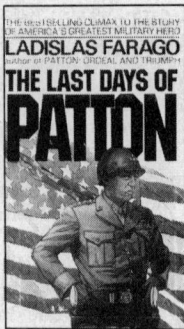

THE LAST DAYS OF PATTON

By Ladislas Farago
(1705) 7-1½ hour cassettes
Rental—$15.50   Purchase—$56.00
Read by John MacDonald

The end of WW II found him at the height of his glory, his tanks poised for more of the lightning thrusts that made him a legend. A year later America's greatest military hero was gone . . . his victories downplayed by the top brass, his life closed in an accident that is still a subject of controversy today.

Ladislas Farago is Patton's supreme biographer. He wrote the classic on which George C. Scott based his film portrayal.

B-O-T has also recorded Farago's *Aftermath, The Broken Sea, The Game of the Foxes,* and of course, the classic *Patton.*

THE LAST LION: WINSTON SPENCER CHURCHILL— VISIONS OF GLORY

By William Manchester
(1902-A) 14-1½ hour cassettes
Rental—$18.50   Purchase—$112.00
(1902-B) 13-1½ hour cassettes
Rental—$18.50   Purchase—$104.00
Read by Peter MacDonald

It is hard to imagine anything new about Churchill. But in this life of the young lion, William Manchester brings us fresh encounters and anecdotes. Alive with examples of Churchill's early powers, *The Last Lion* entertains and instructs.

"Manchester is not only master of detail, but also of 'the big picture.' . . . I daresay most Americans reading *The Last Lion* will relish it immensely . . . " (*National Review*)

Other Manchester titles available from B-O-T include: *American Caesar; Douglas MacArthur 1880-1964* and *The Arms of Krupp.*

LEE: THE LAST YEARS

By Charles Bracelen Flood
(1644) 7-1½ hour cassettes
Rental—$17.50   Purchase—$56.00
Read by Lawrence M. Vanella
A Christopher Enterprises Recording

Robert E. Lee, one of the most famous figures in American history, disappeared from public view after his surrender at Appomattox. He lived only five more years, but during that time he did more than any other man to heal the wounds left from the War between the States.

His forum was the presidency of the then nearly defunct Washington College. Lee created a model university and showed a still-divided nation how compassion, generosity and conciliation could heal.

"An excellent piece of work . . . It brings to life not only Lee but the first years of the Reconstruction period." —John Kenneth Galbraith

Slightly edited for radio presentation.

LIFE WITH FATHER and LIFE WITH MOTHER

By Clarence Day, Jr.
(1141) 7-1½ hour cassettes
Rental—$15.50   Purchase—$56.00
Read by Dan Lazar

Four hundred eighty Madison Avenue, New York, was the home of the Clarence Day family in the 1880's. The times were prosperous and the nation strong, in Clarence Day, Sr.'s view largely because he willed it thus. His prayers reflected this: they turned to shooting matches if God failed to act on schedule.

Father Day's presence dominates each scene just as it has since his son began telling tales about him in the magazines of the 1930's.

LINDBERGH

By Leonard Mosley
(1128) 11-1½ hour cassettes
Rental—$17.50   Purchase—$88.00
Read by James Cunningham

Lindbergh had a love-hate relationship with the American public from the time of his solo flight across the Atlantic in 1927 until his death in Hawaii in 1974. A brilliant aviator, he chose political extremes—which resulted in humiliation when he was not allowed to join a military service in WW II. This book is a provocative narrative of a man who is at ease with machines and the elements, uncomfortable in his dealings with the public, and intimate with his close friends and family.

LINDBERGH ALONE

By Brendan Gill
(1529) 5-1 hour cassettes
Rental—$11.50   Purchase—$40.00
Read by John MacDonald

"The day after which nothing could be the same for him was Friday, May 20, 1927. That morning, alone in a little plane powered by a single engine, Charles A. Lindbergh took off from a muddy runway on the outskirts of New York. His destination was Paris."

So begins Brendan Gill's book about the most extraordinary feat of one of our century's most extraordinary men. With his clarity of vision and his characteristic elegance, Gill gives us a meditation on one man's unprecedented accomplishment, and the world's overwhelming response.

LITTLE FLOWER: The Life and Times of Fiorello LaGuardia

By Lawrence Elliott
(2022) 6-1½ hour cassettes
Rental—$16.50   Purchase—$48.00
Read by by Dick Estell
A Christopher Enterprises Recording

During Fiorello LaGuardia's 12 years as mayor of New York City, he provided what may have been the best reform government in American municipal history. He used his office to rescue a city burdened by the Depression and WW II.

Lawrence Elliott's biography of this mercurial son of Italian immigrants reveals the mayor as a hot-tempered and colorful man, but one of character and courage.

"This lively biography, rich in anecdote, not only profiles LaGuardia himself, but also provides a fascinating look at the times in which he lived." (*E.R.S. Reviews*)

**Interval delivery convenience
See page 2**

A LITTLE LEARNING

By Evelyn Waugh
(2058) 7-1½ hour cassettes
Rental—$15.50   Purchase—$56.00
Read by Ken Scott

A Little Learning is the first and only volume of an autobiography that Evelyn Waugh never completed. It covers his life from infancy to early manhood, thus we know him at Oxford and as a schoolmaster in North Wales. His journals gave him the real-life material for later novels, including *Brideshead Revisited* and *Decline and Fall.*

It was in these years that Waugh perfected his style, so graceful it appeared effortless. Asked once how he did it, he answered "Oh, I just put down the words and push them around a bit."

LONE COWBOY: MY LIFE STORY

By Will James
(1750) 9-1½ hour cassettes
Rental—$16.50   Purchase—$72.00
Read by Michael Prichard

Dear Folks

Here's a long story for you with no names in it to speak of—so, you won't be bothered by the names of the creeks and cow camps you might never heard of—and of riders you wouldn't know—but if you have been in the cow country and are acquainted with the lay of it—you'll have a lot of fun recognizing the spots where I drifted thru. If you don't know the cow country I think you'll like to come out and get lost in it for a spell. You'll know it by the time you ride with me thru these pages—the whole West from the Far North to the South.

There's more than plain riding and covering territory in this story—there's the sunshine, rains, blizzards and crosses of life on the range, from the times I first remember—my raising amongst cowboys and trappers—my teachings from them, the open country and animals. More teachings after I'd growed up while always sitting on a horse—sowing my wild oats—reaping 'em—cutting my wisdom teeth on the sharp edges of experience, and then finally living out to ride for High Points.

Here's a gentle horse for you. Climb on and follow me.

Will James

LONG BEFORE FORTY

By C.S. Forester
(1346) 7-1½ hour cassettes
Rental—$15.50   Purchase—$56.00
Read by Richard Green

Before C.S. Forester achieved literary success with his famous saga of Captain Horatio Hornblower and the great romantic novels such as *The African Queen,* he had a difficult time making his start as an author. *Long Before Forty* is the account of his lonely struggle to learn how to write. The concluding section, "Some Personal Notes," is a memoir of his creation of the famous Captain Hornblower.

LOVE IS ETERNAL

By Irving Stone
(1634-A) 8-1½ hour cassettes
Rental—$15.50   Purchase—$64.00
(1634-B) 7-1½ hour cassettes
Rental—$15.50   Purchase—$56.00
Read by Flo Gibson

This deeply moving story of Mary Todd and Abraham Lincoln contrasts their occasional melancholia with their more frequent humor and abiding love. Life with Lincoln was not easy; before he became a saint, he was a practical politician with all the frustration and compromise endemic to the trade. But Mary Todd was up to the task, and her steadiness was the foundation on which he built.

"Mr. Stone is an expert at his craft. He writes a vigorous, dramatic prose, and he knows how to make his story move." *(Saturday Review)*

LUST FOR LIFE

By Irving Stone
(1188) 12-1½ hour cassettes
Rental—$17.50   Purchase—$96.00
Read by Michael Prichard

Lust for Life is a fictionalized biography of the Dutch painter, Vincent Van Gogh and is based primarily on Van Gogh's three volumes of letters to his brother Theo. Van Gogh was a violent, clumsy and passionate man who was driven to the extremity of exhaustion by his fervor to get life—the essence of it—into paint. Irving Stone treats the artist with great compassion and gives us a portrait that is sympathetic but fair.

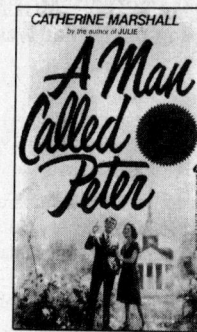

A MAN CALLED PETER

By Catherine Marshall
(1533) 7-1½ hour cassettes
Rental—$15.50   Purchase—$56.00
Read by Alice Ian

A Man Called Peter is a book about love—the compelling love between a dynamic man and his God, and the tender, romantic love between a sensitive man and the girl he marries.

The extraordinary life of Peter Marshall is a gripping adventure—a poor Scottish immigrant, he becomes Chaplain of the United States Senate and as such one of the most revered men in America and an inspiration to Americans of all faiths.

"The best stories are those that really happen. None of the novels concerning the ministry written during the last few years touches the heart and appeals to the mind in the way that Catherine Marshall does in telling the story of her husband's life." *(Chicago Tribune)*

MARY, QUEEN OF SCOTS

By Antonia Fraser
(1826-A) 11-1½ hour cassettes
Rental—$17.50   Purchase—$88.00
(1826-B) 10-1½ hour cassettes
Rental—$16.50   Purchase—$80.00
Read by Flo Gibson

Mary Stuart is one of history's enigmas. She inspired devotion in her followers but hatred in Elizabeth's court. All this, and only 105 pounds!

In *Mary, Queen of Scots,* Antonia Fraser reveals to the listener an intensely feminine, regal, yet tragic figure—a woman more moved about on history's stage than responsible for her own actions.

" . . . this excellent and lively biography is . . . a work not of sentiment but of scholarship and sympathy." *(The London Times)*

Antonia Fraser's *Quiet as a Nun* is also available from B-O-T.

MEN TO MATCH MY MOUNTAINS
The Opening of the Far West, 1840-1900

By Irving Stone
(1631) 14-1½ hour cassettes
Rental—$18.50   Purchase—$112.00
Read by John MacDonald

Colorado's towering minarets, the vast deserts of Utah and Nevada, California's pinnacled Sierra . . . these formidable barriers were all but impassable in the early 1800's. Men challenged them out of vanity, for glory or wealth, sometimes in hope of refuge. The Donner party died, Fremont prevailed, the golden spike was driven, farms pushed into the wilderness. And suddenly the wild was gone. But not the mountains, and not the harsh and brutal weather, which keep us mindful of what this real estate cost.

"Nature did not give in easily and the challenge demanded the utmost from the challengers. *Men to Match My Mountains* will convince you that your forefathers had that utmost." *(Chicago Sunday Tribune)*

MILTON THE PURITAN:
PORTRAIT OF A MIND

By A.L. Rowse
(1921) 10-1½ hour cassettes
Rental—$16.50   Purchase—$80.00
Read by Stuart Courtney

John Milton was the complete intellectual, a man of astonishing range and command. Like many polymaths, he believed that truth was his alone.

Milton sought to impose order, his own order, on the world. To this end he created one of history's greatest epics, *Paradise Lost*, on the most significant and enduring of human themes.

This book is A.L. Rowse's study of Milton's mind, of his intellectual outfit, of the line he took about the issues that led to the English Civil War and its consequences. Milton was a controversial figure in his own time and remains so. His mind and ideas come to life in this remarkable book.

MIRROR OF THE SEA

By Joseph Conrad
(1952) 6-1½ hour cassettes
Rental—$14.50   Purchase—$48.00
Read by Wolfram Kandinsky

In 1878, Joseph Conrad signed aboard a British freighter and began a 17-year odyssey. Mirror of the Sea is his factual account of this period.

He describes the ocean's moods, her anger and charm, how men deal with her. Conrad had no illusions about the sea or the men who worked its commerce. He saw the ocean as metaphor against which men could measure themselves.

"For Mirror of the Sea we would make bold to predict a very long life. We see it being discovered and re-discovered as the years roll on." *(The London Times)*

MOONSHINE: A LIFE
IN PURSUIT OF WHITE LIQUOR

By Alec Wilkinson
(2111) 4-1 hour cassettes
Rental—$9.50   Purchase—$32.00
Read by Grover Gardner

In *Moonshine,* Alec Wilkinson gives us a vivid portrait of an American original—a modern day "revenuer," Garland Bunting. Bunting works the rural back-country of North Carolina, in an area that has always been enormously productive of moonshine, notoriously hard on revenue agents.

"Articulate, canny, imaginative, Bunting clearly enjoys his life, and in this book he and it are vividly portrayed. Wilkinson has celebrated a contemporary who is at the same time a figure out of history . . . a book with humor, energy, compassion." *(Publishers Source)*

THE MOTTLED LIZARD

By Elspeth Huxley
(1784) 10-1½ hour cassettes
Rental—$16.50   Purchase—$80.00
Read by Wanda McCaddon

This sequel to *The Flame Trees of Thika* continues the story of Elspeth Huxley's childhood in Kenya. British settlers, called to serve in WW I, return to their neglected farms and ranches.

For Tilly and Robin it is back to the struggle. For their daughter, now 11, it is back to the ponies, lessons at home, wild pets (this time a cheetah named Rupert), and hunting trips wth Njombo, the Kikuyu headman.

But more is happening. The child narrator is growing into a woman. We lose the wide-eyed child narrator of Thika but gain in her place a thoughtful and prescient observer of the rapidly changing continent.

MY EARLY LIFE:
A ROVING COMMISSION

By Winston S. Churchill
(1854) 9-1½ hour cassettes
Rental—$16.50   Purchase—$72.00
Read by Rupert Keenlyside

When we think of Churchill, a picture comes to mind of a defiant bulldog, well along in years, cigar firmly clenched, brandy at hand, the famous "V for Victory" salute. At the height of his powers in WW II, Churchill was in his sixties.

But once upon a time he was young and in this immensely absorbing story, written when he was barely 30, we learn first hand what it means to be driven by destiny.

His actions were always a little larger than life and his escapades, mainly fighting, were wild and reckless. He loved the glory of war, and after every campaign wrote a book.

The result was that by the time he was 25 he was rich and famous. He was also filled with purpose (politics) and ambition (the top). This is the story of how he began.

**For faster credit card
ordering call 1-800-626-3333**

MY FATHER, MY SON

*By Admiral Elmo Zumwalt, Jr. and
Lt. Elmo Zumwalt III*
(2160) 8-1 hour cassettes
Rental—$16.50   Purchase—$64.00
Read by Dick Estell
A Christopher Enterprises Recording

Admiral Elmo Zumwalt, Jr. was Chief of Naval Operations during the Vietnam War. As such, his purview included "brown water navy," an elite force of volunteers who roamed the waterways in fast attack boats. Among boat commanders was his son and namesake, Elmo Zumwalt, III.

Young Zumwalt may have thought his major hazard was enemy fire, but in fact it was not. Like many other Americans who worked the defoliated jungles, he developed cancer. His enemy was Agent Orange.

The irony is that his father ordered its use, and *My Father, My Son* is the story of how one family has dealt with tragedy. Told in the voices of father and son, the book inspires, for it is about people who believe they can triumph over any adversity.

Slightly edited for radio presentation.

MY FIFTY YEARS IN THE NAVY

By Charles C. Clark
(1938) 8-1 hour cassettes
Rental—$14.50   Purchase—$64.00
Read by John MacDonald

Rear Admiral Charles C. Clark commanded the battleship *Oregon* when she raced from San Francisco to the Caribbean via Cape Horn to join the battle of Santiago in 1898.

The voyage was a tremendous achievement "nothing having approached it in the history of battleships." It captured the imagination of the American people and made Clark a hero.

"The Spanish-American War climaxed his life, as it does this book. And in his story we learn how our senior service steamed into the 20th century. Anecdotal and entertaining." (*E.R.S. Reviews*)

Rental Section At-a-Glance

MY ISLAND HOME

By James Norman Hall
(1432) 8-1¹/₂ hour cassettes
Rental—$15.50   Purchase—$64.00
Read by Larry McKeever

In this autobiography the co-author of *Mutiny on the Bounty, Pitcairn's Island* and other tales of adventure in the South Pacific tells his story in a delightfully casual style. From the "woodshed poet" writing youthful lines on the walls of the family outhouse in Colfax, Iowa, through his career with both the infantry and air services in WW I, to his life on the Island of Tahiti and long friendship with Charles Nordhoff, Hall holds the interest of his audience.

Almost everyone is familiar with Hall's work, but few know that his life was more exciting than the historical events he writes about. *My Island Home* is a candid recounting of his adventures, told in a frank and modest manner.

MY LIFE AND HARD TIMES

By James Thurber
(1227) 3-1 hour cassettes
Rental—$8.50   Purchase—$24.00
Read by Wolfram Kandinsky

With humor at once tolerant and cynical, James Thurber talks about his early life. Thurber's sophisticated urbanity collides with his Midwestern directness in a collection of autobiographical stories like none other. More than just an amusing book, *My Life and Hard Times* is happily critical of those things we take too seriously—like ourselves.

MY THEODOSIA

By Anya Seton
(1245) 10-1¹/₂ hour cassettes
Rental—$16.50   Purchase—$80.00
Read by Wanda McCaddon

Aaron Burr's daughter, Theodosia, was dedicated to him with single-mindedness. Better than anyone else in the world, she understood her father. It was to her he unburdened himself and in this reconstruction of Theodosia's life we see him clearly mirrored. Anya Seton treats the unusual relationship in a factual and open manner, sparing us the pedantry of psycho-history. Theodosia Burr emerges as a strong and loyal individual, one who never flinched in the face of what she believed to be her duty.

For other Anya Seton titles, please refer to our Index.

MY WICKED, WICKED WAYS

By Errol Flynn
(1172) 12-1¹/₂ hour cassettes
Rental—$17.50   Purchase—$96.00
Read by Dan Lazar

Hero to millions who loved him as Robin Hood and Captain Blood, Errol Flynn lived a life that surpassed any adventure he ever filmed. Many of his exploits were made public for the first time in this autobiography, completed just a few months before his death at age 50.

Surprisingly candid, this book reveals an introspective and enigmatic personality previously hidden behind a hedonistic facade.

These brashly written memoirs of his full and consuming life create a self-portrait that is as colorful as it is entertaining.

THE NATURE OF ALEXANDER

By Mary Renault
(1496) 7-1¹/₂ hour cassettes
Rental—$15.50   Purchase—$56.00
Read by Peter MacDonald

What made Alexander "the Great?" It is a question to ponder and Mary Renault helps us come to grips with it in this exceptionally well-written and popular biography of one of history's legendary heroes.

Between the ages of 20 when he succeeded his murdered father and 33 when he died, Alexander became master of almost all the then-known world. That he was a leader, soldier and much else, and a genius of a sort rare at any time in history seems undoubted.

Other Renault titles available from B-O-T are listed in our Index.

NEW YORK JEW

By Alfred Kazin
(2086) 11-1¹/₂ hour cassettes
Rental—$17.50   Purchase—$88.00
Read by Michael Prichard

In his lifetime Alfred Kazin has been many things . . . student, scholar, journalist, critic, activist. But he has also maintained contact with his private self, his spiritual and intellectual self, and in this book we share this wellspring of his creativity.

Kazin got his start with the *New Republic*, later served at *Fortune* with James Agee in the reign of Henry Luce. He knew wartime London; traveled extensively after the war in Italy, Germany, Russia and Israel. His moves along the continuum have always pushed him in one direction—toward truth.

"New York itself is a central character in his book as in his live—a life superbly told, in a book of permanent importance to anyone who cares about American writing and writers." (*Publisher's Source*)

NEWSPAPER DAYS

By H.L. Mencken
(1025) 8-1 hour cassettes
Rental—$14.50   Purchase—$64.00
Read by Daniel Grace

Newspaper Days records the seven years Mencken spent as reporter, drama critic and editor of the *Baltimore Herald*. Mencken's recollections are recounted with the ascerbic humor and wit that made him one of America's foremost journalists. Yet in *Newspaper Days* Mencken reveals an unexpected private gentleness. *Newspaper Days* is the second installment of H.L. Mencken's three volume collection which includes *Happy Days* and *Heathen Days*.

NICHOLAS AND ALEXANDRA

By Robert K. Massie
(1845-A) 9-1½ hour cassettes
Rental—$16.50   Purchase—$72.00
(1845-B) 9-1½ hour cassettes
Rental—$16.50   Purchase—$72.00
Read by Wolfram Kandinsky

Nicholas and Alexandra were the last of the Romanovs, remembered by us today chiefly as the parents who with their four daughters and son were murdered by the Bolsheviks.

The times were not propitious when Nicholas came to power.

It is doubtful Nicholas could have survived the times, even with luck, but fate seemed against him. His son's hemophilia was a great burden; worse was Rasputin, an unprincipled Siberian mystic. On top of it all came the great war in 1914. When Russian armies suffered staggering defeats, the whole structure began to crumble.

"Massie gives the tantalizing 'what ifs' of history a full airing in this satisfying follow-up to *Peter the Great*, another acknowledged master-work." *(Journal of Literary Reviews)*

ORIENT EXPRESS

By John Dos Passos
(1341) 6-1 hour cassettes
Rental—$12.50   Purchase—$48.00
Read by Erik Bauersfeld

John Dos Passos was born in Chicago in 1896, was educated both here and abroad, and graduated from Harvard in 1916. He then traveled to Spain, but soon joined the French Ambulance Service, later transferring to the U.S. Medical Corps. These experiences furnished him fuel for his early books and the resultant *Three Soldiers*, published in 1921, was received with popular and critical acclaim. He followed it with *Manhattan Transfer*, which did in prose for New York what Carl Sandburg did in poetry for Chicago. Dos Passos then treated himself to a trip through Russia and the Levant. He kept a journal and published it in 1927 as *Orient Express*.

THE ORIGIN

By Irving Stone
(1547-A) 9-1½ hour cassettes
Rental—$16.50   Purchase—$72.00
(1547-B) 11-1½ hour cassettes
Rental—$17.50   Purchase—$88.00
Read by Dan Lazar

At the age of 22, in 1832, Charles Darwin was a charming, lighthearted young man without a career or future. A recent graduate of Cambridge, he had decided not to follow in his family's tradition of medicine, and was about to enter the clergy, when out of the blue a letter arrived inviting him to sail on *H.M.S. Beagle* as a naturalist. The voyage would girdle the globe, and the man who returned, young no longer, would change radically the way mankind perceived itself and the world.

"Stone's success with such an intractable subject is a testimony to the power of an art that he has promoted assiduously for many years." *(Science)*

ORTHODOXY

By G.K. Chesterton
(1441) 8-1 hour cassettes
Rental—$14.50   Purchase—$64.00
Read by Robert Mundy

Before diving into G.K. Chesterton's book, it is important to know that he was born in 1874, was raised in the Church of England, and converted to Roman Catholicism in his full maturity. Such a conversion was controversial in the extreme, and Chesterton waved the flag of his religion in the face of a secular British press and public.

Although Orthodoxy is a work of theology, it is also, according to Chesterton, "unavoidably autobiographical." In his characteristically elegant and pithy prose, Chesterton resolves the myriad paradoxes of his belief and constructs a convincing credo that is cogently argued, persuasive and always amusing.

OUR KATE

By Catherine Cookson
(2001) 7-1½ hour cassettes
Rental—$15.50   Purchase—$56.00
Read by Penelope Dellaporta

Catherine Cookson novels are set in and around the North-East of England, past and present. This, her autobiography, makes plain how it is she knows her background and her characters so well.

The Our Kate of the title is not Catherine Cookson, but her mother.

Our Kate is about living with hardship and poverty. The story is told from the viewpoint of a highly sensitive child, later the mature woman, whose zest for life and unquenchable sense of humor made Catherine Cookson the warm, engaging writer she is today.

OUT OF AFRICA

By Isak Dinesen
(1856) 9-1½ hour cassettes
Rental—$16.50   Purchase—$72.00
Read by Wanda McCaddon

In 1921, the year that Baroness Karen Blixen found herself stranded by her divorce on a Kenyan mountain farm, most women in her circumstances would have fled back to civilization.

But instead of returning to her native Denmark, the 35-year-old Blixen stayed on and ran the farm.

In 1931 coffee prices collapsed and she was forced to leave. She returned to Denmark where she poured her memories into a passionate love letter to the life that would hold her in thrall till the end of her days. *Out of Africa*, published in 1937 under the pseudonym of Isak Dinesen, became a classic.

PAPER LION

By George Plimpton
(1001) 10-1½ hour cassettes
Rental—$16.50   Purchase—$80.00
Read by Jake Gardiner

Paper Lion recounts the adventures of George Plimpton, professional writer and weekend athlete, who joined the Detroit Lions in their summer training camp. For four weeks, while being groomed as quarterback, Plimpton shared all the hazards and hard work. Combining humor, sports lore, mayhem and excitement, *Paper Lion* is a quasi-insider's look at the world of big-time athletics.

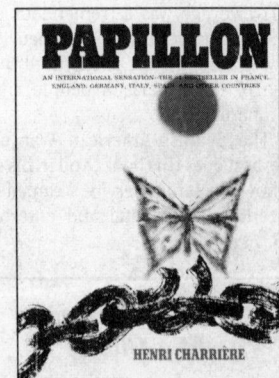

PAPILLON

By Henri Charrière
(1116) 12-1½ hour cassettes
Rental—$17.50   Purchase—$96.00
Read by Michael Prichard

Henri Charrière was a Frenchman who was convicted in 1931 of a murder he did not commit. Sentenced to life imprisonment, he spent 12 years in the penal colony of French Guiana. After eight unsuccessful attempts to escape, he finally got away to Venezuela. More than 20 years later, when he was 60, Charrière wrote this story.

THE PASSIONS OF THE MIND

By Irving Stone
(1225-A) 14-1½ hour cassettes
Rental—$18.50   Purchase—$112.00
(1225-B) 13-1½ hour cassettes
Rental—$18.50   Purchase—$104.00
Read by Wolfram Kandinsky

When Freud was a young man in Vienna his world was the human mind.

Freud's early work was in harmony with his times. But as his insights grew, he could not remain within bounds. His full powers were matchless, and Irving Stone brings them to life in this evocation of a seminal worker's life and thought.

"A stunning job of research. A well-documented, honest biography of an exceedingly important man." *(Saturday Review)*

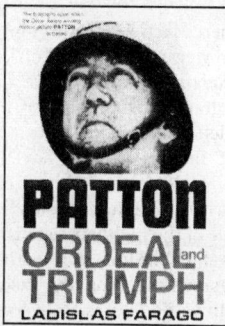

PATTON: ORDEAL AND TRIUMPH

By Ladislas Farago
(1701-A) 9-1½ hour cassettes
Rental—$16.50   Purchase—$72.00
(1701-B) 12-1½ hour cassettes
Rental—$17.50   Purchase—$96.00
Read by John MacDonald

In the vast panorama of WW II, George Patton had few peers as a tactical commander. But the record is less clear about his value as a strategist.

Ladislas Farago sets out Patton's contributions to Western strategy. He follows Patton from the early days in North Africa to the final battle in Europe. He concludes the world would have been more secure, and millions of Europeans would be West of the Curtain if Eisenhower and others had followed Patton's advice and counsel.

"On closing Patton we have the feeling that here was a prophet we failed to heed . . . to our continuing cost and sorrow." *(E.R.S. Reviews)*

A PECULIAR TREASURE

By Edna Ferber
(1628) 11-1½ hour cassettes
Rental—$17.50   Purchase—$88.00
Read by Flo Gibson

Sparkling with humor and insight, this brilliant autobiography, published in 1938, reads as if it were written yesterday.

"Here is her dramatic story, told with wit and humor and compassion, intensity and pride, and always with brilliant reporting." *(New York Times)*

Edna Ferber began her writing career as a newspaper reporter in Chicago and Milwaukee. She was catapulted into the "literary hall of fame" in 1924 when her book *Ice Palace* was awarded the Pulitzer Prize.

B-O-T has available the following books by Edna Ferber: *So Big, Cimarron, Giant* and *Ice Palace*.

THE PERSIAN BOY

By Mary Renault
(1821) 11-1½ hour cassettes
Rental—$17.50   Purchase—$88.00
Read by Peter MacDonald

The sequel to Mary Renault's earlier novel about Alexander the Great, *Fire from Heaven. The Persian Boy* follows the story of Alexander from his victory over the Persian King Darius to his death seven years later.

"A special brand of historical fiction, at once imaginative, dramatic, seductive and scrupulous." *(Saturday Review)*

Also by Mary Renault: *Fire from Heaven; The Last of the Wine; The Mask of Apollo*.

PETER THE GREAT

By Robert K. Massie
(1406-A) 11-1½ hour cassettes
Rental—$17.50   Purchase—$88.00
(1406-B) 9-1½ hour cassettes
Rental—$16.50   Purchase—$72.00
(1406-C) 12¹¹½ hour cassettes
Rental—$17.50   Purchase—$96.00
Read by Wolfram Kandinsky

In this magnificent biography by the author of Nicholas and Alexandra, Robert Massie depicts the life and times of one of civilization's most extraordinary rulers, Peter I, Czar of Russia. The first Czar to travel outside his own country, he was insatiably curious and fired by Western ideas.

Peter wanted to bring Russia out of its stifling medievalism and was driven to change everything: government, society, the economy. He created the Russian Navy, established schools, hospitals, museums, libraries. He was responsible for printing the first newspaper in the country; he edited and published books.

"The author is a clear, entirely unpretentious master of narrative history." *(Newsweek)*

PLAIN SPEAKING: AN ORAL BIOGRAPHY OF HARRY S. TRUMAN

By Merle Miller
(1148) 10-1½ hour cassettes
Rental—$16.50   Purchase—$80.00
Read by Michael Prichard

In the summer of 1961, Merle Miller arrived in Independence to interview Harry S. Truman for a projected television series. Nine months later, he had hundreds of hours of taped conversations with Truman and his closest associates. The television series was cancelled, but Miller had been captivated and *Plain Speaking*, a compilation of Truman's political views and personal philosophy in his own words, is the exquisite result.

PORTRAIT OF A PRESIDENT: JOHN F. KENNEDY IN PROFILE

By William Manchester
(1678) 7-1 hour cassettes
Rental—$13.50   Purchase—$56.00
Read by John MacDonald

This is an inside look at the man who was our 35th president, John Fitzgerald Kennedy. Manchester was his friend, so he gives him to us close up, life size, warts and all. In an epilogue in this revised edition, the author discusses the man, his time, and his place in history.

"It is fascinating, appealing and, like all great drama, enchanting." *(New Republic)*

Other Manchester titles available from B-O-T include: *American Caesar, The Arms of Krupp* and *Disturber of the Peace: The Life and Riotous Times of H.L. Mencken*.

THE PRESIDENT'S LADY

By Irving Stone
(1632) 9-1½ hour cassettes
Rental—$16.50   Purchase—$72.00
Read by John MacDonald

Andrew Jackson is one of the most colorful characters in American history. Jackson's principal source of strength was his wife Rachel, as dedicated to him as he was to his own career. But Rachel herself was tainted by a prior marriage, one that ended with bitterness and recrimination. Jackson never permitted his wife to be slighted: his protection was her brightest shield.

"No writer of fiction could desire more fascinating and romantic characters than Mr. Stone draws from history for this biographical novel." *(New York Herald Tribune)*

**For quick ordering
1-800-626-3333**

PRINCE OF THIEVES

By Brian D. Boyer
(1038) 8-1 hour cassettes
Rental—$14.50   Purchase—$64.00
Read by Dan Lazar

In the jargon of the criminal underworld, a master forger is called "the Prince of Thieves." Such a man is Peter "Tony" Milano. When free-lance writer Brian Boyer first heard of Tony Milano, he suspected that the story of his career might make a provocative novel. He interviewed Milano, and eventually turned hours of his taped recollections into the *Prince of Thieves*, a fictionalized biography of the world's greatest forger.

RANCH LIFE AND THE HUNTING TRAIL

By Theodore Roosevelt
(1888) 8-1 hour cassettes
Rental—$14.50   Purchase—$64.00
Read by Larry McKeever

No American president has been closer to the working life of the West than Theodore Roosevelt. From 1884 to 1886 he built up his ranch on the little Missouri in Dakota Territory.

He met the unique characters of the Bad Lands—mountain men, buffalo hunters, Indians and cowboys—and watched them change as the West filled up with people. Theodore Roosevelt tried his hand at everything from routine labor to a stint as a deputy sheriff (he tracked and caught three horse thieves).

"Whether describing cowboys at work or his own hunts for elk, antelope and bear, this book expresses his lifelong delight in physical hardihood and tests of nerve." *(Editorial Review Service)*

RAW MATERIAL

By Alan Sillitoe
(1295) 6-1 hour cassettes
Rental—$12.50   Purchase—$48.00
Read by Richard Green

Alan Sillitoe is best known for *The Loneliness of the Long Distance Runner*. In *Raw Material*, we meet Sillitoe's impoverished Midlands forebears and learn why Sillitoe believes family relationships are the basis of all security, love and perhaps all truth. For him, these relationships are the artistic "raw material" of his work; thus the family becomes not only the edifice of his life, but also grist for his mill.

THE REAGANS
A Political Portrait

By Peter Hannaford
(1901) 11-1½ hour cassettes
Rental—$17.50   Purchase—$88.00
Read by Michael Prichard

Peter Hannaford was probably the man "most inside" during Ronald Reagan's historic campaign for the presidency of the United States. He was partner in Deaver and Hannaford, Inc., the public relations firm working with Ronald Reagan.

With his shrewd insight into Reagan's management style and methods, he has created a book that's at once an important political reference work and an intimate portrait of Ronald and Nancy Reagan.

THE RED MONARCH—SCENES FROM THE LIFE OF STALIN

By Yuri Krotkov
(1409) 7-1 hour cassettes
Rental—$13.50   Purchase—$56.00
Read by Justin Hecht

This series of sketches captures Stalin with irony, humor and pathos. The author calls his fictionalized version of Stalin "artistic documentation" in the spirit of reality based on research, personal experience, and conversations with others.

Yuri Krotkov, a Soviet Georgian, as was Stalin, was a prominent dramatist and screen writer in the Soviet Union before his defection. As a member of the Russian intelligentsia, he was in the confidence of top-ranking Soviet and party officials in Moscow. Following his arrival in the United States, he held teaching positions at George Washington University, Johns Hopkins University and Oberlin College.

THE RIGHT PLACE AT THE RIGHT TIME

By Robert MacNeil
(1896) 8-1½ hour cassettes
Rental—$15.50   Purchase—$64.00
Read by Robert MacNeil

Robert MacNeil is known by millions of television viewers as one-half of *The MacNeil/Lehrer Report*, the innovative PBS nightly news program that has won every major award for excellence in broadcast journalism.

But in this candid, adventure-filled memoir, MacNeil reveals his rarely seen and richly varied off-camera personality as he recalls some of the highlights of his career. The blunders and blind luck along with the scoops, the dangerous missions, the exclusive interviews with world figures as diverse as Charlie Chaplin and the Ayatollah Khomeini.

The New Yorker says " . . . wonderful stories . . . " while The New Republic finds *The Right Place at the Right Time* " . . . irresistibly readable . . . "

A ROCKEFELLER FAMILY PORTRAIT: FROM JOHN D. TO NELSON

By William Manchester
(1677) 7-1 hour cassettes
Rental—$13.50   Purchase—$56.00
Read by Christopher Hurt

This American portrait focuses on three generations . . . John D., his son Junior, and his grandson Nelson. Manchester traces John D.'s influences on his family: his philanthropy, his fundamentalist religion, his hard-headed business sense, and his dislike of publicity.

"Well researched . . . filled with perceptive and quotable comments . . . presents a generally admiring account of the royal family of United States capitalism." *(Chicago Sunday Tribune)*

Manchester began his career in letters as a writer of fiction. But a chance conversation with John F. Kennedy changed his direction. Kennedy told him: "In turbulent times people are interested in events, not in parables of them."

**Books on Tape™'s service
is 100% guaranteed**

ROYAL WEB

By Ladislas Farago and Andrew Sinclair
(1706) 7-1½ hour cassettes
Rental—$15.50   Purchase—$56.00
Read by John MacDonald

History teaches there was one Victoria, but really there were two, for the Queen was also a mother, and her eldest daughter carried her name.

She was the Princess Victoria, who in marriage chose Frederick of Prussia—solid, conservative, royal. Their first born son was Wilhelm, "Kaiser Bill," a sort of comic opera Teddy Roosevelt. If he didn't claim to have started WW I, it was only because Germany didn't win.

That war ended the "royal web" by which the old queen hoped to insure a peaceful Europe. She contemplated a confederation of cousins, largely hers, ruling the civilized world and its possessions. It didn't play the way she hoped, but it enjoyed a limited and ironic run: as a network for gathering wartime intelligence, it worked well.

RUDYARD KIPLING

By Lord Birkenhead
(1362) 11-1½ hour cassettes
Rental—$17.50   Purchase—$88.00
Read by Richard Green

Rudyard Kipling is a masterpiece of historical biography which was completed about 1950. Regrettably, the Kipling heirs forbade its publication until 1977. Birkenhead's book takes us back to the late 1800's, when England ruled the world and her last frontier was India. Kipling defined that world to itself, shaped our language and gave our parents, however ephemerally, some conception of themselves. Kipling's genius surmounts the criticism of his detractors, and we come to understand and appreciate one of the most influential men of letters in the last 100 years.

SHAKESPEARE THE MAN

By A.L. Rowse
(1090) 7-1½ hour cassettes
Rental—$15.50   Purchase—$56.00
Read by Richard Green

A.L. Rowse, a leading historian of the Elizabethan Age, brings scholarship and historical methodology to bear on the puzzle of Shakespeare, the man. The result is a narrative of Shakespeare's life as he moved from his Stratford boyhood to fame and success in London. There he encountered the "Dark Lady" and wooed her with his love sonnets. Rowse claims to have solved the mystery of her identity, but more than that helps us comprehend Shakespeare's genius and the times in which he lived.

SLIDE RULE: The Autobiography of An Engineer

By Nevil Shute
(1975) 8-1 hour cassettes
Rental—$14.50   Purchase—$64.00
Read by Grover Gardner

Nevil Shute best describes this autobiography in his own words.

"Most of my adult life, perhaps all the worthwhile part of it, has been spent messing about with airplanes. For thirty years there was a period when airplanes would fly when you wanted them to, but there were still fresh things to be learned on every flight, a period when airplanes were small and so easily built that experiments were cheap and new designs could fly within six months of the first glimmer in the mind of the designer.

"That halcyon period started about 1910 and it was in full flower after WW I when I was a young man; it died with WW II when airplanes had grown too costly and too complicated for individuals to build or even to operate. I count myself lucky that that fleeting period coincided with my youth and my young manhood, and that I had a part in it."

A SORT OF LIFE

By Graham Greene
(1590) 7-1 hour cassettes
Rental—$13.50   Purchase—$56.00
Read by Ian Whitcomb

This story of the author's childhood and youth is the first installment of his autobiography. Its sequel, *Ways of Escape,* carries Greene forward into his late middle years.

Greene grew up in England between the two world wars. He seemed a typical member of his social class, public school and Oxford educated. But the similarity was only skin deep.

Underneath the veneer, Greene was churning with discontent. It drove him to the brink of suicide; he regained stability in analysis, but was left with a streak of discontent and rootlessness. Travel and writing released him from his melancholy; he stitched together "a sort of life."

Greene wrote some of the most popular and highly regarded novels of the 20th century, among them *The Third Man* and *The Quiet American. Monsieur Quixote,* a more recent work, and *Ways of Escape,* the second part of his autobiography, are available from B-O-T.

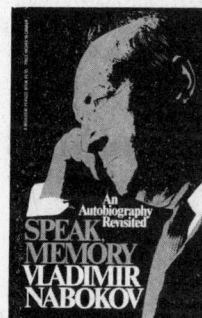

SPEAK, MEMORY

By Vladimir Nabokov
(2047) 7-1½ hour cassettes
Rental—$15.50   Purchase—$56.00
Read by John McDonald

This is the candid, revealing and powerful autobiography of one of the greatest prose masters of the twentieth century. Vladimir Nabokov describes it as a "systematically correlated assemblage of personal recollections ranging geographically from St. Petersburg to St. Nazaire, and covering 37 years, from August 1903 to May 1940."

"He has repeatedly fleshed the bare bones of historical data with recollections and anecdotes, delivered with a felicity of style that makes *Speak, Memory* a constant pleasure to read." *(Harper's)*

THE STORY OF MY LIFE

By Helen Keller
(9109) 4-1 hour cassettes
Rental—$10.50   Purchase—$32.00
Read by Cindy Hardin
A Jimcin Recording

Before she was two years old a serious illness destroyed Helen Keller's sight and hearing. At seven, alone and withdrawn, she was rescued by Anne Sullivan, her teacher and friend. By the time she was 16, Helen could speak well enough to attend preparatory school. Later she went to Radcliffe, from which she graduated with honors in 1904.

Enthusiastic and untiring, Helen Keller's life is deservedly inspirational and stands before all of as as an example of what we can accomplish, given fortitude and purpose.

THE SUMMING UP

By W. Somerset Maugham
(1247) 8-1 hour cassettes
Rental—$14.50   Purchase—$64.00
Read by Eric Bauersfeld

The Summing Up is rare among literary autobiographies for its honesty. In this book, Maugham sorts out 40 years of thoughts and ideas. He analyzes his work as dramatist and novelist, describing exactly how he goes about each project. *The Summing Up* provides insights from a major modern literary craftsman whose reputation continues to grow with time.

SWEET PROMISED LAND

By Robert Laxalt
(1647) 5-1 hour cassettes
Rental—$11.50   Purchase—$40.00
Read by Grover Gardner

Dominique Laxalt came to the United States early in this century and settled in Nevada where he worked nearly all his life as a shepherd. He married; Paul Laxalt, the senator, and Robert, a journalist, are his sons.

In his old age, and for his first and only visit, he returned to his boyhood home in the Pyrenees. His son, Robert, accompanied him, and this is the story of their trip.

"A beautiful story. The dignified father of the Laxalt clan is an unforgettable figure." *(Book Review World)*

T.E. LAWRENCE IN ARABIA AND AFTER

By Basil H. Liddell Hart
(1492) 12-1½ hour cassettes
Rental—$17.50   Purchase—$96.00
Read by Rupert Keenlyside

"Lawrence of Arabia" is not a man so much as a myth, and one's expectation is that on examination the man will be smaller than his story. But Liddell Hart proves the opposite.

Lawrence built his legend by leading the Arabs against their Turkish overlords (Turkey was allied with Germany in WW I). His exploits, highly irregular and individualistic, had a romantic aura that captured the public imagination.

"This excellent biography, superbly written and full of action and adventure, proves Lawrence was an authentic hero. The story is also a first-rate history, not only of WW I, but of the political consequences that are still festering 60 years later." *(Publishers Source)*

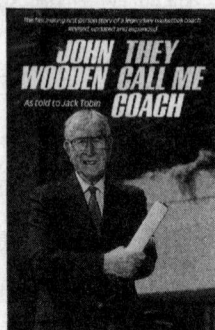

THEY CALL ME COACH

By John Wooden as told to Jack Tobin
(2009) 8-1 hour cassettes
Rental—$14.50   Purchase—$64.00
Read by Larry McKeever

When *They Call Me Coach* first appeared, it was hailed as a classic by fans and critics alike. The personal chronicle of a basketball legend—-the man who coached the UCLA Bruins to ten NCAA championships and the only person to be installed in the Basketball Hall of Fame as both player and coach—it is also an intimate and absorbing account of what it takes to build winning teams and shape winning lives.

"*They Call Me Coach* is grass-roots America, a story bigger than basketball. One of those rare sports books that is must reading for everyone." *(Chicago Tribune)*

THOSE WHO LOVE

By Irving Stone
(1635-A)) 11-1½ hour cassettes
Rental—$17.50   Purchase—$88.00
(1635-B) 9-1½ hour cassettes
Rental—$16.50   Purchase—$72.00
Read by Grover Gardner

John and Abigail Adams shared an ardent compulsion to put words and ideas on paper.

It is the private correspondence between husband and wife that gives this book its unique approach and makes it so special. Listening in on the private conversations of the Adams family, we are introduced to their unique view of America and how it developed.

TWENTIETH CENTURY JOURNEY: THE NIGHTMARE YEARS

By William L. Shirer
(1725-A) 10-1½ hour cassettes
Rental—$16.50   Purchase—$80.00
(1725-B) 10-1½ hour cassettes
Rental—$16.50   Purchase—$80.00
Read by Larry McKeever

At the Nuremberg rallies, when crowds roared their reverence for Hitler, William Shirer was there. In Munich, as Chamberlain abandoned the Czechs; in Vienna during the Anschluss; in Berlin, when Germany blitzed Poland . . . Shirer was there.

If ever a journalist was at the right place at the right time, it was Shirer. In this second volume of his memoirs, he provides an eyewitness and intensely personal interpretation of Hitler. Shirer knew Goring, Goebbels, Himmler, Hess, Heydrich and Eichmann, and with them often observed Hitler at first hand . . . close enough, he noted, "to kill him."

"*The Nightmare Years* is one of the greatest firsthand accounts ever written about the dramatic origins of WW II." *(Book Forum)*

FREE rental from Books on Tape™
See page 3

TWENTIETH CENTURY JOURNEY: THE START

By William L. Shirer
(1568-A) 6-1½ hour cassettes
Rental—$14.50   Purchase—$48.00
(1568-B) 6-1½ hour cassettes
Rental—$14.50   Purchase—$48.00
Read by Grover Gardner

Born in Chicago just after the turn of the century, raised in Cedar Rapids, William Shirer arrived in Paris when he was 21. His pioneering broadcasts from Nazi Germany and his best-selling books including *The Rise and Fall of the Third Reich* made him famous. *The Start* tells us how a young and unknown midwesterner began his trek toward the pinnacle of his profession.

"Shirer's *20th Century Journey* is rich, evocative history; it is a fascinating memoir, full of superb anecdotes about the great and near great; it is subtle autobiography that modestly offers insights into the process by which a naive American youth became a sophisticated European correspondent and ultimately one of the premier chroniclers and analysts of our time." *(Publisher's Source)*

UP FROM SLAVERY

By Booker T. Washington
(9126) 8-1 hour cassettes
Rental—$14.50   Purchase—$64.00
Read by Walter Covell
A Jimcin Recording

Booker T. Washington's autobiography describes his rise from slavery to national eminence as an educator. Born in 1856, the son of a slave woman and a white man, he became the most influential black leader of his time in the United States.

Washington founded the Tuskegee Institute, a vocational school for blacks in Alabama. An advisor on racial problems and policies for two presidents—Theodore Roosevelt and William Howard Taft—he helped make possible the early appointment of several blacks to federal office.

"A classic, important document of racial self-awareness—a cornerstone as well in the development of white society's awareness of the Negro condition." *(Editorial Review Service)*

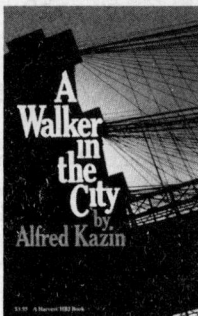

A WALKER IN THE CITY

By Alfred Kazin
(2046) 6-1 hour cassettes
Rental—$12.50   Purchase—$48.00
Read by Michael Prichard

A Walker in the City is a book about an American walking into the world. The American is Alfred Kazin as a young man, and the world he walks into is, first of all, Brownsville in east Brooklyn, a neighborhood then inhabited by Jewish immigrants from eastern Europe, surrounded by the vast alluring "beyond."

"There is certainly no recent autobiographer with so exact and lyric a memory. Before the reader has finished . . . he has come to see the whole texture of life in this tenement realm which is revealed as full of lush and varied richness as an Arabian bazaar . . . " *(The New York Times Book Review)*

Rental Section At-a-Glance

THE WAY OF A TRANSGRESSOR

By Negley Farson
(2098-A) 7-1½ hour cassettes
Rental—$15.50   Purchase—$56.00
(2098-B) 7-1½ hour cassettes
Rental—$15.50   Purchase—$56.00
Read by Ron Shoop

A best seller when it first appeared in 1936 and a book with continuing appeal, *The Way of a Transgressor* is Negley Farson's story of his life as an athlete, aviator and reporter in the early decades of this century. Farson had something to prove: His aristocratic family lost its fortune and he had to make his own. He wanted everything in life, and he pretty nearly got it.

Farson was in France during the first war, in Russia during the revolution. He lived on a houseboat in British Columbia, fished the Caucuses, sold stories to keep alive. He was on a first name basis with most of the men who made headlines under Wilson, Hoover and Roosevelt.

"I know of no international journalist who has written a personal chronicle so exciting, so authentic and romantic, yet so revelatory of what forces have been surging through the world." —Sinclair Lewis

WAYS OF ESCAPE

By Graham Greene
(1589) 7-1½ hour cassettes
Rental—$15.50   Purchase—$56.00
Read by Ian Whitcomb

Graham Greene's unrelenting effort to fight depression and boredom through writing continues in *Ways of Escape,* an autobiographical account of the author's life from the age of 25 to 75.

The book is wonderfully educative reading for any would-be author. It is also an incisive and fascinating travel journal.

Ways of Escape ends with Greene at 75 years of age. His epilogue tells of an individual—"the other"—who has impersonated him in all parts of the globe for 25 years. He ponders whether his imposter is not really himself. His "ways of escape" have proven so successful that the characters he has made so vital for his readers are more real to him than he is to himself.

WEST WITH THE NIGHT

By Beryl Markham
(2096) 7-1½ hour cassettes
Rental—$15.50   Purchase—$56.00
Read by Donada Peters

Beryl Markham was born in England in 1902 but grew up in Kenya. She knew colonial Africa in a way we can only imagine.

Always competitive, Markham started out training race horses. Her interest soon turned to aviation, and she carried mail, passengers and supplies to fields in the Sudan, Kenya and Rhodesia. She flew the Atlantic from east to west, solo, an aviation first. But it is her work as an author that remains.

Hemingway commended her book, but could not have know that this adventurous young woman would speak to a whole new generation. She had the wisdom to write just once, and her book shines with the vitality and intelligence that illuminated her life.

Books of related interest in the B-O-T library include: *Out of Africa* by Isak Dinesen and *Out in the Midday Sun* by Elspeth Huxley.

WHAT SHALL WE WEAR TO THIS PARTY?

By Sloan Wilson
(1033) 12-1½ hour cassettes
Rental—$17.50   Purchase—$96.00
Read by Scott Forbes

Sloan Wilson, author of *The Man in the Gray Flannel Suit,* put a label on middle America during an era in our national passage. *What Shall We Wear to This Party?* holds a mirror up to more current times. Wilson's pen etches the 1930's, student high-jinks at Ivy League colleges, service in "the War," marriage and children, a career at Time, Inc., the inevitable breaking of those bonds, and the painful growth, personal and professional, that lay ahead. This autobiography speaks for Wilson and his generation.

THE WHITE RAJAH

By Nicholas Monsarrat
(1094) 10-1½ hour cassettes
Rental—$16.50   Purchase—$80.00
Read by Richard Green

The White Rajah is based on the life of James Brooke (the White Rajah of Sarawak, 1802-1868). The book's hero, Richard Marriott, is a baronet's illegitimate son who becomes a pirate. In the Dutch East Indies he helps the Rajah of Makassang defeat his priestly enemies. Marriott marries the Rajah's beautiful daughter and in due course assumes the jeweled throne itself. Hardly believable, but it did happen.

THE WINTHROP WOMAN

By Anya Seton
(1357-A) 10-1½ hour cassettes
Rental—$16.50   Purchase—$80.00
(1357-B) 10-1½ hour cassettes
Rental—$16.50   Purchase—$80.00
Read by Penelope Dellaporta

This novel, based on the life of Elizabeth Winthrop, a niece of Governor Winthrop of the Massachusetts Bay Colony, is intensely vivid and alive.

"The Winthrop Woman is that rare literary accomplishment—living history. Really good fictionalized history (like this) often gives closer reality to a period than do factual records." *(Chicago Sunday Tribune)*

Also from Seton: *Devil Water, Green Darkness* and *My Theodosia."*

A WRITER'S CAPITAL

By Louis Auchincloss
(1583) 5-1 hour cassettes
Rental—$11.50   Purchase—$40.00
Read by Justin Hecht

In this exceptional memoir, Louis Auchincloss writes with candor of his early years, and of the people, places and circumstances from which he has drawn his fictional "capital." Examining his growth as a writer, he shares with the listener reflections on family, teachers, mentors and friends, all with the care and precision that we have come to expect from the author of *The Partners, Portrait in Brownstone* and *The Rector of Justin.*

THE YEARS WITH ROSS

By James Thurber
(1040) 8-1 hour cassettes
Rental—$14.50   Purchase—$64.00
Read by Daniel Grace

Ross is Harold Ross, founder of *The New Yorker.* Ross was talented, rude, sensitive, self-pitying and compulsive, but was saved by his sense of quality in writing and writers. Thurber treats Ross with affection, but (as they say) he removes no warts. Thurber himself was one of the pillars on which Ross built *The New Yorker,* and in this book introduces us to the personalities and events from a fabulous era.

ZELDA

By Nancy Milford
(1003) 10-1½ hour cassettes
Rental—$16.50   Purchase—$80.00
Read by Angela Cheyne

In the lives of certain people we catch the echo of an era and in the story of Zelda Sayer Fitzgerald, Scott Fitzgerald's wife and collaborator, Nancy Milford vividly choreographs the twenties. The author wrote this book over a period of several years, when she was a young woman just out of college. Because Zelda is tied to our youthful visions, only a sensitive young artist could have given us such a portrait. It presents Zelda complete, from her radiant beauty and vitality to the pitiful isolation of her later years and a conclusion that is anguishing and tragic.

**TOLL FREE credit card
order line 1-800-626-3333**

MasterCard   VISA

THE ADVENTURES OF HUCKLEBERRY FINN

By Mark Twain
(1062) 7-1½ hour cassettes
Rental—$15.50   Purchase—$56.00
Read by Michael Prichard

The Adventures of Huckleberry Finn recounts the adventures of a boy growing up in the half-settled Missouri of the 1840's. Huck's father was an irresponsible drunk and Huck was left to shift for himself at an early age. He lived by his wits and set in motion projects of great imagination. H.L. Mencken used to read *The Adventures of Huckleberry Finn* once every year, and considered it the finest book ever written by an American author.

THE ADVENTURES OF SHERLOCK HOLMES

By Sir Arthur Conan Doyle
(1109) 7-1½ hour cassettes
Rental—$15.50   Purchase—$56.00
Read by Richard Green

The deerstalker cap and cape-backed coat . . . the calabash pipe . . . the grace of gaslit Victorian London . . . the fog on Baker Street. Such a combination of images can add up to only one conclusion, my dear Watson: the great Sherlock Holmes! Sir Arthur Conan Doyle created one of those fictional characters that escapes the confines of the printed page and becomes "real" to millions of fans. Included on this recording are: "A Scandal in Bohemia," "The Red-Headed League," "A Case of Identity," "The Boscombe Valley Mystery," "The Five Orange Pips," "The Man with the Twisted Lip," "The Adventure of the Blue Carbuncle," "The Speckled Band," "The Engineer's Thumb," "The Noble Bachelor," "The Beryl Coronet" and "The Copper Beeches."

THE ADVENTURES OF TOM SAWYER

By Mark Twain
(1158) 6-1½ hour cassettes
Rental—$14.50   Purchase—$48.00
Read by Michael Prichard

The Adventures of Tom Sawyer is an amusing, nostalgic look at boyhood on the Mississippi River in the mid-nineteenth century, and is based on Mark Twain's memories of his youth in the river town of Hannibal, Missouri. Many of the story's characters and episodes are constructed from the author's early adventures, and Tom Sawyer is probably Mark Twain in mufti. The book is also an insight into Twain's character: he believed that in this complex world innocence was to be found only in the heart of a boy.

ALICE DUGDALE

By Anthony Trollope
(9155) 3-1 hour cassettes
Rental—$9.50   Purchase—$24.00
Read by Sheila Lash
A Jimcin Recording

"Have you ever read novels of Anthony Trollope?" asked Nathaniel Hawthorne. "They precisely suit my taste: solid, substantial, written on the strength of beef and through the inspiration of ale . . . " Trollope was loved by the readers of his day because he portrayed the men and women of the 19th century with affection, understanding, humor and sympathy. *Alice Dugdale* is one of his most sympathetic heroines. Her problem is age-old . . . Major Rossiter doesn't know if he wants a girl intelligent and strong, or one beautiful, fashionable and dull.

ALICE IN WONDERLAND and THROUGH THE LOOKING GLASS

By Lewis Carroll
(9162) 6-1 hour cassettes
Rental—$12.50   Purchase—$48.00
Read by Cindy Hardin
A Jimcin Recording

NEW

Lewis Carroll, who never married, was a minister in the Church of England and professor of mathematics at Christ Church College.

In his diary of July 4, 1862, Carroll described "an expedition up the river to Godstowe with the three Liddells," daughters of the college dean, "on which occasion I told them the fairy tale of 'Alice's Adventures under Ground,' which I undertook to write out for Alice."

That afternoon changed childhood for generations to come. Carroll's talent for mathematical puzzles and paradox, for creating a charming and significant nonsense world, has made *Alice in Wonderland* and *Through the Looking Glass* as much a part of growing up as Mary Janes.

THE AMBASSADORS

By Henry James
(9527) 13-1½ hour cassettes
Rental—$19.50   Purchase—$104.00
Read by Walter Zimmerman
A Jimcin Recording

When Chadwick Newsome lingers too long in Paris, his mother, a wealthy New England widow, sends her fiance, Lambert Strether, to fetch him home. But men are men and Paris after all is Paris. Newsome extends his stay and Strether himself finds Parisian life delightful and intriguing.

Published in 1903, *The Ambassadors* is regarded as a masterpiece of American fiction for its exceptional structure, its moral significance and its depiction of the contrasting New and Old World cultures. Henry James considered this his finest novel.

THE AMERICAN

By Henry James
(9145) 11-1½ hour cassettes
Rental—$18.50   Purchase—$88.00
Read by Jim Killavey
A Jimcin Recording

Leon Edel writes of this novel: "Behind its melodrama and its simple romance is the history of man's dream of better worlds, travel to strange lands, and marriage to high and noble ladies. At the same time the book reveals a deep affection for American innocence and a deep awareness that such innocence carries with it a fund of ignorance. Its novelty lay in its 'international' character, and it is spoken of as the first truly international novel." Henry James was born into a distinguished New York family in 1843. From childhood his interests were more worldly and sophisticated than those held even by his peers. His eyes turned naturally to Europe, where he lived and wrote for a decade before settling in England in 1876.

AMERICAN NOTES

By Charles Dickens
(1042) 7-1½ hour cassettes
Rental—$15.50   Purchase—$56.00
Read by Angela Cheyne

Dickens made three trips to the United States, the first in 1842, when he was 30 and already famous. This book is the result of that trip, and starts dockside in London. It is great history, told in a witty and conversational style. In Dickens' irreverence we trace the first stirrings of our own national literary paternity and acknowledge the debt owed by Twain, Mencken and others to Dickens, the foremost man of letters of his day.

ANNA KARENINA

By Leo Tolstoy
(9531-A) 10-1½ hour cassettes
Rental—$16.50   Purchase—$80.00
(9531-B) 10-1½ hour cassettes
Rental—$16.50   Purchase—$80.00
(9531-C) 10-1½ hour cassettes
Rental—$16.50   Purchase—$80.00
Read by Jill Masters

Tolstoy was born in 1828 to a family of aristocratic landowners and was steeped in the traditions of the Russian nobility.

The story of Anna follows her romance with the young Russian soldier Count Alexey Vronsky. Meeting by chance in Moscow, Vronsky returns with Anna to St. Petersburg, where rumors of their relationship soon reach her husband.

Anna soon learns that moral choices have hard edges. Her education in ethics includes instruction in tragedy and death.

AROUND THE WORLD IN EIGHTY DAYS

By Jules Verne
(9060) 7-1 hour cassettes
Rental—$13.50   Purchase—$56.00
Read by Walter Covell
A Jimcin Recording

One day in the Reformer's Club in London, in 1872, Phileas Fogg takes up a wager to journey round the world in eighty days. He is accompanied by his valet, Passepartout, and a detective named Fix, who has been assigned by the Reformer's Club to observe his movements. Showing fortitude and endless resourcefulness, Fogg and his companions narrowly escape from barbarians, hostile mobs and schemers during their journey. Does Fogg win the bet?

THE ASPERN PAPERS

By Henry James
(9509) 5-1 hour cassettes
Rental—$11.50   Purchase—$40.00
Read by Walter Zimmerman
A Jimcin Recording

The Aspern Papers posits a love affair between Jeffrey Aspern, a romantic poet of the early 19th century, deceased at the time of the story, and a beautiful young woman whom he called "Julianna." In reality, Julianna has become an aged and reclusive spinster, Miss Bordereaux, who lives in seclusion in a barricaded villa in Venice with her niece, Miss Tina. An American editor, the principal character in this story, who is a leading scholar of Jeffrey Aspern, tracks Miss Bordereaux to her Venice redoubt, where he believes she has secreted valuable papers left to her by Jeffrey Aspern. The confrontation between the old world and the new, between European culture and American, Miss Bordereaux and her niece, serve to illustrate James' theme that culture can be neither acquired nor transplanted, but must be grown, one leaf and one branch at a time, in home soil.

THE AWAKENING

By Kate Chopin
(9062) 6-1 hour cassettes
Rental—$13.50   Purchase—$48.00
Read by Walter Zimmerman
A Jimcin Recording

First published in 1899, *The Awakening* shocked its readers because it was so far ahead of its time. It is the story of Edna Pontellier, a lovely young woman who has married into upper class Creole society. She has a well-to-do and surprisingly understanding husband. She also loves and is proud of her sons. Yet within her is a conflicting need for independence and a desire to experience the full potential of life. Unable to control this passion, Edna abandons the decorous and conventional role common to society and makes for herself a controversial and ultimately destructive life.

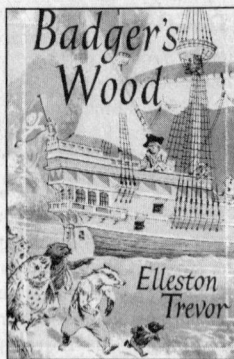

BADGER'S WOOD

By Elleston Trevor
(1689) 4-1 hour cassettes
Rental—$9.50   Purchase—$32.00
Read by Wanda McCaddon

This is a book about the denizens of Deep Wood—Old Stripe the Badger, Potter the Otter, Woo Owl, little Digger Mole and their neighbors of copse and river and treetop.

It is also a book about friendship and courage and individuality—and high adventure. For what starts out as a domestic upset (who broke Potter's wheel and raided Mole's bean patch?) quickly becomes a breathless drama of piracy in which the animals' skill, daring and resourcefulness are put to the test.

Children will enjoy the human quirks and foibles of the adventurers, gobble up the nautical details of boat building, salvage, and midnight raids, and cheer the ending which turns foes into friends.

BARCHESTER TOWERS

By Anthony Trollope
(9523-A) 8-1½ hour cassettes
Rental—$16.50   Purchase—$64.00
(9523-B) 9-1½ hour cassettes
Rental—$17.50   Purchase—$72.00
Read by Walter Zimmerman
A Jimcin Recording

The appointment of a new bishop in the cathedral city of Barchester has left opposing religious factions awash in intrigues and jealousies. This, however, is only the beginning for there are three other persons who intend to wield the real power in the diocese.

Interwoven in this novel is the captivating love story of a young widow who is pursued by a hypocritical priest she despises while ignored by the man she loves.

Barchester Towers is the sequel to *The Warden*, also recorded by Jimcin for B-O-T subscribers.

BARRY LYNDON

By William Makepeace Thackeray
(1026) 8-1½ hour cassettes
Rental—$15.50   Purchase—$64.00
Read by Dan Lazar

Our generation is finding Victorians had more to them than imperialist ambitions and repressed sexuality. Among other things, their novelists treated language with far more precision than our novelists today. Thackeray himself, though troubled by financial insecurity and tormented by his wife's mental illness, was a meticulous wordsmith who infused his characters with life and wit. For that reason, *Barry Lyndon* is one of literature's most believable creations . . . moral scoundrel but mannered gent.

THE BEAST IN THE JUNGLE and Other Stories

By Henry James
(9117) 8-1 hour cassettes
Rental—$15.50   Purchase—$64.00
Read by Donna Barkman
A Jimcin Recording

Henry James is at his best in short story or novella. The reason: no other form demands such discipline and compression.

These three stories treat his favorite subjects. For example, "The Beast in the Jungle" is the tale of a man's habitual obsession with himself and his deserved fate. "An International Episode" contains vignettes of upper-class life in the 1870's. "The Pupil" narrates a son's long history of parental betrayals and rejections.

Henry James was born on April 15, 1843 in New York City. He was part of a distinguished American family that included William James, his brother, later to become famous as a psychologist and philosopher.

BELOVED WAS BAHAMAS: A STEER TO REMEMBER

By Harriet E. Weaver
(1446) 6-1 hour cassettes
Rental—$12.50   Purchase—$48.00
Read by Roses Prichard

In 1964, the magnificent redwood country of Northern California was ravaged by a spectacular flood. *Beloved was Bahamas* is based on a true incident from the historic storm: the amazing rescue of a 900-pound pet steer and its return to its owner, a 15 year-old boy. Harriet E. Weaver tells a dramatic and tender story—about a boy, his pet and the devotion each had for the other.

BENITO CERENO

By Herman Melville
(9035) 4-1 hour cassettes
Rental—$10.50   Purchase—$32.00
Read by John Chatty
A Jimcin Recording

The mysterious, suspenseful *Benito Cereno* is based on a chapter in the journal of a Massachusetts sea captain, Amasa Delano, whose narrative of voyages and travels was published in 1817. In 1799, Captain Delano, commander of an American sealer, seeks shelter in a harbor of an uninhabited island off the coast of Chile. While anchored there, a Spanish merchant ship, the *San Dominick,* comes ghosting through the entrance. Mutiny, escape, pursuit and capture lead to Lima where a trial takes place.

THE BIG BOW MYSTERY

By Israel Zangwell
(9048) 5-1 hour cassettes
Rental—$12.50   Purchase—$40.00
Read by Walter Covell
A Jimcin Recording

Oliver Constance, one of the most dynamic and high-minded orators of his day, is found dead in chambers. No one can tell whether his death is a murder or suicide. A cast—ranging from aesthetes to pragmatists, from charmers to misanthropes, from simpletons to schemers, and from seasoned detectives to Scotland Yard bunglers—knock against each other trying to solve the case. True to form, this mystery hangs fire until the very end.

BLACK BEAUTY

By Anna Sewell
(9058) 6-1 hour cassettes
Rental—$13.50   Purchase—$48.00
Read by John Chatty
A Jimcin Recording

Black Beauty is a well-bred colt, trained to be a gentleman's horse. After a careless accident scars him, Beauty is sold again and again, each time descending lower on the social scales of horse and man. At the last moment he is saved from the knacker by the intervention of two kindly ladies who purchase him. The book ends with Beauty being assured that his life from that point on will be full and content.

THE BOTTLE IMP AND OTHER STORIES

By Robert Lewis Stevenson
(9159) 7-1 hour cassettes
Rental—$14.50   Purchase—$56.00
Read by Jim Killavey and John Chatty
A Jimcin Recording

Robert Lewis Stevenson is best known for adventure stories like *Treasure Island and Dr. Jekyll and Mr. Hyde.* His lucid prose, sense of pace and skill set a new standard for the adventure story and influenced many writers including by his own acknowledgement Graham Greene. Few remember the power of his short stories, but they come across beautifully in this collection. Included are "The Bottle Imp," "The Body Snatcher," "The Beach at Falesa," "A Lodging for the Night" and "Thrawn Janet."

THE BOUNTY TRILOGY—PART I MUTINY ON THE BOUNTY

By Charles Nordhoff and James Norman Hall
(1149-A) 8-1½ hour cassettes
Rental—$15.50   Purchase—$64.00
Read by Jonathan Reese

The Bounty Trilogy is the perfect example of what the historical novel should be—an important historical incident brought to life in a book. This novel retells the story of the mutiny aboard the English vessel *Bounty* on its return voyage from the South Seas in 1789. The first volume describes the actual mutiny against her captain, Mr. Bligh, and the subsequent trial of the mutineers in England.

THE BOUNTY TRILOGY— PARTS II & III MEN AGAINST THE SEA and PITCAIRN'S ISLAND

By Charles Nordhoff and James Norman Hall
(1149-B) 11-1½ hour cassettes
Rental—$17.50   Purchase—$88.00
Read by Jonathan Reese

The second volume, *Men Against the Sea,* is the incredible account of the 3600-mile voyage taken by Captain Bligh and 18 loyal men who were set adrift by the mutineers in the ship's longboat. The third volume, *Pitcairn's Island,* is the narrative of those mutineers who escaped capture and found refuge on an idyllic Pacific Island.

FREE rental from Books on Tape™
See page 3

THE BROTHERS KARAMAZOV

By Fyodor Dostoyevsky
(9161-A) 10-1½ hour cassettes
Rental—$17.50   Purchase—$80.00
(9161-B) 9-1½ hour cassettes
Rental—$17.50   Purchase—$72.00
(9161-C) 9-1½ hour cassettes
Rental—$17.50   Purchase—$72.00
Read by Walter Covell
A Jimcin Recording

Dostoyevsky studied human nature with precision and with passion. He plumbed the depths, his own and others, and never winced at what he found, even when it was beyond his understanding. This extraordinary novel is a recital of his findings, told in the story of four brothers—Dmitri, pleasure-seeking, impatient, unruly; Ivan, brilliant and morose; Alyosha, gentle, loving, honest; and the illegitimate Smerdyakov, sly, silent, cruel. What gives this story its dramatic grip is the part these brothers play in their father's murder. "Dostoyevsky writes like Rembrandt paints. His portraits are so powerful that I judge him to be the greatest of all novelists." —Andre Gide

CALL IT COURAGE

By Armstrong Sperry
(2117) 7-1½ hour cassettes
Rental—$15.50   Purchase—$56.00
Read by Dan Lazar

The Polynesian tradition of courage is as old as the race, so when a chief's son shows fear, the village drives him out. Thus it is that Mafutu, a youth terrified of the sea, sets out on a voyage of discovery.

What he finds, of course, is his courage, and the story of how it comes to him won the Newberry Medal in 1941 as "the year's most distinguished contribution to American literature for children."

Armstrong Sperry wrote books for and about young people. His stories are timeless and absorbing, perfect for family outings or for youngsters who like their heroes believable.

THE CALL OF THE WILD and Other Stories

By Jack London
(9006) 7-1 hour cassettes
Rental—$14.50   Purchase—$56.00
Read by Walter Zimmerman and Jim Roberts
A Jimcin Recording

Buck is a courageous and valiant dog, half St. Bernard and half Scottish shepherd. Kidnapped from his comfortable life on a California estate and thrown into the wild north woods, Buck must fight for survival. He relies more and more on his instincts and turns almost wild. Yet, at one of his worst moments, he receives unexpected kindness from a human and becomes devoted to his new master in a way that is both touching and profound.

CAMILLE

By Alexandre Dumas (the younger)
(9506) 7-1 hour cassettes
Rental—$14.50   Purchase—$56.00
Read by Jim Roberts
A Jimcin Recording

Dumas, the younger, illegitimate son of the gifted father who wrote *The Three Musketeers* and *The Count of Monte Cristo*, gave one immortal work to posterity . . . *Camille*. It achieved fame as a novel, great notoriety as a play, and in its operatic version, adapted by Giuseppe Verdi, it became *La Traviata*.

Camille is the lady of the camellias, Margherita Gauthier, a Parisienne of high fashion who finds real love only in Armando Duval. The two escape to a tranquil country setting, but Armando's father secretly persuades Margherita to give him up. This she does, in a display of sentiment so convincing that Armando takes his leave in high dudgeon, which reduces Margherita to fatal despair. Armando's father relents, but too late, and in one of the tenderest scenes in literature, Armando returns to find her dying.

CANDIDE

By Francois Marie Arouet de Voltaire
(9042) 4-1 hour cassettes
Rental—$10.50   Purchase—$32.00
Read by Jim Roberts
A Jimcin Recording

One of the world's best known satires, *Candide* refutes the optimistic but shallow "All's for the best in this best of all possible worlds." Candide's tutor, the philosophic Dr. Pangloss, embodies this creed, maintaining it in spite of all evidence to the contrary. A standard entry in world lit courses, Candide is as funny and absurd today as when it was written more than 200 years ago.

CAPTAIN BLOOD

By Rafael Sabatini
(1550) 8-1½ hour cassettes
Rental—$15.50   Purchase—$64.00
Read by Dan Lazar

In *Scaramouche* and *Captain Blood,* the two books for which he is best known, Raphael Sabatini created characters struck from the mold of hero—classical swashbucklers full of fire and dash. Peter Blood is a gentlemanly freelance who by a turn of fate becomes prisoner of the English, captive on an island stronghold. His escape and subsequent adventures have captivated generations of readers and in Dan Lazar's narrative take on a new dimension of verisimilitude.

CARMEN AND OTHER STORIES

By Prosper Mérimée
(9090) 4-1 hour cassettes
Rental—$10.50   Purchase—$32.00
Read by Walter Covell
A Jimcin Recording

Prosper Mérimée was born in France in 1803 and died in 1870. He would be unknown to us today except for his story of Carmen, on which Bizet based his opera of the same name.

"Carmen" is a powerful and dramatic story that tells of Don Jose, a handsome young cavalryman, and his love for the beautiful and clever gypsy girl, Carmen. Subscribers who know only the story as they have heard it from Bizet will be delighted with Mérimée's restrained style, and will enjoy equally the other stories in this reading, including "Mateo Falcone," "The Taking of the Redoubt" and "The Venus of Ille," this last an extraordinary ghost tale.

CHILDREN OF THE FROST

By Jack London
(9130) 7-1 hour cassettes
Rental—$14.50   Purchase—$56.00
Read by Walter Zimmerman
A Jimcin Recording

Jack London (1876-1916), one of America's most popular storytellers, drew heavily upon his diverse, often turbulent personal experiences for his enormous output. London grew up in Oakland, was an oyster pirate at 15, a sailor at 17, odd-jobbed everywhere, eventually working up to a prospecting stint in Alaska.

Children of the Frost is a collection of ten stories based entirely upon Indian themes. Like his other books, this one drew immediate praise and continues to be popular today. Particularly good for family groups or younger readers.

THE CHIMES and THE HOLLY TREE

By Charles Dickens
(9501) 5-1 hour cassettes
Rental—$12.50   Purchase—$40.00
Read by Cindy Hardin and Walter Covell
A Jimcin Recording

The Chimes and *The Holly Tree* are two of Dickens' festive stories, and with *A Christmas Carol* form a trilogy. In *The Holly Tree*, the narrator is an old man who relates his Christmas story, which is that he came close to forsaking his bride. Only by a providential snowstorm which confined him to an inn and delayed his departure, was the tragedy prevented. *The Chimes* celebrates New Year's Eve rather than Christmas. It tells us that whatever our state, there is always reason to be grateful.

A CHRISTMAS CAROL

By Charles Dickens
(1897) 3-1 hour cassettes
Rental—$8.50   Purchase—$24.00
Read by Richard Green

This full-length classic is Charles Dickens' famous tale of the tight-fisted Ebenezer Scrooge, who is forced just in time to relearn the meaning of the 'Christmas Spirit.' A family favorite.

CLASSIC GHOST STORIES

By A Collection
(9063) 8-1½ hour cassettes
Rental—$16.50   Purchase—$64.00
Read by Walter Zimmerman and Cindy Hardin
A Jimcin Recording

This potpourri of stories brings us some of the best short mysteries in literature, and contrasts ghost stories of different lands and languages. Titles include: "Mrs. Zant and The Ghost" by Wilkie Collins; "The Red Room" by H.G. Wells; "Old Mrs. Jones" by Clara Riddell; "The Moonlit Road," "The Middle Toe of the Right Foot" and "The Stranger" by Ambrose Bierce; "Green Tea" by Amelia Edwards; "The Signalman" and "The Trial for Murder" by Charles Dickens; "The Apparition of Mrs. Veal" by Daniel Defoe and "The Furnished Room" by O. Henry.

CLASSIC GHOST STORIES—VOL. II

By A Collection
(9113) 7-1½ hour cassettes
Rental—$16.50   Purchase—$56.00
Read by Various Readers
A Jimcin Recording

This second volume offers more of the world's best mysteries and ghost stories. Titles include: "The Hall Bedroom" by Mary E. Wilkins Freeman; "The Story of the Bagman's Uncle" and "The Haunted House" by Charles Dickens; "The Familiar" by Joseph Sheridan LeFanu; "Staley Fleming's Hallucination" and "An Inhabitant of Carcosa" by Ambrose Bierce; "The Old Nurse's Story" by Elizabeth Guskell; "The Philosophy of Relative Existences" by Frank Stockton; "The Phantom Hag" by Guy de Maupassant; "The Doll's Ghost" by F. Marion Crawford; "Hertford O'Donnell's Warning" by Charlotte Riddell; "Ghost Story" by E.T. Hoffmann; "A Ghost Story" by Mark Twain; "The Canterville Ghost" by Oscar Wilde; "The Phantom Woman," "The Spectre Bride" and "The Old Mansion"—all three anonymous.

CLASSIC GHOST STORIES—VOL. III

By A Collection
(9122) 8-1½ hour cassettes
Rental—$16.50   Purchase—$64.00
Read by Various Readers
A Jimcin Recording

Our third volume contains a lucky thirteen of the world's best mystery and ghost stories. Titles include: "Mr. Justice Harbottle" by J.S. LeFanu; "The Seventh Man" by Arthur Quiller-Couch; "Some Haunted Houses" by Ambrose Bierce; "Miss Dulane and My Lord" by Wilkie Collins; "The Tapestried Chamber" by Sir Walter Scott; "The Open Door" by Margaret Oliphant; "The Ghostly Rental" and "Sir Edmond Orme" by Henry James; "Eveline's Visitant" by Elizabeth Braddon; "The Dead Woman's Photograph," anonymous; "Conn Kilrea" by Mrs. J.H. Riddell; "The Castle of the King" by Bram Stoker; and "The Ghost, The Gallant, The Gael and the Goblin" by W.S. Gilbert.

THE COMPLETE GHOST STORIES OF CHARLES DICKENS

Edited by Peter Haining
(2000) 12-1½ hour cassettes
Rental—$17.50   Purchase—$96.00
Read by Jill Masters

Charles Dickens' fascination with ghosts and the macabre is traced to his childhood, to the grim and goulish stories told him by his nursemaid, Mary Weller, whom he referred to as Mercy, "though she had none on me." Along with the horrors of the "penny dreadful" magazine, *The Terrific Register*—a publication which made Dickens "unspeakably miserable and frightened the very wits out of my head"—the stories recounted by Weller were so powerful as to color Dickens' imagination and shape much of the enduring fiction he created.

In this collection, Peter Haining brings together all Dickens' ghost stories—twenty in all—including several long-lost tales. From the blood-curdling story of "Captain Murderer and the Devil's Bargain" to the revelation of "The Single-Man," from "A Christmas Carol" to "The Queer Chair" to the "Madman's Manuscript"—here are chilling histories of coincidence, insanity and revenge.

**Give a Books on Tape™
Gift Certificate
Call 1-800-626-3333**

CONFESSIONS OF AN ENGLISH OPIUM-EATER

NEW

By Thomas De Quincey
(9173) 4-1 hour cassettes
Rental—$10.50   Purchase—$32.00
Read by Jim Killavey
A Jimcin Recording

Thomas De Quincey (1785-1859) is a central figure of English Romanticism. *Confessions of an English Opium-Eater,* his best-known work, is an account of his early life and opium addiction. It is prose which is by turns witty, conversational and nightmarish.

De Quincy lived his full three score years and ten. But few would have predicted it, for his father and numerous of his siblings were carried off by tuberculosis. He owed his survival to opium: its powers kept the disease at bay, but in trade it kept De Quincy its slave.

When the physical life hangs by a thread, nature often compensates with another gift. With him, it was intellect and this offering is on the best-seller list to this day.

A CONNECTICUT YANKEE IN KING ARTHUR'S COURT

By Mark Twain
(1192) 10-1½ hour cassettes
Rental—$16.50   Purchase—$80.00
Read by Michael Prichard

The tale begins when the "yankee," a skilled mechanic in a 19th century New England arms factory, is struck on the head during a quarrel, and awakens to find himself being taken as a prisoner to the Camelot of 528 A.D. With his 19th century know-how, the "yankee" sets out to modernize the Kingdom, but is opposed by a jealous court magician. Clever enough, but buried beneath Twain's humor is a serious social satire.

THE COSSACKS

By Leo Tolstoy
(9103) 8-1 hour cassettes
Rental—$15.50   Purchase—$64.00
Read by Walter Zimmerman
A Jimcin Recording

The Cossacks is one of the finest portrayals in all Russian literature. Written in part in 1852 while Tolstoy was serving in the army of the Caucasus (though not published until 1862 . . . three years before the first installment of his epic *War and Peace*), this novel is rich in the descriptions of that superb region.

In a uniquely Russian form, this story is the old romantic European drama of "The Noble Savage." The young hero, Olenin, an educated aristocrat like Tolstoy, comes to the Caucasus to find himself. Olenin falls in love with a young Cossack girl, Maryanka, She shreds his cherished control and refinement, and the desires she awakes in him take his emotions by storm.

THE COUNTRY OF THE POINTED FIRS

By Sarah Orne Jewett
(9077) 5-1 hour cassettes
Rental—$12.50   Purchase—$40.00
Read by Cindy Hardin
A Jimcin Recording

This superlative work by Sarah Orne Jewett, a late 19th century writer, shows great literary skill, artistry and charm. *The Country of the Pointed Firs* depicts the close personal and family relationships in a small New England village. In its appreciation of the natural beauty and restorative powers of a small community, it is similar to Thoreau's *Walden*.

Ahead of its time with an important social message, and written in the careful prose that marked 19th century literature, *The Country of the Pointed Firs* is an exciting and memorable narrative creation.

CRIME AND PUNISHMENT

By Fyodor Dostoevsky
(9120-A) 9-1½ hour cassettes
Rental—$17.50   Purchase—$72.00
(9120-B) 8-1½ hour cassettes
Rental—$16.50   Purchase—$64.00
Read by Walter Zimmerman
A Jimcin Recording

No work of literary fiction exceeds *Crime and Punishment* for its evocation of the deepest essence of tragedy, pity and terror.

Raskolnikov, a student in St. Petersburg, murders an old woman, a money-lender, and her sister to prove his theory that violence purifies the strong. But no sooner is the deed done than Raskolnikov's remorse lays siege to his resolve. What follows is one of the greatest psychological studies in world literature.

B-O-T has also recorded Dostoevsky's *Notes from the Underground.*

THE CRIME OF SYLVESTRE BONNARD

By Anatole France
(9522) 8-1 hour cassettes
Rental—$15.50   Purchase—$64.00
Read by Walter Covell
A Jimcin Recording

Anatole France (1844-1924) got a foot into two cultures as well as two centuries. But even at his best he never quite made it into English, and his ideas and style reflect a culture other than our own.

What France did well was to write about people. He had great sympathy and warmth, and his writing reflects this. Thus he is able to take Sylvestre Bonnard, a retiring philologist and almost an anti-hero, and involve us successfully in the significant minutiae of his life.

THE CRUISE OF THE DAZZLER

By Jack London
(9170) 4-1 hour cassettes
Rental—$10.50   Purchase—$32.00
Read by Jim Killavey
A Jimcin Recording

NEW

When Joe Bronson runs away to sea, he finds other members of the crew are about to launch a violent attack. It's the last thing he needs, and it makes him wonder what he's doing in a situation like this.

Jack London was born in California in 1876. When he was a boy, he joined oyster pirates on San Francisco Bay. At 17 he shipped out as a seaman. By 24 he was writing for magazines; at 30 he was famous.

The Call of the Wild, White Fang and *Martin Eden* are other Jack London selections recorded by Books on Tape. London's biography, *Sailor on Horseback* by Irving Stone, is also available.

DAISY MILLER and THE REAL THING

By Henry James
(9520) 4-1 hour cassettes
Rental—$10.50   Purchase—$32.00
Read by Walter Zimmerman
A Jimcin Recording

Henry James was as careful about naming his characters as are brand-new parents. His innocent young heroine, a blossom of American civilization, reminded him of the wildflowers that covered the American fields in June . . . hardy and bright, but uncultivated.

James created Daisy as a "child of nature and freedom." She deliberately defied European conventions and for her troubles became the literary toast of two continents. Not incidentally, she made her creator instantly famous.

The Real Thing, published in 1892, is one of James' most reprinted tales; a fable of the reality of the imagination and the insubstantiality of the "real."

DAVID COPPERFIELD

By Charles Dickens
(1076-A) 10-1½ hour cassettes
Rental—$16.50   Purchase—$80.00
(1076-B) 12-1½ hour cassettes
Rental—$17.50   Purchase—$96.00
Read by Angela Cheyne

It is not surprising that Charles Dickens thought of *David Copperfield* as his "favorite child": the book is Dickens' most autobiographical novel. The author drew many of the story's unique characters from his family and acquaintances. Numerous adventures in David's life are also products of Dickens' youthful experiences.

Dickens lived a life much like "Copperfield." He came from a large family submerged in poverty and won his way up by great energy and effort. Thus the story has power and compassion and lives today as it did when it emerged fresh from the pen of its author.

THE DEATH OF IVAN ILYICH and MASTER AND MAN

By Leo Tolstoy
(9059) 5-1 hour cassettes
Rental—$12.50   Purchase—$40.00
Read by Walter Zimmerman
A Jimcin Recording

The Death of Ivan Ilyich is a masterpiece of 19th century fiction. Its conclusion, which triumphantly shows the bond between the dying man and his family, celebrates the enormous gaps that can be closed by love and understanding.

Master and Man is one of Tolstoy's best stories. It has the added fascination of keeping us in suspense to the end. The merchant Brekhunov attempts to save his servant, a task he approaches as if it were a business deal—what benefits his servant will also benefit him. However, things do not work out entirely as he plans, and the story takes on a larger significance.

THE DEERSLAYER

By James Fenimore Cooper
(9529-A) 8-1½ hour cassettes
Rental—$16.50   Purchase—$64.00
(9529-B) 8-1½ hour cassettes
Rental—$16.50   Purchase—$64.00
Read by Walter Zimmerman
A Jimcin Recording

In this epic set in the wilds of colonial New York, a 20 year-old frontiersman, Natty Bumppo, brought up among the Delaware Indians and known as Leather Stocking, helps defend a settler's family during the warfare between the Delawares and the Hurons.

This is the first of Cooper's Leather-Stocking tales in terms of the hero's personal chronology—last in point of publication. Cooper's fame as a novelist rests on these five works of the Leather-Stocking series which give a broad and noble picture of the woodsman and the Indian.

Also available on B-O-T is Cooper's *The Spy.*

DR. JEKYLL AND MR. HYDE

By Robert Louis Stevenson

and THE TURN OF THE SCREW

By Henry James
(1070) 7-1 hour cassettes
Rental—$13.50   Purchase—$56.00
Read by Angela Cheyne

Dr. Jekyll and Mr. Hyde is the story of a wealthy physician who, with the help of chemical formulations, as a young man begins to live a double life. Yet in completing this transformation Dr. Jekyll unleashes the dark, evil side of his nature, as manifested in Mr. Hyde. Alas, the alter ego is not only hideous and compelling, but ultimately fatal.

The Turn of The Screw is a story of evil more refined. Two children see apparitions; these visions corrupt them but leave the question . . . are the apparitions evil, or the children themselves?

THE DOOR IN THE WALL AND OTHER STORIES

By H.G. Wells
(1472) 5-1 hour cassettes
Rental—$11.50   Purchase—$40.00
Read by Justin Hecht

"The Door in the Wall" is the story of a promising public figure used up by his job and obsessed by a vision (or experience?) of an enchanted garden he had known as a child. It is a tale all of us know, the attempt to recover a period when our lives were simpler and complications lay far in the future.

Other titles are: "The Star," "A Dream of Armageddon," "The Cone," "A Moonlight Fable," "The Diamond Maker," "The Lord of the Dynamos," and Wells' durably celebrated story of true freedom and the human spirit: "The Country of the Blind."

DRACULA

By Bram Stoker
(1391) 10-1½ hour cassettes
Rental—$16.50   Purchase—$80.00
Read by Charles Garst

A young Englishman is bound for the remote castle of an obscure count whose estates are folded deep in the mountains of Transylvania. He travels by carriage, staying the nights at rustic inns.

It is 100 years ago, and time is frozen in a winter that knows no release. Heavy snows bog the road, slowing and finally stopping the carriage. Wolves suddenly materialize from the forest, terrifying horses and passenger. Only the driver remains impassive: by superior will he forces the animals back. On plunge the travelers, deeper into the darkness, the woods, the unknown.

First published in 1897, *Dracula* has become synonymous with perversion and evil.

EMMA

By Jane Austen
(9124) 13-1½ hour cassettes
Rental—$19.50   Purchase—$104.00
Read by Jill Masters
A Jimcin Recording

Full of irony, this comedy of manners satirizes the self-deceptions of vanity. *Emma* presents a picture of mixed family and social life as did *Pride and Prejudice,* though mellowed by a riper humor.

Emma is recognizable as a vamp, a pretty and capricious young woman who defines the limits of reality by banging against them. Because Jane Austen shares with us her sense of Emma's pretensions, we are amused and tolerant of this foolish but ripening girl.

"Emma equals *Pride and Prejudice* in its rich humor and vivid portraiture of character. It is a never ending delight in human absurdities, which the fascinated reader shares from chapter to chapter." *(Readers Digest of Books)*

THE ETERNAL HUSBAND

By Fyodor Dostoevsky
(9139) 6-1 hour cassettes
Rental—$13.50   Purchase—$48.00
Read by Jim Killavey
A Jimcin Recording

Fyodor Dostoevsky, 19th century Russian novelist, is one of the towering figures of world literature.

The Eternal Husband is a psychological study of a betrayed husband who seeks revenge on his wife's seducer. In this title Dostoevsky once again with rare psychological and philosophical insight plumbs the depths and complexities of the human soul.

ETHAN FROME

By Edith Wharton
(1381) 4-1 hour cassettes
Rental—$9.50   Purchase—$32.00
Read by Wanda McCaddon

Considered to be the finest of Edith Wharton's many novels and short stories, *Ethan Frome* departs from her usual milieu of fashionable turn-of-the-century society to evolve, in its author's words, "the lonely lives in half-deserted New England villages, before the coming of the motor and the telephone."

This is the tragic story of three such lives, those of the young farmer, Ethan Frome; his wife, Zenobia (Zeena); and Mattie Silver, Zeena's cousin, whom Ethan loves. The grim irony of their fate is unraveled by way of flashback which illustrates for us a tragedy of misspent lives and wasted talent. Ethan Frome, with his 19th century values, is slowly being crushed by a 20th century which has no use for him.

THE EUROPEANS

By Henry James
(9086) 7-1 hour cassettes
Rental—$14.50   Purchase—$56.00
Read by Diane Burroughs
A Jimcin Recording

Henry James was born in 1843 and lived until 1916. He was a dominant figure in American letters, and rose above the wealth and affluence of his inherited circumstances to build for himself a meaningful life as one of our greatest prose stylists.

The Europeans concerns an expatriate American, Eugenia, and her artist brother, Felix Young. Eugenia is the morganatic wife of a German prince, but she is to be repudiated in favor of a state marriage; thus she leaves for Boston to make an appropriate match of her own.

EVE'S RANSOM

By George Gissing
(9095) 7-1 hour cassettes
Rental—$14.50   Purchase—$56.00
Read by Jill Masters
A Jimcin Recording

George Gissing was an "author's author," widely discussed and intimately known by the literary greats of his era. But his popular following was small and his books never achieved wide circulation or the popularity they merit.

Eve's Ransom, written in 1895, is the story of a bizarre triangle of love. An educated but unsuccessful man, Hilliard, is trapped in grimy Birmingham until he receives a modest windfall, totally unexpected. He goes in search of a woman whose picture he had seen in his landlady's photo album . . . A sure formula for disaster.

THE EXTRAORDINARY ADVENTURES OF ARSÈNE LUPIN

By Maurice Leblanc
(9097) 6-1 hour cassettes
Rental—$13.50   Purchase—$48.00
Read by Walter Covell
A Jimcin Recording

Maurice Leblanc, a writer of detective fiction in the first quarter of this century, created Arsène Lupin, a sort of French Robin Hood. An inventive genius, a master of disguise and an accomplished actor, Lupin operates only in the choice chateaux and salons. He scorns sham and with great disdain leaves his card in a baron's residence. The card reads "Arsène Lupin, gentleman-burglar, will return when the furniture is genuine."

The stories include: "The Arrest of Arsene Lupin," "Arsène Lupin in Person," "The Escape of Arsène Lupin," "The Mysterious Traveller," "The Queen's Necklace," "The Seven of Hearts," "Madame Imbert's Safe," "The Black Pearl" and "Sherlock Holmes Arrives Too Late."

THE EYES OF THE PANTHER
and Other Stories

By Ambrose Bierce
(9121) 4-1 hour cassettes
Rental—$10.50   Purchase—$32.00
Read by Walter Zimmerman and
Donna Barkman
A Jimcin Recording

Ambrose Bierce overlapped Edgar Allan Poe and Oscar Wilde. He matched Poe for the macabre, Wilde for the perverse. He disappeared in Mexico in 1913 when he was 71, a suitable close to a paradoxical career.

This collection contains nine of " . . . Bierce's keenly-crafted short stories and fables [and] substantiate his turn-of-the-century popularity as master of the macabre." *(Booklist)*

Titles include "The Eyes of the Panther," "A Watcher by the Dead," "The Death of Halpern Frayser," "Moxon's Master," "Mysterious Disappearances," "The Suitable Surroundings," "The Famous Gilson Bequest" and "The Secret of Macarger's Gulch."

FAR FROM THE MADDING CROWD

By Thomas Hardy
(9138) 12-1½ hour cassettes
Rental—$17.50 Purchase—$96.00
Read by Jill Masters

Thomas Hardy brings us an England that once existed but is no more. It is rural, traditional, pastoral—a society of mannered conduct that flows like a deep river where powerful currents eddy and swirl.

"In this powerful novel of love and disillusion, Hardy's heroine is torn between the three men in her life. Passionate but capricious, her romantic involvements have fascinated generations of readers." *(Book Review Service)*

FATHERS AND SONS

By Ivan Turgenev
(9053) 8-1 hour cassettes
Rental—$15.50 Purchase—$64.00
Read by Walter Zimmerman
A Jimcin Recording

This book deals with Russia in transition from a formal and authoritarian society to one where all beliefs and relationships are questioned. Young people are at the intellectual throats of their parents, who of course fail to understand what is happening. Turgenev coined the word "nihilist" to describe Basarov, the young man who dominates *Fathers and Sons*. Basarov's facade is revolutionary, but his heart is not. The warmth of his nature triumphs over the chill of his intellect, and Basarov emerges as one of the most rounded and successful characters in all literature.

FAVORITE CHILDREN'S STORIES

By A Collection
(9104) 8-1 hour cassettes
Rental—$15.50 Purchase—$64.00
Read by Various Readers
A Jimcin Recording

The title says it all! The 26 stories are: "Dick Whittington and His Cat," "Hok Lee and the Dwarfs," "The Magic Swan," "Childe Roland," "The Happy Prince," "The Remarkable Rocket" and "The Selfish Giant" by Oscar Wilde, "The Magic Wishbone" by Charles Dickens. "The Well of the World's End," "The Story of the Three Bears," "The Six Sillies" and "Squirrel Nutkin" by Beatrix Potter, "The King of the Golden River" by John Rushkin, "How the Whale Got His Throat," "The Beginning of the Armadillos," "The Elephant's Child" and "The Cat that Walked by Himself" by Rudyard Kipling; "The Gorgon's Head" by Nathaniel Hawthorne; "The Fisherman and his Wife," "The Twelve Dancing Princesses," "The Bremen Town Musicians" and "The Six Servants" by the brothers Grimm; "The Emperor's New Clothes," "The Tinder Box," "The Ugly Duckling" and "The Wild Swans" by Hans Christian Andersen. [Note: Restricted to sales and rentals in the U.S.]

THE FIRST MEN IN THE MOON

By H.G. Wells
(9511) 8-1 hour cassettes
Rental—$15.50 Purchase—$64.00
Read by Walter Covell
A Jimcin Recording

Wells was born in England in 1866. He was trained as a scientist, specifically as a biologist, and in his long lifetime became a historian and novelist as well as the father of modern science fiction.

The First Men in the Moon is the story of two men: Bedford, the narrator of the tale, and Cavor, the somewhat absent-minded scientist. They reach the moon; the inhabitants attack them; one man escapes back to earth.

FIRST PERSON RURAL and SECOND PERSON RURAL

By Noel Perrin
(1434) 8-1 hour cassettes
Rental—$14.50 Purchase—$64.00
Read by Bob Erickson

Noel Perrin is a teacher, writer and farmer. He was a Guggenheim Fellow and Fulbright Professor at Warsaw University, Poland. For the past 15 years he has subsisted handily on a Vermont farm.

Because he was transplanted from New York 15 years ago, Perrin has something to tell us city folk about the transition and he does it in a fresh and very funny way. In addition to these two books, Perrin has written for *The New Yorker*, *Country Journal* and *Vermont Life*.

THE FOOD OF THE GODS

By H.G. Wells
(9079) 6-1½ hour cassettes
Rental—$15.50 Purchase—$48.00
Read by Walter Covell
A Jimcin Recording

It all began with the research of two scientists, Mr. Bensington and Professor Redwood, into the principles of growth in living matter. The fruit of their labors was a substance known as Herakleophorbia IV, but their own private term for it was "The Food of the Gods," because of its very special properties.

Their tests produced a day-old chicken as big as a buzzard. And when the substance was consumed by rats, they grew bigger than horses. Then they started feeding the "food" to babies . . .

THE FOUR MILLION

By O. Henry
(9026) 6-1 hour cassettes
Rental—$13.50 Purchase—$48.00
Read by Various Readers
A Jimcin Recording

O. Henry was the pseudonym for William Sydney Porter, master of the short story. His empathy ran deep and he wrote in the language of the man in the street.

The Four Million was published in 1906. It takes inspiration from the then population of New York, our capital city, and serves up slices of the Big Apple, frequently humorous. The promise of a new century energizes everyone from Eastside tenement dwellers to the denizens of Fifth Avenue.

FRANKENSTEIN

By Mary Shelley
(1301) 8-1 hour cassettes
Rental—$14.50 Purchase—$64.00
Read by Dan Lazar

At 166 plus, *Frankenstein* is still going strong. This "King of the Monster" stories is all the more remarkable because it was written by a young woman, the 21-year-old bride of Percy Bysshe Shelley.

FROM THE EARTH TO THE MOON

By Jules Verne
(9020) 5-1 hour cassettes
Rental—$12.50 Purchase—$40.00
Read by Jim Roberts
A Jimcin Recording

Although *From the Earth to the Moon* was written in the 1860's, Jules Verne foresaw space launches from a desolate part of Florida, and he was in many ways accurate about the speeds and times involved for such flights. Verne understood the difficulties of space travel. His solutions are resourceful and alive with details. In addition, the story is good-natured satire of popular myths about America—thus the book is not only futuristic but historic as well.

FROSTY: A RACCOON TO REMEMBER and INDOMITABLE

By Harriet E. Weaver
(1445) 5-1½ hour cassettes
Rental—$12.50   Purchase—$40.00
Read by Roses Prichard

For 20 years Harriet Weaver was the only female ranger in California's Big Basin Redwood Park. A month-old orphaned coon kit, Frosty, became her boisterous charge. Impish, intelligent, and above all, mischievous, the newcomer made each day a challenge and a celebration of life.

Indomitable was a salmon—a member of Prairie Creek Hatchery's Class of '64. Then the entire class vanished from the watershed. Their disappearance remained a mystery until a morning of utter amazement two months later.

THE GAMBLER

By Fyodor Dostoevsky
(9136) 7-1 hour cassettes
Rental—$14.50   Purchase—$56.00
Read by Walter Zimmerman
A Jimcin Recording

In *The Gambler*, Dostoevsky writes from the point of view of an addict about his own addiction. Dostoevsky himself was no stranger to passionate commitments, whether voluntary or not. Thus he was ideally suited to tell this story with sympathy and understanding. The heroine of *The Gambler* is modeled after the tempestuous Apollinaria Suslov—Dostoevsky's mistress.

"It is impossible to appreciate Dostoevsky without sampling his entire range. Moreover, many of his shorter works are masterpieces in their own right. *The Gambler* is an excellent example." *(Editorial Review Serivce)*

THE GHOST OF GUIR HOUSE

By Charles Willing Beale
(9089) 5-1 hour cassettes
Rental—$12.50   Purchase—$40.00
Read by Jim Roberts
A Jimcin Recording

The Ghost of Guir House is a tale of the supernatural written in 1895. The author owned a successful hotel-resort in North Carolina Beale was a convivial host; one of his customs was to tell ghost stories in the evenings on the veranda.

In this story, Paul Henley, a New Yorker, receives a misdirected letter from a young woman addressed to a "P. Henley." The intended addressee is recently deceased, but apparently had long correspondence with the lady. In her letter she suggests they finally meet.

Paul travels to a remote Carolina siding where he meets the beautiful and fascinating Dorothy Guir.

"Eerie, strange and remarkably believable." (Publishers Reviews)

GHOST STORIES OF AN ANTIQUARY

By Montague Rhodes James
(9052) 5-1 hour cassettes
Rental—$12.50   Purchase—$40.00
Read by Walter Covell
A Jimcin Recording

These tales of the supernatural surpass most in the malevolence of their plots, and the vindictiveness of the ghosts, who have the uncomfortable habit of operating in the daytime. Stories include: "Canon Alberic's Scrapbook"; "The Mezzotint"; "The Ash Tree"; "Number 13"; "Count Magnus"; "Oh, Whistle, and I'll Come to You, My Lad"; "Lost Hearts" and "The Treasure of Abbot Thomas." We need hardly say that these stories are best listened to in daylight, so you can see the ghosts when they come to get you!

THE GOD OF HIS FATHERS

By Jack London
(9098) 6-1 hour cassettes
Rental—$13.50   Purchase—$48.00
Read by John Chatty
A Jimcin Recording

Jack London is best known for his novels, but short stories got him started. He drew on his experiences in Alaska and the far North for inspiration.

In addition to "The God of his Fathers," this volume includes "The Great Interrogation," "Which Men Remember," "Siwash," "The Man with the Gash," "Jan the Unrepentant," "Grit of Women," "Where the Trail Forks," "A Daughter of Aurora," "At the Rainbow's End" and "The Scorn of Women."

GREAT AMERICAN ESSAYS

By A Collection
(9134) 7-1 hour cassettes
Rental—$14.50   Purchase—$56.00
Read by Walter Covell, Walter Zimmerman and Jim Killavey
A Jimcin Recording

The essay has lost out in recent years to anchormen and the op-ed page, but in its prime it packed a wallop.

This collection includes: Ralph Waldo Emerson's "Self-Reliance"; Henry David Thoreau's "Walking" and "Civil Disobedience"; Mark Twain's "Hunting the Deceitful Turkey" and "Reply to a Begging Letter"; and Thomas Paine's "The American Crisis."

Other titles are: Alexander Hamilton's "The Union and Its New Constitution"; P.T. Barnum's "The Art of Publicity"; John Burroughs' "A Life of Fear"; Bradford Torry's "A Short Month"; Eugene Field's "Other People's Dogs"; and James Russell Lowell's "Abraham Lincoln."

GREAT AMERICAN SHORT STORIES

By A Collection
(9054) 7-1½ hour cassettes
Rental—$16.50   Purchase—$56.00
Read by Various readers
A Jimcin Recording

This collection of favorite short stories by America's greatest writers provides a standard against which to judge current examples of the short story form. Selections include: "Bartleby the Scrivener" by Herman Melville; "The Blue Hotel" and "The Open Boat" by Stephen Crane; "The Minister's Black Veil" and "The Ambitious Guest" by Nathaniel Hawthorne; "The One Million Pound Bank Note" and "Baker's Bluejay Yarn" by Mark Twain; "The Princess and the Puma" by O. Henry; "Under the Lion's Paw" by Hamlin Garland; "The Law of Life" by Jack London; "An Occurrence at Owl Creek Bridge" and "The Man and the Snake" by Ambrose Bierce; "Paul's Case" by Willa Cather; "MS Found in a Bottle by Edgar Allan Poe; "The Outcast of Poker Flat" and "Tennessee's Partner" by Bret Harte.

Books on Tape™'s service is 100% guaranteed

GREAT AMERICAN SHORT STORIES VOL. II

By A Collection
(9111) 7-1½ hour cassettes
Rental—$16.50 Purchase—$56.00
Read by Various Readers
A Jimcin Recording

Our second volume of classic short stories includes the following titles: "Marjorie Daw" by Thomas Bailey Aldrich; "The Mc-Williams and the Burglar Alarm" and "Mrs. McWilliams and the Lightning" by Mark Twain; "The Phonograph and the Graft" and "The Lotus and the Bottle" by O. Henry; "The Wild Horse of Tartary" by Clara Morris; "The Legend of the Rose of the Alhambra" and "The Phantom Island" by Washington Irving; "The Great Stone Face" and "My Kinsman, Major Molineau" by Nathaniel Hawthorne; "Chickamauga" and "The Coup de Grace" by Ambrose Bierce; "The Premature Burial" and "The Oblong Box" by Edgar Allan Poe; "A Mystery of Heroism" by Stephen Crane; "The Descent of Man" by Edith Wharton; "The Boy Who Drew Cats" by Lafcadio Hearn; and "The Altar of the Dead" by Henry James.

GREAT AMERICAN SHORT STORIES VOL. III

By A Collection
(9114) 7-1½ hour cassettes
Rental—$16.50 Purchase—$$56.00
Read by Various readers
A Jimcin Recording

This popular collection contains the following titles: "The Bride Comes to Yellow Sky" by Stephen Crane; "Mrs. Higgonbotham's Catastrophe" and "The Birthmark" by Nathaniel Hawthorne; "Editha" by William Dean Howells; "The Courting of Sister Wisby" by Sarah Orne Jewett; "The Damned Thing" and "Beyond the Wall" by Ambrose Bierce; "The Gold Bug" by Edgar Allan Poe; "Jimmy Rose" and "The Fiddler" by Herman Melville; "The Stout Gentleman" by Washington Irving; "Even Unto Death" by Jack London; "Louisa" by Mary E. Wilkins Freeman; "Mliss" by Bret Harte; "The Bar Sinister" by Richard Harding Davis; "The Ghostly Kiss" by Lafcadio Hearn; and "The Californian's Tale" by Mark Twain.

GREAT EXPECTATIONS

By Charles Dickens
(1075) 12-1½ hour cassettes
Rental—$17.50 Purchase—$96.00
Read by Angela Cheyne

Considered by critics to be among Dicken's best-constructed stories, *Great Expectations* deals with a major theme of the Victorian social novel: the hero's movement upward through the class structure. Pip, an orphan, helps an escaped prisoner hiding in a marsh. Miss Havisham, an eccentric recluse, is deserted on her wedding day. From these two events, Dickens weaves an unusual story of gratitude set on by vindictiveness.

GREAT FRENCH and RUSSIAN STORIES

By A Collection
(9055) 7-1½ hour cassettes
Rental—$16.50 Purchase—$56.00
Read by Walter Zimmerman, Cindy Hardin and Jim Roberts
A Jimcin Recording

This collection provides a wide selection of literary masterworks from the 19th century. Stories describe conditions in France and Russia at the time, provide unique insights into human nature and are a continuing source of entertainment. Titles include: "Love," "Regret," "A Piece of String," "The Necklace," "The False Jewels," "Useless Beauty," "In the Moonlight" and "Love's Awakening" by Guy de Maupassant; "The Thief" and "The Wedding" by Fyodor Dostoevsky; "The Mysterious Mansion" and "Christ in Flanders" by Honore de Balzac; "The Kiss" and "The Lottery Ticket" by Anton Chekov; "The Overcoat" by Nicolai Gogol; "Zodmirsky's Duel" by Alexander Dumas; "The Shot" by Alexander Pushkin and "The Long Exile" by Leo Tolstoy.

GREAT FRENCH AND RUSSIAN SHORT STORIES— VOL. II

By A Collection
(9119) 8-1½ hour cassettes
Rental—$16.50 Purchase—$64.00
Read by Walter Zimmerman
A Jimcin Recording

Our first collection proved so popular that we recorded another. This second volume offers 18 works by important 19th century French and Russian writers. Titles include: "Where Love is, There God is Also," "How Much Land Does a Man Need?" and "The Raid" by Leo Tolstoy; "The Queen of Spades," "The Blizzard" and "Lady into Lassie" by Alexander Pushkin; "Boule de Suif," "How He Got the Legion of Honor," "Waiter, A Bock!," "The Signal," "Growing Old," "Consideration" and "The Hole" by Guy de Maupassant; "A Simple Soul" by Gustave Flaubert; "The Dream of a Ridiculous Man" by Fyodor Dostoevsky; "The Woman and the Cat" by Marcel Prevost; "A Piece of Bread" by Francois Coppee; and "The Last Lesson" by Alphonse Daudet.

GREEN MANSIONS

By W.H. Hudson
(9069) 6-1½ hour cassettes
Rental—$15.50 Purchase—$48.00
Read by Jim Roberts
A Jimcin Recording

W.H. Hudson was born in 1841 in Buenos Aires and seems to have been a sort of permanent displaced person. He moved to London in 1869 and wrote a series of remarkable books, most with a wilderness background.

In 1904, when he was 63, he focused on an Indian legend and gave us *Green Mansions*, a memorable romance of the jungle, and the book by which he is now chiefly remembered.

GULLIVER'S TRAVELS

By Jonathan Swift
(9174) 8-1½ hour cassettes
Rental—$16.50 Purchase—$64.00
Read by Walter Covell
A Jimcin Recording

Swift was trained for the Church but for years did not achieve a suitable post. He supported himself as a private secretary.

The break came with the publication of *A Tale of a Tub*, published in 1704 when Swift was 37. He continued to draw a living from minor church positions, but increasingly gained recognition for his writing.

Swift went to England as a political journalist for the Tories. But on the death of George I in 1714, he returned to Ireland, much scorned. He retreated into church work, gradually recovered his spirits and in 1725 published *Gulliver's Travels*, his best known title.

For a fascinating biography of Swift, please ask for the Books on Tape recording of *Jonathan Swift: Major Prophet* by A.L. Rowse.

HARD TIMES

By Charles Dickens
(9528) 9-1/2 hour cassettes
Rental—$17.50   Purchase—$72.00
Read by Jill Masters
A Jimcin Recording

By Charles Dickens
(2029) 8-1/2 hour cassettes
Rental—$17.50   Purchase—$64.00
Read by Dick Estell
A Christopher Enterprises Recording

We have two recordings of *Hard Times* to choose from. Please indicate selection by number.

In Hard Times, written in 1854, Dickens indicts the insensitivity and greed rampant in Victorian industrial society. Industries imprison the workers; schools and church bend their wards.

Gradgrind's children, Tom and Louisa, are dutiful offspring. So when Louisa marries banker Josiah Bounderby, the alliance seems predestined. But appearances deceive, and Louisa rebels against husband and father. Gradgrind realizes the error of his ways, and the book closes in an aura of forgiveness and with a sense of the possible.

THE HAUNTED HOTEL

By Wilkie Collins
(9131) 7-1 hour cassettes
Rental—$14.50   Purchase—$56.00
Read by Walter Covell
A Jimcin Recording

Collins' output includes 25 novels, more than 30 short stories and novelettes, over a dozen plays and sporadic bits of journalism. As was the practice with Victorian novelists, Collins wrote his fair share of ghost stories. *The Haunted Hotel,* however, was the first novel in which the supernatural is of central interest.

Wilkie Collins also penned one of the first in the genre of the detective novel, *The Moonstone,* also available from B-O-T.

THE HAUNTED HOUSE AT LATCHFORD

By Charlotte Riddell
(9108) 6-1 hour cassettes
Rental—$13.50   Purchase—$48.00
Read by Walter Covell
A Jimcin Recording

Because in the late 19th century women were thought to be the more spiritually sensitive sex, it was expected that they would produce some of the best ghost stories of the era. Charlotte Riddell was famous and her fiction was an expected feature of London's Christmas annuals. This classic Victorian novel of the supernatural was published for the 1873 yuletide season.

Death visits the house at Latchford and in its wake the tenant's will proves baleful and obscure. Suddenly the house, once friendly, oppresses; and the heirs, largely innocent, become prey.

THE HISTORY OF RASSELAS, PRINCE OF ABISSINIA

By Samuel Johnson
(9101) 5-1 hour cassettes
Rental—$12.50   Purchase—$40.00
Read by Walter Zimmerman
A Jimcin Recording

Samuel Johnson is an author who is known to us today principally because James Boswell immortalized him in his *Life of Johnson.*

Johnson was a polymath: he knew all things about all things. In a word, he was verbose.

Nevertheless, *The History of Rasselas* is one of his major accomplishments and even today is readable and entertaining. It was published in 1759 and deals with the flight into Egypt of a young prince who tires of a life of ease and seeks to plumb the eternal verities.

THE HOUND OF THE BASKERVILLES

By Sir Arthur Conan Doyle
(9503) 6-1 hour cassettes
Rental—$13.50   Purchase—$48.00
Read by Walter Covell
A Jimcin Recording

As a story of place and mood *The Hound of the Baskervilles* has few peers. Long after the reading ends, listeners will carry with them vivid memories, as if they had been there, of unpopulated regions of bracken and bog, and of the fog sending its tendrils, chilly and cold, up against the cold stones of an isolated manor house. Then there is the hound itself, almost more terrifying in prospect than when it appears.

THE HOUSE OF MIRTH

By Edith Wharton
(1384) 10-1/2 hour cassettes
Rental—$16.50   Purchase—$80.00
Read by Penelope Dellaporta

The House of Mirth stands as the work that established Edith Wharton's literary reputation. In it she discovered her major subject: the fashionable New York society in which she had been raised. She described its power to debase both people and ideals. This theme forms the dramatic core of this deftly styled book.

A brilliant portrayal of human frailty, Louis Auchincloss termed *The House of Mirth* "uniquely authentic among American novels of manners."

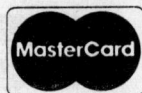

THE HOUSE OF SEVEN GABLES

By Nathaniel Hawthorne
(9110) 8-1½ hour cassettes
Rental—$16.50   Purchase—$64.00
Read by Donna Barkman
A Jimcin Recording

An old mansion in Salem, moss-covered and gabled, broods over the destiny of a distinguished but troubled New England family—the Pynchons. A haunting centuries-old curse, a forceful probing of national and personal guilt, a romance between the young heroine and an attractive stranger—all intertwine in this work that Henry James declared "the closest approach we are likely to have to the Great American Novel."

"The story moves in soft September light, melting like a happy dream of Shakespeare." —Van Wyck Brooks.

Other Hawthorne titles offered by B-O-T include *The Scarlet Letter* and *Tanglewood Tales.*

THE HOUSE OF THE DEAD

By Fydor Dostoevsky
(9158) 10-1½ hour cassettes
Rental—$17.50   Purchase—$80.00
Read by Walter Covell
A Jimcin Recording

In 1849, at the age of 28, Fydor Dostoevsky was sentenced to four years at hard labor in Siberia. Among thieves and murderers, like Russians before him and since, he survived stupefying and mindless degradation. But he never lost faith in the human qualities of his fellow inmates, and from his prison experience he emerged spiritually strengthened.

The House of the Dead, presented in fictional form as the memoirs of a man condemned to ten years of penal servitude for murdering his wife, is in essence the account of this period of Dostoevsky's life.

AN INLAND VOYAGE

By Robert Louis Stevenson
(9502) 5-1 hour cassettes
Rental—$12.50   Purchase—$40.00
Read by Walter Zimmerman
A Jimcin Recording

In An Inland Voyage, Stevenson is at his best. The book was inspired by a canoe trip he made with a friend in 1876 on the rivers of northern France. As we travel with him, we meet a rich variety of characters, portrayed with unspoiled relish by the vivacious and energetic young author. It is charming to discover that boat clubs flourished on the continent a century ago, and that friendship and hospitality were as common among sportsmen then as they are today.

THE INNOCENTS ABROAD

By Mark Twain
(1855-A) 7-1½ hour cassettes
Rental—$15.50   Purchase—$56.00
(1855-B) 7-1½ hour cassettes
Rental—$15.50   Purchase—$56.00
Read by Michael Prichard

One of the funniest and most famous travel books ever written, *The Innocents Abroad* is Mark Twain's story of his encounter with the "Old-World."

Twain's satire is double-edged, slicing chauvinists and cosmopolites alike. Twain used his travelogue to search out the archetypal differences between American and Europeans to define the American identity.

It also contains one of the funniest lines in literature. When an Arab boatman charged Twain seven dollars for a paddle on the Red Sea, Twain said, "No wonder Jesus walked!"

THE INVISIBLE MAN

By H.G. Wells
and SELECTED SHORT STORIES

By Edgar Allan Poe
(1082) 8-1 hour cassettes
Rental—$14.50   Purchase—$64.00
Read by William Shephard

In *The Invisible Man,* a scientist discovers the secret of invisibility, which deranges him. He holds his countrymen powerless for a period of time but in reality is as terrified as they. In the short stories, Edgar Allan Poe is concerned with the possibilities of evil, particularly when it is personal, man to man. Stories include: "The Telltale Heart," "A Cask of Amontillado," "The Fall of the House of Usher," "The Black Cat," "Ligeia" and "The Pit and the Pendulum."

THE ISLAND OF DR. MOREAU

By H.G. Wells
(9009) 5-1 hour cassettes
Rental—$12.50   Purchase—$40.00
Read by Jim Roberts
A Jimcin Recording

A short, muzzle-jawed and loathsome creature carries a man aboard a mysterious ship, and thus begins, with the first of mounting chills, *The Island of Dr. Moreau.* This creature is the servant of Montgomery, a warped scientist who with a cargo of animals is bound for a deserted island. And to that out-of-the-way place the unwilling passenger is himself consigned, the unwanted and soon terrified intruder on a series of ghastly experiments. Those macabre experiments, the mad ambitions of the scientist who performs them, and the agonies they produce in their distorted victims combine to make Wells's story one of the most gripping of its kind.

IVANHOE

By Sir Walter Scott
(9160-A) 7-1½ hour cassettes
Rental—$16.50   Purchase—$56.00
(9160-B) 7-1½ hour cassettes
Rental—$16.50   Purchase—$56.00
Read by Jim Killavey
A Jimcin Recording

Sir Walter Scott gathered a popular audience, larger than any writer before. A great innovator, he created one of the outstanding literary forms of the past two hundred years—the historic novel. His books still glow with color and spectacle, with romance, action and suspense.

In *Ivanhoe* Scott brings to life 12th century England. The disinherited knight Ivanhoe, his fair lady Rowena, Richard the Lion-Hearted and Robin Hood—these are people shaped by the forces of tradition, molded by their nation's history. Through them the past of England comes alive—a past of crusades, chivalry and courtly love.

**TOLL FREE credit card
order line 1-800-626-3333**

JANE EYRE

By Charlotte Bronte
(9092-A) 8-1½ hour cassettes
Rental—$16.50   Purchase—$64.00
(9092-B) 7-1½ hour cassettes
Rental—$16.50   Purchase—$56.00
Read by Donna Barkham
A Jimcin Recording

Jane Eyre is an orphan child who knows only abuse and misery from her mistress. As a young girl she is sent off to boarding school where her good character and diligent habits win her friends and respect. In time Jane herself becomes a teacher at the school.

Seeking wider horizons, Jane takes employment at Thornfield where she comes under the spell of Edward Rochester, its owner, a man of savage temperament and desperate unhappiness. The reason for both is linked to a mysterious crone who is kept locked away on the third floor of the mansion.

JONATHAN WILD

By Henry Fielding
(9143) 6-1½ hour cassettes
Rental—$15.50   Purchase—$48.00
Read by Jill Masters
A Jimcin Recording

Jonathan Wild, a social satire set in the 1700's, shows us a "great man"—not a good man. Henry Fielding makes it clear that a "great man" is a pure villain and that greatness and goodness are never found in one person.

Jonathan Wild is a thief and a cheat. He plots to ruin Heartfree, an honest fellow. Wild gets help wherever he turns, thus goodness and prudence are undone in a world which values corruption and pride more than harmony.

JOSEPH ANDREWS

By Henry Fielding
(9518) 9-1½ hour cassettes
Rental—$17.50   Purchase—$72.00
Read by Jill Masters
A Jimcin Recording

A comic epic often called the first realistic novel of English literature, *Joseph Andrews* is a vivid picture of English life in the 18th century. Fielding spurned the sentimentality of his times, choosing instead to puncture the vanities of human nature with satire.

Joseph Andrews is a footman to Lady Booby after Sir Thomas Booby's death. When Andrews rejects the widow Booby's advances, she discharges him. He sets out from London to see his sweetheart, Fanny. On the way he is robbed and beaten, but a charitable parson comes to his aid and travels with him. Their tribulations on the journey provide the theme of the story.

A JOURNAL OF THE PLAGUE YEAR

By Daniel Defoe
(1030) 8-1 hour cassettes
Rental—$14.50   Purchase—$64.00
Read by Dan Lazar

Daniel Defoe's classic account of a city under siege by the Black Plague carries the listener across four centuries and steeps him in the terror of assault by a relentless and implacable foe. Silent, mysterious, lethal, its cause locked in a science yet unborn, the Black Death killed one third of Europe's population with democratic disregard of age, position or entitlement.

JUDE THE OBSCURE

By Thomas Hardy
(9526) 12-1½ hour cassettes
Rental—$18.50   Purchase—$96.00
Read by Jill Masters
A Jimcin Recording

Jude the Obscure, Hardy's last novel, is generally acknowledged to be his finest. Yet its publication in 1896 elicited a protest as noisy as that which greeted D.H. Lawrence's *Lady Chatterley's Lover* 32 years later. Attacks by the press, abusive letters and a bishop's solemn burning of the book all seem unbelievable today, but their effect was serious.

"Mr. Hardy's rebellious views of life and religion and leanings toward naturalistic methods are given full play in this story of a peasant scholar's foiled ambition, which from beginning to end is somber and in many of the incidents extremely painful." *(Best Fiction)*

THE JUNGLE BOOK

By Rudyard Kipling
(9041) 6-1 hour cassettes
Rental—$13.50   Purchase—$48.00
Read by Cindy Hardin,
Walter Zimmerman and Walter Covell
A Jimcin Recording

Rudyard Kipling was the most popular living English author during Queen Victoria's reign. His stories won him enormous wealth and fame.

The Jungle Book explores the theme of man's innocence in nature. He gives us animals that embody vices as well as virtues. Included are seven stories: "Mowgli's Brothers," "Kaa's Hunting," "Tiger-Tiger!," "The White Seal," "Rikki-Tikki-Tavi," "Toomai of the Elephants" and "Servants of the Queen."

KEPT IN THE DARK

By Anthony Trollope
(9067) 6-1½ hour cassettes
Rental—$15.50   Purchase—$48.00
Read by Jill Masters
A Jimcin Recording

Kept in the Dark gives us a lean, psychological portrait of the destructive effect of past secrets on a marriage. The husband is George Western, self willed and fatally proud. His wife, Cecilia, possesses a complicated mixture of pride and submissiveness that leads her inexorably to deceit. These difficulties are compounded by hypocritical friends and the reappearance of Cecilia's egotistical former suitor, Sir Francis Geraldine. *Kept in the Dark* is one of the finest examples of Trollope's mastery of the Victorian novel.

KIDNAPPED

By Robert Louis Stevenson
(1071) 7-1 hour cassettes
Rental—$13.50   Purchase—$56.00
Read by Angela Cheyne

Kidnapped is a memoir of the activities of David Balfour in the year 1751. Young Balfour is cheated of his inheritance by his malicious Uncle Ebenezer who has him kidnapped and put on a ship bound for the Carolinas. Not many days underway, the ship runs into a small boat in the fog. Only one man is rescued from the smaller vessel. He is Alan Breck, a Scotsman returning from political exile in France. Balfour and Breck are thrown together on their voyage, and thus begins a tale of events which includes shipwreck, murder, flight and intrigue.

RUDYARD KIPLING
KIM

KIM

By Rudyard Kipling
(9107) 8-1½ hour cassettes
Rental—$16.50   Purchase—$64.00
Read by Walter Covell
A Jimcin Recording

The most popular of Kipling's novels and one of the finest adventure stories in literature, *Kim* is the narrative of an orphan boy, the son of an Irish soldier, who grows up in India.

Kim is a survivor. By trade a beggar, he roams back alleys and bazaars, blind to his identity. But unknown to him the blood of empire runs in his veins, and when he meets his father's regiment he finds his true identity.

First as an urchin, later as a schoolboy and then secret agent, Kim gives us a point of identity for a trek through 19th century India. A story of fantasy fulfilled, it is as appealing today as when it was written.

KING SOLOMON'S MINES

By H. Rider Haggard
(1872) 6-1½ hour cassettes
Rental—$14.50   Purchase—$48.00
Read by Ian Whitcomb

"There at the end of the long stone table, holding in his skeleton fingers a great white spear, sat Death himself . . . " Such is the image that our guide and narrator Allan Quatermain encounters as he and his companion approach the mysterious and deadly entrance to King Solomon's Mines.

On an ocean liner bound for Natal, Quatermain is engaged as guide. Supplied with arms and determination, the explorers set out through Africa's beautiful but often inhospitable terrain. The trek culminates in the discovery of these lost and lethal mines.

For quick ordering
1-800-626-3333

THE KREUTZER SONATA and FAMILY HAPPINESS

By Leo Tolstoy
(9087) 8-1 hour cassettes
Rental—$15.50   Purchase—$64.00
Read by Walter Zimmerman
A Jimcin Recording

As a novelist Tolstoy is not all of a piece, and as a man he is full of contradictions, none more evident than those revealed in *The Kreutzer Sonata*. This macabre story concerns the murder of a wife by her husband. Chained to the crime by his conscience, the narrator is filled with an intense self-loathing not so much for the murder as for his inability to explain away its consequences.

In *Family Happiness*, Tolstoy reveals an understanding of the paths of marital communication, which similarly form such a superb conclusion in *War and Peace*.

THE LADY OF THE BARGE

By W.W. Jacobs
(9068) 5-1 hour cassettes
Rental—$12.50   Purchase—$40.00
Read by Walter Covell
A Jimcin Recording

The Lady of the Barge by W.W. Jacobs is a collection of 12 short stories by one of England's acknowledged masters. They range from the light humor of the title story to one of the most famous horror stories ever written—"The Monkey's Paw." Other titles are: "Bill's Paper Chase," "The Well," "Cupboard Love," "In the Library," "Captain Rogers," "A Tiger's Skin," "A Mixed Proposal," "An Adulteration Act," "A Golden Venture" and "Three at Table."

THE LADY OR THE TIGER and Other Stories

By Richard Stockton
(9072) 5-1 hour cassettes
Rental—$12.50   Purchase—$40.00
Read by Walter Zimmerman,
Jim Roberts and Cindy Hardin
A Jimcin Recording

Frank Richard Stockton was born in 1834 in Philadelphia. He was an author who wrote primarily for children, and is remembered now almost entirely for three of the stories that appear in this collection, "The Lady or the Tiger," "The Discourager of Hesitancy" and "Mr. Tolman." These stories may be said to include the reader in their final solution because none is properly "concluded." The listener is left to resolve them for himself.

Other stories include: "Our Archery Club," "The Griffon and the Miner Canon," "His Wife's Deceased Sister," "The Transferred Ghost," "Our Story" and "Old Pypes and the Dryad."

LADY SUSAN

By Jane Austen
(9144) 3-1 hour cassettes
Rental—$9.50   Purchase—$24.00
Read by Cindy Hardin
A Jimcin Recording

The plot is simple: Lady Susan, a clever and ruthless widow, determines that her daughter is going to marry a man whom both detest. Lady Susan sets her own sights on her sister-in-law's brother, all the while keeping an old affair simmering on the back burner.

But people refuse to play the roles they are assigned and in the end her daughter gets the sister-in-law's brother, the old affair runs out of steam and all that is left for Lady Susan is the man intended for her daughter, the one neither can abide!

THE LAST OF THE MOHICANS

By James Fenimore Cooper
(9112) 11-1½ hour cassettes
Rental—$18.50   Purchase—$88.00
Read by Jim Killavey
A Jimcin Recording

Cooper wrote five "leather-stocking tales," of which this is the second and most famous. Here the white frontiersman Hawkeye (aka Peter Bumppo and Leather Stocking) is nobly matched with Uncas, the Indian of the title.

THE LEGEND OF SLEEPY HOLLOW and Other Stories

By Washington Irving
(9507) 7-1 hour cassettes
Rental—$14.50   Purchase—$56.00
Read by Cindy Hardin
A Jimcin Recording

"The Legend of Sleepy Hollow" introduces Ichabod Crane, one of literature's most memorable characters. He is a Yankee schoolmaster, tall and stringy, living with the Dutch folk of Sleepy Hollow on the Hudson. He courts Katrina Van Tassel, daughter of a rich Dutch farmer, but his suit is preposterous and makes him an object of ridicule in the Hollow. All this culminates one night when Katrina's true love, Brom Bones, gotten up as the Headless Horseman, pursues Ichabod over pitch-black country roads.

LIFE ON THE MISSISSIPPI

By Mark Twain
(1069) 8-1½ hour cassettes
Rental—$13.50   Purchase—$64.00
Read by Michael Prichard

Life on the Mississippi was first published when Mark Twain was nearly 50 years old. He wrote it originally as a series of articles titled "Old Times on the Mississippi." It is fresh with enthusiasm for his early life on the river. On hearing it today who can fail to respond to its message of freedom, independent existence and expanding horizons?

THE LIGHT THAT FAILED

By Rudyard Kipling
(9065) 6-1½ hour cassettes
Rental—$15.50   Purchase—$48.00
Read by Donna Barkman
A Jimcin Recording

Published in 1891, *The Light That Failed* tells the story of Dick Heldar. Dick is a lonely and insecure child who grows up to become a war artist. He follows the British Army in battle, and gives us some of the best verbal descriptions of the desert and desert warfare ever written. These military conflicts serve as counterpoint to the artist's internal struggles.

LORD JIM

By Joseph Conrad
(1249) 10-1½ hour cassettes
Rental—$16.50   Purchase—$80.00
Read by Wolfram Kandinsky

Lord Jim is the story of a would-be-hero who deserts what he thinks is a sinking ship. Haunted thereafter by shame, he feels a constant need to explain himself. Jim is a man whose will is weak and behavior craven. Conrad uses Jim as a device to probe the nature of man. He concludes there is a Gresham's law of conduct, wherein the bad drives out the good.

LOST HORIZON

By James Hilton
(1146) 7-1 hour cassettes
Rental—$13.50   Purchase—$56.00
Read by Dan Grace

Lost Horizon is the tale of three men and a woman seeking escape from a political upheaval in the Orient. Their airplane crashed high on a Tibetan plateau. They are saved by a party of natives and taken to Shangri-La.

Finding themselves prisoners at first, then visitors soon becoming willing captives until they discover the secret of that hidden paradise. Their escape is heroic but filled with tragedy.

THE LOST STRADIVARIUS

By J. Meade Falkner
(9088) 6-1 hour cassettes
Rental—$12.50   Purchase—$48.00
Read by Donna Barkman
and Jim Roberts

The Lost Stradivarius is a story of arcane and mysterious spiritual phenomena, equally an exploration of the occult and turn-of-the-century England.

John Meade Falkner was an author who wore at least two hats, for he was by occupation the chairman of Armstrong, Whitworth and Co, Ltd., then the largest British munitions manufacturer. He was knowledgeable and learned, and it was perhaps to seek release from his industrial vocation that he turned to the pen and not only the pen, but stories of evil lurking scarce-concealed in this world.

THE LUCK OF ROARING CAMP and Other Stories

By Bret Harte
(9073) 6-1 hour cassettes
Rental—$13.50   Purchase—$48.00
Read by Jack Bensen,
Walter Zimmerman, Jim Roberts
A Jimcin Recording

With these tales of California's gold rush days, Bret Harte became one of the earliest and most important writers of the American West.

In "The Luck of Roaring Camp" a prostitute dies, leaving a newborn son in the care of hardbitten minors. Named "Luck," the child unlocks emotions the miners never knew they had.

MADAME BOVARY

By Gustave Flaubert
(9129) 9-1½ hour cassettes
Rental—$17.50   Purchase—$72.00
Read by Walter Zimmerman
A Jimcin Recording

Flaubert's genius lay in his infinite capacity for taking pains, and *Madame Bovary*, so true in its characterization, so vivid in its setting, is testimony to the realism of his work.

Perhaps no book in the history of the novel has received more attention than this tale of a provincial woman who cannot bear the discrepancy between her romantic dreams and the dull routine of her daily life.

MAGGIE: A GIRL OF THE STREETS

By Steven Crane
(9140) 3-1 hour cassettes
Rental—$9.50   Purchase—$24.00
Read by Jim Killavey
A Jimcin Recording

Stephen Crane was just 20 when he began his brief career as a journalist in New York. He soon abandoned newspaper work for the broader vistas of fiction.

Nonetheless, it was as a reporter that he found material for his first novel, *Maggie: A Girl of the Streets*, published in 1893. The book is an unflinching picture of the New York slums and is a landmark of literary naturalism.

MAIN STREET

By Sinclair Lewis
(2028-A) 6-1½ hour cassettes
Rental—$16.50   Purchase—$48.00
(2028-B) 7-1½ hour cassettes
Rental—$16.50   Purchase—$56.00
Read by Dick Estell
A Christopher Enterprises Recording

The lonely predicament of Carol Kennicott, caught between her desires for social reform and individual happiness, reflects the position in which America's turn-of-the-century, "emancipated woman" found herself.

MAIN-TRAVELLED ROADS

By Hamlin Garland
(9100) 7-1 hour cassettes
Rental—$14.50   Purchase—$56.00
Read by Walter Zimmerman
and Donald White
A Jimcin Recording

Born on a Wisconsin farm in 1860, Hamlin Garland wrote of Midwestern farm life in the 1880's. His stories won a Pulitzer prize and his fiction foreshadowed the work of Stephen Crane and Theodore Dresier.

Deeply influenced by Whitman's *Leaves of Grass,* Garland wrote "with full intention of telling the truth . . . has a higher quality than beauty."

THE MAN IN THE IRON MASK

By Alexandre Dumas
(9137) 6-1½ hour cassettes
Rental—$15.50   Purchase—$48.00
Read by Walter Covell
A Jimcin Recording

Louis XIII had to be a Solomon; his queen produced twin male heirs—two sons of equal age with equal pretensions. Louis feared for France. One prince is peace and safety for the state, two are civil war and anarchy.

One son had to go. Louis could not kill him—but he could hide him—in an iron mask. Such is the quality of paternal mercy.

This book was originally written as part of a sequel to *The Three Musketeers.* But in time it developed a life of its own and in recent years has alwyas been published as a separate novel that stands on its own merits.

THE MAN THAT CORRUPTED HADLEYBURG and Other Stories

By Mark Twain
(9091) 7-1 hour cassettes
Rental—$14.50   Purchase—$56.00
Read by Walter Zimmerman, Jack Bensen
and Cindy Hardin
A Jimcin Recording

One of the demons Twain always set out to slay was the legend that the citizens of this republic are inherently more virtuous than others. By the invention of an elaborate hoax, a kind of giant practical joke, Twain has his hero turn Hadleyburg inside out and in the process teach the hypocrites who dwelt there a lesson in humility and moral realism.

Other stories include: "Baker's Bluejay Yarn," "The Story of the Bad Little Boy," "The Notorious Jumping Frog of Calaveras County," "Extracts from Adam's Diary," "Eve's Diary," "How I Edited an Agricultural Paper," "The Man Who Put Up at Gadsby's," "Journalism in Tennessee," "The Joke that Made Ed's Fortune," "Edward Mills and George Benton: A Tale" and "Cannibalism in the Cars."

THE MAN WHO WOULD BE KING and Other Stories

By Rudyard Kipling
(9514) 6-1 hour cassettes
Rental—$13.50   Purchase—$48.00
Read by Walter Covell
A Jimcin Recording

"The Man Who Would be King" is the story of two British adventurers who set off to conquer a small kingdom in Afghanistan. Only one of the men returns . . . and in such terribly mutilated condition that the newspaper-man-narrator scarcely recognizes him.

Other stories include: "The Drums of the Fore and Aft," "Wee Willie Winkie," "Baa, Baa, Black Sheep," "Namgay Doola," "Moti Guj Mutineer," "A Conference of the Powers" and "The Head of the District.

THE MAN WITHOUT A COUNTRY and Other Stories

By A Collection
(9037) 6-1 hour cassettes
Rental—$13.50   Purchase—$48.00
Read by Jim Roberts
A Jimcin Recording

"The Man Without a Country" is the most famous work of Edward Everett Hale, an American author who lived from 1822 to 1909. For a psychologically truthful story of what it is like to be driven from the tribe, nothing ranks ahead of "The Man Without a Country."

Other stories include: "My Double and How He Undid Me" and "The Last Voyage of the Resolute" by Edward Everett Hale, "Love of Life" by Jack London, "William Wilson" by Edgar Allan Poe, "The Man and the Snake" by Ambrose Bierce, "Young Goodman Brown" by Nathaniel Hawthorne and "The Joke that Made Ed's Fortune" by Mark Twain.

MANON LESCAUT

By Antoine Francois Prévost d'Exiles
(9516) 7-1 hour cassettes
Rental—$14.50   Purchase—$56.00
Read by Walter Covell
A Jimcin Recording

L'Abbe Antoine Prévost led nearly as exciting a life as his swashbuckling heroes. At different times he was a Jesuit novice, soldier and priest of the Benedictine order.

The young Chevalier des Grieux, a student of philosophy at Amiens, meets Manon as she is entering a convent. He frees her and they flee to Paris where they live extravagantly. The Chevalier becomes a card cheat to support Manon. Later, robbed of their possessions, Manon becomes mistress to an old and wealthy nobleman who bestows many gifts. Manon and her lover run away with the money and jewels, are apprehended by the police and imprisoned. Exile to the penal colony in Louisiana swiftly follows in this exuberantly romantic tale of love and life.

MANSFIELD PARK

By Jane Austen
(9530) 13-1½ hour cassettes
Rental—$19.50   Purchase—$104.00
Read by Jill Masters
A Jimcin Recording

One of the gifts from the 19th century to ours is the writing of Jane Austen. Her graceful and delicate perceptions are far different from those offered us today.

In *Mansfield Park* she creates a household of young people, among them Fanny Price. During an era when upbringing was nearly everything, Fanny has the bad luck to be the poor relation in a wealthy family. Against a lovely and witty rival, she brings only natural goodness as a weapon in her battle for the man she loves.

Other Jane Austen titles recorded by B-O-T include *Northanger Abbey, Persuasion, Pride and Prejudice* and *Sense and Sensibility*.

MARTIN EDEN

By Jack London
(9151) 10-1½ hour cassettes
Rental—$17.50   Purchase—$80.00
Read by Jim Killavey
A Jimcin Recording

Martin Eden is Jack London's most vital and original character. Why? Because it is autobiography, thinly disguised. Like the author, Eden grows up poor in San Francisco, takes to the sea, struggles for an education and literary fame. Who else do we know who did this?

The book is preceded by an introduction in which Andrew Sinclair, the noted critic, contrasts Eden's life with that of his creator. He judged that London was in a depressed state when he wrote the book and offers that as a reason for London's lack of charity toward Eden.

"London's putative autobiography in the land of make believe . . . halfway between a howl and a hoo-haw." (*E.R.S. Reviews*)

THE MASTER OF BALLANTRAE

By Robert Louis Stevenson
(9512) 6-1½ hour cassettes
Rental—$15.50   Purchase—$48.00
Read by John Chatty
A Jimcin Recording

Stevenson was plagued from childhood with poor health, specifically tuberculosis. In his travels he was on the lookout for a better climate, also for the romance and adventure he always felt were just around the corner. When excitement lagged, he invented it.

The Master of Ballantrae is a case in point. Set against the background of Scotland's revolt against England in the 1740's, the story concerns a lifelong family feud between the Master of Ballantrae and his younger brother.

MASTER OF THE WORLD

By Jules Verne
(9001) 5-1 hour cassettes
Rental—$12.50   Purchase—$40.00
Read by Jim Killavey
A Jimcin Recording

Imagine yourself in the Blue Ridge Mountains 100 years ago when suddenly the earth begins to shake. Relatives in Pennsylvania read portents in the sky, and a sea monster (really a high speed submarine, a ship thought then to be impossible) is sighted off New England.

Then comes a letter addressed "To the Old and New Worlds" from "On Board the 'Terror.' "

It is clear that a mad genius is loose, and investigator John Strock sets out with two companions to capture this megalomaniac.

Other Verne titles available from B-O-T are *Around the World in Eighty Days* and *From the Earth to the Moon*.

THE MAYOR OF CASTERBRIDGE

By Thomas Hardy
(9521) 9-1½ hour cassettes
Rental—$17.50   Purchase—$72.00
Read by Jill Masters
A Jimcin Recording

In *The Mayor of Casterbridge*, a young farm laborer, dead drunk, sells his wife and child to another man for five pounds. Simultaneously freed of any restraints and goaded by a hidden guilt, he goes on to become a fabulously rich grain merchant and Mayor of Casterbridge in the bargain. At this point his wife and child reappear and his life, which he thought so secure, begins to unravel.

Thomas Hardy was born in 1840. Like Kipling and H.G. Wells, he bridged the Victorian and the pre-modern eras.

MELVILLE: SIX SHORT NOVELS

By Herman Melville
(1008) 8-1 hour cassettes
Rental—$14.50   Purchase—$64.00
Read by Dan Lazar

These six short novels show Melville to have been not just a brooding genius, but also a writer possessed of wit and humor. He dealt not only with life's tragic possibilities, but also the comic.

Included in this selection are: "Billy Budd," "Bartleby the Scrivener," "The Apple Tree Table," "The Piazza," "I and My Chimney" and "The Happy Failure."

**Special 10% discount
See page 2**

THE MEMOIRS OF SHERLOCK HOLMES

By Sir Arthur Conan Doyle
(1308) 8-1 hour cassettes
Rental—$14.50   Purchase—$64.00
Read by Richard Green

The Memoirs of Sherlock Holmes is a collection of 11 short stories about the famous detective as told by his friend, Dr. Watson. Sir Arthur Conan Doyle draws us into a world of hansom cabs and train rides to country mansions where Holmes deftly solves the unsolvable—through his inimitable logic, cunning and powers of observation. Stories included on this recording are: "The Adventures of Silver Blaze," "The Yellow Face," "The Stockbroker's Clerk," "The Gloria Scott," "The Musgrave Ritual," "The Reigate Squire," "The Crooked Man," "The Resident Patient," "The Greek Interpreter," "The Naval Treaty" and "The Final Problem."

THE MERRY ADVENTURES OF ROBIN HOOD

By Howard Pyle
(9044) 8-1½ hour cassettes
Rental—$16.50   Purchase—$64.00
Read by John Chatty
A Jimcin Recording

Relive the adventures as Robin and his cohorts—Friar Tuck, Little John, Will Scarlet—cavort about Sherwood Forest for the sheer joy and fun of it. However, all is not sport. There is the Sheriff of Nottingham, a villain, who sees Robin as competition. He will stop at nothing to rid the forest of Robin Hood, and one is left asking: who won this game, and how would it have been reported by today's press?

MOBY DICK

By Herman Melville
(1934-A) 9-1½ hour cassettes
Rental—$16.50   Purchase—$72.00
(1934-B) 9-1½ hour cassettes
Rental—$16.50   Purchase—$72.00
Read by Walter Zimmerman

"It is a fabric that should be woven of ships' cables and hawsers. A Polar wind blows through it, and birds of prey hover over it."

So spoke Melville of his masterpiece; and into his tale of Captain Ahab's obsessive quest of the white whale he poured all of his own youthful experience backed by a minute study of the literature of whales and whaling.

But into it also went other experiences, other reading, other insights . . . the "power of blackness" and the deepest dreams and obsessions of mankind.

MOLL FLANDERS

By Daniel Defoe
(1504) 9-1½ hour cassettes
Rental—$16.50   Purchase—$72.00
Read by Wanda McCaddon

Moll Flanders capped a career as harlot and thief with penitence. Her story remains today (as it has for 200 years) the liveliest and most candid record of a bawd's progress. This account of the rising fortunes of a London street urchin, who connived her way into many beds and much wealth, is set in the free-for-all society of 17th century England. Her record of scandalous adventure rings with an earthy, candid humor seldom matched in modern fiction.

MONSIEUR BEAUCAIRE and Other Stories

By Booth Tarkington
(9066) 4-1 hour cassettes
Rental—$10.50   Purchase—$32.00
Read by Jim Roberts
A Jimcin Recording

Booth Tarkington's stories are noted for their romantic and sentimental qualities, yet like most romantics, he has a strong vein of cynicism. These conflicting traits are exemplified in "Monsieur Beaucaire" and "The Beautiful Lady," both of which deal with foreign characters in exotic scenes. Tarkington urges an appreciation of honesty, generosity and kindness above wealth and rank, a virtuous prescription to be sure, but one difficult to ingest. Included in this collection is "Mrs. Protheroe," one of his best stories.

MONSIEUR MAURICE

By Amelia Edwards and

A PHANTOM LOVER

By Vernon Lee
(9093) 5-1 hour cassettes
Rental—$12.50   Purchase—$40.00
Read by Cindy Hardin
and Walter Covell
A Jimcin Recording

Amelia Edwards, author of *Monsieur Maurice*, was a popular journalist-novelist of the 1860's. A writer of history, poetry, novels and short stories, she was also on the staff of the *Saturday Review*. For years a regular contributor to Dickens' magazines, she often furnished the Christmas issue's ghost story.

An expatriate in Italy, Vernon Lee (a pseudonym for Violet Page) was preeminent in many areas: biography, poetry, political philosophy as well as fiction. Remarkable for quality as well as versatility, she deserves our attention.

A Phantom Lover, which first appeared in 1886, is British in its setting and approach. Its intended ambiguities and subtleties are in the manner of the early Henry James.

MOONSTONE

By Wilkie Collins
(9127-A) 8-1½ hour cassettes
Rental—$16.50   Purchase—$64.00
(9127-B) 7-1½ hour cassettes
Rental—$16.50   Purchase—$56.00
Read by Walter Zimmerman
Walter Covell and Jill Masters
A Jimcin Recording

"His eyes, of a steely light grey, has a very disconcerting trick, when they encountered your eyes, of looking as if they expected something more than you were aware of yourself." And thus our introduction to the celebrated Sergeant Cuff, quite possibly the first detective in English fiction.

Published in 1868, and presented to readers as "a romance," *The Moonstone* has since become a classic in the genre of the mystery/detective story. The book concerns the disappearance of a sizable diamond, the Moonstone, that once adorned a rare Hindu idol, and has since come into the possession of an English officer.

MY LADY'S MONEY

By Wilkie Collins
(9070) 6-1 hour cassettes
Rental—$13.50   Purchase—$48.00
Read by Jim Roberts
A Jimcin Recording

Wilkie Collins was born in England in 1824 and studied successfully to become a lawyer. On completion of his schooling he adopted literature as his profession and before he was 30 became a good friend of Charles Dickens, editing with Dickens the magazine *Household Words*. It was in this magazine that Collins published the first story ever to deal seriously with the detection of crime. It was "The Woman in White."

My Lady's Money was published in mid-career, and is a perfect vignette of its time. The regularity of the era, the sense of place and time, and comfortable circumstances of the author all combine to make *My Lady's Money* a memorable and enchanting work.

THE MYSTERY OF THE YELLOW ROOM

By Gaston Leroux
(9118) 8-1 hour cassettes
Rental—$15.50   Purchase—$64.00
Read by Walter Covell
A Jimcin Recording

This novel—the classic French detective story—was written in 1907 by Gaston Leroux, once a reporter who covered the famous trials of his time. (He also wrote *The Phantom of the Opera.)*

Match your wits with his rival detectives—one amateur, one professional—as they try to crack the mystery: Mademoiselle Stangerson retires to bed in the Yellow Room. Suddenly revolver shots echo through the house and she screams for help. Her father and a servant run to the locked room where they find the wounded girl—alone. The only other exit, a window—barred. How had the assailant escaped?

NICHOLAS NICKLEBY

By Charles Dickens
(1242-A) 8-1½ hour cassettes
Rental—$15.50   Purchase—$64.00
(1242-B) 9-1½ hour cassettes
Rental—$16.50   Purchase—$72.00
(1242-C) 8-1½ hour cassettes
Rental—$15.50   Purchase—$64.00
Read by Wanda McCaddon

The third novel to come from the pen of England's most famous novelist, *Nicholas Nickleby* exuberantly fused the humor and absurdity of *Pickwick Papers,* his first novel, with the indignation, emotion and dramatic power that stamped *Oliver Twist,* his second. In *Nicholas Nickleby,* Dickens appears for the first time in his dual roles of comic genius and social reformer.

THE NIGGER OF THE NARCISSUS and HEART OF DARKNESS

By Joseph Conrad
(1098) 7-1½ hour cassettes
Rental—$15.50   Purchase—$56.00
Read by Wolfram Kandinsky

The Nigger of the Narcissus is the story of a voyage from an Eastern port, but at another level the voyage becomes a symbol and is merely the stage on which Waite, a dying Negro, plays out the drama of his demise. Waite's death brings out the best and worst in his crewmates . . . pity and humanity on one hand, selfishness and jealousy on the other . . . *Heart of Darkness* is centered around the death of the powerful white trader Kurtz aboard a river steamer in the Belgian Congo. It is one of the greatest portraits in all fiction of moral deterioration and reversion to savagery.

NORTHANGER ABBEY

By Jane Austen
(9031) 8-1 hour cassettes
Rental—$15.50   Purchase—$64.00
Read by Nancy Dow
A Jimcin Recording

Catherine Morland, a young woman who feels destined to become a heroine (like the ones in Gothic romances), is from a small provincial village. She is invited by a wealthy neighbor to accompany her to Bath, one of the most fashionable watering places of the day. At Bath she is carried away with affairs of the heart which labor clumsily toward unsatisfactory conclusions. Jane Austen seems to be telling us that when we court dreams we wake to foolishness. In *Northanger Abbey,* Jane Austen's cool, ironic humor, stylish prose and beautifully constructed plots are still capable of charming a new generation of readers.

JOSEPH CONRAD
NOSTROMO
MODERN LIBRARY

NOSTROMO

By Joseph Conrad
(1081-A) 7-1½ hour cassettes
Rental—$15.50   Purchase—$56.00
(1081-B) 7-1½ hour cassettes
Rental—$15.50   Purchase—$56.00
Read by Wolfram Kandinsky

Set in the civil-war-torn South American Republic of Costaguana, *Nostromo* is a complex of personal stories. Like everything Conrad wrote, it involves conflicts of heroic proportions and tragic consequences. It is also timeless.

Conrad's device is to pose a cast of characters, each person living his own illusions, next to *Nostromo,* a "natural" man. Greed and cupidity cancel each other out, while fidelity and discipline bring one through.

**Special 10% discount
See page 2**

NOTES FROM THE UNDERGROUND

By Fyodor Dostoevsky
(9034) 6-1 hour cassettes
Rental—$13.50   Purchase—$48.00
Read by Walter Zimmerman
A Jimcin Recording

By the time Dostoevsky was 40, he had spent four years in prison and a further four years in the army as punishment for his part in a political conspiracy. His health was broken. He was gaunt, fervid, anxiety-ridden and close to bankruptcy. It was in this state he wrote *Notes from the Underground,* a masterpiece of the psychology of the outsider. The book relates the experiences of a singular young man who spurns the rule of God and man.

THE OREGON TRAIL

By Francis Parkman
(1483) 8-1½ hour cassettes
Rental—$15.50   Purchase—$64.00
Read by Dan Lazar

Francis Parkman was the son of a Unitarian minister. Born in Boston in 1823, graduated from Harvard, he took advantage of an opportunity to "go West" in 1846. The great contrast of the raw and dynamic frontier with the tame and settled Northeast opened flood gates of creativity in him, and he wrote vividly of life on the trail.

The Oregon Trail captures the flavor of an era with great authenticity and color, and makes it possible for us to journey into that land of long ago.

AN OUTCAST OF THE ISLANDS

By Joseph Conrad
(1095) 8-1½ hour cassettes
Rental—$15.50   Purchase—$64.00
Read by Wolfram Kandinsky

An Outcast of the Islands is the story of a self deluded South Seas trader who, for reasons that are as false as his own self-assessment, marries a Malay woman. Ostracized by his own society, in time he earns the contempt of the natives. Hence, he truly becomes "an outcast of the islands."

OLIVER TWIST

By Charles Dickens
(1074) 10-1½ hour cassettes
Rental—$16.50   Purchase—$80.00
Read by Angela Cheyne

One of Dickens' most popular and moving novels, *Oliver Twist* deals with a world Dickens himself knew only too well—a world of debtors, prisons, alms houses and poverty.

Oliver is born in a workhouse. Apprenticed to an undertaker, he runs away to London where the "Artful Dodger," Jack Dawkins, takes the starving boy into a den of thieves. Among this motley crew, Oliver meets the sinister Bill Sikes, his pitiful and tragic Nancy and the master criminal Fagin.

PERSUASION

By Jane Austen
(9083) 6-1½ hour cassettes
Rental—$15.50   Purchase—$48.00
Read by Jill Masters
A Jimcin Recording

Jane Austen was born in 1775 and died unmarried in her early forties. The daughter of a rector, she lived a comfortable upper middle-class life which was made eventful only through her active imagination.

In *Persuasion,* the book's heroine, Anne Elliot, was earlier engaged to Frederick Wentworth, a young naval officer, now become a captain. Anne is 27, and the early bloom of youth is past when she and Captain Wentworth are thrown together again.

This book is often thought to be the story of Jane Austen's own lost love. In it, she seems mellowed and more philosophical, touched perhaps by the sentiment of a story in which she saw herself as heroine but in whose happy outcome she had premonition that she would never play a part.

PETER PAN

By J.M. Barrie
(9172) 6-1½ hour cassettes
Rental—$15.50   Purchase—$48.00
Read by John Chatty

This is the story of Peter Pan, the boy who does not want to grow up, of Tinker Bell the fairy and of the Darling children—Wendy, John and Michael.

Their great adventure begins on the night that Peter flies into the Darling home looking for his shadow and teaches Wendy, John and Michael how to fly back to Neverland, where adventures happen every day.

J.M. Barrie was born near Dundee, Scotland in 1860. He was a journalist and novelist and began writing for the stage in 1892. *Peter Pan* was first produced on the London stage on December 27, 1904.

THE PICKWICK PAPERS

By Charles Dickens
(9176-A) 8-1½ hour cassettes
Rental—$16.50   Purchase—$64.00
(9176-B) 8-1½ hour cassettes
Rental—$16.50   Purchase—$64.00
(9176-C) 9-1½ hour cassettes
Rental—$17.50   Purchase—$72.00
Read by Walter Zimmerman
A Jimcin Recording

The adventures of the immortal Pickwick Club, headed by the good Mr. Pickwick Club, headed by the good Mr. Pickwick himself, abetted by his faithful manservant, Sam Weller, for the basis of Dicken's first great literary achievement.

Following the intrepidly bumbling Pickwickians along the highways and byways of old England, Dickens creates a vivid world of highwaymen, duels, lawsuits, jails, romantic imbroglios—but a world too, of deeply affecting human warmth and generosity.

"Superbly vigorous, filled with a host of indelible character creations, *Pickwick Papers* has never ceased to enjoy the popularity it won originally in 1838." *(Publisher's Source)*

THE PICTURE OF DORIAN GRAY

By Oscar Wilde
(1390) 8-1 hour cassettes
Rental—$14.50   Purchase—$64.00
Read by Dan Lazar

Oscar Wilde was a man who always drew the public spotlight, Beneath his affections lurked real talent, which he turned to serious purpose with his only novel, The *Picture of Dorian Gray*. It is the tale of a young man's quest for eternal youth and beauty, a quest that ends in scandal, depravity and death.

PINOCCHIO

By Carlo Collodi
(9179) 5-1 hour cassettes
Rental—$12.50   Purchase—$40.00
Read by Donna Collette
A Jimcin Recording

This is the classical tale of the mischievous puppet who longs to be a flesh-and-blood little boy. Join Pinocchio and Jiminy Cricket as they journey from Geppetto's toy shop to mysterious Treasure Island and meet with Monstro the Whale.

Carlo Collodi was the pseudonym of Italian journalist Carlo Lorenzini (1826-1890). He also wrote didactic tales for children, the most famous being this ageless story which was first published in 1883.

THE PIONEERS

By James Fenimore Cooper
(9156-A) 7-1½ hour cassettes
Rental—$16.50   Purchase—$56.00
(9156-B) 6-1½ hour cassettes
Rental—$15.50   Purchase—$48.00
Read by Jim Killavey
A Jimcin Recording

The Pioneers was immediately popular when it was published in 1823, and even today this novel of pioneer life has lost little of its appeal.

Although complete in itself, *The Pioneers* is fourth in a series of five novels with the collective title *The Leatherstocking Tales.* The saga begins with *The Deerslayer,* in which we meet Natty Bumppo, young and foolish. In the next book, *The Last of the Mohicans,* Natty is older and already a master of hairbreadth escapes. He is in his prime in *The Pathfinder,* while in this novel, *The Pioneers,* Natty shows his years. He is already "the foremost in that band of pioneers who is opening the way for the march of the nation across the continent," a line that foreshadows the last book in the series, *The Prairie.*

The Deerslayer and *The Last of the Mohicans* are available on cassette from Books on Tape.

PRIDE AND PREJUDICE

By Jane Austen
(1388) 9-1½ hour cassettes
Rental—$16.50   Purchase—$72.00
Read by Jane Bullen

Pride and Prejudice has delighted generations of readers with its ingenious plot, brilliant dialogue, inventive assortment of unique characters and wealth of humor. The central theme is the romantic clash of two opinionated young people. In one corner, we have Elizabeth Bennet, our highly vivacious heroine; in the other, the arrogant but captivating Mr. Darcy. Their destinies interweave in a timeless pattern of courtship, love, property and marriage.

THE PRINCE AND THE PAUPER

By Mark Twain
(1228) 8-1 hour cassettes
Rental—$14.50   Purchase—$64.00
Read by Michael Prichard

On the same day in 16th century London were born Tom Canty, destined to become a street beggar, and Edward Tudor, son of Henry VII, a future king. Several years later young Canty invades the royal precincts hoping to see the Prince. The boys exchange garments and discover they are identical in appearance. Mistaken for the beggar boy, Prince Edward is thrown into the streets. Tom Canty, too frightened to confess his true identity, assumes the mantle of Prince of Wales.

THE PRISONER OF ZENDA

By Anthony Hope
(9013) 6-1 hour cassettes
Rental—$13.50   Purchase—$48.00
Read by Jim Roberts
A Jimcin Recording

The Prisoner of Zenda was published in 1894. Its hero, Rudolf Rassendyll, an indolent young Englishman, decides to visit the kingdom of Ruritania to witness the coronation of its new king. He discovers the crown prince is nearly his exact double. On coronation day, the king is taken prisoner by his evil brother, Ruppert. Rudolf Rassendyll is suddenly compelled to impersonate the monarch. Did Hope write this book after reading *The Prince and the Pauper?*

PUDD'NHEAD WILSON

By Mark Twain
(9078) 6-1 hour cassettes
Rental—$13.50   Purchase—$48.00
Read by Jim Roberts
A Jimcin Recording

Pudd'nhead Wilson is a novel, a mystery and a satire. Written as a chronicle, it describes events occurring over 25 years in Dawson's Landing, Missouri.

A slave woman's child is swapped for a judge's son. Take Southern prejudice, a switch in identities, a bizarre murder and the exuberant characters of Twain's youth, mix them with his mature wit and social sensibilities, and you have a first rate yarn.

THE RED BADGE OF COURAGE
and Other Stories

By Stephen Crane
(1108) 8-1 hour cassettes
Rental—$14.50   Purchase—$64.00
Read by Michael Prichard

The setting is the Civil War . . . the hero is Henry Flemming, who, swept up in the current of events, joins the Union Army. He plunges heedlessly into battle, at first loses his courage, then later regains it for the crucial confrontation. One of the most realistic war stories ever written, *The Red Badge of Courage* gives a striking depiction of how soldiers behave under fire.

Other stories are: "The Blue Hotel," "The Open Boat" and "The Bride Comes to Yellow Sky."

THE RETURN OF THE NATIVE

By Thomas Hardy
(9524) 11-1½ hour cassettes
Rental—$18.50   Purchase—$88.00
Read by Jill Masters
A Jimcin Recording

A masterpiece of dramatic tension, *The Return of the Native* is set in pastoral England.

Following the ancient model of Greek tragedy, Hardy created this forerunner of the 20th century psychological novel. It concerns a sophisticated diamond merchant who chucks his career to become a schoolteacher. He learns the hard way that "you can't go home again."

ROBINSON CRUSOE

By Daniel Defoe
(1017) 8-1½ hour cassettes
Rental—$15.50   Purchase—$64.00
Read by Dan Lazar

When *Robinson Crusoe* was first published in 1719, it was such an immediate success that a second printing was called for three weeks later. Defoe took the true story of a sailor, Alexander Selkirk, who was cast away on an island in 1703, and skillfully embroidered the truth with a wealth of imaginative detail. In addition to providing ageless entertainment, *Robinson Crusoe* contains a message of self-reliance that is probably more needed today than when it was first written.

ROUGHING IT

By Mark Twain
(1998-A) 6-1½ hour cassettes
Rental—$14.50   Purchase—$48.00
(1998-B) 7-1½ hour cassettes
Rental—$15.50   Purchase—$56.00
Read by Michael Prichard

In his youth Mark Twain drifted through the West. He worked as a civil servant, gold prospector, reporter, lecturer. *Roughing It* is Twain's record—fact and impression—of those early years.

Twain tried his luck at everything. He disputed with vigilantes; crossed Slade the Terrible, whose equally terrible wife shot not from the hip but from the petticoat; met people famous and obscure, from Brigham Young, the ambitious Mormon leader, to Hank Erickson, a farmer who sought advice on turnips from Horace Greeley fulminated against him because he could not decipher the answer.

SAPHO

By Alphonse Daudet
(9517) 7-1 hour cassettes
Rental—$14.50   Purchase—$56.00
Read by Walter Covell
A Jimcin Recording

This naturalistic novel of manners which depicts Bohemian life in Paris in the late 19th century was published in 1884. Daudet's style is clear, graceful and humorous.

Jean Gaussin, a consular student, takes up with a group of Parisian artists. As will happen with romantic and inexperienced young men, he falls in love with Fanny Legrand, a woman far more knowledgeable and sophisticated than he. Fanny is a skillful lover, and in educating Jean, she makes him her slave. The consequences of this dependence can be imagined, and Jean's career carroms like a squash ball off the racquets of circumstance.

SCARAMOUCHE

By Rafael Sabatini
(1349) 10-1½ hour cassettes
Rental—$16.50   Purchase—$80.00
Read by Doug Brown

Born of an Italian father and English mother, Rafael Sabatini was fluent in six languages but wrote in English. After *Scaramouche* he was discovered by Hollywood and popular movies were made of several of his books, notably *Captain Blood* and *The Sea Hawk*. Deservedly he was a self-made man.

Scaramouche is not only an exciting story of intrigue and romance in the early days of the French Revolution. It is also meticulously researched.

"A plot of cunning construction. Filled with suspense and deeds of great imagination." *(Editorial Review Services)*

THE SCARLET LETTER

By Nathaniel Hawthorne
(9010) 8-1 hour cassettes
Rental—$15.50   Purchase—$64.00
Read by John Chatty   and Cindy Hardin
A Jimcin Recording

Because Hester Prynne commits adultery and refuses to name her lover, she must wear a scarlet "A" on the breast of her gown for the rest of her life. In the course of the book, a complex interrelationship develops between Hester, her lover, her husband and the daughter of her adulterous union.

**TOLL FREE credit card
order line 1-800-626-3333**

THE SCARLET PIMPERNEL

By Baroness Orczy
(9106) 8-1/2 hour cassettes
Rental—$16.50   Purchase—$64.00
Read by Walter Zimmerman
A Jimcin Recording

The Scarlet Pimpernel is a romantic adventure set during the French Revolution and the ensuing Reign of Terror.

Inspired by a clandestine leader, a small band of titled Englishmen helps innocent victims escape. The hero, a man of many disguises, not only defies but taunts the French authorities: he leaves a blood red flower, a scarlet pimpernel, at the scene of each of his rescues.

THE SEA WOLF

By Jack London
(9022) 7-1/2 hour cassettes
Rental—$16.50   Purchase—$56.00
Read by John Chatty
and Cindy Hardin
A Jimcin Recording

In this saga of the sea, Jack London creates a gripping, heroic struggle between two contrasting types, Wolf Larson and Humphrey Van Weyden. The book begins when Van Weyden's ship sinks in San Francisco Harbor. Rescued by Larson, Van Weyden is forced to serve as cook's scullion. Larson heads for the Bering Sea, where Van Weyden finds human cruelty is matched only by nature.

THE SECOND JUNGLE BOOK

By Rudyard Kipling
(9128) 8-1 hour cassettes
Rental—$15.50   Purchase—$64.00
Read by Cindy Hardin
and Walter Zimmerman
A Jimcin Recording

Though traditionally viewed as classics of children's literature, *The Jungle Books* are equally charming to people of all ages. *The Second Jungle Book* is a continuation of the first and contains these stories: "How Fear Came," "The Miracle of Purun Bhagat," "Letting in the Jungle," "The Undertakers," "The King's Ankus," "Quiquern," "Red Dog," and "The Spring Running." All concern the adventures of Mowgli, the man-cub, and his memorable jungle companions.

Rudyard Kipling was born in 1865 in Bombay, India, and was raised on tales of native lore. He had a rare understanding of the jungle's allure, and nothing ever erased it.

THE SECRET GARDEN

By Frances Hodgson Burnett
(1648) 6-1/2 hour cassettes
Rental—$14.50   Purchase—$48.00
Read by Penelope Dellaporta

First published in 1911, the spell of *The Secret Garden* is still strong. This enchanting children's classic is the story of the awakening of friendship in two children who have been deprived of love and attention.

Mary Lennox is orphaned and sent to live with her reclusive uncle in his house on the Yorkshire moors. There she meets her cousin Colin, a bedridden youth who has been shunnedby his father. And during her exploration of the manor grounds, she discovers a walled-in garden, locked and neglected for the previous ten years.

When the father returns from an extended journey, he finds two healthy children who have discovered the joy of companionship.

SENSE AND SENSIBILITY

By Jane Austen
(9071) 10-1/2 hour cassettes
Rental—$17.50   Purchase—$80.00
Read by Jill Masters
A Jimcin Recording

Sense and Sensibility has more twists to its plot than should be allowed, and is far too complex for reconstruction here. Suffice it to say that in Elinor and Marianne Dashwood we are presented with contrasting qualities of character, the one practical and conventional, the other emotional and sentimental. The outcome turns on these young women mastering their primary characteristics and finding true happiness when in the one sense gives way to sensibility, and in the other sensibility to sense.

THE SIGN OF THE FOUR

By Sir Arthur Conan Doyle
(9508) 5-1 hour cassettes
Rental—$12.50   Purchase—$40.00
Read by Walter Covell
A Jimcin Recording

Arthur Conan Doyle was born in 1859 in Edinburgh, Scotland, He was trained for medicine, which he entered in 1882. Fortunately his practice was not successful and he began writing to fill out the time. His first Sherlock Holmes novel was *A Study in Scarlet*. Holmes appeared in 56 short stories and three novels: *The Sign of the Four, The Hound of the Baskervilles,* and *The Valley of Fear.* Doyle produced books on other topics, but their importance fades by comparison . . . In *The Sign of the Four,* in which Sherlock Holmes solves the mystery of the Indian Treasure for Miss Mary Marston, he remains as always enjoyable if enigmatic.

SILAS MARNER: THE WEAVER OF RAVELOE

By George Eliot
(9085) 8-1 hour cassettes
Rental—$15.50   Purchase—$64.00
Read by Donna Barkman
A Jimcin Recording

George Eliot was the pen name of Mary Ann Evans, an unusual woman at any time, particularly so for her day. She was born in 1819, received an excellent education, lived a full life, and wrote widely and successfully. Her best remembered book is *Silas Marner.*

Silas Marner becomes a compendium of virtues whose lot is to care for a small golden-haired girl whose mother freezes to death in the snow outside his cottage.

SMOKE

By Ivan Turgenev
(9505) 7-1 hour cassettes
Rental—$14.50   Purchase—$56.00
Read by Walter Zimmerman
A Jimcin Recording

Grigory Litvinoff, the son of a poor Russian farmer, travels to Europe to learn methods more progressive than those used on the farms of his countrymen. On return, Litvinoff stops at the home of his fiancée and her mother. There he meets his early love, Irina, who still enchants him.

Turgenev was born in 1818 and lived during turbulent times. But he never politicized his writings: thus his books are true to his vision and remain alive for us today.

SMOKEY THE COWHORSE

By Will James
(1378) 5-1/2 hour cassettes
Rental—$13.50   Purchase—$40.00
Read by Dan Lazar

If you'd like to meet a real cow puncher, you'll enjoy Clint, the bronc peeler. He'll tell you all about his favorite pony, Smoky, who lived a full horse's life in cow country in the early 1900's. Will James, himself a cowboy and rancher, tells this story with the warmth that only love of an animal can inspire.

THE SON OF THE WOLF

By Jack London
(9105) 6-1 hour cassettes
Rental—$13.50 Purchase—$48.00
Read by John Chatty and Jim Roberts
A Jimcin Recording

Jack London loved the North; thus it is fitting that his career was launched with these tales of the Yukon.

The contest between nature and the individual is a favorite London theme. He lays out the keys for survival: determination, ingenuity, courage. And his work became like the men and women of whom he wrote—violent, bold, primitive.

The nine stories in this collection include: "The White Silence," "The Son of the Wolf," "The Men of Forty Mile," "In a Far Country," "To the Man on Trial," "The Priestly Prerogative," "The Wisdom of the Trail," "The Wife of a King" and "An Odyssey of the North."

THE SPY

By James Fenimore Cooper
(9074) 7-1 hour cassettes
Rental—$14.50 Purchase—$56.00
Read by Jim Roberts
A Jimcin Recording

Published in 1821, *The Spy* took for its theme the American Revolutionary War. Cooper vividly describes the conflicting interests of British and Americans in this tale of valor, fortitude and danger.

Harvey Birch is the hero, a true American and patriot. Birch's various disguises and incredible escapes rivet our attention. He is one of the most memorable characters in American literature, drawn so realistically that many men claimed to be the actual person Cooper had dipicted. Flight and hot pursuit, contrasting styles of gentlemen and country folk, and the exciting historical events surrounding our revolution make this story as stirring today as it was on its publication more than a century and a half ago.

A STUDY IN SCARLET

By Sir Arthur Conan Doyle
(9504) 5-1 hour cassettes
Rental—$12.50 Purchase—$40.00
Read by Walter Covell
A Jimcin Recording

All Holmes stories are important to the Baker Street Irregulars, but this one ranks particularly high in their hagiography. Reason: Dr. Watson is introduced, and with this perfect foil to Holmes's gigantic abilities, the author and his characters attain a more relaxed relationship.

THE SUICIDE CLUB AND OTHER STORIES

By Robert Lewis Stevenson
(9150) 4-1 hour cassettes
Rental—$10.50 Purchase—$32.00
Read by Jim Killavey
A Jimcin Recording

They're desperate men who yearn for death but cannot bring themselves to suicide. He's a monstrous scoundrel who caters to their sick fancies. For forty pounds they can join the Suicide Club and their morbid desires will be satisfied.

They gather each night to watch the cards being dealt out. To the man who gets the ace of spades—death. To the one who receives the ace of clubs—murder!

Other stories include: "Story of the Young Man with the Cream Tarts," "Story of the Physician and the Saragtoga Trunk," "The Adventures of the Hansom Cab," "The Sire de Maletroit's Door" and "Markheim."

THE SWISS FAMILY ROBINSON

By Johann David Wyss
(1110) 8-1½ hour cassettes
Rental—$15.50 Purchase—$64.00
Read by Dan Lazar

The Swiss Family Robnison is a story of family cooperation and mutual support set on an exotic distant island. The tale, the most famous imitation of Defoe's *Robinson Crusoe*, was concocted by Johann Wyss's father for the enjoyment of his sons. The sons pooled their talents in writing, illustrating and editing to produce this popular classic. *The Swiss Family Robinson* is an ideal selection to share with children, at home, on vacation, or on a long weekend.

A TALE OF TWO CITIES

By Charles Dickens
(1073) 8-1½ hour cassettes
Rental—$15.50 Purchase—$64.00
Read by Angela Cheyne

This novel of the French Revolution, told by the most popular English author of his century, gives us an idea of the revulsion Britain felt for France's egalitarian spasm. It was not just the overthrow of the monarchy, nor the establishment of new principles of government, but the ruthless, fratricidal and murderous consequences they deplored.

For quick ordering
1-800-626-3333

TALES OF SPACE AND TIME

By H.G. Wells
(9061) 6-1½ hour cassettes
Rental—$15.50 Purchase—$48.00
Read by Walter Covell and Ivor Hugh
A Jimcin Recording

H.G. Wells was born in 1866 and died 80 years later, just at the end of World War II. He lived to see 20th century science surpass much of the science fiction he had imagined.

In this collection, Wells lets his imagination run backward in time as well as forward. Titles include: "The Crystal Egg: The Star," "Stories of the Stone Age," "A Story of the Days to Come" and "The Man Who Could Work Miracles."

TALES OF TERROR AND THE SUPERNATURAL

By A Collection
(9002) 7-1½ hour cassettes
Rental—$16.50 Purchase—$56.00
Read by Various Readers
A Jimcin Recording

A collection of 16 short stories. Titles include: "Hop Frog" and "The Shadow" by Edgar Allan Poe, "La Horla" and "The Wolf" by Guy de Maupassant, "The Judge's House" and "Dracula's Guest" by Bram Stoker, "The Wondersmith" and "What Was It" by Fitz-James O'Brien, "The Boarded Window" by Ambrose Bierce, "History of the Young Man with Spectacles" by Arthur Machen, "The Adventure of the German Student" by Washington Irving, "The Upper Berth" by F. Marion Crawford, "Dr. Heidegger's Experiment" by Nathaniel Hawthorne. "The Country of the Blind" by H.G. Wells, "Sir Dominic Sarsfield" by J. Sheridan LeFanu and "The Three Strangers" by Thomas Hardy.

TALES OF THE OCCULT

By Various Authors
(9147) 7-1½ hour cassettes
Rental—$16.50 Purchase—$56.00
Read by Walter Zimmerman, Jim Killavey, Walter Covell and Cindy Hardin
A Jimcin Recording

Stories include "The Great God Pan" by Arthur Machen, "A Pair of Hands" by Sir Arthur Quiller-Couch, "The Yellow Sign" by Robert Chambers, "The Voice in the Night" by William Hope Hodgson, "The Willows" by Algernon Blackwood and "Oil of Dog" and "John Barine's Watch," both by Ambrose Bierce.

The collection continues with "The Ghosts" by Lorn Dunsany, "The Legend of the Arabian Astrologer" by Washington Irving, "The Tarn" by Hugh Walpole, "A Strange Christmas Game" by Mrs. J.H. Riddell, "The Mark of the Beast" by Rudyard Kipling and "Pollock and the Porroh Man" by H.G. Wells.

Note: Sale and rental of recordings of this book are restricted to the United States.

TALES OF THE SUPERNATURAL

By Sir Arthur Conan Doyle
(9132) 6-1 hour cassettes
Rental—$13.50   Purchase—$48.00
Read by Walter Covell
A Jimcin Recording

These 15 stories deal with spiritualism, Egyptian magic, psychometry, and other occult domains.

This collection includes "The Bully of Brocas Court," "The Captain of the Polestar," "The Brown Hand," "The Leather Funnel," "Lot No. 249," "J. Habakuk Jephson's Statement," "The Great Keinplatz Experiment," "A Literary Mosaic," "Playing with Fire," "The Ring of Thoth," "The Los Amigos Fiasco," "The Silver Hatchet," "John Barrington Cowles," "Selecting a Ghost" and "The American's Tale."

TALES OF UNREST

By Joseph Conrad
(9081) 6-1½ hour cassettes
Rental—$15.50   Purchase—$48.00
Read by Walter Zimmerman
A Jimcin Recording

Tales of Unrest is a collection of five short stories. They include "The Lagoon"; "An Outpost of Progress," an ironic account of the struggles of two Englishmen who have been transported to a trading post in the remotest interior of Africa; "The Idiots," a family tragedy; "The Return," the story of an upper-class English couple and the progressive destruction of their marriage; and "Karain: A Memory," a postscript to "The Lagoon."

Conrad's entire work was concerned with the destinies of men and how individuals react to the pressures of life and circumstance.

TANGLEWOOD TALES

By Nathaniel Hawthorne
(9039) 7-1 hour cassettes
Rental—$14.50   Purchase—$56.00
Read by Walter Covell
and Walter Zimmerman
A Jimcin Recording

Tanglewood Tales use the Greek classics as their source. Nathaniel Hawthorne has taken the most striking and exciting ones and adapted them for children. From the original stories he has selected episodes that illustrate conceptions held by the original authors. Titles include: "The Minotaur," "The Pygmies," "The Dragon's Teeth," "Circe's Palace," "The Pomegranate Seeds" and "The Golden Fleece."

TESS OF THE D'URBERVILLES

By Thomas Hardy
(9075) 12-1½ hour cassettes
Rental—$18.50   Purchase—$96.00
Read by Jill Masters
A Jimcin Recording

Often labeled Hardy's masterpiece, *Tess of the D'Urbervilles* is a story told at three levels. First, it is a romantic and tragic tale of love gone astray. Second, it is an indictment of the class system so beloved of all Victorians. And third, it is an inquiry into what deities or fates control the destinies of humans.

Hardy is a masterful storyteller, and Tess a captivating heroine. Who can fail to sympathize with a girl who is poor but pure, whose own innocence leads her into circumstances of frightful desperation?

THIRD PERSON RURAL

By Noel Perrin

and THE ADVENTURES OF JONATHAN CORNCOB, LOYAL AMERICAN REFUGEE

By Himself, edited and introduced by Noel Perrin
(1920) 6-1½ hour cassettes
Rental—$14.50   Purchase—$48.00
Read by Grover Gardner

Third Person Rural is Noel Perrin's third set of essays on Vermont farm life. An English professor at Dartmouth College, Perrin refers to his occasional bouts in the country as "a working class farmer who mows fields on contract to summer people, sells wood and stacks it for them."

The Adventures of Jonathan Corncob, author unknown, is a rare satire of the American Revolution. Discovered and introduced by Noel Perrin, this book was originally published in London in 1787 (it has never before been published in America), and is one of very few Revolutionary War novels to have survived. Bawdy, chauvinistic, anti-heroic and funny, Jonathan Corncob was the black humor of the 18th century.

THE $30,000 BEQUEST
and Other Stories

By Mark Twain
(9125) 4-1 hour cassettes
Rental—$10.50   Purchase—$32.00
Read by Jim Killavey and
Walter Zimmerman
A Jimcin Recording

Saladin Foster and his wife Electra are jolted out of their tranquility by the stunning news that a distant relative has left them $30,000. The one condition is that the couple must be able to prove "that they had taken no notice of the gift by spoken word or by letter, had made no inquiries concerning the moribund's progress toward the everlasting tropics, and had not attended the funeral."

Other stories are: "Experience of the Mc-Williamses with Membranous Croup," "The Facts in the Great Beef Contract," "My Watch," "The Canvasser's Tale," "The Professor's Yarn," "The Invalid's Story," "Cecil Rhodes and the Shard" and "A Story Without an End."

THOMAS HARDY:
SELECTED SHORT STORIES

By Thomas Hardy
(9903) 5-1 hour cassettes
Rental—$11.50   Purchase—$40.00
Read by Richard Morant
A Talking Tape Recording

Thomas Hardy was born in 1840 near Dorchester in that part of England he called Wessex. With stories sometimes from his own imagination and sometimes from local tradition, Hardy's work, like Dickens or Trollope, creates a strong sense of mood and location.

Hardy hoped to be remembered for his poetry, but ours is not a poetic age. Thus his claim to a new generation of readers rests on his prose. We find great similarities between his era, a time of change, and our own.

This collection of short stories shows Hardy at his best and includes: "The Three Strangers," "The Withered Arm," "The Fiddler of the Reels," "An Imaginative Woman" and "Barbara of the House of Grebe."

THREE BY ZOLA

By Emile Zola
(9019) 4-1 hour cassettes
Rental—$10.50   Purchase—$32.00
Read by Walter Covell
A Jimcin Recording

These three stories provide an excellent introduction to the author. In "Captain Burle," Zola deals with loyalty and its affect on the careers of military officers. This was an important topic to Frenchmen of his era . . . " The Miller's Daughter" also treats loyalty, but this time in the context of family. The miller is torn between protecting his country's soldiers and his family . . . " The Death of Oliver Becaille" addresses the problems of when life ends and when death begins. In all three stories, Zola puts us on the horns of dilemma.

TOM SAWYER ABROAD

By Mark Twain
(1246) 6-1 hour cassettes
Rental—$12.50   Purchase—$48.00
Read by Michael Prichard

In Tom Sawyer Abroad, published in 1894, Tom, Huck Finn and Jim are examining a balloon in St. Louis when it unexpectedly takes off, swooping them over the Atlantic to Africa. There, wild lions, Bedouins, sand storms and mirages test their courage, which abounds, and their common sense, on occasion absent. By the time they sail up again from Mt. Sinai, they have been through a series of adventures that make their escapades at home look tame. *Tom Sawyer Abroad* is first-rate family entertainment.

TRAVELS WITH A DONKEY

By Robert Louis Stevenson
(9513) 4-1 hour cassettes
Rental—$10.50   Purchase—$32.00
Read by Walter Covell
A Jimcin Recording

Stevenson was set down in the middle of the 19th century and expired before its end. His life was short but brilliant. One of his principal means of fulfillment and discovery was travel.

In *Travels with a Donkey,* full title *Travels with a Donkey in the Cevennes,* he toured that lovely portion of France in 1878 with a donkey as his sole companion. The story is brisk and light, and moves along with Stevenson's sharp and memorable observations.

TREASURE ISLAND

By Robert Louis Stevenson
(1072) 7-1 hour cassettes
Rental—$13.50   Purchase—$56.00
Read by Angela Cheyne

Since its publication in 1883, *Treasure Island* has remained one of the great tales of mutiny. Its primary malefactor, Long John Silver, has become synonymous with evil. The story is told through the eyes of Jim Hawkins, a young man who first encounters tales of buried treasure while working at his father's taver. The action moves from the Admiral Benbow Inn to the high seas and on to secret islands. Never did virtue so reward a young man as Hawkins has been rewarded, made immortal by the gifts of an immortal storyteller.

TYPEE

By Herman Melville
(9164) 8-1½ hour cassettes
Rental—$16.50   Purchase—$64.00
Read by John Chatty
A Jimcin Recording

NEW

Typee was Herman Melville's first book. It is an idyll of four months among primitive South Sea islanders. It won him great fame during his life.

Melville always mixes his own extraordinary personal experiences with later research to produce powerful and imaginative works. *Typee* shocked its original audience with a truthful account of Polynesian tribal life. It also defined the author: caught in its glare like a fly in amber, he stands frozen before the exotic, sharply focused on it, yet forced to remain forever alien.

"A vivid picture of a civilized man in contact with the exotic dream-like life of the tropics." *(Readers Encyclopedia)*

TYPHOON and ALMAYER'S FOLLY

By Joseph Conrad
(1091) 7-1½ hour cassettes
Rental—$15.50   Purchase—$56.00
Read by Wolfram Kandinsky

Typhoon is the tale of an old steamer and an ageless captain. The drama unfolds against a sea gone wild. Unimaginative and imperturbable, Captain MacWhirr faces down the storm, a rebellion in steerage and an insubordinate mate. The story is a deep affirmation of simple and conservative virtues.

Conrad's first novel, *Almayer's Folly* is set in the South Seas. It examines the failure of a man to appraise his own capacity, and the tragedy this brings on others.

THE VICAR OF WAKEFIELD

By Oliver Goldsmith
(9149) 5-1½ hour cassettes
Rental—$14.50   Purchase—$40.00
Read by Walter Zimmerman
A Jimcin Recording

Called by Lord Byron "the most exquisite of all romance in miniature," *The Vicar of Wakefield* is the story of a simple reverend who, losing his fortune, moves his family to a new part of the country and tries to live according to his beliefs.

He and his family make an Arcadian picture of affectionate accord. That is until the idyll is rudely disturbed by a notorious seducer. But in those days before television, what else was there to do?

As an author of the eighteenth century, "Goldsmith's style is the perfection of classical English." *(Best Fiction)*

VICTORY and THE SECRET SHARER

By Joseph Conrad
(1698) 10-1½ hour cassettes
Rental—$16.50   Purchase—$80.00
Read by Wolfram Kandinsky

In *Victory,* drifting and searching for some meaning or value in his life, Axel Heyst retreats to a tropical island in the East Indies where he finds Lena. In this psychological romance between a man—honest, decent, disinterested in material gain—and a woman who was unused to such traits in men, a suspenseful drama is played out involving three bandits and their innocent victims.

The Secret Sharer, one of the great short stories in English, is the tale of a ship captain faced with the responsibility of command struggling to come to terms with self-doubt and anxiety. The first mate, Legatt, in the brig for committing a criminal act, fulfills the captain's need for someone who will empathize with his (the captain's) predicament, in effect a "secret sharer."

WALDEN

By Henry David Thoreau
(1023) 8-1½ hour cassettes
Rental—$15.50   Purchase—$64.00
Read by Dan Lazar

Walden grew from a journal Thoreau kept while he lived in a simple hut by Walden Pond from July 1845 to September 1847. His journal not only describes the seasons and natural inhabitants at Walden, but also the illusions permeating civilized life, and the conflict between the ideals of living and the methods of making a living. *Walden* contains an intimate, beautiful tribute to nature, and Thoreau's treatment of the concepts of self-reliance and common sense is a classic expression of a philosophy that is uniquely American.

FREE rental from Books on Tape™
See page 3

WAR AND PEACE

By Leo Tolstoy
(1352-A) 11-1½ hour cassettes
Rental—$17.50   Purchase—$88.00
(1352-B) 12-1½ hour cassettes
Rental—$17.50   Purchase—$96.00
(1352-C) 13-1½ hour cassettes
Rental—$18.50   Purchase—$104.00
(1352-D) 11-1½ hour cassettes
Rental—$17.50   Purchase—$88.00
Read by Walter Zimmerman

Written about the time of our own Civil War, *War and Peace* concerns another violent conflict, the invasion of Russia by Napoleon in 1812. While Tolstoy himself was born 16 years later, he grew up in a Russia that was still recovering from Napoleon's carnage and his outlook was certainly conditioned by the men he met and the stories he heard.

One finishes *War and Peace* in a state of exhilaration. We have come to know and care deeply about the lives, loves and fates of the teeming personalities who populate Tolstoy's masterpiece and who henceforth will walk with us on our journeys of imagination.

THE WAR OF THE WORLDS (abrid.) and THE TIME MACHINE

By H.G. Wells
(9007) 7-1 hour cassettes
Rental—$14.50   Purchase—$56.00
Read by Walter Zimmerman and
Jim Roberts
A Jimcin Recording

The War of the Worlds is H.G. Wells' classic chiller about a Martian attack on the Earth. It inspired Orson Welles' 1938 radio dramatization that threw the country into widespread panic. It remains a singular and entertaining example of early science fiction.

The Time Machine is the first science fiction story dealing with time travel. Masterfully thought out and filled with a fascinating wealth of inventiveness.

THE WARDEN

By Anthony Trollope
(9510) 8-1 hour cassettes
Rental—$15.50   Purchase—$64.00
Read by Jill Masters
A Jimcin Recording

Anthony Trollope was born in 1815 in London to a father who, though a barrister, became impecunious through speculation. In 19th century England, indebtedness was taken seriously and the family fled to Belgium where Anthony's mother supported her brood by writing. In all, she wrote a total of 114 volumes, so Anthony came by his prolixity, as it were, by a gift of nature.

The Warden, published in 1855, is the story of reform run amok. The Reverend Septimus Harding, a gentle and unprepossessing church functionary, is made precentor of the local cathedral and warden of a charitable foundation which maintains 12 elderly church laborers. The old men are kept in very modest circumstances while the residual income goes to Harding.

WASHINGTON SQUARE

By Henry James
(9102) 8-1 hour cassettes
Rental—$15.50   Purchase—$64.00
Read by Donna Barkman
A Jimcin Recording

The setting is New York City in the 1850's (one of the few Jamesian novels set in his native land). The story centers on an heiress who lacks beauty and wit, her proud father, and her fortune-hunting suitor.

The force of this outstanding short novel lies in paradox. The father accurately appraises the suitor and forbids the marriage. His judgment is correct: his fault is to call the trifler a trifler. Paradox is carried further when out of love comes cruelty, out of innocence, treachery.

WEIRD STORIES

By Charlotte Riddell
(9096) 6-1 hour cassettes
Rental—$13.50   Purchase—$48.00
Read by Jill Masters
A Jimcin Recording

First appearing in 1882, this collection by Charlotte Riddell established her as a leading Victorian author of supernatural fiction. She achieved her effect by using commonplace settings into which the horrors crept.

Stories include: "Walnut-Tree House," "The Open Door," "Nut Bush Farm," "The Old House in Vauxhall Walk," "Sandy the Tinker" and "The Last of Squire Ennismore."

WHITE FANG

By Jack London
(9076) 8-1 hour cassettes
Rental—$15.50   Purchase—$64.00
Read by John Chatty
A Jimcin Recording

As with *The Call of the Wild, White Fang* explores a world where animals and men depend on each other for survival.

This story of a dog who is part wolf has lasted because Jack London gives each of his animals a personality. London's narratives are more than epics of hardship and survival: they are morality plays in which virtuous good triumphs over scrofulous evil.

WIDDERSHINS: THE FIRST BOOK OF GHOST STORIES

By Oliver Onions
(9099) 7-1 hour cassettes
Rental—$14.50   Purchase—$56.00
Read by Diane Burroughs
A Jimcin Recording

The English author Oliver Onions, born in 1873 and known in private life as George Oliver, was noted for his ghost stories. The supernatural beings in these tales are memorable, with understandable but complex psychological patterns and a dimension that extends beyond mortal compass.

Included in this collection is "The Beckoning Fair One," one of the great ghost stories of all time. Algernon Blackwood called it the best ghost story in English; H.P. Lovecraft and other writers and critics have concurred.

Other stories include: "Phantas," "Rooum," "Benlian," "The Accident," "The Lost Thyrsus" and "The Cigarette Case."

THE WIND IN THE ROSEBUSH

By Mary E. Wilkins Freeman
(9116) 5-1 hour cassettes
Rental—$12.50   Purchase—$40.00
Read by Cindy Hardin
A Jimcin Recording

Mary E. Wilkins Freeman is best known as a writer of New England "local color" stories. She received the William Dean Howells medal for fiction in 1925. Her stories sympathetically portray the plight of women in the 1890's.

Freeman is equally convincing when her theme is the supernatural. In this collection she speaks to us of the arcane in a voice original, haunting and authentic. Try these on a stormy winter night: "The Wind in the Rosebush," "The Shadows on the Wall," "Luella Miller," "The Southwest Chamber," "The Vacant Lot" and "The Lost Ghost."

THE WIND IN THE WILLOWS

By Kenneth Grahame
(1389) 7-1 hour cassettes
Rental—$13.50   Purchase—$56.00
Read by Dan Lazar

A simple-hearted Mole, a Water Rat with a flair for poetry, and a wealthy, boastful Toad with a passion for motor cars are the principal characters in Grahame's tale. In this animal story concerned with the small creatures of field, woods and river bank, the author shows an enduring depth of feeling for his subjects. Through his deft blending of fantasy and reality, we enter a world, complete in itself, that contains creatures of unique individuality and delineation.

THE WIZARD OF OZ and THE LAND OF OZ

By L. Frank Baum
(9064) 6-1½ hour cassettes
Rental—$15.50   Purchase—$48.00
Read by Cindy Hardin, Walter Zimmerman and Jim Roberts
A Jimcin Recording

Most of us remember *The Wizard of Oz* as the film with Judy Garland and Bert Lahr. But the film was based on an immensely popular series of Oz novels written between 1900 and 1913. In these books, Oz is a utopia beyond the rainbow where threats are turned back with valor and ingenuity.

Their success is due to the way they induce children to look for the element of wonder in the world around them. Additionally, they have an easy optimism not prevalent in children's stories of that time. *The Wizard of Oz* and *The Land of Oz* are two early samples of the Oz legend.

WOMEN IN LITERATURE: THE SHORT STORY

By A Collection
(9057) 8-1 hour cassettes
Rental—$15.50   Purchase—$64.00
Read by Cindy Hardin and Walter Zimmerman
A Jimcin Recording

These stories, all written around the turn of the century, deal with the situation in which women found themselves as the Victorian era drew to a close.

Titles include: "The Story of an Hour," "Desiree's Baby," "Wiser than the Gods" and "Silk Stockings" by Kate Chopin; "The Other Two" and "The Mission of Jane" by Edith Wharton; "A Wagner Matinee" and "The Sculptor's Funeral" by Willa Cather; "A Village Singer" and "The Revolt of Mother" by Mary E. Wilkins Freeman; "A White Heron" by Sarah Orne Jewett; "The Marquise" by George Sand; "Turkey Red" by Frances Gilchrist Wood and "A Christmas Guest" by Selma Lagerloff.

WUTHERING HEIGHTS

By Emily Bronte
(1475) 9-1½ hour cassettes
Rental—$16.50   Purchase—$72.00
Read by Wanda McCaddon

Wuthering Heights is a story of love turning in on itself and the violence and misery that result from thwarted longing. A book of immense power, it is filled with the raw beauty of the moors and a deep compassion for the destinies of men and women . . . a compassion made all the more extraordinary by the fact that it came from the heart of a frail, inexperienced girl who lived out her lonely life in the moorland wilderness and died a year after this great novel was published.

YOUTH and THE END OF THE TETHER

By Joseph Conrad
(1527) 7-1 hour cassettes
Rental—$13.50   Purchase—$56.00
Read by Wolfram Kandinsky

Both of these stories sprang from Joseph Conrad's own experience sailing in the Far East with the Merchant Navy.

"For it can hardly be denied that it is not their own desserts that men are most proud of, but rather of their prodigious luck, of their marvelous fortune," wrote Conrad of *Youth*. In it he captures a young man's exhilaration in the face of danger and the unknown.

The End of the Tether is in a different mold. Captain Whalley, aging but still afloat, compromises his principles without understanding what can follow. But life, like the sea, is unsparing, and the captain's fate arrives in due course, served up with Conrad's own brand of uncompromising logic.

ZADIG

By Francois Voltaire
(9094) 3-1 hour cassettes
Rental—$9.50   Purchase—$24.00
Read by Walter Covell
A Jimcin Recording

In his preface Voltaire wrote: " . . . I the undersigned, who have passed myself off as a man of learning and even wit, have read this manuscript which, in spite of myself, I have found curious, amusing, moral, philosophic, worthy of pleasing even those who hate novels."

Right on all counts. *Zadig* is the story of an educated, charming and sensible young man living in Babylon who escapes great dilemmas by remaining calmly sensible while serving as an adviser to kings, princes and judges. As in *Candide,* Voltaire satirizes without mercy.

**For Visa and MasterCard
order line 1-800-626-3333**

D·H
LAWRENCE
Aaron's Rod

AARON'S ROD

NEW

By D.H. Lawrence
(2151) 8-1½ hour cassettes
Rental—$15.50   Purchase—$64.00
Read by Richard Brown

After twelve years in a troubled marriage, Aaron has had enough. He leaves not only wife and children, but also the mining community in which he was raised. Confident in his abilities as a musician, he heads south. Then he meets another woman.

Aaron's Rod is one of Lawrence's most intensely self-revealing novels. He explores the interplay of dominance and submission in the complex relationship called "love."

David Herbert Lawrence was born in Nottinghamshire, England, in 1885. His first novel, *The White Peacock*, appeared in 1911. His books were always brilliant, always controversial. He died of tuberculosis in Venice in 1930 at the age of 44.

ACTS OF LOVE

By Elia Kazan
(1433) 9-1½ hour cassettes
Rental—$16.50   Purchase—$72.00
Read by Michael Owens

Elia Kazan's career proves that talent can be multi-faceted. Kazan won an Oscar for his theatrical work and has written several best-selling novels, all to critical acclaim.

Acts of Love explores the dilemma of a young woman who tries to live her life through others. She marries, only to find her husband's father infinitely more compelling than his son.

"This novel explores contemporary attitudes towards a problem as old as history." *(Editorial Review Service)*

**Collector's Editions™
from Books on Tape™
See page 3**

ADULTERY & OTHER CHOICES

By Andre Dubus
(1436) 7-1 hour cassettes
Rental—$13.50   Purchase—$56.00
Read by Dan Lazar

Adultery & Other Choices is our second collection of Andre Dubus' work. In it, we follow the fortunes, fantasies and modest adventures of Paul Clement, a sensitive, small-town Louisiana boy, as he grows to manhood.

Manhood, in his case, means a stint as an enlisted man in the U.S. Marines, with the ritual ragging and closed community codes, the physical trials and emotional flashpoints.

THE AERODROME

NEW

By Rex Warner
(2095) 6-1½ hour cassettes
Rental—$14.50   Purchase—$48.00
Read by Rodney Lay

The Aerodrome was first published in 1941, a time of enormous peril in Britain. Understandably it took a while for the book to catch on.

But when it took root, it flowered mightily. To this day it receives praise not only for its inherent drama and excitement, but for its political and human statements as well.

The Aerodrome is an allegory that pits the order and ruthlessness of a military organization against the sensible muddle of a middle-class village. In the author's view, adaptability is all; judged by this test, the military cannot get its bat up.

"Probably the only work of its time to understand the appeal of fascism and the less confident though finally stronger answer of democracy." *(E.R.S. Reviews)*

THE AFFAIR

By C.P. Snow
(1417) 8-1½ hour cassettes
Rental—$15.50   Purchase—$64.00
Read by John MacDonald

The Affair is perhaps the most celebrated of C.P. Snow's books, a runaway best seller and a great hit in its stage adaption. This novel brings Lewis Eliot back to his old Cambridge College.

Donald Howard, a young research associate, falsifies data and is deprived of his Fellowship. Bitter and friendless, he is deserted by all but his wife. She turns to Eliot for help, and he mobilizes support for Howard.

"Snow's message: the search for the truth is a moral responsibility as well as a scientific one. His explication is a literary joy to behold." *(San Francisco Chronicle)*

THE AFRICAN QUEEN

By C.S. Forester
(1350) 6-1 hour cassettes
Rental—$12.50   Purchase—$48.00
Read by Richard Green

This novel is about an action in WWI between German forces and what might be called British irregulars.

Rose Sayer, sister of an English missionary in German Central Africa, seems an unlikely heroine until her brother dies and she takes responsibility for her own life. With a gin drinking engineer, Allnutt, the indomitable Miss Sayer sets out on *The African Queen,* a leaky thirty-foot river boat, to strike a blow for England and avenge her brother's death.

THE AGE OF INNOCENCE

By Edith Wharton
(1382) 8-1½ hour cassettes
Rental—$15.50   Purchase—$64.00
Read by Flo Gibson

The Age of Innocence is Edith Wharton's Pulitzer prize-winning tale of the manners and morals of New York society in the later 1800's . . . a world she knew well.

Newland Archer is a young attorney, hand some and eligible. Torn between his socally acceptable fiancee and the more earthy attractions of Countess Olenska, Archer is truly on the horns of a dilemma.

"The plot is unobvious, delicately developed, with a fine finale that exquisitely satisfies one's sense of fitness, and as always with Mrs. Wharton, the drama of character is greater than that of event." *(Publishers Weekly)*

AIR BRIDGE

By Hammond Innes
(1801) 7-1½ hour cassettes
Rental—$15.50   Purchase—$56.00
Read by Ron Shoop

Neil Fraser, former WW II hero, is a top notch mercenary pilot. But now he is on the run, and in need of a plane. Bill Saeton has risen from the flames of war with the dream of an air freight fleet.

Fraser needs a plane. Saeton needs Fraser. One would murder his best friend to get what he wants, but this is where the other draws the line.

"Authentic and excellent . . . His plot, characters and suspense live up to the setting." *(San Francisco Chronicle)*

Other Innes titles offered by B-O-T include *The Big Footprints, Campbell's Kingdom, The Doomed Oasis* and *The Naked Land.*

ALL MY FRIENDS ARE GOING TO BE STRANGERS

By Larry McMurtry
(1974) 7-1½ hour cassettes
Rental—$15.50   Purchase—$56.00
Read by Wolfram Kandinsky

Danny Deck is a promising younger writer whose nearly fatal mistake is to cut himself off from his roots. He drifts from his native Texas to California and back, falls in love, looks for ties that will bind him to people and places.

What saves Danny is his discovery that his true country is the borderland—"a thin strip between the country of the normal and the country of the strange." He finds his home is not entirely in Texas or Hollywood, but partially in both. In deed, Danny sounds somthing like his creator.

"Acute, elegiac, funny and dangerously tender . . . indelible people and brilliant set piece scenes." *(Time)*

ALL THE BEST PEOPLE

By Sloan Wilson
(1397) 12-1½ hour cassettes
Rental—$17.50   Purchase—$96.00
Read by Dan Lazar

Sloan Wilson has written a chronicle of two members of the upper-middle class, Dana Campbell and Caroline Stauffer, whose parents are part owners of a fashionable resort hotel on Lake George in the 1920's and 1930's. As he did in *The Man in the Gray Flannel Suit*, Wilson again explores the sensitive underbelly of American success. His descriptions of the frustrations of sex from teenage petting to the vicissitudes of the marriage bed are lush as well as relevant.

Other Sloan Wilson titles available to our subscribers include *The Man in the Gray Flannel Suit* and *What Shall We Wear to This Party*, Wilson's highly personal and detailed autobiography.

THE ALTERATION

By Kingsley Amis
(1121) 8-1 hour cassettes
Rental—$14.50   Purchase—$64.00
Read by Richard Green

The year is 1976 and we are alive in an all Catholic world. The Reformation never took place because Martin Luther made a deal with Rome and became Pope Martin I. The "alteration" proposed to Hubert Anvil, brilliant 10-year-old boy soprano, is that most feared by all males. Pope John XXIV wishes Hubert to preserve the purity of his voice to glorify the Church on a permanent basis; Hubert wishes to share his talent but he has some disquieting thoughts about Pope John's proposal.

AMERICA AMERICA

By Elia Kazan
(1916) 4-1 hour cassettes
Rental—$9.50   Purchase—$32.00
Read by by Dan Lazar

"America, America!" These words are the vision of a young man, Starvos Topouzoglou, 20 years old and ablaze with the dream of a new, far-off world. Nothing can stand in his way.

America America is about immigration, the tyranny of our ancestors' homelands and the obsessive drive that brought our grandfathers to this country. It is difficult for us to imagine the realities of our heritage, but Elia Kazan shows us how the America we know today emerged from our forefathers' drive for a life of greater freedom and opportunity.

"An astonishingly moving narrative . . . beautiful." *(The New York Times)*

AND QUIET FLOWS THE DON

By Mikhail Sholokhov
(1185-A) 9-1½ hour cassettes
Rental—$16.50   Purchase—$72.00
(1185-B) 6-1½ hour cassettes
Rental—$14.50   Purchase—$48.00
Read by Wolfram Kandinsky

And Quiet Flows the Don is the immortal portrayal of a Cossack village—beginning in the days of peace under the Czar, carrying on through war and revolution. Mikhail Sholokhov centers the story around Gregor Melekhov, a young man of the village. Gregor's life in the home of his father, his unhappy marriage, and his fortunes in the revolution are not only a magnificent narrative in themselves, but also a microcosm of the tumultuous world of the Cossacks.

"If one is going to talk about the best Russian novel of the 20th Century, it may be necessary to go no further than *And Quiet Flows the Don*." —Norman Mailer

ANECDOTES OF DESTINY

By Isak Dinesen
(1859) 8-1 hour cassettes
Rental—$14.50   Purchase—$64.00
Read by Wanda McCaddon

As a young woman early in this century, Karen Blixen—whom we know as Isak Dinesen—managed a 6,000-acre hill farm in Kenya where she was doctor, judge and friend to native Kikuyu and Masai who lived on her land.

In middle age, back in her native Denmark, Blixen turned to weaving what may be described as adventures of the mind.

THE ANGELIC AVENGER

By Isak Dinesen
(1858) 8-1½ hour cassettes
Rental—$15.50   Purchase—$64.00
Read by Donada Peters

In the opening moments of this story, Lucan Belleden, a governess nearing spinsterhood, is nervously awaiting—and steeling herself to reject—an offer of marriage from her pompous, middle-aged employer. What she gets, couched in the most highflown and exalted sentiments, is an offer of quite another kind! Lucan takes flight down the ivy, and Isak Dinesen launches us into a colorful adventure, spiced by ironic and mordant humor.

ANIMAL FARM

By George Orwell
(1539) 3-1 hour cassettes
Rental—$8.50   Purchase—$24.00
Read by Richard Green

Animal Farm was George Orwell's satirical shot at the then-new totalitarianism of the left. It is so accurate that no one has been able to do it better or more effectively, or even come close. Who can forget "All Animals Are Created Equal, But Some Are More Equal Than Others." By putting wisdom in the mouths of animals, Orwell uses an age-old artifice and proves again how the pen can be mightier than the sword.

ARABELLA

By Georgette Heyer
(1605) 7-1½ hour cassettes
Rental—$15.50   Purchase—$56.00
Read by Flo Gibson

Silk, velvet, satin and lace; trimmings of ermine and jewels. These are only dreams for Arabella Tallant, the eldest daughter of a poor country vicar.

But fortune favors this young woman. It arrives one day in the matronly form of Lady Bridlington, Arabella's distant but very wealthy godmother, who asks the girl to join her in London.

Georgette Heyer's regency romances set the style for hundreds of imitators. Other popular Heyer romances can be found in the Index at the back of our catalog under the author's name.

FREE rental from Books on Tape™ See page 3

THE ARRANGEMENT

By Elia Kazan
(1917-A) 8-1½ hour cassettes
Rental—$16.50   Purchase—$64.00
(1917-B) 6-1½ hour cassettes
Rental—$14.50   Purchase—$48.00
Read by Dan Lazar

This is Eddie Anderson's story. He's successful, well-off, with a nice home, and an attentive wife. But he's restless. So he has a mistress, and now she wants to change that arrangement. How Eddie got in this mess and how he tries to get out is the story of this best-selling book.

Elia Kazan won two Academy Awards for directing before turning to writing.

"The Arrangement is about those 'arrangements' by which we live, in marriage, out of marriage, between marriages. It is an earth-shaking book and the earth it shakes is the plot on which we're standing." *(Publisher's Source)*

THE ASSASSINS

By Elia Kazan
(1918) 8-1½ hour cassettes
Rental—$14.50   Purchase—$64.00
Read by Dan Lazar

Master Sergeant Cesario Flores is a troubled man. A career non com, he feels safe in his well-ordered life. So when his precious daughter Juana joins the tuned-in, dropped-out generation, Flores breaks into little pieces . . . with murder the result.

The Assassins is set in the United States during the '70s, a violent time at home and abroad. It's about two specific murders, but more than that it focuses on a murderous way of life. *America, America* and *The Arrangement,* both best sellers from Elia Kazan, are also available on cassette from Books on Tape

THE AUTOBIOGRAPHY OF MISS JANE PITTMAN

By Ernest J. Gaines
(1487) 7-1½ hour cassettes
Rental—$15.50   Purchase—$56.00
Read by Roses Prichard

This is a novel in the guise of the tape recorded recollection of a 110-year old black woman who was born a slave but has lived to see the black militancy of the 1960's.

The secret of this book's success is the characterization of Miss Jane. She is a master of her people's language. But more than that, she is unsurpassed as a storyteller.

"Ernest Gaines has written a book that comes down on the side of time, on the side of the future." *(Editorial Review Service)*

B-O-T has also recorded Gaines' *Of Love and Dust, In My Father's House* and *Bloodline.*

BACK EAST

By Ellen Pall
(2032) 7-1 hour cassettes
Rental—$13.50   Purchase—$56.00
Read by Donada Peters

Melanie is a songwriter in LA who's sick of California. She returns to New York to resume her career and reestablish ties with her family. But life takes an unexpected turn.

We are drawn to Melanie. She is a woman whose acceptance of how we live is delivered in the ironic tones that only a chastened heart could muster.

"Ellen Pall, with graceful prose and honest vision, moves towards a deeply earned affirmation of living, of forging ahead, despite obstacles that come viciously, or worse, disguised as love." —Andre Dubus

"Pall's moving story is spiked by the arid wit of the narrator . . . Surprise follows surprise in the life of a heroine one cares about and wishes well." *(Publishers Weekly)*

BARRIER ISLAND

By John D. MacDonald
(1898) 7-1 hour cassettes
Rental—$13.50   Purchase—$56.00
Read by Michael Prichard

A luxury cruiser comfortably offshore, float plane landing close by. What could be more idyllic . . . or misleading. When the two parties meet they exchange more than greeting—money and threats, for example—but part with the promise of favors.

But promises are for breaking if Tucker Loomis changes his mind. Which he may do, given the size of his latest scheme: to get the federal government to buy the island from him at many times its real value. He'll go to any length to make sure that nothing comes between him and his payoff.

B-O-T has recorded all of John D. MacDonald's Travis McGee novels as well as *Condominium* and *One More Sunday.*

BECH: A BOOK

By John Updike
(1277) 6-1 hour cassettes
Rental—$12.50   Purchase—$48.00
Read by Wolfram Kandinsky

In *Bech: A Book,* John Updike delineates a famous writer who, at young middle-age, has already published his best work and now watches helplessly as "his reputation grows while his powers decline."

Bech's final cross, if we may, is his induction into the National Academy of Arts and Letters . . . a reminder that when we start collecting honors, our most productive work, whether personal or corporate, is usually wrapped in the folds of an unkind history.

THE BEGGAR MAID:
Stories of Flo and Rose

By Alice Munro
(1484) 9-1 hour cassettes
Rental—$15.50   Purchase—$72.00
Read by Jeanne Hopson

The "beggar maid" is Rose, a young woman from the wrong side of a small town. Given drive and ambition by Flo, her stepmother, Rose climbs the ladder of success . . . a university degree, love, a dream marriage.

But Rose finds it's not what she wants. Success palls, the marriage fails. On her own and awake to her truest instincts, Rose achieves fame and fortune as an actress and media star. The greatest drama in her life, however, is a later confrontation with Flo.

Alice Munro was born in Wingham, Ontario. She received Canada's highest literary prize for *The Beggar Maid.* Other books of hers recorded by B-O-T include *Something I've Been Meaning to Tell You* and *Lives of Girls and Women.*

A BELL FOR ADANO

By John Hersey
(1304) 8-1 hour cassettes
Rental—$14.50   Purchase—$64.00
Read by Dan Lazar

A Bell for Adano was John Hersey's first novel and won a Pulitzer Prize. It tells the story of an Italian village during WW II, liberated by American forces and then administered by them. The story fits the traditional view Americans take of themselves—tough hombres, but hearts of gold.

If this book is reminiscent of times past, it nevertheless holds up to us the ideal that our fighting men have carried with them into battle through most of the history of this nation.

THE BELLS OF BICETRE

By Georges Simenon
(1513) 8-1 hour cassettes
Rental—$14.50   Purchase—$64.00
Read by Michael Prichard

Here Simenon analyzes the effect of a stroke on a man in the prime of his life. Rene Maugras has risen from obscurity to publisher of a highly influential Paris newspaper. Then suddenly he finds himself in a Paris hospital, speechless and paralyzed, yet surprisingly clear of mind. For the first time in his life he is forced to reflect.

As Simenon charts the stages of illness and recovery, we feel our perspectives alter with Maugras.

BENT'S FORT

By David S. Lavender
(1700) 12-1½ hour cassettes
Rental—$17.50   Purchase—$96.00
Read by Michael Prichard

In 1833 the Bent brothers, men of formidable will and courage, built a great adobe castle on the banks of the Arkansas. They called it Bent's Fort, and it symbolized America's expan sion into the Southwest.

Kit Carson and Blackfoot Smith, Old Bill Williams and John Fremont manned the fort. From it they opened New Mexico, Arizona and California. Old Mexico, slumbering in the decline of empire, lost out.

"There have been many good books about the old Santa Fe Trail . . . but none to match the blend of narrative power, pictorial sense and awareness of the great American melodrama that mark Bent's Fort." *(New York Herald Tribune)*

**Special 10% discount
See page 2**

THE BIG PICK-UP

By Elleston Trevor
(1426) 7-1½ hour cassettes
Rental—$15.50   Purchase—$56.00
Read by Robert Mundy

The Big Pick-Up is a gripping and uncompromising story of WW II. Set entirely in France, Elleston Trevor's powerful novel revolves around a ragged platoon of war-weary and humiliated British soldiers retreating from the German onslaught. With their morale collapsing, with enemy tanks behind them and enemy dive-bombers overhead, they trek to Dunkirk and the expected safety of evacuation.

Dunkirk was a disaster, but the army's salvation by a flotilla of little boats was a miracle.

BILLY PHELAN'S GREATEST GAME

By William Kennedy
(2027) 6-1½ hour cassettes
Rental—$14.50   Purchase—$48.00
Read by Wolfram Kandinsky

Billy Phelan's Greatest Game is the second in William Kennedy's brilliant cycle of novels known as the Albany Trilogy. Billy Phelan, a slightly tarnished poker player, pool hustler, and small-time bookie, moves through the lurid nighttime glare of a tough Depression-era town. A resourceful man full of Irish pluck, Billy works the fringes of Albany sporting life with his own particular style and private code of honor until he finds himself in the dangerous position of potential go-between in the kidnapping of a political boss's son.

Legs, the first part of the Albany Trilogy and the last *Ironweed,* are also available from Books on Tape.

THE BIRD IN THE TREE

By Elizabeth Goudge
(1458) 8-1½ hour cassettes
Rental—$15.50   Purchase—$64.00
Read by Wanda McCaddon

"I love these people too much to let them be unhappy for long," wrote Elizabeth Goudge of her favorite fictional characters, the Eliot family.

Goudge carries the Eliot family saga through two more books, *Pilgrim's Inn* and *The Heart of the Family,* but it is in this first book that we learn the strange history of the family home, so central to the story that it becomes almost a character in its own right.

"You will love this Hampshire coast, the little village and above all, the kind old house. What matters most is that forgotten stretch of marshland, where a man's spirit may rest and grow whole again." *(Boston Transcript)*

THE BISHOP'S APRON

By W. Somerset Maugham
(2115) 6-1 hour cassettes
Rental—$12.50   Purchase—$48.00
Read by Gary Martin

Canon Spratte is an important man . . . most of all in his own mind. He is the son of a Lord Chancellor of England, which alone should insure him the position to which he knows he is entitled. He deserves to be the next Bishop of Sheffield.

"Spratte never concealed from the world that he rated himself highly. He esteemed bashfulness a sign of bad manners, and used to say that a man who pretended not to know his own value was a fool." He knows theoretically that others might not share his good opinion of himself, but he is amazed to find his own family among them.

W. Somerset Maugham was trained as a physician, and he must have enjoyed cutting people up. Other of his dissections available from B-O-T include *Cakes and Ale, The Merry-Go-Round* and *The Moon and Sixpence.*

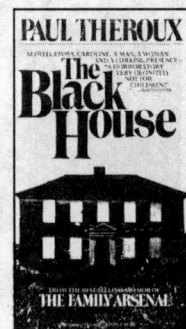

THE BLACK HOUSE

By Paul Theroux
(1866) 6-1½ hour cassettes
Rental—$14.50   Purchase—$48.00
Read by Michael Prichard

The Mundays have taken their failing marriage to the solace of a quaint old country house. Here, in peace and quiet, they may be able to restore themselves. Then a strange, beautiful apparition enters their life. A deliciously cruel reign of terror begins . . . a fatal triangle with more-than-natural consequences.

"Alfred, Emma, Caroline. A man, a woman and a lurking presence—a horror story very definitely not for children!" *(Boston Globe)*

Fans of Paul Theroux will also enjoy other titles available from B-O-T including *The Great Railway Bazaar, Kingdom by the Sea* and *The Old Patagonian Express.*

BLOODLINE

By Ernest J. Gaines
(1489) 7-1 hour cassettes
Rental—$13.50   Purchase—$56.00
Read by Dan Lazar

In this collection of five short stories, the author of *The Autobiography of Miss Jane Pittman* deals with the culture and tradition of the Southern Negro.

Other Ernest J. Gaines titles recorded by B-O-T include *The Autobiography of Miss Jane Pittman, Of Love and Dust* and *In My Father's House.*

THE BLUE HILLS

By Elizabeth Goudge
(1461) 7-1 hour cassettes
Rental—$13.50   Purchase—$56.00
Read by Donada Peters

In *The Blue Hills,* Elizabeth Goudge takes us back to her beloved cathedral town of Torminster in the early years of this century. It is the day of young Hugh Anthony's birthday picnic. A procession of landaus and victorias, plus one motor car, are bound for the Blue Hills and Hugh's picnic.

Whatever the reason, each vehicle gets mysteriously lost on its way to the Blue Hills, and by the time the travellers meet again over tea and iced birthday cake, they have had such adventures. Adventures such that none of them is the same person. They are wiser, nicer and much happier.

Other titles available from B-O-T include *The Bird in the Tree, The Castle on the Hill* and *The Child from the Sea.*

THE BULL FROM THE SEA

By Mary Renault
(1819) 7-1½ hour cassettes
Rental—$15.50   Purchase—$56.00
Read by Peter McDonald

Theseus, King of Athens, returns in triumph from Crete, after slaying the Minotaur, to mount the throne left empty by the death of his father, Aigeus.

Theseus is torn between his genius for kingship and his craving for adventure. He joins the forays of the pirate prince, Pirithoos. While exploring Euxine, Theseus captures a warrior priestess, Hippolyta. She becomes the love of his life and the key to his fate.

"The bull of Marathon, the battle of the Lapits and Kentaurs, and the moon-goddess cult of Pontos are but a portion of the legendary material that Mary Renault weaves into the fabric of great historical fiction." *(Publisher's Source)*

Other Renault titles available from B-O-T include *Fire From Heaven,* the life of Alexander the Great as a youth; its sequel, *The Persian Boy.*

BULLET PARK

By John Cheever
(1781) 7-1 hour cassettes
Rental—$13.50   Purchase—$56.00
Read by Michael Prichard

Eliot Nailles and Paul Hammer meet, presumably by chance, on Sunday at church in Bullet Park. Nailles is open, no secrets. Hammer is, dangerously for him, not what he seems.

The third crucial character, Tony Nailles, is the one who holds the bag. How he got into it and how in the nick of time he appears to get out is the crux of this tale.

Other John Cheever titles available from Books on Tape include *The Wapshot Chronicle* and *The Wapshot Scandal.*

BURMESE DAYS

By George Orwell
(1535) 8-1½ hour cassettes
Rental—$15.50   Purchase—$64.00
Read by Robert Mundy

Burmese Days is George Orwell's distillation of six years with the Indian Imperial Police. It is an honest and evocative novel based on life in upper Burma in the 1920's when Britain's rule was still unchallenged.

Flory, a middle-aged Englishman, has grown soft in the foreign service. He is not ready for love, though it takes him when he meets Elizabeth Lackerstein. She is a beautiful English girl, recently orphaned, and her need for a protector undoes him.

"This is a superior novel, not less so because it tells an absorbing story. Orwell has made his people and his background vividly real. And he knows of what he writes." *(The New York Times)*

**For quick ordering
1-800-626-3333**

THE BURNING SHORE

By Elleston Trevor
(1690) 5-1½ hour cassettes
Rental—$13.50   Purchase—$40.00
Read by Michael Prichard

The Burning Shore is set in Malaya, where Hugh Copland is appointed manager of a jungle airstrip menaced by Communist guerillas. He soon becomes dangerously involved in a struggle for power between the Sultan of Tamarah and elusive enemies.

" . . . nicely calculated to give pleasure in the best sense of the word . . . the more the author writes, the better he does." *(Eastern Daily Press)*

Trevor's *The Sibling, The Flight of the Phoenix* and *The Big Pick-Up* are also available from B-O-T.

BURY HIM AMONG KINGS

By Elleston Trevor
(1191) 10-1½ hour cassettes
Rental—$16.50   Purchase—$80.00
Read by Victor Rumbello

Elleston Trevor has chosen WW I and the lives of a variety of English soldiers for the setting and characters of this insightful novel. The narrative concerns two brothers from the British aristocracy—Aubrey and Victor Talbot. With them in the trenches of France, we share vicerally in their dangers and discomforts.

"A captivating drama of the abrupt end of innocence where love and trust still exist amidst the blood and horror." *(Book Review Service)*

BY THE GREEN OF THE SPRING

By John Masters
(1740-A) 9-1½ hour cassettes
Rental—$16.50   Purchase—$72.00
(1740-B) 10-1½ hour cassettes
Rental—$16.50   Purchase—$80.00
Read by Walter Zimmerman

By the Green of the Spring is the third and final volume in John Master's trilogy Loss of Eden.

The trilogy, starting with *Now God Be Thanked,* depicts the impact of WW I on British life. *Heart of War* carries the saga into the conflict's desperate middle years. *By the Green of the Spring* brings the war to its close and casts the survivors (half the war-time generation was killed) on the barren shores of peace.

"An impressive, large-scale work. Masters never shifts his focus from the human element . . . his storytelling gifts, convincing characterization and skilled organization have never been more tellingly displayed." *(John Barkham Reviews)*

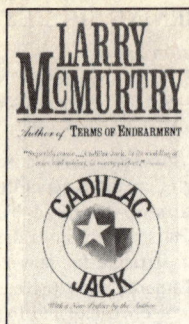

CADILLAC JACK

By Larry McMurtry
(1684) 10-1½ hour cassettes
Rental—$16.50   Purchase—$80.00
Read by Wolfram Kandinsky

Larry McMurtry has a genius for conjuring up the eccentrics who people America's heartland. None is more grittily memorable than the hero of *Cadillac Jack*, a rodeo cowboy turned antique dealer whose gypsy life centers on his classic Cadillac. In it he wanders the Texas flatlands, roams back roads looking for flea markets, samples Washington's political high life.

The cast of characters includes a beautiful social climber, a high-rolling Texan, Washington politicians, and the kind of attractive young women who seem to have their minds on something else when they're making love. Richly comic, strangely moving, this is one of McMurtry's most original novels.

"McMurtry understands a homeless, wandering America . . . Cadillac Jack is a cowboy, but a cowboy who rounds up junk instead of cows. His search for beauty in the rag-and-bone shops is a parable of the great American search for fulfillment." *(Chicago Tribune Book World)*

CAKES AND ALE and UP AT THE VILLA

By W. Somerset Maugham
(1215) 7-1½ hour cassettes
Rental—$14.50   Purchase—$56.00
Read by Erik Bauersfeld

Cakes and Ale is a short novel which cynically dissects the English literary world. On its first appearance, critics believed it to be a satire of Thomas Hardy. Whether true or not, Maugham's characterizations are sharp and clear and the novel scores as polished, sophisticated and amusing.

Up at the Villa is the story of a beautiful young English widow who is living in a village outside Florence, recovering from the recent death of her husband. It being Italy and she being female, she receives proposals of marriage from two men on the same evening. Startling as she finds the proposals, she is even more shocked by the corpse Maugham has in store for her in her bedroom!

CAMPBELL'S KINGDOM

By Hammond Innes
(1802) 7-1½ hour cassettes
Rental—$15.50   Purchase—$56.00
Read by Charles Garst

At 36, Bruce Wetheral, a London insurance clerk, finds he hasn't much time to live. A few hours later he also learns that he has become sole heir to his grandfather's failing Canadian enterprise.

Campbell's land—perched at 7,000 feet in the Canadian Rockies—may contain vast resources of oil. The old man's partners offer him a moderate sum for control. He declines the offer and launches his own search for Rocky Mountain "Black Gold."

"The art of writing thoroughly well-documented and ably-written thrillers is perfectly understood by Innes, whose work stands in a class by itself." —V.S. Pritchett

CASH McCALL

By Cameron Hawley
(1545) 12-1½ hour cassettes
Rental—$17.50   Purchase—$96.00
Read by John MacDonald

This is Cameron Hawley's revealing novel of business and the associated worlds of law and finance. Cash McCall is a vastly intriguing man, a 20th century adventurer who carries on his successful buying and selling of companies behind a suspiciously secret screen of anonymity.

But this is more than a novel of high finance. It is no less an eloquent love story, a discerning journey into the hearts and minds of business wives. Above all else, *Cash McCall* is an intelligent commentary on the morals and motives of our time.

THE CASTLE ON THE HILL

By Elizabeth Goudge
(1723) 15-1½ hour cassettes
Rental—$18.50   Purchase—$120.00
Read by Wanda McCaddon

It is the summer of 1940 and England is fighting for her life. In a rural corner of England the vagaries of war bring together a group of people wrestling the enemy within—fear, despair, loss of faith.

This is Elizabeth Goudge at her best. In this compelling drama of human trial and triumph, she takes us from London air raids to country sunsets and weaves a story of courage and understanding from the threads of history.

THE CAT

By Georges Simenon
(1516) 5-1 hour cassettes
Rental—$11.50   Purchase—$40.00
Read by Michael Prichard

Why are Emile and Marguerite Bouin still married? They cannot stand each other. This is evident from the moment we meet them, isolated and wordless before a beautiful fire. Their only correspondence is an occasional invective jotted on a scrap of paper—this discreetly flicked across the room to the recipient's lap.

A bizarre situation to be sure, but ideal for Simenon. Taking marriage born of a desperate need for companionship and following it to its devastation eight years later, Simenon patiently makes hate almost as alluring as love.

CATCH-22

By Joseph Heller
(1501) 12-1½ hour cassettes
Rental—$17.50   Purchase—$96.00
Read by Wolfram Kandinsky

This satire of the American air war in Italy is comedy all the way to its conclusion. But in Snowden's freezing death we are brought sharply up to Heller's message: life is good but fragile, death is random and violent, wars are insane and evil. With Yossarian as our guide, we find why it is that logic and reason always fail in the face of something Heller called "Catch-22."

CAT'S CRADLE

By Kurt Vonnegut Jr.
(1113) 6-1 hour cassettes
Rental—$12.50   Purchase—$48.00
Read by Dan Lazar

The setting for this relatively short novel is the Caribbean Island of San Lorenzo, and it is here that we meet Felix Hoenikker, a physicist and one of the fathers of the atomic bomb. He has just made another discovery—"ice nine"—a substance that can turn all the liquid in the world into a solid block of ice.

Supporting characters include a crazy religious prophet, a bicycle salesman from Indiana, a Caribbean beauty and her dictator father.

**Give a Books on Tape™
Gift Certificate
Call 1-800-626-3333**

THE CENTAUR

By John Updike
(1655) 9-1 hour cassettes
Rental—$15.50   Purchase—$72.00
Read by John MacDonald

According to Greek mythology, a centaur is one of a race of monsters having the head, arms and trunk of a man and the body and legs of a horse. This story retells the myth of Chiron, the noblest and wisest of them all, who gave up his immortality on behalf of Prometheus. In the retelling, Olympus becomes Olinger High School, where Chiron teaches general science; Prometheus is his 15-year-old son. Updike skillfully alternates past and present perspectives to translate the centaur's search into the events of three winter days spent in Pennsylvania in 1947.

A graduate of Harvard and 3-time recipient of a Pulitzer Prize for literature, John Updike was awarded the National Book Award for Fiction for *The Centaur.*

CHARITY GIRL

By Georgette Heyer
(1603) 6-1½ hour cassettes
Rental—$14.50   Purchase—$48.00
Read by Flo Gibson

Ah, the opportunities available to the capricious rich! With good looks, wealth and influence, their young may dally in carefree fashion. Little is their concern beyond the proprieties that acccompany the baggage of a family name.

The young Viscount Desford had few concerns until his father, the Earl of Wroxton, urged him to marry. Desford obediently falls in love, but with the wrong woman, a beauty but low born.

CHARLES RYDER'S SCHOOL DAYS AND OTHER STORIES

By Evelyn Waugh
(2073) 6-1 hour cassettes
Rental—$12.50   Purchase—$48.00
Read by Octavius Black

Brideshead Revisited was Evelyn Waugh's masterpiece, but its narrator, Charles Ryder, always eluded us. Now he comes into focus.

"Charles Ryder's School Days," the first story in this collection, was probably intended as the first chapter of a novel dealing with Ryder's early years. Waugh drew liberally on his own diaries for this portrait, as a reading of his autobiography, *A Little Learning* (available from B-O-T) makes clear.

One of the finest writers of this century . . . witty, funny, profound." *(Reviews for Readers)*

THE CHILD BUYER

By John Hersey
(1305) 8-1 hour cassettes
Rental—$14.50   Purchase—$64.00
Read by Dan Lazar

This is a story of an investigation into the activities of Mr. Wissey Jones, a stranger who comes to the town of Pequot on urgent defense business.

His business is to buy for his corporation children of a certain sort, in this case a ten-year-old named Barry Rudd, a budding genius of potentially critical value. A hearing is held and questions are asked: Exactly why does Mr. Jones' company buy children, and will it succeed in buying Barry?

THE CHILD FROM THE SEA

By Elizabeth Goudge
(1144-A) 10-1½ hour cassettes
Rental—$16.50   Purchase—$80.00
(1144-B) 9-1½ hour cassettes
Rental—$16.50   Purchase—$72.00
Read by Penelope Dellaporta

The Child from the Sea is the story of Lucy Walter, a child of transcendent beauty and spirituality. Born in 17th century England, Lucy grows up to become the secret wife of Charles II. Against the drama of the times and the machinations of the court, such a union had scant hope for success, but as a love match, the marriage remains a beautiful and tender romance.

"Suspensful . . . Powerful . . . The Child from the Sea casts a magic spell." *(Cleveland Plain Dealer)*

Other memorable Goudge stories available from B-O-T are: *The Heart of the Family, Pilgrim's Inn, The Castle on the Hill* and *A Christmas Book.*

CHILD OF THE MORNING

By Pauline Gedge
(1824-A) 8-1½ hour cassettes
Rental—$15.50   Purchase—$64.00
(1824-B) 7-1½ hour cassettes
Rental—$15.50   Purchase—$56.00
Read by Donada Peters

Thirty-five hundred years ago a woman sat on the throne of the Pharoahs of Egypt. She was Hatshepsut, chosen by her father to follow him—in defiance of the royal male succession—as ruler of the vast kingdom.

Child of the Morning tells the story of this brilliant and beautiful woman, who wore the kilts of a man and the regalia of a king. Her 22-year reign was one of superb administration, exploration, peace and the beautification of her empire.

Yet dark forces were at work to destroy her and erase her name from history.

CHILLY SCENES OF WINTER

By Ann Beattie
(1164) 8-1½ hour cassettes
Rental—$15.50   Purchase—$64.00
Read by Michael Prichard

The hero of Ann Beattie's *Chilly Scenes of Winter* is Charles, 27 years old, working a nine-to-five job that he can't afford to leave. His life is stale and flat. He endures a grotesquely crazy mother and an idiot stepfather. His only release is pizza and beer with his old buddy Sam. Charles exists in a dream world, fantasizing his reunion with Laura, the woman he loves and had an affair with 10 years before.

CHOIRBOYS

By Joseph Wambaugh
(1024) 8-1½ hour cassettes
Rental—$15.50   Purchase—$64.00
Read by Daniel Grace

Perhaps none of Joseph Wambaugh's works explore the conflicts in a policeman's life more thoroughly than *The Choirboys.* Wambaugh introduces us to the five teams of policemen who form the nightwatch patrol. In pre-dawn hours, these men gather for liquor and sex, sessions they euphemistically call "choir practice." Ultimately this off-duty entertainment becomes more of a threat than the danger they face on the beat. XXX for sex and violence.

THE CHOSEN

By Chaim Potok
(1996) 6-1½ hour cassettes
Rental—$14.50   Purchase—$56.00
Read by Wolfram Kandinsky

The Talmud says that a person should do two things for himself: one is to acquire a teacher, the other is to choose a friend. The Greeks say that two friends are like one body with two souls.

Set in New York toward the end of WW II, this is the story of two teenage Jewish boys, one the son of a Zionist, the other of a Russian Hassidic. They turn to each other in a fine show of male bonding.

A CHRISTMAS BOOK

By Elizabeth Goudge
(1847) 6-1½ hour cassettes
Rental—$14.50   Purchase—$48.00
Read by Wanda McCaddon

This anthology from the author of *The Bird in the Tree, Pilgrim's Inn* and *The Heart of the Family* offers nine pieces celebrating the spirit of Christmas with "an amazing visitation of joy, a singing in the soul, a new power of generosity or insight or endurance."

The settings of Elizabeth Goudge's stories—two of them new tales, seven selections from her novels—range in locale from her beloved English countryside to the Holy Land, and through time from before the birth of Christ to the present.

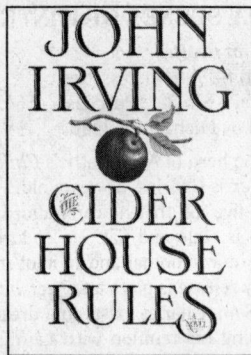

THE CIDER HOUSE RULES

By John Irving
(1927-A) 8-1½ hour cassettes
Rental—$15.50   Purchase—$64.00
(1927-B) 9-1½ hour cassettes
Rental—$16.50   Purchase—$72.00
Read by Grover Gardner

To call St. Cloud a village in the 1920's is to overstate the case—it's a train station, an orphanage and an abandoned lumber camp. But the place is surprisingly busy, with a steady stream of pregnant women arriving at the station and walking up the long hill to Dr. Wilbur Larch's office at the orphanage.

Dr. Larch, to use the local parlance, does both the Lord's work and the Devil's: he delivers unwanted babies and finds homes for them, he also performs abortions. To Dr. Larch these are not two kinds of work but one.

This is a novel about orphans and Maine apple orchards and 19th century American morals. Beyond that, it deals with fragility of rules and rituals in everyday life. It also warns that, for basics like falling in love or saving lives, rules seem to offer little validity or comfort.

CIMARRON

By Edna Ferber
(1627) 8-1½ hour cassettes
Rental—$15.50   Purchase—$64.00
Read by Flo Gibson

Restless Yancey Cravat, a pioneer newspaper editor and lawyer, settles in Osage, a muddy town thrown together overnight when the Oklahoma territory opens in 1889. To this place he brings his wife Sabra, a woman both conventional and well-bred.

Against all odds, Sabra develops a brilliant business sense. She makes a success of the newspaper, a success that ultimately leads her to Congress. Through Sabra's eyes we see the violent frontier collide with resentful Indians, the sodbusters tame the prairie, and the sudden fortune of a lucky few.

"A ripping yarn . . . a gorgeous piece of work." *(Saturday Review of Literature)*

THE CLAN OF THE CAVE BEAR

By Jean M. Auel
(1597-A) 8-1½ hour cassettes
Rental—$15.50   Purchase—$64.00
(1597-B) 8-1½ hour cassettes
Rental—$15.50   Purchase—$64.00
Read by Donada Peters

It is 30,000 years ago, the final Ice Age of the Pleistocene Epoch. The earth is peopled by Neanderthals—squat, bow-legged, nonverbal, they live in clans, exist by foraging, and are ruled by taboos. The Cro-Magnons, the people who will replace them, are just emerging.

When an earthquake destroys a Cro-Magnon dwelling, they tame the prairie, and the sudden fortune of a lucky few.

"A ripping yarn . . . a gorgeous piece of work." *(Saturday Review of Literature)*

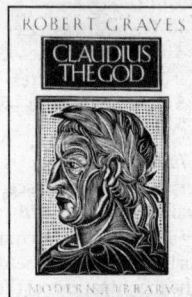

CLAUDIUS THE GOD

By Robert Graves
(2079-A) 7-1½ hour cassettes
Rental—$15.50   Purchase—$56.00
(2079-B) 7-1½ hour cassettes
Rental—$15.50   Purchase—$56.00
Read by David Case

With the same brilliance that characterized *I, Claudius*, Robert Graves continues the tumultuous life of the Roman who became emperor in spite of himself and his handicaps.

Claudius the God captures the vitality, splendor and decadence of Rome just entering its decline. It is a superb re-creation of a colorful moment in history, and through the eyes of the bemused and wry Claudius, a compelling and ironic account of human nature.

"This book, with or without its predecessor, is amusing and illuminating to a high degree." *(The New York Times)*

I, Claudius, Goodbye to All That, Homer's Daughter and *They Hanged My Saintly Billy* are additional Robert Graves' titles available from B-O-T.

THE CLERGYMAN'S DAUGHTER

By George Orwell
(1536) 7-1½ hour cassettes
Rental—$15.50   Purchase—$56.00
Read by Richard Green

Dorothy Hare, the clergyman's daughter of this title, grows up subservient to her tyrannical father. But submission has its limit and Dorothy rebels, or at least her psyche does. She blacks out and reappears as a vagrant amnesiac whose adventures show us life, such as it is, from the underside.

George Orwell's two remarkable classics, *Animal Farm* and *1984*, are available through B-O-T.

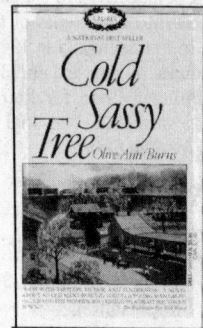

COLD SASSY TREE

By Olive Ann Burns
(2125) 11-1½ hour cassettes
Rental—$19.50   Purchase—$88.00
Read by Dick Estell
A Christopher Enterprises Recording

Cold Sassy, Georgia, had never been a whirlpool of excitement. If the preacher's wifes' petticoats showed, the ladies could make the talk last a week.

But on July 5, 1906, things took a scandalous turn. That was the day E. Rucker Blakeslee, proprietor of the general store and barely three weeks a widower, eloped with miss Love Simpson—a woman half his age and, worse yet, a Yankee!

"Rich with emotion, humor and tenderness . . . a novel about an old man growing young, a young man growing up, and the modern age coming to a small Southern town." *(The Washington Post Book World)*

Slightly edited for radio presentation.

Interval delivery convenience
See page 2

THE COLLECTED STORIES OF EDITH WHARTON

Edited by R.W.B. Lewis
(1385-A) 12-1½ hour cassettes
Rental—$17.50   Purchase—$96.00
(1385-B) 12-1½ hour cassettes
Rental—$17.50   Purchase—$96.00
(1385-C) 12-1½ hour cassettes
Rental—$17.50   Purchase—$96.00
(1385-D) 9-1½ hour cassettes
Rental—$16.50   Purchase—$72.00
(1385-E) 10-1½ hour cassettes
Rental—$16.50   Purchase—$80.00
Read by Flo Gibson

Edith Wharton wrote during the first three decades of this century, yet her prose remains remarkably contemporary. Her characters accurately reflect the attitudes of her era, but their hurts are as real as our own. Nor did she skirt the grim issues of her day. As an example, she used the Lizzie Borden murder case as the foundation of her novella *Confession.*

Edith Wharton was the first woman ever to be awarded both the Gold Medal of the National Institute of Arts and Letters, and the honorary degree of Doctor of Letters from Yale University.

COMING UP FOR AIR

By George Orwell
(1538) 8-1 hour cassettes
Rental—$14.50   Purchase—$64.00
Read by Richard Green

Coming Up for Air is about coping. Orwell hooks a character from among the struggling middle class and, close-up, lets us watch him wiggle. George (Tubby) Bowling is a "fat, middle-aged bloke with false teeth and a red face." He sells insurance, a task at which he grimly excels. The father of two ingrates and husband to a slattern, he dutifully makes mortgage payments on their dreary home. As the years roll by, he comes to feel like a hostage to his family. He regards them as wardens, himself a prisoner. Bowling is a splendid example of Thoreau's observation that "most men lead lives of quiet desperation."

CONDOMINIUM

By John D. MacDonald
(1077) 10-1½ hour cassettes
Rental—$16.50   Purchase—$80.00
Read by Michael Prichard

Condominium is set in the Florida Keys, home of the "condo culture." Martin Liss, a developer, embodies greed and indifference. He victimizes condo residents. He shatters their dreams of a luxurious life by continuing price increases and their very lives are threatened by an approaching hurricane.

"John D. MacDonald's portrayal of the 'condo culture' and those who prey on and profit from it is accurate, ironic and insightful." *(Book Review Digest)*

THE CONFESSIONS OF NAT TURNER

By William Styron
(1877) 12-1½ hour cassettes
Rental—$17.50   Purchase—$96.00
Read by Wolfram Kandinsky

Turner's Rebellion took place in the long hot summer of 1831, in the state of Virginia. When it was over, 59 white people were dead; the insurgents were rounded up and either hanged or worse; and Nat Turner, a preacher, confessed to his part in the only effective revolt in the annals of American Negro slavery.

In his introduction of this Pulitzer Prize winner, Styron says "it has been my own intention to try to re-create a man and his era, and to produce a work that is less an 'historical novel' in conventional terms than a meditation on history."

THE CONSCIENCE OF THE RICH

By C.P. Snow
(1412) 7-1½ hour cassettes
Rental—$15.50   Purchase—$56.00
Read by Robert Mundy

In this third novel of his Strangers and Brothers series, Lewis Eliot returns as narrator and guides us into the private, affluent world of a prominent Anglo-Jewish family, the Marches.

The story sets the generations against each other. A son struggles with his inherited wealth, the fact of his Jewishness, and family obligations within an English society.

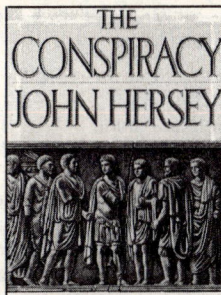

THE CONSPIRACY JOHN HERSEY

THE CONSPIRACY

By John Hersey
(1306) 8-1 hour cassettes
Rental—$14.50   Purchase—$64.00
Read by Dan Lazar

Nero's secret police believe they have come on the first hints of a plot against the emperor's life. Once promising and gifted friend of poets, pupil of the great Seneca, Nero has bloodied himself and grown fat on power. Crass, mediocre men—the military and the secret police—now have his ear. While he and his court give themselves to pleasures increasingly perverse and dissipated, the secret police close in on (or do they foment, or imagine?) the conspiracy of the men of letters.

THE CONSUL'S FILE

By Paul Theroux
(1865) 7-1 hour cassettes
Rental—$13.50   Purchase—$56.00
Read by Michael Prichard

When Paul Theroux's consul arrives in postcolonial Malaysia, his first act is to examine the "secret" files. Imagine when he finds the insects got there first! What pages remain have little writing, less information. Actually, most of the pages are empty.

"The sharp underlying focus is on how uprooted individuals connect or fail to connect with each other and with the places where they have ended up. Sometimes bizarre calamity is the result, sometimes social comedy . . ." *(The Christian Science Monitor)*

B-O-T has also recorded Theroux's *The Great Railway Bazaar, Jungle Lovers* and *The Old Patagonian Express.*

CORRIDORS OF POWER

By C.P. Snow
(1418) 8-1½ hour cassettes
Rental—$15.50   Purchase—$64.00
Read by John MacDonald

Corridors of Power is a novel of high politics, one of the finest of our day on that subject. The chief figure is Roger Quaife, a tough, adroit and ruthless English politician who wants to do something worthwhile with power once he has won it. He decides to take Great Britain out of the nuclear arms race.

The ninth novel in C.P. Snow's Strangers and Brothers series, *Corridors of Power* is narrated by Lewis Eliot, who is a civil servant advisor to Roger Quaife, and a friend. The story Eliot tells raises questions larger than the story itself: How much can one man do, in politics? How much of our life is settled for us, without our knowing it, in the corridors?

THE COUP

By John Updike
(1282) 8-1½ hour cassettes
Rental—$15.50   Purchase—$64.00
Read by Wolfram Kandinsky

John Updike is one of America's most versatile men of letters. His characterization of Rabbit Angstrom in *Rabbit Run, Rabbit Redux* and *Rabbit is Rich* has made the author richer than Rabbit.

But in *The Coup,* Updike disects a modern African state called Kush. Narrated tongue-in-cheek by Kush's exiled president, Colonel Felix Ellellou, Updike proves he is an equal opportunity employer when it comes to slicing up bunkum, whether black or white, first world or third.

COUPLES

By John Updike
(1353) 12-1½ hour cassettes
Rental—$17.50   Purchase—$96.00
Read by John MacDonald

In *Couples*, John Updike explores the psychosexual natures of a group of young middle-class marrieds in Tarbox, Massachusetts. Against the background of general philandering and deceit, couples develop deep attachments punctuated by occasional frenzies of passion and intrigue.

Regarded as on of America's best authors, Updike, a Pulitzer Prize winner, writes with painful insight about the state of marital fidelity in the modern age.

X-rated for sex and language.

THE COURT MARTIAL OF GEORGE ARMSTRONG CUSTER

By Douglas C. Jones
(1124) 7-1½ hour cassettes
Rental—$15.50   Purchase—$56.00
Read by James Cunningham

An imaginary historical novel, *The Court Martial of George Armstrong Custer* focuses on a trial that never occurred. One hundred years ago, Custer and the Seventh Cavalry perished in a battle against renegade Indians. Did Custer endanger the lives of his troops in a foolhardy attack? Was he an opportunist anticipating a political career? Or was he victimized by plans handed down by inept superiors?

Douglas C. Jones proposes Custer survived the massacre and is court-martialed for his actions. Suspense increases right up to the verdict.

A CREED FOR THE THIRD MILLENNIUM

By Colleen McCullough
(1608) 11-1½ hour cassettes
Rental—$17.50   Purchase—$88.00
Read by Penelope Dellaporta

Dr. Joshua Christian is a clinical psychologist with a modest small-town practice. To his patients he brings strength and comfort, for Dr. Christian is one of those rare professionals who loves his work and the people whom he meets in it.

Enter Dr. Judith Carriol, an official from the powerful new Department of the Environment. Ambitious and Machiavellian, Judith recognizes in Joshua a person she can manipulate to attain her own ends.

"Speaks to the unending conflict between self and selflessness . . . a theme touched on by generations of novelists, handled here with great skill by Ms. McCullough on her third outing." *(Editorial Review Service)*

CRESS DELAHANTY

By Jessamyn West
(1203) 6-1½ hour cassettes
Rental—$14.50   Purchase—$48.00
Read by Roses Prichard

Cress Delahanty is a gawky, noisy, cruel but loving female adolescent. Jessamyn West's narrative is a series of short stories, set on a ranch in Southern California, covering Cress's life between the ages of 12 and 16.

Cress shares the joys and disappointments of all adolescents—puppy love, pimples, schoolgirl crushes . . . anyone who has a daughter will recognize this as a truthful and exquisite work of art.

CRIMSON RAMBLERS OF THE WORLD, FAREWELL

By Jessamyn West
(1210) 6-1½ hour cassettes
Rental—$14.50   Purchase—$48.00
Read by Roses Prichard

In this collection of short stories, we find a wide range of Jessamyn West's work . . . tragedy, joy, suspense, romance, even a narrative of the Canadian wilderness.

Titles include: "Hunting for Hoot Owls," "Night Piece for Julia," "The Day of the Hawks," "Child of the Century," and the title story, "Crimson Ramblers of the World, Farewell.

CROWNED HEADS

By Thomas Tryon
(1102) 10-1½ hour cassettes
Rental—$16.50   Purchase—$80.00
Read by Dan Lazar

Crowned Heads takes us into the interlocking lives of four film stars. First we meet Fedora, longest-reining beauty of them all. Sexy Lorna comes next. We find her n a secluded resort trying to heal herself after many jobs, many men, and much trouble.

Bobbitt is a former kiddie star no is his thirties and still "adorable." And Willie, for decades a worldwide symbol of elegance and wit, is alone in his Hollywood showplace mourning his past until the future breaks in.

CRY OF THE PANTHER

By James P. McMullen
(2053) 10-1½ hour cassettes
Rental—$16.50   Purchase—$80.00
Read by Grover Gardner

After Vietnam, with shrapnel in his back and the jungle in his brain, James McMullen got into his car and headed as far south as he could go—the Everglades—the one place in America most like Nam.

In the glades he became one of the "jungle vets," those who sought refuge by disappearing into America's hills and swamps. In Vietnam, McMullen had tracked and been tracked by other men. In the glades, he began to track the Florida panther. And as the "gentle embrace of the untamed" claimed him, he traded one obsession for another.

Saving the panther from extinction became his mission, and with it the realization that the cat was the symbol of his own self-spirit and his own endangered species.

CRY, THE BELOVED COUNTRY

By Alan Paton
(1331) 6-1½ hour cassettes
Rental—$14.50   Purchase—$48.00
Read by Richard Green

An old Zulu parson, from the hills above Ixopo, sets out for Johannesburg, "the city of evil," looking for his son. He finds his boy in prison, charged with the murder of a white man who had devoted his life to justice for the black race.

"This is an indictment of a social system that drives native races to resentment and crime. It is also the story of a beautiful and tragic land and of its landscapes, its people and of its bitter racial unrest." *(Book Review Service)*

**TOLL FREE credit card
order line 1-800-626-3333**

MasterCard   VISA

THE CRYING GAME

By John Braine
(1467) 8-1½ hour cassettes
Rental—$15.50   Purchase—$64.00
Read by Stuart Courtney

The Crying Game is a satirical parable from the author of *Room at the Top*. Frank Batcombe, a conservative North county journalist newly arrived in London, works as a reporter for a national newspaper. A chance encounter changes his life.

His stylish cousin, Adam Keelby, a successful public relations entrepreneur, insists Frank join him in his fashionable quarters in Hampstead.

Suddenly doors open for Frank. Desirable women crowd around and he gets wind of a political scandal that can make his journalistic career.

THE CUSTOM OF THE COUNTRY

By Edith Wharton
(1383) 10-1½ hour cassettes
Rental—$16.50   Purchase—$80.00
Read by Flo Gibson

In a culture dominated by men who refuse to take women seriously, excluding them from the real business of life, Undine Spragg strikes out to discover how far beauty and daring can carry her. She uses her attractiveness like a blunt instrument and clubs her way up the social ladder with a series of increasingly advantageous marriages.

She is the small town girl made good, the rustic who outsmarts New York society and moves on the continental princelings. There seems to be no limit to her conquests, but happiness evade her. We can predict her fall, but are powerless to intervene.

"Brilliantly written. It should be read as a parable." *(Saturday Review)*

Also available from B-O-T are Edith Wharton's *The Age of Innocence* and *Ethan Frome*.

THE DAHOMEAN

By Frank Yerby
(1401) 11-1½ hour cassettes
Rental—$17.50   Purchase—$88.00
Read by Dan Lazar

Frank Yerby, one of our most popular and prolific authors, uses *The Dahomean* to examine the intricate culture of the West African kingdom of Dahomey in the early 19th century. His principal character is Nyasanu, who becomes a powerful chieftain in his own country. But increased political responsibilities bring great dangers and Nyasanu, despite his rank, falls victim to the slave trade.

That a king should become a slave is the ironic engine that drives this story about the capacity men of all races have for villainy.

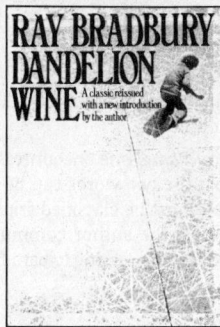

DANDELION WINE

By Ray Bradbury
(1474) 8-1 hour cassettes
Rental—$14.50   Purchase—$64.00
Read by Michael Prichard

In 1957, Ray Bradbury, already famous for stories of fantasy and science fiction, delighted and surprised readers with the lyrical realism of *Dandelion Wine*.

The place is Green Town, Illinois, the year 1928. Douglas Spaulding is twelve. The people parading through his life that summer belong to an America of trolley cars and electric runabouts and of dandelion wine bottled in the summer for the winter's sipping. It is during this summer that Douglas first realizes he is alive, really alive, and that someday he will die. It is this summer when the magic of childhood just begins to be perceived by the child growing up.

"One of the warmest, most refreshing, most appealing evocations of a bygone day that I have ever read or ever hope to read." *(Sunday Tribune,* Chicago)

THE DARK LADY

By Louis Auchincloss
(1112) 8-1 hour cassettes
Rental—$14.50   Purchase—$64.00
Read by Dan Lazar

The Dark Lady is Louis Auchincloss' novel of two women allied in a successful assault on fame, wealth and political power. One is Elesina Dart, a beauty of good background who has gone through two marriages and an erratic theatrical career. The other is Ivy Trask, a shrewd middle-aged fashion editor and social arbiter.

Ivy salvages Elesina from failure and alcohol and embarks on a grand plan to marry her into a world of affluence and power. The offices, penthouses and suburban estates of New York are the setting for the three decades spanned by this story.

A DAY OF PLEASURE

By Isaac Bashevis Singer
(1365) 4-1 hour cassettes
Rental—$9.50   Purchase—$32.00
Read by Peter MacDonald

A Day of Pleasure is about growing up in a pre-WW I ghetto in Warsaw. Suitable for children as well as adults, these stories explore the boyhood mysteries of urban life. Rich in strong religious faith, close family ties and a brilliant recollection of lost innocence in times irretrievably gone by.

This is a collection of 19 stories (14 of which are also in Singer's *In My Father's Court*).

THE DEATH OF WILLIAM POSTERS

By Alan Sillitoe
(1066) 7-1½ hour cassettes
Rental—$15.50   Purchase—$56.00
Read by Richard Green

The Death of William Posters introduces Frank Dauley, a 27-year-old factory worker who finds himself looking ahead to a life at the lathe. Reluctant to settle for shop work, Dauley breaks away to search for new beginnings. Like the author and his hero, we must find our own answer to these questions: what is life for? Should we stay where we are, or is there greener grass on the other side of the road?

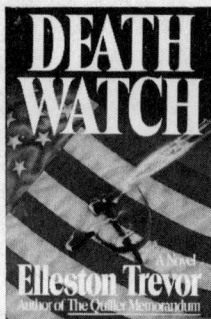

DEATH WATCH

By Elleston Trevor
(1984) 7-1 hour cassettes
Rental—$13.50   Purchase—$56.00
Read by Carl Schmidt

In a Moscow laboratory a genetic accident kills everything in sight. While the scientists responsible try to destroy the mutation, a group of men in the highest echelons of the Kremlin formulate another plan for it.

At the same time, the United States leaks word to the Soviets of an ultimate weapon that does not exist. When the Russians hear of it, the death watch begins.

A tight, tense, powerful story of allies and enemies, spies and traitors, megalomaniacs and people caught in the web of circumstances, *Death Watch* targets in on one of man's greatest fears: the breakdown of civilization.

Originally recorded for radio and is slightly abridged.

DELIVERANCE IN SHANGHAI

By Jerome Agel and Eugene Boe
(1272) 9-1½ hour cassettes
Rental—$16.50   Purchase—$72.00
Read by Rupert Keenlyside

The winds of war blew twenty thousand frantic European Jews to the far East—to the wickedest city on earth—Shanghai, "the Paris of the Orient." *Deliverance in Shanghai* is the story of those men, women and children who traded German subjugation for Japanese.

Though fictional, *Deliverance in Shanghai* is based on exclusive interviews with survivors of the Shanghai ghetto, on the translation many unpublished documents, and on the journals of Americans stationed in Shanghai during and immediately after the war.

"Brightly written, tightly plotted, heartrending and totally absorbing, this book presents a new and true corner of World War II. I found it astonishing." —Isaac Asimov.

DELTA OF VENUS

By Anais Nin
(1129) 7-1½ hour cassettes
Rental—$15.50   Purchase—$56.00
Read by Violet Cielo

In *Delta of Venus* one encounters poetic pornography, if the two words can be joined. While the book must be classified triple X for sex and language, the author communicates an authentic vision of crossing to paradise on a bridge of perversion.

THE DESERT ROSE

By Larry McMurtry
(1940) 8-1 hour cassettes
Rental—$14.50   Purchase—$64.00
Read by Roses Prichard

Harmony is a fading flower. When she arrived in Vegas 20 years ago, she was just 17 and had " . . . the best legs in town . . . maybe the best bust!" But now she's 39 and all that's left are memories, pet peacocks, and a cancelled Visa.

But in a falling down life, Harmony herself is a triumph—an unabashed romantic who sees the silver lining in every cloud. She finds life a joy, thus brings joy into the lives she touches.

"The author captures Las Vegas whole . . . its glittering facade, its 24-hour-a-day supermarkets, its calculated appeal to everyone's American Dream. McMurtry presents his characters with a sympathy and compassion that makes us care about their destinies." *(The Los Angeles Times Book Review)*

THE DEVIL'S ALTERNATIVE

By Frederick Forsyth
(1844) 10-1½ hour cassettes
Rental—$16.50   Purchase—$80.00
Read by Ken Ohst

The brief paragraph on the front page of Lloyd's list of shipping news went pretty much unnoticed.

But there is one reader, Andrew Drake, senior clerk in a London firm of chartered shipbrokers, for whom that paragraph will have more than passing interest. As it turns out, the man discovered unconscious and near-dead in the Black Sea off the coast of Turkey is a refugee Ukrainian partisan.

Drake meets the survivor and suddenly finds he is party to international terror and intrigue.

"A good long—possibly prophetic—read, and exciting enough to make you sweat." *(The Daily Mail)*

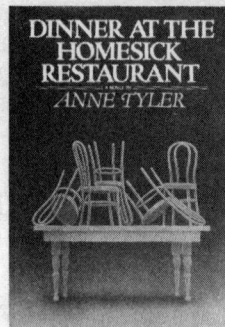

DINNER AT THE HOMESICK RESTAURANT

By Anne Tyler
(1999) 9-1½ hour cassettes
Rental—$16.50   Purchase—$72.00
Read by Jill Masters

Dinner at the Homesick Restaurant is a profoundly felt and deeply moving story about two brothers and a sister deserted by their father, raised by their angry mother, moving through the calamities and exaltations of their difficult youth into separate strategies for survival, and finally into a shared humanity.

The novel opens as the mother, Pearl Tylkl, is dying. What the passing of time does to the Tulls—what happens after Pearl's funeral when they assemble for the last time at Ezra's table—is at the heart of this luminous, most accomplished novel by the writer whom John Updike has called "wickedly good" and Jonathan Yardley, "pure magic."

DISAPPEARANCES

By Howard Frank Mosher
(1978) 9-1 hour cassettes
Rental—$15.50   Purchase—$72.00
Read by Ron Shoop

The time: 1932, just before the repeal of Prohibition and just shy of Wild Bill's fourteenth birthday. The place: Vermont, near the Canadian border.

Bill's dad, desperate to preserve his cattle herd through a bitter winter, resorts to smuggling whiskey—a traditional family occupation. He takes his son on a voyage that will remain etched in the reader's mind: A journey into the demonic and spellbinding past. What they find is the genuine stuff of legends.

"This bounding, inchoate, exuberant book is everything a first novel should be. Mosher revels in an abundance of material, yet is exactly accurate about a thousand details of farming, timbering and whiskey-running life on the Vermont-Canadian border." —Edward Hoagland

DISTORTIONS

By Ann Beattie
(1200) 6-1½ hour cassettes
Rental—$14.50   Purchase—$48.00
Read by Nancy Dannevik

Distortions is a collection of 19 short stories, many of which previously appeared in print, mostly in *The New Yorker*. The author's list of characters is diverse: a lifeguard who wants to "introspect," a suburban couple and a spaceman, a wife who stops talking to her husband but gets up in the middle of the night to mail letters to him.

These people, so different on the surface, all lead lives distorted by dreams, devoid of passion, imagination and vitality. Ann Beattie's style—clipped, cool and concise—gives us cameo portraits of her characters, freezing them in time and space, accentuating the emptiness of their lives.

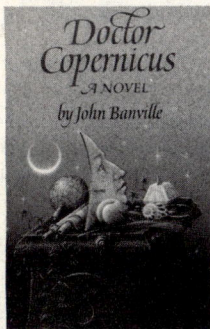

DOCTOR COPERNICUS

By John Banville
(2129) 7-1½ hour cassettes
Rental—$15.50   Purchase—$56.00
Read by Grover Gardner

When Nicolas Copernicus (1473-1543) proved that the earth was not the center of the universe, man's conception of his cosmos and his God broke down. That shattering situation, with the great astronomer at its hub, and the toll it took on him, his church, and his world, is what John Banville skillfully reveals in this novel.

Set in a fascinating, remote world, *Doctor Copernicus* transcends its context, making it at once an historical and a very modern novel.

"Banville is superb . . . There are not many historical novels of which it can be said that they illuminate both the time that forms their subject matter and the time in which they are read: *Doctor Copernicus* is among the very best." *(The Economist)*

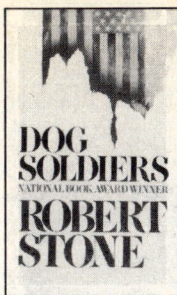

DOG SOLDIERS

By Robert Stone
(1970) 8-1½ hour cassettes
Rental—$15.50   Purchase—$64.00
Read by Paul Shay

A dog soldier is a renegade, and this story is full of them. One is John Converse: loving the chaos in Nam, he sets up a major heroin deal. Converse's friend Hicks takes the drugs to California, where he makes a connection with Marge, Converse's wife. What follows makes combat look tame.

"Stone details an American drama of greed and violence in a world where life is cheap and the price of survival dangerously high." *(Time)*

THE DON FLOWS HOME TO THE SEA

By Mikhail Sholokhov
(1186-A) 11-1½ hour cassettes
Rental—$17.50   Purchase—$88.00
(1186-B) 11-1½ hour cassettes
Rental—$17.50   Purchase—$88.00
Read by Wolfram Kandinsky

The Don Flows Home to the Sea continues the story begun in *And Quiet Flows the Don*. It begins with the period immediately after the Russian Revolution of 1917 and carries on through the end of the civil war in 1921. It follows the fortunes of a group of Cossacks and their women—torn between the intense individualism of their Cossack background and the socialism of the new society.

Russia's most popular writer, Mikhail Sholokhov was awarded the Nobel Prize for literature in 1965.

"As massive and as violent, and perhaps as mad as Russia itself . . . Sholokhov is considered by all odds the finest writer Russia has had since the revolution." *(Dallas News)*

DRUNK WITH LOVE

By Ellen Gilchrist
(2135) 8-1 hour cassettes
Rental—$14.50   Purchase—$64.00
Read by Ruth Stokesberry

Ellen Gilchrist, whose short stories won the 1984 American Book Award for Fiction, offers up new proof of her creative talent in *Drunk with Love*.

This collection of short stories includes "Drunk with Love," "Nineteen Forty-one," "The Expansion of the Universe," "Adoration" and "Traceleen at Dawn."

"*Drunk with Love* goes beyond tradition. Running the gamut from dieting to murder, the stories introduce a whole new generation of characters—outrageous and tragic—that are unmistakably Gilchrist creations." *(E.R.S. Reviews)*

DON'T STOP THE CARNIVAL

By Herman Wouk
(1380) 10-1½ hour cassettes
Rental—$16.50   Purchase—$80.00
Read by Michael Prichard

Don't Stop the Carnival is Herman Wouk's comedy about living out your fantasies on an exotic Caribbean island. Norman Paperman, a successful Broadway publicity agent, has long dreamed of escaping his high-pressure Manhattan life. In a fit of bravado, he chucks it all and buys an old hotel on tiny, primitive, lush Amerigo island.

To anybody who has ever dreamed of escape to an island paradise, this book says "DON'T!"

THE DRIFT FENCE

By Zane Grey
(1311) 7-1 hour cassettes
Rental—$13.50   Purchase—$56.00
Read by Dan Lazar

When the first drift fence is built across a free cattle range, anger overflows. Jim Traft, the tenderfoot in charge of building the fence, finds himself in deep trouble. It takes all his wits to stay alive, let alone complete the fence. But with courage and tenacity Traft finishes his work and lives to see it bring a new order to the range.

THE DWELLING PLACE

By Catherine Cookson
(1886) 8-1½ hour cassettes
Rental—$15.50   Purchase—$64.00
Read by Mary Woods

Cissie Brodie is a fighter, but this may be too much. Her mother and father are gone. She is left alone with her several brothers and sisters, and her whole sense of duty pushed her to find an answer that will save the family from the workhouse.

Enter the local Lord, a man not above extending his help to the deserving poor . . . but what is the price? The alternative is a man who declares he is a true protector . . . but Cissie senses his motives are less than pure.

Fanny McBride, The Fifteen Streets and *The Whip* are other Catherine Cookson titles available from B-O-T.

THE EAGLE AND THE RAVEN

By Pauline Gedge
(1825-A) 9-1½ hour cassettes
Rental—$16.50   Purchase—$72.00
(1825-B) 7-1½ hour cassettes
Rental—$15.50   Purchase—$56.00
(1825-C) 9-1½ hour cassettes
Rental—$16.50   Purchase—$72.00
Read by Donada Peters

In the first century A.D., the Celts were Britain's fiercest warriors. They lived in tribes, to which they gave aggressive loyalty. Under the tribal code, women hunted and fought alongside men.

The Eagle and the Raven spans three generations. First is Caradoc, a king's son, who unites the people of the Raven and leads them against Rome. Eurgain, his wife, alone for months at a time, betrays Caradoc with his best friend. Gladys, Caradoc's warrior sister, falls in love with the Roman general who is her captor. Aricia, queen of the north joined Rome. Finally Boudicca, a strong-willed woman, carries to its conclusion the cause that is Caradoc's legacy.

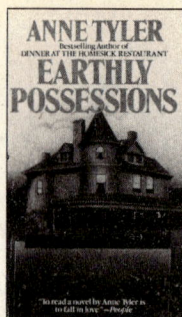

EARTHLY POSSESSIONS

By Anne Tyler
(1997) 8-1 hour cassettes
Rental—$14.50   Purchase—$64.00
Read by Jean Hobson

Charlotte has been meaning to run away from home: from the ceaseless looking-after and the immense faith it takes just to keep everything going. This is the story of her attempt.

"Among our novelists, Anne Tyler occupies a somewhat lonely place, polishing brighter and brighter a craft many novelists no longer deem essential . . . the unfolding of character." *(The New York Times)*

Dinner at the Homesick Restaurant is another Tyler title available on cassette from B-O-T.

EDEN BURNING

By Belva Plain
(1985) 10-1½ hour cassettes
Rental—$16.50   Purchase—$80.00
Read by Jeanne Hopson

Eden Burning is the story of two men and one woman—a triangle as old as time, made modern by the characters and their setting.

Eden is St. Felice, a lush Caribbean island with extremes of privilege and want. Patrick, the fiery black prime minister, seeks a better life for his people. Francis, scion of a prominent New York family, feels the tug of that other island. And Tee—fifteen years old when we meet her, wise beyond her years—runs at life with a reckless passion.

"A superb story in the hands of a masterful storyteller. Violence, political upheaval, clandestine love—they're all here in this great romantic saga." *(E.R.S. Reviews)*

FREE rental from Books on Tape™
See page 3

THE EMBEZZLER

By Louis Auchincloss
(1167) 7-1½ hour cassettes
Rental—$15.50   Purchase—$56.00
Read by Dan Lazar

Auchincloss' story is told in the form of memoirs by the leading participants in the story. Guy Prime, convicted of misappropriating bonds during the depression, first gives his apologia which is followed by the narratives of his closest friend, Rex Geer, and Prime's wife Angelica, who marries Geer after Primes's self-exile.

The three overlapping and mutually contradictory versions create patterns of deception and ambiguity, resulting in a tantalizing psychological mystery that probes the wellsprings of human motivation.

ENEMIES: A LOVE STORY

By Isaac Bashevis Singer
(1366) 8-1 hour cassettes
Rental—$14.50   Purchase—$64.00
Read by Wolfram Kandinsky

Isaac Bashevis Singer is a Nobel Prize-winning author who, in this book, takes as his subject a survivor from the terror of WW II. Herman Broder, whose family was wiped out in the Nazi holocaust in Poland, escaped death by hiding in a village hayloft for two years. When we meet him he is living in an apartment in the Coney Island section of Brooklyn with his cloistered wife, Yadwiga, a Polish peasant girl who helped him escape. He is also deeply involved with Masha Torshiner.

Suddenly Herman learns that his first wife, Tamara, has survived and is now in America. Soon all three women know the truth about one another's roles in Herman's life. Tamara, Yadwiga and Masha each proposes her own solution to the dilemma.

ENGLISH CREEK

By Ivan Doig
(2120) 10-1½ hour cassettes
Rental—$16.50   Purchase—$80.00
Read by Paul Shay

In the days of arriving summer, on a rangeland green across northern Montana, Jick McCaskill comes of age late in the depression. Jick is 14, able now to claim a man's place in the life of family, town and ranch.

His father is a roustabout turned forest ranger, his mother, practical and peppery mate. His brother Alec, his idol, is 18, set on marriage and life as a cowboy. Alec's choices throw the McCaskills into conflict, and through Jicks' eyes we see a family at a turning point—"where all four of our lives made their bend."

"*English Creek* is a portrait of a time and place that at once inspires and fulfills a longing for an explicable past. It is a novel as luminously American as Cather's writing, Wyeth's painting and Copland's music." *(Publisher's Source)*

EVENING IN BYZANTIUM

By Irwin Shaw
(1152) 8-1½ hour cassettes
Rental—$15.50   Purchase—$64.00
Read by Wolfram Kandinsky

The setting is Cannes, the time its annual Film Festival and the hero 48-year-old Jesse Craig, a successful but fading producer. His story is told in flashbacks: a shattered marriage, two daughters whom he scarcely knows, his mistress, a familiar world disintegrating around him.

Evening in Byzantium lets us into the glamorous world of the modern film industry. At the same time we get a whiff of what's behind the facade.

"Shaw knows what happens to people in this industry. So will you, after this book." *(Book Review Services)*

EVERGREEN

By Belva Plain
(2102-A) 8-1½ hour cassettes
Rental—$17.50   Purchase—$64.00
(2102-B) 8-1½ hour cassettes
Rental—$17.50   Purchase—$64.00
Read by Dick Estell
A Christopher Enterprises Recording

The dramatic saga of Anna Friedman, beautiful and bewitching, who had come to New York at the turn of the century from a Polish *stetl.* Yearning for a better life, she leaves the sweatshops to find work as a maid in the home of the elegant Werners.

Anna is torn between the love of two men—aristocratic Paul Werner, scion of the German-Jewish banking family and Joseph Friedman, an immigrant as poor as herself.

It is Joseph she marries, and through an act of passion that will follow her always, Anna lifts them from poverty to the real estate-based fortune that founds the Friedman dynasty.

This is Anna's story—her marriage, her children, her deceit. It is also a novel of grand sweep and power following the generations of the Friedman family.

Slightly edited for radio presentation.

EXCEPT FOR THEE AND ME

By Jessamyn West
(1236) 7-1½ hour cassettes
Rental—$15.50   Purchase—$56.00
Read by Roses Prichard

Except for Thee and Me is the companion book to *The Friendly Persuasion.* Here we find Jess and Eliza Birdwell, the Quaker couple of our earlier acquaintance, looking back at their years of marriage. The story moves from the time when their lives were dominated by a patriarchal father to the happy years of building a home. We relive the turbulence of the Civil War and, at the narrative's end, join the Birdwells at a Christmas gathering, surrounded by their numerous offspring.

"This beautifully written and historically accurate book brings to live a part of the American West seldom celebrated." *(Editorial Reviews)*

EXODUS

By Leon Uris
(1297-A) 9-1½ hour cassettes
Rental—$16.50   Purchase—$72.00
(1297-B) 8-1½ hour cassettes
Rental—$15.50   Purchase—$64.00
Read by Dan Lazar

The time is 1946; the British on Cyprus have set up a more "humane" concentration camp for the Jewish refugees of WW II. And the agents of the Mussad Allyah Bet—the Palestinian "illegal immigration"—are determined to set their people free.

Described as one of the most eloquent and powerful novels about the Jews written in our time, it directs our attention to questions still unresolved, questions being answered in the violence and bloodshed of the Middle East.

"An enthralling book, both for the richness of its detail and for the range of its historical content." *(Chicago Sunday Tribune)*

Also available from B-O-T are Uris' *QB VII* and *Trinity.*

THE EXPLORER

By W. Somerset Maugham
(1742) 6-1½ hour cassettes
Rental—$14.50   Purchase—$48.00
Read by Jill Masters

"Hamlyn's Purlieu, a palatial estate, had belonged to the Allertons for three hundred years. And with each generation the Allertons grew prouder. But at length Purlieu came into the hands of Fred Allerton: and the house, determined now, it seemed, to wreak their malice."

The Explorer is the story of the Allertons, Fred and his children, as they deal with the loss of their birthright. Fred squanders the family fortune and dishonors the family name. His children, Lucy and George, try to pick up the pieces when what they assume is theirs is taken from them.

A FAIR DAY'S WORK and THE TIME BEFORE THIS

By Nicholas Monsarrat
(1179) 7-1 hour cassettes
Rental—$13.50   Purchase—$56.00
Read by Richard Green

Two novels by the author of *The Cruel Sea,* both serious but widely separate in theme. *A Fair Day's Work* pivots on a wildcat strike that cripples the liner *Good Hope.* At berth in Liverpool, the festive passengers and determined strikers offer memorable contrasts . . . *The Time Before This* tackles a grimmer subject: extermination by thermonuclear war. Focus is on Grant Shepherd, a visionary loner, who discovers evidence in Canada's vast wilderness that a sophisticated civilization dwelt there before us. He attributes its demise to nuclear holocaust, "because it discovered more than it knew how to use." Will these words be our own epitaph?

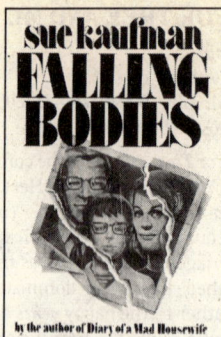

FALLING BODIES

By Sue Kaufman
(1268) 8-1 hour cassettes
Rental—$15.50   Purchase—$64.00
Read by Nancy Dannevik

Statistically speaking, fourteen years is a long time to be married to anyone these days. Perhaps Emma Sohier was lucky to have chalked up that many. All seemed well until her "rough" year: the year her mother died and Emma herself landed in the hospital with FUO—fever of unknown origin. Her husband turned kinky, and her son started picking through New York City garbage pails.

Sue Kaufman wrote *Diary of a Mad Housewife* which has also been recorded by B-O-T.

THE FAMILY ARSENAL

By Paul Theroux
(1868) 8-1½ hour cassettes
Rental—$15.50   Purchase—$64.00
Read by Michael Prichard

Deptford is a seedy riverside district in London. Anonymous in its decay lives a group that might pass for a family: Valentine Hood, ex-American consul; Mayo, a thief working with the IRA Provisionals; and two street-wise waifs—Murf, who makes bombs, and the girl Brodie, who plants them.

Hood throws in with these characters and immediately finds himself tangled up in murder and mayhem. His solo activities, meshing perilously with the IRA's planned English offensive, draw more players into the game. Urban struggle, Hood learns, is a family affair.

Theroux fans will also want to listen to *The Great Railway Bazaar, Kingdom by the Sea* and *The Old Patagonian Express.*

FANNY McBRIDE

By Catherine Cookson
(1884) 8-1 hour cassettes
Rental—$14.50   Purchase—$64.00
Read by Mary Woods

Widowed in middle age, Fanny McBride survives with her good sense and great spirits intact. No longer able to seek the protection of her husband, she now faces all of life's challenges alone.

But Fanny finds there are tragedies beyond losing her mate, and when her children are threatened she discovers resources of courage and energy she never knew existed.

"A compassionate testament to the strength of the human spirit . . . a story hard to put down and impossible to forget." *(The Commonwealth Insider)*

THE FAR COUNTRY

By Nevil Shute
(1937) 8-1½ hour cassettes
Rental—$15.50   Purchase—$64.00
Read by Christopher Hurt

Jennifer fled the drab monotony of postwar London. When she landed in Australia, it was like coming home. She loved it and when she met Carl, she had every reason to stay.

But the two of them came from quite different worlds, and it is the story of their building a life together that Nevil Shute tells in his matchless way. With warmth and understanding, and with his natural affection for the people he creates, the author brings to life his characters and the pioneer country in which they live.

"New lives for old . . . on a fresh, vital, expanding frontier! This is the exciting background of this heartlifting novel by a master weaver of romance and adventure." *(Boston Herald)*

For quick ordering
1-800-626-3333

FEATHERS IN THE FIRE

By Catherine Cookson
(1887) 7-1½ hour cassettes
Rental—$15.50 Purchase—$56.00
Read by Mary Woods

A tenant farm in nineteenth century England provides the setting for this story of love, loss and redemption.

Davy Armstrong struggles hard for his place at Cock Shield Farm. He finds himself at odds with the owner, a man of mordant temper and villainous pride, whom the gods humble by sending him a son, born crippled. Davy's trials include the love of two women. One he scorns, the other, marries.

"Catherine Cookson writes with conviction about the north of England. Her novels have a powerful narrative style combining human warmth, pathos, comedy and tragedy." *(Novels and Novelists)*

THE FIFTEEN STREETS

By Catherine Cookson
(1883) 8-1 hour cassettes
Rental—$14.50 Purchase—$64.00
Read by Mary Woods

Northern England's Tyneside district is the backdrop against which the O'Brien family breaks free.

One man cuts the family's cycle of ignorance and want. He finds courage through the love of a very special woman, but must learn if such a love can survive in *The Fifteen Streets*.

"Sensitive, compelling. Catherine Cookson's feeling for character and uncluttered portrayal of human emotion rises above the commonplace." *(Book Review Service)*

FIFTH BUSINESS

By Robertson Davies
(1283) 10-1 hour cassettes
Rental—$15.50 Purchase—$80.00
Read by Dan Lazar

Dunstan Ramsay is a quiet and devoted professor of history, retiring after 45 years of service to a Canadian boys' school. In writing his memoirs, Ramsay reveals the unique role he played during his life, or rather, lives. For Ramsay is a man twice born. A man who returned from the trenches of WW I and was destined to live within the borderline between history and myth, reality and surreality. *Fifth Business* is volume I of a trilogy which included *The Manticore* and *World of Wonders*, all recorded by B-O-T.

FINDING A GIRL IN AMERICA

By Andre Dubus
(1437) 8-1 hour cassettes
Rental—$14.50 Purchase—$64.00
Read by Dan Lazar

Andre Dubus writes contemporary American fiction. *Finding a Girl in America* is a collection of stories set in the New England coastal region, an area the author knows well. We are reintroduced to Hank Allison, who first appeared in *Adultery & Other Choices*.

Allison's life is clouded by a failed marriage, concern for his daughter and his difficulties with new relationships. He fights through these problems and emerges as a man of healing insight, one who is capable of change, growth and love.

Other Dubus titles available from B-O-T include *Separate Flights* and *Adultery & Other Choices*.

THE FIXER

By Bernard Malamud
(1834) 8-1½ hour cassettes
Rental—$16.50 Purchase—$64.00
Read by Wolfram Kandinsky

Yakov Bok is an ordinary man accused of "ritual murder" and persecuted by agents of a remote and all-powerful state. But when he is at last pushed too far, he triumphs over almost incredible brutality and becomes a moral giant.

The Fixer brought both a Pulitzer Prize and the National Book Award to Bernard Malamud. He has been acclaimed by the *Los Angeles Times* as a writer "whose work will be read in this country long after most of the best sellers of this era are forgotten."

"*The Fixer* upholds the tradition of immediacy which gave the novel much of its importance and its vitality in the past, which is its chief claim to our attention in the present, and its strongest hope for the future."
—National Book Award Citation

FLIGHT

By Edmund Fuller
(1257) 7-1 hour cassettes
Rental—$13.50 Purchase—$56.00
Read by Dan Lazar

With only a little more than a month to go until graduation, Greg Warren, to all appearances a normal 19-year-old, suddenly leaves his New England boys' school and decamps for Italy. His uncle, Samuel Tilden, a middle-aged widowed teacher at the same school, goes after him—wanting to help the boy and find some answers for himself.

FLIGHT OF THE INTRUDER

By Stephen Coonts
(2097) 9-1½ hour cassettes
Rental—$16.50 Purchase—$72.00
Read by Michael Prichard

Stephen Coonts flew A-6's in Viet Nam. He has the credentials to write this story, which helps explain its long stay on the best seller list.

A-6's were called Intruders. Their pilots tackled assignments of dazzling complexity and flew them with daring and dispatch. But they paid a price . . . in lost lives, disillusion, incredible tension.

They had one reward—exhilaration—worth the whole candle. You share the airmen's special brand of comradery, the one stabilizing force in an otherwise precarious life, that only an insider knows.

"Documentary and dramatic, *Flight of the Intruder* is to the novel what *Top Gun* was to film." *(E.R.S. Reviews)*

THE FLIGHT OF THE PHOENIX

By Elleston Trevor
(1157) 7-1 hour cassettes
Rental—$13.50 Purchase—$56.00
Read by Richard Green

A cargo plane crash lands in the Central Libyan desert during a violent sandstorm. Twelve men and a monkey survive. They stare without hope into the desert sky: search planes will not seek their unscheduled flight. One man proposes the impossible—to build from the wreckage an aircraft capable of flying them 200 miles to the nearest oasis. But the pilot refuses to cooperate and this struggle becomes the pivot for survival or death. *The Flight of the Phoenix* launched Elleston Trevor's remarkable career.

Tervor writes not only under his own name but also as Adam Hall, creator of the award-winning Quiller stories.

FONG AND THE INDIANS

By Paul Theroux
(1869) 7-1 hour cassettes
Rental—$13.50   Purchase—$56.00
Read by Michael Prichard

The Indians who plot against Fong don't live in teepees. They are his rival traders in a mythical East African country who compete with him for the black market.

Fong is an anti-hero. He survives, but it is always by the skin of his teeth and for the wrong reasons.

"Theroux has created a lovable non-hero and underscored brilliantly the foibles of a topsey-turvey world in which only the innocent loser can possibly win." *(Boston Post)*

THE FOURTH PROTOCOL

By Frederick Forsyth
(1768) 10-1½ hour cassettes
Rental—$16.50   Purchase—$80.00
Read by Rupert Keenlyside

A million dollar robbery in London is flawlessly conceived and meticulously executed.

The robbery is not for money alone. It masks a more sinister plot. The game is to stage an "accident" that will change the face of British politics and shatter the Western Alliance.

Enter John Preston, special agent. He suspects treachery among the Queen's most trusted advisors. Hours melt to minutes, then seconds, as Preston closes on his elusive and deadly foe.

THE FOXES OF HARROW

By Frank Yerby
(1403) 12-1½ hour cassettes
Rental—$17.50   Purchase—$96.00
Read by Dan Lazar

Stephen Fox arrived in New Orleans in 1825 on a pig boat, with a ten-dollar gold piece, a pearl stick pin—and a dream. Tall, red-haired, with a face that looked like Lucifer's so soon after the fall that the angel-look was still on it, Fox saw his chance and took it. He gambled and won . . . and built "Harrow," the greatest manor house and plantation in Louisiana.

Yerby has overlooked none of the color and atmosphere of New Orleans through the troubled days between 1825 and the Civil War.

B-O-T has also recorded Yerby's *Judas, My Brother; The Dahomean* and *A Rose for Ana Maria.*

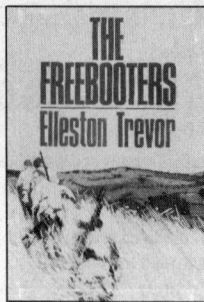

THE FREEBOOTERS

By Elleston Trevor
(1789) 8-1 hour cassettes
Rental—$14.50   Purchase—$64.00
Read by Christopher Hurt

In the middle of a hundred thousand square miles of East African bush, a British regiment hunkers down inside a ring of barbed wire. They are ordered not to respond to provocation.

This is a story of fighting men who give up because they are not allowed to fight, a story of mutiny, desertion and escape through hostile territory. These men are freebooters and their inspiration is not hate but love . . . because one of them has met a girl . . . and must find her again.

Other Elleston Trevor titles available from Books on Tape include *The Burning Shore, The Flight of the Phoenix* and *Gale Force.*

(Note: A story or related interested is *Freedom Observed* by Gwyn Griffin.)

FREEDOM OBSERVED

By Gwyn Griffin
(1173) 9-1½ hour cassettes
Rental—$16.50   Purchase—$72.00
Read by Wolfram Kandinsky

Freedom Observed drops us into Sebangerisque, a former French colony in West Africa. It is busily imposing upon itself a domestic rule considerably more brutal than that from which it has recently escaped. We join a small group of whites traveling from one part of the country to another. Told with unflinching realism, the story of their passage reminds the reader that the step from civilization to savagery is but a short one and that freedom by another name is license.

FRENCHMAN'S CREEK

By Daphne du Maurier
(1881) 7-1½ hour caysettes
Rental—$15.50   Purchase—$56.00
Read by Wanda McCaddon

England during the Restoration provides the setting for du Maurier's fanciful tale of a titled lady and a daring pirate. *Frenchman's Creek* blends adventure, romance and wit to give us a satisfying story and a complete change from the endless progression of espionage and spy thrillers.

"A beautifully written tale of captivating enchantment. Recommended." *(Library Journal)*

A FRIEND OF KAFKA

By Isaac Bashevis Singer
(1367) 8-1½ hour cassettes
Rental—$15.50   Purchase—$64.00
Read by Wolfram Kandinsky

A Friend of Kafka is a collection of twenty-one short stories, all originally published in *The New Yorker, Harper's, Commentary, The Saturday Evening Post,* and other leading national magazines. Singer's people are the dispossessed of the modern world, European Jews who have fled their homelands and taken up new lives in cities ranging from Buenos Aires to New York.

"All his tales are unfailingly entertaining, but Singer's reputation as a master storyteller rests on his ability as a teacher . . . we follow the narratives of his knowledge with a sense of personal discovery and delight at our new perception . . . " *(The New York Times* Book Review)

THE FRIENDLY PERSUASION

By Jessamyn West
(1168) 8-1 hour cassettes
Rental—$14.50   Purchase—$64.0
Read by Roses Prichard

The Friendly Persuasion has had many editions and millions of admirers. It is the story of the Birdwell family of Indiana—pious Quakers with an inexhaustible relish for life. The eight Birdwells live according to the dictates of William Penn . . . but the Civil War interrupts their tranquil existence and tests their strength and faith.

**TOLL FREE credit card
order line 1-800-626-3333**

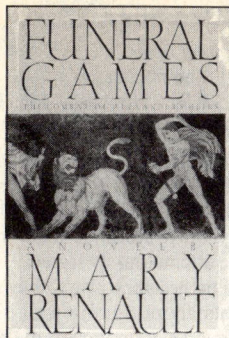

FUNERAL GAMES

By Mary Renault
(1823) 8-1½ hour cassettes
Rental—$15.50   Purchase—$64.00
Read by Christopher Hurt

In the sweltering midsummer heat of the palace at Babylon, Alexander the Great, master of half the known world, lies dying. His only heirs are his unborn child and his simpleton half-brother. He sinks into a coma without having named his successor.

When Homer's heroes fell, their fellow warriors held funeral games, racing and wrestling for rich prizes to honor the dead. Now Alexander's generals, no longer united by his magnetic presence, begin their struggle for the glittering prize of his vast dominions.

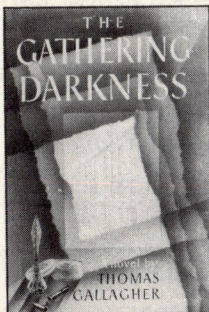

THE GATHERING DARKNESS

By Thomas Gallagher
(1973) 7-1½ hour cassettes
Rental—$15.50   Purchase—$56.00
Read by John McDonald

It is 1929, and the market is already wobbly. When John McPeek plays it, he loses more than money: he loses his family and very nearly his life.

He and his wife Cathy cash in their special understanding and balance. Hard, cold money—or rather the loss of it—slowly extinguishes their love and trust.

"Describes a scene to which we can all relate." *(Publisher's Souce)*
Other Thomas Gallagher titles recorded by B-O-T include *Assault in Norway, The Monogamist, Paddy's Lament* and *The X-Craft Raid.*

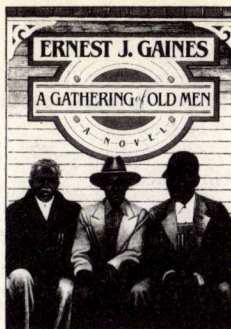

A GATHERING OF OLD MEN

By Ernest J. Gaines
(2104) 7-1 hour cassettes
Rental—$13.50   Purchase—$56.00
Read by Ron Shoop

Beau Boutan, a Cajun farmer, is shot dead. Candy Marshall, the headstrong young plantation owner, tells everyone that she killed Beau. But when the sheriff arrives, he finds a dozen aging black men each claiming to have done the deed.

The sheriff fails to break the circle of protection thrown around the real murderer. He realizes that these men are not afraid of Boutan family vengeance, and welcome a chance to get even after whole lifetimes of oppression.

"Ernest J. Gaines makes it clear that dignity and fortitude are virtues available to men and women of all races at all times . . . profound and moving." *(E.R.S. Reviews)*
The Autobiography of Miss Jane Pittman is another Gaines novel that has been recorded by B-O-T.

GEORGE PASSANT
(Formerly titled:
Strangers and Brothers)

By C.P. Snow
(1411) 8-1½ hour cassettes
Rental—$15.50   Purchase—$64.00
Read by Robert Mundy

The second novel in C.P. Snow's multi-volume work titled *Strangers and Brothers, George Passant* follows *Time of Hope.* The story is set in an English provincial town where Lewis Eliot, the narrator, is training in law. George Passant is his friend and mentor, an idealistic lawyer and a man of principle and courage.

"The successive revelations of (Passant's) character . . . and the turmoil in Eliot's mind as he considers these revelations stir the reader into making his own analysis of Passant's motivations. Snow is thought-provoking and entertaining at the same time." *(Chicago Sunday Tribune)*

GIANT

By Edna Ferber
(1629) 10-1½ hour cassettes
Rental—$16.50   Purchase—$80.00
Read by Flo Gibson

Leslie Lynnton, beautiful and spirited, trades Virginia for Texas with her husband, Bick Benedict, owner of the Reata Ranch empire. Vast fortunes in cattle and oil contrast with the plight of Mexican laborers, but Texas emerges as tempestuous, exhilarating, exasperating and, above all, "alive."

"Marvelous reading—wealth piled upon wealth, wonder on wonder in a stunning splendiferous pyramid of ostentation." *(The New York Times Book Review)*
For other Ferber titles, please refer to the Index in the back of our catalog.

THE GIRL

By Catherine Cookson
(1891) 7-1½ hour cassettes
Rental—$15.50   Purchase—$56.00
Read by Mary Woods

Hannah Boyle was barely eight when she and her mother trudged the twenty-three miles from Newcastle to Hexham. Her mother delivered Hannah to the man she claimed was Hannah's father. And she left a letter in safe keeping with the church, a letter that was to be given to Hannah on her wedding day. Then she died.

Protected by her father from her stepmother, who could only bring herself to refer to Hannah as "the girl," Hannah becomes an educated, accomplished young woman. But she makes a loveless match and nearly disintegrates when she reads her mother's letter.

Fanny McBride, The Fifteen Streets and *The Whip* are among the other Catherine Cookson titles available from B-O-T.

GIRL 20

By Kingsley Amis
(1100) 8-1 hour cassettes
Rental—$14.50   Purchase—$64.00
Read by Richard Green

Life in London means glamour, fashion, finance and art. Consider then an aging conductor, husband in an unsatisfactory marriage, father to an unhappy brood. When a young woman responds to his overtures, he breaks the marriage and bursts the family . . . alas, everyone loses in this drama, for nothing puts people together again.

Kingsley Amis is one of England's finest men of letters. Try *Lucky Jim, The Green Man* or others listed in our Index under the author's name.

GIRLS AT PLAY

By Paul Theroux
(1863) 8-1 hour cassettes
Rental—$14.50   Purchase—$64.00
Read by Michael Prichard

Set in the green chaos of East Africa, *Girls at Play* concerns the ambitions of three women, teachers at a remote girls school. They are the only white women in the region and each in her own way is doomed.

Miss Poole, the headmistress and a colonial, attempts to order the society along Christian principles. Bettyjean Lebow is an American Peace Corps volunteer from San Diego.

Heather Monkhouse left a dull job in London only to be fired from her first teaching position in Nairobi. Trapped at the school, each struggles to realize her own vision of Africa, and to survive.

" . . . This is a well-controlled, well-shaped and penetrating novel showing the hand of a born writer . . ." *(The Times (London) Saturday Review)*

THE GLASS BLOWERS

By Daphne du Maurier
(1880) 9-1½ hour cassettes
Rental—$16.50   Purchase—$72.00
Read by Donada Peters

We asked our reader, Donada Peters, to review this book for us and she wrote:

"A historical romance without the romance, *The Glass Blowers* follows the fortunes of a large family of merchant craftsmen 200 years ago in revolutionary France. The heroes and heroines of the story are Daphne du Maurier's own ancestors, who were master glass makers during the reigns of Louis XV and XVI.

"I found it an absolutely absorbing story, and given its basis in fact, a valuable addition to my own understanding of the period."

GOAT SONG

By Frank Yerby
(1404) 11-1½ hour cassettes
Rental—$17.50   Purchase—$88.00
Read by Dan Lazar

Frank Yerby is one of the most prolific and popular of American authors. His novels frequently explore widely diverse historical incidents, and *Goat Song* takes us back 25 centuries to that age of Greece when Sparta was dominant. The principal character is Ariston, a well-born young Spartan, whose series of adventures mature him physically and psychology.

Other Frank Yerby titles available from B-O-T include *The Dahomean; Judas, My Brother; The Foxes of Harrow* and *A Rose for Ana Maria.*

GOD IS AN ENGLISHMAN

By R.F Delderfield
(1462-A) 13-1½ hour cassettes
Rental—$18.50   Purchase—$104.00
(1462-B) 9-1½ hour cassettes
Rental—$16.50   Purchase—$72.00
Read by Ian Whitcomb

Adam Swann, scion of an army family, returns home in 1858 after service with Her Majesty's Army in the Crimea and India, determined to build his fortune in the dog-eat-dog world of Victorian commerce. Swann is captivated by Henrietta, the high-spirited daughter of a local mill owner. The two share adventures, reversal and fortune.

Swann's adventures are continued in *Theirs Was the Kingdom.*

"Mr. Delderfield writes with vigor, unceasing narrative drive and a high degree of craftsmanship." *(The New York Times Book Review)*

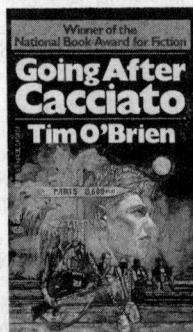

Winner of the National Book Award for Fiction
Going After Cacciato
Tim O'Brien

PARIS 8600

GOING AFTER CACCIATO

By Tim O'Brien
(1842) 7-1½ hour cassettes
Rental—$15.50   Purchase—$56.00
Read by John McDonald

Cacciato is one dumb soldier. He walks away from the Vietnam War. Across mountains, deserts and swamps, he plans to hike 8600 miles form Vietnam to Paris. He's after peace and freedom. But that's insane. Isn't it? So a squad of his buddies goes after him. They're told to bring him back . . . or else.

Going After Cacciato gives us the grunt, day by day. It brings Vietnam home. It won a National Book Award for fiction.

"Incomparable! Every war has its chroniclers of fear and flight, its Stephen Cranes and Joseph Hellers. Tim O'Brien joins their number." *(Philadelphia Inquirer)*

THE GOLDEN SOAK

By Hammond Innes
(1809) 7-1½ hour cassettes
Rental—$15.50   Purchase—$56.00
Read by H. Alan Cornell

Alec Falls attempts desperately to regain his fortune by tackling the region's fabled McIlroy's Monster: a mine with enough promise of trapped ore to destroy as many men as it seduces into attempting its secrets.

The mine becomes Alec's obsession. As he plunges blindly into the morass, his character gradually erodes along with his hopes of hitting "the big strike."

For other Innes titles, please refer to the Index.

GOOD AS GOLD

By Joseph Heller
(1503) 9-1½ hour cassettes
Rental—$16.50   Purchase—$72.00
Read by Dan Lazar

Meet Bruce Gold, 48 and ready for a change. He settles on government service.

There is a hitch, however: to land the job, Gold must bring to the marriage couch Andrea Conover, the darling daughter of an influential Washington anti-Semite, whose chief delight is baiting Bruce. And Andrea will not marry Bruce until he has the government job.

"This is a great pleasure . . . an indelible central figure in a stunning cast of characters!" *(San Francisco Chronicle)*

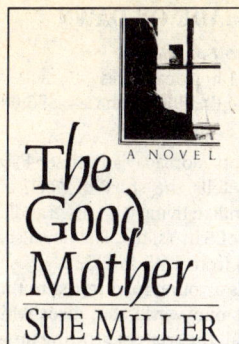

THE GOOD MOTHER

By Sue Miller
(2078) 9-1½ hour cassettes
Rental—$16.50   Purchase—$72.00
Read by Donada Peters

Anna Dunlap is being torn in two . . . by love for her daughter, Molly, and by passion for her lover, a painter with liberal ideas about personal freedom. To Anna it looks like these two flowers come from the same plant. What she can't understand is how they are causing her such pain. It's a classic problem, hers to solve . . . which, remarkably, she does.

This story is about conflict not between good and evil but between two powerful sets of feelings, the erotic and the maternal. We share Anna's dilemma over the loyalties that divide her. But we also share her growing strength as well, the stubborn emergence of courage, acceptance and hope . . . the classic attributes of the good mother.

"A very gifted first novel." —John Fowles

GRENDEL

By John Gardner
(1747) 5-1 hour cassettes
Rental—$11.50   Purchase—$40.00
Read by Wolfram Kandinsky

The first monster ever to appear in English literature tells his side of the story in *Grendel.*

It is comic, grotesque, at times sad, and peopled with fantastic characters and a stranger literally from another world. Beowulf, defender of mankind.

In the stories of Beowulf, Grendel, devourer of men, signifies the dread that lies beyond human knowledge. But the truth is even darker . . . Grendel haunts the warrior feast-hall because he is in love with an ideal vision of man and God, a vision betrayed when humanity fails his test.

Other titles by John Gardner available from B-O-T include *October Light* and *Sunlight Dialogues.*

GROWING UP RICH

By Ann Bernays
(1166) 8-1½ hour cassettes
Rental—$15.50   Purchase—$64.00
Read by Nancy Dannevik

A young princess of upper class New York Jewish society at a twist of fate is removed from her family to an adopted one, from privilege not so much to poverty as to ordinariness, and from Manhattan to Brookline, Massachusetts. The book turns on how an adolescent copes with change and strikes an echo in our own remembrance of those far distant years.

"Excellent writing . . . and a story that will stay in your heart." *(Editorial Reviews)*

THE HAJ

By Leon Uris
(1619-A) 7-1½ hour cassettes
Rental—$15.50   Purchase—$56.00
(1619-B) 8-1½ hour cassettes
Rental—$15.50   Purchase—$64.00
Read by Michael Prichard

Until the Jews came, the village of Tabah was little changed from one Arab generation to another. Then everything changed forever.

Tabah was ruled by Haj Ibrahim, a man who had mastered the complex ways of his people. Forced to leave Tabah during the struggle for Palestine, his family flees to a refugee camp near Jericho. There the Haj fights against the refugee system in a struggle at once lonely, gallant and doomed.

B-O-T listeners will also enjoy Leon Uris's *Exodus, QB VII* and *Trinity.*

HARVEST ON THE DON

By Mikhail Sholokhov
(1790) 11-1½ hour cassettes
Rental—$17.50   Purchase—$88.00
Read by Wolfram Kandinsky

In *Harvest on the Don*, Mikhail Sholokhov continues the dramatic story of the impact of revolution on the people of his native Russia. In *And Quiet Flows the Don* and *The Don Flows Home to the Sea,* Sholokhov tells of the violent and tumultuous days of the revolution and the civil war.

In this novel we see the same Don village, Gremyachy Log, whose people have lived for generations according to medieval ritual, torn from the ancient ways.

To Gremyachy Log has come Davidov, representative of the Party's drive to revolutionize village agriculture. The peasants see a vision of a better life in the plans of this man. Yet to-the-death opposition lurks just beneath the surface.

THE HEART OF A MAN

By Georges Simenon
(1506) 6-1 hour cassettes
Rental—$12.50   Purchase—$48.00
Read by Michael Prichard

The Heart of a Man is the story of a master artist. Emile Maugin is the most celebrated actor in France. At the height of his success, he is stunned by a blunt warning from his doctor. Suddenly confronted with his mortality, he finds himself vulnerable as never before.

"Maugin's appetite for live, his competing emotions, are compellingly portrayed." *(Book Review Service)*

For a complete list of Simenon books recorded by B-O-T, please refer to our Index.

THE HEART OF THE FAMILY

By Elizabeth Goudge
(1460) 9-1½ hour cassettes
Rental—$16.50   Purchase—$72.00
Read by Wanda McCaddon

In this unusual story of a family and the strangers it takes to its heart, Elizabeth Goudge reintroduces us to the Eliots, a clan we grow to love and cherish.

"The author's exquisite portrayal of children, grownups, animals and the English countryside gives it the refreshing charm for which she is famous." *(Library Journal)*

A sequel to *Pilgrim's Inn, The Heart of the Family* is the third in Goudge's trilogy about the Eliot family.

THE HEART OF WAR

By John Masters
(1715-A) 9-1½ hour cassettes
Rental—$15.50   Purchase—$72.00
(1715-B) 10-1½ hour cassettes
Rental—$16.50   Purchase—$80.00
Read by Walter Zimmerman

The middle years of WW II were desperate for the English. We forgot how their world looked to them then, but it was largely hostile.

Britain never broke, but some British bent . . . an adjutant sleeps with his commander's wife, a pilot weeps for his fallen foes, a woman donated herself along with the coffee and biscuits . . . this is their story.

"In this sequel to *Now God Be Thanked,* John Masters, a novelist who won his spurs in military service, shows his grip of war behind the lines as well as at the front." *(Publisher's Source)*

**FREE rental from
Books on Tape™
See page 3**

HER VICTORY

By Alan Sillitoe
(1767-A) 7-1½ hour cassettes
Rental—$15.50   Purchase—$56.00
(1767-B) 7-1½ hour cassettes
Rental—$15.50   Purchase—$56.00
Read by Penelope Dellaporta

Her Victory is a fine achievement, as was *The Widower's Son,* another novel from his more recent period. Both deal with those times when one feels overloaded with the accumulated burdens of life. Sillitoe's characters perform a chiropractic function: they put things back in place.

"*Her Victory* is a celebration of the human spirit and a memorable love story for our times." *(Book Review Service)*

HERITAGE

By Peter Driscoll
(1697-A) 7-1½ hour cassettes
Rental—$15.50   Purchase—$56.00
(1697-B) 8-1½ hour cassettes
Rental—$15.50   Purchase—$64.00
Read by Rupert Keenlyside

The Lombard family—tight-knit, wealthy, conservative—finds its loyalties split when massacre, terrorism and torture cripple their beloved Algeria. Colonialism is dead—so are a lot of colonials.

Jean-Claude, the eldest son, is a brooding introvert, viciously anti-Arab. Emile, passionately liberal, marries an Arab girl and joins the rebels. Paule, their lovely young sister, breaks down under the butchery, while Robert, the soldier, fails his own personal loyalty test.

As the terror grows, members of the family take different sides in a fratricidal struggle that can be resolved only by the death of one brother.

THE HERO

By W. Somerset Maugham
(1741) 6-1½ hour cassettes
Rental—$14.50   Purchase—$48.00
Read by Jill Masters

Five years change a man, and when they have been spent in the bush fighting Boers, the changes are profound. So when Jamie Parson comes home with captain's pips and a Victoria Cross, he is no longer the boy he was. But not to his parents and Mary, his sweetheart . . . they expect him to fit in.

Jamie can't, and shortly breaks off with Mary. Happiness remains a shadow, illusive as the Boers, and Jamie finds the moral struggle as relentless as the military.

The Explorer and *Mrs. Craddock* are both recent additions to B-O-T's collection of W. Somerset Maugham titles.

HOMECOMING

By C.P. Snow
(1416) 8-1½ hour cassettes
Rental—$15.50   Purchase—$64.00
Read by John MacDonald

C.P. Snow forged three careers in one lifetime: scientist, civil servant and author. He wrote about power from the inside, and his broad experience reveals itself in a compassion that, in today's phrase, we would call "nonjudgmental."

His master work the *Strangers and Brothers* series, follows Lewis Eliot's career from student days to the peerage. In this installment we accompany Lewis through an unhappy marriage to a neurotic woman, her death, and his affair with and eventual marriage to a woman more suited to his style.

"(This) story accents not the events themselves but their psychological effect upon the persons involved. Crisp, carefully fashioned prose; for the discriminating." *(Booklist)*

HOMER'S DAUGHTER

By Robert Graves
(1979) 6-1½ hour cassettes
Rental—$14.50   Purchase—$48.00
Read by Lindy Nettleton

In *Homer's Daughter* Robert Graves recreates the *Odyssey.* He bases his story on Samuel Butler's argument that the author of the *Odyssey* was not the blind and bearded Homer of legend, but a young woman who calls herself Nausicaa in Graves' story.

"Here," he says, "is the story of a high-spirited and religious-minded Sicilian girl who saves her father's throne from usurpation, herself from a distasteful marriage, and her two younger brothers from butchery by boldly making things happen, instead of sitting still and hoping for the best."

Goodbye to All That and *They Hanged My Saintly Billy,* both by Robert Graves, have been recorded on cassette by B-O-T.

HONORABLE MEN

NEW

By Louis Auchincloss
(2124) 8-1½ hour cassettes
Rental—$15.50   Purchase—$64.00
Read by Grover Gardner

Honorable Men explores the circumstances under which America's "best and brightest," or at least richest and most socially secure, came to grief over the moral issues of the 1960's.

Chip Benedict appears to have everything: wealth, good looks, education. Called to serve in WW II, he returns a hero and eventually becomes chairman of the family firm.

Despite his many gifts, Chip is morally flawed. Thus when it comes to choosing sides on the issue of Vietnam, he faces a decision that challenges his character at its deepest level.

HOUSE MADE OF DAWN

By N. Scott Momaday
(1019) 7-1 hour cassettes
Rental—$12.50   Purchase—$56.00
Read by Scott Forbes

N. Scott Momaday's Pulitzer Prize-winning novel tells the story of Abel, a young American Indian living with his grandfather in the pueblo of San Ysidro. The novel spans the seven years from 1945 to 1952.

Abel is a young man trying to find himself not in one world, but two: white and Indian. To all the trials of growing up is added cultural ambiguity.

"*House Made of Dawn* is a brilliant exposition of the mind and soul of the American Indian and an important contribution to American literature." *(Digest Reviews)*

THE HOUSE OF GOD

By Samuel Shem, M.D.
(1594) 9-1½ hour cassettes
Rental—$16.50   Purchase—$72.00
Read by Bob Erickson

To the world-famous teaching hospital ("the House of God") come six impassioned interns—each planning to be the savior for whom the medical world waits.

One is Roy Basch, Rhodes Scholar and recent graduate of the Best Medical School. His lofty ideals sag as he copes with repugnant day-to-day realities. Dodging hospital politics but enduring endless hours of work and vital responsibility, he works his way through an internship that is bizarre but has at least recognizable particles of truth.

"Wonderfully wild, ribald, erotic . . . in the same spirit as *Catch-22* or *M*A*S*H.*" *(Seattle Times)*

X-rated for ribaldry.

HUD
(Published as:
Horseman, Pass By)

By Larry McMurtry
(1719) 7-1 hour cassettes
Rental—$13.50   Purchase—$56.00
Read by Wolfram Kandinsky

We missed the movie, but the book struck us as more about Lonnie than Hud. Told from a 17-year-old's point of view, Hud emerges as ruthless, cold and mean. He is the kind of fellow we love to hate.

A McMurtry book is very special. *Horseman, Pass By* won overwhelming acclaim, and subsequent novels have established the author as one of our most brilliant contemporary novelists.

Also available from B-O-T are McMurtry's *The Last Picture Show, Leaving Cheyenne* and *Terms of Endearment.*

THE HUNT FOR RED OCTOBER

By Tom Clancy
(1929) 12-1½ hour cassettes
Rental—$17.50 Purchase—$96.00
Read by John MacDonald

The Soviet's most valuable ship—a new ballistic-missile submarine with their most trusted and skilled naval officer at the helm—is attempting to defect to the United States. It is high treason on an unprecedented scale, and the Soviet Atlantic fleet's mission is to seek and destroy her at any cost.

If the U.S. fleet can locate the *Red October* and get her safely to port, it will be the intelligence coup of all time. But the submarine has a million square miles in which to hide and the deadly game of hide-and-seek is on.

"The Hunt for Red October is a thriller that stands in a category all alone. With his rich imagination and grasp of advanced technology, Clancy has created a dramatic and realistic adventure. Highly recommended." *(Publisher's Source)*

THE HURRICANE

By Charles Nordhoff and James Norman Hall
(1256) 7-1 hour cassettes
Rental—$13.50 Purchase—$56.00
Read by Jonathan Reese

The Hurricane is a fine romance, enriched by genuine appreciation of the South Sea Islands and their people. Written by the authors of *Mutiny on the Bounty,* it's a sympathetic tale of Polynesian life seen through the eyes of Dr. Kersaint, a French medical officer.

But even paradise has a serpent, and in Polynesia it is called "hurricane."

THE HURRICANE YEARS

By Cameron Hawley
(1546-A) 8-1½ hour cassettes
Rental—$15.50 Purchase—$64.00
(1546-B) 7-1½ hour cassettes
Rental—$15.50 Purchase—$56.00
Read by John MacDonald

After graduation from college, Cameron Hawley went to work in the advertising business. Before turning full time to writing, he held positions ranging from account manager to director of scientific research.

In *The Hurricane Years,* Hawley addresses the question: "Why do men knock themselves out for a corporation? And knock themselves out they do, particularly in mid-career. "the hurricane years," when stress takes its greatest toll.

" . . . engrossing . . . keeps you reading." *(Book World)*

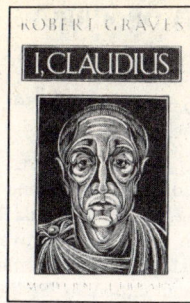

I, CLAUDIUS

By Robert Graves
(2059) 12-1½ hour cassettes
Rental—$17.50 Purchase—$96.00
Read by David Case

NEW

Tiberius Claudius Drusus Nero Germanicus lived from 10 B.C. to 54 A.D. Physically weak, a stammerer, Claudius was ignored. He survived because of his infirmities. Imagine his agenda when he became emperor!

Written in the form of Claudius' autobiography, this book recounts the events of a scandalous era. Public morality disappeared, corruption flourished high and low. The Barbarians found Rome ripe for the picking. No wonder . . . it was soft to the core.

Robert Graves, the author, speaks to us from another era. He survived the trenches of WW I to create books of uncommon diversity and insight. His autobiography, *Goodbye to All That,* is available from B-O-T, as is *They Hanged My Saintly Billy.*

I COME AS A THIEF

By Louis Auchincloss
(1198) 7-1 hour cassettes
Rental—$13.50 Purchase—$56.00
Read by Jonathan Reese

Tony Lowder, a promising New York lawyer, stands on the threshold of a successful social and professional career. The only barrier is money. Ethics give way to ambition and Lowder accepts a bribe for delaying legal action against a brokerage firm. The lesson is that if man has the freedom to sin he has a matching obligation to atone.

ICE BROTHERS

By Sloan Wilson
(2011-A) 7-1½ hour cassettes
Rental—$17.50 Purchase—$56.00
(2011-B) 8-1½ hour cassettes
Rental—$17.50 Purchase—$64.00
Read by Dick Estell
A Christopher Enterprises Recording

In *Ice Brothers* Sloan Wilson recreates WW II with the insight of maturity and the perspective of hindsight. A Greenland patrol and the crew of the Coast Guard ice trawler Arluk are a microcosm of that war—all wars—in that they transcend time and place.

It is an exciting and lovely novel—one that all who ever served in WW II will recognize as true and that those who have not, will identify with for its essential humanness.
Slightly edited for radio presentation.

ICE PALACE

By Edna Ferber
(1630) 10-1½ hour cassettes
Rental—$16.50 Purchase—$80.00
Read by Flo Gibson

This is the story of Alaska before statehood, in all its glory, beauty and bleakness . . . where men pitted themselves against the elements and the wilds, only to find the greatest threat is from "outside."

Edna Ferber is one of the best-selling novelists of this century. Her Pulitzer Prize novel *So Big* has been recorded by B-O-T, as have other of her novels which are listed in the Index under her name.

IN MY FATHER'S COURT

By Isaac Bashevis Singer
(1368) 7-1½ hour cassettes
Rental—$15.50 Purchase—$56.00
Read by Wolfram Kandinsky

In My Father's Court is an account of a time and place now lost —a Jewish ghetto in rural Poland in the three years prior to WW I.

These rich memoirs of Isaac Bashevis Singer, who has been awarded the Nobel Prize for Literature, are warm and faithful evocations of human nature, emotions, and deep religious feeling. The author grew up in old-time Jewish Warsaw. His recollections of that experience, of his family, and of a rabbinical court—an ancient institution among the Jews—are the essence of this work.

IN MY FATHER'S HOUSE

By Ernest J. Gaines
(1488) 6-1 hour cassettes
Rental—$12.50 Purchase—$48.00
Read by Wolfram Kandinsky

"Gaines tells a story not just about black men, but about all men." *(Digest Reviews)*

In addition to *In My Father's House,* B-O-T has also recorded Gaines' *The Autobiography of Miss Jane Pittman* and *Of Love and Dust.*

IN THE WET

By Nevil Shute
(1778) 9-1½ hour cassettes
Rental—$16.50   Purchase—$72.00
Read by Stuart Courtney

Originally published in 1953, *In the Wet* is Nevil Shute's speculative glance into the future of the British Empire. An elderly clergyman stationed in the Australian bush is called to the bedside of a dying derelict. In his delirium Stevie tells a story of England in 1983 through the medium of a quadroon air pilot in the service of Queen Elizabeth II.

"Devotees of Mr. Shute will enjoy this fine story. Shute still remains master of an easy style that practically reads itself." *(Canadian Forum)*

IN THEIR WISDOM

By C.P. Snow
(1424) 8-1½ hour cassettes
Rental—$15.50   Purchase—$64.00
Read by John MacDonald

C.P. Snow was elevated to the House of Lords in 1964. It was as a member of Lords that he conceived the idea for this portrait of judicial corruption.

Lord Massie, having outlived his contemporaries and estranged from his only daughter, Jenny, leaves his considerable fortune to his housekeeper's son. Jenny swiftly contests. But she is bullied into actions that threaten to discredit both Jenny and her father.

AN INDECENT OBSESSION

By Colleen McCullough
(1549) 8-1½ hour cassettes
Rental—$15.50   Purchase—$64.00
Read by Wanda McCaddon

The time is late 1945, the setting Base Fifteen, a military hospital in the Pacific. The war is over and the remaining staff and patients await evacuation. In the smallest and most remote ward five men—human flotsam the war has thrown together—cling like a precarious family around the strong and caring figure of their nurse, Sister Honour Langtry.

Into this uneasy equilibrium comes a sixth patient, Sergeant Michael Wilson. Aiming only to avoid involvement, Wilson ironically falls in love with Langtry.

In addition to *An Indecent Obsession*, itself a best seller, B-O-T has recorded McCullough's enormously popular saga *The Thorn Birds*.

AN INFINITY OF MIRRORS

By Richard Condon
(1170) 8-1½ hour cassettes
Rental—$15.50   Purchase—$64.00
Read by Penelope Dellaporta

An *Infinity of Mirrors* takes place between 1932 and 1944 in Paris and Berlin. A beautiful young French Jew, Paula Bernheim, and a Prussian officer, Wilhelm von Rhode, meet and fall in love. Within a few months they are married and settled in Berlin—just as Hitler's rise to power begins.

The story of what happens to this young couple serves as a microcosm for the European convulsion, as Hitler's poisonous brand of anti-Semitism invades every strata of society.

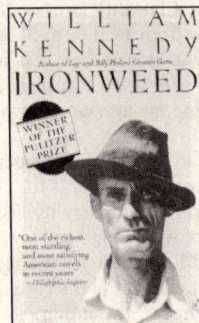

IRONWEED

By William Kennedy
(2008) 8-1 hour cassettes
Rental—$14.50   Purchase—$64.00
Read by Wolfram Kandinsky

Francis Phelan, ex-ballplayer, part-time gravedigger, full-time drunk, has hit bottom. Years ago he left Albany in a hurry after killing a scab during a trolley workers' strike. He ran away again after accidentally—and fatally—dropping his infant son.

Now, in 1938, Francis is back in town, roaming the old familiar streets with his hobo pal, Helen, trying to make peace with the ghosts of the past and the present . . .

"A powerfully affecting work, abounding in humor and heartbreak." *(Chicago Tribune Bookworld)*

AN ISAAC BASHEVIS SINGER READER

By Isaac Bashevis Singer
(1369) 10-1½ hour cassettes
Rental—$16.50   Purchase—$80.00
Read by Wolfram Kandinsky

This collection by Singer, awarded the Nobel Prize in 1977, contains 13 short stories, 4 memoirs and the complete novel *The Magician of Lublin,* a "tale about Yasha Mazur, who makes a living in the circuses and theaters of 19th century Poland. He can skate on the high wire, eat fire . . . and, above all, charm any woman." *(Time)*

Short stories included are: "Gimpel the Fool," "The Mirror," "The Unseen," "The Man Who Came Back," "Short Friday," "Yentl the Yeshiva Boy," "Blood," "The Fast," "The Seance," "The Slaughterer," "The Lecture," "Getzel the Mondey," and "A Friend of Kafka." Memoirs include: "My Father's Friedn," "Dreamers," "A Wedding," and "Had He Been a Kohen."

JAMAICA INN

By Daphne du Maurier
(1879) 8-1½ hour cassettes
Rental—$15.50   Purchase—$64.00
Read by Wanda McCaddon

When young Mary Yellan finds herself marooned in a mouldering inn on the bleak Cornish moors it takes all her wits and courage to survive.

Jamaica Inn is a moody, candlelit manse. Accessible only by horse or foot, it commands the high road that threads a waste of blackened heather and marsh.

Jamaica Inn is one of Daphne du Maurier's most famous novels. Adapted for film by Alfred Hitchcock in 1939, it was the first of her books to be brought to the screen.

THE JEALOUS GOD

By John Braine
(1468) 9-1 hour cassettes
Rental—$15.50   Purchase—$72.00
Read by Christopher Hurt

The jealous god of John Braine's fourth novel is the censorious conscience of a young schoolmaster, Vincent Durgarven. Educated in a severely pious atmosphere, Vincent struggles to fulfill his mother's wish that he become a priest. More the product of duty than conviction, these efforts shatter when Laura, a lovely, black-haired girl, appears in the Charbury Public Library. Vincent's obsession with her soon dominates his life.

John Braine's career as a novelist began with the successful publication of *Room at the Top.* B-O-T also offers his instructive and entertaining *Writing A Novel.*

JUDAS, MY BROTHER

By Frank Yerby
(1402) 13-1½ hour cassettes
Rental—$18.50   Purchase—$104.00
Read by Dan Lazar

Judas, My Brother is one of Frank Yerby's most famous and respected novels. Through the adventures of Nathan, a young Jew of great vitality, Yerby puts forward a plausible account of the beginnings of Christianity.

Born in the years immediately preceding Christ, Nathan lives through that watershed era and emerges transformed by the intensity of his experience. Torn by the conflict between skepticism and faith, Nathan represents the eternal dilemma each man must confront and solve for himself.

JUNGLE LOVERS

By Paul Theroux
(1864) 7-1½ hour cassettes
Rental—$15.50   Purchase—$56.00
Read by Michael Prichard

Africa is a familiar setting to Paul Theroux's readers. For many years, first as a Peace Corps volunteer, later independently, he lived and taught in Central and East Africa.

In *Jungle Lovers,* a Massachusetts salesman enters a small African country caught up in the throes of revolution. An entrepreneur, he immediately opens an insurance brokerage. Going further, he marries a local business woman and with her sets up housekeeping in a local brothel.

" . . . (this) is a first-rate performance—informative, colorful and insightful. His portrait of modern Malawi is as good as one could want . . . " *(Book World)*

KATIE MULHOLLAND

By Catherine Cookson
(1885-A) 7-1½ hour cassettes
Rental—$15.50   Purchase—$56.00
(1885-B) 7-1½ hour cassettes
Rental—$15.50   Purchase—$56.00
Read by Penelope Dellaporta

The offspring of working class people in a very class conscious England and at fifteen the model of a young nymph, Katie finds work in one of the great houses. There her industry attracts Bernard Rosier, the master, an accomplished seducer who uses force with Katie when charm fails.

Deflowered but not defeated, Katie vows to challenge the Rosiers on their own terms. How she does this, how she forges a financial empire and founds her own dynasty, is the stuff of this story.

Catherine Cookson titles recorded by B-O-T include *Fanny McBride, The Fifteen Streets* and *The Whip.*

KEEP THE ASPIDISTRA FLYING

By George Orwell
(1537) 6-1 hour cassettes
Rental—$12.50   Purchase—$48.00
Read by Richard Green

The chief character in this early but exceptionally fine novel of Orwell's is Gordon Comstock, a writer who rebels against the twin British middle-class preoccupations: money and respectability.

"Not pretty, but powerful, accurate, and fair. This book projects as do few others the desperate ingredients and blind rage of the educated moneyless. And Orwell's power is wielded responsibly. Neither the rebels nor the hucksters are romanticized, nor is life—which wins in the end." *(Chicago Sunday Tribune)*

KEPLER

NEW

By John Banville
(2137) 8-1 hour cassettes
Rental—$14.50   Purchase—$64.00
Read by Grover Gardner

Johannes Kepler, master mathematician and astronomer, developed his theories in 16th century pre-Renaissance Germany. His work laid the foundation on which his successors, notably Isaac Newton, built the modern picture of the universe that held until Einstein.

The author shows us a Rabelaisian world . . . chaotic, muddled, and dirty. Kepler's famly mirrored this disorder, and he retreated into his own cerebrations for relief.

Kepler took the theories of his time and stood them on their head. He extracted truth from superstition and the story, in Banville's hands, is a triumph, heroic and exuberant." *(E.R.S. Reviews).*

**Give the perfect gift
from Books on Tape™
See page 2**

THE KILLING GROUND

By Elleston Trevor
(1543) 8-1 hour cassettes
Rental—$14.50   Purchase—$64.00
Read by Christopher Hurt

"The battle of Falaise," wrote General Eisenhower in 1944, "will be the greatest killing-ground of the war." He was not far off the mark, for at Falaise the invasion ended and a new advance began that carried the Allied armies to Berlin.

Elleston Trevor depicts the men of a tank squadron as they cross the silent, darkened Channel, storm the "invincible" coast, and sweep into Falaise. His book is a classic story of men at war.

"The technical detail is unobtrusive, but convincingly adequate; the dialogue is sharply revealing of character; and the characters themselves are created with compassionate warmth." *(The Times Literary Supplement)*

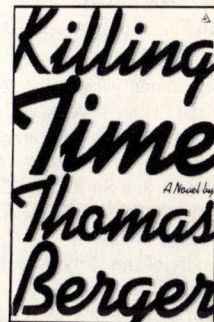

KILLING TIME

NEW

By Thomas Berger
(2148) 8-1½ hour cassettes
Rental—$15.50   Purchase—$64.00
Read by Ron Shoop

Killing Time is a psychological novel about crime. The hero, Joseph Detweiler, is the world's most courteous, sensitive, sincere and likable killer. He is even innocent of the fact that a crime has been committed.

This tough and bizarre story breaks all the rules. It is not a whodunit, because the killer is already known. It is not a detective story or a sociological treatise on crime, because it is told from the point of view of the criminal.

"Detweiler is one of the most complex characters in modern fiction . . . the eeriest thing about him is that he is wholly believable, which is to say, of course, that Thomas Berger is a magnificent novelist." *(National Review)*

THE KING MUST DIE

By Mary Renault
(1820) 9-1½ hour cassettes
Rental—$16.50   Purchase—$72.00
Read by Peter McDonald

Mary Renault is best known for her books about Alexander the Great, but her work was not limited to him. She knew the whole civilization of Ancient Greece and blended myths with archeology in a great display of historical imagination. *The King Must Die* is one of her best.

A Book-of-the-Month Club selection, *The King Must Die* retells the Theseus legend—son of Persius, King of Athens, sent to reclaim the dynasty from a stifling matriarchy.

"Astonishing, sophisticated, brilliant and breathtaking." *(E.R.S. Reviews)*

THE KING'S GENERAL

By Daphne du Maurier
(1882) 10-1½ hour cassettes
Rental—$16.50   Purchase—$80.00
Read by Donada Peters

Menabilly stands bare and desolate on the Cornish coast, its ivy-covered walls hiding the secret which two people will carry to their graves: Honor Harris, so injured as a girl that she can never walk, and Sir Richard Grenvile, the King's General in the West, resentful, proud, bitter to the end.

To tell more of the story here would be unfair. Only du Maurier is able to do justice to the hairbreadth escapes and exciting events which punctuate this tale of 300 years ago, told as if it happened yesterday.

KWAIDAN

By Lafcadio Hearn
(9171) 3-1 hour cassettes
Rental—$9.50   Purchase—$24.00
Read by Walter Covell
A Jimcin Recording

Kwaidan is a collection of weird, ghostly legends and beliefs of old Japan. Hearn spent 14 years in Japan, translating into English with superb effect the atmosphere of the tales which he avidly collected.

Based on Japanese literature and folklore, *Kwaidan* contains 17 stories. The stories of Loichi, the blind *biwa* player who was called to perform for the dead; of Muso, the journeying priest who encountered a man-eating goblin; of the samurai who outwitted the ghost of a dead man. All these plus 14 other spooky tales are included in this collection.

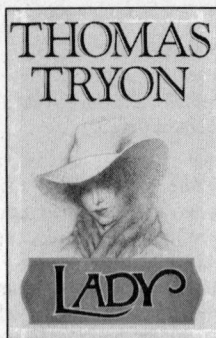

LADY

By Thomas Tryon
(1103) 8-1½ hour cassettes
Rental—$15.50   Purchase—$64.00
Read by Dan Lazar

Lady re-creates a small New England town of the 1930's and 40's. Seen through the eyes of an eight-year-old boy, Woody, we meet Lady, a charming widow, owner of an imposing home on the Green. As does Woody, we come to care for and love his "special friend."

But there is more to Lady than meets the eye, and we share Woody's fear as he closes in on Lady's terrible secret.

LADY CHATTERLEY'S LOVER

By D.H. Lawrence
(2050) 9-1½ hour cassettes
Rental—$16.50   Purchase—$72.00
Read by Richard Brown

This is the story of Constance Chatterley, a lovely young woman whose parts are all in good working order. Not so her husband, Clifford. He wears repression like armor.

So when Constance is thrown into contact with Oliver Mellors, her husband's gamekeeper, the results are explosive. He restores her sexuality and with it her zest in life and living.

When the book was published in 1928, it caused a sensation. Lawrence wrote of physical love with a lack of inhibition that startled his readers, but his scenes evoked lyrical tenderness and joy. They still do. This edition, banned in the United States until 1959, was the first complete and unexpurgated text of Lawrence's finest and most famous novel.

"The most tender, poignant and liberated love story of all time." *(Reviews for Readers)*

A LAST LAMP BURNING

By Gwyn Griffin
(1208) 15-1½ hour cassettes
Rental—$18.50   Purchase—$120.00
Read by Wolfram Kandinsky

Gwyn Griffin selected postwar Naples as the location of this powerful drama of greed, lust and corruption. A Neapolitan family, whose members range in material possessions from squalor to great wealth, anxiously awaits the death of a well-to-do bachelor uncle.

As in *An Operational Necessity* and *Freedom Observed,* Griffin drops individuals into situations of great tension and lets events dictate their destinies.

THE LAST OF THE WINE

By Mary Renault
(1495) 11-1½ hour cassettes
Rental—$17.50   Purchase—$88.00
Read by Peter MacDonald

The Last of the Wine is Mary Renault's superb historical novel of Athens in the days of the Third Peloponnesian War. Written as an autobiography, it is the story of Alexias, son of an aristocratic officer.

At the heart of Alexias' story is his love for Lysis, another of Socrates' noble proteges with whom he lives out the romantic ideal of those times. It is their lot to see Athens drained by war and manipulated by oligarchs. In restoring freedom to the city, Alexias and his friends risk their lives and treasures.

Other Renault titles recorded by B-O-T include *Fire from Heaven, The Mask of Apollo* and *The Nature of Alexander.*

THE LAST PICTURE SHOW

By Larry McMurtry
(1721) 6-1½ hour cassettes
Rental—$14.50   Purchase—$48.00
Read by Wolfram Kandinsky

It was Sam the Lion, the rough-edged yet protective old sentimentalist who gave Thalia its poolhall, its all-night cafe, and, most cherished in the reverie of the towns' restless youth, its own picture show. Set in the north-central Texas of the late 1950's, *The Last Picture Show* is an unforgettable novel of youth and dreams, and of harsh, dry reality.

Later made into an award-winning motion picture, *The Last Picture Show* demonstrates Larry McMurtry's talents as a writer and observer.

LAST TALES

By Isak Dinesen
(1860) 10-1½ hour cassettes
Rental—$16.50   Purchase—$80.00
Read by Wanda McCaddon

The 12 tales in this volume represent the last things that Dinesen wrote prior to her death in 1962. The first seven stories are from an unfinished novel, *Albondocani,* which occupied the author for many years. These are followed by two new Gothic Tales and—of note to those who enjoyed *Winter's Tales*—three new Winter's Tales, each delivered in the fluid, magnetic style that continually draws us to her work.

In addition to *Last Tales* and *Winter's Tales,* B-O-T has available *Out of Africa,* perhaps Isak Dinesen's most famous book.

LAST THINGS

By C.P. Snow
(1420) 9-1½ hour cassettes
Rental—$16.50   Purchase—$72.00
Read by John MacDonald

Last Things is the culmination of C.P. Snow's Strangers and Brothers sequence. Sir Lewis Eliot agonizes over a tempting offer to accept a peerage and join the new Labour Government as a prominent minister. After he has reached a difficult decision he suffers a recurrence of his eye trouble, returns to the hospital, where, during an operation, his heart actually stops beating. This encounter with death leads Sir Lewis to re-evaluate his own life and achievements and to adopt a fresh slant on the achievements of others.

LAUGHING WHITEFISH

By Robert Traver
(1363) 7-1½ hour cassettes
Rental—$15.50   Purchase—$56.00
Read by Wolfram Kandinsky

Willy Poe is a newcomer to Michigan's Upper Peninsula—a shy, lonely young lawyer yearning to meet the girl who will call him William. On a lovely day in July in 1873 he meets her. Her name is Laughing Whitefish.

She presents him with as exciting, challenging and hopeless a case as ever set a precedent. At issue is an elemental question of raw justice: can Laughing Whitefish, a Chippewa Indian, collect a debt owed her father? She has unimpeachable proof—a tattered document giving Marji a share in the fabulous Jackson iron ore mine. And no one denies the validity or authenticity of the document . . . but an Indian?

LEGS

By William Kennedy
(2026) 8-1½ hour cassettes
Rental—$15.50   Purchase—$64.00
Read by Wolfram Kandinsky

Legs inaugurated William Kennedy's cycle of novels set in Albany, New York. True to both life and myth Legs evokes the flamboyant career of the legendary gangster Jack "Legs" Diamond, who was finally murdered in Albany.

Through the equivocal eyes of Diamond's attorney, Marcus Gorman (who scraps a promising political career for the elemental excitement of the criminal underworld), we watch as Legs and his showgirl mistress, Kiki Roberts, blaze their gaudy trail across the tabloid pages of the 1920s and 1930s.

"Pure literary excitement . . . easy to read and hard to put down. I enjoyed it from beginning to end and wished it were longer." —Joseph Heller

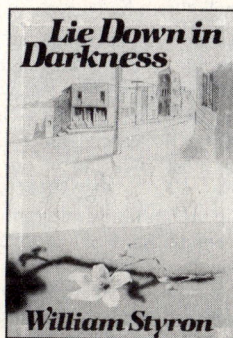

LIE DOWN IN DARKNESS

By William Styron
(1873) 14-1½ hour cassettes
Rental—$18.50   Purchase—$112.00
Read by Wolfram Kandinsky

The South looms dark and ominous in the background of William Styron's first novel, *Lie Down in Darkness.* The author captures the region's biblical rhetoric, racial conflicts and headlong industrialization.

"Styron has done brilliant justice to the Southern tradition from which his talents derive . . . a triumph of characterization." *(The New York Times)*

Lie Down in Darkness was awarded the Prix de Rome of the American Academy of Arts and Letters.

THE LIGHT AND THE DARK

By C.P. Snow
(1413) 9-1½ hour cassettes
Rental—$16.50   Purchase—$72.00
Read by Robert Mundy

Lewis Eliot is the narrator in each of Snow's 11-novel Strangers and Brothers series. In this fourth book, Eliot helps his friend Roy Calvert win an appointment at Cambridge. Calvert is a brilliant but erratic young linguist. Despite great intelligence, he is flawed . . . spiritually tormented and morally maladjusted.

"This is the way a novel of university life should be written—slowly, richly, without partisanship, reformatory fanaticism, or that curious chip-on-the-shoulder emotion which ruins most American fiction having to do with the academic world." *(Saturday Review of Literature)*

THE LITTLE SAINT

By Georges Simenon
(1515) 6-1 hour cassettes
Rental—$12.50   Purchase—$48.00
Read by Michael Prichard

Louis Cuchas does not have an easy life. His father sells fruits and vegetables; there will be no patrimony.

But what Louis lacks in material blessings he more than makes up with his sunny and cheerful nature. His nickname: "The Little Saint."

Louis transforms his gifts of character into artistic expression. He becomes a successful painter. His radiance shines through his work.

"The Little Saint may be the most joyous novel Simenon has written . . . his story is lively, realistic, genial and magnetic." *(Saturday Review)*

LIVES OF GIRLS AND WOMEN

By Alice Munro
(1485) 7-1½ hour cassettes
Rental—$15.50   Purchase—$56.00
Read by Jeanne Hopson

A rekindling of our own remembrances springs from this realistic narrative by Del Jordan of her passage through the many phases of growing up in the 1940's and 1950's. Looking back, she recalls an era that was high on hope.

Alice Munro, one of the most skilled writers in Canada today, twice received her country's highest literary prize, the Governor General's Award.

B-O-T has also recorded Munro's *The Beggar Maid* and *Something I've Been Meaning to Tell You.*

**For quick ordering
1-800-626-3333**

LIZA OF LAMBETH

By W. Somerset Maugham
(1240) 5-1 hour cassettes
Rental—$11.50   Purchase—$40.00
Read by Wanda McCaddon

Liza of Lambeth is Maugham's first novel, and such is its power that it remains as vital today as when first written. Liza is a warm-hearted young girl, stifled by life in the London tenement. Liza has been bred to it and externally can cope. But the heart is the problem: it craves love and affection.

"A fine book . . . shows all the promise of the author's later stories." (*Editorial Reviews*)

LONE STAR RANGER

By Zane Grey
(1314) 8-1 hour cassettes
Rental—$14.50   Purchase—$64.00
Read by Dan Lazar

This Zane Grey western takes place in Texas in the 1870's. After killing a man in self-defense, Buck Duane becomes an outlaw, living among the gunfighters and rustlers along the Texas border. In a camp on the Mexican side, he tries to rescue a young girl held prisoner, bringing down the wrath of her captors, and forcing him to live the life of a loner, pursued by both honest men and outlaws. Eventually, a sympathetic ranger wins a pardon for Duane, who then becomes a ranger himself. The tale is full of action and suspense—the outcome always hanging tensely in the balance.

**Books on Tape™'s service
is 100% guaranteed**

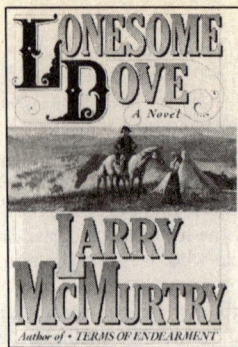

LONESOME DOVE

By Larry McMurtry
(1552-A) 7-1½ hour cassettes
Rental—$15.50   Purchase—$56.00
(1552-B) 11-1½ hour cassettes
Rental—$17.50   Purchase—$88.00
(1552-C) 9-1½ hour cassettes
Rental—$16.50   Purchase—$72.00
Read by Wolfram Kandinsky

A love story, an adventure, an American epic, *Lonesome Dove* embraces all the West—legend and fact, heroes and outlaws, whores and ladies, Indians and settlers—in a novel that recreates the central American experience, the most enduring of our national myths.

Set in the late nineteenth century, *Lonesome Dove* is the story of a cattle drive from Texas to Montana—and much more. The drive is a risk, sure; but it's part of the American Dream, a chance to carve a new life out of the last remaining wilderness.

"Once again, McMurtry spins a yarn about the West—and also about the nature of friendship, of folly, of responsibility, of moral codes and of men and their destinies." (*The Wall Street Journal*)

THE LONG MARCH

By William Styron
(1874) 3-1 hour cassettes
Rental—$8.50   Purchase—$24.00
Read by Wolfram Kandinsky

In the blaze of a Carolina summer, among the poison ivy and loblolly pines, eight Marines are killed almost casually by misfired mortar shells. Deciding that his battalion has been "doping off," Colonel Templeton calls for a 36-mile forced march to inculcate discipline. *The Long March* is a searing account of this ferocious ordeal—and of the two officers who resist.

First published in 1953, this remarkable short novel established the author as a major new American writer.

Styron's best-selling novel *Sophie's Choice* has also been recorded by B-O-T.

LOST PUEBLO

By Zane Grey
(1312) 8-1 hour cassettes
Rental—$14.50   Purchase—$64.00
Read by Dan Lazar

Lost Pueblo is a tale of romance in the Old West. The heroine is Jane Endicott—a spirited young woman who travels to Arizona with her father. She falls in love with this rough and rugged frontier—not to mention the eligible young cowboys.

Her father, rushing in where angels fear to tread, tries to match her with the son of an old friend. Complications arise.

"Zane Grey is unrivalled in his mastery of the western scene . . . this is a charming and vintage story." (*Book Review Service*)

LOTUSLAND
A Story of Southern California

By Ian Whitcomb
(1482) 8-1½ hour cassettes
Rental—$15.50   Purchase—$64.00
Read by Ian Whitcomb

Through a remarkable series of coincidences Ian Whitcomb—author, entertainer, musician—meets one of the living legends of jazz. What follows is an amazingly energetic and humorous tour through the early dreams of Nirvana, beginning in the Venice of 1917. With Whitcomb as guide, we see how the city of anything goes has finally become the place where everything went.

Whitcomb is a writer, crooner, pop historian, pianist and ukulelist extraordinaire who is best known to B-O-T subscribers for his gifted narration (*Fire from Heaven* by Mary Renault, *The March to Tunis* by Alan Moorehead). *Lotusland* is Whitcomb's first novel.

LOVIN' MOLLY
(Published as:
Leaving Cheyenne)

By Larry McMurtry
(1720) 6-1½ hour cassettes
Rental—$14.50   Purchase—$48.00
Read by Wolfram Kandinsky

This Cheyenne is not a place on the map . . . it's a part of life. And Larry McMurtry's story traces a bittersweet three-sided affair. Molly Taylor stands at the apex and bears each suitor a son. This offbeat relationship is not without its tensions, resolved when the three finally "leave Cheyenne." All of us know what the passing years do to young hopes and dreams. But McMurtry gives us a vision of the ideal cowboy and a dream of friendship that goes beyond sex.

Leaving Cheyenne was filmed as *Lovin' Molly.* McMurtry also wrote *Horseman, Pass By,* which became the film *Hud* and *The Last Picture Show,* which when transmogrified became the Academy Award winning film of the same name.

LUCKY JIM

By Kingsley Amis
(1195) 6-1½ hour cassettes
Rental—$14.50   Purchase—$48.00
Read by Richard Green

Kingsley Amis has written a marvelously funny novel describing the attempt of England's postwar generation to break from that country's traditional class structure. When it appeared in England, *Lucky Jim* provoked a heated controversy in which everyone took sides. Even Somerset Maugham reviewed the book, happily with great favor: "Mr. Kingsley Amis is so talented, his observations so keen, that you cannot fail to be convinced that the young men he so brilliantly describes truly represent the classes with which his novel is concerned."

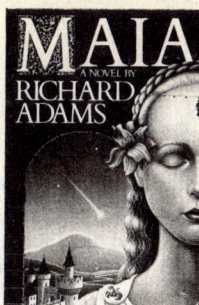

MAIA

By Richard Adams
(2090-A) 12-1½ hour cassettes
Rental—$17.50   Purchase—$96.00
(2090-B) 12-1½ hour cassettes
Rental—$17.50   Purchase—$96.00
(2090-C) 9-1½ hour cassettes
Rental—$16.50   Purchase—$72.00
Read by Bill Kelsey

Maia, eldest daughter in a poor fisherman's family, grows up in a remote corner of the Belkan Empire. She leads a quiet, sheltered life until . . . impossible for her to have imagined, and entirely through the duplicitous act of another . . . she is sold into bondage as a concubine.

Thrust into a world wicked and depraved, Maia survives. She inspires confidence and gathers power. At a time of great crisis within the Empire, Maia stands alone as the one who can prevent its destruction. She gains national fame . . . yet remains caught up in danger and despair.

"*Maia* is Richard Adams' most remarkable creation . . . a heroine to love, in a book that enthralls." *(Publisher's Source)*

Shardik is another Richard Adams' story recorded unabridged by B-O-T.

THE MAKING OF A SAINT

By W. Somerset Maugham
(1939) 6-1½ hour cassettes
Rental—$14.50   Purchase—$64.00
Read by Octavius Black

The Making of a Saint, published in 1898, was W. Somerset Maugham's second novel. He always regarded it as his black sheep, even tried to suppress its republication.

His disaffection is not easy to understand. The book enjoyed a good reception and continues to be well reviewed. It remains today, as it was on publication, an intense and highly colored novel of plot and counterplot, passion and intrigue.

"A fine story of 15th century Italy. Intrigue and assassination were standard issue and targets as likely to be clerical as courtly . . . in this ferment of sinners, the Saint was a miracle." *(E.R.S. Reviews)*

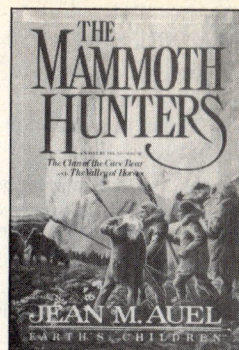

THE MAMMOTH HUNTERS

By Jean M. Auel
(1764-A) 11-1½ hour cassettes
Rental—$17.50   Purchase—$88.00
(1764-B) 10-1½ hour cassettes
Rental—$16.50   Purchase—$80.00
Read by Donada Peters

In this third of the acclaimed Earth's Children novels, Ayla, the independent heroine of *The Clan of the Cave Bear* and *The Valley of Horses,* sets out from the valley on Whinney, the horse she tamed.

With her is Jondalar, tall, handsome and yellow-haired, the man she nursed back to health and came to love. Together they meet the Manutoi—the Mammoth Hunters—people like Ayla. Among them is Ranec, an artistic, magnetic master carver of ivory.

Ayla finds herself torn between Ranec and Jondalar, the latter a powerful lover but insecure and wildly jealous. It is not until the great mammoth hunt, when Ayla's life is threatened, that a fateful decision is made.

THE MAN FROM ST. PETERSBURG

By Ken Follett
(1572) 8-1½ hour cassettes
Rental—$15.50   Purchase—$64.00
Read by Richard Green

The year is 1914, the season summer, and Europe is tottering toward WW I. That encounter—undertaken so casually—will destroy the flower of English, French and German manhood, free Russia from the Czars, but chain her ineluctably to a new tyranny, and set the stage for WW II.

In *The Man from St. Petersburg,* we play a two-sided game: first with the author as his characters leap down from the stage to take on a life of their own; and second with conjecture. Because of all the wars that might have gone another way to the greater glory of life and humankind, WW I came closest and was most manageable.

THE MAN IN THE GRAY FLANNEL SUIT

By Sloan Wilson
(1394) 10-1 hour cassettes
Rental—$15.50   Purchase—$80.00
Read by Dan Lazar

This book speaks for a whole generation of Americans. They were the ones who suffered through the depression, fought WW II and then found themselves non-coms in America's corporate army. The strains of conformity, the straits of marriage, the stress of children and the striving for success are all faithfully recounted here.

This generation of Americans believed passionately that the good life had its roots in material well-being, and when their personal experiences came unraveled, they had little understanding of where to turn.

THE MAN IN THE YELLOW RAFT

By C.S. Forester
(1621) 6-1 hour cassettes
Rental—$12.50   Purchase—$48.00
Read by Stuart Courtney

The Man in the Yellow Raft is a collection of eight stories about the American destroyer *Boon* and the men who served on her during WW II. The stories have a point: they remind us that courage and clear-thinking in the midst of great danger go hand in hand and are the keys to survival. Not only is cowardice disgraceful, it is frequently lethal.

"With great insight into the character of men and their behavior in naval warfare, Forester gives us a story of how battle must have looked to those who fought it." *(E.R.S. Services)*

THE MAN ON A DONKEY

By Hilda Prescott
(1900-A) 9-1½ hour cassettes
Rental—$16.50   Purchase—$72.00
(1900-B) 10-1½ hour cassettes
Rental—$16.50   Purchase—$88.00
Read by Dan Lazar

England, seemingly so serene, has been visited through her history by rebellion, insurrection and riot. None was more obscure, possibly more dangerous, than the 16th century religious upheaval called "the Pilgrimage of Grace."

It occurred in the midst of Reformation, a time of great torment and passion. The story is humanized, told through the experiences of characters who are historically accurate, made real to us by our identification with them.

"A stirring narrative of English life in more courtly but more brutal days." *(Editorial Review Service)*

THE MAN WHO LOVED CAT DANCING

By Marilyn Durham
(1018) 8-1 hour cassettes
Rental—$14.50   Purchase—$64.00
Read by Dan Lazar

This story blazes through Wyoming territory in the 1880's. We plunge into the lives of a fugitive U.S. Army officer planning a desperate train robbery. Characters include his three diverse accomplices, a runaway white woman, and the lovely Indian girl, Cat Dancing, mother of the officer's children. Listener satisfaction is guaranteed!

"Some stories nearly break your heart. This is one." *(Digest Reviews)*

MANHATTAN TRANSFER

By John Dos Passos
(1340) 10-1½ hour cassettes
Rental—$16.50   Purchase—$80.00
Read by Michael Prichard

Generally acknowledged to be Dos Passos' finest novel, *Manhattan Transfer* is a tapestry of many fragments of the New York scene. Characters appear and disappear like threads in a design, and like any great composition the whole is much more than the sum of its parts.

"Dos Passos displays his power, his architectonic ability, and a poetic sense of rhythms, color, sounds and smells." *(Boston Transcript)*

B-O-T has also recorded Dos Passos' *Orient Express* and *Three Soldiers*.

MANTICORE

By Robertson Davies
(1284) 6-1½ hour cassettes
Rental—$14.50   Purchase—$48.00
Read by Dan Lazar

David Staunton, a Canadian, enters Jungian analysis in Switzerland to help him cope with his father's strange death. As the analysis proceeds, David learns surprising things not only about himself but also about his father, about the schoolmaster Dunstan Ramsay, about the libidinous Liesl, about the warped and gifted Magnus Eisengrim. This novel is part two of the trilogy that also includes *Fifth Business* and *World of Wonders*.

"Lucid, concise, beautifully phrased, rich in drama . . . this novel is a synthesis of narrative and idea that never ceases to be superior entertainment as well." *(Library Journal)*

**For faster credit card
ordering call 1-800-626-3333**

MARJORIE MORNINGSTAR

By Herman Wouk
(1321-A) 8-1½ hour cassettes
Rental—$15.50   Purchase—$64.00
(1321-B) 10-1½ hour cassettes
Rental—$16.50   Purchase—$80.00
Read by Michael Prichard

In *Marjorie Morningstar* the focus is on rebellion. A boy and a girl, both raised in Jewish families proud of their ancestry and culture, deny their background, symbolized by changing their names. Marjorie Morgenstern becomes Marjorie Morningstar and Sal Ehrman, with whom she falls in love, becomes Noel Airman. This fictional biography depicts her struggle to become a successful actress.

Wouk received the Pulitzer Prize in 1952 for *The Caine Mutiny*. Also available from B-O-T are Wouk's *Winds of War* and *War and Remembrance*.

THE MARRAKESH ONE-TWO

By Richard Grenier
(1935) 8-1½ hour cassettes
Rental—$14.50   Purchase—$64.00
Read by Michael Prichard

It all begins as Burt Nelson, struggling with the mysteries of the Arab mind, tries to complete a film version of the life of Mohammed. But things keep getting in the way—a bloody but failed coup in Morocco, a confrontation with Colonel Kaddafi, a hijacking.

Richard Grenier has had careers as screenwriter, critic and foreign correspondent. His work has appeared in *The New York Times, The New Republic, The American Spectator*.

"Grenier's Arab world, with its blood lusts, assassinations, coups d'etat, hijackings, is depicted with murderous realism and antic pleasure. Immensely entertaining." —Daniel Monahan

MARRY ME

By John Updike
(1133) 7-1½ hour cassettes
Rental—$15.50   Purchase—$56.00
Read by Wolfram Kandinsky

In *Marry Me*, Updike has chosen as his theme the cliché of adultery in the suburbs. Jerry Conant and Sally Mathias are the couple. Inevitably their "affair" has repercussions on themselves, their spouses and their several small children. The story concludes not with a clearly drawn moral, but rather with a special Updike dilemma: By what demons are nice people driven to create such chaos and destruction in their own lives and in the lives of those they love?

"Marital infidelity is no joke, and Updike treats it with the attention it deserves." *(Editorial Review Service)*

THE MASK OF APOLLO

By Mary Renault
(1494) 10-1½ hour cassettes
Rental—$16.50   Purchase—$80.00
Read by Peter MacDonald

The Mask of Apollo is set in an Athens that has been fragmented by its war with Sparta. It is an ancient world where Greek Sicily is emerging as a fractious, tyrannical and powerful state. Out on this turbulent stage steps an actor, Mary Renault's hero, Nikeratos. This gifted man takes us through the Greece of his day; we meet the leading playwrights and politicians.

Ultimately we become involved with a larger story, that of Dion, a man of noble birth, a friend of Plato, and one who for a time gives promise of becoming a philosopher king.

THE MASSACRE AT FALL CREEK

By Jessamyn West
(1250) 9-1½ hour cassettes
Rental—$16.50   Purchase—$72.00
Read by Roses Prichard

This story concerns an America coming to terms with itself, specifically the conflict between whites and Indians in the wooded hills of the midwest. Unable to make a lasting accommodation and undercut with mutual distrust, settlers and natives clash with murderous treachery and hatred. When the killing stops, the search for justice begins. And as the story unfolds, we meet a young frontier city lawyer, Charlie Fort, and his frontier sweetheart, Hannah Cape. It is in the passion of these two young people that the story resolves itself.

THE MASTERS

By C.P. Snow
(1414) 9-1½ hour cassettes
Rental—$16.50   Purchase—$72.00
Read by Robert Mundy

Thirteen Fellows at a Cambridge college gather to elect a new master. The old master is dying and the new one must come from their group. The candidates plot and scheme against each other, as lethal as scorpions in a box.

In this book, the fifth in the *Strangers and Brothers* series, Lewis Eliot, again the narrator, observes and comments, but like the author makes no moral judgment.

"It is written in beautiful English . . . a novel, obedient to its form, and rich with understanding of the motives of men." *(Commonweal)*

MEMOIRS OF HECATE COUNTY

By Edmund Wilson
(1519) 10-1½ hour cassettes
Rental—$17.50   Purchase—$80.00
Read by Wolfram Kandinsky

Edmund Wilson was one of our premier men of letters. His two classics . . . *To the Finland Station* and *Memoirs of Hecate County* . . . marked him as a literary leader during a time when competition for this accolade was fierce.

Memoirs of Hecate County is Wilson's round-up of "what it meant to be at home in America." Defining the American experience was a serious literary occupation in the thirties, the decade of Wilson's maturation, and he gives the subject a searching and profound view.

"Such civilized writing and observations are rare in the U.S. nowadays, and on its merits *Memoirs of Hecate County* is certainly the best contemporary chronicle, so far, of its place and period." *(Time)*

THE MERRY-GO-ROUND

By W. Somerset Maugham
(2061) 9-1½ hour cassettes
Rental—$16.50   Purchase—$72.00
Read by Penelope Dellaporta

Somerset Maugham was one of the world's most prolific and popular authors. He wrote with great facility and at one time had four plays running simultaneously in four different London theatres. He was trained as a doctor, and he must have been good: his observations are truthful and free of sentiment. His books are a tonic.

The "merry-go-round" was his term for London at the turn of the century. His narrator, Miss Ley, is a shrewd and amusing elderly spinster, something like Maugham in drag. A born commentator, she acts like a Greek chorus. The world may be mad, she seems to say, but it is amusing.

B-O-T offers a number of other Maugham selections, including *Mrs. Craddock, The Razor's Edge, The Narrow Corner* and *Liza of Lambeth.*

MESSAGE FROM ABSALOM

By Anne Armstrong Thompson
(1226) 7-1 hour cassettes
Rental—$13.50   Purchase—$56.00
Read by Nancy Dannevik

The heroine of Anne Armstrong Thompson's lush, romantic thriller is an ex-CIA agent. The action begins when a CIA operative smuggles her a code message with instructions that she must take it to the president of the United States and trust no one else. This she does—but not without horrifying obstacles—from near rape and torture in Communist Bulgaria, to being held hostage on a plane hijacked to the desert by Palestinian guerrillas. The action is swift and exciting.

MICKELSSON'S GHOST

By John Gardner
(1748-A) 11-1½ hour cassettes
Rental—$17.50   Purchase—$88.00
(1748-B) 10-1½ hour cassettes
Rental—$16.50   Purchase—$80.00
Read by Jack Hrkach

Peter Mickelsson is professor of philosophy at a small college in Pennsylvania. Once considered a brilliant philosopher in his own right, Mickelsson has now slipped into a debt- and alcohol-ridden state in which he is haunted by ghosts. In a desperate effort to escape the mounting chaos, he buys a ramshackle farmhouse in the mountains.

This retreat offers little solace, however. His own ghosts follow him and are soon joined by the real ghosts who inhabit the lonely farmhouse. Confronted with the gradual re-enactment of a long-ago murder, Mickelsson faces the ultimate test of his courage, sanity and will to survive.

B-O-T has recorded other Gardner books which are listed in the Index under the author's name.

MISCHIEF

By Ben Travers
(1771) 6-1½ hour cassettes
Rental—$14.50   Purchase—$48.00
Read by Flo Gibson

Mischief is the quick-witted, farcical story of the calamitous marriage between Reggy—the middle-aged protective husband—and his impulsive and lovely young wife, Eleanor. The humor is delightfully British . . . a combination of 1920's bedroom farce and a tongue-in-cheek poke at the proprietaries that govern "civilized" man.

"Think of Feydeau, of Keystone Comedies, of Wodehouse, perhaps faintly, of Saki and read *Mischief* with delight. It is preposterous and hilarious." —Emily Kimbrough.

THE MONOGAMIST

By Thomas Gallagher
(1270) 6-1 hour cassettes
Rental—$12.50   Purchase—$48.00
Read by John MacDonald

John Wisher is a man who can not bring himself to live a double life. When *The Monogamist* opens, he has been married for 25 years. His family is grown and his business has prospered. He has carved out his life like a single monolithic block.

Then he meets a young and provocative woman. He falls in live, yet he still loves his wife.

"A profoundly moving and perceptive story . . . The gift of the Irish storyteller lies in Gallagher's writing, and to it he has added the richness of a searching mind." *(New York Herald Tribune Book Review)*

A MONTH OF SUNDAYS

By John Updike
(1279) 5-1½ hour cassettes
Rental—$13.50   Purchase—$40.00
Read by Wolfram Kandinsky

After years of dutifully ministering to his flock, the Reverend Thomas Marshfield, 41, begins fleecing the ewes. When his fervid trysts with the seductive church organist, the richest elder's romance-starved wife, and other susceptible supplicants are exposed, the errant preacher is shipped off for a month's retreat at a desert spa for troubled clergymen. The rules for this "enforced" rest demand that afternoons be spent alone at an obligatory typewriter, where he confesses orgies of oriental voluptuousness.

THE MOON AND SIXPENCE

By W. Somerset Maugham
(1079) 8-1 hour cassettes
Rental—$14.50   Purchase—$64.00
Read by Richard Green

Maugham, with his impeccable taste and style, deftly portrays a 19th century gentleman who abandons his profession and family to pursue his art in Paris. This book was inspired by Maugham's admiration for Gauguin. It presents a complex character as it explores artistic and social impulses of that time.

MORGAN'S PASSING

NEW

By Anne Tyler
(2087) 7-1½ hour cassettes
Rental—$15.50   Purchase—$56.00
Read by Mary Woods

Halfway through a puppet show, Cinderella flops over. The Prince asks if there is a doctor in the house. Remarkably there is: Morgan appears and on cue delivers "Cinderella's" baby in the back seat of a car. Then he disappears.

Later, with his life in shambles, he needs new roles to play, new lives to enter. The Prince, Cinderella, and the baby girl he delivered years ago obsess him, and he stalks them with an eye for an opening.

What happens when Morgan drops his mask, attaches himself to this couple, disrupts their existence, leaves havoc in his wake, is at the heart of this wonderfully imagined novel.

Dinner at the Homesick Restaurant is another Anne Tyler novel recorded by B-O-T.

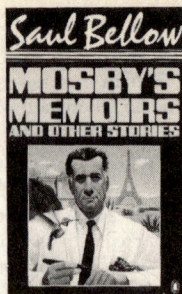

MOSBY'S MEMOIRS AND OTHER STORIES

By Saul Bellow
(1968) 7-1½ hour cassettes
Rental—$15.50   Purchase—$56.00
Read by Wolfram Kandinsky

The only joke in the human comedy is its name. What's funny about people contesting their fate, breaking their teeth on the traps?

Saul Bellow is an observer of this spectacle, not disinterested, but not sweated and bloody, either. His characters may contend, the author remains aloof.

"A fine collection, deeply moving, written by one of the greatest literary artists that America has produced" says the *Louisville Times* about this book by the winner of the Nobel Prize for Literature in 1976. Stories include "Leaving the Yellow House," "The Old System," "Looking for Mr. Green," "The Gonzaga Manuscripts," "A Father-to-Be" and "Mosby's Memoirs."

MRS. CRADDOCK

By W. Somerset Maugham
(1744) 8-1½ hour cassettes
Rental—$15.50   Purchase—$64.00
Read by Jill Masters

It is the end of the 19th century and Victoria's reign is coming to an end. It is also the end of an era, but no one knows. The landed gentry, so soon to lose their power, are the last to suspect.

Bertha Ley is mistress of Court Ley, a great spread of land. She marries Edward Craddock, a man beneath her station, but quite the essence of new order. A gentleman farmer, he is steady and a doer who turns Court Ley into an efficient farm. But Bertha wants passion and ardor: she gets reality.

"Bertha's tragedy is in her expectations—life would be so simple without them. Her assaults on the amiable Craddock are as rational as beating a flounder for not flying." *(Literary Observer)*

MRS DALLOWAY

By Virginia Woolf
(1786) 6-1 hour cassettes
Rental—$14.50   Purchase—$48.00
Read by Wanda McCaddon

Clarissa Dalloway, in her fifties, wife of an English MP, emerges from her house in Westminster one fine June morning to buy flowers for her party. And by that simple act she entwines her life with the lives of others who will hear, with her, Big Ben toll away the hours of their destinies that day.

"Clarissa's day captures in a definite matrix the drift of thought and feeling in a period, the point of view of a class, and seems almost to indicate the strength and weakness of a civilization." *(The New York Times)*

Other books by Virginia Woolf recorded by B-O-T include: *A Room of One's Own* and, in combination, *To the Lighthouse/The London Scene.*

MY COUSIN RACHEL

By Daphne du Maurier
(1143) 8-1½ hour cassettes
Rental—$15.50   Purchase—$64.00
Read by Richard Green

Philip Ashley and his Uncle Ambrose share a happy bachelor existence on the family estate in Cornwall until ill health sends Ambrose to Italy. There he meets and marries a distant cousin, Rachel. After his death Rachel journeys to Cornwall where Philip's initial reluctance to meet her is dispelled by her charm. But rumors concerning Rachel's conduct in Italy persist and soon Philip is desperate to know if the woman he is falling in love with could really be the poisoner of his beloved Uncle Ambrose.

MY ENEMY'S ENEMY

By Kingsley Amis
(1135) 6-1 hour cassettes
Rental—$12.50   Purchase—$48.00
Read by Richard Green

A selection of seven short stories set in post WW II England, *My Enemy's Enemy* is social satire at its ironic best. Three of these stories, dealing with members of a British Signal Unit at the end of the war, are humorous in their analysis of the moral and social climate of that time. Three of the remaining stories focus on some peculiarities of civilian life, and the last piece constitutes an unusual venture into science fiction.

MYSTERIES OF MOTION

By Hortense Calisher
(1922-A) 7-1½ hour cassettes
Rental—$15.50   Purchase—$56.00
(1922-B) 9-1½ hour cassettes
Rental—$16.50   Purchase—$72.00
Read by Donada Peters

In Cabin Six the half-dozen men and women—and one stowaway—who are passengers on the first American space shuttle for civilians are entering the space age as we all are, with our personal histories at our backs.

Tom Gilpin, social reformer and cult hero; Veronica, the sexual explorer; Mulenberg, the businessman; William Wert, the diplomat who will be head man on arrival; Soraya, survivor of Iran's revolution; Lievering, possible survivor of the death camps—share all their secret histories.

"Reader," says Tom Gilpin, "ride with us. Not for our sake alone, not for yours . . . (but) for the sake of that once gentle brown humus from which we all come."

THE NAKED LAND

By Hammond Innes
(1803) 7-1½ hour cassettes
Rental—$15.50   Purchase—$56.00
Read by Christopher Hurt

Hammond Innes cut his teeth as a writer during the Great Depression when he worked for a London daily. Inspired equally by geography and literature, he developed an early interest in writing about far-off places.

In The Naked Land, Innes sets his story in French Morocco, land of the Berbers, where murderous tribesmen compete for an arid and inaccessible piece of land known as Kasbah Foum.

"The Naked Land is an exciting and handsomely written a novel as Innes has given us yet." *(Chicago Tribune)*

THE NAPOLEON OF NOTTING HILL

By G.K. Chesterton
(1444) 8-1 hour cassettes
Rental—$14.50   Purchase—$64.00
Read by Stuart Courtney

In *The Napoleon of Notting Hill,* Chesterton examines the question "What if the Crown of England devolved upon a common man?"

He selects Auberon Quin, and a more common individual it is difficult to imagine. That is, to all appearances . . . except that deep within Quin burns a desire for the exceptional, a love of individuality, and a deep and abiding humorous tolerance.

Other G.K. Chesterton books include *Heretics, Orthodoxy* and *What I Saw in America.*

THE NARROW CORNER

By W. Somerset Maugham
(1216) 8-1 hour cassettes
Rental—$14.50   Purchase—$64.00
Read by Erik Bauersfeld

Three men voyaging together in a small vessel—an exiled doctor, a disreputable sea captain, and a young man fleeing from justice—are driven to take shelter on a small island in the Malay Archipelago. Their lives are soon shattered by a strange, exotic girl of English parentage, but oriental in her mystery. The story contains humor and wit, exact and incisive observation of character and an ironical philosophy that mark this tale as another Maugham classic.

THE NEW MEN

By C.P. Snow
(1415) 7-1½ hour cassettes
Rental—$15.50   Purchase—$56.00
Read by Robert Mundy

This sixth novel in the Strangers and Brothers series focuses on a group of nuclear scientists and high government officials working together in England during the war.

"Mr. Snow's particular strength and peculiar distinctions are in the depiction of the problems and paradoxes of power as they are decided by the clashes of temperament in committees, or among other groups of men. He celebrates, and he analyzes bureaucratic man: the administrator, the scientist, the don, the ruler who is also ruled . . . " *(The London Times Literary Supplement)*

NICKEL MOUNTAIN

By John Gardner
(1005) 8-1 hour cassettes
Rental—$14.50   Purchase—$64.00
Read by Dan Lazar

The hero of *Nickel Mountain* is Henry Soames, a fat, gentle, middle-aged man who runs a diner deep in the forests of the Catskills. He is assisted by a young girl who has become pregnant by a rich man's errant son. Henry Soames marries her out of kindness. Quietly, delicately, author John Gardner reveals what these two are to each other as the years pass. Together they experience the universal rituals of courtship, marriage, birth, loss of innocence and the acceptance of death. *Nickel Mountain* is a love story which celebrates what is most decent in human nature.

NIGHTWORK

By Irwin Shaw
(1222) 9-1½ hour cassettes
Rental—$16.50   Purchase—$72.00
Read by Wolfram Kandinsky

Irwin Shaw is at his storytelling best in this tale. Set against glamorous backdrops such as St. Moritz, Rome and Paris, this is the narrative of two con men—one amateur (whose stolen bankroll sets the whole thing in motion) and one a debonair professional, whose schemes are wild and hugely profitable. The lesser characters are a diverse group—beautiful and obliging women, an improbable crew working on a porno film, and a likeable Italian wine dealer with Fascist enemies.

1984

By George Orwell
(1540) 7-1½ hour cassettes
Rental—$15.50   Purchase—$56.00
Read by Richard Green

The world has suffered many disillusionments before, but few times has its hounded denizens been more uniformly beset than in the years following WW II. Here we had finished a war of liberation, fought on the most massive scale imaginable, and at its conclusion delivered over to Russian or Chinese Communist control hundreds of millions of unconsenting citizens.

Many saw the magnitude of this error, but it was Orwell who pointed out what we might become in combating the menace to our freedom. In his vision of 1984, we have grown as ruthless and manipulative as our enemies, callously uncaring of personal and individual freedoms, all in the name of the freedom and democracy we profess to defend.

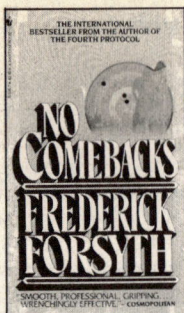

NO COMEBACKS and THE SHEPHERD

NEW

By Frederick Forsyth
(2085) 7-1½ hour cassettes
Rental—$15.50   Purchase—$56.00
Read by Richard Brown

In *The Shepherd*, a young pilot has just completed his mission over Germany. He heads for home, for England. Suddenly his radio goes dead. A dense fog shrouds him. His compass fails. All seems lost . . . then he sees another plane—a mysterious old WW II bomber—flying just below him, as if trying to make contact.

No Comebacks is a collection of ten crisp, suspenseful, serpentine tales of betrayal, blackmail, murder and revenge—told as only Frederick Forsyth can tell them. *Kirkus Reviews* called it "masterful," while *Publishers Weekly* thinks *No Comebacks* is "chillingly effective."

NOP'S TRIALS

By Donald McCaig
(2002) 6-1½ hour cassettes
Rental—$14.50   Purchase—$48.00
Read by Ron Shoop

Here is the story of a family and two remarkable individuals—Lewis Burkholder, a farmer in Virginia, and his young Border Collie, Nop. When the dog is stolen, Nop embarks on an ordeal of peril and hardship that he survives only through courage, and love. The same qualities in Lewis enable him to search relentlessly for his sheep dog—a search that takes him far from home and touches forgotten corners of his life.

"*Nop's Trials* held me in fascinated suspense to the last page. Poignant, authentic and beautiful . . . This insight into animal and human nature is masterly."—James Herriot

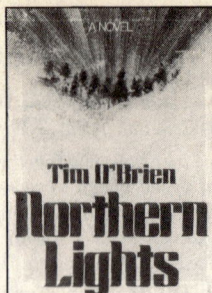

NORTHERN LIGHTS

By Tim O'Brien
(1841) 8-1½ hour cassettes
Rental—$15.50   Purchase—$64.00
Read by John MacDonald

Set in the rugged Arrowhead country of Minnesota, *Northern Lights* is the story of Paul and Harvey Perry—two brothers who act out the dreams of their dead father. Their rivalry spins out of control and ends in a final test of endurance and survival. *Northern Lights* is a novel of fundamentals: men at war with their own natures, their images of a good life, their memories, and the elements.

Books on Tape has also recorded O'Brien's award-winning *If I Die in a Combat Zone* and *Going After Cacciato*.

NOW GOD BE THANKED

By John Masters
(1714-A) 9-1½ hour cassettes
Rental—$16.50   Purchase—$72.00
(1714-B) 9-1½ hour cassettes
Rental—$16.50   Purchase—$72.00
Read by Walter Zimmerman

Now God Be Thanked is the first volume in a trilogy, Loss of Eden, which depicts the impact of WW I on British life. It is a saga of the mingled fortunes of four families: the aristocratic Durand Beaulieus, the industrial Strattons and Rowlands, and the reprobate Gorses.

"The cast is huge, the sweep of events swift and far-flung. John Masters has planned nothing less than a dissection of English life at its most crucial moment of change. The abiding vitality of the characters, their essential humanity, and the feel of that long vanished England of 1914-15 are real and true." *(New York Times Book Review)*

OBASAN

By Joy Kogawa
(1942) 7-1½ hour cassettes
Rental—$15.50   Purchase—$56.00
Read by Jill Masters

Joy Kogawa is a gifted poet and writer. She is also Nisei, the child of Japanese immigrant parents. Obasan, her first novel, recovers the truth about what happened to her, her family and her people in Canada during WW II. Winner of the Before Columbus Foundation's 1982 prize, Obasan reminds us of the indignities and injustice we visited on our loyal Japanese-American citizens.

"This quiet first novel burns in your hand. Rage mellows into sorrow; sorrow illumines love. It is love the you come away with, finally, in *Obasan*." *(Washington Post)*

"A very moving vision of an affront to democratic principles . . . *a tour de force*, a deeply felt novel." *(The New York Book Review)*

THE OCCUPYING POWER

By Gwyn Griffin
(1578) 10-1½ hour cassettes
Rental—$16.50   Purchase—$80.00
Read by Wolfram Kandinsky

The Island of Baressa, a modest, oval splotch of land, was one of Italy's earliest and most embarrassing colonial acquisitions. Merely 95 miles long, half that in width, this reclusive parcel escaped Mussolini's military attention.

But not the British. On an August afternoon in 1940, commanded by Major Euan Lemonfield, an assault force secures the island. What follows is an occupation that marries high moral purpose to puritanical force and hypocrisy.

"Engrossing, entertaining, edifying. A real page-turner." *(Life Magazine)*

OCTOBER LIGHT

By John Gardner
(1746) 12-1½ hour cassettes
Rental—$17.50   Purchase—$96.00
Read by Grover Gardner

James Page is a crusty old Vermonter. One day, pissed at the world, he blasts his sister's television with a shotgun. She locks herself in her bedroom where she holds out with a box of apples from the attic and a trashy novel from under the bed.

Thus their dilapidated farmhouse turns into a battleground. Their anger is a crucible that strips away years of shame and guilt. Not only are the passions liberated, but a number of ghosts as well.

"The author is like a Columbus who sails bravely into the unknown—but Gardner's voyage is into the psyche, probably more dangerous than any sea monsters the mariners faced." *(Editorial Review Services)*

OF LOVE AND DUST

By Ernest J. Gaines
(1490) 7-1 hour cassettes
Rental—$13.50   Purchase—$56.00
Read by Dan Lazar

Ernest J. Gaines is best known for his prize-winning *Autobiography of Miss Jane Pittman,* but *Of Love and Dust* has equal power and fascination. It zeros in on an explosion in the making between two men, one black and one white, trapped in the vise of Southern back country prejudice.

When young Marcus is bonded out of jail, he is sent to the Hebert Plantation to work in the fields. He treats Sidney Bonbon, the Cajun overseer, with contempt and Bonbon retaliates by working him nearly to death. Marcus decides to take his revenge.

Other Gaines titles recorded by B-O-T include: *In My Father's House, The Autobiography of Miss Jane Pittman and Bloodline.*

OF THE FARM

By John Updike
(1656) 5-1 hour cassettes
Rental—$11.50   Purchase—$40.00
Read by Jack Hrkach

Joey Robinson is a 35-year-old advertising executive employed in Manhattan. *Of The Farm* recounts his visit to the farm where he grew up and where his mother now lives alone. Accompanied by his newly acquired second wife, Peggy, and an 11-year-old stepson, Joey spends three days reassessing and evaluating the course his life has run. But for Joey and Peggy, the delicate balance of love and sex is threatened by a dangerous new awareness.

"Very clearly and very completely a small masterpiece." *(The New York Times)*

THE OLD STAG

By Henry Williamson
(1849) 7-1 hour cassettes
Rental—$13.50   Purchase—$56.00
Read by Donada Peters

Our reader, Donada Peters, writes: "Henry Williamson was a conservationist ahead of his time and one of the leading nature writers of this century, so we should expect this early collection of hunting stories to contain some surprises—and they do!"

In a good number of these stories the quarry, through cunning and courage, gets clean away and moreover exacts a satisfying revenge on the hunters—animal or human. Williamson deals equally with the two-and four-footed protaganists of his tales. He " . . . breaks down the barriers between ourselves and animals, and makes us ex perience their lives with an extraordinary and touching lucidity."

ON THE BEACH

By Nevil Shute
(1183) 8-1 hour cassettes
Rental—$14.50   Purchase—$64.00
Read by Richard Green

The time is 1963. China and Russia have engaged in an all-out nuclear war against each other. The fighting actually begins in Albania, spreads to Tel Aviv, prompting Egypt to unleash a direct assault on London and Washington. The result of this military activity is the total destruction of all life in the Northern Hemisphere.

On The Beach tells the story of the last survivors in Australia, waiting resignedly for the globegirdling bands of radiation to work their way south and swallow the final remaining life on earth.

ON THE BLACK HILL

By Bruce Chatwin
(1969) 6-1½ hour cassettes
Rental—$14.50   Purchase—$48.00
Read by Justin Hect

Lewis and Benjamin Jones, identical twins, farm The Vision, a property in the Welsh Borders, with the green fields of England on one side and the black hills of Wales on the other. Here they are born in 1900, and here for eighty years they share one life—eat the same food, sleep in the same bed, swing an axe in the same trajectory.

On the Black Hill is the story of their intertwined double drama—and how they sense the salvation that is theirs in the "abiding city on the hill."

Bruce Chatwin has charterd the passage of the twentieth century from the viewpoint of people who live out their lives in small circumstances.

ONE MAN'S WEST

By David S. Lavender
(1699) 8-1½ hour cassettes
Rental—$15.50   Purchase—$64.00
Read by Michael Prichard

When Lavender was growing up in Colorado in the thirties, something unique in the nation's experience was ending. Great ranches were breaking up, miners were forced onto the dole, a whole way of life came grinding to a halt. Though few of us knew it, pioneers were passing into history.

"His story is realistic and readable . . . he puts on record some of the most engaging characters in the modern literature of the West." *(The New York Times)*

ONE MORE SUNDAY

By John D. MacDonald
(1946) 10-1½ hour cassettes
Rental—$16.50   Purchase—$80.00
Read by Michael Prichard

In *One More Sunday,* John D. Mac-Donald turns a skeptical eye toward the practices of corporate religion. Meadows Center is a sprawling, heavily-guarded community of homes, commerce and worship. It also provides a base of operation for the Eternal Church of the Believer.

MacDonald has no quarrel with religion, organized or not. But he is quick to label quackery for what it is.

"To diggers a thousand years from now . . . the works of John D. MacDonald would be a treasure on the order of the tomb of Tutankhamen."—Kurt Vonnegut, Jr.

THE 158-POUND MARRIAGE

By John Irving
(1360) 8-1 hour cassettes
Rental—$14.50   Purchase—$64.00
Read by Dan Lazar

The 158-Pound Marriage is an erotic and ironic love story by the author of the best selling *The World According to Garp.* John Irving looks beyond the eye-catching gyrations of the mating dance, beyond the theatrics of body contact and love, to the morning-after complications. *The 158-Pound Marriage* is everything you've always known about sex and were afraid to admit.

FREE rental from Books on Tape™
See page 3

OONA O'

By Thomas Gallagher
(1361) 6-1 hour cassettes
Rental—$12.50   Purchase—$48.00
Read by Dan Lazar

Oona O'Hagen is courageous, fanciful and witty; she has endless capacity for spontaneity and joy. She is, in short, what many people strive to become themselves, or to meet and marry: direct, honest and genuine. The story of this unlikely but wholly believable girl, her married lover, her baby—and what happened to them—is unforgettable.

Thomas Gallagher is an author with whom B-O-T subscribers are well acquainted. He wrote the enormously popular *Assault in Norway*, *The X-Craft Raid* and *Fire at Sea*.

AN OPERATIONAL NECESSITY

By Gwyn Griffin
(1092) 12-1½ hour cassettes
Rental—$17.50   Purchase—$96.00
Read by Wolfram Kandinsky

An Operational Necessity explores the complex moral issues of naval warfare. Disheartened and desperate, a German U-boat crew machine guns the survivors of a torpedoed freighter. Captured as they near neutral sanctuary, the U-boat officers are returned to an allied tribunal. During the trial the officers face their accuser, Gaston, the lone survivor.

The German officers emerge as young and inexperienced, caught between their compassion for the survivors and the welfare of their own crew. The reader confronts the question of personal obedience versus individual ethics until, in the conclusion, the court delivers its final verdict.

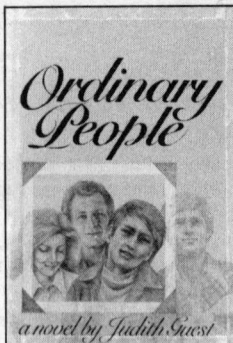

ORDINARY PEOPLE

By Judith Guest
(1925) 6-1½ hour cassettes
Rental—$14.50   Purchase—$48.00
Read by Roses Prichard

This is the story of the Jarrett family. Calvin is a determined, successful provider; Beth, an organized efficient wife. They had two sons, Conrad and Buck. Now they have one. They are ordinary people. And they are coming apart.

Ordinary People is the critically acclaimed novel by the author of *Second Heaven*. Its subsequent adaptation as a film won Academy Awards for Best Direction and Best Picture.

"A poem of a book . . . leaves us with a sense of having lived, for a while, with a family we care for." *(Mademoiselle)*

THE PARTNERS

By Louis Auchincloss
(1233) 8-1 hour cassettes
Rental—$14.50   Purchase—$64.00
Read by Dan Lazar

The Partners is a knowledgeable characterization of lawyers and of the people in whose service they gain riches and prestige. It is the story of a small but distinguished New York firm and particularly of one of the senior partners, Beekman Ehninger. *The Partners* is also a group portrait of men—and women, in what is mostly a man's world—whose common bond is their work. Within that bond each one pursues different answers to the search for money, power, love, revenge, or a meaning in life.

THE PENTHOUSE

By Elleston Trevor
(2084) 7-1½ hour cassettes
Rental—$15.50   Purchase—$56.00
Read by Mary Woods

At nine o'clock on a mild October night two men are shot in the lobby of Manhattan's luxury Park Tower. Minutes later, a police chief listens to a voice on the telephone from the penthouse. "I've jammed the elevators and stacked forty pounds of nitro against the stairway door. Break it open and you'll blow this building right across Central Park."

Tina St. Clair, beautiful and rich, hears the same words . . . but she is only inches away from the speaker, trapped in her apartment by this crazy who wants to love her. She has never had to fight for anything in her life . . . but she had better fight now!

"Trevor is greatly talented. One never doubts the absolute reality of every page he writes." *(The Times, London)*

THE PEREGRINE'S SAGA

By Henry Williamson
(1848) 7-1 hour cassettes
Rental—$13.50   Purchase—$56.00
Read by Donada Peters

In *The Peregrine's Saga*, the young author, recovering like many of his generation from the scars of WW I, escapes to the Devon countryside of a still rural England and becomes a wandering observer and chronicler of the intertwined lives of field, cliff and hedgerow.

"The non-human actors in these dramas ring true with the respect, love, precise observation and profound understanding a master naturalist and master craftsman brings to their delineation."—Donada Peters

This is one of the first books Henry Williamson wrote in a 50-year career as naturalist, novelist, essayist and short story writer—a book that was to win him the Hawthornden Prize.

PILGRIM'S INN

By Elizabeth Goudge
(1459) 10-1½ hour cassettes
Rental—$16.50   Purchase—$80.00
Read by Wanda MaCaddon

The second novel in Elizabeth Goudge's trilogy about the Eliot family, *Pilgrim's Inn* takes up their story after WW II, but focuses on Lucilla's soldier son George, his beautiful wife Nadine, and their five children. At the heart of the story is their acquisition of an ancient pilgrim's inn on the river. Under the author's skillful hand the inn develops a life of its own that touches not only its new owners but also those strangers who on their pilgrimages stop there for a rest.

"Affirms the hope that good will triumph providing we are willing to exercise the necessary discipline." *(San Francisco Chronicle)*

A PLACE FOR THE WICKED *NEW*

By Elleston Trevor
(2143) 8-1 hour cassettes
Rental—$14.50   Purchase—$64.00
Read by Peter McDonald

For a small group of friends a flight to the South of France marks the beginning of a well-earned holiday, the fourth they have spent at the Villa Mimosa in Antibes. It is a place they have come to love—the sun, the sea, the palms. But this year it will be different.

It only takes a split second of panic on one of their parts to compromise all of them. The easy camaraderie that once bound them together cracks and falls away. All are prisoners of fear and guilt—and there is no one to rescue them but themselves.

"Call it a psychological thriller. It is skillfully deployed, very gripping and totally convincing. What will each of them do? You won't want to put it down until you have found out." *(Evening Standard, London)*

PLAGUE SHIP

By Frank G. Slaughter
(2014) 7-1½ hour cassettes
Rental—$17.50   Purchase—$56.00
Read by Dick Estell
A Christopher Enterprises Recording

High in the Andes an archaeologist stumbles on an ancient tomb, unwittingly releasing the germs from a civilization doomed by plague over 5000 years ago.

What happens when this deadly organism, for which there is no antidote, reappear forms the basis of this sensational novel. Frank Slaughter tells of the complex, high-stakes world of intraglobal medicine, taking us behind the public deeds to the private people whose courage can make the difference between a footnote today . . . and a headline tomorrow.

THE POORHOUSE FAIR

By John Updike
(1654) 6-1 hour cassettes
Rental—$12.50   Purchase—$48.00
Read by Jack Hrkach

The Poorhouse Fair was John Updike's first full length novel, published four years after he graduated from Harvard. It concerns the events surrounding a fair put on by members of a poorhouse and is an allegory about charity. Short and succinct, it speaks to those fears all of us have of growing not old, but dependent.

"Since the successful poetic novel—for lack of a more precise term—has long been the most rarefied form of prose fiction, John Updike, the poet and short story writer, has done a startling thing in his first novel . . . by producing, with almost academic precision, a classic, if not flawless, example of one." (Whitney Balliett, writing in *The New Yorker*)

PORTRAIT IN BROWNSTONE

By Louis Auchincloss
(1118) 8-1½ hour cassettes
Rental—$15.50   Purchase—$64.00
Read by Dan Lazar

Portrait in Brownstone begins with cousin Geraldine's suicide in 1950 and concludes with son Hugh's wedding a year later. In the interval, Ida Dennison Hartley journeys into the past to retrieve the childhood values and traditions she needs to order her present and protect her family's future. Louis Auchincloss uses this novel of manners to chronicle the world of the socially prestigious and economically powerful Dennisons of New York City throughout the first half of the century.

POWERS OF ATTORNEY

By Louis Auchincloss
(1234) 8-1 hour cassettes
Rental—$14.50   Purchase—$64.00
Read by Dan Lazar

Louis Auchincloss, a practicing attorney himself, here presents 12 short stories all centering on members of the fictional law firm of Tower, Tilney and Webb. The main interest in most of the stories is the vying for position and the search for status that take place within the firm itself. Often a certain character appears in several different stories, each time with a different facet of his personality emphasized. In these stories Auchincloss is clearly on home turf.

**Interval delivery convenience
See page 2**

THE PRAISE SINGER

By Mary Renault
(1822) 7-1½ hour cassettes
Rental—$15.50   Purchase—$56.00
Read by Grover Gardner

In this novel of ancient Greece, Mary Renault turns to the world of the poet—the bard who since the time of Homer had sung his verses from memory for the occasions of the court.

This is the life of Simonides, who lived in sixth-century Greece during the age of the tyrants. Renault builds a rich and full recreation of that ancient world. "Mary Renault has again worked her magic to create a historical landscape filled with the kind of passions and politics that persist to this day." *(Publisher's Source)*

Books on Tape's selection of Mary Renault titles include *The Bull from the Sea, Fire From Heaven, Funeral Games* and *The Persian Boy.*

PRESERVE AND PROTECT

By Allen Drury
(1237) 12-1½ hour cassettes
Rental—$17.50   Purchase—$96.00
Read by Dan Lazar

The setting is Washington, D.C. The action begins when President Harley Hudson is killed in an air crash. The Speaker of the House becomes President and calls for a National Committee to select new nominees for the coming election.

The theme of this novel is violence in American life—a violence promoted and condoned by politicians who are fools, dupes or knaves. The narrative moves quickly, full of the excitement and intrigue for which Allen Drury is well known.

PRIZZI'S HONOR

By Richard Condon
(1788) 7-1½ hour cassettes
Rental—$15.50   Purchase—$56.00
Read by Christopher Hurt

Prizzi's Honor is no ordinary story of boy-meets-girl. Charley Partanna is a faithful lieutenant for the Prizzis, New York's most powerful Mafia family. The object of his affections is Irene Walker, a Los Angeles-based tax consultant. But it's her freelancing that pays—she's a hit man for the Mob. She has also cheated the Prizzis out of an unforgivably large sum of money.

This is very dangerous moonlighting indeed, and eventually it places Charley's oldest loyalties in conflict with his newest one. Which wins?

"His best book since *The Manchurian Candidate* . . . he mixes caricature and character as easily as Charley hacks off thumbs." *(Chicago Tribune Book World)*

PURE AS A LILY

By Catherine Cookson
(1889) 7-1½ hour cassettes
Rental—$15.50   Purchase—$56.00
Read by Mary Woods

Life was not easy during the Depression, and nowhere was it harder than in the north of England. For young Mary Walton, there seemed to be no way out—her father chronically unemployed, her mother a whine, her brother irresponsible.

Then Mary became housekeeper for a rich widower and life took on a happier hue.

Catherine Cookson never releases her characters entirely from their early circumstances, and in this book she gives us enough sweep so we can participate with Mary as she works out her destiny.

PURSUIT

By Robert L. Fish
(1407) 10-1½ hour cassettes
Rental—$16.50   Purchase—$80.00
Read by Dan Lazar

The year is 1944. The German defense is collapsing. As the Allies cross into Poland, Colonel Helmut von Schraeder, the "Monster" of the Miadanek death camp, uses plastic surgery to assume the identity of a Jewish prisoner and escape retribution.

As Benjamin Grossman, he is released at the end of the war, only to find his route to freedom blocked by a turn of events that leads him to Israel. There his talents bring him to national leadership and recognition. His marriage to a beautiful Israeli and the birth of their son give him partial relief from his bitter frustration. But the past rises dangerously to haunt him.

Q.B. VII

By Leon Uris
(1298) 10-1½ hour cassettes
Rental—$16.50   Purchase—$80.00
Read by Dan Lazar

Q.B. VII stands for Queen's Bench Number Seven—a courtroom in the conservative London Law Court. It is here that Leon Uris sets the stage for one of the most electrifying legal battles in British history. Two principal characters people this scenario. One is Adam Kelno—a brilliant surgeon and Polish nationalist, once imprisoned in a concentration camp during WW II. The other is Abraham Cady—a bright, spirited American novelist. In one of Cady's books, he casually mentions Dr. Kelno's name in relationship to experimental sterilization surgeries conducted on Jewish inmates of the concentration camp. Adam Kelno sues Abraham Cady for libel—and the drama unfolds.

THE QUEEN OF A DISTANT COUNTRY

By John Braine
(1470) 8-1 hour cassettes
Rental—$ Purchase—$14.50
Read by 64.00

Stuart Courtney   The brilliant author of *Room at the Top* probes the obsessive passion of a young man for a vital older woman and the painful ordeal which must follow—the exorcism of desire, the shattering of bonds, the shaking off of a profound and powerful influence.

"A masterful exploration of the many forms of love. Compulsively readable . . . shows us what an outstandingly good writer he is; flashes of descriptive power, subtleties of insight and intuition abound." *(The Sunday Times of London)*

RABBIT IS RICH

By John Updike
(1695) 12-1½ hour cassettes
Rental—$17.50   Purchase—$96.00
Read by Michael Prichard

John Updike continues to probe the yearning frustrations and pain of suburban America in this third encounter with the Angstroms, Harry ("Rabbit"), Janice and their son Nelson.

Rabbit, basically decent but no intellectual, is ten years down the road from *Rabbit Redux*. Updike's hero, now a middle-aged Toyota dealer, still seeks peace and contentment—items not standard equipment in his life.

Rabbit is Rich won the literary Triple Crown: the Pulitzer prize, American Book Award, and a commendatory scroll from the National Book Critics Circle. "For Updike is now indisputable at the top of his craft. No one else using the English language over the past 2-1½ decades has written so well in so may ways as he." *(Time)*

RABBIT REDUX

By John Updike
(1281) 10-1½ hour cassettes
Rental—$16.50   Purchase—$80.00
Read by Wolfram Kandinsky

The year is 1969, the end of a revolutionary decade, when men walked the moon and controversies raged over the Vietnam War, civil rights, women's liberation, morality and its decline. A liberated Rabbit Angstrom loses his wife to a hotshot used car salesman dripping with Vitalis and acquires a menage that includes his teenage son, a spaced-out white chick, and an evangelical black man. Rabbit lives a life that is bent, a normal life refracted in a funhouse mirror. He courts complications, all the more bizarre for their believability.

RABBIT RUN

By John Updike
(1280) 8-1½ hour cassettes
Rental—$15.50   Purchase—$64.00
Read by Wolfram Kandinsky

To millions of Americans, Rabbit Angstrom is like a member of the family. They have followed hin through *Rabbit Run, Rabbit Redux,* and (most recently) *Rabbit is Rich.* We meet him for the first time in this novel, when he is age 22, and a salesman in the local department store. Married to the second best sweetheart of his high school years, he is the father of a preschool son and husband to an alcoholic wife. The unrelieved squalor and tragedy of their lives remind us that there are such people, and that salvation, after all, is a personal undertaking.

RAINTREE COUNTY

By Ross Lockridge, Jr.
(1351-A) 10-1½ hour cassettes
Rental—$16.50   Purchase—$80.00
(1351-B) 10-1½ hour cassettes
Rental—$16.50   Purchase—$80.00
(1351-C) 11-1½ hour cassettes
Rental—$17.50   Purchase—$88.00
Read by Wolfram Kandinsky

In 1948, three young authors published first novels that indelibly changed the landscape of American letters . . . *The Naked and the Dead* by Norman Mailer; *The Young Lions* by Irwin Shaw; and *Raintree County* by Ross Lockridge, Jr. Whereas Mailer and Shaw went on to write many other novels, Lockridge died by his own hand at the age of 34 in 1948—the year of his single but magnificent work.

This panoramic epic of the 19th century in Raintree County, Indiana (particularly of the Civil War and its effects), was produced after six years of research, writing and revision. It continues to command attention and respect as a stylistically unique work of considerable force, and was made into a brilliant motion picture starring Elizabeth Taylor and Montgomery Clift.

RANDOM WINDS

By Belva Plain
(2083-A) 7-1½ hour cassettes
Rental—$15.50 Purchase—$56.00
(2083-B) 7-1½ hour cassettes
Rental—$15.50 Purchase—$56.00
Read by Ruth Stokesberry

Random Winds is an epochal saga about a family of physicians—first Enoch, the dedicated country doctor; then Martin, his son, a brilliant neurosurgeon; and Claire, his flamboyant, unconventional daughter.

The story moves from a turn-of-the-century village in upstate New York to privileged estates outside London, from the bedsides of the rural poor to the frenetic emergency room of a New York hospital, from war-torn London to hideaways on the French Riviera. It tells of the trials and triumphs of a dynamic family struggling to hold its center, and of love beyond anyone's power to deny.

"Belva Plain creates vivid people and involves us with them. She is at the top of the novelist's profession." *(Editorial Review Service)*

Evergreen, another best seller by Belva Plain, is available on cassette from B-O-T.

THE RAZOR'S EDGE

By W. Somerset Maugham
(1087) 8-1½ hour cassettes
Rental—$15.50 Purchase—$64.00
Read by Richard Green

This is the story of a young man in search of himself. It is set in Paris, the Riviera and the East, all areas the author knows well. As the record of a journey of human spirit, it stands with *Of Human Bondage* as one of the great English novels of our time.

The Razor's Edge has twice been adapted successfully to the screen—in 1946, starring Tyrone Power, and again in 1984 with Bill Murray as the young Amerian Larry Darrell.

REBECCA

By Daphne du Maurier
(1296) 10-1½ hour cassettes
Rental—$16.50 Purchase—$80.00
Read by Jane Bullen

A young woman, after a brief courtship, becomes the wife of an English aristocrat, Maxim de Winter. The two are deeply in love, but the memory of Max's first wife, Rebecca, still lingers on at Manderley, their country mansion. The beauty and charm of the first wife haunt the new wife, whose unfamiliarity with life in the grand manner makes her seem a poor choice in comparison. It is only in the revelation of Rebecca's death that the new mistress of Manderley finds the happiness which almost eluded her.

THE RECTOR OF JUSTIN

By Louis Auchincloss
(1050) 7-1½ hour cassettes
Rental—$15.50 Purchase—$56.00
Read by Dan Lazar

In this novel, the rector of a New England Episcopal private school for boys, 80-year-old Dr. Frank Prescott, is seen through the eyes of those whose lives he has touched. His powerful personality creates disciples or enemies. He is ultimately successful in building his school but fails in the perfection for which he aims. *The Rector of Justin* has been called the American answer to "Goodbye, Mr. Chips."

RED SKY AT MORNING

By Richard Bradford
(1032) 7-1 hour cassettes
Rental—$12.50 Purchase—$56.00
Read by Dan Lazar

Richard Bradford takes us back in time to WW II. When his father goes off to war, the hero, Josh Arnold, and his mother leave Mobile to settle in a small New Mexico town for the duration. The clash of cultures, personalities and events remain with us long after we close the book.

RED STORM RISING

By Tom Clancy
(2024-A) 10-1½ hour cassettes
Rental—$16.50 Purchase—$80.00
(2024-B) 10-1½ hour cassettes
Rental—$16.50 Purchase—$80.00
Read by Michael Prichard

When Moslem fundamentalists blow up a key Soviet oil complex, making an already critical oil shortage calamitous, the Russians figure they are going to have to take things into their own hands.

They plan to seize the Persian Gulf, more ambitiously to neutralize NATO. Thus begins Red Storm, an audacious gamble that uses diplomatic maneuver to cloak a crash military build-up.

When Soviet tanks begin to roll, the West is caught off guard. What looks like a thrust turns into an all-out shooting war, possibly the climactic battle for control of the globe.

**TOLL FREE credit card
order line 1-800-626-3333**

MasterCard   VISA

REGENCY BUCK

By Georgette Heyer
(1601) 9-1½ hour cassettes
Rental—$16.50 Purchase—$72.00
Read by Flo Gibson

Georgette Heyer is the queen of Regency romances, and nowhere is her ruling talent better displayed than in *Regency Buck*.

Her heroine, Judith Taverner, is lovely, vivacious and daring. But she meets her match in her guardian, the lofty consequential Lord Worth. Judith challenges him in a duel of wits.

This historical novel is reminiscent of Jane Austen in its subtle humor and sure sense of character and plot. "Nowhere is the society, the flavor and the cant of Regency England more knowingly and delightfully portrayed than in the novels of Georgette Heyer." (Philadelphia Bulletin)

RIDERS OF THE PURPLE SAGE

By Zane Grey
(1450) 7-1½ hour cassettes
Rental—$15.50 Purchase—$56.00
Read by Dan Lazar

Zane Grey is the all-time bestselling author of westerns, and here is the most popular of his thrilling tales. It is a picturesque romance set in the unspoiled grandeur of Utah when Mormon authority rules unchallenged. Jane Withersteen befriends a young rider on her range, Bernie Venters, a non-Mormon. Angered Elders resent this alliance, and put pressure on Jane to break with Bernie. Jane resists, and the Elders try to break her will. Enter Lassiter, a loner from the North who comes to her aid bearing a fearsome reputation as a deadly hand with a gun. Beneath his tough exterior, Lassiter proves to have a tender heart, and therein lies the story.

RIVER OF THE SUN

By James Ramsey Ullman
(1011) 9-1½ hour cassettes
Rental—$16.50 Purchase—$72.00
Read by Michael Prichard

River of the Sun is set in the Amazon River Basin during the days following WW II. The characters are a group of men and one woman on an expedition searching for a legendary river. This tributary of the Amazon is in an area reported to be rich in oil. The descriptions of the sullen natives, the oppressive jungle, and the endless, swollen river are excellent. The plot encompasses a mystery, a love affair and a hairraising escape.

B-O-T has also recorded Ullman's *Down the Colorado with Major Powell* and *The Age of Mountaineering*.

THE ROBE

By Lloyd Douglas
(1356-A) 8-1½ hour cassettes
Rental—$15.50   Purchase—$64.00
(1356-B) 8-1½ hour cassettes
Rental—$15.50   Purchase—$64.00
Read by Bob Erickson

When asked about the nature of his books, Lloyd Douglas once replied, "If my novels are entertaining I am glad, but they are not written so much for the purpose of entertaining as of inspiration."

The Robe is a fine example of this. Here we are given the story of the young Roman soldier, Marcellus, who was witness to the crucifixion of Jesus Christ. The flowing narrative draws clear lines to contemporary examples of human crises, and our own measures of the "rightness" of our actions.

"Easily his most brilliant parable." *(Saturday Review of Literature)*

THE ROMANCE OF ATLANTIS

By Taylor Caldwell
(1430) 7-1½ hour cassettes
Rental—$15.50   Purchase—$56.00
Read by Roses Prichard

The Romance of Atlantis brings to life all the dazzling splendor of that lost kingdom. However, Atlantis is threatened by powerful neighboring states. Tension increases when the ruler of an adjacent kingdom bids to marry the empress. If she marries him, Atlantis would be safe from invasion. Yet, such a marriage contradicts the deepest feelings of her heart, the secret wisdom of her lineage, and her sacred trust as queen. We will not spoil your enjoyment of this novel by telling the conclusion!

ROUND THE BEND

By Nevil Shute
(1777) 9-1½ hour cassettes
Rental—$15.50   Purchase—$72.00
Read by Christopher Hurt

Tom Cutter is in love with airplanes and has been from his boyhood. He can remain in England, an employee in another man's aviation business, or he can set out on his own.

With little more than personal grit and an antique aircraft, Cutter organizes an independent flying service on the Persian Gulf. He sees opportunities everywhere, also dangers.

"In Cutter's growth from provincial conservative to worldly entrepreneur, Shute brings us a fine portrayal of a man willing to accept pain and danger in his search for personal growth." *(Editorial Review Service)*

RULE BRITANNIA

By Daphne du Maurier
(1205) 8-1½ hour cassettes
Rental—$14.50   Purchase—$64.00
Read by Jane Bullen

Rule Britannia is a satire that looks to the future—to that moment in history when Britain's last hope for survival is a union with the U.S. Driven by a failing economy and a hopelessly divided population, Britain accepts the idea of the formation of USUK. But when marriage begins to look like a military takeover, (U.S. Marines, ration cards, roadblocks, American warships) the Brits rebel.

SAND PEBBLES

By Richard McKenna
(1526-A) 9-1½ hour cassettes
Rental—$16.50   Purchase—$72.00
(1526-B) 7-1½ hour cassettes
Rental—$15.50   Purchase—$56.00
Read by Wolfram Kandinsky

It helps to remember that China was a basket case in 1900. Disease, faminie, opium, pirates, pestilence, warlords, rickshaws, Tongs, slaves—they really existed. Western nations found no law there, so they made their own.

Enter Jake Holman, crewman on *Sao Pablo*, a gunboat far up the Yangtze. Jake is Navy through and through—but with a difference. He loves China and its people, and that is where the conflict starts.

"A natural storyteller with an eye for character and an expert grasp of historical setting, McKenna's skill as a novelist is firmly established. As a story of violence and humor, tragedy and courage, it holds the reader engrossed from the first line to the last." *(Naval Institute Press)*

**Collector's Editions™
from Books on Tape™
See page 3**

SAKI (H.H. MUNRO): SELECTED SHORT STORIES

By H.H. Munro
(9901) 6-1 hour cassettes
Rental—$12.50   Purchase—$48.00
Read by Hugh Burden
A Talking Tape Recording

Saki was the cup-bearer in the Rubáiyat of Omar Khayyám: he brought pleasure to those he served.

H.H. Munro was born in Burma in 1870 and taken to England at the age of two. He became famous for his short stories, particularly his satires.

Short stories in this collection include "Sredni Vashtar," "The Story-Teller," "Morlvera," "The She-Wolf," "The Open Window," "The Music on the Hill," "Mrs. Packletide's Tiger," "The Story of St. Vespaluus," "Tobermory," "The Schartz Metterklume Method," "The Hounds of Fate," "The Mouse," "The Brogue," "Laura" and "The Lumber-Room" among others.

"There is no greater compliment to be paid the right kind of friend than to hand him Saki, without comment."—Christopher Morley.

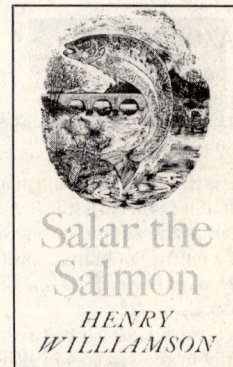

SALAR THE SALMON

By Henry Williamson
(1850) 8-1 hour cassettes
Rental—$14.50   Purchase—$64.00
Read by Donada Peters

In Latin "salar" means "leaper" and to the Romans who first came to England the name perfectly described the magnificent sea-run salmon that fought their way up rivers and streams.

In Henry Williamson's great nature story, Salar is a five-year-old salmon returning to the stream of his birth. He faces great dangers—cruising lampreys, poachers with their cruel nets and spears, sharp-eyed otters, cascading falls—all between Salar and his goal in the spawning sands.

"No lover of the country can fail to be thrilled. The author has the power given to few of seeing life from the point of view of the animal's he describes." *(Guardian)*

THE SAVAGE KINGDOM

By Zane Grey
(1313) 5-1 hour cassettes
Rental—$11.50   Purchase—$40.00
Read by Dan Lazar

The Savage Kingdom is made up of three stories—about animals and their relationship with men. In "Tappan's Burro," a prospector risks his life to save a sickly animal. "The Wolf Tracker" is the story of a killer wolf, "Old Gray." Cowboys and hunters take to his trail but no one can catch him . . . until a mysterious trapper by the name of Brink takes up the quest. "Strange Partners of Two Fold Bay" is about whales and men—and the uncanny intelligence possessed by dolphins and killer whales. It serves as an early outcry against the senseless slaughter of the great whales.

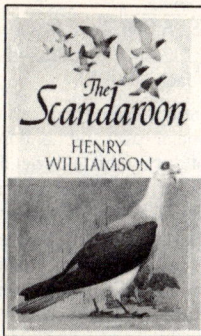

THE SCANDAROON

By Henry Williamson
(1852) 4-1 hour cassettes
Rental—$9.50   Purchase—$32.00
Read by Donada Peters

Scandaroons are a variety of homing pigeon. The name derives from Iskanderun, a seaport in Syria, called after Alexander the Great, so the bird of this title carries a noble tradition. The story is set in rural Devon shortly after WW I.

During that war, pigeons carried messages from outposts to home base. They probably looked for a peaceful retirement, but their ancient enemies, the falcons and hawks, had other ideas. Thus the story is about conflicts within nature and their reverberations in man.

Salar the Salmon and *Tarka the Otter* are other Williamson titles available from B-O-T.

SCORPION ON A STONE

By Gwyn Griffin
(1582) 8-1 hour cassettes
Rental—$14.50   Purchase—$64.00
Read by Wolfram Kandinsky

Gwyn Griffin is one of the great undiscovered authors of the 20th century. Subscribers find it hard to believe that this collection of stories has an impact as great as his longer novels: *An Operational Necessity, Master of this Vessel, Freedom Observed* and *Last Lamp Burning.*

Gwyn Griffin's brilliant evocation of life in the African continent stems from his long and varied experience there. As a young man he worked as a Sudanese cotton planter. During WW II, he served with the British African Colonial Troops and later became superintendent of Colonial Police. He was educated in England, traveled widely through Africa, and lived in Australia and the Canary Islands.

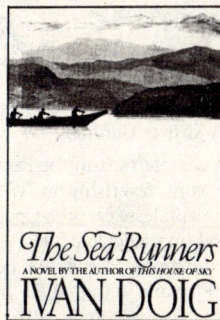

THE SEA RUNNERS

By Ivan Doig
(2145) 8-1 hour cassettes
Rental—$14.50   Purchase—$64.00
Read by Paul Shay

In 1853, in the farthest outpost of the Czar's empire, many of the laborers were indentured servants—seven-year men no better off than slaves. In New Archangel, now Sitka, four of them, all Scandinavians, stole a canoe and pointed it south toward Astoria, in Oregon, twelve hundred miles away.

This adventurous story pits its characters against the sea and ultimately against each other. The four sea runners—glib, gangly Melander, silent Karlsson, the thief Braff, and sour, doubting Wennberg—must weather the worst the ill-named Pacific can throw at them. And must, day upon day, guided as much by instinct as by map, simply paddle, stroke upon stroke, toward the mouth of the Columbia River.

This House of Sky and *English Creek* are other Ivan Doig titles recorded by B-O-T.

THE SEARCH

By C.P. Snow
(1422) 7-1½ hour cassettes
Rental—$14.50   Purchase—$56.00
Read by Rupert Keenlyside

The first novel by the author of the Strangers and Brothers series, *The Search* concerns the life of a young research scientist. Snow brings his career experience with science-in-government to the fore, as we watch the scientist maneuver for financial support and prestige. Like the author, the protagonist abandons science because his interest in subjective human muddle has become stronger than his quest for scientific knowledge.

"C.P. Snow must now be regarded . . . as one of the most important English novelists of this century." (Bookman)

SEPARATE FLIGHTS

By Andre Dubus
(1435) 8-1 hour cassettes
Rental—$14.50   Purchase—$64.00
Read by Dan Lazar

On its publication, *Separate Flights* won the *Boston Globe's* Lawrence L. Winship Award as the outstanding book of New England origin. This Dubus sampler includes a novella and seven short stories. Themes range from violence and confrontation to tenderness and affection. To quote from *The Los Angeles Times,* "Dubus has been compared with Chekov . . . this collection restores faith in the survival of the short story.

Additional recordings of Dubus books can be found in our Index.

SET THIS HOUSE ON FIRE

By William Styron
(1530-A) 9-1½ hour cassettes
Rental—$16.50   Purchase—$72.00
(1530-B) 9-1½ hour cassettes
Rental—$16.50   Purchase—$72.00
Read by Wolfram Kandinsky

The narrator, Peter Leverett, a government employee returning to the U.S., stops in the Italian village of Sambuco to see his old schoolmate Mason Flagg. But the next morning Flagg is found dead at the base of a cliff, a peasant girl has been beaten to death, and Cass Kinsolving, a drunken American painter, is gone.

Though the case has been written off as a murder followed by a suicide, Peter doesn't believe it. His search takes him through the Mediterranean and back to America as well.

"This is not a book for the squeamish. For seldom in modern fiction have we had such a relentlessly powerful examination of human depravity." *(Chicago Daily News)*

SETTING FREE THE BEARS

By John Irving
(1358) 8-1½ hour cassettes
Rental—$15.50   Purchase—$64.00
Read by Dan Lazar

This funny and moving novel juxtaposes selected events in WW II with the rebellion of youth in the last 1960's. One spring day in Vienna, Graff, an earnest young Austrian student who has just failed his exams, meets Siggy, a wildly eccentric motorcycle mechanic and philosopher. Together they roam the countryside astride a 700cc Royal Enfield racer. Lovely long-limbed Gallen soon joins them. Moving rapidly from incident to incident in the best picaresque tradition, the drama climaxes in "the great zoo bust" as all forms of beast—including human—break free.

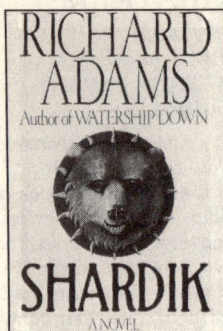

SHARDIK

By Richard Adams
(1387-A) 7-1½ hour cassettes
Rental—$15.50   Purchase—$56.00
(1387-B) 7-1½ hour cassettes
Rental—$15.50   Purchase—$56.00
Read by Dan Lazar

Shardik is an epic of classical proportions. It deals with the long-awaited reincarnation of the gigantic bear, Lord Shardik, the Power of God. A very real bear . . . they take the bear's arrival as a divine portent.

Shardik himself dominates the story. The myth that surrounds him touches everyone. Kelderek, the hunter who discovers the bear and saves its life, becomes first devotee then prophet, then priest-king of a vast empire.

But Shardik leads him back to a wilderness. And Kelderek discovers in failure the true meaning of Shardik's liberating revelation.

SHELL GAME

By Douglas Terman
(1274-A) 7-1½ hour cassettes
Rental—$15.50   Purchase—$56.00
(1274-B) 7-1½ hour cassettes
Rental—$15.50   Purchase—$56.00
Read by Michael Prichard

A high-voltage thriller set in Cuba during the missile crisis, *Shell Game* combines political espionage and dramatic adventure. The story is so real and life-like that fact and fiction seem to merge.

And as a tale of two brothers divided by love and war, it exposes what may be in reality the most deadly deception of the nuclear age. What if, as Terman suggests, the Soviets removed only the missle casings and not the missiles themselves?

"*Shell Game* is a first-class thriller. It marks the coming of age, I think, of a great suspense novelist." —Ken Follett

THE SHOOT

By Elleston Trevor
(2130) 5-1½ hour cassettes
Rental—$13.50   Purchase—$40.00
Read by Grover Gardner

On a remote rock in the Pacific a scientific team works feverishly on "White Lance," an experimental space probe powered by a volatile and unpredictable fuel.

The technical crews are considerably stressed. For one thing, their most recent launch has failed. For another their chief, Dr. James Chapel, a pacifist, feels threatened by a nearby ICBM training unit. This exacerbates Chapel's quirky perfectionism, disturbing his men. His wife, who has her reasons, takes up with the ICBM unit commander and goes beyond just admiring his rocket.

"*The Shoot* succeeds as a drama of tension, of men striving against their own limitations in a field where there is no margin for error." *(Reviews for Readers)*

Deathwatch, The Big Pick-up and *The Burning Shore* are a few Elleston Trevor titles recorded by Books on Tape.

A SIGNIFICANT EXPERIENCE

By Gwyn Griffin
(1581) 3-1 hour cassettes
Rental—$8.50   Purchase—$24.00
Read by Wolfram Kandinsky

"Have you ever read a novel by Gwyn Griffin? If not, you have missed an unusual reading experience unlike any to be encountered in the works of other contemporary writers." Thus wrote Orville Prescott in *The New York Times* on the occasion of this book's publication.

In this brilliantly written novella, an ingenuous young cadet at a British regimental training facility in Egypt becomes the victim of a brutal disciplinary action inflicted by officers of the old school.

SLAPSTICK and MOTHER NIGHT

By Kurt Vonnegut, Jr.
(1160) 8-1 hour cassettes
Rental—$14.50   Purchase—$64.00
Read by Dan Lazar

Slapstick has its foundation in the author's relationship with his sister. His sardonic humor permeates this tale of Eliza and Wilbur Swain who live in a future time and share a joint mind which they conceal as long as they can. *Mother Night* relates to war crime "confessions" of Howard W. Campbell, Jr., an American by birth, a Nazi by reputation and a former U.S. counter-intelligence agent in fact. Vonnegut's moral: "We are what we pretend to be, so be careful of pretense."

THE SLEEP OF REASON

By C.P. Snow
(1419) 11-1½ hour cassettes
Rental—$17.50   Purchase—$88.00
Read by Jack Hrkach

The time is 1963; the locations, and English provincial town and London.

Out of duty to his old friend, the lawyer George Passant, Lewis Eliot agrees to help in a murder trial. The case is shocking: two lesbians are charged with torturing and killing an 8-year-old boy. As the trial progresses, Snow brings alive all the people caught up in the tragedy—fascinating in their difference under pressure. And he examines the broader questions implied: of responsibility, of freedom, of choice, of hope.

"A profoundly moving book, easily one of the more insightful glimpses into the human predicament set down in print." *(Worchester Review)*

A SLIPPING-DOWN LIFE

By Anne Tyler
(2031) 6-1 hour cassettes
Rental—$12.50   Purchase—$48.00
Read by Mary Woods

Drum Casey surprised Evie like the discovery of an island surprises a drowning person . . . If it wasn't love between them, it was at least dry land . . .

Anne Tyler's novels are a rare mixture of laughter and tears. Critics have praised her fine gift for characterizations and her skill at blending touching insight and powerful emotions to create superb entertainment.

"A taste of Anne Tyler is a splendid addiction." *(The New York Times)*

Books on Tape has also recorded *Dinner at the Homesick Restaurant* and *Earthly Possessions*—both best sellers from Anne Tyler.

Special 10% discount
See page 2

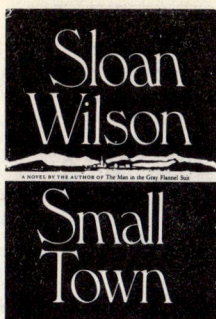

SMALL TOWN

By Sloan Wilson
(2101) 11-1½ hour cassettes
Rental—$17.50   Purchase—$88.00
Read by Ron Shoop

Small Town is a story of the passions that lie just below the surface of a deceptively placid upstate New York village. What has fists clenched is a simmering triangle between Ben Winslow, a middle-aged widower; his son Ebon; and Winslow's young sister-in-law, Annie.

Their relationships shift and blur, but never their feelings. The arrival of Annie's Irish father, amiable but drunk, brings everything to a head. The resulting confrontation nearly blows the community apart.

"Sloan Wilson never tells a dull story and this is one of his best." *(Reviews for Readers)*

All the Best People, Ice Brother, The Man in the Gray Flannel Suit and *A Summer Place* are other Sloan Wilson titles available from Books on Tape.

THE SNOW WAS BLACK

By Georges Simenon
(1505) 7-1 hour cassettes
Rental—$13.50   Purchase—$56.00
Read by Michael Prichard

This hair-raising novel is a masterpiece of psychological suspense. It is the unforgettable story of Frank Friedmaier, only son of a brothel madam, who grows up in a bordello in postwar Europe.

It points to the sinister influences that goad a man down the torturous path of evil, and to the endless possibilities of self-discovery and regeneration that can pull him back from the brink. B-O-T has also recorded Simenon's *Maigret's Christmas, The Watchmaker* and *The Iron Staircase,* plus others listed in our index.

SO BIG

By Edna Ferber
(1626) 7-1½ hour cassettes
Rental—$15.50   Purchase—$56.00
Read by Flo Gibson

Selina Peake De Jong is a memorable literary heroine . . . strong, proud, devoted equally to her son Dirk and what she sees as "the pursuit of beauty." When fortune casts her as the wife of a young farmer in the vast midwestern plains, she tackles the role with customary zest.

The plot turns on her relationship with Dirk and his failure to fulfill his early promise. In Selina, Edna Ferber catches the hope and attention all parents lavish on their children and helps us understand why those we love are truly "hostages to fortune."

So Big won the Pulitzer Prize and launched Edna Ferber on her career.

SO FAR FROM HEAVEN

By Richard Bradford
(1099) 8-1 hour cassettes
Rental—$14.50   Purchase—$64.00
Read by Dan Lazar

So Far From Heaven is the story of the Tafoya clan, a Chicano family with a flair for misadventure. The Tafoyas include a physicianphilosopher, a radical daughter with a degree from Bryn Mawr, a clumsily stupid son, and a Governor of New Mexico. From these elements Bradford creates a story as funny and tender as *Red Sky at Morning,* also set in New Mexico, also well worth reading.

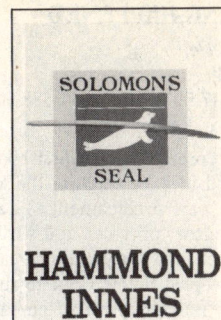

SOLOMONS SEAL

By Hammond Innes
(1813) 8-1½ hour cassettes
Rental—$15.50   Purchase—$64.00
Read by Dan Lazar

A beautiful young heiress, Perenna Holland, falls on hard times. She enlists Roy Slingsby, estate agent and *bon vivant,* to sell the family manse.

Once into the assignment, he uncovers an album of stamps with a singular story to tell.

Slingsby sets out to trace its origin. He joins a ship where the cargo is contraband, sails to an island seething with rebellion and finds the stamps are tied to a dark secret in Perenna's family. How will she take this information?

"With all the power, suspense and authenticity that has attracted millions of readers to his work, *Solomons Seal* is a stirring novel of adventure in the grand manner of Hammond Innes." *(Publisher's Source)*

SOMEBODY'S DARLING

By Larry McMurty
(1743) 8-1½ hour cassettes
Rental—$15.50   Purchase—$64.00
Read by Wolfram Kandinsky

Jill Peel is the first woman to make Hollywood's bigtime as a director. She has other interests as well—Joe Percy, a veteran screenwriter whose mainstay is his love for Jill, and Owens Oarson, an opportunist who studs her to advance his own career.

All three travel in a world of easy sex and available drugs, of astronomical salaries and artistic compromise—until one tragic day, on location, the fairytale comes to an end.

Besides the recent Pulitzer Prize winning *Lonesome Dove,* Books on Tape has also recorded Larry McMurtry's *The Desert Rose, Terms of Endearment, Hud* and *The Last Picture Show.*

SOMETHING HAPPENED

By Joseph Heller
(1447) 11-1½ hour cassettes
Rental—$17.50   Purchase—$88.00
Read by Dan Lazar

This is Joseph Heller's first book after *Catch-22,* and in it he explores the wartime generation's new predicament . . . as husband, progenitor, provider and survivalist. What happened to all the youthful dreams and those who peopled them? Gone to ruin. Because Heller isan architect of our age, his comments on the rubble contain more irony than perhaps he realizes.

SOMETHING I'VE BEEN MEANING TO TELL YOU

By Alice Munro
(1486) 6-1½ hour cassettes
Rental—$14.50   Purchase—$48.00
Read by Jeanne Hopson

Something I've Been Meaning to Tell You is a collection of 13 varied stories addressing the questions, fears, doubts and observations of childhood and adolescence.

"All the aspects of the feminine charade are touched on in these stories, and some of them are indeed 'lit with piercing glances into the life of things." *(Canadian Forum)*

B-O-T has recorded other Munro titles including *The Beggar Maid* and *Lives of Girls and Women.*

SOMETHING TO HIDE and SMITH & JONES

By Nicholas Monsarrat
(1243) 6-1½ hour cassettes
Rental—$14.50   Purchase—$48.00
Read by Stuart Courtney

A middle-aged accountant driving to his lakeside cottage gives a lift to a forlorn teenager. She is pregnant, tells conflicting stories of her predicament, and asks to spend the night. He agrees . . . with consequences!

"Almost completely unlike anything else Monsarrat has ever written, here he shows complete mastery of Greek tragedy by successfully casting it into modern-day form and life." *(Best Sellers)*

Smith and Jones, embassy officials, are sent to a frozen, hostile capital. Frustrated and unstable, the two defect to the alien land. Why they go and what happens to them is revealed in Monsarrat's spare, swift-moving narrative about individualism versus patriotism, national and personal security.

SOPHIE'S CHOICE

By William Styron
(1878-A) 9-1½ hour cassettes
Rental—$16.50   Purchase—$72.00
(1878-B) 10-1½ hour cassettes
Rental—$16.50   Purchase—$80.00
Read by Wolfram Kandinsky

Choice: Stingo, our young Southern narrator. Manuscript reader for a major publisher . . . or . . . a genuine novelist soaking up the experiences that one day will re-emerge as stories fo great power and precision.

Choice: Nathan Landau. A charming sophisticate possessed of great intelligence . . . or . . . a classic schizophrenic, a manic depressive with a consuming distrust of his lover's fidelity.

Choice: Sophie Zawistowska, the Polish Catholic immigrant, forever stamped with her decision in a Nazi Concentration Camp. Having already chosen between her homeland and freedom, she must ultimately choose between life alone and death in the arms of her lover.

Sophie's Choice: William Styron's summit achievement in fiction. Winner of an American Book Award, the film *Sophie's Choice* starred Meryl Streep.

THE SPY WHO DIED OF BOREDOM

By George Mikes
(1028) 8-1 hour cassettes
Rental—$14.50   Purchase—$64.00
Read by Dan Lazar

Entertainment of the first chop for those who enjoy a sophisticated and witty lampoon of the spy business. Posted to London, a young Russian undercover agent determines that British secrets will fall to him from the lips of British secretaries whom he seduces. He sets for himself a prodigious pace, and we are treated to a humorous interpretation of coexistence. In this battle of East vs. West, the outcome is a draw.

THE STAND

By Stephen King
(2163-A) 11-1½ hour cassettes
Rental—$17.50   Purchase—$88.00
(2163-B) 12-1½ hour cassettes
Rental—$17.50   Purchase—$96.00
Read by Grover Gardner

NEW

The old Chevy came out of the Texas dusk at near walking speed, a Pandora's box of nightmare and death. Up ahead the lights of Bill Hapscomb's Texaco station glimmered . . . the box was about to be opened . . . the dance of death about to begin.

But the survivors of that dance have something much worse than death to fear, because the dark man is on his way. He is Randy Flagg, the Walkin' Dude, the man with no face. He is a drifter with a hundred different names. His is the majid man, the living image of Satan and his hour is at hand.

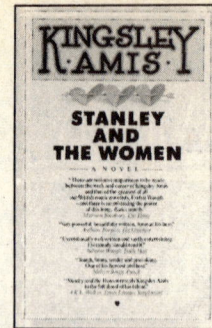

STANLEY AND THE WOMEN

By Kingsley Amis
(1765) 6-1½ hour cassettes
Rental—$14.50   Purchase—$48.00
Read by Richard Green

The hero of Kingsley Amis's comedy is Stanley Duke. Attractive, prosperous and happily remarried, Stanley leads a life that is positively enviable—that is, until it becomes apparent that his teenage son, Steve, is going mad.

It isn't that Steve suddenly tears up a copy of Bellow's *Herzog,* or cranks his stereo to ear-shattering levels . . . that's normal. It's his pursuit by cosmic forces that concerns his father. Stanley's confrontation with his son's madness give Amis the opportunity to pull off a comic masterpiece.

"Tough, funny, tender and provoking. One of his fiercest and best." *(Punch)*

A START IN LIFE

By Alan Sillitoe
(1083) 9-1½ hour cassettes
Rental—$16.50   Purchase—$72.00
Read by Richard Green

A Start in Life chronicles the young manhood of a vigorous non-conformist, Michael Cullen. Born a bastard, Cullen refuses to stand in the "working class ranks" and batters his way up. In the course of his picaresque adventures he makes a great deal of money and a great deal of love. Although *A Start in Life* is traditional in form, its author is thoroughly modern. Alan Sillitoe peoples this story with familiar 20th century types—communists, drop-outs and liberated young women.

**For quick ordering
1-800-626-3333**

THE STATE OF STONY LONESOME

By Jessamyn West
(1977) 5-1 hour cassettes
Rental—$11.50   Purchase—$40.00
Read by Roses Prichard

Zen is a gambler, drinker and womanizer. In his mid-thirties, lean, handsome, disarmingly direct, he appears to be—depending on one's point of view—dashing and attractive or a soul headed for perdition.

Ginerva is a lovely girl, still in her teens. But in the theatre of her imagination, romance and propriety frequently clash. The problem is Zen, with whom she is secretly and most improperly in love. Because Zen is not only old enough to be her father . . . he is in fact her uncle.

"Jessamyn West balances tension, humor and wisdom in a bittersweet nostalgia." *(Publisher's Source)*

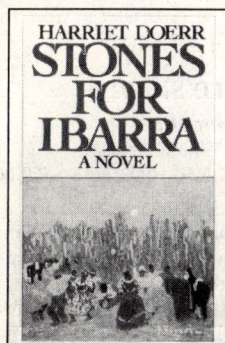

STONES FOR IBARRA

By Harriet Doerr
(1766) 6-1½ hour cassettes
Rental—$14.50   Purchase—$48.00
Read by Jeanne Hobson

Richard and Sara Everton mortgage, sell and borrow, leave friends and country to settle in the Mexican village of Ibarra. They intend to spend the rest of their lives here, in a place neither of them has seen, to speak a language neither of them know. Their dream is to reopen Richard's grandfather's abandoned copper mine. In a few short months work is advancing in the mine and their home is ready—then Richard learns he has six years to live.

Richard's determination to make the mine and village prosper matches Sara's effort to deny the diagnosis. While Richard measures time, she rejects its passage.

This novel, Harriet Doerr's first, was written when she was in her seventies. It won the American Book Award.

THE STRODE VENTURER

By Hammond Innes
(1808) 7-1½ hour cassettes
Rental—$15.50   Purchase—$56.00
Read by Dan Lazar

The Strode Venturer, ploughing distant seas, bridges two very different worlds—the island paradise of Addu Atoll and the commercial world of London.

Everything is very much business as usual, but at Strode House a coterie of directors plots against the family. Nowhere is disaster closer than in the Maldives, where the Adduans, an isolated seafaring people, have literally bet their future on the company.

Peter Strode, wanderer, the odd man out in a family interested only in power and money, makes the cause of the Adduans his own. Volatile, impulsive, full of driving enthusiasm, he sets out to save these people and restore his father's company. Only death can deflect him from his purpose.

SUMITRA'S STORY

By Rukshana Smith
(1775) 7-1 hour cassettes
Rental—$13.50   Purchase—$56.00
Read by Jill Masters

Sumitra's Story is about a young Asian girl growing up in Britain in recent years, and the confusion engendered by her situation.

Many of her family and friends blame everything on the color of their skin, Sumitra hears them say, "If I were black, I'd have got rehoused by now!," "If I was colored, they'd have given me that job!" And Indians blame the fact that they are brown for not getting jobs and houses.

Is this, Sumitra wonders, a device to cover up inadequacy? In order to preserve the myth of difference, people seem to line up in rows of black, brown or white and hurl their prejudices at each other. That way they never have to meet, never discover that beneath their skin they are all the same.

THE SUMMER OF KATYA

By Trevanian
(1967) 8-1 hour cassettes
Rental—$14.50   Purchase—$64.00
Read by Grover Gardner

It is the summer of 1914. Golden days that look to roll on forever . . . who could hear the guns of August?

Deep in the Basque countryside, a young doctor signs on at a clinic. His first case is simple, the consequences complex . . . for he meets a young woman, Katya, with whom he falls deeply in love.

Trevanian is the author of *The Eiger Sanction, Shibumi* and *The Main,* all best sellers that receive continuing acclaim.

"Trevanian is in a class by himself . . . beyond any doubt superior." *(John Barkham Reviews)*

A SUMMER PLACE

By Sloan Wilson
(1395) 7-1½ hour cassettes
Rental—$15.50   Purchase—$56.00
Read by Justin Hecht

The summer place from which Sloan Wilson's novel takes its title is an island off the coast of Maine. On this island one summer, Ken Jorgenson and Sylvia Raymond meet. The story of what happens to them, to the people they marry and to their children, who years later meet on the island, is the central thread of a novel about how marriages are made on earth: some out of fear, some out of pride, some out of desperation, and some, when there is strength and self-knowledge, out of love.

Sloan Wilson is best known as the author of *The Man in the Gray Flannel Suit.*

THE SUNDOWNERS

By Jon Cleary
(1376) 8-1½ hour cassettes
Rental—$15.50   Purchase—$64.00
Read by Mark Howell

The author, an Australian himself, conceived of *The Sundowners* as "A novel in which the people weren't troubled by neuroses and didn't blame the world for their own shortcomings." With his great admiration for the self-reliant Australians, Cleary vividly and often poetically etches the saga of the Carmodys.

This is a sundowner family in the rural Australia of the 1920's, always on the move from job to job, heading toward the horizon.

"*The Sundowners* has a nostalgic warmth that makes it out of the ordinary." *(The New York Times)*

SUNLIGHT DIALOGUES

By John Gardner
(1745-A)) 11-1½ hour cassettes
Rental—$17.50   Purchase—$88.00
(1745-B) 11-1½ hour cassettes
Rental—$17.50   Purchase—$88.00
Read by Grover Gardner

It is 1966 . . . remember? In upstate New York, Fred Clumly, a civic-minded police chief, is trying to hold his force and his city together. He feels beleaguered. The foundations are shaking.

So when a vagrant hippie, "the Sunlight Man," shows up, Clumly enjoys throwing him in the slammer.

Later, when the Sunlight Man escapes and a murder follows, Clumly is suffused with self-righteous elation. He looks forward to tracking down the degenerate who represents all those things that are undermining America.

"A masterpiece of comic irony . . . a profound examination of the massive changes that swept the country in the sixties." *(Saturday Review)*

SYLVESTER or
THE WICKED UNCLE

By Georgette Heyer
((1604)) 8-1½ hour cassettes
Rental—$15.50   Purchase—$64.00
Read by Flo Gibson

It is the predicament of Sylvester, heir to the Dukedom of Salford, that an inheritance comes to him at the tender age of 19. While he quickly learns skills such as estate management, it is predictable that he will be untutored in affairs of the heart. Then Sylvester meets Phoebe Marlow—young, hoydenish and opportunistic.

Sylvester is another addition to an engaging series of historical romances from the pen of Georgette Heyer. For a complete list of her books recorded by B-O-T, please refer to our Index.

TALES FROM A
TROUBLED LAND

By Alan Paton
(1333) 3-1 hour cassettes
Rental—$8.50   Purchase—$24.00
Read by Stuart Courtney

Paton's theme is the tragedy of apartheid in his native South Africa. His characters are torn between affection for the land and grief for its divided people.

Paton's first career was in social service. He worked as director of a reformatory for African boys, and the 10 short stories in *Tales from a Troubled Land* deal primarily with incidents from this time. Titles include "Life for a Life," "Sponono," "Ha'Penny," "The Waste Land," "The Worst Thing of His Life," "The Elephant Shooter," "Debbie Go Home," "Death of a Tsotsi," "The Divided House" and "A Drink in the Passage."

TALES OF MOORLAND
AND ESTUARY

By Henry Williamson
(1851) 6-1½ hour cassettes
Rental—$14.50   Purchase—$48.00
Read by Donada Peters

Henry Williamson was one of the great nature writers of the century. His area of observation was North Devon—its coast and moors, its inhabitants in all their forms. He regarded animals and men with compassion and wrote about them in clear, memorable prose.

These twelve stories range from the eerie "A Winter's Tale," about a stranded hiker's night in a fog-shrouded farmhouse, to the satiric observation of "The White Stoat," an albino weasel's encounter with a Cockney interloper; and from "The Crake," a Melvillean saga of a fisherman's duel with the sea, to "The Yellow Boots," a chilling tale of a bizarre convict hunt on the moors.

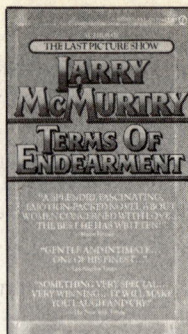

TERMS OF ENDEARMENT

By Larry McMurtry
(1945) 10-1½ hour cassettes
Rental—$16.50   Purchase—$80.00
Read by Roses Prichard

One of Larry McMurtry's most sensitive and compelling portrayals of human relationships, *Terms of Endearment* is a story of love, its occasional absence and the emotional tensions we generate in its maintenance.

At the story's center is a Aurora Greenway, a woman who makes the world revolve around her. Shrewd yet inwardly tender, spirited but vulnerable, she attracts a series of dedicated protectors. But in the final analysis she learns about love not from a person but from an event—in this case loss, specifically the death of her daughter.

"A vivid and richly detailed novel about ourselves and those we love . . . about time—about the disorder that seeps into human relationships, the erosion of hope, the loss of illusions, the transmissions of essential values from generation to generation—and about the way that women keep life going in spite of the odds." *(The New Republic)*

THEATRE

By W. Somerset Maugham
(1178) 8-1 hour cassettes
Rental—$14.50   Purchase—$64.00
Read by Bernard Mayes

Theatre is W. Somerset Maugham's tale about London's theatrical world. Julia Lambert, a brilliant actress in her forties, projects stage values into her own personal life. Julia seeks variety in her numerous affairs, but always emerges unscathed and unattached. Emotions and commitments not dictated in a script seem beyond her grasp.

"*Theatre* is a superb entainment—a skillful discourse on vanity, jealousy, spite and sexual possessiveness." *(Editorial Review Service)*

THEIRS WAS THE KINGDOM

By R.F. Delderfield
(1463-A) 12-1½ hour cassettes
Rental—$17.50   Purchase—$96.00
(1463-B) 13-1½ hour cassettes
Rental—$18.50   Purchase—$104.00
Read by Robert Mundy

Theirs Was the Kingdom is Delderfield's magisterial sequel to *God is an Englishman*. The saga of the Swann family continues through the years leading up to Queen Victoria's jubilee.

Again, Adam Swann is the central character, but the focus frequently switches to his devoted wife, Henrietta, and to the adventures—mostly amorous—of their brood of children. Alex becomes a career soldier. Stella marries into the landed gentry, and the aesthetic Giles improbably falls in love with a madcap heiress, while George, in the face of his father's overt skepticism, develops the first motorpowered transport vehicle.

"Rich and rewarding . . . has the spirit of the time." *(Best Sellers)*

THESE OLD SHADES

By Georgette Heyer
(1602) 9-1½ hour cassettes
Rental—$16.50   Purchase—$72.00
Read by   Wanda McCaddon

The Duke of Avon is merely indulging himself when he rescues a handsome youth from a cruel older brother.

But what the Duke doesn't know is that this boy will soon engage his heart as well . . . for physical appearances aside, the lad is actually a young girl. As she blossoms into a stunning beauty, the Duke finds himself drawn to her.

"Nowhere is the society, the flavor and the cant of the regency period more knowingly and delightfully portrayed than in the novels of Georgette Heyer." *(The Philadelphia Bulletin)*

THEY HANGED MY SAINTLY BILLY

By Robert Graves
(1903) 8-1½ hour cassettes
Rental—$15.50   Purchase—$64.00
Read by John MacDonald

They Hanged My Saintly Billy is about William Palmer, a surgeon and racehorse owner, thief and philanderer. But was he a poisoner?

Using interviews with Palmer's friends and enemies, as well as trial transcripts, Graves' novel has all the immediacy and passion of contemporary life. Palmer's salty life and notorious death make compelling reading.

"My novel is full of sex, drink, incest, suicides, dope, horseracing, murder, scandalous legal procedure, cross-examinations, inquests and ends with a good public hanging—attended by 30,000 . . . Nobody can now can now call me a specialized writer." —Robert Graves

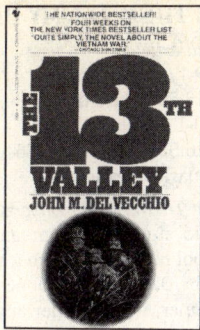

THE 13TH VALLEY

By John M. Del Vecchio
(2010-A) 11-1½ hour cassettes
Rental—$17.50   Purchase—$88.00
(2010-B) 10-1½ hour cassettes
Rental—$16.5   Purchase—$80.00
Read by Paul Shay

"Powerful . . . a diverse group of men, gathered together to make war, proceed to transcend racial and ethnic differences, become brothers in combat, suffer horribly, fight an apocalyptic battle and win . . . There have been a number of excellent books but none has managed to communicate in such detail the day-to-day pain, discomfort, frustration and exhiliration of the American military experience in Vietnam." *(The New York Times Book Review)*

Rental Section At-a-Glance

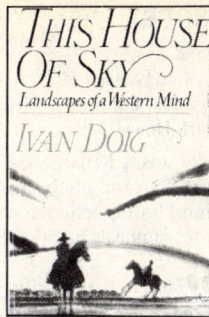

THIS HOUSE OF SKY

By Ivan Doig
(2113) 8-1½ hour cassettes
Rental—$15.50   Purchase—$64.00
Read by Paul Shay

Ivan Doig grew up in the rugged Montana wilderness with his father, Charlie, and his grandmother, Bessie Ringer. He lived among sheepherders and the characters in small-town saloons and valley ranches as he tagged along with his restless father.

Doig puts us in touch with the land and its influence on us, also with ties to our family and those who shaped our values in the search for intimacy, independence and love.

"From this beautifully written, deeply felt book we recognize that other step toward the universal. The language begins in western territory and experience but in the hands of an artist it touches all landscapes and all life. Doig is such an artist." *(The Los Angeles Times)*

THE THORN BIRDS

By Colleen McCullough
(1117-A) 9-1½ hour cassettes
Rental—$16.50   Purchase—$72.00
(1117-B) 9-1½ hour cassettes
Rental—$16.50   Purchase—$72.00
Read by Penelope Dellaporta

The *Thorn Birds* is a robust and romantic saga that begins in the green hills of New Zealand and moves quickly to Australian sheep country. It spans the years between 1915 and 1969 and chronicles three generations of Cleary women—Fiona, Meggie and Justine.

"The interweaving of love stories from one generation to the next, the dramatic plotting, the sense of steadily mounting tension, the believable characterizations are well-nigh irresistible." *(Publishers Weekly)*

THE THREE IMPOSTERS

By Arthur Machen
(9142) 6-1 hour cassettes
Rental—$13.50   Purchase—$48.00
Read by Jim Killavey
A Jimcin Recording

In this extraordinary novel, the author sees Victorian London as a fantasy land, filled with intrigue, mysteries and marvels. Each day he finds adventure in a kalideoscope of coincidence, chance meetings, anecdotes and encounters.

But is this story dream or nightmare, horror or delight? It is at least a strange excursion to the edge of reality, possibly beyond. For at the root of this apparently straightforward story of prosaic, rather stuffy Londoners lies a pervasive of evil. Respectablility, Machen seems to say, is merely a screen for unimaginable horrors lurking right beneath the well-shined, sturdy shoes of your neighbor.

THREE SOLDIERS

By John Dos Passos
(1339) 11-1½ hour cassettes
Rental—$17.50   Purchase—$88.00
Read by Jascha Kessler

John Dos Passos' theme is universal: an indictment against war. Almost a pacifist novel, it ironically contributed to America's near fatal delay in rearming for WW II.

The three central characters in this story meet in an American army training camp during WW I: Dan Fuselli, an Italian-American; Chrisfield, an Indiana farm boy; and John Andrews, the college man, a sensitive aspiring composer, in whom we see the author.

"*Three Soldiers* is engrossing . . . finely imagined and powerfully created." *(Literary Review)*

B-O-T has also recorded Dos Passos' *Orient Express* and his *U.S.A. Trilogy.*

**For Visa and MasterCard
order line 1-800-626-3333**

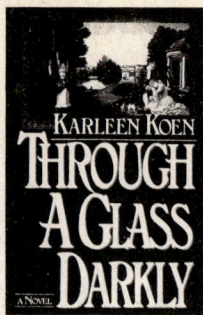

THROUGH A GLASS DARKLY

By Karleen Koen
(2131-A) 8-1½ hour cassettes
Rental—$15.50   Purchase—$64.00
(2131-B) 7-1½ hour cassettes
Rental—$15.50   Purchase—$56.00
(2131-C) 8-1½ hour cassettes
Rental—$15.50   Purchase—$64.00
Read by Donada Peters

Set in the upper-class families of 18th century England and France, *Through a Glass Darkly* tells the story of Barbara Alderley, a beautiful and passionate heroine; the grandmother she adores; the mother she despises . . . and the man she loves.

At 15, Barbara finds herself betrothed to a man 27 years her senior. Marriage propels her into a glittering, cynical society: the casual adulteries and violent politics of the age of Richelieu, Pope and Swift; of buildings by Christopher Wren; of greed, elegance, excess and cruelty. Barbara navigates these dangers with great skill; her beauty takes on polish and sophistication.

Through a Glass Darkly was a major selection of the Book of the Month Club. Writing about it, Jean M. Auel, author of *Clan of the Cave Bear,* said: "Rarely has a book so completely captured an era . . . it is rich, stunning, thoroughly believable . . . and kept me turning the pages."

Rental Section At-a-Glance

TIME OF HOPE

By C.P. Snow
(1410) 8-1½ hour cassettes
Rental—$15.50   Purchase—$64.00
Read by Mark Howell

C.P. Snow was a Renaissance man . . . scientist, artist, servant of the people. His greatest and most lasting achievement was the 11-volume series of novels he titled *Strangers and Brothers.*

Time of Hope is first in this series. It introduces us to Lewis Eliot, the narrator, who appears in subsequent novels.

Like Snow, Eliot is a man without connections who achieves professional status. A lawyer, Eliot tells us his own life story from 1914, at the age of nine, to 1933. After a brilliant start, he is nearly brought to ruin by his marriage and finds himself involved in a moral struggle from which there is no easy exit.

THE TIMES ARE NEVER SO BAD

By Andre Dubus
(1894) 6-1 hour cassettes
Rental—$12.50   Purchase—$48.00
Read by Ron Shoop

Ordinary lives, lives that brush against us every day, that's Dubus territory. It's rendered in the unblinking realism for which he is famous, and which, in this collection of short fiction, focuses on the twisting deformations of love that police, with irony, call "domestic disturbances."

Andre Dubus is a well established author whose beat is the northeast. He knows it and its people, it nuances and their problems. He writes with great honesty and conviction about people and their lives.

" . . . luminous with honesty and generosity. Dubus is interested in essential things—in the shadowy powers that circle our lives and in the slender resources of faith and love with which we try to keep them at bay." —Tobias Wolff

Adultery & Other Choices, Finding a Girl in America and *Separate Flights,* other Dubus titles, are all recorded by B-O-T.

TO SERVE THEM ALL MY DAYS

By R.F. Delderfield
(1465-A) 10-1½ hour cassettes
Rental—$16.50   Purchase—$80.00
(1465-B) 10-1½ hour cassettes
Rental—$16.50   Purchase—$64.00
Read by Stuart Courtney

To Serve Them All My Days is R.F. Delderfield's epic study of life at an English boarding school between the two wars. It is a story related by David Powlett-Jones, the son of a Welsh miner, whose father and brother died in a pit accident, a socialist whose politics mellow as he ages. The victim of severe shell-shock after three nightmarish years of service in the battlefields of the First World War, David is advised by a doctor to take up a teaching post at Bamfylde School in the rural south west of England.

Not least, *To Serve Them All My Days* provides behind-the-scenes glimpses of the struggles for power that rage in an enclosed environment where personalities must inevitabley clash.

TO THE LIGHTHOUSE (Fiction) and THE LONDON SCENE (Non-Fiction)

By Virginia Woolf
(1787) 7-1½ hour cassettes
Rental—$15.50   Purchase—$56.00
Read by Wanda McCaddon

To The Lighthouse is a haunting psychological portrait of the Ramsay family and their friends who gather for a brief vacation in the Ramsay summer home on the Hebrides Isle of Skye.

There is talk of a boating trip to the lighthouse at the island's end. But the year is 1914, a World War intervenes, and it is a somber group that finally assembles to make the ritual journey.

The five brief essays that comprise *The London Scene* conjure up the invisible magic known as London. The author lifts the city's docks, its abbeys and cathedrals, the houses of its great men, Oxford Street, and the House of Commons above the commonplace.

TOO LATE THE PHALAROPE

By Alan Paton
(1332) 7-1 hour cassettes
Rental—$13.50   Purchase—$56.00
Read by Richard Green

Too Late the Phalarope is set in South Africa, as well as its predecessor, *Cry, the Beloved Country.* And like that earlier novel, *Too Late the Phalarope* uses the lives of ordinary people to illustrate the inhuman quality of South African apartheid.

Racial segregation is odious in concept, impossible in application. To prove it, Paton tells us the story of Pieter, a white policeman, who has an affair with a naive girl. He is betrayed and reported, and thus brings shame on himself and his family.

THE TOUCH

By F. Paul Wilson
(2082) 8-1½ hour cassettes
Rental—$15.50   Purchase—$64.00
Read by Ron Shoop

After a dozen years in practice, Alan Bulmer, M.D., finds he can cure people by touching them. At first he doesn't believe what his senses are telling him . . . but there is no other explanation.

When Alan gives himself over to this mysterious power, he revels in it. But he cannot cure jealousy, and soon the world is against him. How can he put his life together again?

F. Paul Wilson is himself a practicing physician. His early book, *The Keep* was a best seller and won a wide literary reputation. *The Keep* is also available from Books on Tape.

THE TRAIN

By Georges Simenon
(1512) 4-1 hour cassettes
Rental—$9.50   Purchase—$32.00
Read by Michael Prichard

One of Georges Simenon's most persuasive and moving novels, *The Train* introduces us to Marcel, a timid young man, full of self doubt, who is catapulted into the pandemonium of war. When the Germans invade Belgium, he joins the stampede for trains running south.

This is the break of his life for which he has unconsciously waited. Separated from his family, he meets Anna, a Czech Jewess, with whom he finds real love for the first time.

As the train moves through a surrealistic landscape, all inhibitions fall away. But the moment is brief, and realities inevitably reassert themselves.

For other Simenon titles please refer to the Index under the author's name.

TRINITY

By Leon Uris
(1096-A) 10-1½ hour cassettes
Rental—$16.50   Purchase—$80.00
(1096-B) 9-1½ hour cassettes
Rental—$16.50   Purchase—$72.00
Read by Dan Lazar

Trinity is Leon Uris' phenomenally successful novel. written on the scale of a massive panorama, it is the story of the period on Irish history from the 1840's to the Easter Rising of 1916. This turbulent drams tells of Ireland's past, explains its present unrest, and gives insight into its future.

"Leon Uris uses history as the raw material for legend in his powerful novel *Trinity*, a tale packed with romance and adventure that finally explains just what the hell the Irish are fighting about in their endless war." *(Philadelphia Sunday Bulletin)*

Other recorded books in our Uris collection are: *Exodus* and *Q.B. VII.*

THE TROLL GARDEN

By Willa Cather
(9084) 6-1 hour cassettes
Rental—$13.50   Purchase—$48.00
Read by Donna Barkham
A Jimcin Recording

Born in 1873, Willa Cather grew up in a Nebraska that was vastly different from the prosperous state we know today. Then the country was unbroken, the land in the process of being settled by immigrants, and a rough and ready ethos prevailed.

Cather's important novels were to come later *(O Pioneers, My Antonia, Death Comes for the Archbishop)*, but her graceful style and intelligent sensibilities were well formed by the time she wrote her first book of short pieces.

Stories include: "Flavia and her Artists," "The Sculptor's Funeral," "The Garden Lodge," "A Death in the Dessert," "The Marriage of Phaedra," "A Wagner Matinee," and "Paul's Case."

UNDER THE TONTO RIM

By Zane Grey
(1315) 8-1 hour cassettes
Rental—$14.50   Purchase—$64.00
Read by Dan Lazar

Lucy Watson, a young schoolteacher, is appointed welfare instructor in a community of isolated backwoods folk. She quickly overcomes their fears, and achieves popularity by the practical results of her work. She is especially successful with a strong, uncouth beehunter. Zane Grey's handling of these primitive characters is robust and understanding.

"Zane Grey is a gifted artist who draws scenes of the southwest in unforgettable stories." *(E.R.S. Reviews)*

THE UNDERSTUDY

By Elia Kazan
(1919) 9-1½ hour cassettes
Rental—$16.50   Purchase—$72.00
Read by Dan Lazar

The Understudy, swirls through a wealth of environments: the Broadway stage, a mind-blown safari in east Africa, a Hollywood film studio, a closing-night cast party in Boston, New York's underworld and its straight analog, the television industry.

Drawing on his experience as a director, Elia Kazan enhances the meaning of "arrangement" to encompass the sexual accommodations most people live by . . . and lie about.

Kazan's films have become classics. *Viva Zapata!, East of Eden* and *A Streetcar Named Desire* secured his reputation, and he won Academy Awards for *Gentlemen's Agreement* and *On the Waterfront.*

Books on Tape has recorded Kazan's successful *America, America, Acts of Love* and *The Arrangement.*

THE U.S.A. TRILOGY

John Dos Passos

He describes the trilogy in his own words in the following paragraph.

"U.S.A. is the slice of a continent. U.S.A. is a group of holding companies, some aggregations of trade unions, a set of laws bound in calf, a radio network, a chain of moving picture theatres, a column of stock quotations rubbed out and written in by a Western Union boy on a blackboard, a public library full of old newspapers and dogeared history books with protests scrawled on the margins in pencil. U.S.A. is the world's greatest river valley fringed with mountains and hills. U.S.A. is a set of bigmouthed officials with too many bank accounts. U.S.A. is a lot of men buried in their uniforms in Arlington Cemetery. U.S.A. is the letters at the end of an address when you are away from home. But mostly U.S.A. is the speech of the people."

THE 42ND PARALLEL: (Part I of The U.S.A. Trilogy)

By John Dos Passos
(1342) 10-1½ hour cassettes
Rental—$16.50   Purchase—$80.00
Read by Michael Prichard

The novel's subject is America, as represented by her great men, her popular culture, the autobiographical evocations of an unseen author, and the lives of vividly created fictional characters.

1919: Part II of The U.S.A. Trilogy)

By John Dos Passos
(1343) 11-1½ hour cassettes
Rental—$17.50   Purchase—$88.00
Read by Michael Prichard

"The obscenity of the war, 'Mr. Wilson's War,' is Dos Passos' theme, and since the war is the most important political event of the century, he rises to his theme with a brilliance that does not conceal the fury behind it." (From the introduction by Alfred Kazin.)

THE BIG MONEY: (Part III of The U.S.A. Trilogy)

By John Dos Passos
(1344) 13-1½ hour cassettes
Rental—$18.50   Purchase—$104.00
Read by Michael Prichard

America in the boom years of the twenties. Hog-wild material prosperity rules the land and cripples the national life.

"Dos Passos' subject is indeed democracy, but his belief—especially as he goes into the final volume of his trilogy—is that the force of circumstances that is 20th century life is too strong for the average man, who will probably never rise above mass culture, mass superstition, mass slogans." (From the introduction by Alfred Kazin.)

B-O-T has also recorded John Dos Passos' *Manhattan Transfer* and *Three Soldiers.*

THE V.I.P.

By Elleston Trevor
(1735) 6-1½ hour cassettes
Rental—$14.50   Purchase—$48.00
Read by Jill Masters

In the aftermath of WW II, Nikolas II, King of Slavakia, brought his nation from ashes to the forefront of world politics. But now he is in exile, debauched, promiscuous and bitter. When Slavakia wants him back, he is willing—but is he ready to accept the challenge?

Thus begins Elleston Trevor's tale of politics and deception. A story of love and will set against the background of the Cold War, it is about a man of power, the pressures he copes with and the decisions he must make.

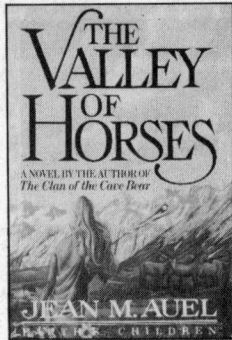

THE VALLEY OF HORSES

By Jean M. Auel
(1726-A) 9-1½ hour cassettes
Rental—$16.50   Purchase—$72.00
(1726-B) 8-1½ hour cassettes
Rental—$15.50   Purchase—$64.00
Read by Donada Peters

In this second novel of the Earth's Children saga, Ayla, the unforgettable heroine of *The Clan of the Cave Bear*, sets out solo into a world far from friendly.

She is in search of Others like herself . . . and in search of love. Driven by energies she scarcely understands, she explores where the Clan never dared to travel.

In a hidden valley she finds not only a herd of steppe horses, but also a unique kinship with animals as vulnerable as herself. Still, nothing prepares her for the emotional turmoil she feels when she rescues a young man, Jondalar—the first of the Others she has seen—from almost certain death.

**Give a Books on Tape™
Gift Certificate
Call 1-800-626-3333**

VANISHING ANIMALS and OTHER STORIES

By Mary Morris
(1471) 6-1 hour cassettes
Rental—$12.50   Purchase—$48.00
Read by Nancy Dannevik

Twelve beautifully crafted stories by one of America's rising talents in fiction, Mary Morris, are collected in *Vanishing Animals and Other Stories*. She writes with delicate wit and compassion of the familiar dilemmas of childhood and adolescene, of troubling memories and irretrievable moments, of contemporary loves, of lonely newcomers.

Most of her stories are reminiscences in an uneasy vein. She knows what threatens us and how we fear. She also knows and subtly dramatizes the intriguingly beautiful resilience of the ever-adaptable human spirit.

VARIETY OF MEN

By C.P. Snow
(1423) 6-1½ hour cassettes
Rental—$14.50
Read by John MacDonald

The nine men here portrayed have stamped this century with their work or personality. At first glance they seem very different: Robert Frost and Josef Stalin, Winston Churchill and Albert Einstein. But C.P. Snow relates them to each other by parallels he finds in their natures. With the exception of Stalin, he has kown them all, thus he brings to their portraits a genuine warmth and vividness.

His other subjects include G.H. Hardy, Cambridge mathematician; H.C. Wells, founder of modern science fiction; Lloyd George, England's great radical politician; and Dag Hammarskjold, Secretary General of the United Nations before his untimely death and one of history's great humanitarians.

"C.P. Snow combines his gifts as a novelist with his intimate knowledge of the worlds of science, literature and government to bring us a uique and important book. Personal, witty, continually flashing with insight." *(E.R.S. Services)*

THE VIRGINIAN

By Owen Wister
(1294) 10-1½ hour cassettes
Rental—$16.50
Read by Dan Lazar

When Owen Wister wrote *The Virginian* in 1902, it became the cowboy book against which all others were compared. Set in Wyoming in the 1880's, it nonetheless contains the phrase, "When you say that, SMILE!"

Wister experienced firsthand all he describes. His book links us to an era that forms a vital part of our national legend. *The Virginian* was a major publishing event, half historical novel, half western, and remains a unique reminder of how far we have come since it was written.

VON RYAN'S EXPRESS

By David Westheimer
(2081) 7-1½ hour cassettes
Rental—$15.50   Purchase—$56.00
Read by Michael Prichard

NEW

A thousand British and American POWs learn to hate the American colonel who singlehandedly shapes them up. His strict discipline brings order to the camp; it also earns him a derisive "von." When Italy surrenders, German guards herd the men into boxcars for shipment to the Reich. Ryan has other ideas. He reckons to take the train to Switzerland . . . and freedom.

"A taut, exciting and well-keyed war novel . . . Ryan is a difficult hero to like, but he is a hero nonetheless. An exciting, authentic book." *(Book Week)*

VOYAGE TO SOMEWHERE

By Sloan Wilson
(1393) 8-1 hour cassettes
Rental—$14.50   Purchase—$64.00
Read by Penelope Dellaporta

What *The Cruel Sea* did for the war in the Atlantic, *Voyage to Somewhere* does for war in the Pacific.

Men at sea on war patrol are in constant danger, even when they feel most secure. And it is Sloan Wilson's purpose to show us that heroism can be found far back in the ranks, even on a lowly supply ship.

"Moving, exciting, shocking, sad, *Voyage to Somewhere* recreates for a new generation the kind of man whose response to the pressures of war brought us victory in the Pacific." *(Publisher's Source)*

THE WAPSHOT CHRONICLE

By John Cheever
(1674) 8-1½ hour cassettes
Rental—$15.50   Purchase—$64.00
Read by Michael Prichard

In 1957, when *The Wapshot Chronicle* was published, John Cheever was already recognized as a writer of superb short stories. But *The Wapshot Chronicle*, which won the 1958 National Book Award, established him as a major novelist. Seven years later, *The Wapshot Scandal* confirmed his standing.

Together, these novels present the complete story of the Wapshot inheritance, from the early twentieth century to the 1960's and from a small Massachusetts village to New York and Europe.

"*The Wapshot Chronicle* has been a beautifully rewarding experience for me . . . it is a compelling book. Character after character is perfectly rendered with warmth and detachment. Episode after episode is a model of narrative virtuosity." —Robert Penn Warren.

THE WAPSHOT SCANDAL

By John Cheever
(1749) 7-1½ hour cassettes
Rental—$15.50   Purchase—$56.00
Read by Michael Prichard

Where *The Wapshot Chronicle* leaves off, *The Wapshot Scandal* takes over and completes the tale of the Wapshot family.

''This second novel . . . about the Wapshot family is a delectable and glorious piece of fiction, especially in the three main strands of its subject matter: the pitiful lust of a well-meaning upperclass woman; the harm done by a scientist who lacks a grounding in the humanities; the humor inherent in old age. If it is a portrait of paradise, the author has included a fair leavening of serpents.'' —Glenway Wescott

WAR AND REMEMBRANCE

By Herman Wouk
(1575-A) 11-1½ hour cassettes
Rental—$17.50   Purchase—$88.00
(1575-B) 12-1½ hour cassettes
Rental—$17.50   Purchase—$96.00
(1575-C) 11-1½ hour cassettes
Rental—$17.50   Purchase—$88.00
Read by Michael Prichard

Prologue to *War and Remembrance* was *The Winds of War,* first published in 1971, and subject of a major television special program. The earlier book took Pug Henry, a Navy captain, and his family up to Pearl Harbor. This book carries the story on to Hiroshima.

More than history and much more than a novel, *War and Remembrance* has a purpose, a theme, and a message. Its purpose is to show (in Pug Henry's words) "Either war is finished, or we are." Its theme is that light triumphs over dark, good over evil.

"Wherever the machinery of WW II grinds lives together or hurls them apart . . . Mr. Wouk takes us there . . . A journey of extraordinary emotional riches." *(The New York Times Book Review)*

THE WAR LOVER

By John Hersey
(1175) 10-1½ hour cassettes
Rental—$16.50   Purchase—$80.00
Read by Dan Lazar

The War Lover is Buzz Morrow, a pilot who glorifies war and his military duties. Hersey makes the point that wars exist precisely because there are men like Buzz who revel in them. At the same time, he gives us a detailed account of a Flying Fortress crew based in England during WW II. The language is rough and expressive, revealing the loyalties, humor, and camaraderie existing in this wartime atmosphere.

THE WATER-METHOD MAN

By John Irving
(1359) 8-1½ hour cassettes
Rental—$15.50   Purchase—$64.00
Read by Dan Lazar

Bogus Trumpeter, a wayward knight-errant in the battle of the sexes, has a serious problem. And he has only his "weapon" to blame. Due to a birth defect, or a nonspecific kind of infection, or a strain of venereal disease, Trumpeter suffers from a recurring urinary tract blockage. Four alternatives present themselves as possible solutions to his problem: drugs, no sex, surgery or "the water method." As if this were not enough, Trumpeter's life is further complicated by a wife who wants out and a mistress who wants a baby. Pure John Irving!

WELCOME TO THE MONKEY HOUSE

By Kurt Vonnegut, Jr.
(1194) 7-1½ hour cassettes
Rental—$15.50   Purchase—$56.00
Read by   Dan Lazar

Welcome to the Monkey House is a collection of stories and essays first appearing as magazine articles in *Atlantic, Esquire* and *Playboy.* Vonnegut was uncertain about their reception in hard cover form, prompting this statement in the preface: "The contents of this book are samples of work I sold in order to finance the writing of the novels. Here one finds the fruits of Free Enterprise." The stories are much better than that—stretching "funny" beyond the normal bounds of humor.

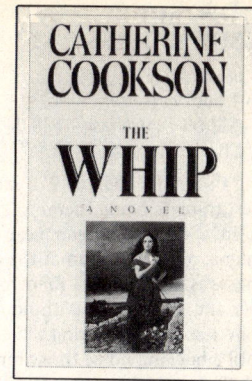

THE WHIP

By Catherine Cookson
(1892) 10-1½ hour cassettes
Rental—$16.50   Purchase—$80.00
Read by Mary Woods

The Whip is set in Tyneside, a region in northern England where the rugged country and rough weather once made life little more than a battle for survival.

But Emma Molinero, orphan daughter of an itinerant carnival performer, is beyond that kind of struggle. She is a woman whose fiery independence and skill at performing with the whips—her father's only legacy—make her a figure of mysterious but commanding fascination to the villagers among whom she lives.

"*The Whip* is Miss Cookson's finest novel to date . . . a richly detailed, totally absorbing story that will surely add many new readers to the millions who are already devoted Catherine Cookson fans." *(Publisher's Source)*

THE WIDOWER'S SON

By Alan Sillitoe
(1130) 7-1½ hour cassettes
Rental—$15.50   Purchase—$56.00
Read by   Richard Green

The Widower's Son is a *tour de force* from the author of *The Loneliness of the Long Distance Runner.* A young man, the son of a sergeant, adopts his father's discipline and rises far above his origins.

He succeeds brilliantly as a gunnery officer in WW II, entirely devoted to duty, self-discipline and order. Yet, these virtues do not serve him as well in peacetime life, and in his marriage to a brigadier general's daughter he comes close to the brink of disaster.

WILL JAMES' BOOK OF COWBOY STORIES

By Will James
(1377) 6-1 hour cassettes
Rental—$12.50   Purchase—$48.00
Read by Charles Garst

Loping through a book by Will James is the next best thing to being there.

Born in a covered wagon near Great Falls, Montana, and an orphan at the age of three, James was adopted by a French Canadian trapper and prospector. With no formal schooling or lessons in drawing, "he was a cowboy until a bucking horse threw him into writing," as *Time* magazine once said of him. He looked more like an Irish scholar than a cowpuncher, but he wrote as he talked . . . in a natural, easy-going way.

THE WINDS OF WAR

By Herman Wouk
(1574-A) 10-1½ hour cassettes
Rental—$16.50   Purchase—$80.00
(1574-B) 9-1½ hour cassettes
Rental—$16.50   Purchase—$72.00
(1574-C) 9-1½ hour cassettes
Rental—$16.50   Purchase—$72.00
Read by Michael Prichard

In this magnetic and compelling drama, Herman Wouk re-creates the first two years of WW II, before the United States was officially involved.

The Winds of War examines the world at that time through the eyes of a 49-year-old naval commander, Victor Henry, military attache to President Roosevelt.

Henry is posted to Pearl Harbor in the Fall of 1941. All looks peaceful in Hawaii. Japan appears indecisive, Europe is half a world away, the American Navy dominates the Pacific—until that fateful hour on December 7 when we plunged irretrievably into a maelstrom of conflict.

"First rate storytelling . . . it succeeds most admirably in that always tricky business of combining true history with fiction, and actual characters with fictional ones." (*The New York Times*)

Rental Section At-a-Glance

WINTER'S TALES

By Isak Dinesen
(1857) 8-1½ hour cassettes
Rental—$15.50   Purchase—$64.00
Read by   Wanda McCaddon

"The tale is the original form of literature . . . tales are written the way one speaks. I also hope that my tales can be told, for thus they have been conceived, and such is my natural form of expression, when I write." — Isak Dinesen, writing as Karen Blixen, in 1942 following the Danish publication of *Winter's Tales.*

These tales include the following titles: "The Young Man with the Carnation," "Sorrow-acre," "The Heroine," "The Sailorboy's Tale," "The Pearls," "The Invincible Slaveowners," "The Dreaming Child," "Alkmene," "The Fish," "Peter and Rosa" and "A Consolatory Tale."

B-O-T also offers Dinesen's *Anecdotes of Destiny* and *Out of Africa.*

THE WITCHES OF EASTWICK
a novel by JOHN UPDIKE

THE WITCHES OF EASTWICK

By John Updike
(1912) 9-1½ hour cassettes
Rental—$16.50   Purchase—$72.00
Read by Donada Peters

Many of us have known witches, and some of us have lived with them . . . but none like Jane, Sukie and Alexandra, a real coven. Artists, they sculpt, write and play . . . but that is all for the surface. Their beings are submerged . . . and malignant.

Most men quail, but not Darryl Van Horne. A wealthy stranger who arrives in town, he goes them one better . . . he sets up as an alchemist.

In John Updike's hands this material takes on a life of its own. Updike examines how women cope when they are alone . . . and how deprivation turns them into what they were afraid of becoming.

WITHOUT ARMOR

By James Hilton
(1211) 7-1½ hour cassettes
Rental—$15.50   Purchase—$56.00
Read by Erik Bauersfeld

Without Armor was published in America six months after *Lost Horizon,* yet before *Lost Horizon* began to win popularity—thus it missed the wider appeal it might otherwise have had. Set in Russia, it is the story of Ainsely Fothergill, an Englishman who served as a British spy and was exiled to Siberia for eight years. The book reminds us that James Hilton was one of the best storytellers of our era, and that a good story never loses it appeal.

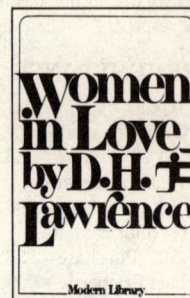

Women in Love by D.H. Lawrence
Modern Library

WOMEN IN LOVE

By D.H. Lawrence
(2132-A) 8-1½ hour cassettes
Rental—$15.50   Purchase—$64.00
(2132-B) 6-1½ hour cassettes
Rental—$14.50   Purchase—$48.00
Read by Richard Brown

Women in Love is perhaps D.H. Lawrence's most profound statement about men and women and about man and nature.

The story is a parable of two sisters, Ursula and Gudrun, a study in contrasts. For example, their love affairs . . . Gudrun and Gerald's, icy and sterile; Ursula and Birkin's, fruitful and transcendent.

One of the most controversial writers of the 20th century, Lawrence was born in England in 1885, the son of a coal miner and a school teacher. This misalliance was in some measure responsible for Lawrence's deeply divided nature. His relatively short life was a search for meaning; his books reflect the intensity of his vision.

Lady Chatterly's Lover, Lawrence's best known novel, is available in a full-length reading from Books on Tape.

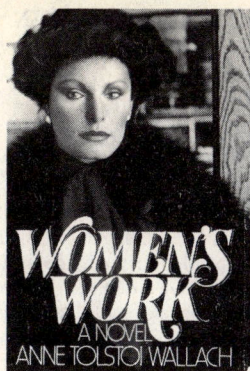

WOMEN'S WORK

By Anne Tolstoi Wallach
(1610) 10-1½ hour cassettes
Rental—$16.50   Purchase—$80.00
Read by Penelope Dellaporta

Women's Work is a vivid account of the difficulties faced by women executives, told with a flair for personalities, a good sense of humor, and considerable intelligence. The heroine is Domina Drexler, the talented creative director in a successful ad agency. Despite her ability, the agency's directors derail her projects and withhold their support.

The author, herself a successful New York business woman, brings to life the frustrations women face in today's competitive corporate world.

THE WORLD ACCORDING TO GARP

By John Irving
(2165-A) 8-1½ hour cassettes
Rental—$15.50   Purchase—$64.00
(2165-B) 7-1½ hour cassettes
Rental—$15.50   Purchase—$64.00
Read by Michael Prichard

Journey through generations and across two continents with the astonishing family of T.S. Garp, bastard son of a belligerent mother. Garp loves, lusts, labors and triumphs in a world of assassins, wrestlers, feminist fanatics, tantalizing teen-age babysitters, adoring children and a wayward wife.

His life is comic, tragic, violent and tender, his world outrageous. And it is as real as our own.

"Like all great works of art, Irving's novel seems always to have been there, a diamond sleeping in the dark, chipped out at last for our enrichment and delight." *(Cosmopolitan)*

Books on Tape™'s service is 100% guaranteed

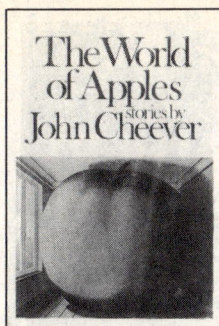

THE WORLD OF APPLES

By John Cheever
(1776) 6-1 hour cassettes
Rental—$12.50   Purchase—$48.00
Read by Michael Prichard

Innocent, old-fashioned, self-aware, Cheever's people are summoned by strange and improbable events to ponder the values they have been taught to trust . . . decency, common sense, nostalgia, even Truth. Stunned by these encounters, they nevertheless survive.

A worn out poet finds peace in his heart as he lays his Lermontov medal at the foot of the sacred angel; a prosperous suburbanite contemplates his predicament when his wife joins the cast of a nude show; a guileless and romantic well digger, anxious for a bride, visits Russia, falls in love and returns home "singing the unreality blues"; and a miserably married man fantasizes a beautiful lover who comes to him for strength, love and counsel while he tends the charcoal grill in the backyard.

"These dazzling stories—each one singular and enchanting—constitutes a major collection from an important American writer." *(E.R.S. Services)*

WORLD OF WONDERS

By Robertson Davies
(1285) 8-1½ hour cassettes
Rental—$15.50   Purchase—$64.00
Read by Dan Lazar

World of Wonders is the third volume of a trilogy in which *Fifth Business* and *The Manticore* are the first two. The author is one of Canada's most distinguished men of letters whose theme in these works is the contrast between art and life, illusion and reality. We meet Magnus Eisengrim, a celebrated magician, on location for a film at a remote Swiss castle. On hand are a famous Swedish director and the mysterious hostess, Liesel, in whose company we hear Magnus tell his life story. It is a story of contrast and paradox, out of which we are asked to choose what is truth, what is image.

THE WRECK OF THE MARY DEARE

By Hammond Innes
(1804) 10-1 hour cassettes
Rental—$15.50   Purchase—$80.00
Read by Christopher Hurt

Dusk is at hand as a Biscay gale shoves waves and weather into the Channel. John Sands, standing watch aboard the *Sea Witch*, spots a freighter, low in the water but making adequate weigh. She slips round Ushant and heads into the darkness.

Next morning the storm is gone, but not the freighter. There she is, the *Mary Deare*, abandoned and nearing the Channel Reefs. Sands goes aboard . . . but what a rescue, what a crazy ship, and what a story!

THE YOUNG LIONS

By Irwin Shaw
(1207-A) 10-1½ hour cassettes
Rental—$16.50   Purchase—$80.00
(1207-B) 9-1½ hour cassettes
Rental—$16.50   Purchase—$72.00
Read by Wolfram Kandinsky

Irwin Shaw was a noted playwright and author of short stories when his first novel, *The Young Lions*, was published in 1948. The work was a best seller and established Shaw as a major American novelist. Set in WW II, the book traces three young men, two Americans and a German, from 1938 to 1945 when they meet as soldiers in a Bavarian forest. The outcome, as in any tragedy, is foreordained, but it leaves the reader with a deep appreciation of the tensions of those times and what it meant to be in combat, in earnest, in a war where the issues were clearly drawn.

YOUNGBLOOD HAWKE

By Herman Wouk
(1379-A) 15-1½ hour cassettes
Rental—$18.50   Purchase—$120.00
(1379-B) 11-1½ hour cassettes
Rental—$16.50   Purchase—$88.00
Read by   Michael Prichard

A powerful novel about an aspiring young author's assault on the citadel of New York publishing. Hawke launched his career with an oversized manuscript that becomes an instant success. Toasted by critics and swept along on a tide of popularity, he gives himself over to the lush life that gilds artistic success.

This story makes us the companion of a young writer caught up in the glamour and intrigue of "life at the top" in New York. It suggests the life and career of Thomas Wolfe.

ACROSS THE WIDE MISSOURI

By Bernard DeVoto
(1354) 11-1½ hour cassettes
Rental—$17.50   Purchase—$88.00
Read by Larry McKeever

The Missouri, not the Mississippi, marked the jumping off point for mountain men and trappers in 1840. They ranged unexplored mountains and rivers as they searched out beaver and pushed back horizons. But on their heels came farmers and ranchers, lesser breeds, and in two short decades the frontier was gone forever.

Winner of the Pulitzer prize for history, DeVoto's book "is documented carefully; his notes and bibliography are in themselves enough to start any interested reader off on half a lifetime of reading in the field." *(San Francisco Chronicle)*

AFTERMATH

By Ladislas Farago
(1704-A) 8-1½ hour cassettes
Rental—$15.50   Purchase—$64.00
(1704-B) 7-1½ hour cassettes
Rental—$15.50   Purchase—$56.00
Read by Wolfram Kandinsky

An international sensation on publication, *Aftermath* is the story of Ladislas Farago's hunt for and subsequent confrontation with Martin Bormann, former head of the Nazi Party chancery and secretary to the Fuhrer.

Backed by interviews, documents and secret files, the author tells how Hitler's vast fortune found its way to South America; of Peron's complicity in aiding the Nazi war criminals; of the FBI's search for Bormann in 1948. Aftermath skillfully follows the escape, life in exile and activities of the former Reichsleiter.

Farago's *The Game of the Foxes* has also been recorded by B-O-T.

THE AGE OF FIGHTING SAIL

By C.S. Forester
(1622) 8-1 hour cassettes
Rental—$14.50   Purchase—$64.00
Read by Bill Kelsey

On June 18, 1812, the United States declared war on Britain, a whelp attacking its mother. The slogan "Free Trade and Sailors' Rights" said it all: we had it with British interference in our trade and shipping.

But it's one thing to tangle with a bigger dog, another to whip it. How we brought it off is the story told in this book.

"*The Age of Fighting Sail* is a history of the War of 1812—the war that made America a world power and, paradoxically, an isolationist one." *(E.R.S. Reviews)*

ALBERT SPEER: THE END OF A MYTH

NEW

By Matthias Schmidt
(2152) 8-1½ hour cassettes
Rental—$15.50   Purchase—$64.00
Read by Richard Wulf

Did the master builder of the Third Reich, Albert Speer, really not know about the Nazi extermination camps? What did he conceal from Allied interrogators, and from the millions who bought his memoirs, *Inside the Third Reich?*

Here is the chilling, documented tale about the "hero" of the Nuremberg Trials. In this book, which was an immediate best-seller in Europe, historian Matthias Schmidt interweaves documentary evidence with his own interviews with Speer's former colleagues. He unravels the most carefully crafted falsification in modern history—Albert Speer's memoirs dangerously polluted history. Schmidt's book purifies the record." —David Irving.

Speer's *Inside the Third Reich* and *Spandau: The Secret Diaries* are also available from B-O-T.

AMERICA IN SEARCH OF ITSELF: The Making of the President 1956-1980

By Theodore H. White
(1534-A) 8-1½ hour cassettes
Rental—$14.50   Purchase—$64.00
(1534-B) 7-1½ hour cassettes
Rental—$14.50   Purchase—$56.00
Read by Grover Gardner

In this, the last of his prize-winning series on American presidential politics, Theodore H. White explains the transformation of American politics over the past 25 years.

White sets the stage by describing the forces molding American politics . . . from television to the Great Inflation. He revisits elections, from Dwight D. Eisenhower to Ronald Reagan, and suggests how future contests might develop. He argues that events shape the man rather than vice versa: "I have learned that such men are cast up by events and forces larger than individuals."

"A clear and uncluttered look at the tumultuous decades that we find ourselves in." *(Editorial Review Service)*

APPEASEMENT: A STUDY IN POLITICAL DECLINE

By A.L. Rowse
(1562) 5-1 hour cassettes
Rental—$11.50   Purchase—$40.00
Read by Stuart Courtney

Appeasement is a vitriolic essay in which the author takes to task those responsible for Britain's policy of appeasement in the 1930's.

Rowse particularly castigates Chamberlain and his circle for Munich and explains how so many people could have been so wrong. He blames them for their ignorance of modern history and for holding a Victorian system of values in which Empire was more important than Europe.

Other A.L. Rowse titles in the B-O-T catalog are listed in the Index under the author's name.

THE ARMADA

By Garrett Mattingly
(1068) 9-1½ hour cassettes
Rental—$16.50   Purchase—$72.00
Read by James Cunningham

In The Armada, Garrett Mattingly has written far more than a history of the defeat of the Spanish fleet in 1588. Meticulous in describing its disastrous fate, he also discusses the profound effects of Philip's decision on every kingdom in Europe. A Book Society choice in England, a selection of the History Book Club and Book-of-the Month Club in the United States, *The Armada* received the National Book Award for non-fiction and a Pulitzer special citation.

THE ARMY OF THE POTOMAC—PART I MR. LINCOLN'S ARMY

By Bruce Catton
(1139-A) 9-1½ hour cassettes
Rental—$16.50   Purchase—$72.00
Read by James Cunningham

This is the first volume of Catton's award-winning trilogy, *The Army of the Potomac.* The army springs to life in accounts gathered from diaries and letters of ordinary foot soldiers who discovered that their skylarking "picture book" war was grim and deadly, as wars must ever be. *Mr. Lincoln's Army* never forgets—as histories frequently do—that wars were fought by men, and for battles to come alive, they must be told in the words of those who did the fighting.

Interval delivery convenience See page 2

THE ARMY OF THE POTOMAC—PART II GLORY ROAD

By Bruce Catton
(1139-B) 10-1½ hour cassettes
Rental—$16.50 Purchase—$80.00
Read by James Cunningham

Glory Road recounts the campaigns of late 1862 and early 1863, highlighting the fierce encounters at Fredericksburg, Chancellorsville and Gettysburg. Excerpts from letters, diaries, recollections and official reports give reality to the descriptions of battles, camps and citizen soldiers. *Glory Road* is a vivid account not only of military campaigns, but also of the internal upheaval of the North at war.

THE ARMY OF THE POTOMAC—PART III A STILLNESS AT APPOMATTOX

By Bruce Catton
(1139-C) 11-1½ hour cassettes
Rental—$16.50 Purchase—$88.00
Read by James Cunningham

This final volume in the author's trilogy describes the last year of the Civil War, after Grant became commander of the armies. In his review of this book, David Donald said, "What Mr. Catton has done is write the life history of an army . . . but these superb volumes are not merely accurate and provocative history; the combination of literary brilliance and deep human compassion makes them a memorable and moving saga of Americans at war."

ASSAULT IN NORWAY

By Thomas Gallagher
(1045) 8-1 hour cassettes
Rental—$14.50 Purchase—$64.00
Read by Dan Lazar

Assault in Norway is the true story of an Allied attack in the fall of 1942 on a German strategic materials plant located in Nazi-occupied Norway. A venturous group of ten Norwegian patriots, rigorously trained by British Intelligence, is assigned to disable and destroy the "heavy water" production plant at Vemork, Norway. Despite Nazi guards, numbing winter weather and delaying mishaps, the team assiduously pursues its mission. Gallagher tells in dramatic detail the steps the Allies took to cripple Nazi efforts towards the production of a nuclear bomb.

AT DAWN WE SLEPT
The Untold Story of Pearl Harbor

By Gordon W. Prange
(1976-A) 10-1½ hour cassettes
Rental—$16.50 Purchase—$72.00
(1976-B) 8-1½ hour cassettes
Rental—$15.50 Purchase—$64.00
(1976-C) 8-1½ hour cassettes
Rental—$15.50 Purchase—$64.00
Read by John MacDonald

Gordon Prange devoted his life to understanding our war with Japan. He saw Pearl Harbor for what it was: a military classic, one of the great surprise attacks in history. He also saw it as a warning to keep us from an even more dread opening blow.

Prange was well suited to his task. As former chief of the Historical Section in Japan under General MacArthur, he interviewed virtually every surviving Japanese officer who took part in the Pearl Harbor operation, as well as every important U.S. source.

"Prange's personal meetings with people on both sides enable him to tell the story in such personal terms that the reader is bound to feel its power . . . it is impossible to forget such an account." *(The New York Times Book Review)*

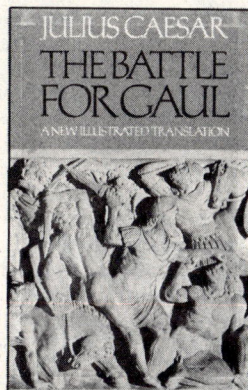

THE BATTLE FOR GAUL

By Julius Caesar
(1438) 8-1½ hour cassettes
Rental—$15.50 Purchase—$64.00
Read by Bob Erickson

Julius Caesar was for a few years the undisputed master of the Roman world—devoted to expanding Roman supremacy and his own fame. *The Battle for Gaul* contains seven books of Caesar's *Commentaries* on his campaign in Gaul from 58 to 50 B.C. in their original narrative sequence.

These unparalleled accounts of war in Western Europe in the closing years of the Roman republic are clear and exciting. We feel the immediacy of the moment as we listen to Caesar's dramatic story of his daring expedition into Germany and unprecedented bridging of the Rhine, the decimation of two Roman legions in a forest ambush, and the heroic last defense of 80,000 Gauls in central France.

THE BATTLE FOR THE WEST— THERMOPYLAE

By Ernle Bradford
(1730) 8-1 hour cassettes
Rental—$14.50 Purchase—$64.00
Read by Walter Zimmerman

The whole of the East is on the move. Day after day, armies of men tramp the dusty roads of Asia Minor . . . Persians with shields and stabbing swords, Arabs on camels, mountain men from the Causasus, Libyan charioteers, horsemen from central Iran.

Over this vast projection of imperial force stands the Emperor Xerxes, ringed round by his immaculate royal guard. The year is 480 B.C., and Xerxes has given the order to invade Europe.

"This account is a memorial to those ancient Greeks who, so many centuries ago, ensured that their patterns of freedom and individual liberty should survive in the West." *(Book Review Service)*

BATTLES LOST AND WON

By Hanson W. Baldwin
(1015) 12-1½ hour cassettes
Rental—$17.50 Purchase—$96.00
Read by Daniel Grace

Hanson Baldwin, the author of *Battles Lost and Won,* was military editor and analyst of *The New York Times* from 1942 through 1968. He reviews 11 great campaigns of WW II. The battles selected "present a cross-section of the world's greatest war—from the Polish campaign, where blitzkrieg was born, to Okinawa, 'the last battle,' where the kamikaze portended the coming menace of the missile." *Battles Lost and Won* combines the emotional and dramatic immediacy of tremendous events with the knowledge and wisdom of subsequent years.

BEHIND RUSSIAN LINES

By Sandy Gall
(1832) 8-1 hour cassettes
Rental—$14.50 Purchase—$64.00
Read by John MacDonald

In the summer of 1942, Sandy Gall set off for Afghanistan on the hardest assignment of his life. During his career as a reporter he had covered wars and revolutions but he had never been required to walk all the way to an assignment and back again—dodging Russian bombs *en route.*

He and a film crew hiked from Pakistan to the Panjsher Valley—a two-week trek. Their goal was the stronghold of the resistance leader Masud. When Russian fighters pounded the Panjsher as prelude to a full-scale ground attack, Gall and his team fled with their prized documentary.

"An enthralling book . . . Gall's dramatic adventures behind Russian Lines are a tribute to the Afghan freedom fighters." *(Readers Reviews)*

THE BIG SHOW

By Pierre Clostermann
(2157) 7-1½ hour cassettes
Rental—$15.50 Purchase—$56.00
Read by Gary Martin

Pierre Clostermann joined the Free French Forces in 1941 as a fighter pilot and later served as squadron leader in the RAF. Whether he is describing a deadly duel with a Focke-Wulf or the excitement of a 400-mile-an-hour strafing run at treetop level, Clostermann lets the reader share his experience.

In the cramped cockpit of a flashing Spitfire you live the dangers, strains and exhilaration of 420 sorties against Nazi air and ground forces.

"The Big Show is no backward look but flying and fighting as it really happened . . . recorded at the end of each day's heated action with all the skill, speed and daring." (*Reviews for Readers*)

BLACK NIGHT, WHITE SNOW

By Harrison Salisbury
(1275-A) 10-1½ hour cassettes
Rental—$16.50 Purchase—$80.00
(1275-B) 10-1½ hour cassettes
Rental—$16.50 Purchase—$80.00
Read by Wolfram Kandinsky

The fall of the Romanov dynasty and the triumph of Lenin's revolution catapulted Russia into the 20th century. *Black Night, White Snow* gives us a panoramic narrative that is fast moving and impeccably researched. Calling on documents, letters, reports, diaries, memoirs, novels and newspapers of that time, Salisbury gives us fresh facts about the revolution.

Harrison Salisbury has spent nearly half a lifetime in Russia. His heralded series, *Russia Reviewed,* brought him the Pulitzer Prize for journalism in 1955.

Other Salisbury titles available from B-O-T include: *The 900 Days: The Siege of Leningrad* and *The War Between Russia and China.*

BLENHEIM

By David Green
(1392) 6-1 hour cassettes
Rental—$12.50 Purchase—$48.00
Read by Stuart Courtney

In August 1704, during the war of the Spanish succession, an army of Britons and Austians under Marlborough and Prince Eugene defeated an army of French and Bavarian soldiers near the village of Blenheim, in West Germany. In consideration of his military services, a princely mansion was erected for the Duke of Marlborough and named Blenheim Palace.

David Green has used contemporary records and unpublished letters of the time in his recreation of this famous battle, which brought to a close the ten-year string of French victories. He then traces Marlborough's triumphal return to London and the building of Blenheim Palace.

BLOODY AACHEN

By Charles Whiting
(1659) 5-1 hour cassettes
Rental—$11.50 Purchase—$40.00
Read by Justin Hecht

Aachen. For more than 1,000 years it stood as an imperial city, symbol of German nationalism. But in September 1944, as Allied forces pressed forward and the Third Reich neared collapse, Aachen earned a new place in history as the first German city ever besieged by the U.S. Army.

"Bloody Aachen is more than a story of a military operation. It also tells of people in a Catholic city who opposed the Hitler regime and remained behind—against orders and against odds—determined to defend their homes; of men, women and children who fought to survive in the ruins and unwittingly, aided their Nazi enemy." (*Publisher's Source*)

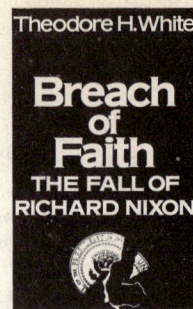

Theodore H. White
Breach of Faith
THE FALL OF RICHARD NIXON

BREACH OF FAITH: THE FALL OF RICHARD NIXON

By Theodore H. White
(2134) 12-1½ hour cassettes
Rental—$17.50 Purchase—$96.00
Read by John MacDonald

The Nixon crisis of 1973-1974 threatened the nation in ways we did not immediately understand. Stripped of drama and confusion, however, the problem was that our President had placed himself above the law. The nation had to decide whether that could be allowed.

Theodore H. White starts this story with the last days of Richard Nixon in the White House—as those closest recognized that he had deceived them and that they must force him out.

He follows the thread of manipulation back to its origin 20 years earlier and shows how the Nixon team came to see politics as war in which no quarter was given, in which the White House was a command post where ordinary rules did not apply, where power could be used without restraint.

"Absolutely fascinating as history and narrative . . . and as classical tragedy." (*E.R.S. Reviews*)

THE BROKEN SEAL

By Ladislas Farago
(1702) 12-1½ hour cassettes
Rental—$17.50 Purchase—$96.00
Read by Wolfram Kandinsky

Was there a conspiracy in the White House to maneuver the Japanese into war? Were the commanders in Hawaii derelict in their duty? Exactly how much did the United States know about Japanese intentions on the eve of Pearl Harbor?

Here for the first time is the whole secret history of Japanese and American code-breaking operations between 1921 and 1941—a fascinating progression of clandestine events that culminated at Pearl Harbor.

For much of his life, Ladislas Farago was involved with intelligence. During WW II he served as Chief, Research and Planning, U.S. Naval Intelligence, Special Warfare Branch.

THE CENTENNIAL HISTORY OF THE CIVIL WAR—PART I THE COMING FURY

By Bruce Catton
(1202-A) 14-1½ hour cassettes
Rental—$18.50   Purchase—$112.00
Read by Michael Prichard

The Coming Fury is the first book in Bruce Catton's trilogy, *The Centennial History of the Civil War*. As in his earlier trilogy, *The Army of the Potomac*, Catton proves himself a master in combining readability with an enormous number of facts. He draws heavily on battlefield correspondence and published recollections of survivors. The material is vivid in detail. *The Coming Fury* opens with the Democratic convention of 1860 and ends with the Battle of Bull Run in July, 1861, the first major encounter of the Civil War.

THE CENTENNIAL HISTORY OF THE CIVIL WAR—PART II TERRIBLE SWIFT SWORD

By Bruce Catton
(1202-B) 13-1½ hour cassettes
Rental—$18.50   Purchase—$104.00
Read by Michael Prichard

Terrible Swift Sword is Part II of Bruce Catton's trilogy of the Civil War. In it, he examines two turning points which changed the scope and meaning of the war. First, he describes how events seemed to take charge, and then how the sweeping force of all-out conflict changed the war's purpose, making it into a war for human freedom. It was this enlargement of the war to end slavery that "in the end pushed America's own horizon all the way out to infinity."

THE CENTENNIAL HISTORY OF THE CIVIL WAR—PART III NEVER CALL RETREAT

By Bruce Catton
(1202-C) 13-1½ hour cassettes
Rental—$18.50   Purchase—$104.00
Read by Michael Prichard

Never Call Retreat is Bruce Catton's third volume in his epic trilogy, *The Centennial History of the Civil War*. It chronicles the relentless bloodletting from Fredericksburg through each succeeding and increasingly bitter campaign to the final clash of the great armies. More than just another military history, *Never Call Retreat* describes the impact of Lincoln's assassination and the tenuous beginnings of the gigantic task of reconstruction, a task which continues to this day.

CHARLIE COMPANY

By Peter Cochrane
(1785) 7-1 hour cassettes
Rental—$13.50   Purchase—$56.00
Read by Rupert Keenlyside

Of the many books about WW II, *Charlie Company* is something special. It is the story of the Cameron Highlanders.

Peter Cochrane joined the company as a young platoon commander in 1940. He won the DSO for his part in the North African campaign.

From his own experience Cochrane resurrects a small group of soldiers of whom any country would be proud. What emerges is war with all its horrors, but balanced by humor and the wonderful spirit of exceptional men.

"A truly remarkable story of heroism and endurance . . . a deeply moving book." —Ian Chapman.

CHARLIE COMPANY: WHAT VIETNAM DID TO US

By Peter Goldman and Tony Fuller
(2118) 8-1½ hour cassettes
Rental—$15.50   Purchase—$64.00
Read by John MacDonald

There were no homecoming parades for the million men and women who served in the longest war America ever fought . . . the only war it has ever lost. This is a book about 65 of those nearly forgotten men who soldiered in the late 1960's in a gook-hunting, dirt-eating, dog-soldiering infantry unit called Charlie Company.

They were boys then, 19 or 20 years old on the average. The Army snatched them up out of small towns, suited them up as soldiers and sent them off to a place they could not locate on a map to fight a war they did not understand.

Charlie Company is not a military history. It is not a record of great battles or a moral commentary. It is instead a chess game viewed by the pawns. It is a collective memoir of the war and the homecoming, filtered through time and pain, anger and guilt, bitterness and forgetfulness.

"An absorbing book by two distinguished journalists. Their chronicles provide a meaningful dimension to the Vietnam tragedy that may enlighten future generations of the real costs of war." —Tim O'Brien

COUNTERCOUP: STRUGGLE FOR CONTROL OF IRAN

By Kermit Roosevelt
(1278) 7-1 hour cassettes
Rental—$13.50   Purchase—$56.00
Read by Justin Hecht

It was typical June weather in Washington: hot and humid. Kermit Roosevelt, grandson of Theodore Roosevelt and a veteran of the OSS, was hurrying to a meeting with John Foster Dulles at the State Department. That meeting in 1953 was to lead to one of the greatest triumphs in America's covert operations in foreign affairs. For at that time it was believed that Iran, under the leadership of Prime Minister Mossadegh, was slipping under Russian domination. At the meeting in Dulles' office, Kermit Roosevelt was given the go-ahead to mastermind the overthrow of Mossadegh and return the Shah to the Peacock throne.

CRIMSONED PRAIRIE

By S.L.A. Marshall
(1177) 6-1½ hour cassettes
Rental—$13.50   Purchase—$48.00
Read by Michael Prichard

Crimsoned Prairie is the story of the Indian wars on the Great Plains told by one of America's foremost writers on military affairs. The long war between America's neglected post-Civil War Army and the Sioux, Cheyenne and other Plains Indians has been covered in many books, but this is the first to provide a thorough-going analysis of military tactics.

Special 10% discount
See page 2

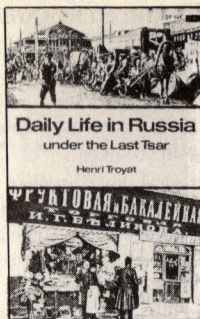

DAILY LIFE IN RUSSIA: Under the Last Tsar

By Henri Troyat
(1833) 7-1/2 hour cassettes
Rental—$15.50   Purchase—$56.00
Read by Wolfram Kandinsky

This book is a vivid account of life in Moscow, "the most Russian of Russian cities," in 1903, a year before Russia's disastrous war with Japan and two yars before the failed 1905 revolution.

Henry Troyat tells his story through the eyes of a fictional young Englishman visiting a prosperous Russian merchant family. He sees Moscow as it was, from public entertainments to private, from family gatherings to the devotions of the Orthodox.

"Sets the stage for the revolution that took place 15 years later." *(Reports for Readers)*

Troyat's biographies *Catherine the Great* and *Ivan the Terrible* are also available from B-O-T.

THE DAY LINCOLN WAS SHOT

By Jim Bishop
(2041) 6-1/2 hour cassettes
Rental—$14.50   Purchase—$48.00
Read by Allen Cornell

On April 14, 1865 John Wilkes Booth, an actor and as improbable a character as Lee Harvey Oswald or Sirhan Sirhan, shot Abraham Lincoln in the head, from behind, as the president enjoyed an evening at Ford Theater. Lincoln died the next morning.

The Day Lincoln Was Shot is a moment by moment account of the last 24 hours of the president's life. From 7:00 a.m. Friday until 7:22 a.m. Saturday, the moment Lincoln took his last breath, Jim Bishop narrates the chain of events that changed the course of Reconstruction. Lincoln's approach to the South, statesmanlike and generous, never had a chance after his death, and hopes for a compassionate reconciliation between the two sides were buried with him.

"Reads like a novel—holds you in suspense like a detective story." *(Pittsburgh Press)*

DEATH OF A DIVISION

By Charles Whiting
(1658) 5-1 hour cassettes
Rental—$10.50   Purchase—$40.00
Read by Christopher Hurt

Bearing the proud nickname "The Golden Lions," the U.S. 106th Infantry Division was routed on the night of December 6, 1944, in what was described by the official historian as "the most serious reverse suffered by American arms during the operations of 1944-5 in the European theater." The division historian himself put it more colorfully: "Panic, sheer unreasoning panic, flamed the road all day and into the night. Everyone, it seemed, who had any excuse, and many who had none, were going West that day."

Charles Whiting is a military historian whose books include *Bloody Aachen* and *Massacre at Malmedy,* both available from B-O-T.

DISPATCHES

By Michael Herr
(1932) 6-1/2 hour cassettes
Rental—$13.50   Purchase—$48.00
Read by Christopher Hurt

Michael Herr experienced Vietnam firsthand—not as a soldier but as a war correspondent for *Esquire* magazine. Dispatches is his personal journal chronicling his journey through that nightmare.

"I was overwhelmed . . . it summons up the very essence of that war—I believe it may be the best personal journal about war, any war, that any writer has ever accomplished." *(Chicago Tribune)*

A DISTANT MIRROR

By Barbara W. Tuchman
(1737-A) 12-1/2 hour cassettes
Rental—$17.50   Purchase—$96.00
(1737-B) 8-1/2 hour cassettes
Rental—$15.50   Purchase—$64.00
Read by Larry McKeever

The 14th century gives us two contradictory images: on one hand crusades and castles, cathedrals and chivalry; on the other, ferocity and spiritual agony—a world plunged into chaos.

Barbara Tuchman dispels the myths and shows us the era in its rhythms, and in the grain and texture of domestic life . . . what childhood was like, what marriage meant, how money, taxes and war dominated the lives of serf, noble and clergy.

"Beautifully written, careful and thorough in its scholarship . . . What Tuchman does superbly is tell how it was . . . No one has ever done this better." *(The New York Times Review of Books)*

EARLY NARRATIVES OF THE NORTHWEST 1634-1699

Edited by Louise Phelps Kellogg
(1429) 9-1/2 hour cassettes
Rental—$16.50   Purchase—$72.00
Read by Grover Gardner

Early Narratives of the Northwest is a jeweled collection of stories by 17th century adventurers who discovered the Great Lakes, the plains of Illinois and the astonishing Mississippi River.

These journals cover the voyages of Joliet and Marquette, La Salle, Tonty and others who pioneered trade and missionary work in the Great Lakes area. "The narratives of the early Frenchmen who traversed the Old Northwest possess a charm that will always appeal to the student of history." *(Nation)*

EISENHOWER AT WAR

By David Eisenhower
(2158-A) 9-1½ hour cassettes
Rental—$16.50   Purchase—$72.00
(2158-B) 10-1½ hour cassettes
Rental—$16.50   Purchase—$80.00
(2158-C) 8-1½ hour cassettes
Rental—$15.50   Purchase—$64.00
Read by John MacDonald

Eisenhower at War reshapes our thinking about WW II in Europe and its legacy—the divided continent with which the world has precariously lived. This book also revises established portraits of the wartime leaders: Roosevelt, Churchill, Marshall, Montgomery and Eisenhower himself, of whom his grandson draws a far more complex and subtle portrait than seen before.

David Eisenhower reconsiders such settled issues as the Tehran Conference, the Allied decision to invade France, the Market-Garden disaster, the loss of Warsaw, Berlin and Prague, the Yalta Conference, and above all, the Soviet role in the defeat in Germany and the Allied response.

Based on voluminous primary sources and amplified by his personal knowledge of his grandfather's conduct during the war, Eisenhower's account illuminates a great historical moment in a new and brighter light.

ELIZABETH AND ESSEX

By Lytton Strachey
(1814) 6-1½ hour cassettes
Rental—$14.50   Purchase—$48.00
Read by Jill Masters

When the Earl of Essex succeeded his stepfather, the Earl of Leicester, as Queen Elizabeth's favorite, he was 21 and the Queen was in her mid-50's. She was imperious and demanding; he was spoiled and ambitious, but shrewd and with an eye toward the main chance.

Their relationship is an ideal subject for Lytton Strachey's sardonic but not unsympathetic analysis.

"Elizabeth and Essex shared common traits of ego and vanity, and they exercised a fascination for each other. Their relationship, a struggle for dominance with all the overtones of repressed sexuality, is all the more fascinating for the difference in their ages." *(E.R.S. Services)*

THE ELIZABETHANS AND AMERICA

By A.L. Rowse
(1556) 7-1½ hour cassettes
Rental—$15.50   Purchase—$56.00
Read by Jill Masters

Why should A.L. Rowse want to follow *The England of Elizabeth* and *The Expansion of Elizabethan England* with a book about *The Elizabethans and America?* Simply because it was the English who put their stamp on us, and not just any English, but the Elizabethans.

England staged a renaissance under the Virgin Queen. Everything flowered, particularly the institutions of government. Elizabeth midwifed the notion that individuals had inherent worth, that citizens were free, and that the right to govern flowed from them.

"We take our inheritance for granted, but it could have been different. Rowse helps us appreciate how chancey it was and by what a narrow margin the experiment worked in America." *(E.R.S. Services)*

THE ENGLAND OF ELIZABETH

By A.L. Rowse
(1555-A) 10-1½ hour cassettes
Rental—$16.50   Purchase—$80.00
(1555-B) 10-1½ hour cassettes
Rental—$16.50   Purchase—$80.00
Read by Jill Masters

The England of Elizabeth is A.L. Rowse's celebrated account in the era of the Virgin Queen. Like all great monarchs, she unified her country. Her influence was pervasive, and she put her stamp on the age.

Profound changes were at work during her reign. Throughout Europe the Catholic Church was being challenged in what later came to be called the Reformation, and in England a new group of people, neither aristocrats nor commoners, identified only as "gentry," sought political representation.

"Magnificent . . . one of those books in which knowledge becomes vitalized and turns into literature." *(The Chicago Sunday Tribune)*

ESCAPE FROM SINGAPORE— 1942

By Ian Skidmore
(1292) 6-1 hour cassettes
Rental—$12.50   Purchase—$48.00
Read by Richard Green

Escape from Singapore—1942 is the narrative of a minor but heroic detail of WW II. A small band of British soldiers refuses to obey an order to surrender to the Japanese at Singapore. One step ahead of the enemy, they take a tiny sailing canoe across the Bay of Bengal to Ceylon. The journey takes 36 days and nearly ends in disaster. A thrilling story of victory from out of the jaws of defeat.

THE EXPANSION OF ELIZABETHAN ENGLAND

By A.L. Rowse
(1557) 15-1½ hour cassettes
Rental—$18.50   Purchase—$120.00
Read by Jill Masters

Elizabeth ruled from 1558 to 1603. It is moot whether she inspired the tremendous increase in national energy or whether it would have occured without her. But it is certain that England started its 400-year run as a great power during her reign.

The Elizabethans marched forward on all fronts. Howard defeated the Armada; Drake and Raleigh found far-off lands; Shakespeare wrote his plays. Man was the measure of all things, and the "island race" prospered as never before.

"Rowse is a master, and anyone who wants to understand the origins of our modern world will love this book." *(E.R.S. Services)*

THE FACE OF BATTLE

By John Keegan
(1302) 10-1½ hour cassettes
Rental—$16.50   Purchase—$80.00
Read by Victor Rumbellow

What is it like to be in battle? John Keegan, a senior instructor at Sandhurst, the British Military Academy, speaks for soldiers who were present in the fray.

For examples Keegan selects Agincourt in 1415, Waterloo in 1815, and the Somme in 1916. What is common about them, what different? Agincourt was hand-to-hand combat, thrust and cut, fearful and personal encounter. At Waterloo, 400 years later, the battle was still largely personal. As it swayed back and forth, men on opposite sides came to recognize the same individuals they had fought off in previous charges.

Keegan closes his book with the Somme. For him it stands as the distillation of wars in the industrial age: long distance killing of faceless men by others who merely activate the instruments of destruction.

For faster credit card ordering call 1-800-626-3333

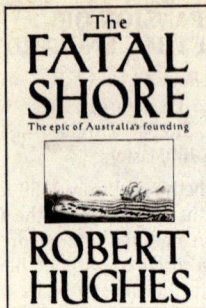

THE FATAL SHORE

By Robert Hughes
(2136-A) 11-1½ hour cassettes
Rental—$17.50   Purchase—$88.00
(2136-B) 10-1½ hour cassettes
Rental—$17.50   Purchase—$80.00
Read by Richard Brown

The Fatal Shore is a fascinating account of Australia's origins in the massive social experiment called "transport." A simple idea, transport called for the removal of criminals, thus the removal of crime.

The first fleet carrying 736 convicts, arrived at Botany Bay in 1788. eighty years and 100,000 convicts later, in 1868, the last ship dropped anchor. During this period the continent served as an enormous jail. But, against all odds, the inmates reformed themselves and Britain found she had on her hands not a jail, but a flourishing colony. How had it happened?

"Splendid . . . the narrative drive of *Mutiny on the Bounty*, the insight of de Tocqueville." —Arthur M. Schlesinger, Jr.

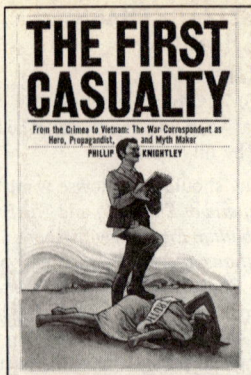

THE FIRST CASUALTY

By Phillip Knightley
(1125) 14-1½ hour cassettes
Rental—$18.50   Purchase—$112.00
Read by James Cunningham

"The first casualty when war comes is truth," pronounced Hiram Johnson to the United States Senate in 1917. To test the validity of that remark, Phillip Knightley, a special correspondent for the *London Times* compiled an account of war correspondents in action for the past 120 years. It suggests that our attitudes toward history are molded by what we read in war-time and that what we read too often bears little resemblance to reality.

FOCH: THE MAN OF ORLEANS

By Basil H. Liddell Hart
(2093-A) 7-1½ hour cassettes
Rental—$15.50   Purchase—$56.00
(2093-B) 6-1½ hour cassettes
Rental—$14.50   Purchase—$48.00
Read by Bill Kelsey

Foch was hailed as a savior in WW I, and for all the wrong reasons. He was irrationally aggressive, overly dedicated to the offensive, stolid and unimaginative. Yet he ended up in charge of all Allied armies and presided over five million deaths.

Basil H. Liddell Hart explains his purpose. "It is my strongest hope that this book will not be regarded as an attack on Foch. It certainly brings out his too absorbing devotion to the offensive in the theory and practice of war—and the grave consequences [in human life] not only to France but to her Allies. But, this question apart, the book is really an analysis of the limitations which high command suffered under the conditions of the World War."

FREE AS A RUNNING FOX

By T.D. Calnan
(1345) 8-1½ hour cassettes
Rental—$15.50   Purchase—$64.00
Read by Dan Lazar

T.D. Calnan was a pilot in the R.A.F. during WW II. One assignment, a reconaissance patrol, seemed particularly easy, and he writes:

"My altimeter read 31,000 feet and I was flying just 500 feet underneath the critical condensation level. My Spitfire was leaving no give-away trail of white vapor . . . nothing below would have the speed to catch me, so I felt safe."

But safe he was not, and the flight ended in disaster. Shot down, badly burned, Calnan was captured, then sent to prison camp. But he was not passive, and his attempts to get free were heroic.

FROM TIME IMMEMORIAL: The Origins of the Arab-Jewish Conflict over Palestine

By Joan Peters
(1992-A) 8-1½ hour cassettes
Rental—$15.50   Purchase—$64.00
(1992-B) 6-1½ hour cassettes
Rental—$14.50   Purchase—$48.00
Read by Mary Woods

If Joan Peters is right—and there is a real possibility she may be—then our policies are frequently at odds with the facts.

Peters shatters the widely-held belief that Arabs and Jews co-existed for centuries in the Arab World. She claims that Jews, along with other non-Muslims, were second-class citizens, oppressed for more than a millennium. She also claims that this hostility continues to underlie every Arab action toward the State of Israel.

"This book is an historical event . . . could well change the course of events in the Middle East." —Barbara W. Tuchman

FULL CIRCLE

By J.E. Johnson
(2063) 7-1½ hour cassettes
Rental—$15.50   Purchase—$56.00
Read by Gary Martin

Air fighting began in WW I when single, fabric-covered airplanes scouted "the other side of the hill." Pilots and observers initially waved to each other, later duelled with rifles and revolvers. Soon the two-seaters carried machine guns and began to fly in pairs. Pairs grew into squadrons and team fighting was born with German circuses (so called because their planes sported paint jobs as radical as today's dragsters) against British wings.

Today the supersonic interceptor flies alone, as did the first scouts, and within half a century the story of air fighting has come full circle.

Air Vice-Marshall Johnson was the top-scoring Allied fighter pilot of WW II, and an exchange pilot with the USAF in Korea. His narrative chronicles the achievements of the great fighter pilots of both wars.

GALLIPOLI

By Alan Moorehead
(1989) 9-1½ hour cassettes
Rental—$16.50   Purchase—$72.00
Read by Bill Kelsey

In Gallipoli, Alan Moorehead describes the great amphibious campaign of WW I. Winston Churchill, then First Lord of the Admiralty, was its strongest proponent. He was blamed for the fiasco that followed: a plan so admirable in concept yet so abominable in its execution.

The idea was to relieve pressure on the Western Front. An Anglo-French campaign to force the Dardanelles was designed to link up the Allies and sever Turkey from the other Central Powers.

But the idea stalled in planning and was delayed in execution. Results were disastrous. Turkish artillery and machine guns scythed down British troops. The failure cost Churchill his post: he served the remainder of the war as an officer in the trenches in France.

**Give a Books on Tape™
Gift Certificate
Call 1-800-626-3333**

THE GAME OF THE FOXES

By Ladislas Farago
(1703-A) 12-1½ hour cassettes
Rental—$17.50   Purchase—$96.00
(1703-B) 11-1½ hour cassettes
Rental—$17.50   Purchase—$88.00
Read by Wolfram Kandinsky

Those of us who have always felt that during WW II we were protected by J. Edgar Hoover and the F.B.I. may learn much from this account of German espionage in the U.S. and Great Britain.

Germany's intelligence service, the Abwehr, specialized in cloak and dagger. For example, German spies burrowed into communication centers in Washington and London, stole our super secret Norden bomb sight, succeeded even in tapping the Roosevelt-Churchill hot line.

"Farago has pieced together a fascinating chronology of Nazi spying inside and outside the U.S. and England between 1920 and 1945." *(Newsweek)*

THE GERMAN GENERALS TALK

By Basil H. Liddell Hart
(1454) 7-1½ hour cassettes
Rental—$15.50   Purchase—$56.00
Read by Justin Hecht

Like many of his brother officers, Liddell Hart served in both World Wars. Many German generals were junior officers on the Western front in the first encounter, master planners in the second.

In 1945 Liddell Hart had an unparalleled opportunity to meet with his opposite numbers to obtain their spontaneous impressions of the war.

"A 'must' for the historian, it is also a stimulating excursion for the casual rambler through the highways and byways of history." *(The New York Times)*

THE GHOST OF NAPOLEON

By B.H. Liddell Hart
(2122) 5-1 hour cassettes
Rental—$11.50   Purchase—$40.00
Read by Bill Kelsey

B.H. Liddell Hart believes that "thought working on thought is the most influential process in history. Yet, being intangible, it is less perceptible than the effects of action, and has always received far less attention than it deserves."

In *The Ghost of Napoleon,* Liddell Hart concentrates on two of these intellections, each of which vitally affected the course of history in the last two centuries. One was responsible for the triumphs of Revolutionary France and for Napoleon's empire; the other, for that ruinous conflict called WW I.

Liddell Hart is to military subjects what Peter Drucker is to business. Liddell Hart's thoughts can be examined at leisure in the B-O-T library. Two of his best are *The Soviet Army* and *Great Captains Unveiled.*

THE GREAT CRASH

By John Kenneth Galbraith
(2035) 7-1 hour cassettes
Rental—$13.50   Purchase—$56.00
Read by John MacDonald

The great crash here still refers to the stock market bust of 1929. But you can't crash from down, and everyone tends to forget how much Americans enjoyed the twenties, and how speculative was the age.

This is history—amusing and engrossing, but also serious and careful. The author has a further end in mind. All great booms are fed by operators who make leverage a way of life. Galbraith assesses the national mood of nearly 60 years ago, and leaves it to us to answer the question: will history repeat itself?

GREAT RIVER, WIDE LAND

By Armstrong Sperry
(2154) 7-1 hour cassettes
Rental—$13.50   Purchase—$56.00
Read by Paul Shay

"The Rio Grande! Watch is as it slithers across the wide land, this brown serpent of a river. Giant sloth and mastodon, primitive huntsmen, Spaniards in armor, friars with cross upheld—all drank of its waters.

"Indifferent to man-made marvels, the ageless Rio Grande pursues its course through mountain, mesa and desert, through the land of little rain and plenty of time, through mystery and color and grandeur, on its way to the sea."

Sperry was a prize-winning author who devoted his considerable talent to acquainting young people with stories, many factual, that introduced his readers to heroic vitures. *All Sail Set, Call It Courage* and *Pacific Islands Speaking* are all Armstrong Sperry titles available from B-O-T.

THE GREAT SIEGE

By Ernie Bradford
(1877) 6-1 hour cassettes
Rental—$12.50   Purchase—$48.00
Read by Walter Zimmerman

Modern day Malta is still the main British naval base in the Mediterranean and a NATO headquarters, but its role as a fortress is centuries old.

Ernie Bradford first visited Malta in 1942, at a time when it was enduring the second major siege in its history. He returned again in 1951 to research this study of the great siege of 1565 when Suleiman the Magnificent envisioned the important role Malta was destined to fulfill.

Hannibal, The Mediterranean, The Shield and the Sword and *Ulysses Found* are Bradford titles also available on cassette from B-O-T.

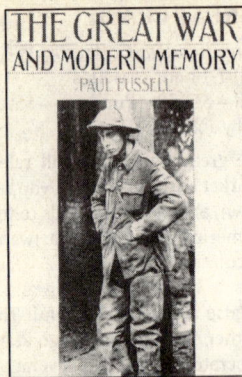

THE GREAT WAR AND MODERN MEMORY

By Paul Fussell
(1672) 11-1½ hour cassettes
Rental—$17.50   Purchase—$88.00
Read by Christopher Hurt

The Great War and Modern Memory is an absorbing exploration of the ongoing consequences of WW I.

Slaughter on the Western Front reached epidemic proportions and left in its wake a generation of cynics. Irony became the dominant literary mode.

Reflecting this change in attitude, writers like Siegfried Sasson, Robert Graves, Wilfred Owen and David Jones created a radical iconography and forced new images of violence into the language. Their writings, together with journalist's accounts and the private letters and diaries of ordinary soldiers, stamped the collective consciousness of the twentieth century. In this pioneering study, Fussell presents war as the harsh reality it is.

A GREATER THAN NAPOLEON

By B.H. Liddell Hart
(1544) 7-1 hour cassettes
Rental—$13.50   Purchase—$56.00
Read by John MacDonald

Publius Cornelius Scipio Africanus, a Roman general who lived in the 2nd century B.C., defeated Hannibal in the Punic Wars. In the Second Punic War, Scipio conquered Spain and ended the war by beating Hannibal in Africa. He returned home in triumph and was named Africanus after the country he conquered.

In his preface, B.H. Liddell Hart states, "The reason for this book is that, apart from the romance of Scipio's personality and his political importance as a founder of Rome's world dominion, his military work has great value . . . the art of generalship does not age, and it is because Scipio's battles are rich in stratagems and ruses that his story provides an unfailing object lesson even today."

THE GREATEST ACES

By Edward H. Sims
(1502) 7-1½ hour cassettes
Rental—$15.50   Purchase—$56.00
Read by Justin Hecht

This unique book is a thrilling, minute-by-minute account of the greatest aerial missions as recalled by the top WW II aces of the R.A.F., U.S.A.A.F. and the Luftwaffe.

There is Douglas Bader, one of the best of the R.A.F. fighter pilots despite two artificial legs; Adolf Galland of the Luftwaffe, who, subsequent to being shot down in France one morning, took off in another Messerschmitt that afternoon; another German ace, Hans-Joachim Marseille, the young "Pilot of Africa" who would steal into the British fighters' own formations to down several Hurricanes before the enemy could react; and Robert S. Johnson, the American who heroically defended Liberator and Flying Fortress formations.

THE GUNS OF AUGUST

By Barbara W. Tuchman
(1733-A) 8-1½ hour cassettes
Rental—$15.50   Purchase—$64.00
(1733-B) 6-1½ hour cassettes
Rental—$14.50   Purchase—$48.00
Read by Jack Hrkach

In her terse drama of this event, Barbara Tuchman analyzes the first 30 days of battle in the summer of 1914—a month which determined the course of WW I and ultimately the political shape of our present world. Tuchman begins with the funeral of Edward VII and traces each step that led to the inevitable clash. And inevitable it was, for this war had been planned by each side for a generation.

"The Guns of August is an epic never flagging in suspense, and Barbara Tuchman is a first-rate scholar and writer . . . its lessons are still valid today, a reminder to presidents, prime ministers and generals of war's treacheries and pitfalls." *(Christian Science Monitor and Washington Post)*

B-O-T has also recorded Tuchman's *The Zimmerman Telegram.*

HANNIBAL

By Ernle Bradford
(1731) 6-1 hour cassettes
Rental—$12.50   Purchase—$48.00
Read by Walter Zimmerman

During the second century B.C., the North African city of Carthage was a powerful commercial center. One of its leading citizens was Hannibal. Carthagian excursions into Roman territory led to the Punic Wars and Hannibal was called into service.

Ernle Bradford examines the campaign during the Second Punic War when Hannibal set out to invade Italy with a small force of select troops, crossing the Alps with a full baggage train intending to take Rome. For sixteen years the campaign continued and Bradford examines the tactics of the major battles and traces the reasons why Hannibal failed to conquer the Romans.

Ulysses Found and *The Battle for the West—Thermopylae,* both by Bradford, are also available from B-O-T.

HIROSHIMA

By John Hersey
(1307) 4-1 hour cassettes
Rental—$9.50   Purchase—$32.00
Read by Dan Lazar

Hiroshima is the story of six human beings who survived the first atomic bomb. With simplicity of genius, John Hersey tells what these six—a clerk, a widowed seamstress, a physician, a Methodist minister, a young surgeon and a German Catholic priest—were doing at 8:15 a.m. on August 6, 1945, when Hiroshima was destroyed. Then he follows the course of their lives hour by hour, day by day, in the classic piece that Lewis Gannett called "the best reporting to come out of this war."

THE HISTORY OF THE SECOND WORLD WAR

By Basil H. Liddell Hart
(1147-A) 12-1½ hour cassettes
Rental—$17.50   Purchase—$96.00
(1147-B) 12-1½ hour cassettes
Rental—$17.50   Purchase—$96.00
Read by Bernard Mayes

Basil H. Liddell Hart, English military strategist and historian, served as a captain during WW I, and later developed a theory of mobile warfare. A prophet without honor in his own country, his theories were adopted with dispatch by the Germans, who called them "blitzkrieg." Thus, this analysis of WW II is one of the few written by a man who was primarily a military expert.

"[This] is military history on a grand scale, and should become one of the classic accounts of the war." *(Library Journal)*

Other fascinating studies by Liddell Hart available from B-O-T are: *The Rommel Papers* and *The German Generals Talk.*

HOMAGE TO CATALONIA

By George Orwell
(1105) 8-1 hour cassettes
Rental—$14.50   Purchase—$64.00
Read by Richard Green

In 1936 Eric Blair, a novelist, critic and political satirist known by the pseudonym George Orwell, went to Spain to write about the Spanish Civil War. This book is his eyewitness account of that conflict. Nothing written since is as moving and alive with the terrors and triumphs of that time past. Orwell battled totalitarianism through his novels *Animal Farm* and *1984,* but for immediacy and passion nothing surpasses this chronicle.

I WAS A STRANGER

By General Sir John Winthrop Hackett
(1862) 6-1½ hour cassettes
Rental—$14.50   Purchase—$48.00
Read by John MacDonald

In one of the most unusual true stories of escape to come out of WW II, General Hackett shares the long-held secret of his stay in the home of members of the Dutch resistance.

When British troops were withdrawn after the Battle of Arnhem late in 1944, the general, badly wounded, had to be left behind. Hidden in the home of the de Nooij family, he recuperated until he was strong enough to make his escape.

"This is the story of a family that untiringly nursed an Allied officer back to health while hiding him from the enemy. It is also another view of the disaster at Arnhem, and how men in battle stand up to losing." *(E.R.S. Reviews)*

IF I DIE IN A COMBAT ZONE

By Tim O'Brien
(1840) 6-1 hour cassettes
Rental—$12.50   Purchase—$48.00
Read by John MacDonald

"Snipers yesterday, snipers today. What's the difference?" All they could do was keep their heads down. It wouldn't be any use to shoot back . . . you have to know which way to shoot first.

Tim O'Brien chronicles the dislocation a young American feels when he is yanked out of his Mom-and-apple pie midwestern home and thrown face first into the pit that was war-time Vietnam. The author lived this tale twice, the first time in Nam, the second when he wrote it for us.

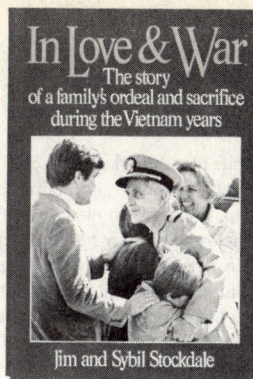

IN LOVE AND WAR

By Jim and Sybil Stockdale
(1466) 12-1½ hour cassettes
Rental—$17.50   Purchase—$96.00
Read by Christopher Hurt
and Mary Woods

On September 9, 1965, James Stockdale was shot down on a bombing run over North Vietnam. Captured, he remained in a Hanoi prison for seven years as the highest ranking POW.

Two struggles began. One was his battle to survive. The other was Sybil Stockdale's—trying to raise a family alone and live without her husband. Both rose to the challenge.

"Admiral Stockdale, one of the heroes of our time, is, it turns out, married to an equally remarkable heroine. Their story of astonishing bravery demonstrates that the Vietnam War was an occasion for noble service at home as well as in Indochina." —George Will

IN SEARCH OF HISTORY

By Theodore White
(1425-A) 8-1½ hour cassettes
Rental—$15.50   Purchase—$64.00
(1425-B) 9-1½ hour cassettes
Rental—$16.50   Purchase—$72.00
Read by Don Lazar

Theodore White's autobiography is the story of a man who literally covered the world, who understood that world and wrote about it brilliantly. *In Search of History* is a marvelous rags-to-riches autobiography, thoughtful, dramatic and funny, filled with perceptive details about events and personalities.

In White's parade of men and events, we meet Douglas MacArthur, both as outcast and conqueror; listen to a troubled Eisenhower preparing to lay aside his uniform and plunge into politics; visit Mao Tse-tung in his cave in Hunan; and trace the power-curve of America's greatness across the glory years at home and abroad.

INFAMY: PEARL HARBOR AND ITS AFTERMATH

By John Toland
(1971) 8-1½ hour cassettes
Rental—$15.50   Purchase—$64.00
Read by Jill Masters

The events of Sunday morning, December 7, 1941, have always been shrouded in mystery. The bombs had scarcely stopped falling before Americans of every stripe were calling for an investigation.

Infamy is John Toland's contribution to the literature. It is a fascinating and disturbing chronicle that confronts the most important questions. Was there a "winds execute" message? Why were Short and Kimmel not given vital information from the broken Japanese codes? Could Roosevelt have known of the approaching carrier force and have made a decision not to act?

"This is history at its best: a story of spies and suspense, widespread irresponsibility, and an international diplomatic game whose players tragically miscalculated the odds—at an untold cost in lives." *(Reviews for Readers)*

INSIDE THE THIRD REICH

By Albert Speer
(1309-A) 10-1½ hour cassettes
Rental—$16.50   Purchase—$80.00
(1309-B) 9-1½ hour cassettes
Rental—$16.50   Purchase—$72.00
Read by Michael Prichard

Speer was an ambitious young architect who caught Hitler's eye. Hitler's grandiose dreams of a greater German empire included architecture on a super-colossal scale, and he saw Speer as his planner.

When the war came, Hitler moved Speer to more immediate tasks and made him Minister of Armaments and War Production. From his vantage point within the inner circle, Speer gives us an intimate assessment of the Nazi elite during the war.

"Not only the most significant personal German account to come out of the war but the most revealing document of the Hitler phenomenon yet writen." *(The New York Times Book Review)*

Note: available for rent to all our customers, but for sale to libraries only.

**Collector's Editions™
from Books on Tape™
See page 3**

IRAN: THE UNTOLD STORY

By Mohamed Heikal
(1694) 6-1½ hour cassettes
Rental—$14.50   Purchase—$48.00
Read by Bob Erickson

One of the best-informed men in the Middle East, Mohamed Heikal met and interviewed most of the principal figures in the Iranian conflict, including the late Shah and Ayatollah Khomeini.

Heikal tells us what happened in the last days of the Shah's regime. He discloses for the first time what Khomeini's forces knew about American intentions and how they uncovered our secrets.

The author is a working journalist. He served as a minister of foreign affairs and minister of information for Gamel Abdel Nasser and was editor of Al Ahram, the leading newspaper of the Arab world, prior to his arrest by Anwar Sadat in 1981.

THE JOURNALS OF LEWIS AND CLARK

Edited by Bernard DeVoto
(1355) 14-1½ hour cassettes
Rental$—18.50   Purchase$—112.00
Read by Bob Erickson

Anxious to strengthen claims of the United States to the Oregon country and to stimulate commerce in the West, Thomas Jefferson authorized an expedition to locate a practical land/water route to the Pacific. He chose his private secretary, the young Captain Meriwether Lewis, to lead the expedition with the assistance of George Rogers Clark. Setting out in May 1804, the expedition established a new route to the Pacific, and arrived back in St. Louis in September 1806.

This condensation of the Lewis and Clark journals has been edited for the general reader by Bernard DeVoto, the gifted historian of America's frontier.

THE JUNGLE IS NEUTRAL

By F. Spencer Chapman
(1782) 10-1½ hour cassettes
Rental—$16.50   Purchase—$80.00
Read by Rupert Keenlyside

For more than three years, Colonel Spencer Chapman lived in the Malayan jungle, training Chinese Guerillas, harassing Japs, undertaking the most hazardous marches. Twice he was captured, twice he escaped. He suffered black-water fever, pneumonia and tick-typhus, in addition to almost chronic malaria.

Yet the jungle provides food and water, and unlimited cover for friend or foe. It is the attitude of mind that determines whether you go under or survive. The jungle is neutral.

A true story of WW II, "as a tale of endeavor and endurance it will not be surpassed." —Bernard Fergusson

THE KILLER ANGELS

By Michael Shaara
(1961) 9-1½ hour cassettes
Rental—$16.50   Purchase—$72.00
Read by Ken Ohst

In four bloody and courageous days, two armies fought for their conflicting dreams of Gettysburg. And as men died on those Pennsylvania fields so did our national innocence.

The Killer Angels won the Pulitzer Prize. Shaara said he told the story "from the viewpoints of Lee, Longstreet and others who fought there. Stephen Crane said that cold history was not enough; he wanted to know what it was like to be there. In order to live it he had to write it. This book was written for much the same reason."

This book was originally recorded for broadcast and is slightly abridged.

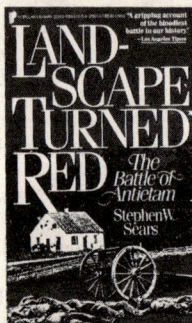

LANDSCAPE TURNED RED

By Stephen Sears
(2021) 10-1½ hour cassettes
Rental—$18.50   Purchase—$80.00
Read by Dick Estell
A Christopher Enterprises Recording

September 17, 1862: Antietam. It was the bloodiest day in American history, and with the possible exception of Gettysburg, the most pivotal battle of the Civil War.

"Draws on a new body of material . . . an exact historian, Mr. Sears has the novelist's eye for illuminating all that was awesome and pitiable in that furious encounter." *(The New York Times)*

Winner of the 1983 Fletcher Pratt Award from the New York Civil War Round Table.

Slightly edited for radio presentation.

THE LAST HAPPY HOUR

By Charles Hackett
(1174) 8-1 hour cassettes
Rental—$14.50   Purchase—$64.00
Read by Jonathan Reese

What is the Army to do with men who have genius IQs? Such soldiers more often than not are misfits: posting them to innoculous billets is S.O.P.

The Last Happy Hour tells of three brilliant but incompetent officers who are removed from combat during WW II. Stationed on a French tugboat permanently moored in an English port, the three ride it out for the duration in circumstances of manic comedy. After 30 years the men find themselves reunited, a circumstance which provides the framework for this tale.

THE LAST PARALLEL

By By Martin Russ
(1151) 8-1½ hour cassettes
Rental—$15.50   Purchase—$64.00
Read by Dan Lazar

Martin Russ was one of those unusual young men who wanted to serve in Korea as a Marine. In this book he relives his experiences—as a boot, in the line and even R&R's which he probably now blushes to recall!

The Last Parallel opens in a West Coast embarkation camp in August of 1952 and closes with Russ's discharge in September 1953. During the intervening 13 months we are reminded that Korea cost just as many lives as Vietnam, but that the soldiers who fought there were a different breed.

LIFE AND DEATH IN SHANGHAI

By Nien Cheng
(2109-A) 8-1/2 hour cassettes
Rental—$15.50   Purchase—$64.00
(2109-B) 8-1/2 hour cassettes
Rental—$15.50   Purchase—$64.00
Read by Penelope Dellaporta

In August 1966, at the beginning of the Cultural Revolution, a group of Red Guards ransacked the home of Nien Cheng, widow of a former Kuomintang diplomat. A few weeks later she was arrested. She remained in solitary confinement of nearly seven years.

A main selection of the Book of the Month Club, *Life and Death in Shanghai* is Cheng's powerful account of those harrowing years. A sharp observer, she draws sympathetic and remarkably unembittered portraits of the people she encountered and lived among.

"For all its suffering and sadness *Life and Death in Shanghai* is an exhilarating book, affording the privilege of intimacy with a wonderful writer and a courageous woman who embodies the nobility of the human spirit." *(Publisher's Source)*

MI 5: BRITISH SECURITY SERVICE

By Nigel West
(1792) 10-1/2 hour cassettes
Rental—$16.50   Purchase—$80.00
Read by Rupert Keenlyside

Nigel West's book traces the history of MI 5 from its modest beginnings in 1909 until 1945. The focus is on its role in WW II, recalling the enemy agents rounded up in Britain; the manipulation of the Axis espionage networks by the use of 'turned' Abwehr agents and the all-important check on its success provided by the intercepted German signals decoded at Bletchley.

Laced with true anecdotes as bizarre and readable as espionage thrillers, this book is based on interviews of Nazi and Soviet agents, counter-intelligence officers, case officers and, most remarkably, more than a dozen of the double agents.

THE MAKING OF THE PRESIDENT 1960

By Theodore H. White
(2110-A) 7-1/2 hour cassettes
Rental—$15.50   Purchase—$56.00
(2110-B) 6-1/2 hour cassettes
Rental—$14.50   Purchase—$48.00
Read by Grover Gardner

"White, a journalist who makes contemporary history come alive, takes the cold ashes of a political campaign and injects such a sense of immediacy that one feels again the tensions, uncertainties and emotional partisanship . . . a permanent contribution to the study of our democratic procedures." *(Kirkus Reviews)*

"Competent, penetrating, complete . . . the classic record of Kennedy vs. Nixon, this century's most dramatic presidential contest." *(Christian Science Monitor)*

America in Search of Itself and *In Search of History* are both Theodore H. White titles available from B-O-T.

THE MARCH TO TUNIS

By Alan Moorehead
(1029) 10-1 hour cassettes
Rental—$15.50   Purchase—$80.00
(1034) 8-1/2 hour cassettes
Rental—$15.50   Purchase—$64.00
(1037) 6-1/2 hour cassettes
Rental—$14.50   Purchase—$48.00
Read by Ian Whitcomb

Alan Moorehead is one of those gifted individuals who weaves the details of an event into memorable and coherent tapestry. In *The March to Tunis*, he recounts a campaign that pitted British and Americans against Italians and Germans, and both sides against the burning sands.

The fantastic scope of the desert campaign, the vast open spaces, the trackless dunes stretching off forever, the hardships by day and dangers by night.

"It is a fine piece of journalism. His quick eyes can size up a military weakness . . . but they do not miss the rediculous . . . or the bizarre . . . *(Manchester Guardian)*

MARINES DON'T HOLD THEIR HORSES

By Ian Skidmore
(2105) 5-1 hour cassettes
Rental—$11.50   Purchase—$40.00
Read by Bill Kelsey

WW II produced many heroes whose exploits were not known to the public. One of these was Alan Warren, a Colonel of British marines. He took the war behind enemy lines and, when captured, was a thorn in the flesh of his Japanese guards.

Colonel Warren spent three years in prison camps along the River Kwai. Though prisoners died every day, "Cocky" Warren stood his ground and raised morale to the highest possible level. As one contemporary said of him, "He was a master of time and space, fearless, upright, downright and straightforward."

"His story, clearly told, is a tribute to a courageous man and a valuable addition to military history." *(Publisher's Source)*

Other Ian Skidmore titles available from B-O-T include *Escape from Singapore-1942, Island Fling* and *Lifeboat V.C.*

MASSACRE AT MALMEDY

By Charles Whiting
(1657) 8-1 hour cassettes
Rental—$14.50   Purchase—$64.00
Read by Grover Gardner

In December of 1944, during the final flush of the German breakout in the Bulge, several SS divisions led by Colonel Johann Peiper swarmed the American encampment at Malmedy, in the Ardennes. American prisoners, wounded and unwounded, were summarily executed, as were many Belgian civilians, under the charge that the village had harbored American troops.

Colonel Peiper and a number of his lieutenants were subsequently charged for their roles in the massacre, and sentenced to hang. But incredibly, as with the majority of convicted war criminals, they were spared.

" . . . for those who recall the fears and turmoil of December 1944, it is a terribly real remembrance of dreadful events." *(Best Sellers)*

**Interval delivery convenience
See page 2**

THE MEDITERRANEAN

By Ernle Bradford
(1728-A) 8-1½ hour cassettes
Rental—$15.50   Purchase—$64.00
(1728-B) 8-1½ hour cassettes
Rental—$15.50   Purchase—$64.00
Read by Walter Zimmerman

Bounded by Europe, Africa and Asia, the Mediterranean is the crossroads from which our civilization evolved. Across its waters men sailed, traded and fought, while on its shores they built, conquered and dreamed.

Ernle Bradford is a sailor-historian who cruised the Mediterranean for many years. He believes that to understand its history one must first understand its geography, and he sees the interplay between east and west across the Mediterranean as the yeast of our culture.

Other Bradford titles recorded by B-O-T include *Ulysses Found* and *The Battle for the West—Thermopylae.*

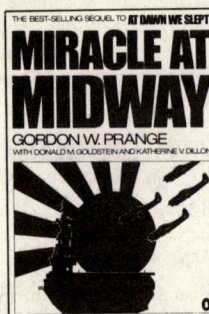

MIRACLE AT MIDWAY

By Gordon W. Prange
(2070) 11-1½ hour cassettes
Rental—$17.50   Purchase—$88.00
Read by Grover Gardner

Seven months after blitzing Pearl Harbor, the Japanese commander, Admiral Yamamoto, prepared to finish his work. He targeted a smaller United States force commanded by Chester Nimitz, a junior admiral. Given the superiority of the Japanese fleet, Yamamoto had every reason to expect victory.

But we had broken the Japanese code and Nimitz learned of Yamamoto's plans. He responded with tactics of beautiful flexibility. The Japanese, ablaze with confidence, suffered a crippling reverse. Midway put our navy back on its feet.

Based on original archival research as well as exclusive interviews with survivors on both sides, this book is a majestic sequel to *At Dawn We Slept*, also by Gordon W. Prange, also available from Books on Tape.

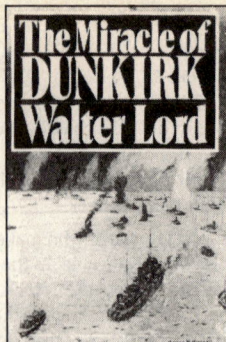

THE MIRACLE OF DUNKIRK

By Walter Lord
(1951) 7-1½ hour cassettes
Rental—$15.50   Purchase—$56.00
Read by John MacDonald

This is the story of the greatest rescue of all time. On May 24, 1940, some 400,000 Allied troups lay pinned against the coast of Flanders near the French port of Dunkirk. Hitler's advancing tanks were only ten miles away.

By June 4 more than 338,000 of these men had been evacuated safely to England. It was a crucial turning point in WW II, aptly called by Winston Churchill "a miracle of deliverance."

Rich in fresh information from the British archives, new material uncovered in France and Germany, and above all, the reports of some 500 participants, *The Miracle of Dunkirk* stands as a definitive account of this WW II epic event.

"Walter Lord is a writer who can take a chunk of momentous contemporary history in his teeth and shake it into a lively, well-researched narrative." (*The New York Times Book Review*)

MOLLIE AND OTHER WAR PIECES

By A.J. Liebling
(1972) 8-1½ hour cassettes
Rental—$15.50   Purchase—$64.00
Read by Wolfram Kandinsky

Liebling was war correspondent for *The New Yorker* magazine. In this volume he collected the best of his reporting on WW II and added a retrospective evaluation on the major event of his generation.

These war experiences, in Liebling's hands, become an instrument of communication and a means by which the reader can better understand what appears to have been the cataclysm of the century.

"Liebling was one of the great literary journalists of our time. It is a commentary on Liebling's stature that his colleagues, whose functions Liebling frequently criticized, are among those who most value his perennial freshness, his humor, his waspishness and his deep sense of humanity." (*Publisher's Source*)

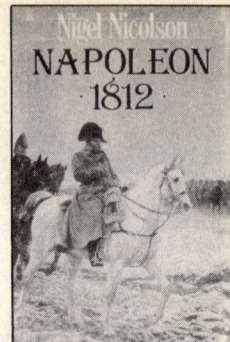

NAPOLEON: 1812

By Nigel Nicolson
(1904) 8-1 hour cassettes
Rental—$14.50   Purchase—$56.00
Read by Peter McDonald

Napoleon's invasion of Russia occupied only six months, June to December 1812, but during that period nearly half a million men died. At the start Napoleon was at the height of his power, at the end at his nadir.

Why did he invade Russia? Why, in spite of his early successes and the capture of Moscow, did he fail?

Nigel Nicholson writes that he wanted to " . . . examine the story afresh, consider why one of the greatest commanders in history lost and one of its least gifted won, how Tolstoy misinterpreted the drama and how Hitler, 130 years later, failed to benefit from Napoleon's example . . . and to consider in retrospect the folly and wastage of it all."

NEMESIS: TRUMAN AND JOHNSON IN THE COILS OF WAR IN ASIA

By Robert J. Donovan
(2140) 8-1 hour cassettes
Rental—$14.50   Purchase—$64.00
Read by Grover Gardner

Nemesis is the story of the calamitous experiences suffered by Presidents Truman and Johnson when they intervened in Korea and Vietnam to halt the spread of Communism by armed force.

Caught in the pressures of the Cold War, Truman and Johnson passed through comparable traumas that effectively ended their political power. Their party suffered, too: 1952 and 1968 were winners for Republicans.

As portrayed in *Nemesis*, the tragedy of both wars—and the main lesson it holds for today's involvement—is that initially modest commitments of force are rarely sufficient, but that larger efforts carry the threat of escalation. (Another recent B-O-T recording, *On Strategy* by Colonel H. G. Summers, examines this problem as it applied in Vietnam.

"Filled with anecdote and personality, written with clarity and passion, *Nemesis* is both an important document for today and a fascinating look at our recent history." (*Publisher's Source*)

THE NIGHT OF THE LONG KNIVES

By Max Gallo
(1027) 8-1½ hour cassettes
Rental—$15.50   Purchase—$64.00
Read by Wolfram Kandinsky

Hitler authored many infamous atrocities, but none more coldblooded or less understood than his early roundup and massacre of political dissidents. Max Gallo tells us the story of that bygone event in such a way that the years roll back and pose once again the question that plagues us to this day: What shall the western democracies do in the face of tyranny existing in a neighboring state? A disturbing book, and a very important one.

NIGHT WATCH

By David Atlee Phillips
(2100) 9-1½ hour cassettes
Rental—$16.50   Purchase—$72.00
Read by John MacDonald

For 25 years David Atlee Phillips stood "the night watch" for the CIA. He directed Western Hemisphere Operations when the Chilean government was overthrown (with CIA help) in 1973.

Phillips details his experiences in eighteen countries. Along the way, we learn much about "the company," certainly one of the least understood and most controversial pillars of our defense ever to have been invented.

"Phillips is as skilled a writer as he was a spook, and his astonishingly readable book makes a convincing case for the necessity of an intelligence service such as the CIA." —Joseph C. Goulden.

THE 900 DAYS: THE SIEGE OF LENINGRAD

By Harrison E. Salisbury
(1049-A) 8-1½ hour cassettes
Rental—$15.50   Purchase—$64.00
(1049-B) 10-1½ hour cassettes
Rental—$16.50   Purchase—$80.00
Read by Daniel Grace

C.P. Snow writes: "I have read nothing on Leningrad which moves me so totally, so painfully, as Harrison Salisbury's magnificent book.

The year: 1940. The problem: how to topple England. The answer: blitz Russia in a quick summer campaign, leaving the island kingdom alone and without hope in a fortress Europe dominated by the Third Reich. How Hitler's dreams ran afoul of stubborn Russian resistance is at the heart of this book about history's grimmest siege.

For quick ordering
1-800-626-3333

NOTES FROM CHINA

By Barbara Tuchman
(2128) 3-1 hour cassettes
Rental—$8.50   Purchase—$24.00
Read by Walter Zimmerman

During the summer of 1972, Barbara W. Tuchman spent six weeks visiting eleven cities and a variety of rural settlements in China—and *Notes from China* is the report of what she observed there.

The book, written in conjunction with President Nixon's historic visit, catches the flavor of China's diversity: workers in the city, provincial party bosses, military professionals, political cadres, farmers, scientists and educators.

A final and provocative section, "If Mao Had Come to Washington in 1945," includes the offer made by Mao to meet in Washington with Roosevelt. It speculates on how this meeting—which never took place—could have changed the course of postwar history.

A Distant Mirror, The Guns of August and *The Zimmerman Telegram* are other Tuchman titles available from Books on Tape.

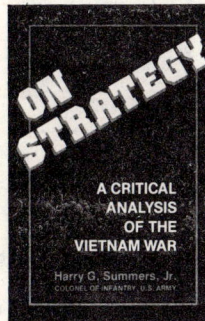

ON STRATEGY

*By Harry G. Summers, Jr.,
Colonel, U.S. Army*
(2025) 7-1 hour cassettes
Rental—$13.50   Purchase—$56.00
Read by John MacDonald

What went wrong in Vietnam? Applying the principles of war to the way we fought there, the author illustrates why our effort was such a disaster.

Some fatal errors: failure to learn from the Korean experience. Surrendering the initiative to the enemy. No comprehension of internal Vietnamese problems. Failure to discern how North Vietnam cloaked its real objectives behind a much inflated insurgency.

Colonel Summers wrote *On Strategy* for the Strategic Studies Institute of the U.S. Army War College, where he lectures. He served in combat in Korea and Vietnam.

"Illuminates a part of American history that is distorted by misunderstanding and emotion." —Hamilton Howze, General, U.S. Army (Ret.)

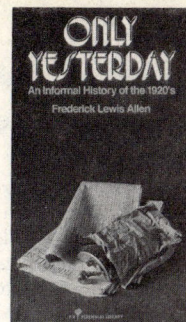

ONLY YESTERDAY

By Frederick Lewis Allen
(2042) 9-1½ hour cassettes
Rental—$16.50   Purchase—$72.00
Read by Larry McKeever

This book is the story of a distinct era in American history—the 11 years between the end of the war with Germany in 1918 and the stock market panic of 1929. Originally published in 1931, it remains popular today.

"Marvelously absorbing . . . *Only Yesterday* sketches the 20's from the collapse of Wilson and the New Freedom to the collapse of Wall Street and the New Era." *(Chicago Daily Tribune)*

OPERATION SEA LION

By Peter Fleming
(2048) 9-1½ hour cassettes
Rental—$16.50   Purchase—$72.00
Read by Richard Brown

In the summer of 1940 the Germans prepared to launch Operation Sea Lion, the invasion of England. The British, barely recovered from Dunkirk, rallied their defenses.

Both sides operated in great secrecy and, because the invasion never took place, the dramatic preparations for what would have been one of the watershed battles of history faded from memory. Not, however, before Peter Fleming rescued this fascinating story from military archives and the recollections of survivors who were involved.

OVERLORD

By Max Hastings
(2141) 10-1½ hour cassettes
Rental—$16.50   Purchase—$80.00
Read by Derek Partridge

On June 6, 1944, American and British armies staged the greatest amphibious landing in history. It began Operation Overlord, the battle for the liberation of Europe. Max Hastings, a war correspondent at the time, mades a study of D-Day and the battle of Normandy; and his book, far from traditional, overturns a host of national legends.

It describes in graphic detail the experience of Normandy, as Hastings follows the men and officers of the British, American and German forces all through the bitter weeks of this battle.

OWAIN GLYNDWR, PRINCE OF WALES

By Ian Skidmore
(1831) 6-1 hour cassettes
Rental—$12.50   Purchase—$48.00
Read by Ralph Coshan

Statesman, law-maker, scholar, military genius and folk legend, Owain Glyndwr is Wales' supreme national hero. This study by Ian Skidmore helps us understand why.

Few stories in British history compare with the career of this Welsh farmer who, in the 14th century, raised an army against the English and became Prince of his own country.

"Skidmore outlines Glyndwr's campaigns in careful detail and succeeds in separating myth and man . . . he brings to light some aspects of Glyndwr's career overlooked by historians . . . a fascinating portrait of an important historical figure." *(E.R.S. Reviews)*

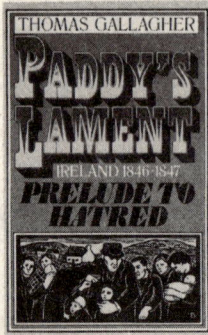

PADDY'S LAMENT
Ireland 1846-1847
Prelude to Hatred

By Thomas Gallagher
(1271) 7-1½ hour cassettes
Rental—$15.50   Purchase—$56.00
Read by John MacDonald

By the mid-19th century, Ireland was a country of 8 million, largely peasants, living as tenants on small plots, and never far from economic disaster. They depended on a single crop: potatoes.

Then tragedy intervened. In the summer of 1846, the potato crop failed. A quarter of the population starved in less than two years.

The history of three nations was changed and a hatred was born, a hatred that cut across the years and tears the daily fabric of life in England and Ireland, even today.

PATTON: A STUDY IN COMMAND

By Herbert Essame
(1291) 8-1½ hour cassettes
Rental—$15.50   Purchase—$64.00
Read by Justin Hecht

In *Patton: A Study in Command,* Essame examines each of Patton's major battles, its place in winning the war and the principles that guided Patton's strategies and decisions. In addition, the author compares Patton with his Allied colleagues, particularly Eisenhower and Montgomery and concludes that he outclassed them "in imagination, technique, and achievement." The portrait painted is that of a man who possessed all of the requirements of generalship. It is probable that Patton would have been pleased with Essame's professional analysis of his operational role.

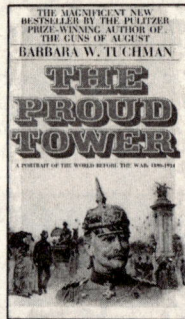

THE PROUD TOWER

By Barbara W. Tuchman
(2069-A) 8-1½ hour cassettes
Rental—$15.50   Purchase—$64.00
(2069-B) 9-1½ hour cassettes
Rental—$16.50   Purchase—$72.00
Read by Walter Zimmerman

What went wrong with the 20th century? It dawned with such hope but in its second decade collapsed into WW I. What can we learn from those prewar years?

Barbara Tuchman concentrates on society rather than the state. Her aim is "to discover the quality of the world from which the Great War came . . . The diplomatic origins are only the fever chart of the patient; they do not tell us what caused the fever. To probe for underlying causes and deeper forces one must operate within the framework of a whole society and try to discover what moved the people in it . . ."

Other works by Tuchman available from B-O-T include *A Distant Mirror, The Guns of August* and *The Zimmerman Telegram.*

PUTTIN' ON OLE MASSA

Edited by Gilbert Osofsky
(1039) 8-1½ hour cassettes
Rental—$15.50   Purchase—$64.00
Read by Michael Prichard

This unusual book is a compilation of slave narratives which have been verified by the editor. Stark and dramatic in their force, they tell of man's unquenchable desire for freedom and the lengths he will go to in order to achieve it. *Puttin' on Ole Massa* is a great testament to the spirit which burns in the hearts of all men.

THE REAL WAR

By Basil H. Liddell Hart
(1453) 12-1½ hour cassettes
Rental—$17.50   Purchase—$96.00
Read by Rupert Keenlyside

The Real War is a history of WW I unlike anything we have ever read. Liddell Hart sets the stage like a masterful dramatist. Bismark, Disraeli, Czar Nicholas and Kaiser Wilhelm emerge from the wings and drive their countries on a collision course.

The action ranges wherever Germany and the Allies lock in combat: Poland, Mesopotamia, Gallipoli, Caporetto, Bagdad, the North Sea and the Mediterranean. The origins of the war, the backroom agonies of the diplomats trying to avert it, the feelings of the generals who conduct it fill the pages of this authoritative study.

"Captain Liddell Hart has synthesized the immensity of the war into a single volume, presenting it tactically, critically, historically—a valuable work." *(Nation)*

THE RISE AND FALL OF ADOLF HITLER

By William A. Shirer
(1890) 4-1 hour cassettes
Rental—$10.50   Purchase—$32.00
Read by Larry McKeever

At daybreak on September 1, 1939, the German army poured across the Polish border while German bombers rained destruction from the skies, WW II had begun—"Hitler's war," as the British say.

As an American correspondent in Berlin, William Shirer had met Hitler, listened to his fiery speeches, and observed him firsthand. *The Rise and Fall of Adolf Hitler* is based on what Shirer saw and on his later research of the massive files captured by the Allies.

"Hitler's conquest was classic. He double crossed his friends, massacred millions, plunged the world into its bloodiest war . . . and buried his own nation in the process. In Hitler, tryanny found nearly perfect exposition." *(E.R.S. Reviews)*

Special 10% discount
See page 2

THE RISE AND FALL OF THE THIRD REICH

By William L. Shirer
(2037-A) 12-1½ hour cassettes
Rental—$17.50   Purchase—$96.00
(2037-B) 12-1½ hour cassettes
Rental—$17.50   Purchase—$96.00
(2037-C) 12-1½ hour cassettes
Rental—$17.50   Purchase—$96.00
(2037-D) 8-1½ hour cassettes
Rental—$15.50   Purchase—$64.00
Read by Larry McKeever

No other powerful empire ever bequeathed to historians such mountains of evidence about its rise and fall as did the Third Reich. The Allied demand for unconditional surrender produced, when the bitter war was over and before the Nazis could destroy their files, an almost hour-to-hour record of the nightmare empire built by Adolf Hitler.

William L. Shirer watched and reported on the Nazis since 1925. He spent five and a half years sifting through this massive documentation. Out of it, and out of his own on-the-spot reporting of Germany and Europe over nearly four decades, he has written what may well be the definitive history of one of the greatest and most frightening chapters in the history of mankind.

ROCK ODYSSEY

By Ian Whitcomb
(1928-A) 7-1½ hour cassettes
Rental—$15.50   Purchase—$56.00
(1928-B) 6-1½ hour cassettes
Rental—$14.50   Purchase—$48.00
Read by Ian Whitcomb

In 1965 Ian Whitcomb's novelty rocker "You Turn Me On" was number eight on the national charts, along with entries from the Beatles, the Rolling Stones, The Beach Boys and the Byrds.

In 1966 he was nowheresville!—a certified rock 'n' roll flash in the pan.

"With survivor's humor Whitcomb tells both his and rock's story from their beginnings . . . he captures the inner workings of the pop music business as only a true insider can." *(Variety)*

"The story of the British invasion, the genesis of folk rock, the blooming of Flower Power, the Summer of Love, and the inner workings of the pop-music biz, all told as only a true insider can." *(Variety)*

THE ROMMEL PAPERS

By Basil H. Liddell Hart
(1093-A) 9-1½ hour cassettes
Rental—$16.50   Purchase—$72.00
(1093-B) 10-1½ hour cassettes
Rental—$16.50   Purchase—$80.00
Read by Wolfram Kandinsky

Field Marshal Erwin Rommel, "the Desert Fox" had a career that reached from the sand of Africa to Normandy's beaches. His audacious campaigns drove his staff to despair and stupefied the opposition.

All of the information included in *The Rommel Papers* was prepared by Rommel himself and collected and edited after the war by Basil H. Liddell Hart. The result is this study of modern combat generalship detailing not only the maneuvers of the battlefield but also the inner workings of Hitler's high command.

A RUMOR OF WAR

By Philip Caputo
(1122) 9-1½ hour cassettes
Rental—$16.50   Purchase—$72.00
Read by Wolfram Kandinsky

This best-selling, unsentimental story, a Book-of-the-Month Club selection, has already become part of the literature of combat. Caputo's clear-sighted narrative helps us understand the psychology of modern half-wars, where friend and foe are almost indistinguishable and every step, in jungle or city, may lead to terror or ambush. In 1965, as a Marine Corps officer, the author landed at Danang and for 16 unforgettable months battled heat, fatigue, disease and VC in a contest that admitted no rules.

THE RUSSIAN REVOLUTION

By Alan Moorehead
(2044) 8-1½ hour cassettes
Rental—$15.50   Purchase—$64.00
Read by Bill Kelsey

WW II's abrupt end brought us many gifts, none stranger than the papers of the German State. These were captured virtually complete, and to this day give up secrets.

One that emerges from Alan Moorehead's research is the extent to which Germany was involved in the Russian Revolution. The ironic result of this clandestine maneuver was Germany's sure defeat on the Eastern front in WW II.

"It all forms a fascinating chapter in the history of our century," states The Book-of-the-Month Club, "and the man ignorant of how that chapter unrolled is minus of the keys to an understanding of his own time and so in part himself—Moorehead hands us that key."

THE SECOND WORLD WAR: VOLUME I THE GATHERING STORM

By Sir Winston Churchill
(1261-A) 10-1½ hour cassettes
Rental—$16.50   Purchase—$80.00
(1261-B) 6-1½ hour cassettes
Rental—$14.50   Purchase—$48.00
Read by Richard Green

Churchill's six-volume undertaking earned for its author the Nobel prize for literature. This first volume covers the period from the Treaty of Versailles to Churchill's appointment as Prime Minister in 1940. During that time the western democracies pursued policies that practically invited aggression.

Churchill constantly warned of danger, and when at last he became Prime Minister in 1940, he felt all his life had been a preparation for this hour.

THE SECOND WORLD WAR: VOLUME II THEIR FINEST HOUR

By Sir Winston Churchill
(1262-A) 7-1½ hour cassettes
Rental—$15.50   Purchase—$56.00
(1262-B) 8-1½ hour cassettes
Rental—$15.50   Purchase—$64.00
Read by Richard Green

The year is 1940 and Britain has her back to the wall. Only a thin strip of sea holds Hitler at bay.

Writing in *The Saturday Review of Literature*, Crane Brinton says, "This is vintage Churchill. The great phrases are here, dramatically, lovingly prepared . . . Mr. Churchill has a central and most dramatic theme: Britain alone against her enemies, alone against our enemies, against the enemies of civilization. He makes the most of this theme with no concessions to the academic notion that the historian is above moral judgements as he is above emotion."

THE SECOND WORLD WAR: VOLUME III THE GRAND ALLIANCE

By Sir Winston Churchill
(1263-A) 9-1½ hour cassettes
Rental—$16.50   Purchase—$72.00
(1263-B) 8-1½ hour cassettes
Rental—$15.50   Purchase—$64.00
Read by Richard Green

This volume carries the history up to the middle of January 1942, and is even more absorbing than its predecessors. The beginning is an admirable survey of the way the war looked after the failure of the Germans in their first all-out attack on Britain.

Included are the bombing of Pearl Harbor and the subsequent great meetings between Roosevelt and Churchill. The sinking of the Bismarck is told magnificently, as might be expected from a man who was at one time the First Lord of the Admiralty.

THE SECOND WORLD WAR: VOLUME IV THE HINGE OF FATE

By Sir Winston Churchill
(1264-A) 10-1½ hour cassettes
Rental—$16.50   Purchase—$80.00
(1264-B) 10-1½ hour cassettes
Rental—$16.50   Purchase—$80.00
Read by Richard Green

The Hinge of Fate begins in the grim winter of January 1942, and concludes during the triumphant spring of May 1943. As Churchill states in the preface, "I have called this volume *The Hinge of Fate* because in it we turn from almost uninterrupted disaster to almost unbroken success."

As with the first three volumes, this is contemporary history based on the kind of access to documents only a man in Churchill's position could have—and written with the pen of an experienced historian.

THE SECOND WORLD WAR: VOLUME V CLOSING THE RING

By Sir Winston Churchill
(1265-A) 7-1½ hour cassettes
Rental—$15.50   Purchase—$56.00
(1265-B) 7-1½ hour cassettes
Rental—$15.50   Purchase—$56.00
Read by Richard Green

Closing the Ring covers the conflict from June 1943 to June 1944, extending from the invasion of Sicily to the eve of D-Day, June 6, 1944. As in the previous volumes, Churchill views the war from the perspective of British Prime Minister and Minister of Defense.

The grave differences between Churchill and his "great friend" Roosevelt are more pronounced here than previously, making the operational unity of the Western Allies look more than ever like a miracle—a miracle that perhaps only Churchill could have accomplished.

THE SECOND WORLD WAR: VOLUME VI TRIUMPH AND TRAGEDY

By Sir Winston Churchill
(1266-A) 7-1½ hour cassettes
Rental—$15.50   Purchase—$56.00
(1266-B) 8-1½ hour cassettes
Rental—$15.50   Purchase—$64.00
Read by Richard Green

Triumph and Tragedy brings to a conclusion this great chronicle of the Second World War. Inevitably, the interest of this volume is in the political tragedy rather than in the military triumph.

Churchill's personal touches and firsthand knowledge of events make these volumes an invaluable contribution to our own personal comprehension of the events that have shaped our age.

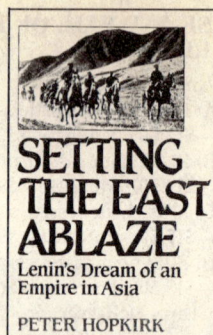

SETTING
THE EAST
ABLAZE
Lenin's Dream of an
Empire in Asia

PETER HOPKIRK

NEW

SETTING THE EAST ABLAZE

By Peter Hopkirk
(2068) 6-1½ hour cassettes
Rental—$14.50   Purchase—$48.00
Read by Richard Brown

Not content with Russia, the Bolsheviks tried to "set the East ablaze" with their heady new gospel of Marxism. This extraordinary tale of intrigue and treachery, barbarism and civil war echoes today in Afghanistan and Central America.

Lenin's dream was to liberate the whole of Asia. But his starting point was British India, the richest of all imperial possessions. So began a brutal undeclared war along Central Asia's Silk Road. It reached into China, Mongolia and Turkey. It involved Chinese warlords, Muslim visionaries, and officers of British Indian intelligence.

"An amazing story, full of adventure, charged with implications for today." (*Far East Economic Review*)

THE SHIELD AND THE SWORD

By Ernle Bradford
(1729) 6-1½ hour cassettes
Rental—$14.50   Purchase—$48.00
Read by Walter Zimmerman

The Knights of St. John, also called the Knights of Malta, trace their origin to Jerusalem where they began in charity and penance. But when they embraced the church militant, they made themselves preeminent in the Mediterranean. They were the master mariners, navigators and builders of their time.

Malta lay astride the sea lanes of antiquity. Thus when the Knights occupied and fortified the island they threatened Turkish expansion. In 1522 the Turks set out to destroy them, a task to which they brought great numerical superiority. Nevertheless, they failed . . . and a legend of invincibility attached to the Knights, a legend which in some measure endures to this day.

THE SINKING OF THE BISMARCK

By William L. Shirer
(2007) 4-1 hour cassettes
Rental—$9.50   Purchase—$32.00
Read by Larry McKeever

At 8:00 a.m. on May 21, 1941, a coded message arrived at the Admiralty in London. The *Bismarck,* the world's most powerful battleship, has been sighted heading for the North Atlantic. Swiftly, the British organize an armada of fighting ships to pursue. Before the *Bismarck* can get a chance to fire on any of the British convoys, she must be sunk.

In this book William L. Shirer reconstructs the one-week chase. The fighting spirit, courage and endurance of both the British and the German officers and crews are vividly described in this dramatic authentic account of the sinking of the *Bismarck.*

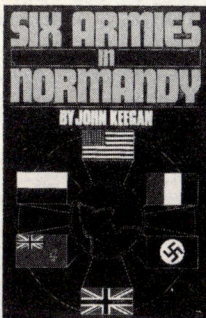

SIX ARMIES IN NORMANDY

By John Keegan
(1933) 9-1½ hour cassettes
Rental—$16.50   Purchase—$72.00
Read by Christopher Hurt

On D-Day, 1944, the armies of six nations converged on the beaches of France and began the final dramatic chapter of WW II.

The Americans, British, Canadians, Poles, Free French and Germans each had specific goals. Politics shaped many military considerations; where one began and the other ended was often unclear.

"The analysis of this historic action is carried out on many levels. Keegan weighs national character, illuminates the strategy of Allied and Axis leaders, and reminds us of the part played by heroism, individual and collective, in the outcome." *(Editorial Review Services)*

SON OF THE MORNING STAR

By Evan S. Connell
(1980-A) 7-1½ hour cassettes
Rental—$15.50   Purchase—$56.00
(1980-B) 7 1-1½ hour cassettes
Rental—$15.50   Purchase—$56.00
Read by Christopher Hurt

George Armstrong Custer, a hero to some, a disaster to others, cut an enigmatic and extravagant figure. One thing everyone agreed—he was fearless. When he first saw the line of Indian camps opposing him, a line more than four miles long, he whooped, "Hurrah, boys, we've got them!" Disregarding a Cheyenne warning, Custer rode to his death—and led to death every man of the Seventh Cavalry who followed.

Evan Connell brings his storyteller skills to this meticulously researched book, part biography of Custer, part history of the Plains Indian Wars. Connell dwells on the rare human details that historians often ignore: he tells of Crazy Horse on a pilgrimage to the burial scaffold of his infant daughter; Lt. Calhoun—who probably mounted the only organized defense at the Little Bighorn—carrying a cake into battle; and of Chief Gall listening to Mendelssohn's Wedding March.

**Books on Tape™'s service
is 100% guaranteed**

THE SOVIET ARMY

By B.H. Liddell Hart
(2056) 12-1½ hour cassettes
Rental—$17.50   Purchase—$96.00
Read by Bill Kelsey

This book traces the evolution of Russia's Army during the first half of the twentieth century. It was written by men who knew their subject: officers who had fought with or against the Russians. It is crammed with gripping, vital information.

Its aim is to review the striking power of the USSR both in the wider perspective of Russian history and in the light of lessons learned in WW II. The authors, many of them distinguished soldiers, cover every aspect of the Soviet Army. The result is a fascinating work of narrative history for all students of military affairs and international relations.

"Russia's ultimate weapon is her manpower. That it can be effectively mobilized is beyond doubt. Liddell Hart and his associates do us a service by describing its reach and limits, thereby helping us gain a better understanding of the world in which we live." *(History Book Club)*

SPANDAU: THE SECRET DIARIES

By Albert Speer
(1310-A) 7-1½ hour cassettes
Rental—$15.50   Purchase—$56.00
(1310-B) 7-1½ hour cassettes
Rental—$15.50   Purchase—$56.00
Read by Michael Prichard

On the first day of October 1966, Albert Speer, onetime Reich Minister for Armaments and War Production, and personal architect and confidant to Hitler, walked out of Spandau Prison, free for the first time since the end of WW II. Waiting for him were the more than 25,000 pages of notes and diaries he had secretly written and smuggled out of Spandau during the course of his 20-year sentence. As Speer himself said, "This [diary] stands in place of a life."

[Note: Available for rent to all our customers, but for sale to libraries only.]

On the first day of October 1966, Albert Speer, onetime Reich Minister for Armaments and War Production, and personal architect and confidant to Hitler, walked out of Spandau Prison, free for the first time since the end of WW II. Waiting for him were the more than 25,000 pages of notes and diaries he had secretly written and smuggled out of Spandau during the course of his 20-year sentence. As Speer himself said, "This [diary] stands in place of a life."

[Note: Available for rent to all our customers, but for sale to libraries only.]

SQUADRON AIRBORNE

By Elleston Trevor
(1707) 6-1/2 hour cassettes
Rental—$14.50   Purchase—$48.00
Read by Christopher Hurt

"Through the fog, an aircraft took shape by degrees, its photograph slowly developed by the strengthening light. Its outline might have been the outline of any object with gaunt angles protruding, meaningless angles that had nothing to do with a tailplane, or an undercarriage, or a propeller. The machine looked no more likely to rise into the air than dead timber . . . "

Yet it was a Spitfire, and Squadron Airborne is the story of those painfully young men who fought the battle of Britain in them during the summer of 1940. Their competence and courage gave Hitler his only defeat of those early war years and won from Churchill an unforgettable tribute: "Never have so many owed so much to so few."

Other Elleston Trevor titles available from B-O-T include *Badger's Wood, The Big Pick-Up, The Flight of the Phoenix* and *Gale Force.*

STILWELL AND THE AMERICAN EXPERIENCE IN CHINA

By Barbara W. Tuchman
(2156-A) 10-1/2 hour cassettes
Rental—$16.50   Purchase—$80.00
(2156-B) 11-1/2 hour cassettes
Rental—$17.50   Purchase—$88.00
Read by Walter Zimmerman

In *Stilwell and the American Experience in China* Barbara W. Tuchman realizes two objectives. First, venturing into the murk of America's defeat in China, she clarifies issues, assigns responsibilities and gives praise and blame—all with the detachment of an historian. Second, Tuchman presents General Stilwell in the round with an intimacy made possible by his unpublished papers

"This book lives up to the criteria Barbara Tuchman once laid down for historical writing: it has 'action, ideas, synthesis and significance.' " *(Saturday Review)*

"The most informative book the American public has ever had on the difficulties and failures of the American relationship with China." —Edwin O. Reischauer, Former U.S. Ambassador to Japan

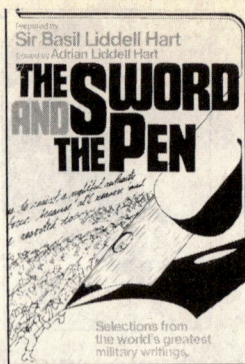

THE SWORD AND THE PEN

By Adrian Liddell Hart
(1303) 8-1/2 hour cassettes
Rental—$15.50   Purchase—$64.00
Read by Victor Rumbellow

Adrian Liddell Hart is the son of Basil H. Liddell Hart, the pre-eminent strategist and historian of WW II. *The Sword and the Pen* is an anthology of the very finest writing on the subject of conflict. It is brought together with admirable skill by Adrian Liddell Hart and introduced in the easy but authoritative style reminiscent of his father.

Ranging centuries and continents, these reflections contain a special wisdom that is bought with precious coin. The men who wrote them paid for their knowledge with the pain, fear and frustration known only to men who have led a soldier's life.

TEN DAYS THAT SHOOK THE WORLD

By John Reed
(1724) 11-1/2 hour cassettes
Rental—$17.50   Purchase—$88.00
Read by Wolfram Kandinsky

John Reed was an American journalist who went to Russia during WW I. He was there in 1917 when Lenin seized power. Reed was far from neutral; he was dedicated to the Bolshevik cause, and in it believed he saw the future.

Despite Reed's partisanship, this book remains a classic of reporting. It served as inspiration for the award-winning film *Reds,* starring Warren Beatty and Diane Keaton.

Of related interest: Harrison Salisbury's *Black Night, White Snow* and Robert Massie's *Nicholas and Alexandra.*

TRIUMPH IN THE WEST: The War Diaries of Lord Alanbrooke Vol. 2

By Sir Arthur Bryant
(1588) 12-1/2 hour cassettes
Rental—$17.50   Purchase—$96.00
Read by Walter Zimmerman

This classic history has been called "the most important of all contemporary personal records of the war." *Triumph in the West* is Sir Arthur Bryant's sequel to *The Turn of the Tide* and is the second and concluding volume in the author's dramatic account of the waging of WW II. Based on the personal diaries of Field-Marshall Lord Alanbrooke, this volume spans the eventful months from September 1943 to Alanbrooke's resignation as Chief of the Imperial General Staff years later.

THE TURN OF THE TIDE: The War Diaries of Lord Alanbrooke Vol. 1

By Sir Arthur Bryant
(1587-A) 9-1/2 hour cassettes
Rental—$16.50   Purchase—$72.00
(1587-B) 11-1/2 hour cassettes
Rental—$17.50   Purchase—$88.00
Read by Walter Zimmerman

Alanbrooke was Churchill's Chief of Staff, and the two volumes based on his war diaries, *Turn of the Tide* and *Triumph in the West,* are indispensable accompaniments to Churchill's WW II memoirs. What Churchill conceived, Alanbrooke had to implement, and as Blake reminds us, "Execution is the chariot of genius."

The war began with a series of disasters for the British. But the ultimate disaster, loss of the British expeditionary force in Europe, did not occur because of the escape from Dunkirk.

Alanbrooke was in charge of the retreat through France. When one reads how deeply the British were committed, how under strength and ill-equipped, one marvels at the generalship that pulled them out.

THE ULTRA SECRET

By F.W. Winterbotham
(1134) 8-1 hour cassettes
Rental—$14.50   Purchase—$64.00
Read by Bernard Mayes

The intelligence project code-named Ultra was a well-kept secret indeed—its existence unknown during WW II and for 25 years thereafter. Yet due to the Ultra, Allied commanders were privy to the most vital directions of the German high command throughout the war, at times intercepting Hitler's orders to his generals even before they were administered. *The Ultra Secret* is out at last, but it leaves one question unanswered: how would the Allies have fared without it?

THE USE OF HISTORY

By A.L. Rowse
(1561) 8-1 hour cassettes
Rental—$14.50   Purchase—$64.00
Read by Stuart Courtney

The Use of History is the key volume in the "Teach Yourself History" project undertaken shortly after the close of WW II by British universities. Rowse's book is an overview of the series.

In his introduction the author says "I am convinced that the most congenial, as well as the most concrete and practical, approach to history is the biographical, through the lives of the great men whose actions have been so much a part of history, and whose careers in turn have been so molded and formed by events."

"Rowse is the leading English historian practicing today, a position he has occupied for the past four decades. His easy and comfortable style with words and people make his work a pleasure." *(Editorial Review Service)*

WAR AS I KNEW IT

By George S. Patton
(1181) 9-1½ hour cassettes
Rental—$16.50   Purchase—$72.00
Read by Jonathan Reese

George Smith Patton, four-star general, conqueror of Palermo and commander of the Third Army in its great sweep across Europe, was characteristically not one to hide anything about himself. In this consolidation of letters written to his wife, we get not a history of the Third Army, but an insight into the problems of modern high command and a fascinating self-portrait of a brilliant professional American soldier.

WAR IN VAL D'ORCIA:
An Italian Wary Diary 1943-44

By Iris Origo
(1941) 7-1½ hour cassettes
Rental—$15.50   Purchase—$56.00
Read by Jill Masters

In 1943, Marchesa Iris Origo, an Anglo-American married to an Italian landowner, found herself raising a young family in the middle of a civil war and a simultaneous foreign invasion.

Worse, she had divided loyalties, since her country of adoption was at war with her country of origin. But her principal concern was not politics, it was survival, and in her journal she noted each day's events.

"The story is tense, with a true, unforced excitement. But the story has a deeper value than drama. The Marchesa and her husband fought a private war for humanity, a war also waged by hundreds of Italian peasants who, at the risk of their lives, gave food and clothing to poor strangers—escaped Allied POW's—for no political cause or ideology, but in charity and pure compassion."—Eric Linklater

WING LEADER

By J.E. Johnson
(1780) 8-1½ hour cassettes
Rental—$15.50   Purchase—$64.00
Read by Rupert Keenlyside

Johnnie Johnson joined the Royal Air Force Volunteer Reserve in 1939 as a week-end flier, and finished the was as the top-scoring Allied fighter pilot with thirty-eight confirmed victories.

Wing Leader is his account of the Battle of Britain, of the bitter fighting over Dieppe, and of the final battle across the skies of France and over the Rhine when, as a group captain, he commanded a British wing of the latest and most powerful Spitfires.

"*Wing Leader* is a magnificent story of fighter pilots—so graphic in its description of aerial combat, so sympathetic in its portraits of fighting men that it will rank with the finest books which have come out of the war." *(Book Review Service)*

THE X-CRAFT RAID

By Thomas Gallagher
(1286) 6-1 hour cassettes
Rental—$12.50   Purchase—$48.00
Read by Jonathan Reese

The X-Craft Raid is Thomas Gallagher's story of the Allied effort during WW II to sink the menacing German Battleship *Tirpitz*. This formidable craft was kept in impregnable Norwegian fiords from which it could sally forth to attack Allied convoys. For the *Tirpitz's* destruction, the Allies designed the X-crafts—mini-submarines, form which divers were to plant destructive charges under the *Tirpitz*. What happened you must hear for yourself!

THE ZIMMERMAN TELEGRAM

By Barbara W. Tuchman
(1732) 7-1 hour cassettes
Rental—$13.50   Purchase—$56.00
Read by John MacDonald

In *The Zimmerman Telegram*, Barbara Tuchman analyzes Woodrow Wilson's decision to join the Allies in the First World War. She introduces us to Kaiser Wilhelm, unable to decide if the Japanese are the yellow peril or the natural allies of Germany; Pancho Villa, who thought Wilson his amigo until the United States refused to support him in a revolution; and Wilson himself, in whom were matched those curious siblings, moral certitude and hidden rage.

"Told with great literary and dramatic talent . . . her book should take a place near the top of studies concerning the entrance of the U.S. into WW I. Its value lies in her brilliant use of well-known materials, her sureness of insight and her grasp of this complicated chapter of diplomatic history." *(The New York Times)*

ALARMS AND DIVERSIONS

By James Thurber
(1639) 8-1½ hour cassettes
Rental—$15.50   Purchase—$64.00
Read by Wolfram Kandinsky

Another collection of Thurberiana, unique in that it contains a peppering of the author's favorites, also an introduction to his "serious comedy." Among the 32 stories lurk joyosities such as "The Lady of Orlon," "The Psychosemanticist Will See You Now, Mr. Thurber," "Get Thee to a Monastery," and "The Moribundant Life, or Grow Old Along with Whom?"

"His writings will be a document of the age they belong to."—T.S. Eliot

AT WIT'S END

By Erma Bombeck
(1165) 5-1 hour cassettes
Rental—$11.50   Purchase—$40.00
Read by Nancy Dannevik

At Wit's End is a collection of articles Erma Bombeck wrote for the Field Newspaper Syndicate. The book contains enough wit to help us get over the shock of recognizing ourselves in the mirror. Bombeck's gift is that she "knows the territory" where of she writes, and it is a terrain with which most of us are at least passingly familiar.

DIARY OF A MAD HOUSEWIFE

By Sue Kaufman
(1267) 7-1½ hour cassettes
Rental—$15.50   Purchase—$56.00
Read by Nancy Dannevik

In this funny but poignant novel, Sue Kaufman puts on stage an American house wife caught in our male-oriented society. She is 36-year-old Tina Balser, mother of two lovely children, wife and helpmate of a handsome and successful husband, doyenne of a bright apartment on Central Park West. But she's not content. On the contrary, she's on the verge of madness and hysteria. She has completely lost sight of her purpose in life, and believes that only by writing a diary—her personal form of self-therapy—can she regain her sanity.

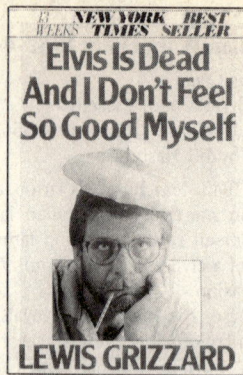

ELVIS IS DEAD AND I DON'T FEEL SO GOOD MYSELF

By Lewis Grizzard
(1396) 8-1 hour cassettes
Rental—$16.50   Purchase—$64.00
Read by Lawrence M. Vanella
A Christopher Enterprises Recording

The 1950's were simple times to grow up. For Lewis Grizzard, gallivanting meant hanging out at the local store eating Zagnut candy bars. About the worst thing a kid ever did was slick back his hair in a ducktail and try gyrating like Elvis.

But the sixties exploded with assassinations, terrorism, free love, Vietnam and drugs. In place of Elvis, the Pied Piper of his generation, scuzzy Liverpudlians performed half-naked or in costumes straight from Zasu Pitts.

"Elvis is Dead and I Don't Feel So Good Myself is Grizzard's account of coping with a changing world. We may not feel so good ourselves, but Grizzard's commentary and humor help make us feel better." *(Publisher's Source)*

FABLES FOR OUR TIME and FURTHER FABLES FOR OUR TIME

By James Thurber
(1637) 4-1 hour cassettes
Rental—$9.50   Purchase—$32.00
Read by Wolfram Kandinsky

Here is a collection of humorous tales in the style of Aesop laced through with barbs of memorable satire. In tales such as "The Rabbits Who Caused All the Trouble," "The Scotty Who Knew Too Much," "The Bat Who Got the Hell Out" and "The Sheep in Wolf's Clothing," we recognize a glimmer of ourselves.

Thurber, one of the cornerstones on which *The New Yorker* was built, was its managing editor and a contributor for many years. *The Saturday Review* wrote of this great American humorist: "His verbal legerdemain—tricks pulled off with the deadest of pans—are a delight to observe."

"Some Thurber titles recorded by B-O-T include: *The Middle-Aged Man on the Flying Trapeze, My Life and Hard Times, Thurber Country,* and the autobiographical *The Years with Ross.*

GOD AND MR. GOMEZ

By Jack Smith
(1861) 7-1 hour cassettes
Rental—$13.50   Purchase—$56.00
Read by Michael Prichard

"A charming account of the building of a dream house in Baja California. Mr. Gomez, on whom all depends, is a delightful character-creation."—Clifton Fadiman.

"Their house took form, first in their imaginations, then on paper. Little things went wrong along the way . . . The building site had away of moving slightly each time they visited it, and by the time the foundation was laid, it had moved to the middle of the road. Gomez got around that by simply moving the road."

"Fortunately, Gomez was always on hand to provide the solution, and the dream house was finally built. In the process, the Smiths came to accept Mr. Gomez's philosophy that all practical problems can be solved with a little time—and a little tequila."

"Jack Smith is a newspaper reporter, magazine writer, and a daily columnist for the *Los Angeles Times.*

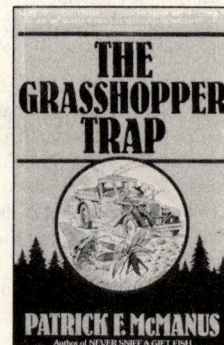

THE GRASSHOPPER TRAP

By Patrick McManus
(2018) 6-1 hour cassettes
Rental—$15.50   Purchase—$48.00
Read by Dick Estell
A Christopher Enterprises Recording

Patrick McManus is at it again in these tales celebrating life in the Great Outdoors. As many of his loyal fans have discovered, you don't have to be a nature lover to love his stories about fishing, hunting and camping—and the silver bullets in between.

This book's chapters reveal the secret art of constructing a grasshopper trap and the countless uses of a skunk ladder, also why wives on Christmas mourn, and why you should never cry snake.

"Describing [him] as an outdoor humorist is like saying Mark Twain wrote books about small boys." *(Atlanta Journal-Constitution)*

Slightly edited for radio presentation.

IF IT MOVES, KISS IT

By Joni Moura and Jackie Sutherland
(1219) 7-1 hour cassettes
Rental—$13.50   Purchase—$56.00
Read by Nancy Dannevik

There was a time when to be a female member of the armed services was a great adventure. This book is about those times. A sequel to *Tender Loving Care,* this volume carries forward the adventures of two nurses who confound the rules of an impersonal military establishment. Somewhat risque.

ISLAND FLING

By Ian Skidmore
(1685) 7-1 hour cassettes
Rental—$13.50   Purchase—$56.00
Read by Rodney Fay

When a tiny Welsh island secedes, the Brits move quickly to suture the breach. But the rebels have law on their side. A loophole allows Sir Huwap Gryfydd, ancestral lord of Tad and an evolutionary throwback to the Dark Ages, to rule his kingdom in the traditional Welsh way. They also have force: a "Dad's Army" of inspired halfwits and suppressed geniuses gets ready to tackle the British Army and police force. Armed only with unconquerable pride and native resolution, they know this will be their finest hour." . . . in the great tradition of British humor."(E.R.S. Services)

"JUST WAIT UNTIL YOU HAVE CHILDREN OF YOUR OWN!"

By Erma Bombeck and Bill Keane
(1299) 3-1 hour cassettes
Rental—$8.50   Purchase—$24.00
Read by Nancy Dannevik

"Just wait until you have children of your own" is one of the classic threats that parents resort to when all else fails. And it takes on added comic force here as two of America's foremost family humorists sketch the teenagers of today. Written primarily from the point of view of parents who see themselves as only slightly older teenagers, the contests between children and their parents are humorous and familiar.

**FREE rental from
Books on Tape™
See page 3**

THE MIDDLE-AGED MAN ON THE FLYING TRAPEZE

By James Thurber
(1155) 6-1 hour cassettes
Rental—$12.50   Purchase—$48.00
Read by Wolfram Kandinsky

This collection of 36 stories including: "The Gentleman is Cold," "Everything is Wild," "Mr. Preble Gets Rid of His Wife," "Hell Only Breaks Loose Once," "If Grant Had Been Drinking at Appomattox," and "How to See a Bad Play." *The London Times* said, "There may be greater humorists writing in America today than James Thurber, but none with quite his individual touch and his flavor. "For a colorful memoir of Thurber's years at *The New Yorker,* enjoy *The Years with Ross* in the Biography section of our catalog.

MY WORLD AND WELCOME TO IT

By James Thurber
(1636) 7-1 hour cassettes
Rental—$13.50   Purchase—$56.00
Read by Wolfram Kandinsky

James Thurber reported the world as he saw it. But what a world! Only Thurber could picture a seal peering nearsightedly over a headboard or a former husband crouched atop the armoire.

Titles in this selection, all vintage Thurber, hint at the range of his whimsy and include "Courtship Through the Ages," "The Secret Life of Walter Mitty," "Interview with a Lemming" and "You Know How the French Are."

"Few writers have re-created daydreams and nightmares as Thurber re-creates them. He manages, somehow, to pin them while the nerve filaments are alive and wriggling . . . " *(The New York Times Book Review)*

NEVER SNIFF A GIFT FISH

By Patrick McManus
(2019) 6-1 hour cassettes
Rental—$15.50   Purchase—$48.00
Read by Dick Estell
A Christopher Enterprises Recording

You need never have held a rifle, worn a backpack, or even thought about putting a worm on a hook to appreciate these tales of a sportsman's life in the great, and often not-so-great, outdoors.

Patrick McManus offers cracker-barrel-wisdom and country insights into the agonies and ecstasies of hunting, fishing and camping. He punctures the myth of masculine mystique, gently exposes the imperfections of man and beast, but always celebrates life in the natural world with wit and warmth.

"McManus writes high-class humor, with echoes of Benchley, Buchwald and Bombeck." *(Kirkus Reviews)*
Slightly edited for radio presentation.

P.G. WODEHOUSE: SELECTED SHORT STORIES

By P.G. Wodehouse
(9902) 6-1 hour cassettes
Rental—$12.50   Purchase—$48.00
Read by Timothy Carlton
A Talking Tape Recording

At the time of his death at the age of 93, P.G. Wodehouse was at work on his 97th novel. This unique writer of social comedy, with hisoutlandish humor and sharp caricatures of English types, was born in 1881 in Guildford, England. In novels and short stories, he created such memorable characters as Psmith and Jeeves, the archetypical Edwardian drone and his butler.

The universality of his appeal is demonstrated in these six stories: "Lord Emsworth and the Girlfriend," "Jeeves and the Yuletide Spirit," "Ukridge's Accident Syndicate," "Mulliner's Buck U Uppo," "Anselm Gets his Chance" and "The Clicking of Cuthbert" (a golfer's delight).

RING LARDNER: BEST SHORT STORIES

By Ring Lardner
(1009) 8-1½ hour cassettes
Rental—$15.50   Purchase—$64.00
Read by Daniel Grace

For a whole generation of readers who have grown to maturity without reading Ring Lardner, this book will introduce one of the great American storytellers. Lardner was a heavy weight author who dealt with light weight themes. His style, sardonic and irreverent, made it difficult for him to be taken seriously by the literary establishment. But in reality, Lardner was one of the foremost experimental writers of his time, and his talent shines out in these stories.

SOME CHAMPIONS

By Ring Lardner
(1035) 7-1 hour cassettes
Rental—$13.50   Purchase—$56.00
Read by Daniel Grace

Ring Lardner has been resurrected as an authentic American humorist. Wit and style flash from this fresh new collection of Lardner improbables. Listening to the stories and there current Lardner themes of innocence and its debarking, of worldliness and its miscues, one realizes the people and times of which Lardnerwrites, while an authentic part of our recent past, are now dead as the dodo. A bracing illustration of the change in our national character, if any is needed.

TENDER LOVING CARE

By Joni Moura and Jackie Sutherland
(1006) 8-1 hour cassettes
Rental—$14.50 Purchase—$64.00
Read by Nancy Dannevik

Imagine two nurses who joined the Air Force 25 years ago. They live in segregated quarters, do not engage in sexual acrobatics or expand their minds with coke, yet have a simply marvelous time cavorting through an all-male world. One of the true delights of the book is seeing that sex can still be treated robustly without resort to unseemliness. *If it Moves, Kiss it* is the sequel to this delightful story. Somewhat risque.

THE THROWBACK

By Tom Sharpe
(1948) 8-1 hour cassettes
Rental—$14.50 Purchase—$64.00
Read by Richard Green

When Lockhart Flawse, idiot savant and illegitimate member of the squirearchy, is denied his proper inheritance, what is he to do?

Flawse isn't sure, but he has plans, and these include gassing, suing, whipping, dynamiting, killing and maiming. His misanthropy is matched only by his incompetence, and fortunately for the locals most of his strategies fail.

Critics say "this is black humor and comic anarchy at its best" *(The Sunday Times,* London), and "Sharpe is funny, bitter, a danger to his public, and should be wildy applauded by all right-thinking men and women." *(The Listener)*

THE THURBER CARNIVAL

By James Thurber
(1640) 7-1½ hour cassettes
Rental—$14.50 Purchase—$56.00
Read by Wolfram Kandinsky

"The writing is, I think, different. In his prose pieces he appears always to have started from the beginning and to have reached the end by way of the middle. It is impossible to read any of the stories from the last line to the first without experiencing a definite sensation of going backward." Appropriate reflections indeed from Thurber's self-penned preface to this collection of stories.

The Thurber Carnival contains selections from previous B-O-T releases: *My World and Welcome to It, The Middle-Aged Man on the Flying Trapeze,* the complete *My Life and Hard Times,* and *Fables for Our Time,* as well as the following never-before-recorded anecdotes, stories, diversions and absurdities from: *Let Your Mind Alone, "Stories Not Collected Before in Book Form"* and *The Owl in the Attic.*

THURBER COUNTRY

By James Thurber
(1190) 7-1 hour cassettes
Rental—$13.50 Purchase—$56.00
Read by Wolfram Kandinsky

James Thurber is one of the greatest and most original American humorists. Perhaps the most amazing aspect of Thurber's genius is that he produced the majority of his famous articles and illustrations with greatly impaired eyesight, which deteriorated with age until he became entirely blind. As with everything else within his life, he viewed this in a positive manner: "My one-eighth vision happily obscures sad and ungainly sights, leaving only the vivid and the radiant . . . *"Thurber Country* is a collection of 25 short stories including: "What's So Funny?," "My Own Ten Rules for a Happy Marriage," "What a Lovely Generalization!," "File and Forget," "What Cocktail Party?" and "See No Weevil."

VINTAGE STUFF

By Tom Sharpe
(1949) 8-1 hour cassettes
Rental—$14.50 Purchase—$64.00
Read by Richard Green

At a third-rate private school for boys, a little education goes a long way and entirely in the wrong direction.

We learn this by meeting Peregrine Roderick Clyde-Browne, a doltish student who takes literally each and every word he hears. Acting without malice, he fuels a long-standing feud between two instructors who share a deep and mutual loathing for each other.

"Needle-Sharpe . . . vintage stuff, all right" says *The London Times* while *Publisher's Weekly* finds *Vintage Stuff* "bawdy, fast, tense and very funny."

WILT

By Tom Sharpe
(1947) 8-1 hour cassettes
Rental—$14.50 Purchase—$64.00
Read by Richard Green

A humble professor at a technical college by day, Henry Wilt at night is often drunk . . . on both alcohol and fantasies of killing his idiotic wife. In a state of fumey intoxication, he tries a practice run. It does not go well.

When he dumps a life-size sex doll down a bore-hole at a building site, he is accused of uxoricide. Worse, his wife has really disappeared—run aground on a pleasure cruise with two sexually ambiguous friends.

"America has deserved Sharpe for some time, and at last we have him. At his best—notably in *Wilt* (lewd but funny)—he is far more satisfying than any other British humorist since Evelyn Waugh." —Roy Blount, Jr.

THE WRONG BOX

*By Robert Louis Stevenson
and Lloyd Osbourne*
(9154) 5-1½ hour cassettes
Rental—$14.50 Purchase—$40.00
Read by Jim Killavey
A Jimcin Recording

Morris and John Finsbury are victims of Uncle Joseph's amiable depletion of their trust fund. But he himself is an unusual asset . . . one of the last few members of a tontine, a sort of survivors insurance bonanza popular in the 19th century. Because they will be beneficiaries, the young men set up as guardians of their uncle's good health.

All does not proceed smoothly. A train accident sets in motion a string of comic events, and a corpse mistaken for Uncle Joseph turns up in the most unlikely places.

Robert Louis Stevenson and his stepson, Lloyd Osbourne, co-authored *The Wrong Box* in 1889. It was made into a successful movie 70 years later, proof of its lasting appeal.

**Give the perfect gift
from Books on Tape™
See page 2**

ACCIDENTAL CRIMES

By John Hutton
(2033) 6-1½ hour cassettes
Rental—$14.50   Purchase—$48.00
Read by Richard Brown

The murder investigation had nothing to do with Conrad. He was a model citizen, even a rather important one. He had, however, been under considerable strain recently: there was the uncertainty about his future, and his relationship with Stephanie, his wife, was not quite what it had once been.

Perhaps that explained why he had lied to the police. It had been such a small untruth, a simple dodge to escape the roadblock across the desolate moorlands where a girl's raped and mutilated body had been found. But it was to have a devastating effect on Conrad's life.

"A compelling novel. John Hutton uses crime to explore the complexities of human personality and the dangerous pitfalls of self-delusion. His psychology is impeccable, his writing sharp and often wryly comic, and his central character a hauntingly believable creation. Highly recommended." *(E.R.S. Reviews)*

ADVISE AND CONSENT

By Allen Drury
(1142-A) 9-1½ hour cassettes
Rental—$16.50   Purchase—$72.00
(1142-B) 11-1½ hour cassettes
Rental—$17.50   Purchase—$88.00
Read by Dan Lazar

Advise and Consent is a study of political animals in their natural habitat and is universally recognized as *the* Washington novel. It begins with Senate confirmation hearings for a liberal Secretary of State, and concludes two weeks later, after debate and controversy have exploded the issue into a major crisis.

"I can recall no other novel in which there is so well presented a President's dilemma when his awful responsibility for the nation's interest conflicts with a personal code of good morals." *(The New York Times)*

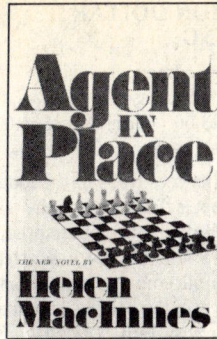

AGENT IN PLACE

By Helen MacInnes
(1374) 9-1½ hour cassettes
Rental—$16.50   Purchase—$72.00
Read by Wanda McCaddon

This sophisticated narrative of spy/counterspy is set in Washington, where the Russians have planted an "agent in place." For nine years he has worked himself quietly into the fabric of government and society. Dedicated and patient, he has everyone's respect. In a plot where amateurs are the villains, professionals are the heros—particularly a team of British and French agents whose job is to foil further Russian intervention.

The story moves from Washington to New York to Menton on the French Riviera, where it concludes in a series of stunning revelations, dismaying setbacks and breathless recoveries. Also offered for Helen MacInnes devotees are *Prelude to Terror, The Snare of the Hunter* and *North from Rome*.

ANATOMY OF A MURDER

By Robert Traver
(1156) 12-1½ hour cassettes
Rental—$17.50   Purchase—$96.00
Read by Wolfram Kandinsky

This novel is a meticulously detailed account of a celebrated murder trial. It concentrates on defense attorney Paul Biegler from the moment he accepts the case until the verdict is brought in. Biegler's client is accused of murdering a man who his wife claims assaulted her. The book leaves us wondering about the guilt and its locus—in this case does it belong to the deadman, to the accused, or to his wife?

THE AQUITAINE PROGRESSION

By Robert Ludlum
(1931-A) 11-1½ hour cassettes
Rental—$17.50   Purchase—$88.00
(1931-B) 9-1½ hour cassettes
Rental—$16.50   Purchase—$72.00
Read by Michael Prichard

It is a real possibility. A group of generals not from one nation taking control in a palace coup, but from most nations taking control of most of the world in a coordinated lightning stroke. What's to stop them?

In *The Aquitaine Progression,* one-man . . . Joel Converse, a battle scarred veteran of the Vietnam war who in the course of business stumbles onto the plot. "This is Ludlum at his best . . . a thrilling international novel and love story." *(Publishers Weekly)*

For other Ludlum novels, please refer to the Index where they are listed under the author's name.

ATLANTIC FURY

By Hammond Innes
(1807) 7-1½ hour cassettes
Rental—$15.50   Purchase—$56.00
Read by Charles Garst

Hammond Innes novels are famous for their thrills and exotic locations. The present selection is no exception. *Atlantic Fury* is set against the wild out-islands of the Hebrides, whose reefs and storms nearly kill the crew of a military landing craft.

A spectacular rescue spirals into a bizarre court martial. It seems the boat's commander is afraud: he tried to bury his crew so he could bury his past. "Authentic and excellent . . . His plot, characters and suspense live up to the setting. "(San Francisco Chronicle)*

THE BARBOZA CREDENTIALS

By Peter Driscoll
(1269) 7-1½ hour cassettes
Rental—$15.50   Purchase—$56.00
Read by Richard Green

Joe Hickey, a retired Rhodesian policeman, operates a lucrative but shady business selling mining equipment to blacklisted countries. His office is in Portuguese Mozambique, and when the colony gains independence, the new government no longer turns a blind eye to his activities. His office is closed, his representative is killed and he finds himself caught between native police and old-guard Portuguese who blackmail him to get a fugitive ex-general out of the country.

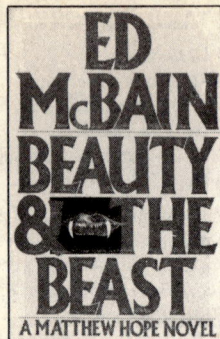

BEAUTY AND THE BEAST

By Ed McBain
(1964) 7-1½ hour cassettes
Rental—$13.50   Purchase—$56.00
Read by Michael Prichard

The first time Matthew Hope sees Michelle Harper is on North Sabal Beach. She's so spectacular he can't help staring. And he can't believe his good luck when she comes to him as a client. Except her story is not pretty . . . she claims her husband beats her.

Thus when Michelle turns up murdered, the police arrest her husband, George. Only one thing is wrong: he says he's innocent.

Somehow, Hope believes him—and takes on the case. He finds it worse than he imagined. The results says *The Sunday Times* (London), is "a strictly X-rated fairy tale" and a "daring, engrossing story . . . " (*Publishers Weekly*)

THE BIG FOOTPRINTS

By Hammond Innes
(1811) 7-1½ hour cassettes
Rental—$15.50   Purchase—$56.00
Read by John MacDonald

Decimated by drought and poacher's bullets, the last of Africa's majestic elephants face extinction. They are pursued by a "great white hunter" who relies on modern technology to process them as food for starving natives.

He is opposed by his former partner who is determined that the beasts shall not pay the price for man's inability to manage his resources wisely.

"Hammond Innes shows great depth of understanding of the complex strands that make up the ecology of a region." (*Best Sellers*)

FREE rental from Books on Tape™
See page 3

THE BILLION DOLLAR SURE THING

By Paul E. Erdman
(1288) 8-1 hour cassettes
Rental—$13.50   Purchase—$64.00
Read by Dan Lazar

Fact sometimes trails in the footsteps of fiction, and so it is that events in the real world have followed much the course predicted by Paul Erdman's famous novel. Written when the first Arab oil embargo sent shock waves through our carefully balanced and delicately tuned economicsystem, *The Billion Dollar Sure Thing* describes a plot to control the world's monetary assets.

BLOOD RELATIVES

By Ed McBain
(2071) 6-1 hour cassettes
Rental—$12.50   Purchase—$48.00
Read by Michael Prichard

It was exactly the sort of case Detective Carella despised. One girl had been raped and murdered, another slashed by a psycho. Patricia Lowery survived the attack and could identify the killer. All Carella needed was the girl's eyewitness testimony and a little luck.

Then Patricia spotted her assailant in a routine line-up and Carella's luck ran out. His witness had fingered a fellow detective who had been on the force for seventeen years.

Books on Tape's selection of Ed McBain thrillers includes *Beauty and the Beast, Goldilocks, Long Time No See* and *Rumpelstiltskin*.

THE BOURNE IDENTITY

By Robert Ludlum
(1760-A) 8-1½ hour cassettes
Rental—$15.50   Purchase—$64.00
(1760-B) 6-1½ hour cassettes
Rental—$14.50   Purchase—$48.00
Read by Michael Prichard

In this best-selling novel by Robert Ludlum, a man is shot, left for dead, later rescued from the sea. Surviving, but with no memory, he is given a name: Jason Bourne. Physically and mentally agile, he retraces his past through a harrowing personal labyrinth. The discovery: he was a trained killer, and now in turn is being hunted by assassins. "His characters are complex and credible, his sleight of plot as cunning as any terrorist conspiracy. It is a Bourne from which no traveler returns unsatisfied." (*Time*)

THE BOURNE SUPREMACY

By Robert Ludlum
(1818-A) 9-1½ hour cassettes
Rental—$16.50   Purchase—$72.00
(1818-B) 8-1½ hour cassettes
Rental—$15.50   Purchase—$64.00
Read by Michael Prichard

David Webb is an ordinary citizen living an ordinary life in a small university town . . . except he is under 24 hour personal surveillance. Of course his memory is gone, but with his wife's loving care his past is on the mend.

Suddenly it returns, but not at his volition. From Hong Kong comes word that the assassin has struck again, that Bourne is back!

But the U.S. government knows he never existed. Webb only posed as Bourne to unearth anotorious killer. Yet someone is killing again in Bourne's name . . . and he must be stopped or stability in the Far East will crumble. The decision is made—Jason Bourne must exist again and hunt his own imposter.

BREAD

By Ed McBain
(2116) 7-1 hour cassettes
Rental—$13.50   Purchase—$56.00
Read by Michael Prichard

It is August, and in the 87th Precinct everything is red hot . . . at 100°, the weather; the police, who have just made the biggest dope bust ever; and Roger Grimm, because someone burned up his warehouse and the cops aren't doing a thing about it. To cool Grimm off, Detectives Steve Carella and Cotton Hawes take on the investigation.

But Steve and Cotton soon realize that they have tumbled on to something bigger than a case of playing with matches. Before long they put the heat on some cold-blooded killers, hoping to get them with the goods before anyone else gets burned.

"Intricate and absorbing . . . one of McBain's best." (*Publishers Weekly*)

Other Ed McBain thrillers recorded by Books on Tape include *Blood Relatives, Long Time No See* and *Where There's Smoke*.

BRIGHT ORANGE FOR THE SHROUD

By John D. MacDonald
(1176) 8-1 hour cassettes
Rental—$14.50   Purchase—$64.00
Read by Michael Prichard

A Travis McGee mystery, this is the story of an immensely clever confidence scheme run by a group of vicious double crossers. An old friend of McGee's is sucked into their trap and bled, financially and physically. Before the story ends, McGee is forced to use dirtier tactics than ever before. He becomes more cunning and heartless than the men he is pursuing. Along the way he discovers an innocent-looking blonde whose treachery includes the blackest arts of love.

BURNT OFFERINGS

By Robert Marasco
(1126) 8-1 hour cassettes
Rental—$14.50   Purchase—$64.00
Read by Dan Lazar

The Rolfes—Ben, Marian, son David and Aunt Elizabeth—are a pleasant family from New York seeking escape from the doldrums of a summer in their Queen's apartment. They find a beautiful old country mansion on Long Island—restful, secluded, with pool and private beach, perfect for the right people.

But their "perfect" summer home hides terrors beyond their wildest imaginings. During that long summer the house becomes a nightmare from which there seems no escape.

BY THE NORTH GATE

By Gwyn Griffin
(1579) 6-1½ hour cassettes
Rental—$14.50   Purchase—$48.00
Read by Wolfram Kandinsky

An unnerving story of personal, political and amorous intrigue, _By the North Gate_ is set in a British military outpost in Northeast Africa after WW II. In an attempt to whip resentment into hysteria, a group of rabid Nationalists seize on the bungled execution of a native terrorist as away to rid themselves of British occupation.

"People and episodes are drawn with unforgettable intensity and although a theme of brutality runs through the story it is indispensable to the book's overall pattern." _(Booklist)_

Other Griffin books recorded by B-O-T include _A Significant Experience_, plus numerous additional titles listed in our Index.

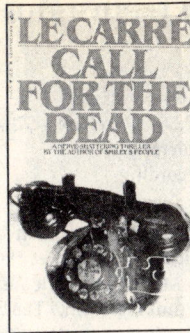

CALL FOR THE DEAD

By John le Carré
(1532) 6-1 hour cassettes
Rental—$12.50   Purchase—$48.00
Read by Rupert Keenlyside

The cast includes a brilliant, twisted former hero of the German underground, a once beautiful woman with a terrifying secret, a suspect British civil servant, and a high-ranking bureaucrat. Also an undercover operative named George Smiley, tired and feeling very used-up. He has seen and done more than he ever wanted to, but he can't refuse this one last call to duty.

"Superb plotting and characters!" _(Best Sellers)_

John le Carré fans will also enjoy _The Honourable Schoolboy, The Little Drummer Girl, Tinker, Tailor, Soldier, Spy_ and _The Spy Who Came in from the Cold._

CARMILLA and GREEN TEA

By J.S. Le Fanu
(9030) 5-1 hour cassettes
Rental—$12.50   Purchase—$40.00
Read by Linda Vars and Walter Covell
A Jimcin Recording

These two stories by an Irish novelist, a master of the Victorian supernatural tale, explore the occult and mysterious.

Carmilla is the story of a vampire and demonstrates the victory of superstition over logic. In _Green Tea_ the personality of the witness is as charged with the supernatural as is the manifestation itself.

CAUSE FOR ALARM   **NEW**

By Eric Ambler
(2102) 6-1½ hour cassettes
Rental—$14.50   Purchase—$48.00
Read by Richard Brown

Italian fascists were a joke, unless they had you in their power. They had Marlow, and he was desperate. He ended up running for his life.

"Exciting chases, hairbreadth escapes, authentically accurate. Excellent!" _(Saturday Review)_

Journey Into Fear is another thriller by Eric Ambler available on audio cassette from B-O-T.

THE CHANCELLOR MANUSCRIPT

By Robert Ludlum
(1757) 11-1½ hour cassettes
Rental—$17.50   Purchase—$88.00
Read by Michael Prichard

Peter Chancellor, a novelist known for his deadly accurate and dangerously controversial political "fictions," makes a dangerous discovery in the course of his research: "J. Edgar Hoover did not die a natural death. He was assassinated."

With a simple pretext for his protagonist's motivation, Ludlum plunges the listener into a veritable whirlwind of plot and counterplot.

" . . . _The Chancellor Manuscript_ seems to justify our worst nightmares of what really goes on in the so-called Intelligence Community in Washington." _(The New York Times Book Review)_

THE CHELSEA MURDERS   **NEW**

By Lionel Davidson
(2030) 6-1½ hour cassettes
Rental—$14.50   Purchase—$48.00
Read by Richard Green

A grotesque figure burst into the girl's room. Its head piled with fake curls, its face concealed behind a smiling mask, it wore the rubber gloves of a surgeon or perhaps a mortuary attendant. It seized the girl from behind and chloroformed, suffocated, and finally, decapitated her.

Hers was only one in a series of horrendous murders by a killer who played games with the police, always mailing them cryptic bits of poetry—baffling clues to the identity of his next victim.

"A milestone in the genre." —Ngaio Marsh

The Menorah Men, The Night of Wenceslas and _The Rose of Tibet_ are all Lionel Davidson mysteries available on cassette from Books on Tape.

THE CHINESE ORANGE MYSTERY

By Ellery Queen
(1104) 8-1 hour cassettes
Rental—$14.50   Purchase—$64.00
Read by Michael Prichard

An unknown dead man is found in the office of a prosperous publisher. His clothes are on backward, and all of the furniture in the room has been reversed. Ellery Queen continues to uncover "backward" clues—leading him to the identity of this puzzling victim.

CINNAMON SKIN

By John D. MacDonald
(1649) 8-1 hour cassettes
Rental—$14.50   Purchase—$64.00
Read by Michael Prichard

In this 20th episode, Travis McGee avenges a tragedy that hits close to home. While his friend Meyer is on a lecture tour, he lends his boat to his newly married niece. But the boat explodes and a Chilean terrorist group claims responsibility. Following a trail that leads from Florida to Mexico, Meyer and McGee uncover evidence of a drug connection as a possible reason for the fatal explosion.

THE CIRCULAR STAIRCASE

By Mary Roberts Rinehart
(9135) 6-1½ hour cassettes
Rental—$15.50   Purchase—$48.00
Read by Cindy Hardin
A Jimcin Recording

A milestone of the mystery genre, *The Circular Staircase* founded in 1908 what Ogden Nash dubbed the Had-I-But-Known school. The focus of these books—the Gothic Heroine—has the worst instincts this side of Lady MacBeth. She always makes the wrong decisions and always trusts the wrong people.

In this case, our heroine, Miss Cornelia Van Gorder, takes a summer house with her niece and nephew. A series of eerie events follow as a criminal tries to retrieve stolen securities hidden in the house and the aunt attempts to solve the mystery.

CLASSIC DETECTIVE STORIES

A Collection
(9082) 9-1½ hour cassettes
Rental—$17.50   Purchase—$72.00
Various Readers
A Jimcin Recording

These detective stories are from the vintage era of mystery writing, which is to say that time when the deductive powers of a human mind were more to be treasured than the laboratory analyses.

Included in this carefully culled selection are the following gems: "The Problem of Cell 13" by Jacques Futrelle, "The Lenton Croft Robberies" by Arthur Morrison, "The Adventure of the Six Napoleons" and "The Adventure of the Empty House" by Sir Arthur Conan Doyle, "The Absent Minded Coterie" by Robert Barr, "Madame Sare" by L.T. Meade, "How He Cut His Stick" by M. Bodkin, "The Glasgow Mystery" and 'The Dublin Mystery" by Baroness Orczy.

CLASSIC DETECTIVE STORIES VOL. II

A Collection
(9115) 9-1½ hour cassettes
Rental—$17.50   Purchase—$72.00
Various Readers
A Jimcin Recording

Here are 14 more intriguing detective stories to challenge your deductive powers: "The Stolen Cigar Case" by Bret Harte, "The Nicobar Bullion Case" and "The Affair of the Tortoise" by Arthur Morrison, "The Blood Red Cross" by L.T. Meade and Robert Eustace. "The Fatal Cipher" by Jocques Futrelle, "The Duchess of Wilshire's Diamonds" by Guy Boothby. "The Mystery of Mrs. Dickenson" by Nicholas Carter, "The Stolen White Elephant" and "A Double-Barrelled Detective Story" by Mark Twain, "The Red-Headed League" and "The Adventure of the Noble Bachelor" by Sir Arthur Conan Doyle, "The Purloined Letter" and "The Murders in the Rue Morgue" by Edgar Allan Poe, and "Mr. Policeman and the Cook" by Wilkie Collins.

CLASSIC DETECTIVE STORIES VOL. III

A Collection
(9146) 7-1½ hour cassettes
Rental—$17.50   Purchase—$56.00
Read by Walter Zimmerman
and Walter Covell
A Jimcin Recording

You have met them before in one form or another, as books, plays or movies, frequently all three, and here they are again—our third collection of classic detective stories, compiled by Jimcin Recordings, and made available especially for B-O-T subscribers.

Classic detectives stories included are: R. Austn Freeman's "The Mandarin's Pearl" and "The Blue Sequin"; Arthur Morrison's "The Ward Lane Tabernacle"; Baroness Orczy's "The Liverpool Mystery" and "The Case of Miss Eliot"; Emile Gaborian's "The Little Old Man of Batignolles"; William Le Quenx's "The Secret of the Fox Hunter"; Anna Katherine Green's "The Staircase at the Heart's Delight"; and Sir Arthur Conan Doyle's "The Adventure of the Naval Treaty."

THE CLUB OF QUEER TRADES

By G.K. Chesterton
(1443) 6-1 hour cassettes
Rental—$12.50   Purchase—$48.00
Read by Stuart Courtney

The Club of Queer Trades is G.K. Chesterton's first mystery. It is the story of a club with a membership requirement that is eccentric and typically English: no one can join unless he has created a brand-new profession.

So what are the new ways to earn a living? One man offers himself as a butt for repartee, another provides suitable romance for lonely souls.

A COAT OF VARNISH

By C.P. Snow
(1493) 8-1½ hour cassettes
Rental—$15.50   Purchase—$64.00
Read by Peter MacDonald

Aylestone Square is a conservative London neighborhood, virtually the last bastion of upper-class gentleness and decorum. It seems an improbable setting for a brutal, vicious killing.

When a shockingly gruesome murder occurs there, it catches everyone by surprise. There is an autopsy scene that makes the hardboiled school of crime writers seem timid and genteel.

A COFFIN FOR DIMITRIOS

NEW

By Eric Ambler
(2106) 8-1 hour cassettes
Rental—$14.50   Purchase—$64.00
Read by Richard Brown

Dimitrios began his career in Turkey by cutting the throat of a moneylender. In Morocco he made a fortune as a white slaver. In Bulgaria he plotted assassinations. In Belgrade he traded state secrets. In Paris he dealt in drugs. Now, in Istanbul, Dimitrios has finally been stopped—by his own murder.

Charles Latimer is obsessed with Dimitrios. A mystery writer in search of a story, Latimer digs into Dimitrios' past . . . and nearly ends up digging his own grave.

THE DAIN CURSE

By Dasheill Hammett
(1443) 7-1 hour cassettes
Rental—$12.50   Purchase—$56.00
Read by Michael Prichard

This is the story of Gabrielle Leggett, a young woman who is generally believed to be suffering from the curse of the mad Dains. She has all the signs—stigma, neuroses, rages . . . and a pistol.

Beginning with a robbery, the plot moves quickly to drugs, obscene rituals and murder, all connected with the temple of a sinister cult.

THE DARK SIDE OF THE ISLAND

By Jack Higgins
(1455) 5-1 hour cassettes
Rental—$11.50   Purchase—$40.00
Read by Mark Howell

The Greek islands, sun-drenched and tranquil, evoke pictures from a tourist brochure. It takes a special imagination to dredge up their blood-soaked history when, as a subject land in WW II, island revolts were crushed by the occupying Germans.

In those days, Hugh Lomax was sent by the British to aid the Greeks in their struggle. He succeeded brilliantly, but on leaving for another assignment was betrayed. Those who collaborated with him were executed and survivors, not unnaturally, held Lomax responsible for the carnage.

DARK NANTUCKET NOON

By Jane Langton
(1591) 8-1 hour cassettes
Rental—$14.50   Purchase—$64.00
Read by Michael Prichard

The brilliant but exceptionally vulnerable young poet, Kitty Clark, goes to Nantucket to view an eclipse of the sun. At the foot of a deserted lighthouse, as the day plunges into darkness, she stumbles over the bloody body of the wife of her ex-lover, the well-known novelist Joe Green. Not only is Kitty found kneeling over the murdered woman, but her knife is found neatly buried in the sand nearby.

THE DARK SIDE OF THE STREET

By Jack Higgins
(1924) 6-1 hour cassettes
Rental—$12.50   Purchase—$48.00
Read by by Rupert Keenlyside

With commando-like precision, someone was breaking Britain's most notorious prisoners out of jail, and delivering convicted spies back to the Communists. His code name was The Baron—there was just one way to trace him: put a secret operative inside the walls and let The Baron get him out.

To do it the Special Branch needed an agent with the cunning mind of a criminal and the cold heart of a killer. That agent was Paul Chavasse. "A great adventure yarn!" *(Boston Globe)*

DARKER THAN AMBER

By John D. MacDonald
(1214) 7-1 hour cassettes
Rental—$13.50   Purchase—$56.00
Read by Michael Prichard

John D. MacDonald is best known as the creator of that famous adventure and folk hero, Travis McGee. In *Darker Than Amber*, McGee and his philosophical cohort Meyer rescue a beautiful Eurasian woman from her "friends. "Her eyes, "just a little darker than amber," pull them into a crisis that nearly finishes them. As the mystery unfolds, McGee follows to its end the trail of a band of murderous profiteers.

A DEADLY SHADE OF GOLD

By John D. MacDonald
(1114) 8-1½ hour cassettes
Rental—$15.50   Purchase—$64.00
Read by Michael Prichard

Travis McGee's buddy, Sam Taggart, turns up for an impromptu visit. Sam shows McGee the gold figurine of an Aztec deity and tells him that he plans to regain possession of 27 additional idols that once belonged to him.

A few hours later Taggart is a corpse with a slit throat. McGee takes custody of the golden idol and Taggart's former girlfriend.

DEATH OF A LITERARY WIDOW

By Robert Barnard
(1843) 6-1 hour cassettes
Rental—$12.50   Purchase—$48.00
Read by Jay Fitts

Here we have the story of Walter Machin, novelist of the working classes. Twice married, he has failed to write books that sell. Then Machin dies.

Left to grieve are two widows who share his house in a pleasant North England town. No sooner have they settled in than Walter's literary reputation begins to flourish. Comfort and serenity now seem to be Machin's unexpected legacy to his widows. Then one of them unexpectedly dies. Into this expanding pool of mortality plunges Greg Hocking, a friend of the widows. His investigation leaves nothing, including the roots of Walter's literary reputation, to rest in peace.

DEATH UNDER SAIL

By C.P. Snow
(1421) 6-1½ hour cassettes
Rental—$14.50   Purchase—$48.00
Read by Ian Whitcomb

Like *A Coat of Varnish*, C.P. Snow's final novel, *Death Under Sail* is a murder mystery of imposing tension. It is not only a top-class and ingenious who-dunnit, but also a superb study of human motivation, a clever and unobtrusive comment on society and the very best example of watertight craftsmanship.

"Even the most jaded of detective-story-readers will find a thrill." *(Observer)*

THE DEEP BLUE GOOD-BY

By John D. MacDonald
(1662) 6-1 hour cassettes
Rental—$12.50   Purchase—$48.00
Read by Michael Prichard

The Deep Blue Good-By introduces John D. MacDonald's alter-ego, the rugged and articulate Travis McGee.

In this initial story, McGee comes to the aid of a lovely lady in soul-deep distress—a lady who has been dragged through so much mud that she may never feel clean again. The plot concerns some precious stones "liberated" by McGee's client's father in India during WW II.

As *The New York Times* stated, MacDonald "is one of the most creative and reliable writers . . . and is a very good writer, not just a good 'mystery' writer."

**Special 10% discount
See page 2**

THE DOGS

By Robert Calder
(1255) 7-1 hour cassettes
Rental—$13.50   Purchase—$56.00
Read by Dan Lazarar

Dr. Chaim Mandleburg, a genetic sorcerer, creates a super-class of German Shepherds that will kill on command or on their own if unsupervised. One of the puppies gets loose, and is adopted by a college professor. The puppy attacks the professor's small son, then escapes to form a wild canine pack. The focus is on the pack, which threatens a terrified rural town. The brutal action reaches its peak on the final hunt. XX-rated for violence.

THE DOOMED OASIS

By Hammond Innes
(1806) 8-1½ hour cassettes
Rental—$15.50   Purchase—$64.00
Read by Jack Hrkach

Charles Whitaker is a Welshman who forsakes his native country for the deserts of Araby. Adapting quickly to this hostile terrain, he soon becomes more Bedouin than British.

Whitaker's illegitimate son, David, sets out to find his father. He in turn is followed by a Welsh solicitor who hopes to reunite the two men. The story moves at two levels: one involves a desperate struggle for desert oil; the second, hardly less intense, for father and son to find each other. Both struggles are resolved at Saraifa, the doomed oasis of the title.

THE DREADFUL LEMON SKY

By John D. MacDonald
(1059) 7-1 hour cassettes
Rental—$13.50   Purchase—$56.00
Read by Michael Prichard

Hero of *The Dreadful Lemon Sky* is Travis McGee, a man of universal interest and independent means who lives on the old houseboat he won in a poker game.

One evening, a young woman shows up with a suitcase full of cash. McGee agrees to be bagman. She tells him what to do if she doesn't return.

When she doesn't, McGee is left alone to deal with an intrigue that involves drugs, fear, passion and death.

DRESS HER IN INDIGO

By John D. MacDonald
(1239) 7-1½ hour cassettes
Rental—$15.50   Purchase—$56.00
Read by Michael Prichard

Travis McGee is again the star of this adventure. This modern-day Sam Spade, accompanied by his friend Meyer, travels to the Mexican village of Oaxaca. There they meet all kinds—the gay, the depraved, the violent as they try to determine the cause of a client's violent and tragic death.

EAST OF DESOLATION

By Jack Higgins
(1457) 6-1 hour cassettes
Rental—$12.50   Purchase—$48.00
Read by Ian Whitcomb

A plane crashes on the Greenland icecap. Joe Martin, a bush pilot, flies insurance investigators to the site. Among his passengers is a beautiful and intriguing woman, Sarah Kelso, widow of the man who was supposed to have been flying the ill-fated plane.

Jack Higgins, who also wrote *The Eagle Has Landed*, sets his story in the desolation of the ice fields of the arctic north. His men and women are hungry with greed, but possess cool daring and courage. Even Higgins' bad guys are good.

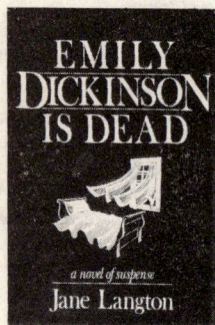

EMILY DICKINSON IS DEAD

By Jane Langton
(2004) 6-1½ hour cassettes
Rental—$14.50   Purchase—$48.00
Read by Ruth Stokesberry

Emily Dickinson noted "Death's tremendous Nearness" in one of her poems. Of course, she'd been dead a hundred years when her admirers came to Amherst to celebrate her at a memorial symposium.

Among them was Homer Kelly, distinguished Thoreau scholar and ex-detective, who had himself dealt with murder, a form of death, in the past. To his amazement he finds himself once again embroiled in sudden death when murder stalks the symposium. *Dark Nantucket Noon*, *The Memorial Hall Murder* and *The Transcendental Murder* are other Jane Langton mysteries recorded by Books on Tape.

THE EMPTY COPPER SEA

By John D. MacDonald
(1318) 8-1 hour cassettes
Rental—$14.50   Purchase—$64.00
Read by Michael Prichard

When Hub Lawless falls overboard off the Florida coast, it's called a drowning. But no one quite believes it. Not Travis McGee, whose old friend Van Harder, skipper of Hub's boat, is blamed for the mishap. Not the insurance company, with whom Lawless had a two million dollar policy. And not Hub's wife, Julie, whose ESP has convinced her that he is dead, but not from drowning. It's all a messy business—and McGee is called upon to sort out all the contradictions and find the truth.

EPITAPH FOR A SPY

By Eric Ambler
(2121) 8-1 hour cassettes
Rental—$14.50   Purchase—$64.00
Read by Richard Brown

Josef Vadassy is the type you wouldn't notice in an empty room. A shy teacher of languages, his life is just a steady, gray stream. Until the day he arrives at a French hotel filled with holiday tourists, is arrested for a crime he hasn't yet committed, and begins his life in the icy undercurrents of international espionage.

"Ambler towers above his newer imitators!" *(The Los Angeles Times)*

Other Eric Ambler thrillers available from Books on Tape include *Cause for Alarm*, *A Coffin for Dimitrios* and *Journey Into Fear*.

THE EXTORTIONERS

By John Creasey
(1330) 6-1 hour cassettes
Rental—$12.50   Purchase—$48.00
Read by Richard Green

Inspector West is up against a clutch of ruthless hoodlums who will stop at nothing to achieve their objective. West's search leads him to the world's most illustrious anthropologists.

With the assistance of his ham-fisted but talented associate, Venables, West uncovers a syndicate illegally operating a mining venture in central Australia . . . an area which contains agreat anthropological discovery. The Inspector emerges solution in hand and reputation intact.

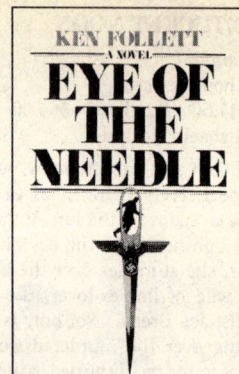

THE EYE OF THE NEEDLE

By Ken Follett
(1400) 7-1½ hour cassettes
Rental—$15.50   Purchase—$56.00
Read by Richard Green

The time is early 1944, the place a secluded area on the east coast of England. To keep the impending invasion of Normandy a secret, American and British forces have constructed a "fake" military site here—complete with imitation ships, plywood airplanes, barracks and equipment. The Germans are meant to "discover" this operation through aerial photographs.

However, a German spy has uncovered the deception and is trying to meet up with a German U-boat to report the Allied plan to the Germans. The whole outcome of the war hangs in the balance.

FIRST STRIKE

By Douglas Terman
(1500) 10-1½ hour cassettes
Rental—$16.50   Purchase—$80.00
Read by Bob Erickson

At an underground factory in Siberia, the Russians have made a replica of a U.S. Navy warhead. In Moscow, Soviet military planners carefully review the latest computer assessment of their chances to survive all-out nuclear war. And the KGB selects its target for high level political subversion . . . a vulnerable U.S. senator with presidential ambitions.

"A winner . . . a whirlwind of a book and shockingly immediate . . . Enough to scare the eyeballs out of any reader who still dwells in international innocence." —Ernest K. Gann

FREE FALL IN CRIMSON

By John D. MacDonald
(1593) 8-1 hour cassettes
Rental—$14.50   Purchase—$64.00
Read by Michael Prichard

Free Fall in Crimson is a Travis McGee mystery that was the choice of four book clubs on its publication. It is the story of an inherited fortune and an unsolved murder. It ranges from Florida to California and involves McGee in everything from motorcycles to movies to hot air balloons. As the pace quickens, McGee moves with increasing assurance and in the book's turbulent climax is fully restored as our reigning folk hero.

FREE FLIGHT

By Douglas Terman
(1646) 8-1/2 hour cassettes
Rental—$15.50   Purchase—$64.00
Read by Bob Erickson

The Russians have won WW III with a brief, horrifying nuclear strike. Greg Mallen, American Air Force officer, is one of the survivors. He sets out on a do-or-die mission to save what is left of humanity.

A national best seller, *Free Flight* was described by *The New York Times* as "A gripping book superbly written!" The *Washington Post* said, "As distinctive and carefully crafted a suspense novel as we are likely to see . . . lean, taut, beautifully articulated.

"THE GEMINI CONTENDERS

By Robert Ludlum
(1756) 10-1/2 hour cassettes
Rental—$16.50   Purchase—$80.00
Read by Michael Prichard

December 9, 1939. Salonika, Greece. Five trucks enter the guarded encampment of the Order of Xenope, a harsh monastic brotherhood.

All instructions and schedules have been meticulously planned. The objective: to deliver a small iron vault into the hands of one Savarone Fontini-Christi, a wealthy and influential padrone of northern Italy. The vault has been buried for over 15 centuries. What are its contents, and why is there such desperate urgency?

THE GIRL IN THE PLAIN BROWN WRAPPER

By John D. MacDonald
(1667) 7-1/2 hour cassettes
Rental—$15.50   Purchase—$56.00
Read by Michael Prichard

While making good his promise to prevent a young girl from committing suicide, Travis McGee encounters an entirely new string of problems of his own. Attempting to salvage someone else's troubled life, McGee soon finds it is enough just to keep his own neck out of the noose! As with all of John D. MacDonald's books, *The Girl in the Plain Brown Wrapper* is filled with the special insights into human fears and desires that millions of readers have come to expect from him.

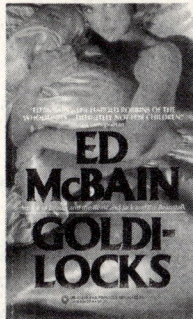

GOLDILOCKS

By Ed McBain
(1962) 6-1 hour cassettes
Rental—$12.50   Purchase—$48.00
Read by Michael Prichard

On the steamy west coast of Florida, in the quiet of their home, a woman and her two little girls have been brutally murdered. The one person who couldn't possibly have a motive for the crime is the only one confessing to it, and he insists on Matthew Hope for his defense. Now Matt finds himself tangled in unravelling three heartless killings in which every half-sister, stepson and first wife seemed to have had a hand. Somebody must be lying—maybe everybody.

"Ed McBain is clearly having fun with attorney Matthew Hope . . . a likable character and an interesting locale . . . the next Hope thriller cannot come too soon for me." *(Omaha World Herald)*

GORKY PARK

By Martin Cruz Smith
(1692) 10-1/2 hour cassettes
Rental—$16.50   Purchase—$$80.00
Read by Wolfram Kandinsky

Three mutilated bodies are discovered in Moscow's Gorky Park, frozen solid in deep snow. When Chief Homicide Investigator Arkady Renko of the local police finds a surly KGB officer already at the site, he suspects that these are no ordinary murders.

Arkady Renko is an anomaly in the cynical Soviet society—too brilliant an investigator and too courageous a man not to solve the Gorky Park murders, no matter the cost.

Gorky Park, coming out of the blue and all unheralded, became a great literary success. Harrison Salisbury stated, "A tour de force, written with equal dexterity and realism. Super!"

GREAT TALES OF MYSTERY

By Various Authors
(9168) 7-1/2 hour cassettes
Rental—$16.50   Purchase—$56.00
Read by Various Readers
A Jimcin Recording

This collection of nine short stories includes: "The Mystery of Marie Roget" by Edgar Allan Poe, "The Queer Feet" by G.K. Chesterton, "The Invisible Man" by G.K. Chesterton, "The Mysterious Death on the Underground Railway" by Baroness Orczy and "The Fated Five Hundred" by Robert Barr.

"The Aluminum Daggar" By R. Austen Freeman, "The Redhill Sisterhood" by Catherine Louisa Pirkis, "The Mystery of Room 666" by Jacques Futrelle, "The Trailer Murder Mystery" by Abraham Lincoln and "The Sheriff of Gullmore" by Melville Davidson Post round out this collection.

GREEN DARKNESS

By Anya Seton
(1184-A) 9-1/2 hour cassettes
Rental—$16.50   Purchase—$72.00
(1184-B) 8-1/2 hour cassettes
Rental—$15.50   Purchase—$64.00
Read by Penelope Dellaporta

This story of troubled love takes place simultaneously during two periods of time: today and 400 years ago. We meet Richard and Celia Marsdon, an attractive young couple, whose family traces its lineage back to medieval England. Richard's growing depression creates a crisis in Celia, and she falls desperately ill. Lying unconscious and near death, Celia's spirit journeys backward to a time four centuries earlier when another Celia loved another Marsdon.

"No one writing today has a greater capacity to make the reader feel the joys and stresses of another age."

"B-O-T has also recorded Seton's *Devil Water*.

THE GREEN MAN

By Kingsley Amis
(1229) 7-1 hour cassettes
Rental—$13.50   Purchase—$56.00
Read by Richard Green

We turn with delight to any book by Kingsley Amis. His mixture of humor, sex and suspense marks *The Green Man* as a premiere B-O-T entry. This sophisticated ghost story takes place in an English medieval coaching inn that has been converted into a class-A restaurant called The Green Man. One of its features is a ghost who remains with you long after the book is completed. A delicious blend of satire, terror, suspense and metaphysics, *The Green Man* is a superbly macabre entertainment treat.

THE GREEN RIPPER

By John D. MacDonald
(1449) 7-1 hour cassettes
Rental—$13.50   Purchase—$56.00
Read by Michael Prichard

In what is nearly his final adventure, Travis McGee falls deeply in love with Gretel, his live-aboard boatmate. Then Gretel is horribly and impersonally murdered.

Desperate and half-demented, McGee sets out to find the killers. The trail leads him to the Church of Apocrypha, an eerily familiar religious cult whose converts are given terrorist training.

The Green Ripper is the most brutal and suspenseful outing of McGee's career, and we find a different kind of "knight errant" emerging from its savagery.

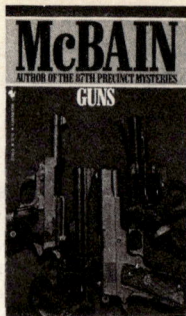

GUNS

By Ed McBain
(2092) 7-1 hour cassettes
Rental—$13.50   Purchase—$56.00
Read by Michael Prichard

Colley Donato, twenty-nine, was just a small-time crook. Then he got very big, very quick. He killed a cop.

Colley and his buddies make a habit of robbing liquor stores in New York—quick cash, easy pickings. But today something is very wrong. The weather is hot, tempers short, and it's their thirteenth job. Colley doesn't like it at all.

He likes it less when two cops come charging down the aisle with guns drawn. As if in slow motion, Colley sees his own gun come up, sees his own finger pull the trigger.

"A crime novel tougher, grittier, even more suspenseful than McBain's famous 87th Precinct series." *(Reviews for Readers)*

HAIL THE CONQUERING HERO

By Frank Yerby
(1405-A) 8-1½ hour cassettes
Rental—$15.50   Purchase—$64.00
(1405-B) 8-1½ hour cassettes
Rental—$15.50   Purchase—$64.00
Read by Dan Lazar

In the imaginary Caribbean republic of Costa Verde, a sinister cabal wields the power. Against them Frank Yerby sets an untested United States ambassador, James Randolph Rush. When Rush discovers trades are under way swapping oil for nuclear weapons, he blows the whistle.

This was his first fictional work to be published nationally and it won a special O. Henry Award.

XXX-rated for language and sex.

HELL IS TOO CROWDED

By Jack Higgins
(1476) 4-1 hour cassettes
Rental—$9.50   Purchase—$32.00
Read by Larry McKeever

The face swimming at him out of the fog. The strange woman appearing suddenly. The invitation to her flat. The offer of a drink . . . that drink was the last thing Matt Brady remembered.

When he woke, police were all around . . . and the body of the girl was lying near him. Of course, they did not believe his story. He was charged with murder and sent to prison.

But few prisons can hold Brady, and he knew he had to get out . . . fast! He had to find out the truth behind this crazy nightmare. Who wanted to frame him? Who wanted him out of the way?

THE HOLCRAFT COVENANT

By Robert Ludlum
(1758) 13-1½ hour cassettes
Rental—$18.50   Purchase—$104.00
Read by Michael Prichard

Noel Holcroft, a young American architect, flies to Geneva where he sees an astonishing document. Drawn up more than 30 years ago by three ostensibly repentant Nazis, it is the key to a $780 million fund sequestered by the trio to aid survivors of the Holocaust. All that is required is Holcroft's signature.

But the document is a lie and the fund's real purpose is to establish a new Nazi Reich. If Holcroft signs the document, he will be validating his own death warrant . . . .but paradoxically, only by signing it can he prevent the plot he has uncovered from reaching its predestined conclusion.

THE HONORABLE SCHOOLBOY

By John le Carré
(1119) 15-1½ hour cassettes
Rental—$18.50   Purchase—$120.00
Read by Wolfram Kandinsky

The Honourable Schoolboy continues the career of spychief George Smiley. Smiley sets out to rebuild the reputation of the British Secret Service, which has been shattered by a high level defection. Smiley recruits Jerry Westerby, the honourable schoolboy of the title, to help him trace funds flowing from Hong Kong to Communist China. Westerby is a pawn in Smiley's bigger game and learns at last what it means to be expendable.

I, THE JURY

By Mickey Spillane
(1835) 4-1½ hour cassettes
Rental—$13.50   Purchase—$32.00
Read by Richard Wulf

Meet Mike Hammer, the toughest private eye in New York City. When his best friend gets the business from a forty-five, Hammer sets out to nail the killer.

Suspects include an ex-bootlegger, the dead man's drug-addicted fiancée, and a voluptuous blond psychiatrist—to name a few. Hammer, alone on his one-man mission of vengeance, does solo duty as fudge, jury and executioner.

"Spillane is a master . . . you always want to turn the next page" *(The New York Times)*

IN CASE OF EMERGENCY

By Georges Simenon
(1510) 5-1 hour cassettes
Rental—$11.50   Purchase—$40.00
Read by Michael Prichard

In this novel of obsession, Lucien Gobillot, a respected criminal lawyer, takes as his mistress a prostitute who celebrates infidelity like a virtue.

Driven by forces he cannot control, Gobellot plumbs the depths of degradation. It is logical he should find murder waiting there.

Also available from B-O-T are Simenon's *The Heart of a Man, The Premier, Maigret Sets a Trap, None of Maigret's Business* and other titles listed in our Index.

IN CONNECTION WITH KILSHAW

By Peter Driscoll
(1078) 8-1 hour cassettes
Rental—$14.50   Purchase—$64.00
Read by Chris Winfield

British Intelligence veteran Harry Finn is sent to Ireland to kill James Campbell Kilshaw, a Protestant extremist leader. This decision, reluctantly arrived at, is expected to defuse a highly inflammable situation and avert a full-scale civil was.

As the threat grows with each passing hour, Finn is caught up in the ancient conflict and soon realizes that even he as an outsider must prepare to fight for his life.

"Driscoll is a good writer and a baffling entertainer, and he has us at his mercy all the way." *(The New Yorker)*

IN THE HOUR BEFORE MIDNIGHT

By Jack Higgins
(1456) 6-1 hour cassettes
Rental—$12.50   Purchase—$48.00
Read by Ian Whitcomb

Stacey Wyatt is a gifted pianist. He is also a competent mercenary soldier. But at the moment, he is sojourning in an Egyptian prison.

Sean Burke has plans to rescue him. Charity is not his motive. He merely needs Stacey for what becomes a deadly intrigue. There is just one hitch.

"An astonishing story of high-action and foreign intrigue. The developing play of confidences leads to an explosive climax unrivaled in the genre . . . " *(Reviewers Weekly)*

THE INCREDULITY OF FATHER BROWN

By G.K. Chesterton
(1837) 8-1 hour cassettes
Rental—$14.50   Purchase—$64.00
Read by Richard Green

"There was a brief period during which Father Brown enjoyed, or rather did not enjoy, something like fame. He was a nine days' wonder in the newspapers; he was even a topic of controversy in the weekly reviews; his exploits were narrated eagerly and accurately in any number of clubs and drawing-rooms . . . his adventures as a detective were even made the subject of short stories appearing in magazines."

Strangely enough, this renown reaches him at a most unwelcome time. Sent to officiate in a dispute in South America, he lands in the middle of a revolution, recognized, attacked and left for dead.

In fact everyone thinks he *is* dead—until he rises from his coffin, creating no end of trouble with the natives . . . for they certainly know a resurrection when they see one!

The Innocence of Father Brown and *The Wisdom of Father Brown* are also available on cassette from Books on Tape.

THE INNOCENCE OF FATHER BROWN

By G.K. Chesterton
(1762) 8-1 hour cassettes
Rental—$14.50   Purchase—$64.00
Read by Richard Green

Shortly after the publication of *Orthodoxy*, G.K. Chesterton moved from London to Beaconsfield, where he met Father O'Connor. It was the combination of Father O'Conner's shrewd insights to the darker side of man's nature with his mild appearance that suggested to Chesterton a character that became the usassuming, pudding-faced Father Brown.

Numerous short stories followed. All of them featuring this priest who appeared to know nothing yet in fact knew more about criminals than they knew about themselves. *The Innocence of Father Brown* is the first collection of thes stories.

"Father Brown is a direct challenge to the conventional detective and in many ways he is more amusing and ingenious." *(Saturday Review)*

INSPECTOR MAIGRET AND THE STRANGLED STRIPPER

By Georges Simenon
(1507) 5-1 hour cassettes
Rental—$11.50   Purchase—$40.00
Read by Michael Prichard

A dancer in a Montmartre bar hears two men planning to murder a countess. After work she takes her story to the police. Later she retraces it. Nevertheless, both she and the countess are soon dead.

Enter Jules Maigret. His famous method is based primarily on intuitive imagination. Maigret immerses himself in the ambience of the crime.

"Well characterized . . . adroitly handled." *(The New York Times)*

INSPECTOR WEST ALONE

By John Creasey
(1329) 7-1½ hour cassettes
Rental—$15.00   Purchase—$56.00
Read by Stuart Courtney

The Inspector has been framed for murder! He is found by the police in an empty house with the body of a dead girl near him, battered with an axe bearing West's fingerprints. And the identification in his wallet is not his own. He risks career, like and the safety of everyone close to him as he untangles this set-up.

John Creasey's *The Extortioners* has also been recorded by B-O-T.

Books on Tape™'s service is 100% guaranteed

THE IRON TIGER

By Jack Higgins
(1477) 6-1 hour cassettes
Rental—$12.50   Purchase—$48.00
Read by Ian Whitcomb

Jack Drummond is an adventurer—a tough ex-Naval pilot who is fed up with too many hot countries and strange cities. He resolves to fly only one more mission.

Dropping off an illegal shipment of arms in Tibel (his last), Drummond is suddenly caught up in a bloody border war. To escape he must fly a boy King and a very beautiful woman to their safety.

But someone has burned his plane and destroyed his supplies. To survive he must take on the entire ChiCom army. Against them he has only a plan. A very desperate plan.

"Higgins is a wonderful storyteller." (*The New York Times*)

JACK AND THE BEANSTALK

By Ed McBain
(1965) 6-1½ hour cassettes
Rental—$14.50   Purchase—$48.00
Read by Michael Prichard

Jack McKinney's mother thought he was a tennis bum. His sister thought he was a rustler. McKinney himself thought he was going to turn a bankrupt snapbean farm into a paying operation.

On a steamy August day, the unemployed 20-year-old plunked down a $4,000 deposit on the farm, promised the remaining $36,000 in cash, and ordered attorney Matthew Hope to push the deal through. Four days later, McKinney was dead—no sign of the cash.

As Hope is drawn deeper into the dead-man's affairs, he runs into a far-from-grieving mother, a sexually provoking sister, and a prostitute who's come into a sudden windfall.

THE KEEP

By F. Paul Wilson
(1797) 10-1½ hour cassettes
Rental—$16.50   Purchase—$80.00
Read by Michael Prichard

An eerie fortress called The Keep stands atop Dinu Pass in the Balkan Alps. A commander of Nazi troops establishes his base within its massive, cross-covered walls. Soon afterward he sends a cryptic message to headquarters in Warsaw: "*Something* is murdering my men.

"An elite SS extermination squad is dispatched to the scene. But it is no match for what waits.

"A battle between good and evil that staggers the imagination, with an ending as dramatic and exciting as any horror fan could wish!"(*Providence Journal*)

Note: Suitable for adult listening.

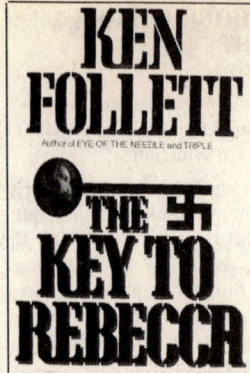

KEN FOLLETT
Author of EYE OF THE NEEDLE and TRIPLE
THE KEY TO REBECCA

THE KEY TO REBECCA

By Ken Follett
(1563) 8-1½ hour cassettes
Rental—$15.50   Purchase—$64.00
Read by Richard Green

Infiltrated into the kaleidoscopic world of wartime Cairo, a lone German agent, Alex Wolff, using a code whose key is buried in Daphne du Maurier's famous novel, *Rebecca*, works to help Rommel gain the city. He is opposed by a singular British intelligence officer. Both men have as companions loneliness and danger; each burns with equal commitment and discipline. Into this steaming cauldron of emotional repression Ken Follett stirs Woman—or rather two women.

"This is surely Ken Follett's finest book."(*E.R.S. Services*)

THE KEYS OF HELL

By Jack Higgins
(1478) 4-1 hour cassettes
Rental—$9.50   Purchase—$32.00
Read by Larry McKeever

Super spy Paul Chavasse is looking forward to a vacation when the Chief says there's a simple little job he'd like Chavasse to do first. Of course nothing the Chief ever wants is simple or little: it is invariably large and lethal. The job: get into Albania and put a dangerous double agent out of commission—permanently. What Chavasse doesn't know is that someone has set a trap for him—someone who has waited a long time for revenge—someone who has planned his destruction—someone who holds the keys to hell!

**FREE rental from
Books on Tape™
See page 3**

THE KOBRA MANIFESTO

By Adam Hall
(1570) 6-1½ hour cassettes
Rental—$14.50   Purchase—$48.00
Read by Michael Prichard

A Yugoslavian plane crashes in the south of France; a fuel tanker explodes at Rome airport; a British diplomat is shot dead in Phnom Penh. In each case Quiller, Adam Hall's relentless British agent, witnesses the violence as he pursues a fanatical terrorist group known only as Kobra.

The Kobra Manifesto is the seventh of Adam Hall's highly acclaimed series of Quiller novels. This chilling novel has all the gloss, pace and tension of Ian Fleming, combined with a detailed knowledge of secret service procedures characteristic of John le Carré.

"Tense, intelligent, harsh, surprising." (*The New York Times*)

THE LAND GOD GAVE TO CAIN

By Hammond Innes
(1805) 7-1½ hour cassettes
Rental—$15.50   Purchase—$56.00
Read by John Voight

Ian Ferguson learns that his father's death was precipitated by an S.O.S. radioed from the Labrador peninsula. The mystery is that the message came from a man believed to be dead, victim of a fiery plane crash during an earlier geological expedition.

Ian sets out across Canada's desolate north. Here he unravels the mystery surrounding the expedition and its bizarre connection with his grandfather's murder some 50 years before.

THE LEAVENWORTH CASE

By Anna Katharine Green
(9148) 8-1½ hour cassettes
Rental—$16.50   Purchase—$64.00
Read by Jim Killavey
A Jimcin Recording

Horatio Leavenworth is a New York merchant whose material wealth is matched by his eminence in the community and reputation for good works. He is also the guardian of two striking nieces who share his Fifth Avenue mansion. Mary, her uncle's favorite, is to inherit his fortune at his death. As this mystery opens, that lamentable event has just occurred. Leavenworth has been shot to death and circumstances point to one of his young wards.

Circumstantial evidence points in one direction; but is that the trail to follow? Not to give anything away, but Yale University used this book in its law school to demonstrate the fallability of such evidence.

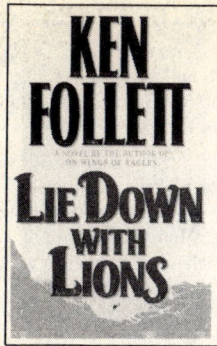

LIE DOWN WITH LIONS

By Ken Follett
(1558) 9-1½ hour cassettes
Rental—$16.50   Purchase—$72.00
Read by Richard Green

Afghanistan is a hard, high, cold and cruel land. It sits on the roof of the world and looks down into Russia, Persia, India. It is a strategic prize, and has been through history. The Russian invasion in 1980 ignited a full scale guerrilla war.

A young English woman, a French physician, and a roving American meet in the remote Valley of the Five Lions. Jean-Pierre brings medical relief, his pregnant wife, Jane, aids the native women, and Ellis, the American, bears a message for the legendary leader of the rebels, Masad.

"Follett builds menace as only he can, setting a hunted pair with a babe in arms in flight across an impassable mountain, clambering over ice-covered crags, pursued by enemy helicopters—as he leads us to a confrontation that echoes all our nightmares."*(Publishers Source)*

THE LIGHT OF DAY

By Eric Ambler
(2138) 8-1 hour cassettes
Rental—$14.50   Purchase—$64.00
Read by Richard Brown

Arthur Simpson was out of his league. Hustling a tourist, a little pimping, a quick hand in a pocket . . . these Simpson could handle. But an international jewel heist was another story.

Of course, Simpson has a choice. He could always say "No"—and spend the rest of his life rotting in a Turkish jail.

"Mr. Ambler had never done better." *(Library Journal)*

Other Ambler thrillers recorded by Books on Tape include *A Coffin for Dimitrios* and *Cause For Alarm.*

THE LITTLE DRUMMER GIRL

By John le Carré
(1910) 13-1½ hour cassettes
Rental—$18.50   Purchase—$104.00
Read by Richard Green

Leaving behind the world of Smiley and his people, le Carré leads us into a new maze of intrigue in this thrilling and complex spy story. The setting is the Middle East in 1977. Seeking revenge for a series of PLO attacks on Jews throughout Europe, Israeli intelligence agents stalk a lethal and elusive terrorist. A young English actress baits the deadly trap.

This best seller "raises both hair and hackles. Le Carré has plunged directly into one of the most anguished and impassioned conflicts on earth." *(Time)*

For a complete list of le Carré books recorded by B-O-T, please refer to our Index.

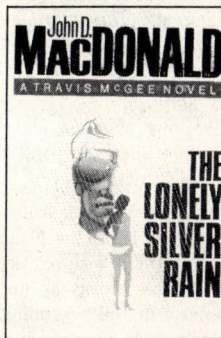

THE LONELY SILVER RAIN

By John D. MacDonald
(1451) 7-1 hour cassettes
Rental—$13.50   Purchase—$56.00
Read by Michael Prichard

The disappearance of a custom-built yacht . . . the brutal murder of a Peruvian debutante . . . the sloppy "accidental death" of a Florida tycoon. These are the pieces of the puzzle Travis McGee must fit together to save his own life.

It is becoming very clear that someone wants to add McGee's name to the list of casualties. McGee figures the only way he can stay off that roster is to sound the alarm, to shatter the uneasy peace that reigns between opposing forces in Miami's underworld.

This is the 21st best-selling Travis McGee adventure in our series of John D. MacDonald novels. See the Index for the complete list.

THE LONG LAVENDER LOOK

By John D. MacDonald
(1668) 6-1½ hour cassettes
Rental—$14.50   Purchase—$48.00
Read by Michael Prichard

While driving along a darkened stretch of Florida road, Travis McGee and friend Meyer encounter a young girl wearing little more than a frightened look as she leaps out from the shadows directly in line with their headlights. A skillful swerve saves the girl but finds McGee and friend upside down in ten feet of swamp water. Not two minutes later they are dodging bullets fired from a speeding pickup. McGee reports these unusual events to the local sheriff and finds himself arrested for murder!

More McGee from B-O-T: *The Dreadful Lemon Sky, Cinnamon Skin, The Deep Blue Good-By* and *Free Fall in Crimson.*

LONG TIME NO SEE

By Ed McBain
(1773) 5-1½ hour cassettes
Rental—$13.50   Purchase—$40.00
Read by Dan Lazar

One cold Novembr night Detectives Carella and Meyer of the 87th Precinct examine the cold body of a murdered blind man, Jimmy Harris. Then they talk to his widow. She is blind, too, but says she can identify the body anyway. She never does. Next day her throat is cut. Was it money . . . a $25,000 insurance policy? Thrills . . . someone with a thing for blind people? Or just hatred?

The more Carella and Meyer dig into the case—from file rooms to massage parlors—the more they become convinced that the key to the crime lies buried in the past—and only one man knows the answer. Somehow the corpse of James Harris must be made to talk.

Beauty and the Beast, Goldilocks and *Jack and the Beanstalk* are all Ed McBain titles available on cassette from Books on Tape.

THE LOOKING GLASS WAR

By John le Carré
(1088) 8-1 hour cassettes
Rental—$14.50   Purchase—$64.00
Read by Wolfram Kandinsky

The Looking Glass War is the story of a former military espionage department in London—a small, obsolete operation left over from WW II. Le Clerc, the department's obsessed director, struggles to keep his operation afloat.

On the flimsiest of pretexts he sends Leiser, a Polish defector and former agent, into East germany. From the beginning we know it isn't going to work. But Leiser is a professional and has a chance to pull it off.

MAIGRET AND THE BUM

By Georges Simenon
(1514) 4-1 hour cassettes
Rental—$9.50   Purchase—$32.00
Read by Michael Prichard

Georges Simenon, writing auto-biographically, once confessed his desire to drop out of society, to sever family ties and disassociate fimself from friends.

His empathy with misfits is reflected in Simenon's police superintendent Jules Maigret. When Maigret learns that a bum's murder is in reality an assassination, he becomes deeply involved in what without him would have been left as an unremarkable event.

Maigret must discover the identity of the man who had been living under the Seine bridge, then find out why anyone would want him dead.

MAIGRET AND THE WINE MERCHANT

By Georges Simenon
(1518) 5-1 hour cassettes
Rental—$11.50   Purchase—$40.00
Read by Michael Prichard

While interrogating a penniless delinquent about a sordid crime, Maigret is called to the scene of an utterly different murder; one of the richest wine merchants in Paris is dead.

"Georges Simenon's Chief Inspector Maigret belongs to the Paris of today as surely as Holmes did to gaslit London." *(The New York Times Book Review)*

More Maigret from B-O-T: *Maigret Sets a Trap, Inspector Maigret and the Strangled Stripper, Maigret's Christmas* and *None of Maigret's Business*

MAIGRET SETS A TRAP

By Georges Simenon
(1508) 5-1 hour cassettes
Rental—$11.50   Purchase—$40.00
Read by Michael Prichard

A human life baits the trap when Inspector Maigret goes after the murderer of five women. All victims have had the same build, all were knifed at night in the streets of Montmartre, all had their clothes slashed.

Consulting with a distinguished psychiatrist, Maigret creates a psychological profile of the killer, and nervously watches waiting for his trap to be sprung. The plan seems to be working—until another totally unexpected crime occurs.

MAIGRET'S BOYHOOD FRIEND

By Georges Simenon
(1517) 6-1 hour cassettes
Rental—$12.50   Purchase—$48.00
Read by Michael Prichard

On a calm day in mid-summer, Maigret receives a visit from a former schoolmate whose detailed account of a murder he has witnessed leaves Maigret curiously puzzled.

As the Superintendent reflects on the story his friend has told him, he compares the mature man with his memories of the boy. While some clues point to his friend as the murderer, Maigret remains doubtful.

Maigret finally discerns the truth as he contrasts the reality of the murder with the inventions of a compulsive deceiver.

"As usual, while other writers flail away at huge lumps of story and end up with rhinestones, Georges Simenon works small and produces a diamond." *(The Saturday Review)*

MAIGRET'S CHRISTMAS

By Georges Simenon
(1223) 10-1½ hour cassettes
Rental—$16.50   Purchase—$80.00
Read by Michael Prichard

Maigret's Christmas is a collection of nine superb stories, Inspector Maigret, appearing in eight of them. Maigret, unlike any other stock detective, works by immersing himself completly in the psychological atmosphere of the case in which he is engaged. Maigret is as famous in Belgium and France as Sherlock Holmes is in England and America—exhibiting equally keen insights into human motivation and oddities of personality.

THE MALTESE FALCON

By Dashiell Hammett
(1258) 7-1 hour cassettes
Rental—$13.50   Purchase—$56.00
Read by Michael Prichard

Sam Spade's partner is murdered while working on a case, and it is Spade's responsibility to find the killer. In his search Spade runs mortal risks as he comes closer to the answer.

When this book was first published, the *London Times* wrote: "This is not only probably the best detective story we have ever read, it is also an exceedingly well-written novel." The years that have passed sice then have only enhanced the book's reputation. It stands today as one of the classics of both suspense literature and American writing.

THE MAN IN LOWER TEN

By Mary Roberts Rinehart
(9163) 5-1 hour cassettes
Rental—$12.50   Purchase—$40.00
Read by Jim Killavey
A Jimcin Recording

Lawrence Blakely, attorney-at-law, sets off by train to deliver valuable documents in a criminal case. Along the way he encounters romance, treachery, a murder in which he is implicated and, finally, a train wreck.

This is Mary Roberts Rinehart's second mystery in the "had-I-but-known" school which she pioneered. It followed closely upon the enormous success of *The Circular Staircase* and proved to be just as popular. *The Circular Staircase* is also available from Books on Tape.

THE MAN WHO WAS THURSDAY

By G.K. Chesterton
(9141) 5-1½ hour cassettes
Rental—$13.50   Purchase—$40.00
Read by Walter Covell
A Jimcin Recording

The Man Who Was Thursday, is an allegorical novel disguised as a detective story. Gabrial Syme, a poet buy also a policemen, lives in an upside-down world. For balance, he joins a group of anarchists, the Supreme Council of Seven, where each member takes a day of the week for his name.

Subscribers who enjoy *The Man Who Was Thursday* may want to sample *Heretics, The Innocence of Father Brown, The Napoleon of Notting Hill* and other Chesterton titles listed in our Index.

THE MANCHURIAN CANDIDATE

By Richard Condon
(1048) 7-1½ hour cassettes
Rental—$15.50   Purchase—$56.00
Read by Daniel Grace

The Manchurian Candidate is the fictional account of a far-from-ordinary G.I. who is brainwashed while held as a Korean POW. He returns to the United States as a programmed, remote-controlled killer. *The Manchurian Candidate* is a remarkable penetration of the human mind, its foibles and its ultimate malleability.

**For Visa and MasterCard
order line 1-800-626-3333**

THE MANDARIN CYPHER

By Adam Hall
(2089) 8-1 hour cassettes
Rental—$14.50   Purchase—$64.00
Read by Grover Gardner

NEW

Quiller is in Hong Kong, where he thinks he's on vacation. But every alleyway leads dead to danger, and Quiller gets the message: he's never off duty.

The plot moves into high gear. Quiller always enjoys his rides, but this one is taxing. He finds a woman as faithless as she is beautiful; he fails to reform her, but enjoys the effort. He takes on villains one, two and three at a time and dispatches them on land with karate and in the South China Sea with its aquatic equivalent.

"Breathless entertainment." *(Associated Press)*

Other Adam Hall thrillers recorded by B-O-T include *The Kobra Manifesto, The Ninth Directive, The Quiller Memorandum* and *The Sinkiang Executive.*

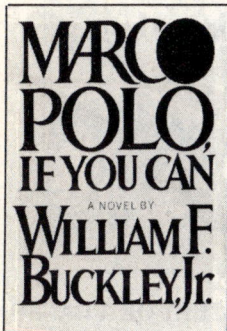

MARCO POLO, IF YOU CAN

By William F. Buckley Jr.
(1643) 8-1 hour cassettes
Rental—$14.50   Purchase—$64.00
Read by Michael Prichard

William F. Buckley, Jr. editor of *National Review*, may be remembered by posterity as the novelist who created Blackford Oaks. In this installment, Buckley used a celebrated incident of 20 years ago to create a fictional adventure consistent with official history.

Oaks has just been cashiered from the Agency, when his boss decides he is the only man for an excptionally dirty piece of work. Oaks agrees to return, but in short order finds himself standing before a secret Soviet military tribunal which has as its subject his execution for spying.

B-O-T also offers its listeners Buckley's *Saving the Queen, Stained Glass, Airborne* and *Who's on First.*

MARTIN HEWITT, INVESTIGATOR

By Arthur Morrison
(9050) 7-1 hour cassettes
Rental—$14.50   Purchase—$56.00
Read by Walter Covell
A Jimcin Recording

Martin Hewitt came to life in 1891 in *The Strand* magazine and appeared episodically through 1905. His personality and methods are in contrast to Sherlock Holmes', but his deductive powers and results rival anything dreamed up by Arthur Conan Doyle.

We first meet Hewitt in the "Lenton Croft Robberies" where his task is to solve three successive thefts where the only clues are three half-burned matches.

Additional stories include "The Case of the Dixon Torpedo," "The Loss of Sammy Crocket," "The Stanway Cameo Mystery," "The Holford Will Case" and (gruesomely) "The Case of the Missing Hand."

THE MATARESE CIRCLE

By Robert Ludlum
(1759-A) 7-1½ hour cassettes
Rental—$15.50   Purchase—$56.00
(1759-B) 7-1½ hour cassettes
Rental—$15.50   Purchase—$56.00
Read by Michael Prichard

The world's top secret agents—the American, Scofield and the Russian, Taleniekov—have each sworn to kill the other. Yet know they must become allies in order to destroy the Matarese, an international circle of killers dedicated to reducing the world to chaos by assassination and terror.

"This is a chase story that will leave readers gasping for breath . . . " *(Booklist)* "It's a blockbuster!" *(The Wall Street Journal)*

THE MATLOCK PAPER

By Robert Ludlum
(1753) 7-1½ hour cassettes
Rental—$15.50   Purchase—$56.00
Read by Michael Prichard

Washington had been working its data banks and computers overtime. Finally, the machines came up with a name: James Barbour Matlock, the perfect man for the assignment.

This assignment was to cause Matlock and his loved ones great pain. But the soundless machines and the faceless men didn't care as long as a conspiracy called Nimrod was distroyed. "A 110% story all in overdrive, extraordinarily readable . . . Ludlum writes better and better." *(Kirkus Reviews)*

A MATTER OF HONOR

By Jeffrey Archer
(2017) 8-1½ hour cassettes
Rental—$17.50   Purchase—$64.00
Read by Dick Estell
A Christopher Enterprises Recording

When Colonel Scott dies, his will points the way to clearing the unspoken secret that shadowed his retirement and turned him from a WW II hero into a disgraced and broken man. It is up to Adam to follow.

The path leads to a Swiss bank and a vault, strongly guarded. It contains a priceless Russian icon, smuggled out of Russia by the last Czar, before passing into the hands of a Nazi war criminal.

As Adam works to clear his father's name, he stumbles across a revelation so explosive, so charged, so unexpected that it could change the balance of power between America and the Soviet Union. Suddenly, Adam is in great danger.

Slightly edited for radio presentation.

THE MEMORIAL HALL MURDER

By Jane Langton
(1592) 8-1 hour cassettes
Rental—$14.50 Purchase—$64.00
Read by Michael Prichard

This gripping story takes place during rehearsals for a Christmas performance of Handel's *Messiah*, and each chapter is introduced by a selection from his masterpiece. When someone bombs Memorial Hall, Hamilton Down, the corpulent and beloved choir master, disappears in the rubble. Fortunately on hand to help the local police set to work is Jane Langton's famous sleuth, Homer Kelly, present at Harvard as visiting lecturer in American Literature. Kelly carefully baits his trap. It snaps shut during the *Messiah's* thrilling finale, a fitting conclusion to the story and a proper orchestration for justice.

THE MENORAH MEN

By Lionel Davidson
(1328) 6-1½ hour cassettes
Rental—$14.50 Purchase—$48.00
Read by Rupert Keenlyside

The Menorah Men, Lionel Davidson's acclaimed best seller, is set in Israel, archaeologist, is persuaded to travel to Israel to decipher a recently discovered scroll. Its contents set him hot on the trail of the long-lost Menorah. Accompanied by Shoshana, a dusky Yemenite soldier who is his chauffeuse, Laing scours the Holy Land in a dangerous search for a priceless buried treasure.

MESSAGE FROM MALAGA

By Helen MacInns
(1372) 11-1½ hour cassettes
Rental—$17.50 Purchase—$88.00
Read by Wanda McCaddon

To the accompaniment of flamenco guitars, a drama of espionage begins in a cafe courtyard in Malaga. For Ian Ferrier, on a vacation visit to his old friend Jeff Reid, it means the starting dicovery that Reid, is more than just a wine exporter; he is in fact a CIA agent who smuggles Cuban refugees into Spain.

When a more important refugee—a high-ranking, defecting KGB agent—arrives, the drama intensifies. Ferrier finds himself alone and responsible for the defector's safety.

**Special 10% discount
See page 2**

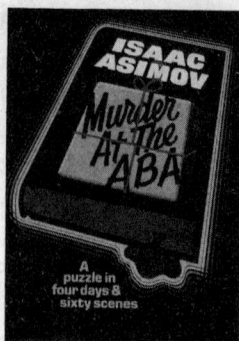

MURDER AT THE ABA

By Issac Asimov
(1054) 8-1 hour cassettes
Rental—$14.50 Purchase—$64.00
Read by Daniel Grace

This is Asimov's first mystery. Set at a recent meeting of the American Booksellers Association, the characters are so realistic that the author was compelled to write a disclaimer about names and events.

To the field of mystery writing, Asimov has brought his usual imaginative excellence and narrative drive. To these are coupled suspense and intrigue as the plot develops.

"Excellent. Asimov is a master of any genre he attempts." *(E.R.S. Reviews)*

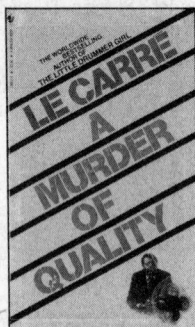

A MURDER OF QUALITY

By John le Carré
(1428) 6-1 hour cassettes
Rental—$12.50 Purchase—$48.00
Read by Rupert Keenlyside

"We're looking for a maniac, a man who kills for pleasure or the price of a meal." Only one man in the Service has a mind of sufficient subtlety to take on the assignment—George Smiley. He steps in to solve a baffling, bloody crime.

One key to the puzzle is a woman as dangerous as she is charming. Another is a tottering but brilliant operative haunted by a perverse secret buried deep in his past. Through them and beyond, Smiley trails his man.

"Le Carré is simply the world's greatest fictional spymaster." *(Newsweek)*

THE MYSTERY OF EDWIN DROOD

By Charles Dickens
(9157) 8-1½ hour cassettes
Rental—$16.50 Purchase—$64.00
Read by Walter Covell
A Jimcin Recording

The Mystery of Edwin Drood is Charles Dicken's contribution to the field of crime and its detection.

When young Edwin Drood disappears, suspicion centers on John Jasper, a drug-addicted choirmaster who hungers after Drood's fiancée. So is Neville Landless, a Ceylonese who has previously quarreled violently with the missing man.

The Mystery of Edwin Drood is further enhanced because it was left unfinished at the author's death. Thus the book has challenged the imagination of generations of readers.

"Certainly one of the most beautiful of his works, if not the most beautiful of all."
—Henry Wadsworth Longfellow

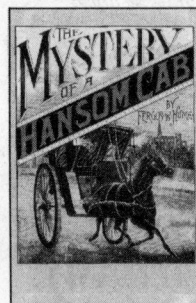

THE MYSTERY OF A HANSOM CAB

By Fergus Hume
(9153) 7-1½ hour cassettes
Rental—$16.50 Purchase—$56.00
Read by Walter Covell
A Jimcin Recording

This unlikely first literary attempt by a young law clerk in Australia, published in Melbourne, became *the* best-selling mystery novel of the nineteenth century, better even than Sherlock Holmes.

In the dead of night, on a dark, lonely street in Melbourne, a cabby discovers that his drunken passenger has been murdered—suffocated with a chloroform saturated handkerchief. The murderer, his motive, even the identity of the victim are unknow.

"The Mystery of a Hansom Cab has been virually forgotten, which itself is a mystery, for the book is ingeniously plotted, fast-paced and engrossing. Its characters are memorable and the atmosphere of Melbourne richly evoked. An outstanding story and a superior tale of suspense." *(Editorial Review Service)*

THE NAIVE AND SENTIMENTAL LOVER

By John le Carré
(1907) 12-1½ hour cassettes
Rental—$16.50   Purchase—$96.00
Read by Rupert Keenlyside

Aldo Cassidy is one of le Carrés most satisfying creations. A successful man of affairs, he is a fool in love. The triangle he gets himself into, with an artist and his wife, would be funny were it not so painful . . . and deadly.

"John le Carré's . . . thrillers placed him in the company of the foremost novelists writing to-day . . .

"Splendid, original . . . le Carré shows how endowed he is with the art of storytelling." *(The Times)* Books on Tape's collection of le Carré titles includes *Tinker, Tailor, Soldier, Spy; The Honourable Schoolboy; Smiley's People* and *The Little Drummer Girl.*

NIGHT OF THE GENERALS

By Hans Hellmut Kirst
(1041) 7-1½ hour cassettes
Rental—$15.50   Purchase—$56.00
Read by Daniel Grace

The author is best known for his *Revolt of Gunner Asch*, a sort of Catch-22 about the German army. *Night of the Generals* is a radical departure from prior themes. Kirst involves three fictional German generals with the brutal slayings of three women in three different cities over 20 years. Crammed with intrigue and suspense, the drama tethers us from start to finish. Highly recommended.

THE NIGHT OF WENCESLAS

By Lionel Davidson
(1326) 6-1 hour cassettes
Rental—$12.50   Purchase—$48.00
Read by Rupert Keenlyside

The Night of Wenceslas, Lionel Davidson's first novel, concerns Nicolas Whistler—24 years old, debt-ridden, thwarted in his attempts to rise in what was once the family business. Nicolas is inveigled to take a trip from London to Prague, ostensibly to smuggle out some industrial secrets. But the secrets are in fact atomic, and Nicolas lets himself in for more than he bargained.

Davidson's award-winning novel is a crisp thriller which offers, as the careful plans unravel, glimpses of the Czech-emigre network in England, and of the inner workings of the British Embassy in Prague.

NIGHTMARE IN PINK

By John D. MacDonald
(1663) 6-1 hour cassettes
Rental—$12.50   Purchase—$48.00
Read by Michael Prichard

Nightmare in Pink is the second Travis McGee adventure. In it McGee tackles a high risk free-lance assignment as a favor to Mike, his old wartime buddy.

Mike's sister Nina needs help. Her fiancée is dead, victim of murder, and the rap laid on him doesn't stop there. Will McGee give Nina a hand?

In the event, he gives her a hand and then some. Her initial coolness quickly turns to passion for the big Floridian. McGee hunts out leads no matter where they take him—to jet-setters, call girls, dopers.

"Another winner from John D. MacDonald. Tightly constructed, entertaining and loaded with action." *(E.R.S. Reviews)*

THE NINTH DIRECTIVE

By Adam Hall
(1209) 8-1 hour cassettes
Rental—$14.50   Purchase—$64.00
Read by Victor Rumbellow

The setting is Thailand. A very important representative of the Queen is scheduled to visit Bangkok on a good-will tour. A threat has been made against his life, and somewhere amidst the golden spires waits a deadly assassin. The top-secret British espionage bureau feels ordinary security precautions are not sufficient, so they call in agent Quiller. He's a cynical loner—but the only man capable of tracking down the would-be killer. The tale is complex, set at a breathless pace!

NONE OF MAIGRET'S BUSINESS

By Georges Simenon
(1509) 5-1 hour cassettes
Rental—$11.50   Purchase—$40.00
Read by Michael Prichard

None of Maigret's Business offers a new perspective on the Chief Inspector of the Paris police. Maigret's famous "method" involves totally immersing himself in the ambience of the crime in question. But this time Maigret, on a medically imposed leave of absence, has to follow a particularly baffling case in the newspapers just like any layman playing ameteur detective.

Unable to endure being sidelined, Maigret solves both his dilemma and the case by sending anonymous "hints" to his stymied subordinate.

NORTH FROM ROME

By Helen MacInnes
(1371) 9-1½ hour cassettes
Rental—$16.50   Purchase—$72.00
Read by Wanda McCaddon

Bill Lammiter, a young American playwright, has lost his girl and is on the point of leaving Rome. Then Lammiter saves a mysterious Italian girl from a beating and the fat is in the fire.

A kidnapping, a battle in a Renaissance villa, a schrewd gamekeeper, a chance snapshot, and a touring preppy contribute to the excitement and suspense, which also prove a testing ground for Lammiter and his sweetheart.

Other books by Helen MacInnes include: *Agent in Place, Prelude to Terror* and *The Snare of the Hunter.*

NORTH STAR

By Hammond Innes
(1810) 7-1½ hour cassettes
Rental—$15.50   Purchase—$56.00
Read by Charles Garst

Michael Randall is a man in a hurry. Desperate to succeed, he seeks his fortune in the oil sands far beneath the North Sea.

At the story's center is the Northstar, an obsolete and dangerous drilling platform anchored precariously off the Shetland Islands. This is where Randall takes his stand.

"Innes is a master storyteller. The vividness of his settings, the shaping of his characters and the control of his plots all contribute to a fantastic body of fiction . . . " *(Reader's Guild Service)*

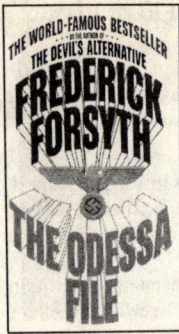

THE ODESSA FILE

By Frederick Forsyth
(1830) 8-1½ hour cassettes
Rental—$15.50   Purchase—$64.00
Read by Richard Green

The O.D.E.S.S.A is a group of SS survivors still active many years after the fall of the Third Reich. Far from being harmless they are ready to launch a new offensive—codename: Werwolf. Its goal: carry out Hitler's "final solution" twenty years after his death.

"In the hands of Frederick Forsyth, the documentary thriller achieves its most sophisticated form . . . The total effect is stunning . . . a brilliant entertainment." (*The Guardian*)

"A highly superior combination of real-life facts and suspense fiction." (*Publishers Weekly*)

The Devil's Alternative and *The Fourth Protocol* are other Frederick Forsyth titles available on cassette from Books on Tape.

THE OLD MAN IN THE CORNER

By Baroness Emmuska Orczy
(9175) 6-1½ hour cassettes
Rental—$15.50   Purchase—$48.00
Read by Walter Covell
A Jimcin Recording

NEW

Ensconced in a cozy corner of a London teashop, a nameless, shabbily dressed old man toys ceaselessly with a bit of string as he unravels the baffling crimes of the day for an admiring lady journalist. Relying solely on his vast Holmesian powers of deduction, the "strange looking" sleuth never deigns to visit the scene of the crime, question a suspect, or examine clues.

Nor does he have faith in conventional police methods and crime-solving capabilities: "There is no such thing as a mystery in connection with any crime, provided intelligence is brought to bear upon its investigation."

This enigmatic old man is the creation of Baroness Ocrzy (1865-1947) who gives us here an even dozen of her finest tales involving the perspicacious armchair detective.

ONE FEARFUL YELLOW EYE

By John D MacDonald
(1665) 6-1½ hour cassettes
Rental—$14.50   Purchase—$48.00
Read by Michael Prichard

An urgent call for help from Gloria Geis involves Travi McGee in a bizarre plot. Six hundred thousand dollars in cash has mysteriously been extorted from her husband during the last painful year of his life. Geis' other heirs accuse her of stealing. Obviously blackmail, but how and why?

"A finely wrought plot with the expected MacDonald action, wisdom and tension." (*Best Sellers*)

Please refer to our Index for other MacDonald books recorded by B-O-T.

THE OSTERMAN WEEKEND

By Robert Ludlum
(1752) 6-1½ hour cassettes
Rental—$14.50   Purchase—$48.00
Read by Michael Prichard

In a quiet suburban town a strange assortment of men and women gather for a momentious weekend. Meanwhile in Zurich, Moscow and Washington, the time machine is already ticking.

But countermeasures are in motion. In Washington, John Tanner bets his life in a gamble to destroy the menacing conspiracy that hangs over us all.

"Shattering . . . it will cost you the night and the cold hours of morning!" (*Cincinnati Enquirer*)

Ludlum titles available from B-O-T include: *The Parsifal Mosaic, The Bourne Identity* and many others listed in our Index.

For quick ordering
1-800-626-3333

PALE GRAY FOR GUILT

By John D. MacDonald
(1666) 6-1½ hour cassettes
Rental—$14.50   Purchase—$48.00
Read by Michael Prichard

We let the dust jacket tell the story: "Tush Bannon was in the way. It wasn't anything he knew or anything he had done. He was just there, in the wrong spot at the wrong time, and the fact that he was a nice guy with a nice wife and three nice kids didn't mean one scream in hell to the jackals who had ganged together to pull him down.

"And they got him, crushed him to hamburger, and walked away counting their change. But one thing they never could have figured . . .

"Tush Bannon was Travis McGee's friend."

The New York Times has called John D. MacDonald "one of the most creative and reliable writers of paperback originals."

PANGOLIN

By Peter Driscoll
(1491) 8-1½ hour cassettes
Rental—$15.50   Purchase—$64.00
Read by Rupert Keenlyside

Alan Pritchard has been a loser all his life. The opportunity to kidnap Rod Kiley, Southeast Asia's chief CIA operative, provides his last opportunity to be some sort of success. Filled with venomous hatred for Kiley (code name: Pangolin), Pritchard goes to work on his plan.

Pangolin is great suspense fiction. It also provides an inside look at the seamy side of life in Hong Kong and other parts of Southeast Asia. The reader feels the sticky heat of August in Kowloon and the awful crowding of the Hong Kong backstreets, riddled with drug traffic and prostitution. This panorama of packed humanity provides an excellent backdrop against which Pritchard and his men play out their desperate game.

THE PARSIFAL MOSAIC

By Robert Ludlum
(1761-A) 9-1½ hour cassettes
Rental—$16.50   Purchase—$72.00
(1761-B) 9-1½ hour cassettes
Rental—$16.50   Purchase—$72.00
Read by Michael Prichard

Conspiracies proliferate in this swiftly-paced thriller. A deceit of enormous consequences—if revealed—threatens to engulf the world in war, and only one man can untangle the knot.

The conclusion to this complex and compelling novel reveals Ludlum's storytelling virtuosity and clearly demonstrates why he holds the ranking position among America's most popular contemporary novelists.

"Ludlum stuffs more surprises into this one than any other six-pack of thrillers combined." (*The New York Times*)

PASSAGE BY NIGHT

By Jack Higgins
(1479) 5-1 hour cassettes
Rental—$11.50   Purchase—$40.00
Read by Larry McKeever

Harry Manning, a freebooter with a past he doesn't like to talk about, runs a charter boat in the Bahamas. Also, he boozes.

When his sweetheart leaves him by dying, Harry can find no relief. Except for the thought of revenge. And because he is Harry, he sets out to settle the score.

"Vengence is not a noble motive, but as this Jack Higgin's parable illustrates, it is a powerful and inspiring companion." (*E.R.S. Reviews*)

THE PASSENGER FROM SCOTLAND YARD

By H.F. Wood
(9133) 9-1½ hour cassettes
Rental—$17.50   Purchase—$72.00
Read by Walter Covell
A Jimcin Recording

Five men sat in a railroad compartment on the mail train from London to Dover. The same five men boarded the Channel steamer and crossed to Calais, where they entrained for Paris. By the time the train reaches Paris, we learn that one man is a detective from Scotland Yard, on the trail of a fortune in stolen gems; one unknown man is a murderer; and another, a corpse!

This impressive introduction leads the listener into a story that has been aptly characterized as the best detective novel between *The Moonstone* and *The Hound of the Baskervilles*.

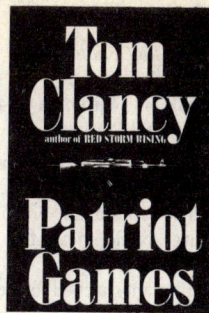

Tom Clancy
author of *RED STORM RISING*

Patriot Games

PATRIOT GAMES

NEW

By Tom Clancy
(2155-A) 8-1½ hour cassettes
Rental—$15.50   Purchase—$64.00
(2155-B) 7-1½ hour cassettes
Rental—$15.50   Purchase—$56.00
Read by Michael Prichard

It is fall. CIA analyst Jack Ryan, historian and former Marine, is vacationing in London with his wife and young daughter. Suddenly, right before his eyes, a terrorist group launches its deadly attack.

Instinctively, he dives forward to break it up, and is shot. It is not until he wakes up in the hospital that he learns whose lives he has saved—the Ulster Liberation Army, an ultra-left splinter of the IRA.

By his impulsive act, he has gained both the gratitude of a nation and the enmity of its most dangerous men—men who do not sit on their hate.

Patriot Games is a prequel to *The Hunt for Red October* and has all the excitement and energy of Clancy's famous first book. *The Hunt for Red October* is available from Books on Tape, as is *Red Storm Rising*, Clancy's brilliant conception of the origin of WW III.

THE PEKIN TARGET

NEW

By Adam Hall
(2112) 6-1½ hour cassettes
Rental—$14.50   Purchase—$48.00
Read by Richard Brown

In Peking ("Pekin" in British usage), the crowds are gathered for the funeral of the Chinese Premier. Quiller reports it: "The British delegates formed a short line along the side of the catafalque as their leader placed the Queen's wreath carefully against it; then suddenly the sky was filled with flowers and the bloodied body of the Secretary of State was hurled against me by the blast as the coffin exploded."

"Quiller takes over where Bond left off." (*Bookseller*)

Other Adam Hall titles available from Books on Tape include *The Quiller Memorandum, The Kobra Manifesto* and *The Mandarin Cypher*.

THE PEOPLE VERSUS KIRK

By Robert Traver
(1691) 9-1 hour cassettes
Rental—$15.50   Purchase—$72.00
Read by John MacDonald

Robert Traver is best known for his memorable *Anatomy of a Murder,* but all of his books exhibit carefully structured plots and fine craftsmanship.

Set in rural Michigan, this tale of a love triangle resolves its tensions in mortal violence. The story is more than a simple whodunit, and the means by which the mystery unravels leads the reader through a complicated maze.

"Powerful and moving. Traver's control is masterful." (*Editorial Review Service*)

A PERFECT SPY

By John le Carré
(2023-A) 8-1½ hour cassettes
Rental—$15.50   Purchase—$64.00
(2023-B) 7-1½ hour cassettes
Rental—$15.50   Purchase—$56.00
Read by Richard Green

A Perfect Spy plumbs the essential nature of espionage as it interweaves the story of a secret international manhunt with the unfolding of a secret life—the life of a man of spectacular gifts, nursed on deceit, schooled in betrayal, incapable of life: a perfect spy.

"*A Perfect Spy* is a magnificent novel whose most remarkable achievement is to immerse us at once in two parallel dramas—each totally gripping, the two togethr producing a force field in which suspense breeds suspense. It is a work that surpasses—in its mermerizing hold on the reader, its richness of story and character, and its moral resonance—any novel we have yet had from John le Carré." (*Publisher's Source*)

THE PIOUS AGENT

By John Braine
(1469) 7-1½ hour cassettes
Rental—$15.50   Purchase—$56.00
Read by Stuart Courtney

Xavier Flynn is the pious agent of John Braine's novel of treachery within the British Secret Service. A devout Roman Catholic, Flynn belongs to a group of agents hired to dispose of England's interior enemies.

Flynn's personal assignment is to search out and eliminate the members of an undercover Trotskyite group, whose survival depends on sabotaging a family-owned, credit-to-private enterprise motorcycle factory.

"Braine is a smooth, sophisticated writer . . . *The Pious Agent* is an exciting and stimulating read." (*The New York Times Book Review*)

PRELUDE TO TERROR

By Helen MacInnes
(1375) 9-1½ hour cassettes
Rental—$16.50   Purchase—$72.00
Read by Jane Bullen

The scene is Vienna, where an American art expert, Colin Grant, has been dispatched by a Texas millionaire to buy a painting by the Dutch master Ruysdael. He is instructed to get the painting "at any cost," but to keep his employer's name a secret. This seemingly simple assignment turns into a nightmare for Grant as he finds himself in the center of a conspiracy to unleash bloody international terrorism.

THE PREMIER

By Georges Simenon
(1511) 5-1 hour cassettes
Rental—$11.50   Purchase—$40.00
Read by Michael Prichard

An elderly French statesman, former premier of the nation, retires to a small farmhouse on the Norman coast. Left alone with his memories, this once-powerful manipulator of people and events contemplates a career in which he traded tranquility for a moment at the summit.

"An intensive, poignant story remarkable for its insight into human worth and human frailty." *(Book-of-the-Month Club)*

Other Simenon books recorded by B-O-T include *In Case of Emergency, None of Maigret's Business* and others listed in our Index.

A PURPLE PLACE FOR DYING

By John D. MacDonald
(1064) 6-1 hour cassettes
Rental—$12.50   Purchase—$48.00
Read by Michael Prichard

A Purple Place for Dying finds Travis McGee witness to a murder he can't prove and a kidnapping nobody believes. McGee becomes a pawn between a wealthy Southwestern patriarch, the law, and a mysterious gang bent on insurance fraud. Just the kind of thing McGee revels in!

THE QUICK RED FOX

By John D. MacDonald
(1664) 6-1 hour cassettes
Rental—$12.50   Purchase—$48.00
Read by Michael Prichard

It was the standard blackmail scheme. For years, sultry Lysa Dean's name on a movie had meant a bonanza at the box office. Now a set of pictures could mean the end of her career.

When first approached for help by lovely Dana Holtzer, Lysa's personal secretary, Travis McGee is thoroughly turned off by the tacky details. But being low on cash, and tenderly attracted by the star's intriguingly remote secretary, McGee sets out to locate his suspects—only to find that they start turning up dead!

QUIET AS A NUN

By Antonia Fraser
(1828) 7-1 hour cassettes
Rental—$14.50   Purchase—$56.00
Read by Wanda McCaddon

In Antonia Fraser's first work of fiction we meet Jemima Shore, a refreshing addition to the considerable list of investigators in the mystery genre. Jemima's first task is to solve a murder in the secluded tower at Blessed Eleanor's Convent in Sussex. The victim—an old school friend—left a puzzling note stating: "Jemima will understand what is going on here. Jemima knows . . . " But Jemima doesn't!

THE QUILLER MEMORANDUM

By Adam Hall
(1145) 7-1 hour cassettes
Rental—$13.50   Purchase—$56.00
Read by Richard Green

This well-drawn tale of espionage is set in West Berlin, 15 years after the end of WW II. Quiller, a British agent who works without gun, cover, or contacts, takes on a neo-Nazi underground organization and its war-criminal leader. In the process, he discovers a complex and malevolent plot, more dangerous to the world than any crime committed during the war.

On its publication *The Quiller Memorandum* received the Edgar Award as best mystery of the year.

THE RETURN OF SHERLOCK HOLMES

By Sir Arthur Conan Doyle
(9051) 8-1½ hour cassettes
Rental—$16.50   Purchase—$64.00
Read by Walter Covell
A Jimcin Recording

If you're not superstitious, try listening to this intriguing collection of 13 stories! The famous detective, who was given his first name after an English cricketer of the time and his second after Oliver Wendell Holmes, has become more real than either.

Stories include . . . The Adventures of: "The Empty House," "The Norwood Builder," "The Dancing Men," "The Solitary Cyclist," "The Priory School," "Black Peter," "Charles Augustus Milverton," "The Golden Pince-Nez," "The Missing Three-Quarter," "The Abbey Grange" and "The Second Stain."

THE RHINEMANN EXCHANGE

By Robert Ludlum
(1754) 11-1½ hour cassettes
Rental—$17.50   Purchase—$88.00
Read by Michael Prichard

David Spaulding is a top-secret American agent on a mission that he himself does not fully understand. Jean Cameron is a beautiful young widow who has been betrayed once by the havoc of war and is determined never to let herself be hurt that way again.

They come together in Buenos Aires, a wartime city of violence and intrigue where representatives of America and Nazi Germany play a deadly game with the fate of the world in perilous balance.

"A heady brew of fear, romance, racy dialogue, high readability and an intricate plot that builds to a bloody crescendo!" *(John Barkham Reviews)*

THE RIVERSIDE VILLAS MURDER

By Kingsley Amis
(1230) 6-1 hour cassettes
Rental—$12.50   Purchase—$48.00
Read by Richard Green

A classic armchair mystery, *The Riverside Villas Murder* has for its hero a 14 year-old boy, Peter Furneaux. Like all 14 year-olds, he is hovering hopefully on the brink between sexual inexperience and initiation, and in this book, under our very eyes, Peter suddenly becomes an adult!

A crime, truly murderous, is committed by an unknown and almost unidentifiable assailant. Only Peter begins to guess at the truth—a dangerous truth—which leads him to the river bank by moonlight. A delightful book, and as with all works by Kingsley Amis, guaranteed to please.

THE ROAD TO GANDOLFO

By Robert Ludlum
(1755) 7-1½ hour cassettes
Rental—$15.50   Purchase—$56.00
Read by Michael Prichard

Here Robert Ludlum combines a motley cast—characters all—with the U.S. Army's latest fall guy in a mad plot to kidnap the most beloved pontiff since John XXIII. The ransom: one American dollar for every Catholic in the world. The problem: Pope Francesco I says: "Gentle souls, why not?" Originally published under the pseudonym Michael Shepherd, *The Road to Gandolfo* marked Robert Ludlum's debut as an author.

The following Ludlum titles are also available from B-O-T: *The Bourne Identity, The Osterman Weekend, The Matarese Circle* and *The Parsifal Mosaic.*

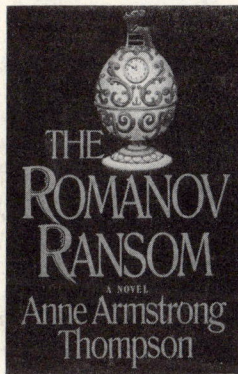

THE ROMANOV RANSOM

By Anne Armstrong Thompson
(1564) 8-1½ hour cassettes
Rental—$15.50   Purchase—$64.00
Read by Wanda McCaddon

Ward Grant is a hard-luck case. Bad enough to be in East Germany, worse to have his cover blown, but unthinkable to be caught and shipped to Lubyanka for interrogation.

Even as American officials demand Grant's release, Russian agents announce the price: a dozen long-vanished, jeweled Faberge Easter eggs made for Czar Nicholas. Enter Henryk Kessel, CIA ace, who skillfully manipulates KGB, Russian emigres, and art dealers in a high stakes gamble to keep Lubyanka from becoming Grant's tomb.

A ROSE FOR ANA MARIA

By Frank Yerby
(1101) 8-1 hour cassettes
Rental—$14.50   Purchase—$64.00
Read by Michael Prichard

Meet Diego, a young Spanish revolutionary living in Paris, who has killed the Spanish consul as a protest against the Spanish government. Diego must flee, of course—he wants to return to Spain to continue his fight against tyranny. So he throws in with another "revolutionary," a young woman named Ana Maria. In exchange for help in fleeing France, they agree to assassinate a highranking Spanish official. Their revolutionary zeal and sexual goatishness overlap as the book moves into its final chapters. X-rated for sex and violence.

THE ROSE OF TIBET

By Lionel Davidson
(1327) 8-1½ hour cassettes
Rental—$15.50   Purchase—$64.00
Read by Rupert Keenlyside

When his brother is mysteriously lost in Tibet, Charles Houston leaves London to find him. His search takes him to India and Sikkim, through a succession of exotic locales, and finally to Tibet where Houston falls in love with MeiHua, the abbess of the monastery of Yamdring.

Lionel Davidson's novel, set during the Communist Chinese invasion of Tibet, is the story of a man who is forced against his will into a desperate fight for his life.

"The sense of physical jeopardy is relentless, the geographical scope boundless, and the plot unremittingly surprising." *(Editorial Review Service)*

Rental Section At-a-Glance

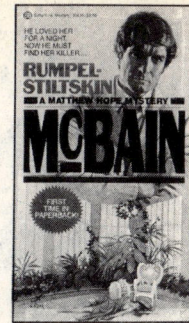

RUMPELSTILTSKIN

By Ed McBain
(1963) 8-1 hour cassettes
Rental—$14.50   Purchase—$64.00
Read by Michael Prichard

She's a rock star of the 60's, hungry for a comeback. He's a divorced lawyer working to put his life back together. Their one-night stand is brief but torrid.

When she is found the next day, brutally murdered, and her six-year-old daughter turns up missing, Matthew Hope inherits love's toughest labor—hunting down a culprit who kidnaps and kills.

"Crackling dialogue, snappy pacing, an abundance of cleverly placed clues, and a gaggle of quirky characters!" *(Philadelphia Inquirer)*

"Expert McBain!" *(The New York Times Book Review)*

SAVAGE DAY

By Jack Higgins
(1480) 5-1 hour cassettes
Rental—$11.50   Purchase—$40.00
Read by Larry McKeever

The British Army has a thankless job in Northern Ireland. Other than endless check points and a stifling police presence, its only hope is to infiltrate the IRA.

Enter Simon Vaughn, a British officer turned gun runner. He is sprung from a Greek prison by the British on condition that he pose as an undercover arms dealer in Northern Ireland. Fresh out of options, Vaughn agrees. He gets more than he bargains for, or wants—$500,000 in hijacked gold, a smuggling operation in Ulster and a murderous manhunt.

"*Savage Day* confirms Higgins' high rank in the field of adventure fiction."*(E.R.S. Services)*

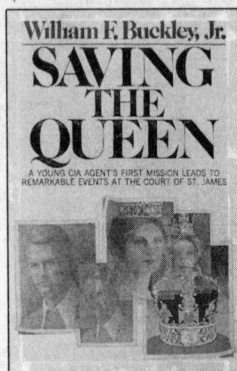

SAVING THE QUEEN

By William F. Buckley, Jr.
(1322) 7-1/2 hour cassettes
Rental—$16.50   Purchase—$56.00
Read by William F. Buckley, Jr.

Blackford Oakes is Yale's answer to James Bond, and as if to prove his protagonist's ability, author Buckley sends Oakes abroad to save the Queen. Turnabout is fair play, and in some of the scenes it seems Oakes himself is the one who is being protected.

THE SCARLATTI INHERITANCE

By Robert Ludlum
(1751) 8-1/2 hour cassettes
Rental—$15.50   Purchase—$64.00
Read by Michael Prichard

It is October 1944. An elite member of the Nazi high command is ready to defect, bringing information vital to the Allied cause. He will deal with no one but Army Intelligence Major Matthew Canfield, who will accept the assignment only if a certain top-secret State Department file is surrendered to him, its seal unbroken.

Canfield is one of the few people in the world who knows what that file contains—a story involving famous figures, momentous events, vast powers, and an incredibly rich, resourceful and determined woman.

"Great, astonishing, the most spellbinding suspense in years!" *(Minneapolis Tribune)*

FREE rental from Books on Tape™
See page 3

THE SCARLET RUSE

By John D. MacDonald
(1670) 6-1/2 hour cassettes
Rental—$14.50   Purchase—$48.00
Read by Michael Prichard

McGee was too busy with his beloved houseboat, the *Busted Flush,* to pay attention to the little old man with his missing postage stamps. Except that they weren't ordinary stamps. No indeed. They were rare stamps, $400,000 worth.

Even that amount doesn't ignite McGee. What does is a generously endowed Amazon named Mary Alice McDermit.

And right behind her came a syndicate killer who wanted to cancel McGee . . . permanently. A killer who knew something about stamps—and even more about McGee.

THE SCORPION SIGNAL

By Adam Hall
(1569) 8-1 hour cassettes
Rental—$14.50   Purchase—$64.00
Read by Robert Mundy

Quiller is older now, embittered, cynical and running on empty. A sorely needed vacation is rudely interrupted with an urgent mission to Moscow.

A reliable British agent, Schrenk, an old partner of Quiller's, has been captured by the Russians and subjected to torture in Lubyanka Prison. Schrenk has managed to escape, but he has disappeared and has made no contact with control in London. Quiller is told to find him.

The Scorpion Signal is a stark and believable spy novel, largely set behind the Iron Curtain.

For a complete list of Adam Hall books recorded by B-O-T, please refer to our Index.

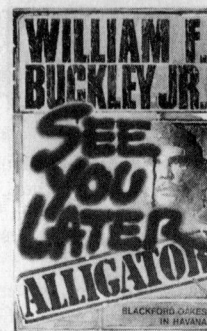

SEE YOU LATER ALLIGATOR

By William F. Buckley, Jr.
(1464) 8-1/2 hour cassettes
Rental—$15.50   Purchase—$64.00
Read by Paul Shay

President John F. Kennedy listens to the secret proposal and approves Operation Alligator. Can anyone tread the deadly, delicate waters of diplomacy between Cuba and the United States better than Blackford Oakes?

Oakes is sent to negotiate a trade and noninvasion agreement initiated by Che Guevara. The story takes off when everyone—the Cuban leaders, the Russians, everyone, that is, except Oakes, discovers that our hero is being used as a pawn in an attempt by the Russians to deploy the missiles in Cuba.

Other Blackford Oakes adventures B-O-T have recorded include *Saving the Queen, Marco Polo, If You Can, The Story of Henri Tod* and *Who's on First.*

SEVEN DAYS IN MAY

By Fletcher Knebel and
Charles W. Bailey II
(1163) 8-1/2 hour cassettes
Rental—$15.50   Purchase—$64.00
Read by Wolfram Kandinsky

Cast in Washington and centered around the Pentagon, the action begins on a quiet Sunday morning as Col. Martin J. "Jiggs" Casey, Director of Research for the Joint Chiefs of Staff, assumes his once-monthly stint as officer of the day. The president's popularity is at an all-time low, due principally to his controversial disarmament treaty with Russia. By Tuesday, Col. Casey accidentally uncovers a fantastic plot to overthrow the president. The conspirators are not a lunatic fringe but the most influential of the Joint Chiefs. The president and a small group of confidential advisors have seven days to avert an unprecedented crisis.

THE SIAMESE TWIN MYSTERY

By Ellery Queen
(1140) 8-1 hour cassettes
Rental—$14.50   Purchase—$64.00
Read by Michael Prichard

The Siamese Twin Mystery finds Ellery and his father, the irascible Inspector Queen, trapped in a mountain retreat by a raging forest fire. The members of the household are a strange lot, and the mysterious murder of the retreat's host indicates to the Queens that not only are they isolated with an odd assortment of characters, but a dangerous killer as well!

THE SIBLING

By Elleston Trevor
(1688) 6-1½ hour cassettes
Rental—$14.50   Purchase—$48.00
Read by Rupert Keenlyside

A brother and sister, whose childhood wickedness surpasses understanding, meet again years later. Fascinated with their power as adults, the evil they share boils into flower.

"Imaginative and well presented . . . realistic dialogue and interior monologue drive this tale speedily to its alarming conclusion." *(Publishers Weekly)*

For other Trevor/Hall titles please refer to our Index.

THE SILVER BEARS

By Paul Erdman
(1289) 8-1 hour cassettes
Rental—$14.50   Purchase—$64.00
Read by Dan Lazar

The Silver Bears involves a Swiss bank controlled by the Mafia, an ancient silver mine rediscovered in Iran, bullion smugglers on the Persian Gulf, and an American speculator living in England.

With his great storytelling gifts and singular experience in world money markets, Paul Erdman takes us through the twists and turns of a complex plot to make a huge fortune in silver. As powerful men manipulate the market, one is reminded of 1979-80, when silver went from $5.00 to $50.00 an ounce— and back again.

THE SINKIANG EXECUTIVE

By Adam Hall
(1571) 6-1½ hour cassettes
Rental—$14.50   Purchase—$48.00
Read by Rupert Keenlyside

Whirling silently through space, satellite cameras pick up a suspicious new Soviet missile complex which at all costs must be properly identified.

The mission is carefully planned and carefully rehearsed. The latest and fastest MiG, which a defecting Soviet pilot has conveniently landed in the West, is to fly at treetop level until well into Soviet airspace and on course for the target. And the return journey? Well, that's up to Quiller.

Quiller fans will also enjoy *The Kobra Manifesto, The Ninth Directive* and *The Quiller Memorandum,* all available from B-O-T.

A SMALL TOWN IN GERMANY

NEW

By John le Carré
(2066) 9-1½ hour cassettes
Rental—$15.50   Purchase—$72.00
Read by Barry Philips

A British diplomat carrying confidential files stolen from the embassy in Bonn suddenly vanishes. And a tough London investigator is assigned to the case.

This is a relentless thriller unlocked by a hidden key that leads to a secret on which England's survival, Germany's future and the fate of the whole world may depend.

"Unique and vivid characters . . . a plot that leads you on, catches you off guard, and culminates in astonishing suspense. Le Carré entertains, informs and satisfies." *(The Denver Post)*

B-O-T's selection of le Carré titles includes *The Honourable Schoolboy, The Little Drummer Girl, The Spy Who Came in From the Cold* and *Tinker, Tailor, Soldier, Spy.*

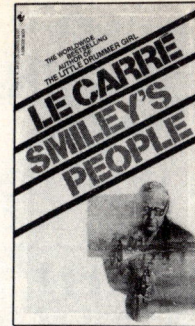

SMILEY'S PEOPLE

By John le Carré
(1909) 12-1½ hour cassettes
Rental—$17.50   Purchase—$96.00
Read by Rupert Keenlyside

At some point George Smiley intends to retire. The problem is, his brain doesn't. So when the Circus asks him to play just one more round, his response is predictable.

Smiley's opponent in this final match is Karla, his opposite number in the Kremlin and top man in Soviet espionage. For years they have dualed at long range—now there is a chance to close.

What happens when they do is perfect le Carré—precise, inevitable, dispassionate. This treatment calls on the listener to supply the emotion, with the result, surely by design, that you finish the story as the author intended, a willing convert to the devoted legion, one of Smiley's life-long people.

THE SNARE OF THE HUNTER

By Helen MacInnes
(1373) 9-1½ hour cassettes
Rental—$16.50   Purchase—$72.00
Read by Penelope Dellaporta

Irina Kusak flees Czechoslovakia to seek her Nobel-laureate father in Austria. She finds herself drawn into a political intrigue with terrifying consequences. Is she the bait in a trap to snare her father? Or is she playing a part in an even more insidious scheme with incredibly high stakes?

Set against the backdrop of peaceful Austrian countryside, Irina's nightmare journey becomes a flight to evade *The Snare of the Hunter.*

SNOW WHITE AND ROSE RED

By Ed McBain
(1966) 8-1 hour cassettes
Rental—$14.50   Purchase—$64.00
Read by Michael Prichard

Shimmering blonde hair framing an exquisite pale face. Deep green eyes, a generous mouth. Matthew Hope took one look and fell in love.

Sarah Whittaker has everything: stunning good looks, youth, money, social standing. Everything, that is, but her freedom. Hope might have lost his heart, but he hasn't lost his wits. He probes Sarah's story of a mother driven by hate to confine her only child to a mental institution and decides she is telling the truth. He takes the case, and in so doing is led into a hall of mirrors in which reality and delusion blur into murder, mutilation and the greatest danger he has ever known.

SOMETHING OF AN ACHIEVEMENT

By Gwyn Griffin
(1580) 6-1½ hour cassettes
Rental—$14.50   Purchase—$48.00
Read by Wolfram Kandinsky

This is the story of Cecil Spurgeon, a middleaged Chief of Rural Police in a British East Africa colony, and his quest to fill the soon-to-be vacant post of deputy commissioner. Spurgeon is a bureaucrat whose ambitions greatly exceed his abilities. When the colony turns violent his career crumbles. Lust, infidelity, mayhem and murder lead to a climax that is brutal but believable.

"Grim and wholly absorbing." *(Chicago Sunday Tribune)*

THE SPANISH CAPE MYSTERY

By Ellery Queen
(1111) 8-1 hour cassettes
Rental—$14.50   Purchase—$64.00
Read by Michael Prichard

The Spanish Cape Mystery is a study in jealousy, revenge and mistaken identity. The setting is a brooding headland called the Spanish Cape. The cast contains the monstrous Captain Kidd, the ill-fated David Cumer and his beautiful niece Rosa, and Rosa's suitors. Into this scene drives Ellery Queen, intent on a holiday. Instead he must solve a baffling kidnap-murder!

THE SPY WHO CAME IN FROM THE COLD

By John le Carré
(1060) 7-1 hour cassettes
Rental—$13.50   Purchase—$56.00
Read by Chris Winfield

Crafted with great power and psychological verisimilitude, this novel tells the story of a 50-year-old British spy who has been too long in the field. Stale, tired and bitter, he accepts one last assignment. The story is elegantly written—completely convincing in its setting and characters.

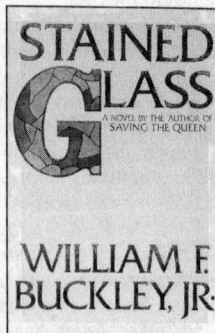

STAINED GLASS

By William F. Buckley, Jr.
(1324) 6-1½ hour cassettes
Rental—$14.50   Purchase—$48.00
Read by Dan Lazar

Blackford Oakes returns! The spy who made *Saving the Queen* so memorable now tackles the problem of Count Axel Wintergrin, whose campaign for a unified Germany is causing panic on both sides of the Iron Curtain. Oakes finds himself deeply involved in cold war cloak and dagger intrigue which features the rise of a German anti-Fuehrer and his campaign to reunify divided Germany—by diplomacy if possible, by the Bomb if necessary. Never has a son of Eli been so severely challenged.

THE STORY OF HENRI TOD

By William F. Buckley, Jr.
(1936) 6-1½ hour cassettes
Rental—$14.50   Purchase—$48.00
Read by Michael Prichard

Berlin, pre-wall. Kruschev gives President Kennedy an ultimatum. Kennedy stalls, but directs the CIA to contact a secret group of German dissidents: the Bruderschaft.

Blackford Oakes, senior agent and the author's alter ego, leads the charge. While Kennedy confers with De Gaulle and Macmillan, Oakes penetrates the Bruderschaft.

"Writing about high noon in the cold war, Buckley has created characters he cares about, as you will, in a novel of style and substance, wit and tragedy, seriousness and surprise." *(Publisher's Guide)*

THE SWISS LEGACY

By Anne Armstrong Thompson
(1189) 8-1 hour cassettes
Rental—$14.50   Purchase—$64.00
Read by Penelope Dellaporta

Carolyn Bruce, while visiting London with her banker husband David, suddenly finds herself a widow when her husband is killed in a very suspicious "accident." Scotland Yard uncovers evidence that David was not the innocent he appeared, rather he was a large-scale embezzler.

It is immediately assumed that Carolyn is an accomplice, and soon old "friends" are chasing, shadowing and propositioning her in an effort to recoup the stolen funds.

"The action is fast, tricky and exciting." *(E.R.S. Reviews)*

A TAN AND SANDY SILENCE

By John D. MacDonald
(1669) 6-1½ hour cassettes
Rental—$14.50   Purchase—$48.00
Read by Michael Prichard

Travis McGee is the strikingly handsome and ever resourceful invention of John D. MacDonald. Born in the author's imagination in 1964, McGee drifted into the world on a 52-foot diesel-powered houseboat, the *Busted Flush,* which he has used as base of operations through many adventures.

In *A Tan and Sandy Silence,* news of a former girlfriend's mysterious disappearance leads McGee to the West Indian island of Grenada. There he takes on a whirlwind plot of double-dealing, shady financing and shifting identities.

"MacDonald is the thinking mystery-lovers' answer to Ian Fleming and Mickey Spillane." *(San Francisco Chronicle)*

TINKER, TAILOR, SOLDIER, SPY

By John le Carré
(1908) 8-1½ hour cassettes
Rental—$15.50   Purchase—$64.00
Read by Richard Green

Somewhere in the uppermost reaches of British Intelligence there lurks a double agent . . . a "mole." He can only be one of five men, each a brilliant top-level agent. And it is to George Smiley, perhaps the most brilliant and talented of the five, that the task falls: find the mole and kill him.

"The plot is as tangled and suspenseful as any action fan could require, and the inductive skill of the diffident, intellectual hero should bring joy to the hearts of the purists." *(The New York Times)*

Other le Carré titles available from B-O-T include *The Little Drummer Girl, Smiley's People* and others listed in our Index.

THE TRANSCENDENTAL MURDER
(Also published as
THE MINUTEMAN MURDER)

By Jane Langton
(1473) 8-1 hour cassettes
Rental—$14.50   Purchase—$64.00
Read by Michael Prichard

"Dying is a wild night and a new road" wrote Emily Dickinson. The sharpness of this poetic vision takes on a new meaning when, during the annual pageant commemorating Paul Revere's ride, a prominent citizen's gruesomely ventilated body (still in Minuteman costume) signals a murderer is on the loose.

Homer Kelly, celebrated Emersonian scholar and legendary ex-homicide detective, happens to be in Concord completing his latest academic opus. When the local constabulary asks him for help, he willingly agrees.

KEN FOLLETT
A NOVEL BY THE AUTHOR OF EYE OF THE NEEDLE

TRIPLE

By Ken Follett
(1448) 8-1½ hour cassettes
Rental—$15.50   Purchase—$64.00
Read by Richard Green

Triple is based on a bizarre, still unexplained and true episode: the 1968 disappearance at sea of a shipment of 200 tons of uranium.

One lone Israeli agent concocts an incredible scenario for the biggest and quietest hijacking in history—all against the formidable forces of the Russian KGB, Egyptian Intelligence, and the Arab extremist Fedayeen. Follett is a master of crafty plot and credible detail—creating a timely and unique thriller guaranteed to capture and hold all imaginations.

THE TURQUOISE LAMENT

By John D. MacDonald
(1671) 6-1½ hour cassettes
Rental—$14.50   Purchase—$48.00
Read by Michael Prichard

In what seems an innocuous beginning, Travis McGee sets out to find a scholar's notebooks which contain plans for a number of million-dollar salvage projects.

His first step is to locate the scholar's relatives, and this being a McGee story, it is predictable that the nearest and dearest will be a daughter, one Pidge.

McGee's attention is distracted by Pidge's story that her husband is trying to kill her and that he has another female stowed away aboard the ship. McGee's ability is challenged almost to the limit, but fortunately for the series, he survives.

"A finely wrought plot, multi-dimensional characters, and plenty of action, are all part of the style which has made Mr. MacDonald one of America's most widely read authors." *(Saturday Review)*

THE WATCHMAKER and
THE IRON STAIRCASE

By Georges Simenon
(1153) 7-1½ hour cassettes
Rental—$15.50   Purchase—$56.00
Read by Michael Prichard

The Watchmaker and *The Iron Staircase* are two fine examples of Georges Simenon's short stories. Simenon is father of the psychological crime novel, and these tales, carefully observant, are excellent examples of his style.

Set in rural New York, *The Watchmaker* investigates the consequences of a volatile father-son relationship. In *The Iron Staircase,* the confrontation is between husband and wife. In both stories, family tensions wring the participants in one of the oldest dramas in the human predicament.

WHERE THERE'S SMOKE

By Ed McBain
(2038) 5-1 hour cassettes
Rental—$11.50   Purchase—$40.00
Read by Michael Prichard

Benjamin Smoke's for hire . . . but not for money. All he asks is a case tough enough to challenge his extraordinary powers. Smoke is looking for something different . . . the perfect crime.

So when someone begins kidnapping corpses from funeral homes, Smoke deals himself in . . . and finds that he's playing with a cunning, brutal psychopath, who's stacked the deck with murderous jokers.

Beauty and the Beast, Goldilocks, Long Time No See, Rumpelstiltskin and *Jack and the Beanstalk* are Ed McBain titles recorded by Books on Tape.

WHISPER OF THE AXE

By Richard Condon
(1204) 6-1½ hour cassettes
Rental—$14.50   Purchase—$48.00
Read by Samantha Neal

Richard Condon presents his scenario for the second (and final) American Revolution. Led by a brilliant black criminal lawyer, Agatha Teel, the revolutionaries plan a mission to "save" society by punishing it—starting with the destruction of 30 cities. In China, hand-picked leaders undergo intensive training in urban warfare, and secret personnel and weaponry are spread throughout the U.S.—the entire vast operation funded through the heroin trade. Could it happen here? Condon colors doomsday with vivid, believable colors.

**Interval delivery convenience
See page 2**

THE WHITE LIE ASSIGNMENT

By Peter Driscoll
(1014) 8-1 hour cassettes
Rental—$14.50   Purchase—$64.00
Read by Ian Whitcomb

The White Lie Assignment is the story of a London photographer's caper with British Intelligence in Communist Albania. Michael Mannis had done a little business with the MI5 intelligence organization before. He is selected for an assignment that will carry him to Albania to take covert photographs of something that may not even exist. The assignment involves only a few white lies about Mannis' background. Mannis soon discovers that the fate of Western Europe may hinge on his photographs—and that one super-power will stop at nothing to get them.

WHO'S ON FIRST

By William F. Buckley, Jr.
(1642) 8-1 hour cassettes
Rental—$14.50   Purchase—$64.00
Read by Michael Prichard

Who's On First is the story of the race between the United States and the Soviet Union to be first to place a satellite in orbit. All of us know who was first, but Buckley's fictional re-creation of the events leading up to that historical fact will keep the listener on edge.

As with all of Buckley's novels of cold war skulduggery, his wit and elan show through in the statements of his insouciant alter ego, Blackie. Buckley spices the dialogue with vignettes between the then CIA Director Allen Dulles and former Secretary of State Dean Acheson.

As *Kirkus Reviews* prophesied, "anyone who can make conferences between Dulles and Acheson sound like vaudeville routines deserves the audience he is bound to get."

THE WILBY CONSPIRACY

By Peter Driscoll
(1053) 8-1 hour cassettes
Rental—$14.50   Purchase—$64.00
Read by Chris Winfield

The Wilby Conspiracy is part thriller, part sociological document. An English mining engineer vacationing with another man's wife in South Africa accidentally befriends a fugitive black man. He quickly finds himself wanted by the police, involved in a black liberation movement, and openly stalked by diabolically efficient secret agents. It was this bestselling novel that established Peter Driscoll as a major figure in stories of international intrigue.

THE WILD ISLAND

By Antonia Fraser
(1829) 7-1 hour cassettes
Rental—$13.50   Purchase—$56.00
Read by Donald Peters

As Jemima Shore, Investigator, arrives at Inverness Station for a Highland holiday, the sun is shining. Paradise, she thinks. But at that moment, she hears a voice: "All this way for a funeral."

So begins an adventure far removed from Jemima's visions of heather-covered hills, crystal-clear streams, romantic men in kilts, fairy-tale castles . . . Instead she is plunged into the strange world of the aristocratic Beauregard family with its tensions, jealousies and violence. The setting is the Wild Island itself, sometimes enchanting but too often frighteningly remote; the streams, not silvery, but brown and sinister; her holiday home with its disturbing influence; the people—none of them quite what they seem

THE WINDOW AT THE WHITE CAT

By Mary Roberts Rinehart
(9152) 5-1½ hour cassettes
Rental—$14.50   Purchase—$40.00
Read by Jim Killavey
A Jimcin Recording

A beautiful girl seeks the help of an attorney when her father vanishes. Before long, her aunt also disappears from a locked house in the dead of the night. The search leads to The White Cat, an infamous establishment frequented by crooked politicians. And then—murder.

The Window at The White Cat is another in the famous "had-I-but-known" school of mysteries founded by Mary Roberts Rinehart with the publication in 1908 of her first work, *The Circular Staircase,* (also available from Books on Tape). The focus of these stories is the Gothic Heroine—*always* in the wrong place at the wrong time trusting the wrong people.

WINTER KILLS

By Richard Condon
(1065) 7-1½ hour cassettes
Rental—$15.50   Purchase—$56.00
Read by Daniel Grace

In *Winter Kills,* Richard Condon probes one of the most significant events in America's 20th century: the assassination of a president. Timothy Kegan is shot in a Philadelphia motorcade; a presidential commission condemns a lone psychopath as the killer.

Fourteen years later, Tim's half-brother, Nick, learns through a deathbed confession that Tim was the victim of a mysterious conspiracy. As Nick attempts to find the real assassin, he encounters oil kings, movie queens, venal police, organized crime, the CIA, labor unions—all eager for power and control. The ending is guaranteed to surprise and horrify!

THE WISDOM OF FATHER BROWN

By G.K. Chesterton
(1763) 8-1 hour cassettes
Rental—$14.50   Purchase—$64.00
Read by Richard Green

From London to Cornwall, then to Italy and France, a short, shabby priest runs to earth bandits, traitors, killers. Why is he so successful?

The reason is that after years spent in the priesthood, Father Brown knows human nature and is not afraid of its dark side. Thus he understands criminal motivation and how to deal with it.

The stories included are "The Absence of Mr. Glass," "The Paradise of Thieves," "The Duel of Dr. Hirsch," "The Man in the Passage," "The Mistakes of the Machine," "The Head of Caesar," "The Purple Wig," "The Perishing of the Pendragons," "The God of the Gongs," "The Salad of Colonel Cray," "The Strange Crime of John Boulnois" and "The Fairy Tale of Father Brown."

THE WOMAN IN WHITE

By Wilkie Collins
(9169-A) 10-1½ hour cassettes
Rental—$17.50   Purchase—$80.00
(9169-B) 9-1½ hour cassettes
Rental—$17.50   Purchase—$72.00
Read by Various Readers
A Jimcin Recording

Who is the "solitary figure of a woman, dressed from head to foot in white garments," whose appearance shattered forever the outward peace of life at Limmeridge House? Is she an apparition . . . a madwoman . . . perhaps a player in some bizarre scheme?

From the moment "the Woman" first appears to Walter Hartright on a moonlit London road, Wilkie Collins' melodrama casts its spell.

The Woman in White was a tremendous success when it first appeared in 1860—cloaks, bonnets and perfumes were named after it. Gladstone put off a theatre party to read it. Thackeray sat up all night to finish it—and now, over 125 years later, it still enthralls.

Rental Section At-a-Glance

WRATH OF THE LION

By Jack Higgins
(1481) 5-1 hour cassettes
Rental—$11.50   Purchase—$40.00
Read by Larry McKeever

It was all a set-up. Neil Mallory—tough, experienced veteran of more wars than he cared to remember—was in a new business now. That was why he watched so carefully when Anne Grant left the bar followed by two strangers.

When he heard her cry out a few minutes later, Mallory knew it was time to rescue her. She was very grateful. So grateful she offered him a job. That was exactly what he was waiting for and that attack on her was all part of a new game of intrigue and violence. She could not know she was the key to everything.

Other Jack Higgins titles from B-O-T are *The Keys to Hell, Passage by Night, Savage Day* and *The Eagle Has Landed.*

YOU'LL NEVER TAKE ME

By Robert Douglas Mead
(1408) 5-1 hour cassettes
Rental—$11.50   Purchase—$40.00
Read by Jack Hrkach

Frank Desper, descended from a French trapper and his Indian wife, is a man well acquainted with the wilds of Minnesota border country.

Insulted in a local bar by a drunken young Finn, who happens to be the son of the sheriff, Desper draws his knife and fights, then flees into the woods he knows so well. In this concise, exciting account, Desper eludes a deadly manhunt, perfects his skill and instincts for survival and undergoes a terrifying transformation.

B-O-T has also recorded Robert Mead's *Ultimate North.*

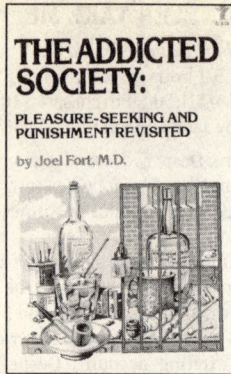

THE ADDICTED SOCIETY: Pleasure-Seeking and Punishment Revisted

By Joel Fort, M.D.
(1956) 5-1 hour cassettes
Rental—$11.50   Purchase—$40.00
Read by Michael Prichard

We are a nation of addicts, says Fort— you, me, everybody. We like to think of addicts as a bunch of "others," people unlike ourselves, airheads who pop, snort and shoot.

But Fort's point is that mainstream addictions are much more subtle, though equally lethal. He asks us to consider the use we make of alcohol, tranquilizers, coffee and tobacco. Dr. Fort is founder of the National Center for Solving Special Social and Health Problems in San Francisco.

"Fort puts his finger on what it is that is sick in our society and is quick to identify the liars and totalitarians in our power structure." *(The Saturday Review)*

AFTER COLLEGE: THE BUSINESS OF GETTING JOBS

By Jack Falvey
(2077) 5-1 hour cassettes
Rental—$11.50   Purchase—$40.00
Read by Tom H. Middleton

Jack Falvey is an independent business consultant and *WSJ* columnist. In *After College: The Business of Getting Jobs,* he levels with every college student about breaking into the job market and making it in the work-a-day world that does *not* await him.

"*After College* is indispensable for college students eager to launch into the marketplace. No other job manual I've ever seen so clearly addresses the major problems of college graduates." —Betty Lehan Harragan, author of *Games Mother Never Taught You*

"A refreshing, opinionated, and useful guide that bridges the gap between college and the real world . . . A pragmatic guide to career exploration and growth outside the Fortune 500." —V.P. Pappas, Editor, *National Business Employment Weekly*

AFTER YALTA

By Lisle A. Rose
(1335) 6-1½ hour cassettes
Rental—$14.50   Purchase—$48.00
Read by Justin Hecht

In his search for the origins of the cold war, Lisle Rose moves beyond international diplomacy to domestic American politics.

He suggests our view of a world polarized between communism and liberal democracy was a magnification of our own divisions, and that with time we will grope our way to a stable relationship with the Russians. "Provocative and stimulating." *(E.R.S.Reviews)*

THE AGE OF DISCONTINUITY

By Peter F. Drucker
(1337) 11-1½ hour cassettes
Rental—$17.50   Purchase—$88.00
Read by Michael Prichard

Peter Drucker, noted philosopher of business and management, anaylzes the major forces at work during the third quarter of the twentieth century.

Drucker cites four major areas of discontinuity. First is an explosion in technology. The result is the rise of major new industries which in turn require enormous infusions of capital and manpower. Second is our entry into a true world economy, and third is the expansion of knowledge based on mass education. Fourth is the rise of pluralistic institutions which challenge our traditional loyalties.

As with his The Effective Executive (also available from B-O-T), *The Age of Discontinuity* helps us understand the times through which we are passing.

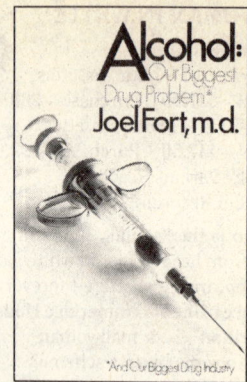

ALCOHOL: Our Biggest Drug Problem

By Joel Fort, M.D.
(1955) 6-1 hour cassettes
Rental—$12.50   Purchase—$48.00
Read by Michael Prichard

Dr. Joel Fort, a leading critic of the Alcohol Lobby, first alerted us to the hazards of alcohol abuse and addiction in 1960. In *Alcohol: Our Biggest Drug Problem,* Dr. Fort discusses the economics and politics of this immense drug culture and biggest legalized drug industry.

Dr. Fort founded the National Center for Solving Special Social and Health Problems.

"At last, common sense about our number one social and health problem. Dr. Fort treats alcohol as a drug in the same context as marijuana, heroin or cocaine." *(Industry Insider)*

ALIVE

By Piers Paul Read
(2016) 8-1½ hour cassettes
Rental—$17.50   Purchase—$64.00
Read by Dick Estell
A Christopher Enterprises Recording

Their plane crashed high in the Andes. Their only shelter was the plane's shattered fuselage, their only supplies a little wine and some bits of candy. In the beginning, there were thirty-two survivors. Then, only twenty-seven, then, nineteen . . . and, in the end, sixteen. This is their story—the greatest modern epic of catastrophe and human endurance. Those who survived clung to life with extraordinary tenacity . . . and made the most difficult decision in order to cheat starvation.

"A masterpiece of narrative . . . It is inconceivable to me that this story could have been better told." —Graham Greene

ANATOMY OF A JURY

By Seymour Wishman
(2133) 9-1 hour cassettes
Rental—$17.50   Purchase—$72.00
Read by Dick Estell
A Christopher Enterprises Recording

A woman is murdered and a suspect arrested. Twelve "ordinary" citizens are gathered to hear the case and reach a verdict. We are at the heart of the American criminal system.

In this unique narrative, novelist and criminal lawyer Seymour Wishman gives us a rare view of how these citizens perform their crucial function. With the cooperation of jurors, drawing on his own experience as a prosecuting and defense attorney and examining existing research on juries, the author reveals in detail why and how the jury reaches its decision. In doing so he tackles the fundamental questions surrounding the America's way of justice.

"For any of us who may one day be judged, for anyone who has served on a jury or will in the future assume that role, *Anatomy of a Jury* is a revealing social drama and a cogent analysis of legal and human forces at work." *(Source Reports)*

ANATOMY OF AN ILLNESS

By Norman Cousins
(1319) 4-1 hour cassettes
Rental—$9.50   Purchase—$32.00
Read by Dan Lazar

This is the best-selling story of recovery from a crippling and supposedly irreversible disease, of a partnership between physician and patient who team to beat back the odds. Norman Cousins is senior lecturer at the School of Medicine, University of California at Los Angeles, and for almost all of his professional life was affiliated with *The Saturday Review of Literature. Anatomy of an Illness* is his personal story.

THE ART OF MANAGING PEOPLE

By Tony Alessandra, Ph.D.
(1799S) 3-1 hour cassettes
Rental—$9.50

This lively professional development seminar hosted by Dr. Tony Alessandra offers techniques for communicating better with others. Learn to recognize differences in people and how to modify your approach appropriately. Learn to take a better look at people; some are "thinkers" who like facts, while others are "feelers" who like intuitions. This is a business-oriented approach to managing yourself and others more productively.

THE ART OF THINKING

By S. Morris Engel, Ph.D.
(1651S) 12-1½ hour cassettes
Rental—$28.50

Dr. Engel is Associate Professor of Philosophy and has earned a well-deserved reputation for presenting his topic in a clear, interesting and entertaining format. For anyone who has ever had an interest in logic and its many pitfalls, Dr. Engel is an excellent guide to take one through the thickets of this important specialty. Highly recommended!

ASSORTED PROSE

By John Updike
(1276) 8-1½ hour cassettes
Rental—$15.50   Purchase—$64.00
Read by Wolfram Kandinsky

Assorted Prose includes Updike's early essays at humor and parody, some reportage for *The New Yorker's* "Talk of the Town," his description of Ted Williams' last appearance in Fenway Park, several semi-autobiographical first person accounts and numerous book reviews. Titles include: "Hub Fans Bid Kid Adieu," "On the Sidewalk, Mr. Ex-Resident," "Drinking from a Cup Made Cinchy," "The Dogwood Tree: A Boyhood," "The Lucid Eye in Silver Town," "My Uncle's Death," "Beerbohn and Others," "Faith in Search of Understanding," "More Love in the Western World."

THE BEST OF THE WALL STREET JOURNAL 1974

By the Editors
(1058) 9-1½ hour cassettes
Rental—$16.50   Purchase—$72.00
Read by Daniel Grace

All right-thinking people from Kansas to the Kremlin read our national daily newspaper and hardly a subscriber to B-O-T will fail to recognize one of his favorite stories in this captivating collage. Comprised of the most talked-about *Journal* stories. *Best of the Wall Street Journal 1974* is a series of short stories that entertains and informs.

Give the perfect gift from Books on Tape™ See page 2

THE BEST OF THE WALL STREET JOURNAL 1981

By the Editors
(1722) 10-1½ hour cassettes
Rental—$16.50   Purchase—$80.00
Read by Wolfram Kandinsky

The Best of the Wall Street Journal 1981 is a collection of 56 feature articles by the staff writers of America's most widely respected daily newspaper. The variety in this satisfying sampler of stories ranges from souffles such as "Is That a Condor? No, It's a Reporter Trying to Hang Glide" and "Singapore Fast Food: Try Pig Intestines—or Maybe a Big Mac" to heavyweight pieces like "Saigon Diary: Vietnam Era Report, Classified for Years, Recounts Tet Attack" and "Losing the Way: Teenage Suicide Toll Points Up the Dangers of Growing Up Rich."

BEYOND CULTURE

By Edward Hall
(2036) 7-1½ hour cassettes
Rental—$15.50   Purchase—$56.00
Read by Donada Peters

"There are two related crises in today's world. The first and most visible is the population/environmental crisis. The second, more subtle but equally lethal, is humankind's relationships to its extensions, institutions, ideas, as well as the relationships among the many individuals and groups that inhabit the globe. If both crises are not resolved, neither will be."

So begins *Beyond Culture*, Edward Hall's acclaimed anthropological study of human culture. "A fascinating book that no one should do himself the disservice of failing to read. *Beyond Culture* not only will increase the reader's knowledge, but also will enlarge his mind." *(Chicago Daily News)*

A BOOK OF COUNTRY THINGS

By Walter Needham and Barrows Mussey
(1370) 4-1 hour cassettes
Rental—$9.50   Purchase—$32.00
Read by Paul Shay

For those of us who yearn for simpler times, this is a book that reminds us how complex the simpler things could be. Dictated from the memoirs of Walter Needham's grandfather, it gives brief and colorful descriptions of carpentry, farming, animal husbandry and domestic sciences and is an accurate picture of life in New England in the 1800's.

"Wise in the self-sufficient ways of country life in the last century." *(Library Journal)*

BORSTAL BOY

By Brendan Behan
(1138) 8-1½ hour cassettes
Rental—$15.50   Purchase—$64.00
Read by Dan Lazar

Brendan Behan was an Irish playwright and novelist, as well as a youthful revolutionary. In 1939, at age 16, he was arrested in Liverpool with a suitcase full of high explosives.

Borstal Boy is the autobiographical record of Behan's experiences from that day through his imprisonment, trial, remand to reform school and final release. Schools for delinquents in England are called Borstal Institutions, and Behan's account of his years as a "Borstal Boy" is told in vigorous, dramatic prose.

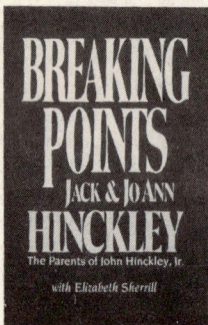

BREAKING POINTS

By Jack and Jo Ann Hinckley
(1542) 8-1½ hour cassettes
Rental—$15.50   Purchase—$64.00
Read by Dan Lazar

"I held my breath until they gave the gunman's name. I was afraid it was my son." This letter and others like it from anxious parents reached Jack and Jo Ann Hinckley after their son John shot President Reagan and three other men in 1981.

Ironically, the Hinckleys had no such fears. They had never recognized the danger signs in John's "typical childhood."

"A terrifying account of the unpredictability with which serious mental illness strikes . . . If out of the Hinckley's tragedy a better public awareness of the reality of mental illness results, then their suffering . . . will not have been in vain." —John A. Talbott, M.D., President, American Psychiatric Association.

CEREMONY OF INNOCENCE

Harvey D. Goldstein, Ph.D.
(1653-AS) 9-1½ hour cassettes
Rental—$18.50
(1653-BS) 8-1½ hour cassettes
Rental—$16.50

Ceremony of Innocence takes us on a tour through the masterpieces of world literature from Genesis to the 19th century, studied as the significant expressions of the human condition. We recognize the unchanging nature of man and track generations of scholars in their search for enduring values.

Our instructor in this stimulating trek is Harvey D. Goldstein, Ph.D., Associate Professor of English and Comparative Literature. He covers his topics with erudition, with love of his subject, and with illuminating insights that went right over our heads when we were in college, but now speak to us in clear and resonant terms.

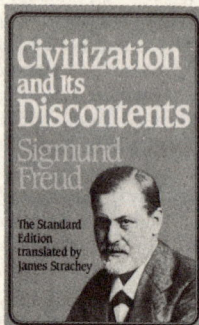

CIVILIZATION AND ITS DISCONTENTS

By Sigmund Freud
(2119) 4-1 hour cassettes
Rental—$9.50   Purchase—$32.00
Read by Michael Prichard

Civilization and Its Discontents is one of the last of Freud's books, written in the decade before his death and first published in German in 1929. In it he states his views on the broad question of man's place in the world, a place Freud defines in terms of ceaseless conflict between the individual's quest for freedom and society's demand for conformity.

Freud's theme is that what works for civilization doesn't necessarily work for man. Man, by nature aggressive and egotistic, seeks self-satisfaction. But culture inhibits his instinctual drives. The result is a pervasive and familiar guilt.

"Freud's great experience richly illuminates the tension between men and their institutions." *(Editorial Review Service)*

COMING INTO THE COUNTRY

By John McPhee
(1990) 10-1½ hour cassettes
Rental—$16.50   Purchase—$80.00
Read by Dan Lazar

Coming into the Country is about Alaska and Alaskans. The book is divided into three parts that deal respectively with wilderness, urban Alaska, and life in the bush.

Coming into the Country unites a vast region of America with one of America's notable literary craftsmen, singularly qualified to do justice to the scale and grandeur of the design. "John McPhee's fans will find his portrait of Alaska to be right at the top of his work." *(Editorial Review Service)*

CONFESSIONS OF A KNIFE

By Richard Selzer
(1577) 7-1 hour cassettes
Rental—$13.50   Purchase—$56.00
Read by Christopher Hurt

Richard Selzer is poet laureate of surgeons in America: a superb literary stylist who explores not only the human body, but the mind and soul as well. These essays are largely autobiographical and extend deep into emotional and medical territory commonly avoided by other writers.

Dr. Selzer's work has been published in *New American Review, Esquire, Harper's,* and other periodicals. In 1975 he won the National Magazine Award for his essays.

B-O-T has recorded another Selzer book, *Mortal Lessons: Notes on the Art of Surgery.*

CREATIVE DIVORCE

By Mel Krantzler
(1398) 8-1 hour cassettes
Rental—$14.50   Purchase—$64.00
Read by Paul Shay

Creative Divorce deals with the gut feelings of men and women facing the need to build new lives in the wake of loneliness, guilt, anger, rejection and a sense of failure.

He outlines a process that goes from the death of the relationship through a period of mourning, to an ultimate rebirth of the individual. Precepts include how to reconcile your expectations of life as a divorced person; learning to live with uncertainty and a new environment; learning to relate openly to children and understanding their need for a positive image of both parents.

**Interval delivery convenience
See page 2**

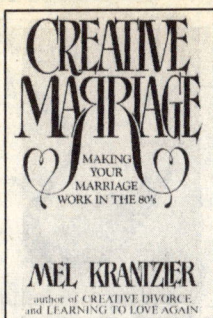

CREATIVE MARRIAGE

By Mel Krantzler
(1541) 11½ hour cassettes
Rental—$17.50   Purchase—$88.00
Read by Paul Shay

Creative Marriage throws new light on one of the oldest, most enduring, most problematic of human relationships. It identifies six natural "passages" or marriages-within-a-marriage that all couples experience.

The couples that recognize and accept these cycles enjoy a harmonious life together. Couples that don't head for splitsville.

"Mel Krantzler's message is this: Your best chance of finding a new marriage is with your existing partner, not with another one." *(Publisher's Source)*

THE CURVE OF BINDING ENERGY

By John McPhee
(1991) 7-1 hour cassettes
Rental—$13.50   Purchase—$56.00
Read by Dan Lazar

"Binding Energy" may be described loosely as the force that holds things together. In physics the term applies to atomic structuring and resultant weaponry. With his customary skill and accuracy, McPhee walks us through atom-land in an easy and uncomplicated stroll.

"McPhee lucidly sets out these life and death issues. He leaves us, as he intends, wondering." *(Reports for Readers)*

THE DISCOVERERS

By Daniel J. Boorstin
(1944-A) 11-1½ hour cassettes
Rental—$17.50   Purchase—$88.00
(1944-B) 7-1½ hour cassettes
Rental—$15.50   Purchase—$56.00
(1944-C) 8-1½ hour cassettes
Rental—$15.50   Purchase—$64.00
Read by Michael Prichard

The Discoverers is a sweeping, original history of man's greatest adventure: his search to discover the world around him.

This is not the usual succession of battles, empires and conquests, but a biography of discoveries and beginnings. Dr. Boorstin explores intriguing questions such as why we were so slow to learn the earth goes around the sun, how we began to think of "species" of plants and animals and why China didn't discover America.

Daniel J. Boorstin was the Librarian of Congress from 1975-1987. Previously he was senior historian of the Smithsonian Institute in Washington, D.C.

DISCOVERY: DEVELOPING VIEWS OF THE EARTH

By John Parker
(1386) 6-1 hour cassettes
Rental—$12.50   Purchase—$48.00
Read by Dan Lazar

Where are we? That deceptively simple question has provided the impetus for hazardous but enlightening exploration ever since our ancestors were seized with the desire to see what lay beyond the next range of hills.

In his fascinating narrative, John Parker recreates the adventures of mariners, merchants, scholars, mapmakers and other travelers. He charts the contributions each has made to the geography of our lands and seas. Like many people at ease with their subjects, Parker makes geography fascinating and understandable.

DR. SCHIFF'S WEIGHT LOSS PLAN FOR HEALTH, BEAUTY AND HAPPINESS

By Martin Schiff, M.D.
(1696) 4-1 hour cassettes
Rental—$9.50   Purchase—$32.00
Read by Martin Schiff, M.D.

Have you been burdened with excess baggage for years? Have you lost weight with every diet under the sun—only to gain it all back sooner or later? Are you disgusted, downhearted and melancholy because you have been on a roller-coaster of "up and down—up and down" for years? Then this "no-diet" weight loss plan developed by Martin Schiff, a medical doctor and weight control specialist, can change your mind forever.

Dr. Schiff's program helps you develop correct eating and thinking habits, set realistic weight loss goals—and achieve them permanently! The pathway to the body is through your mind.

THE DOCTOR'S STORY

By Thomas Gallagher
(2103) 8-1½ hour cassettes
Rental—$15.50   Purchase—$64.00
Read by John MacDonald

The Doctor's Story was published in 1967 in commemoration of the 200th anniversary of the Columbia University College of Physicians and Surgeons.

It is a vivid and comprehensive popular history and covers not only medical education and medical practice, but social, cultural, political and economic life in New York City.

It is a vivid and comprehensive popular history of medical education and medical practice as well as social, cultural, political and economic life in New York City.

Other Gallagher titles recorded by Books on Tape include *Assault in Norway, The Gathering Darkness, The Monogamist* and *Paddy's Lament.*

THE ECONOMICS OF CRISIS

By Eliot Janeway
(1115) 8-1½ hour cassettes
Rental—$15.50   Purchase—$64.00
Read by James Cunningham

This might have been titled *The War Behind The War,* for it concerns policy for management of our economy in WW II. Recalling not only that we were shifting almost overnight from peace to a war footing, but also that we had just completed eight years of grinding Depression, economic policy was necessarily controversial. The book established the author as one of the foremost writers on "the dismal science."

THE EFFECTIVE EXECUTIVE

By Peter Drucker
(1338) 6-1 hour cassettes
Rental—$12.50   Purchase—$48.00
Read by Michael Prichard

The Effective Executive is a pragmatically original guide on how to escape common management traps. Analyzing what makes for effectiveness, Drucker asserts it is an acquired self-discipline that enables the executive not only to avoid what is unproductive, but to perceive and accomplish what really needs doing. Drucker ranges widely to demonstrate the distinctive skill of the executive while providing many fresh insights into old and seemingly obvious situations.

ENCOUNTERS WITH THE ARCHDRUID

By John McPhee
(1995) 7-1 hour cassettes
Rental—$13.50   Purchase—$56.00
Read by Dan Lazar

David Brower is a man with a mission—to save the unspoiled regions of the world. A militant conservationist, he takes on anyone who threatens his vision of our wilderness heritage.

John McPhee arranged for Brower, the Archdruid of the story, to meet on contested turf with three of Brower's chief opponents. Thus we are introduced to spectacular landscapes and spirited encounters—at Sea Island, Georgia; in the Rockies and afloat on the Colorado Riverdeep in the Grand Canyon.

"McPhee presents the confrontations between these remarkable men and their causes with clarity and relish. Witty and fair." *(Editorial Review Services)*

THE FATE OF THE EARTH

By Jonathan Schell
(1595) 7-1½ hour cassettes
Rental—$15.50   Purchase—$56.00
Read by Michael Prichard

When Jonathan Schell heard all that loose talk about attainment of objectives in a limited nuclear war, it was too much for him and he did what all of us would like to do: he wrote a book.

It is very pessimistic. The mere presence of all those weapons is enough to ensure that sometime, somewhere, someone is going to set one off.

Schell makes sure all of us know the horrendous possibilities of a nuclear exchange and all the reasons for bringing such possibilities to a halt.

Everyone agrees. The question is, how do we get these monsters under control?

FATE IS THE HUNTER

By Ernest K. Gann
(2020) 10-1½ hour cassettes
Rental—$19.50   Purchase—$80.00
Read by Dick Estell
A Christopher Enterprises Recording

"This book is an episodic log of some of the more memorable of the author's nearly ten thousand hours aloft in peace and (as a member of the Air Transport Command) in war. It is also an attempt to define by example his belief in the phenomenon of luck—that 'the pattern of anyone's fate is only partly contrived by the individual.' " *(The New Yorker)*

"This fascinating, well-told autobiography is a complete refutation of the comfortable cliche that 'man is master of his fate.' As far as pilots are concerned, fate (or death) is a hunter who is constantly in pursuit of them . . . there is nothing depressing about *Fate Is the Hunter.* There is tension and suspense in it but there is great humor too. Happily, Gann never gets too technical for the layman to understand." *(Saturday Review)*

THE FIRE CAME BY: THE RIDDLE OF THE GREAT SIBERIAN EXPLOSION

By John Baxter and Thomas Atkins
(1199) 5-1 hour cassettes
Rental—$11.50   Purchase—$40.00
Read by Wolfram Kandinsky

One of the great accidents of nature occurred in Siberia in 1908 when a fireball appeared over the horizon and slammed into a remote forest area of Siberia, creating shock waves which were felt half a world away.

The Fire Came By goes into great depth and explores not only what Russian scientists have to say about the affair today, but also enlightened opinions from scientists worldwide, as well as on-the-scene reports and interviews. The book makes the fantastic comprehensible and gives the event a threatening immediacy.

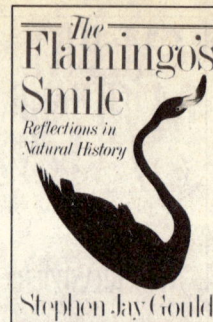

THE FLAMINGO'S SMILE

By Stephen Jay Gould
(2107) 10-1½ hour cassettes
Rental—$16.50   Purchase—$80.00
Read by Grover Gardner

"*The Flamingo's Smile* is about history," writes the author in this volume of essays, " . . . and about what it means to say that life is the product of a contingent past, not the inevitable and predictable result of simple, timeless laws of nature. Quirkiness and meaning are my two not-so-contradictory themes."

Flamingos that feed upside down; flowers and snails that change from male to female; the probability that an errant asteroid sounded the death knell of the dinosaurs and ushered in the evolution of mankind . . . these are only a few of the things that open our eyes to the endless delights of Gould's subject . . . evolutionary theory.

Hen's Teeth and Horse's Toes is another treatise from Stephen Jay Gould recorded by Books on Tape.

FORTUNE'S CHILD: A PORTRAIT OF THE UNITED STATES AS SPENDTHRIFT HEIR

By Lewis H. Lapham
(1565) 12-1½ hour cassettes
Rental—$17.50   Purchase—$96.00
Read by Michael Prichard

Fortune's Child is a collection of 31 pieces by Lewis H. Lapham, editor of *Harper's* magazine and one of the wittiest and most astute analysts of post-WW II America. These essays scrutinize our national pathology of greed and self-aggrandizement. Lapham concludes we have engaged in a dissolute foreign policy, suffered a general loss of courage, humor and clearmindedness and made a steady retreat from the idea of democracy.

FROM BAUHAUS TO OUR HOUSE

By Tom Wolfe
(1836) 4-1 hour cassettes
Rental—$9.50   Purchase—$32.00
Read by Ken Ohst

Walter Groppius, granddaddy of steel and glass, conceived his architectural vision in the rubble of WW I and the decadence of Weimar in the decade after.

His doctrine found fertile soil in America, where it was time to adopt a clearly defined and suitable representative architecture.

Tom Wolfe, author of *The Painted Word* and *The Right Stuff,* treats us to a chronicle of the trends that ultimately brought us the ubiquitous and baffling "glass box" of modern commerce.

"Delightfully witty, biting history of modern architecture . . . scintillating high comedy of big money, manners and massive manipulation of public taste." (*Publishers Weekly*)

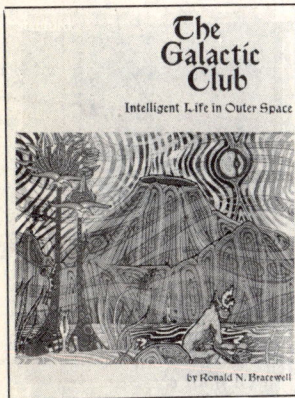

THE GALACTIC CLUB
(Portable Stanford Series

By Ronald N. Bracewell
(1914) 5-1 hour cassettes
Rental—$11.50   Purchase—$40.00
Read by Michael Prichard

Interest in the possibility of life in outerspace is intense. Do we have neighbors? Will we contact them? What will their interest in us be—friendly or hostile? We do not know. This book explores these questions and offers answers culled from disciplines ranging from physics to anthropology.

Professor Bracewell belongs to the American Astronomical Society and the Royal Astronomical Society and is a Fellow of the Institute of Electrical and Electronic Engineers. He joined the Stanford faculty in 1955.

GENERATION OF VIPERS

By Philip Wylie
(1520) 8-1½ hour cassettes
Rental—$15.50   Purchase—$64.00
Read by Ron Shoop

This is the book that made Philip Wylie famous in 1944. Philip Wylie is bitter and caustic. He calls his book "a sermon," but feels no need to be charitable in his attacks.

Wylie pleads for a more rational society, one that is based on sound psychological principles. For those who agree with him, his book is a reaffirmation; for those who don't, it stimulates the cir culation.

"A Rabelaisian catalogue of sin and moral desuetude . . . truly a remarkable book." (*New York Tribune*)

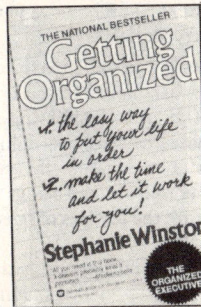

GETTING ORGANIZED

By Stephanie Winston
(1899) 7-1 hour cassettes
Rental—$13.50   Purchase—$56.00
Read by Penelope Dellaporta

You're doing lots more now, but are you doing it as well as you could? Organization—that's what you need! And here's the book that shows you how to get it.

Learn how to maximize your storage space, expand your studio apartment, make the most of your new house or your office, reduce your shopping time and increase your efficiency—even organize the spouse and kids!

Stephanie Winston is founder and director of The Organizing Principle, a New York-based consulting firm. She travels the country on behalf of private clients and corporations, lectures extensively and conducts workshops and classes on the subject of organization. "A clear, clear voice in the wilderness . . . will show you how to break vague but overwhelming discontents into manageable problems." (*McCalls*)

THE GLORY AND THE DREAM:
A NARRATIVE HISTORY
OF AMERICA 1932-1972

By William Manchester
(1680-A) 10-1½ hour cassettes
Rental—$16.50   Purchase—$80.00
(1680-B) 11-1½ hour cassettes
Rental—$17.50   Purchase—$88.00
(1680-C) 12-1½ hour cassettes
Rental—$17.50   Purchase—$96.00
(1680-D) 11-1½ hour cassettes
Rental—$17.50   Purchase—$88.00
(1680-E) 6-1½ hour cassettes
Rental—$14.50   Purchase—$48.00
Read by   Grover Gardner

The Glory and the Dream: A Narrative History of America 1932-1972 is history at its most detailed and finest. It covers an incredible array of "the major events, sensational happenings, and news-making personalities from the Great Depression through the second inauguration of Richard M. Nixon." By no means a stark, dry collection of minutiae, Manchester breathes life into the great periods of America's growth.

"Manchester has an uncanny ability to give his readers an almost tactile sense of the past and to make them feel, 'So that's how it was!' " (*Christian Science Monitor*)

THE GORBACHEV ERA

Edited by Alexander Dallin and Condoleezza Rice
(1567) 8-1 hour cassettes
Rental—$14.50   Purchase—$64.00
Read by Michael Prichard

Who runs the Soviet Union and how? What will change under Gorbachev? What is life in the USSR like today? What forces shaped modern Russia? How is the Soviet economy organized? What are its flaws? And what are Gorbachev's prospects for correcting them?

A group of outstanding Sovietologists met at Stanford University in 1985 to answer these questions. This book is the result.

"*The Gorbachev Era* presents a sober, balanced realistic picture of the Soviet Union today. The contributors are among the most able and best informed specialists on the USSR." —Walter Stoessel, Jr., United States Ambassador to the USSR, 1974-76.

**Books on Tape™'s service
is 100% guaranteed**

THE GRIZZLY BEAR

By Thomas McNamee
(2108) 9-1½ hour cassettes
Rental—$16.50   Purchase—$72.00
Read by Richard Wulf

Much of our considerable fascination with the grizzly bear is perhaps due to our unsettling kinship with it. Man and bear are omnivorous, predatory, intelligent . . . each at the top of his respective food chain. Each has little to fear from any creature . . . except ourselves and the other.

The heroine of this narrative is a female grizzly who has just emerged from hibernation with two wobbly-legged cubs in tow. For seven months, from thaw to freeze, we follow the daily life of this family on their home range in Yellowstone Park.

"In this wise, balanced, brilliantly researched book, Thomas McNamee has given us an outstanding and exemplary work of natural history." *(Publisher's Source)*

THE HEALING HEART

By Norman Cousins
(1609) 4-1 hour cassettes
Rental—$9.50   Purchase—$32.00
Read by Ken Ohst

More people die from heart attacks and heart disease in the United States than from any other malady. Cousins should know: a massive heart attack nearly killed him in 1980.

This dramatic account of that trauma highlights the importance of the patient's role in combating serious illness.

Cousins addresses the problem of panic and helplessness produced by any serious illness. He describes techniques for liberating ourselves from fear, that corrosive companion that always makes a difficult situation worse.

This reading of *The Healing Heart* was originally recorded for radio and is slightly abridged.

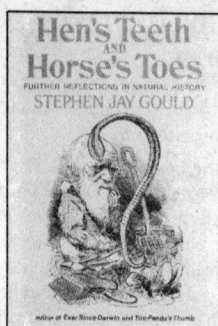

HEN'S TEETH AND HORSE'S TOES

By Stephen Jay Gould
(1623) 10-1½ hour cassettes
Rental—$16.50   Purchase—$80.00
Read by Larry McKeever

What color is a zebra? Does the changing size of Hershey bars hold a lesson of adaptive significance? Did an asteroid bring mass extinction to the earth sixty-five million years ago? Why do animals walk, fly, swim and slither but never roll? Human beings notwithstanding, why are the females of most species larger than males?

Behind each question and each answer lie concepts central to science and in particular to an understanding of evolution, the centerpiece of biology. Science is the art of the doable, and the science of evolutionary biology has changed our view of the world. It is important to remember that natural selection is not a perfecting principle, but a means of making sense of our earth as we find it today.

Stephen Jay Gould, an acclaimed scientist and author, won *Discover* magazine's Scientist of the Year award in 1982. He is a MacArthur Fellow and a member of the faculty at Harvard College.

HERETICS

By G.K. Chesterton
(1442) 8-1 hour cassettes
Rental—$14.50   Purchase—$64.00
Read by Robert Mundy

A collection of 20 free-ranging essays, *Heretics* contains some of Chesterton's most stimulating writing. He enjoyably attacks some of his favorite targets: Nietzsche, George Bernard Shaw, H.G. Wells, hypocrisy, faddism and muddy thinking. He takes to task the English gutter press of the early twentieth century and chides Rudyard Kipling for not having spent enough of his life in England. With equal vigor, Chesterton defends the institutions he holds dear: the family ("a good institution because it is uncongenial"), his country and his Church.

"Eccentric, lucid and entertaining." *(E.R.S. Services)*

THE HITE REPORT: A NATIONWIDE STUDY OF FEMALE SEXUALITY

By Shere Hite
(1316) 12-1½ hour cassettes
Rental—$17.50
Read by Roses Prichard

Shere Hite distributed questionnaires consisting of some 60 questions to 3000 women across the country, from every age and economic group and from all walks of life. Her aim was to reveal the complex nature of female sexuality.

The Hite Report presents what the women who answered said, in their own words and in their own way. The book features dozens of actual quotes from respondents to illustrate the conclusions at which Hite has arrived. (Rental only—not available for purchase.)

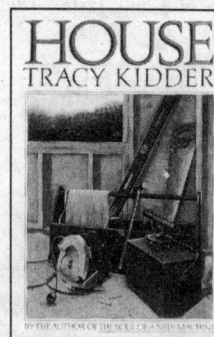

HOUSE

By Tracy Kidder
(1739) 10-1½ hour cassettes
Rental—$16.50   Purchase—$80.00
Read by Larry McKeever

To build a house. It is one of those nearly universal dreams, like falling love. And like falling in love, it is fraught with complication.

In this luminous book, Tracy Kidder follows the construction of a new house from gleam-in-the-eye to moving day. We get to know the ambitious owners, the architect who gives form to their dreams, the carpenters who pound then ails. Kidder delves into their lives and weaves their stories together in this portrait of a project that is the modern expression of an age-oldritual.

"The stuff of real drama . . . In the way that a well-told story of a marriage or a love affair or of a child's coming of age fills you with a sense that you are reading about a fundamental human expeience for the first time, so it is with *House*. Tracy Kidder makes us feel with a splendid intensity the complex web of relationships and emotions that comes into play in the act of bringing a work of architecture to fruition." *(The New York Times Book Review)*

HUGGING THE SHORE

By John Updike
(1930-A) 9-1½ hour cassettes
Rental—$16.50 Purchase—$72.00
(1930-B) 8-1½ hour cassettes
Rental—$15.50 Purchase—$64.00
(1930-C) 8-1½ hour cassettes
Rental—$15.50 Purchase—$64.00
Read by John MacDonald

Since 1960 John Updike has been writing book reviews for *The New Yorker,* and his contributions the last eight years make up the bulk of this volume.

On this collection, James Atlas adds that there is "the sort of ambitious scholarly reappraisal not seen in this country since the death of Edmund Wilson.

"Among the authors discussed in *Hugging the Shore* are Samuel Beckett, Saul Bellow, John Cheever, Isak Dinesen, Gunter Grass, Ernest Hemingway, Franz Kafka, Herman Melville, Vladimir Nabokov, Muriel Spark and Kurt Vonnegut, Jr.

HUMAN OPTIONS

By Norman Cousins
(1624) 7-1 hour cassettes
Rental—$13.50 Purchase—$56.00
Read by Dan Lazar

Anatomy of an Illness was Norman Cousin's first major book. It delivered a message of enormous optimism and hope.

So does *Human Options,* a more recent work. Cousins finds that our era, often called collective, is in fact highly individual. The good news is that choices remain in our hands, and that in many ways the good life is there for us to take.

HUSTLING ON GORKY STREET

By Yuri Brokhin
(1016) 7-1 hour cassettes
Rental—$13.50 Purchase—$56.00
Read by Michael Prichard

The Soviet Union is generally thought to be homogeneous and uniform. But this is not necessarily true. Within its confines, a whole universe of enterprise and opportunity abounds. Often delving into crime, prostitution and drugs, *Hustling on Gorky Street* is an expose of low-life in the Soviet Union . . . fascinating reading. XXX-rated for sex and language.

IN SEARCH OF EXCELLENCE
Lessons from America's Best-Run Companies

By Thomas J. Peters and Robert H. Waterman, Jr.
(1923) 10-1½ hour cassettes
Rental—$16.50 Purchase—$80.00
Read by Michael Prichard

What is the secret to successful business management? Why does one corporation do extraordinarily well while another, similar company wallows in mediocrity?

In Search of Excellence provides some surprisingly simple, straightforward answers to these and many other questions concerning the nature of American business.

"I found it extraordinary in its content, and most importantly, in its ability to be implemented. —Archie J. McGill, Vice-President Business Marketing, AT&T

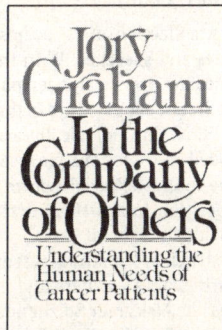

IN THE COMPANY OF OTHERS
Understanding the Human Needs of Cancer Patients

By Jory Graham
(1895) 6-1 hour cassettes
Rental—$12.50 Purchase—$48.00
Read by Wanda McCaddon

Jory Graham had cancer. The "others" of her title are the thousands of Americans who wage a daily war against their disease.

During her years of treatment Graham wrote a syndicated column, "A Time for Living," in which she argued that cancer patients be accepted as self-directed human beings, with the right to make choices about their lives and deaths.

In the Company of Others is an immensely moving book. Jory Graham died in 1983. Her courage and dignity lead us not to sadness and pity, but to respect and admiration.

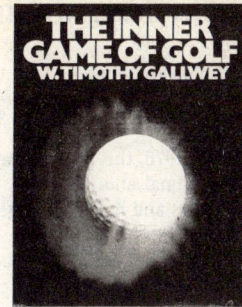

THE INNER GAME OF GOLF

By W. Timothy Gallwey
(2159) 6-1½ hour cassettes
Rental—$14.50 Purchase—$48.00
Read by Ron Shoop

One's mind, emotions and confidence play a much larger role in golf than in almost any other sport. Whether brooding over having flubbed the last drive, dreading the next shot from a sand trap or trying to line up a tricky putt, a golfer is constantly grappling with self-doubt, fear of failure and tension.

The Inner Game of Golf offers no miracles. What it does offer is a method simply helping players to observe, quiet the mind, control anxiety and think positively. It is a function of trusting your body, of practice and of relaxed concentration.

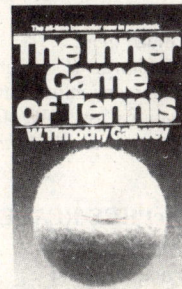

THE INNER GAME OF TENNIS

By W. Timothy Gallwey
(2060) 5-1 hour cassettes
Rental—$11.50 Purchase—$40.00
Read by Ron Shoop

Tim Gallwey's education began as a teacher. He has been a fine technician, but when he began to coach others, he needed more than the moves.

Gallwey probed to find where games were won. The answer came to him: in the mind of the player. His students began to play gracefully and with freedom. They tapped a new sense of energy and were never discouraged by temporary setbacks.

In this watershed book Gallwey explores the limitless potential of mind and body through the medium of tennis. And teaches us how to play the inner game on—and off—the court.

"A startling surprise . . . a how-to sport book with depth and soul." *(Tennis News)*

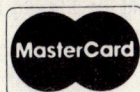

THE INNOVATION MILLIONAIRES

By Gene Bylinsky
(1063) 6-1½ hour cassettes
Rental—$14.50   Purchase—$48.00
Read by Daniel Grace

Published in 1976, this book surveys the careers, both personal and corporate, of today's entrepreneurs and how their ingenious blending of technology and finance produced fortunes for themselves and their backers. Stimulating in the extreme, well-researched and accurate, *The Innovation Millionaires* lets us accompany a select band of individuals on their clamber up the pyramid.

INSIDE MOVES:
Corporate Smarts for Women on the Way Up

By Marilyn Machlowitz, Ph.D.
(1959) 6-1 hour cassettes
Rental—$12.50   Purchase—$48.00
Read by Paul Shay

Inside Moves is good information—not fluff. It tracks the careers of thousands of successful women. *Inside Moves* is a guide to what works, what doesn't and why.

A compilation of Machlowitz's widely-read national columns, *Inside Moves* offers advice and counsel in a number of areas, including the ten laws of fast-track success, the Velvet Ghetto (women's jobs that lead nowhere), the challenge of the two-career relationship, and much more.

Marilyn Machlowitz is an author, lecturer and management consultant with a Ph.D. in organizational psychology from Yale. B-O-T has also recorded *Workaholics* and *Whiz Kids.*

THE JOHN McPHEE READER

By John McPhee
(1944) 12-1½ hour cassettes
Rental—$17.50   Purchase—$96.00
Read by Dan Lazar

Given a free rein at *The New Yorker,* John McPhee chose to write about those subjects that interested him. His investigations have ranged from tennis to oranges to atomic fission to wilderness conservation.

These excerpts from the following stories will introduce you to McPhee's world and to McPhee himself: "A Sense of Where You Are," "The Headmaster," "Oranges," "The Pine Barrens," "A Roomful of Hovings," "Levels of the Game," "The Crofter and the Laird," "Encounters withthe Archdruid," "The Deltoid Pumpkin Seed," "Pieces of the Frame," "The Curve of Binding Energy" and "The Survival of the Bark Canoe."

KIDS AND CASH

By Ken Davis and Tom Taylor
(1641) 7-1½ hour cassettes
Rental—$15.50   Purchase—$56.00
Read by John MacDonald

Kids and Cash provides parents with a simple step-by-step approach for helping children understand and appreciate the value of money.

The book includes a section on the many ways kids can earn money for themselves, and also recounts ways in which several famous people earned money when they were children.

KNOCKING ON THE DOOR
Shorter Writings

By Alan Paton
(1334) 10-1½ hour cassettes
Rental—$16.50   Purchase—$80.00
Read by Stuart Courtney

This is a collection of 70 poems, short stories, articles and speeches. With three exceptions, none have previously been published in the United States; about a third of the pieces first appear here. Chronologically arranged, they are divided into sections corresponding to Paton's life interests: penal reform, literature and opposition to apartheid first within and then outside the Liberal Party.

"One is struck by the strong resemblance in certain particulars to writers and intellectual witnesses like Aleksandr Solzhenitsyn and George Orwell." *(The New York Times)*

LEARNING TO LOVE AGAIN

By Mel Krantzler
(1553) 8-1 hour cassettes
Rental—$14.50   Purchase—$64.00
Read by Paul Shay

Just when you thought it would never happen again. The shock is over. You've made it through the explosive realities that losing love brings. It's over, but your life isn't. You're ready to love again. Or are you?

Are you having trouble finding the "right" man or woman? Are you afraid of making another "mistake"? Do you keep getting involved in short-term relationships? Are you beginning to think finding love is a matter of luck?

Mel Krantzler, author of *Creative Divorce,* gives clear guidelines and challenging steps that lead from loneliness to love: The Remembered Pain Stage, absorbing a blow from the past; The Questing Experimental Stage, surveying the possibilities; The Selective-Distancing Stage, a cautious step forward; and The Creative-Commitment Stage, where enduring love begins.

"Full of energy and advice . . . Hardly a page where some truth doesn't hit home." *(The NewYork Times Book Review)*

LEAVING THE OFFICE BEHIND

By Dr. Barbara Mackoff
(1793) 7-1 hour cassettes
Rental—$13.50   Purchase—$56.00
Read by Donada Peters

Dr. Mackoff, a psychotherapist, examines the problems of people who spend all day being "professional," but then must be interested, caring parents, spouses or lovers on reaching the front door.

Quoting from interviews with professionals in many fields, Mackoff offers a Rx for shifting from work to home. She outlines specific techniques for dealing with an agenda of items that includes unfinished business, arguments with the boss, passing up happy hour, tabling complaints, listening effectively and carving out time for yourself and your partner.

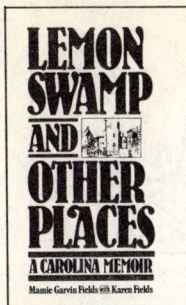

LEMON SWAMP AND OTHER PLACES: A CAROLINA MEMOIR

*By Mamie Garvin Fields
and Karen Elise Garvin*
(2091) 8-1½ hour cassettes
Rental—$15.50 Purchase—$64.00
Read by Mary Woods

Mamie Garvin Fields was born in Charleston, South Carolina in 1888. Though black, her family was gifted and she grew up not among house servants or sharecroppers but among artisans and professionals.

In *Lemon Swamp,* she looks back on this all-but-forgotten community of friends and family, and on the wider social landscape of the segregationist South of her youth.

"*Lemon Swamp,* is wonderful. I think anyone interested in Southern history, black history, Charleston, or the struggles of women in society will find it thoroughly engaging." — Ernest Hollings, U.S. Senator

LIFE AFTER MARRIAGE: DIVORCE AS A NEW BEGINNING

By Mary Ann Singleton
(1131) 7-1 hour cassettes
Rental—$13.50 Purchase—$56.00
Read by Nancy Dannevik

This practical narrative is designed as a self-help for divorced women. The author explores the personal and psychological consequences of divorce, and gives counsel on topics ranging from establishing credit to housekeeping while working while working full time.

Singleton believes that this experience offers opportunity for personal growth and creative living. Her book invites others to share this belief and pursue life after marriage.

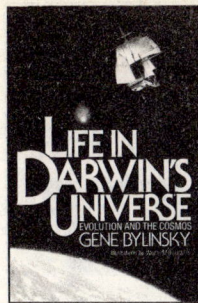

LIFE IN DARWIN'S UNIVERSE

By Gene Bylinsky
(1531) 6-1½ hour cassettes
Rental—$14.50 Purchase—$48.00
Read by Justin Hecht

The unique premise of *Life in Darwin's Universe* is that just as the laws of physics and chemistry apply throughout the cosmos, so must Darwin's principles of evolution.

Bylinsky's journey through time and space gives us a scientific view of what life might be like on uninhabited planets of the galaxies—how the evolutionary push of life might respond to different physical requirements. Bylinsky even speculates on what creatures might have dominated Earth had conditions here been somewhat different.

THE LION AND THE UNICORN

By George Orwell
(2139) 7-1½ hour cassettes
Rental—$15.50 Purchase—$56.00
Read by Donald Monat

"As I write, highly civilized human beings are flying overhead, trying to kill me." So starts this 1941 study of the English national character, so beautifully displayed during a war that tested it to the limit.

Because so many of our own institutions derived from the British, these essays refract them in a different and arresting way. Also, Orwell is valuable because his technique helps us evaluate and process "information" (for which substitute "disinformation").

LIVING THE GOOD LIFE: How to Live Sanely in a Troubled World

By Helen and Scott Nearing
(1981) 6-1½ hour cassettes
Rental—$14.50 Purchase—$48.00
Read by Jill Masters

In 1932, Helen and Scott Nearing moved from New York City to a farm in the Green Mountains of Vermont. Their purpose was to seek a simple life on the land, away from the stresses of depression and city life. *Living the Good Life,* first published in 1954, presents a technical, economic, sociological and psychological report on how they fared.

"A prophet account of the creation of a self-sufficient little Walden in rural Vermont that has been an underground bible for the city-weary." *(Newsweek)*

THE MAGIC ANIMAL

By Philip Wylie
(1522) 8-1½ hour cassettes
Rental—$15.50 Purchase—$64.00
Read by Richard Shoop

Christianity, American materialism, behaviorist psychology, "now" generation . . . Wylie targets these for comment. He contends that man's growing depredation of his natural environment and his ignorance of the laws of ecology and science have left him ill-equipped to live beyond the twentieth century.

"He is in the unfortunate position of one who sees flames crawling over the proscenium and cries 'Fire' in a crowded theatre. The audience applauds politely—and goes on eating its popcorn." *(The New York Times)*

MAKING IT IN AMERICA

By Barry Minkow
(2062) 5-1 hour cassettes
Rental—$11.50 Purchase—$40.00
Read by Ron Shoop

Barry Minkow made a million dollars at age 18 and was a hero. By 21 he had lost it and was a disgrace. This is his story of the rise to riches.

He began working at age 9 and by the time he was 15, he launched his own carpet and drapery cleaning business, ZZZZ Best. Six years later he was broke.

The question is, which was the real Minkow? Despite the author's flaws and failures, the book is a vital and living document.

THE MAKING OF A SURGEON

By William A. Nolen, M.D.
(1693) 8-1 hour cassettes
Rental—$14.50 Purchase—$64.00
Read by Bob Erickson

Dr. Nolen takes us through the surgical residency and introduces us to the very real world where he was intern and chief resident for five years: New York's Bellevue State Hospital. Funny, compassionate, sometimes tragic, Nolen provides an intimate view of life in the wards, labs and operating rooms of a great hospital.

"His book is devastatingly frank . . . a cornucopia of enthralling stories . . . an intensely human record of a young surgeon's apprenticeship." *(Saturday Review)*

**Special 10% discount
See page 2**

MALE CHAUVINISM!
How It Works

By Michael Korda
(1598) 6-1½ hour cassettes
Rental—$14.50   Purchase—$48.00
Read by Wanda McCaddon

Michael Korda writes brilliantly and irreverently about what male chauvinism means, why men act the way they do toward women in business, marriage and sex—ways men are finally being asked to, forced to, abandon.

He includes discussions with successful women such as Barbara Walters and Helen Gurley Brown.

"Here, with unflinching candor, rapier wit, factual case histories, Michael Korda strips bare the means by which American men put down, illuse, dominate American women." —Irving Wallace.

MANAGING TO SUCCEED: SUCCESS STORIES OF THE WALL STREET JOURNAL

Edited by Lawrence A. Armour
(1241) 7-1½ hour cassettes
Rental—$15.50   Purchase—$56.00
Ready by Bob Erickson

Managing to Succeed is not how-to-do-it, but a series of stories about executives who are making a success of running their businesses. Through these case studies, Armour strips the terms "success" and "management" of generalities and presents them as concrete examples that help us see how one can truly manage to succeed.

Armour holds a BA from Dartmouth College and an MBA from Northwestern University. In 1971, his coverage of the collapse of a major brokerage firm won the Deadline Club Award for Financial Journalism.

MAN'S WORLD, WOMAN'S PLACE

By Elizabeth Janeway
(1213) 9-1½ hour cassettes
Rental—$16.50   Purchase—$72.00
Read by Becky Bell Maxwell

In this refreshing study of the role of women in our society, Elizabeth Janeway uses information from historians, sociologists, psychoanalysts and anthropologists. She finds that the idea of women as household drudges is barely three centuries old and, worse, confined largely to the middle class. She examines why society is so reluctant to abandon this notion, and finds the answer lies in a number of well-established social and psychological patterns.

**Collector's Editions™
from Books on Tape™
See page 3**

MARY KAY ON PEOPLE MANAGEMENT

By Mary Kay Ash
(1950) 8-1 hour cassettes
Rental—$14.50   Purchase—$64.00
Read by Roses Prichard

Based simply upon the age-old Golden Rule, *Mary Kay on People Management* is designed to encourage managers to treat staff, customers, suppliers—everyone—with the same care, consideration and concern they would like to receive themselves. It is the management philosophy that turned Ash's storefront cosmetic business into a multi-million dollar corporation in just 20 years.

"Mary Kay's book is terrific! Every manager ought to read it. Her formula is straightforward—care, trust and an unshakable belief that people will shine if given the chance." —Thomas J. Peters, *In Search of Excellence*

MATTERS OF LIFE AND DEATH
Risks vs. Benefits of Medical Care

By Eugene D. Robin, M.D.
(1988) 6-1½ hour cassettes
Rental—$14.50   Purchase—$48.00
Read by Michael Prichard

Matters of Life and Death is a thoughtful, well-reasoned explanation of the practice of medicine. It is not a how-to book. But it will help you make sensible decisions about medicine and medical care.

Dr. Robin treats subjects such as getting the most from your doctor . . . seeing how diagnostic and therapeutic measures are introduced and perpetuated . . . learning why doctors overtest and overtreat . . . discovering what risks are inherent in every medical encounter . . . from a simple blood test to a major operation . . . and finding out how to increase the benefits and decrease the risks of modern medicine for yourself and your family.

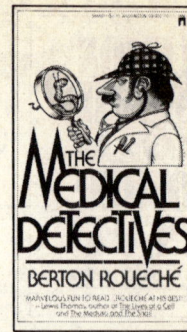

THE MEDICAL DETECTIVES Vol. I

By Berton Roueche
(1551) 10-1½ hour cassettes
Rental—$16.50   Purchase—$80.00
Read by Paul Shay

It all seems routine. You come home from a weekend in the mountains and complain of a headache the next day. Tuesday you have a slight fever and spend the day in bed. But that night, tossing in sweaty sheets, dehydrated, wracked with spasms, you gasp for a doctor and what he prescribes may depend on how alert he has been to the work increasingly done by medical detectives.

These research scientists, laboring alone or in teams, sift through the data supplied by doctors from the front lines of disease. Their solutions are often intuitive and they rely as much on judgment as on what the test tubes show.

"Mysteries, with doctors as the sleuths—and sometimes culprits! . . . highly addictive reading." (*Chicago Sun-Times*)

THE MEDICAL DETECTIVES Vol. II

By Berton Roueche
(1559) 11-1½ hour cassettes
Rental—$17.50   Purchase—$88.00
Read by Paul Shay

As AIDS has most recently taught us, a rare disease can surface without warning and spread like wildfire. Who mans the rampart against such onslaughts?

A legion of interrelated health services, professional and amateur, guard us. Linked by training, interest and technology, they gather data and share resources to disarm these diseases before they get started.

This is the second of two collections that bring together the best of Berton Roueche's *Annals of Medicine* narratives. Originally published in *The New York* magazine, the stories are classics of literary and medical lore.

The Medical Detectives Vol. I is also available from Books on Tape.

MEDITATIONS ON HUNTING

By Jose Ortega y Gasset
(1293) 4-1 hour cassettes
Rental—$9.50 Purchase—$32.00
Read by Victor Rumbellow

Meditations on Hunting is a broad examination of the condition of life. "The life that we are given has its minutes numbered, and in addition it is given to us empty . . . we have to fill it on our own, that is we have to occupy it one way or another . . . " Ortega y Gasset also discusses the evolution of hunting and carefully examines its implications to the hunter—its total absorption of mind and body, its atavistic reverberations, its animalistic fulfillments, and its tonic immersion in nature.

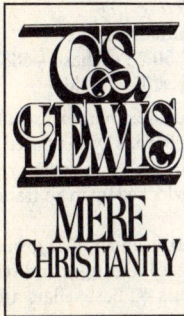

MERE CHRISTIANITY

By C.S. Lewis
(2080) 8-1 hour cassettes
Rental—$16.50 Purchase—$64.00
Read by Michael York
A Christopher Enterprises Recording

C.S. Lewis was professor of Medieval and Renaissance English at Cambridge and a Fellow at Oxford. He earned his spurs with scholarly exactitude.

But his interests were so broad that he defies labelling. If his science fiction tended toward the philosophical, then his philosophy embraced humanism, just as humanism was lit with a strong sense of ethics and morality.

Mere Christianity was published in 1952 and incorporates the author's thoughts about the Christian faith. But what really commends the book, at least to this reviewer, is the strong current of warmth and affection that runs through it.

MINK AND RED HERRING:
The Wayward Pressman's Casebook

By A.J. Liebling
(2003) 9-1 hour cassettes
Rental—$15.50 Purchase—$72.00
Read by Wolfram Kandinsky

As one of the premier journalists of this century, A.J. Liebling is uniquely qualified to comment on the inadequacies of the American press, especially during the late 1940s setting of this book.

"The American Press," Liebling wrote in 1948, "makes me think of a gigantic, supermodern fish cannery, a hundred floors high, capitalized at eleven billion dollars with tens of thousands of workers standing ready at the canning machines, but relying for its raw material on an inadequate number of fishermen in leaky rowboats."

B-O-T has also released Liebling's *Mollie and Other War Pieces*.

MOOD CONTROL

By Gene Bylinsky
(1260) 8-1 hour cassettes
Rental—$14.50 Purchase—$64.00
Read by Michael Prichard

Gene Bylinsky tells us in this compelling book that of all prescriptions written in the U.S., nearly one quarter are for Librium. While rampant depression is itself depressing, the extent of medical response stretches beyond belief. Traveling through this book the reader encounters aphrodisiacs, psychopharmacology, memory aids, and drugs for controlling aggression and rage. While their proposed use is beguiling, and may bring about the end of madness, our concern is the harmful use to which such potent drugs can be put.

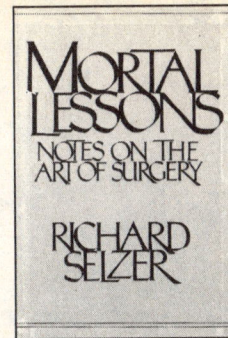

MORTAL LESSONS
Notes on the Art of Surgery

By Richard Selzer, M.D.
(1576) 7-1 hour cassettes
Rental—$13.50 Purchase—$56.00
Read by Christopher Hurt

Richard Selzer is a surgeon by training but an artist by nature. His book inquires deeply into the meaning behind medicine; his method is narrative, anecdote and irony.

"Selzer forces physicians to think about the morality of medicine—and to search for meaning in their rituals of an art 'at once murderous, painful, healing and full of love.' "

Dr. Selzer is a member of the Yale Medical School faculty as well as a practicing physician.

MURDER AND MADNESS
(Portable Stanford Series)

By Donald T. Lunde
(1913) 7-1 hour cassettes
Rental—$13.50 Purchase—$56.00
Read by Michael Prichard

An examination of causes behind murder in the U.S., with comparative looks at violence in other countries. Dr. Lunde reveals new insights into the question of sanity in relation to murder, and suggests alternative approaches for our judicial system to use in dealing with this form of ultimate violence.

The Portable Stanford is published by the Stanford Alumni Association and features articles and opinions by some of Stanford's most distinguished experts on today's vital issues.

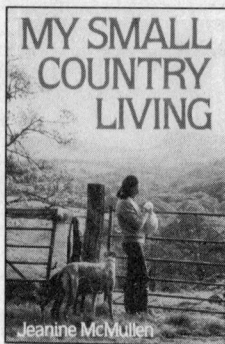

MY SMALL COUNTRY LIVING

By Jeanine McMullen
(1736) 7-1½ hour cassettes
Rental—$15.50   Purchase—$56.00
Read by Jill Masters

Jeanine McMullen was a BBC producer in London, when she went to Wales on assignment. There she fell in love—with Wales, its people, and most of all with the farm that on impulse she decided to buy.

"Magical writing about animals and the country scene with glorious, gusting humor. I loved every word. Jeanine McMullen's book is absorbing, touching and funny and I found something inspiring in her zestful acceptance of life." —James Herriot

THE NEXT 200 YEARS

*By Herman Kahn, William Brown,
Leon Martel*
(1057) 6-1½ hour cassettes
Rental—$14.50   Purchase—$48.00
Read by Michael Prichard

In a closely reasoned and carefully documented study, Herman Kahn and his associates at the Hudson Institute give us their expectations for what the next 200 years (1976-2176) will bring. While no Pollyannas, they nevertheless hold out hope for the species and make us wish we could stick around to see the exciting times ahead.

---

*Rental Section
At-a-Glance*

ON THE DEMOCRATIC IDEA IN AMERICA

By Irving Kristol
(1013) 5-1 hour cassettes
Rental—$11.50   Purchase—$40.00
Read by Michael Prichard

When Irving Kristol wrote this book, the country was still reeling from the turbulence of the sixties and seemed headed ever leftward in pursuit of the Great Society. By calling for are turn to ideas and policies more central to the American experience, Mr. Kristol became one of those who helped engineer the Reagan landslide of 1980. This exposition of his views is important, because it makes us consider which direction we want the country to travel.

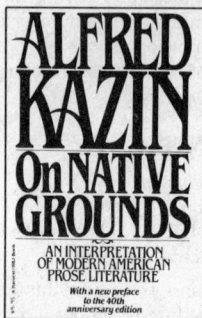

ON NATIVE GROUNDS

By Alfred Kazin
(2099-A) 8-1½ hour cassettes
Rental—$15.50   Purchase—$64.00
(2099-B) 8-1½ hour cassettes
Rental—$15.50   Purchase—$64.00
Read by Michael Prichard

Alfred Kazin is a gifted scholar, author and teacher. He made his reputation with literary criticism that upset tradition. His focus: American authors and their birthright.

Kazin understands what shaped American letters. He also has the courage to state his case without ceremonial and platitudinous apologies to European cultures that are more settled, more sedate, more sedentary.

Writing in 1942, Kazin pointed out that modern American literature was not simply an outgrowth of the revolt against Victorian gentility but a reflection of something greater—the moral transformation of our entire society after the Civil War. He interprets our principal literary figures from 1890 through the 1930's.

"Conceived on a grand scale and as not only a literary but a moral history, it is quite the best and most complete treatment of an arduous and difficult subject." *(The Nation)*

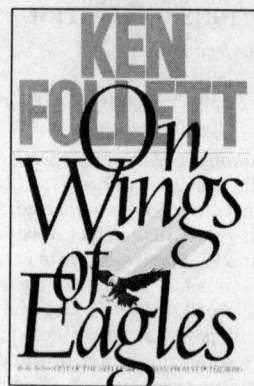

ON WINGS OF EAGLES

By Ken Follett
(1893) 11-1½ hour cassettes
Rental—$17.50   Purchase—$88.00
Read by Rupert Keenlyside

They were all computer executives, employees of Ross Perot's Dallas-based EDS Corporation. Their secret mission: rescue two EDS colleagues locked up in an Iranian prison in 1978.

Ken Follett is on familiar ground in this document of real-life danger and rescue. The ingredients of his #1 best sellers are present: penetration of enemy territory, last-second escape, and a race for the border. But this is real—it actually happened!

"As exciting as any of Follett's thrillers. An impressive nonfiction debut." *(Publishers Weekly)*

THE ONION FIELD

By Joseph Wambaugh
(1007) 10-1½ hour cassettes
Rental—$16.50   Purchase—$80.00
Read by Daniel Grace

The Onion Field is a true story of the 1963 kidnapping of two Los Angeles policemen. The abduction ends in the dead of night in an onion field near Bakersfield. One of the officers is murdered, the other manages to escape only to undergo, as author Joseph Wambaugh puts it, "psychological murder."

"The grisly events of the story are repelling yet hypnotic. Wambaugh follows step by step the wretched triumph of evil over good in this compelling drama.

PACIFIC ISLANDS SPEAKING

By Armstrong Sperry
(2040) 6-1 hour cassettes
Rental—$12.50   Purchase—$48.00
Read by Dan Lazar

NEW

As the Atomic Age shrinks the world in time and distance, the Pacific Islands and their people grow in importance. To deal with these emerging populations, our first task is to understand the forces that have shaped them over the ages.

"If we listen closely, perhaps we shall be able to hear the Pacific Islands speaking—a universal language of the hopes and fears, the dreams and aspirations shared by us all."

All Sail Set is another title by Armstrong Sperry available on cassette from Books on Tape.

THE PANDA'S THUMB

NEW

By Stephen Jay Gould
(2142) 8-1½ hour cassettes
Rental—$15.50   Purchase—$64.00
Read by Larry McKeever

"There is grandeur in this view of life," wrote Charles Darwin in the last line of *The Origin of Species,* "with its several powers, having been originally breathed into a few forms or into one."

In *The Panda's Thumb,* Gould delights and instructs while deepening and extending his examination of evolution, a centerpiece of modern science. Were dinosaurs really dumber than lizards? Why are roughly the same number of men and women born? What do the panda's magical "thumb" and the sea turtle's perilous migration tell us about imperfections that prove the evolutionary rule?

"These questions of life lie on a continuum that touches us all. Seldom have their mysteries been explained with such wit, beauty and elegance." *(Publisher's Source)*

Other studies on natural history by Gould recorded by Books on Tape include *The Flamingo's Smile* and *Hen's Teeth and Horse's Toes.*

PARKINSON'S LAW and THE LAW AND THE PROFITS

By C. Northcote Parkinson
(1150) 8-1 hour cassettes
Rental—$14.50   Purchase—$64.00
Read by Richard Green

When *Fortune Magazine* published an article titled "How Seven Employees Can Be Made to Do the Work of One," a funny critique of managerial bureaucracy, Parkinson's Law was launched.

In *The Law and the Profits,* Parkinson concludes there are limits to the collection of revenue. He advises greatly reduced taxation to bring about an improvement in public services.

PICKED UP PIECES

By John Updike
(1926-A) 7-1½ hour cassettes
Rental—$15.50   Purchase—$56.00
(1926-B) 7-1½ hour cassettes
Rental—$15.50   Purchase—$56.00
Read by John MacDonald

Best known for his Rabbit Angstrom and Henry Bech novels, John Updike proves his mastery of the short form with this selection.

In this compilation of his non-fiction work, Updike discourses on other authors, the future of the novel, feminism, the nobility of Africa and how to improve ones golf swing. He approaches his subjects wholly, grouping the reviews topically, thus giving the collection continuity and a sense of progression.

Born in 1932, Updike made his literary debut in 1954 when *The New Yorker* published one of his poems. He worked for *The New Yorker* as a staff reporter (1955-57), then left to work full time on his poetry, drama, novels and children's books.

THE PINE BARRENS

By John McPhee
(1993) 4-1 hour cassettes
Rental—$9.50   Purchase—$32.00
Read by Dan Lazar

The Pine Barrens is about the vast expanse of bog, swamp and piney woods in central New Jersey. Listening to this book is like having an intelligent and witty guide take you on a personal tour of a region you never knew existed, a region as remote as the moon but as close as your own backyard.

"McPhee captures something of the dreamlike quality of this quiet land, so threatened by the noise and clutter of our mechanical civilization." *(E.R.S. Reviews)*

A PRACTICAL APPROACH TO SUCCESS

By Jim Cathcart and Tony Alessandra, Ph.D.
(1800S) 14-1 hour cassettes
Rental—$28.50

"Most people aim at nothing in life and hit it with amazing accuracy."

Success is a goal greatly valued in our country. Jim Cathcart and Tony Alessandra, along with the University of Southern California, team up to teach us how success can be attained in the business world of human relationships. You will learn that true success can only be measured by total success; in and out of the office.

THE PRESIDENT SPEAKS OFF THE RECORD

By Harold Brayman
(1251) 7-1½ hour cassettes
Rental—$15.50   Purchase—$56.00
Read by Victor Rumbellow

This is a history of the Gridiron Club, an exclusive organization of Washington reporters. For nearly a century this club has hosted dinners at which presidents, cabinet members, party brass and assorted political fauna have taken turns roasting each other.

Harold Brayman is a former Gridiron Club president and is the only writer who has ever received permission to use the club's private records. This recording covers the initial one-third of the book, from Grover Cleveland to Herbert Hoover.

PRISONERS OF SANTO TOMAS

By Celia Lucas
(1650) 7-1½ hour cassettes
Rental—$15.50   Purchase—$56.00
Read by Wanda McCaddon

Among the casualties of war in the Pacific were thousands of American and British civilians who fell into the Japanese net.

Two who survived were a courageous English woman, Isla Corfield, and her teenage daughter Gill. Through three years of privation and despair, Isla kept a diary, recorded secretly in notebooks which she hid. These notebooks give a first hand account of what it was like to live in the nightmare world of internment.

FREE rental from Books on Tape™
See page 3

PROFESSIONAL SELLING TECHNIQUES

By Nido Qubein
(2144) 7-1 hour cassettes
Rental—$13.50   Purchase—$56.00
Read by Grover Gardner

Nido Qubein, one of the nation's most dynamic and successful sales educators has a profound message that can change the way you sell—and the way you live.

Simply put, to compete and succeed in today's sophisticated market, you must be a professional—not merely a professional salesperson, but the type of true "professional" we call to mind when we think of doctors or lawyers. *Professional Selling Techniques* packs powerful strategies you can readily put to work. Qubein examines the six basic ways today's customers are more demanding. He illustrates the 12 vital skills a professional salesperson must master, and he offers a revealing self-test to help you target areas for improvement.

"Qubein takes you behind the simple motivation of many popular books to mobilization beyond enthusiasm to action." *(E.R.S. Reviews)*

THE PROFESSIONAL THIEF

By Edwin H. Sutherland
(1325) 5-1½ hour cassettes
Rental—$13.50   Purchase—$40.00
Read by Mike Owens

This classic text of criminology, written in 1937 by Edwin H. Sutherland, a professor at Indiana University, takes us on a journey into the hidden world of the professional thief.

In our own era of great criminality, this book provides an important flashback and is a valid investigation of the criminal mentality. The evidence here suggests a criminal society exists, further that it resists all attempts at assimilation.

R.F.K. MUST DIE!

By Robert Blair Kaiser
(1399) 15-1½ hour cassettes
Rental—$18.50   Purchase—$120.00
Read by Dan Lazar

On the night of June 4, 1968, Sirhan Bishara Sirhan shot and killed Senator Robert F. Kennedy in a steamy pantry of the Los Angeles Ambassador Hotel. Kennedy and his entourage had been celebrating his victory in the California primary for the Democratic nomination for president.

R.F.K. Must Die! begins on the night of Kennedy's assassination and moves forward chronologically to the end of Sirhan's trial. Comprehensive in scope and meticulous in detail, *R.F.K. Must Die!* reads like a novel.

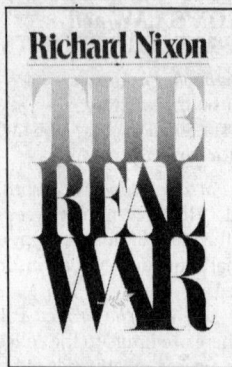

THE REAL WAR

By Richard Nixon
(1548) 9-1½ hour cassettes
Rental—$16.50   Purchase—$72.00
Read by Wolfram Kandinsky

Richard Nixon's vision of history has always been keen and has improved with experience (stand up to Khrushchev, withdraw from Vietnam, recognize mainland China).

As the sixties were an era when the nation's first priority was to address problems within its boundaries, so in the 1980's our agenda must start with security in this world. Nixon spends very little time with might-have-beens and concentrates instead on how we reached our present weakened position and what can be done to improve that position.

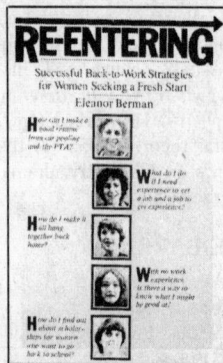

RE-ENTERING

By Eleanor Berman
(1645) 8-1 hour cassettes
Rental—$14.50   Purchase—$64.00
Read by Wanda McCaddon

This book is specifically designed for women whose children are grown, those who want to increase family income, divorcées and widows. It helps homemakers with little or no job experience move toward a rewarding career.

Eleanor Berman is well-qualified to write about the challenges of re-entering, having herself gone back to work after more than a decade. Her new career is in publishing and public relations. *Re-Entering* is her third book.

THE ROAD TO WIGAN PIER

By George Orwell
(1528) 7-1 hour cassettes
Rental—$13.50   Purchase—$56.00
Read by Richard Green

Times were hard for English workers in the thirties when George Orwell dramatized their plight in this documentary expose of the underclasses. *The Road to Wigan Pier* is a trek back through time to an experience suffered by many of our parents and is an unrecognized masterpiece by the author of *1984* and *Animal Farm*. Always courageous and original, Orwell gives us a feeling for what it must have been like to have had to cope with the grinding poverty of half a century ago.

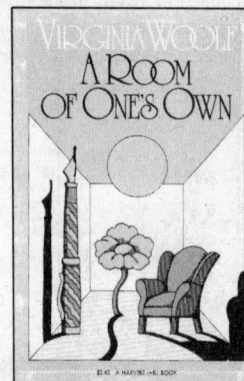

A ROOM OF ONE'S OWN

By Virginia Woolf
(1159) 5-1 hour cassettes
Rental—$11.50   Purchase—$40.00
Read by Penelope Dellaporta

Virginia Woolf is one of the twentieth century's great innovative writers. She was a member of the Bloomsbury group in pre-WW I England.

A Room of One's Own is her investigation of the woman artist as a writer. Speculating on the imaginary life of Shakespeare's equally talented sister, she posits the necessity of "a room of one's own" (and a fixed income) for the writer to pursue her craft.

THE RUSSIANS

By Hedrick Smith
(1132-A) 10-1½ hour cassettes
Rental—$16.50   Purchase—$80.00
(1132-B) 9-1½ hour cassettes
Rental—$16.50   Purchase—$72.00
Read by Wolfram Kandinsky

Hedrick Smith was *The New York Times* bureau chief in Moscow from 1971 to 1974 and won a Pulitzer Prize for international reporting.

Russians are cynical about their government but devoted to their country, friendly to the West but cautious, hopeful of peace but dreading war. They seem to be a people with whom we can deal, but saddled with a difficult rider.

"He has an unerring reporter's eye and ear for small but significant nuances of social and political behavior." *(Saturday Review)*

THE SEARCH FOR A SOUL: TAYLOR CALDWELL'S PSYCHIC LIVES

By Jess Stearn
(1431) 8-1½ hour cassettes
Rental—$15.50   Purchase—$64.00
Read by Roses Prichard

Jess Stearn takes us on a fascinating exploration of psychic phenomena with Taylor Caldwell. Under hypnosis, Caldwell relates her previous existences, all supported by remarkable details. According to Stearn, the extraordinarily precise technical information in Caldwell's novel *Testimony of Two Men* was much the product of a trance.

B-O-T has books of further interest by Jess Stearn, namely, *Edgar Cayce: The Sleeping Prophet* and *Yoga, Youth, and Reincarnation,* and by Taylor Caldwell, *The Romance of Atlantis.*

THE SECRETS OF CONSULTING

By Gerald M. Weinberg
(2161) 8-1 hour cassettes
Rental—$14.50   Purchase—$64.00
Read by Paul Shay

Gerald M. Weinberg draws on his 25 years of experience as author, lecturer and consultant to share his secrets about the often irrational world of consulting. "The irrationality can drive consultants crazy but if consultants can cope with it, it can also drive them rich."

Using memorable rules, laws and principles to make his points, Gerald M. Weinberg offers guidance on how to succeed in this highly competitive profession. Among the topics are pricing and marketing your services, measuring your effectiveness and dealing with client resistance.

". . . an irreverent, funny but true look at those thousands of professionals, as well as con men, who call themselves consultants." —Martin A. Goetz, President, Applied Data Research, Inc.

THE SENSUOUS WOMAN

By "J"
(1212) 4-1 hour cassettes
Rental—$10.50   Purchase—$32.00
Read by Violet Cielo

The first "how to" manual of sexual practice and manipulation, *The Sensuous Woman* is candid, amusing and detailed. Its significance is that it opened for discussion a subject that was taboo prior to its publication, namely, female eroticism and how it can be used to captivate the startled male.

"J" is Joan Terry Garrity. Prior to the great success achieved by this book Garrity had made her way as a literary publicist and freelance writer.

THE SEVEN PILLARS OF WISDOM

By T.E. Lawrence
(1600-A) 9-1½ hour cassettes
Rental—$16.50   Purchase—$72.00
(1600-B)) 10-1½ hour cassettes
Rental—$16.50   Purchase—$80.00
Read by Rupert Keenlyside

T.E. Lawrence was "Lawrence of Arabia," famous for his exploits in WW I. This book is his own vivid and stirring account of the Arabian campaigns.

"No historic figure has turned his eyes inward as Lawrence did, few have had such an immortal tale to tell; and none—not Julius Caesar or Leon Trotsky has applied to the events and characters of historic movement this exquisitely tortured imagination, this sensibility, the mind and heart of an artist." *(The Bookman)*

THE SEVEN SISTERS

NEW

By Anthony Sampson
(2067) 11-1½ hour cassettes
Rental—$17.50   Purchase—$88.00
Read by Paul Shay

The Seven Sisters: Exxon, Gulf, Texaco, Mobil, Socal, British Petroleum and Shell. Is it true that they run our lives?

First published in 1975, updated in 1983, *The Seven Sisters* is rich in political and corporate lore. Firmly international and rooted in the real world, this book forms an important key to understanding how we fare in the arena, not just of big business, but of business that is so big it merges with the national interest.

"Everyone will find something to like in this book. Serious students of the industry will be enlightened. Liberals will love it because it bashes business; conservatives, because it makes governments look stupid. It is a remarkable achievement." *(E.R.S. Reviews)*

THE SEVEN STOREY MOUNTAIN

By Thomas Merton
(1846) 13-1½ hour cassettes
Rental—$18.50   Purchase—$104.00
Read by Wolfram Kandinsky

Writing autobiographically, Thomas Mertonre counts his conversion to Roman Catholicism as a young man. Already enjoying recognition as a poet, he felt the need for spiritual communion in a Trappist monastery in Kentucky.

His story is one of deep conviction and penetrating introspection; his vision is at once private and universal.

"The Seven Storey Mountain is a book that deeply impresses the mind and the heart." *(Commonweal)*

SIGNAL ZERO

By George L. Kirkham
(1097) 7-1 hour cassettes
Rental—$13.50   Purchase—$56.00
Read by Dan Lazar

George Kirkham was comfortable with his theories of criminal behavior and taught them conscientiously to somnolent undergraduates. Then he put in a tour as uniformed officer patrolling the ghetto beat.

Full of suspense and adrenalin, *Signal Zero* gives us a new comprehension of police problems—and great respect for George Kirkham, a professor with the courage to test his social recipes in the pressure cooker of experience.

SO YOU'VE GOT A GREAT IDEA

By Steve Fiffer
(2150) 8-1 hour cassettes
Rental—$14.50   Purchase—$64.00
Read by Larry McKeever

NEW

Have you ever had a million-dollar idea that someone else made a million on? *So You've Got a Great Idea* can help you be that one person who cashes in on an innovative product, service, business or novelty item.

Steve Fiffer shows you how to tell whether your idea is a winner or a clunker and, through entertaining profiles of successful innovators, helps you decide how to follow through.

Having a great idea is one thing; making a great idea make money is what this book is about.

"At any one time, there may be 50 people talking about the same idea; it's the one who stops talking and starts doing who succeeds." —Marvin Rosenblum, inventor of the Spiro Agnew wristwatch.

SOME MUST WATCH WHILE SOME MUST SLEEP (Portable Stanford Series)

By William C. Dement
(1915) 6-1 hour cassettes
Rental—$12.50   Purchase—$48.00
Read by Michael Prichard

One of the nation's leading sleep researchers, Dr. Dement founded the Sleep Laboratory at Stanford in 1963. This is his study of the nature of sleep and what happens when you sleep and dream.

The Portable Stanford is published by the Stanford Alumni Association and features articles and opinions by some of Stanford's most distinguished experts on today's vital issues.

THE SOUL OF A NEW MACHINE

By Tracy Kidder
(2162) 7-1½ hour cassettes
Rental—$15.50   Purchase—$56.00
Read by Grover Gardner

NEW

Everything actually happened. No names have been changed. Nothing controversial has been left out. In 1979 Tracy Kidder went underground into the closely guarded research basement of Data General to observe a crack team of computer wizards about to embark on a crash program to design and build a fast new computer. *The Soul of A New Machine* is the Pulitzer Prize-winning result.

The "Hardy Boys" and the "Microkids" are competitors, most just out of engineering school. Their job: build a minicomputer more powerful than anything on the market.

Kidder watched as they pushed themselves to their physical and intellectual limits . . . twelve-hour days, twenty-hour days, all-night shifts, weekends . . . in an effort to maximize the win by building their machine in record time: one year.

"[This saga . . . provides a lucid description of computer engineering. More important, it is a surprisingly gripping account of people at work . . . a fascinating tale." *(The Wall Street Journal)*

THE STATIONARY ARK

By Gerald Durrell
(1525) 6-1 hour cassettes
Rental—$12.50   Purchase—$48.00
Read by Stuart Courtney

Gerald Durrell helped establish a model zoo on the Isle of Jersey, an experience that caused him to reconsider the whole question of wild animals in human hands.

"On one level this book is about zoos. More profoundly, however, *The Stationary Ark* is about the misuse of wild animals in captivity. Durrell's material reveals a fascinating blind spot in modern zoological thought, namely that we are almost completely ignorant about the important facts of many wild animals' lives." *(Saturday Review)*

STRATEGY FOR TOMORROW

By Hanson W. Baldwin
(1137) 9-1½ hour cassettes
Rental—$16.50   Purchase—$72.00
Read by James Cunningham

Published in 1970, *Strategy for Tomorrow* reminds us how rapidly our world evolves and how fluid are the combinations of power, politics and national self-interest. Much of the work remains valid today, for instance Baldwin's view of the United States as a "colossus under strain."

Baldwin was military affairs editor of *The New York Times,* and brings to his task great experience, knowledge and scholarship.

SUCCESS!

By Michael Korda
(1317) 7-1½ hour cassettes
Rental—$15.50   Purchase—$56.00
Read by Dan Lazar

We have here a hands-on guide to executive success. The author examines all the strategies known to man and weighs them up.

In Korda's game plan, style counts for everything. He advises men and women how to walk, sit and dress, how to communicate effectively, how to get a promotion—even how to look successful when you're on the bottom rung!

SUM AND SUBSTANCE

By Herman Harvey, Ph.D.
(1554) 10-1 hour cassettes
Rental—$15.50   Purchase—$80.00
Read by Herman Harvey et al

Sum and Substance showcases 20 of the great minds of this part of the century as they share declarations of belief and commitment—a permanent, living record of their ideas on a wide range of subjects and opinions, on their values and philosophies as they look back over their accomplishments.

Guests include William Inge, Pulitzer Prize playwright *(Bus Stop);* Jimmy Durante, entertainer; Upton Sinclair, Pulitzer Prize author Jean Renoir, eminent French film producer-director; Aldous Huxley, author of *Brave New World;* and Clifford Odets, playwright of *Country Girl.*

Others are Paul Tillich, leading Protestant theologian; Ruth St. Denis, American creative dancer; Hans Margenthau, contemporary political theorist; Gregor Piatigorsky, solo cellist and teacher; Roy Harris, foremost American composer; Jacques Lipchitz, sculptor and leader of early cubist technique; and Margaret Mead, anthropologist.

The list concludes with Erskine Caldwell, American novelist; Jessie Greenstein, professor of astrophysics at Cal Tech; Stanton Macdonald-Wright, artist and teacher; Adela Rogers St. Johns, famous newspaper woman; Ray Bradbury, author of science fiction; Alfred Kazin, critic and essayist; and Josh White, singer of folk songs.

Note: Interviews are between 20 and 30 minutes, thus some cassettes have only 40 minutes of recording.

Give a Books on Tape™
Gift Certificate
Call 1-800-626-3333

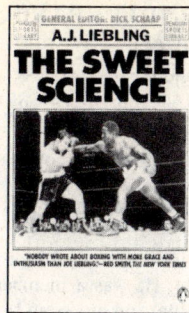

THE SWEET SCIENCE

By A.J. Liebling
(2049) 7-1½ hour cassettes
Rental—$15.50   Purchase—$56.00
Read by Wolfram Kandinsky

A.J. Liebling was one of this century's finest reporters. He practiced at *The New Yorker* where its founder and resident genius, Harold Ross, let him snuffle wherever the scent led . . . investigations of the press, wartime Italy and Europe, low life in New York . . . and boxing, "the sweet science."

The pieces collected here, published in *The New Yorker* between 1951 and 1956, may have been Liebling's metaphor for clearing his mind of wartime excess. He wrote about "heroic transactions" in the ring, and set them in historical perspective for us: the rise of Rocky Marciano and the demise of those who fought him plus the comeback of the nonpareil Sugar Ray Robinson. He muses as well on the varying natures of fight managers, trainers and crowds.

"Funny, acerbic, authoritative—superior sports writing with literary ruffles and flourishes." *(Saturday Review)*

TAKE CHARGE

Dr. Edward Bodaken
and Irene Lurkis
(1652) 10-1 hour cassettes
Rental—$14.00

Take Charge is a unique program designed to stimulate managers at all levels of public and private organizations and is hosted by USC faculty members Drs. Edward Bodaken and Irene Lurkis. Dr. Bodaken is recipient of USC's highest teaching honor.

Among the topics covered are: Awareness, Time Management, Effective Communication, Effective Listening, Handling Information, Interpersonal Relations, Effective Writing, Assertiveness, Overcoming Stress, and Brain Power and Creativity.

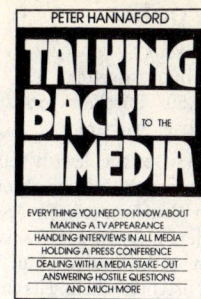

TALKING BACK TO THE MEDIA

By Peter Hannaford
(2065) 6-1 hour cassettes
Rental—$12.50   Purchase—$48.00
Read by Larry McKeever

Talking Back to the Media prepares you for any eventuality involved with facing the media—from doing a radio interview or appearing before TV cameras to coping with a media stakeout or getting through a Congressional hearing.

It tells you how to call a press conference, how to frame answers to hostile questions and how to make the media give *your* side of the story. It covers what recourse you have to protect yourself from a blitz of bad publicity—from writing simple letters or issuing press releases to suing for libel.

Peter Hannaford is a public relations expert and chief executive officer of The Hannaford Company, Inc., a public relations firm based in Washington, D.C. Hannaford was director for public affairs for then-governor Ronald Reagan in Sacramento as well as serving in Reagan's two presidential campaigns.

TERRA NON FIRMA

By James M. Gere and Haresh C. Shah
(1987) 6-1 hour cassettes
Rental—$12.50   Purchase—$48.00
Read by Michael Prichard

In this account of the causes and effects of earthquakes, Professors Gere and Shah, directors of the John A. Blume Earthquake Engineering Center at Stanford University, present the facts behind the headlines.

And they tell us what to do . . . how to react when an earthquake comes, how to protect yourself and your home, how individuals can build to reduce damage and injuries.

"A book for the curious and the cautious, for the renter and the property owner, for the stay-at-home and the traveler whose destination may lie in earthquake country." *(Editorial Review Service)*

THIS IS MY GOD

By Herman Wouk
(1573) 8-1½ hour cassettes
Rental—$15.50   Purchase—$64.00
Read by Michael Prichard

This account of the Jewish people and their faith is as compelling and absorbing as any of Herman Wouk's novels. For Jewish and Christian readers alike, it is informative because Judaism is the source of all Western religion. Many listeners will find its chief value in the highly candid personal statement of faith by a major American author. Wouk's novels and plays have gained him a world audience. His books have been translated into 15 languages, and he has won the Pulitzer Prize for fiction.

TROUT MADNESS

By Robert Traver
(1675) 6-1 hour cassettes
Rental—$12.50   Purchase—$48.00
Read by Bob Erickson

"Being a dissertation of the symptoms and pathology of this incurable disease by one of its victims."

"Here for the delight of all piscophiles are 21 stories accumulated from a lifetime of fishing—tales as true as can reasonably be expected of a fisherman."

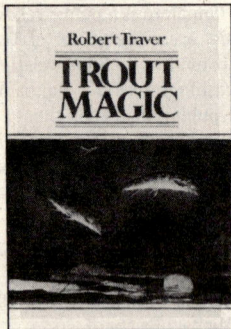

TROUT MAGIC

By Robert Traver
(1738) 6-1 hour cassettes
Rental—$12.50   Purchase—$48.00
Read by Dan Lazar

Trout Magic is a warm and maverick look at trout fishing and its attendant lore. Robert Traver tells of a mysterious dancing fly, speaks pointedly about kiss-and-tell fishermen, debunks fly enthusiasts as the world's greatest snobs, and lets us in on the fishing story *Life* missed.

"There's enough trout magic here to rub off on every reader—man, woman or child—as Robert Traver weaves his inimitable spell. *Trout Magic* is a great catch . . ." *(Publisher's Source)*

THE TRUTH THAT KILLED

By Georgi Markov
(1638) 8-1½ hour cassettes
Rental—$15.50   Purchase—$64.00
Read by Walter Zimmerman

When we heard that a political refugee had been killed in London by an assassin using an umbrella gun, we wondered what was behind it.

This book is the story, and Georgi Markov was the refugee. He was a member of Bulgaria's ruling elite, and moved in the highest circles. When he wrote his memoirs, not complimentary, his life was forfeit.

VISION OR VILLAINY:
Origins of the Owens Valley-
Los Angeles Water Controversy

By Abraham Hoffman
(1687) 7-1½ hour cassettes
Rental—$15.50   Purchase—$56.00
Read by Jack Hrkach

Over 75 years ago the growing city of Los Angeles, amid considerable conflict, appropriated water from a rural area 250 miles away.

"[Hoffman] exposes the often false story of the Owens Valley-Los Angeles controversy. The complex story . . . is a fascination study involving the compromising of ethics because the growing city had to have water." *(American History Review)*

THE WAR BETWEEN
RUSSIA AND CHINA

By Harrison Salisbury
(1220) 7-1 hour cassettes
Rental—$13.50   Purchase—$56.00
Read by James Cunningham

The tensions between Russia and China are widely known and of geologic duration. What makes this book different is Salisbury's analysis of how the United States can act as a third force to balance Communism's two colossi.

Harrison Salisbury is a Pulitzer Prize winning author who was military affairs editor for *The New York Times*.

**FREE rental from
Books on Tape™
See page 3**

WHAT I SAW IN AMERICA

By G.K. Chesterton
(1440) 8-1½ hour cassettes
Rental—$15.50   Purchase—$64.00
Read by Robert Mundy

In 1921 G.K. Chesterton lectured widely in the United States and in the following year published *What I Saw in America*. The first sentence—"I have never managed to lose my old conviction that travel narrows the mind"—gives some inkling of the delights in store. Chesterton offers insights on the architecture of American hotels and the real reasons for Prohibition. His topics include slavery, the Irish in America, the decline of the British Empire, Abraham Lincoln, and the American businessman.

WHEN BAD THINGS HAPPEN
TO GOOD PEOPLE

By Harold Kushner
(1661) 5-1 hour cassettes
Rental—$11.50   Purchase—$40.00
Read by Michael Prichard

As a small town rabbi, Harold Kushner comforted other people in their sorrows. But not until he learned that his son, then 3 years old, would die in his teens did he experience the kind of desolation he had so often seen in others.

Praised by theologians, psychiatrists and counselors, *When Bad Things Happen To Good People* is a very special book. It offers peace of mind and affirms humanity.

" . . . a moving and humane approach to understanding life's windstorms." —Elizabeth Kubler-Ross

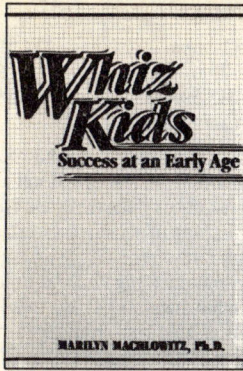

WHIZ KIDS

By Marilyn Machlowitz, Ph.D.
(1960) 6-1 hour cassettes
Rental—$12.50   Purchase—$48.00
Read by Paul Shay

Whiz kids. What makes them tick? Here, lively interviews and incisive analyses provide a portrait of success achieved at an early age.

At once practical and illuminating, *Whiz Kids* offers a comprehensive perspective on the early success, for those who want to raise one—and those who want to be one!

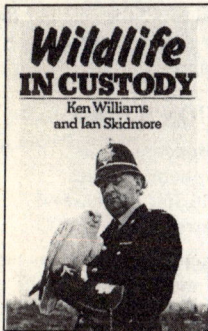

WILDLIFE IN CUSTODY

By Ken Williams and Ian Skidmore
(1683) 7-1 hour cassettes
Rental—$13.50   Purchase—$56.00
Read by Andy Parfitt

There was no question about what Ken Williams would be when he grew up: son of a policeman, grandson of a policeman . . . the path was clear. But it wasn't his first choice.

A born naturalist, Williams hoped to be a gamekeeper, but his father decreed otherwise. So after a stint in the Welsh Guard, he returned to Wales to be a constable in Holyhead —but his days still revolved around the care of wildlife, on and off duty.

With the coming of industry to Anglesey his boyhood dream became a reality. A mining corporation gave him a stretch of woodland and rocky coastline, and his own nature reserve was opened at Penrho. Thousands of tourists, naturalists and ornithologists visit it every year.

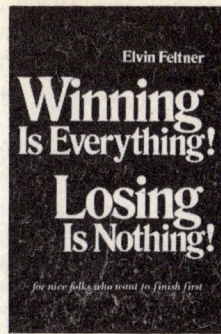

WINNING IS EVERYTHING

By C.E. Feltner, Jr.
(1953) 5-1 hour cassettes
Rental—$11.50   Purchase—$40.00
Read by Michael Prichard

In honest, to-the-point prose, Elvin Feltner details the steps to becoming a winner. He uses scores of examples drawn from personal experience and from the lives of celebrated successes to illustrate his main point: you can learn to win and still love yourself. Nice folks can finish first!

Winning is Everything! Losing is Nothing! combines unshakable faith in human nature with no nonsense business judgment. The result is are freshing approach to the best things in life.

In the authors own words, "You only need leaf through the Guinness Book of World Records to marvel at the limitless scope of human achievement. There's no reason why your achievements or mine cannot be just as amazing. After all, those awesome records were not set by supermen but by human beings like us. What they did, we can do—if we try hard enough."

WORKAHOLICS

By Marilyn Machlowitz, Ph.D.
(1958) 5-1 hour cassettes
Rental—$11.50   Purchase—$40.00
Read by Paul Shay

They head some of our greatest corporations. They count among their number leading scientists, writers, artists, physicians and statesmen.

Whether you are a workaholic or have to cope with one, this survey provides important information . . . the characteristics of workaholics, how a person becomes one, the four types of work addicts, how productive they really are, and, not least, how to live with one.

"Intelligent, perceptive . . . presents facts and observations clearly." *(Publishers Weekly)*

WRITING A NOVEL

By John Braine
(1201) 6-1 hour cassettes
Rental—$12.50   Purchase—$48.00
Read by Victor Rumbellow

Writing a Novel is a sound, entertaining book, written by the author of *Room at the Top*. Braine describes sample novels for beginners to study.

Braine concludes a novelist " . . . should be neutral and invisible . . . civilized and tolerant . . . possessing, above all, intellectual integrity. The writer doesn't have to inhabit a rarified moral or intellectual plane, but he must always be, no matter how imperfectly, the conscience of society."

YOGA, YOUTH, AND REINCARNATION

By Jess Stearn
(1224) 8-1½ hour cassettes
Rental—$15.50   Purchase—$64.00
Read by Dan Lazar

Jess Stearn was an experienced reporter and man of the world who viewed an invitation to a three-month study session of Hatha Yoga with extreme skepticism. But the experience transformed Stearn into a true believer.

Yoga, Youth, and Reincarnation explains how this change came about and commends yoga as a remedy for problems of tension, weight control, sexuality and various other complaints.

ACROSS THE SEA OF STARS

By Arthur C. Clarke
(1254) 8-1 hour cassettes
Rental—$14.50   Purchase—$64.00
Read by Dan Lazar

Across the Sea of Stars is a treasury of science fiction containing 18 of Clarke's finest short stories. In three groupings . . . "Expeditions to Earth," "Tales from the White Hart" and "Reach for Tomorrow," the selections include such memorable tales as "Encounter at Dawn," "The Sentinel," "Armaments Race," "Jupiter Five" and "Time's Arrow."

ASIMOV'S MYSTERIES

By Isaac Asimov
(1136) 8-1 hour cassettes
Rental—$14.50   Purchase—$64.00
Read by Dan Lazar

Asimov's Mysteries consists of 14 short stories designed to please mystery fans and science fiction devotees. Many of the stories, written between 1939 and 1967, are interrelated and several characters appear in more than one story. This collection includes: "The Dying Night," "The Singing Bell," "The Talking Stone," "What's in a Name," "The Dust of Death," "I'm in Marsport without Hilda," "Marooned Off Vesta," "Anniversary," "Obituary," "Starlight," "Pate de Foie Gras," "The Key," "A Loint of Paw" and "The Billiard Ball."

THE BEST OF ISAAC ASIMOV

By Isaac Asimov
(1231) 8-1½ hour cassettes
Rental—$15.50   Purchase—$64.00
Read by Dan Lazar

The Best of Isaac Asimov is a rare collection of the 12 best stories written by Asimov over the past 35 years. The collection includes: "Marooned Off Vesta," "Nightfall," "C-Chute," "The Martian Way," "The Deep," "The Fun They Had," "The Last Question," The Dead Past," "The Dying Night," "Anniversary," "The Billiard Ball" and "Mirror-Image." (Please note that some of these stories are also recorded in *Asimov's Mysteries*.)

CHILDHOOD'S END

By Arthur C. Clarke
(1169) 8-1 hour cassettes
Rental—$14.50   Purchase—$64.00
Read by Dan Lazar

This novel tells the tale of the last generation of mankind on earth. All man's developments in space and travel are stopped by alien "overlords" who take over Earth, establishing a benevolent dictatorship which eliminates poverty, ignorance and disease. This golden age ends abruptly as the overlords bend to the will of a superior intelligence which demands Earth's destruction.

THE COMPLETE ROBOT

By Isaac Asimov
(2094-A) 8-1½ hour cassettes
Rental—$16.50   Purchase—$64.00
(2094-B) 9-1½ hour cassettes
Rental—$17.50   Purchase—$72.00
Read by Larry McKeever

Though Isaac Asimov coined the word "robotics," his robots are close to human. His metal, plastic and (occasionally) organic mechanical men are very much like people we know . . . frequently warm, frequently fallible.

"Here is every last one of Asimov's robot stories, including some never before appearing in a book. Anyone who enjoys Asimov, science fiction, robots, or indeed anyone who cherishes stimulating and entertaining puzzles will love *The Complete Robot*." (*Publisher's Source*)

DEEP RANGE

By Arthur C. Clarke
(1252) 8-1 hour cassettes
Rental—$14.50   Purchase—$64.00
Read by Dan Lazar

This story takes place about 100 years in the future, when the earth's population is fed principally from the sea—on whale products or from plankton farms. Its hero is Walter Franklin, a grounded space engineer now assigned to a submarine patrol tending the whale herds. *Deep Range* vibrates with exciting adventures of the mysterious sea: a fight with a giant squid 12,000 feet down, the search for a great sea serpent, the heroic rescue of a damaged submarine—all vividly and plausibly portrayed.

EARTHLIGHT

By Arthur C. Clarke
(1235) 6-1 hour cassettes
Rental—$12.50   Purchase—$48.00
Read by Dan Lazar

The time: 200 years after man's first landing on the Moon. There are permanent populations established on the Moon, Venus and Mars. Outer space inhabitants have formed a new political entity (The Federation), and between the Federation and Earth a growing rivalry has developed. *Earthlight* is the story of this emerging conflict.

FOUNDATION

By Isaac Asimov
(1816) 6-1 hour cassettes
Rental—$12.50   Purchase—$48.00
Read by Larry McKeever

Foundation is the initial volume of Asimov's *Foundation* series which relates the decline and fall of the Galactic Empire and the attempt by a group of scientists to establish a new and better empire.

Asimov obtained his Ph.D. at Columbia, then taught biochemistry at Boston University's School of Medicine from 1949 to 1958. *Foundation and Empire, The Second Foundation* and *Foundation's Edge* are the second, third and fourth books in the series.

FOUNDATION AND EMPIRE

By Isaac Asimov
(1232) 8-1 hour cassettes
Rental—$14.50   Purchase—$64.00
Read by Dan Lazar

Foundation and Empire is the second section of Asimov's award-winning *Foundation* series. In this narrative, the Galactic Empire established in the previous episode is decaying, consumed by its own immorality and scientific mismanagement. *The Foundation* is formed to fill the void but soon gains equal, if not superior, power to the disintegrating Empire.

FOUNDATION'S EDGE

By Isaac Asimov
(1817) 9-1½ hour cassettes
Rental—$16.50   Purchase—$72.00
Read by Larry McKeever

The Second Foundation was supreme in the realm of mental power, in its ability to control.

It is 498 years since the establishment of the First Foundation. Power struggles sweep the foundations as each drives toward becoming the controlling nucleus in the planned Second Galactic Empire. The destiny of humankind is at stake.

A stirring blend of actions and ideas with future technology and hyperspace travel, this sequel to *The Second Foundation* is as intriguing as its predecessors.

Interval delivery convenience
See page 2

IN THE DAYS OF THE COMET

By H.G. Wells
(9080) 6-1½ hour cassettes
Rental—$15.50   Purchase—$48.00
Read by Walter Covell
A Jimcin Recording

In the Days of the Comet was published in 1906, four years before Halley's Comet made its predicted reappearance. Wells takes as his point of departure the question, "What if the comet were to collide with Earth?" But in Wells' story, the question has already been answered affirmatively, which is to say there has been a collision. This story is about how life goes on. Given the current revival of interest in nuclear holocaust and its aftermath, *In the Days of the Comet* takes on a new timeliness.

JOURNEY TO THE CENTER OF THE EARTH

By Jules Verne
(9023) 8-1½ hour cassettes
Rental—$16.50   Purchase—$64.00
Read by Tom Collette
A Jimcin Recording

As with many things in life, early failure begets later success. Exasperated by his efforts as a playwright in the early 1860's, Jules Verne turned to writing what he considered a new kind of adventure-story for boys.

Journey to the Center of the Earth is the story of Professor Lidenbrock, his nephew Axel and their quest for the secrets contained at the earth's core. Led by Hans, their Icelandic guide, Lidenbrock and Axel explore the mysteries of a never-before-seen subterranean world.

"He was the first writer to welcome change and to proclaim that scientific discovery could be the most wonderful of all adventures. For this reason he will never grow out of date . . . " —Arthur C. Clarke

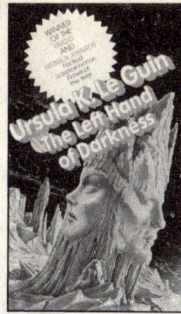

Rental Section At-a-Glance

THE LEFT HAND OF DARKNESS

By Ursula K. LeGuin
(2052) 8-1½ hour cassettes
Rental—$16.50   Purchase—$64.00
Read by Ruth Stokesberry

The Terrans have sent a landing party to Gethan and what they find are a people outside their realm of understanding. Ong Tot Oppong's field notes reveal that "our entire pattern of socio-sexual interaction is non-existent here. The Gethenians do not see one another as men or women. This is almost impossible for our imaginations to accept. There is no division of humanity into strong and weak. One is respected and judged only as a human being . . . it is an appalling experience for a Terran . . . "

"What got me was the quality of the story-telling. She's taken mythology, psychology—the entire creative surround—and woven it into a jewel of a story." —Frank Herbert

The Left Hand of Darkness won an international reputation for its author, Ursula K. LeGuin. It also won Hugo and Nebula prizes when first published.

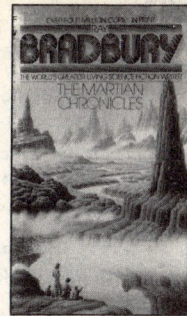

THE MARTIAN CHRONICLES

By Ray Bradbury
(2127) 8-1 hour cassettes
Rental—$14.50   Purchase—$64.00
Read by Michael Prichard

Leaving behind a world on the brink of destruction, man came to Mars and found Martians waiting. While seeking a new beginning, man nevertheless brought with him his oldest fears and deepest desires. Man conquered Mars, but in that instant, Mars conquered him.

"A consummate storyteller, Ray Bradbury is America's preeminent master of the fantastic. Poignant and satiric, eerie and poetic, *The Martian Chronicles* is Bradbury's masterwork, a modern classic that has enchanted millions of readers worldwide." (Publisher's Source)

"There is no writer quite like Ray Bradbury." (The New York Times)

OUT OF THE SILENT PLANET

By C.S. Lewis
(1794) 7-1 hour cassettes
Rental—$13.50   Purchase—$56.00
Read by Grover Gardner

Out of the Silent Planet is the first volume of Lewis' space trilogy which is continued in *Perelandra* and *That Hideous Strength*.

Dr. Ransom, a noted philologist, is kidnapped and flown by spaceship to Malacandra (Mars) where he flees his human captors and establishes communication with the planet's extraordinary inhabitants. What he learns galvanizes his attempt to return to Earth with a message of great urgency.

"A credible and stimulating *tour de force*." (Library Journal)

PERELANDRA

By C.S. Lewis
(1796) 6-1½ hour cassettes
Rental—$14.50   Purchase—$48.00
Read by Grover Gardner

A sharp, sophisticated fantasy, this second book in Lewis' science fiction trilogy deals with an old problem—temptation—in a new world—Perelandra (Venus).

Dr. Ransom is ordered to Perelandra by the supreme being. There he finds a Garden of Eden.

"A story told by a writer of distinguished imagination. It is enriched with learning, a sharp pictorial sense of the extraordinary and metaphysical speculation." *(Observer)*

RENDEZVOUS WITH RAMA

By Arthur C. Clarke
(1253) 8-1 hour cassettes
Rental—$14.50   Purchase—$64.00
Read by Dan Lazar

In 2130, a new celestial body is discovered heading toward the sun. Earthlings name this object "Rama"—a vast cylinder, about 31 miles long and 12 miles across, with a mass of at least ten trillion tons. The spaceship *Endeavor*, directed by Commander Bill Norton, lands on Rama and has three weeks to explore its hollow interior. Inside the vessel they discover a completely self-contained world—a world that has been cruising through space for perhaps more than a million years.

THE SECOND FOUNDATION

By Isaac Asimov
(1196) 8-1 hour cassettes
Rental—$14.50   Purchase—$64.00
Read by Dan Lazar

In *The Second Foundation,* Isaac Asimov addresses the phenomenon of genetic mutation and its potential danger to a civilization. The novel tells of an overwhelmingly powerful mutant human being, born with the ability to mold men's emotions and minds. He has brought down the First Foundation; only the Second Foundation remains.

THE SIRENS OF TITAN

By Kurt Vonnegut, Jr.
(1120) 8-1 hour cassettes
Rental—$14.50   Purchase—$64.00
Read by Dan Lazar

Of all Vonnegut's books, his favorite is *The Sirens of Titan* which he admits was "the only book that was pleasant to write." We meet Malachi Constant, "the richest man in America," who feels a calling to probe the depths of space. He leaves a life of unequaled indulgence to voyage through the solar system. He participates in a Martian invasion of Earth, mates with the wife of an astronaut who is adrift on the tides of time, and from start to finish follows the irresistible lure of the "Sirens of Titan."

THAT HIDEOUS STRENGTH

By C.S. Lewis
(1795) 11-1½ hour cassettes
Rental—$17.50   Purchase—$88.00
Read by Grover Gardner

Jane Studdock has dreams for which she can find no explanation. At the same time her husband Mark joins the National Institute of Coordinated Experiments (N.I.C.E.) which is building a facility on the ancient site of Merlin's tomb. Soon N.I.C.E. dominates their lives, and Mark and Jane find themselves on opposite sides of a conflict between good and evil.

C.S. Lewis ends his celebrated space trilogy with a story of satanic will, and an exploration of the lengths to which love and duty can be stretched. "Well written, fast-paced satirical fantasy." *(Time)*

Note: A number of science fiction titles are so well established as to have become classics. Those additional books are listed in our Classics and Family section.

Allow 4-6 weeks for delivery.

BERLITZ® CASSETTE COURSE
The Language of Travel

With a few foreign words, your trip (and you) can be more interesting. Enjoy the satisfaction of knowing a new language, meeting people, getting involved.

Now you can learn—easily, painlessly—without leaving your home. Berlitz, the company whose name is synonymous with language instruction has a basic Cassette Course for you in French, German, Italian or Spanish.

Here's what your *Berlitz Cassette Course* brings you . . .

1. 90-minute "zero" or beginner's cassette with 10 basic lessons.

2. Two 60-minute cassettes—20 more lessons in all, on what to say when abroad.

3. Two illustrated books featuring the text of all cassettes with explanatory notes, instructions for easy reference.

4. Unique rotating verb finder showing tenses of all key verbs.

5. As an extra bonus, a Berlitz phrase book plus a pocket dictionary for any emergency.

There are 30 lively lessons in all—3-1½ hours of playing (and replaying) time. No grammer—not until you're ready. Just listen and repeat at your own pace—in the privacy of your own home.

$59.95 Each—Sale Only
96115 French
96116 German
96117 Italian
96118 Spanish

BERLITZ® CASSETTEPAKS

For the total travel experience, knowing the language before seeing the country is essential. With Berlitz Cassettepaks—designed with that in mind—travellers can now arrive with the knowledge they need for a more successful and pleasant visit. Each cassettepak includes:

• a 60-minute cassette recording in stereo with the voices of four native speakers who converse first in English and then in the language being learned.

• a 32-page manuscript containing the complete text of the dual language recording and pronunciation tips.

• a 192-page Berlitz Phrasebook, featuring a wide variety of common expressions and vocabulary plus useful facts and helpful travel tips.

$14.95 Each—Sale Only

86213 Latin American Spanish
86215 Serbo-Croatian
86219 French
86220 German
86221 Chinese
86222 Spanish
86223 Italian
86278 Arabic
86279 Portuguese
86285 Japanese
86286 Swedish
86287 Norwegian
86288 Russian
86289 Hebrew
86294 Greek
86295 Dutch
86296 Finnish
86297 Danish

FOREIGN SERVICE INSTITUTE (FSI) COURSES

The most effective in-depth course available for foreign language learning are those developed by the Foreign Service Institute (FSI) for the U.S. State Department. They were created for diplomatic personnel who must learn a foreign language quickly and thoroughly for use at embassies abroad.

The basic concept of the FSI courses is that you learn a foreign language the same way you learned English—by hearing and imitating what you hear. You are given neither endless rules of grammer nor massive vocabularies to memorize. Grammar rules are explained but the emphasis is on listening and repeating.

All Foreign Service Institute language programs are for purchase only.

SPANISHS

101 FSI Programmatic Spanish Vol. I: 12 cassettes (17 hours), 464-page text, and manual, $135

S121 FSI Programmatic Spanish Vol. II: 8 cassettes (12 hours), 614-page text, and manual, $120

S153 Basic Spanish Advanced Level Part A, Units 31-45: 12 cassettes (13 hours), 614-page text, $155

S170 Basic Spanish Advanced Level Part B, Units 46-55: 12 cassettes (12½ hours), 472-page text, $155

GERMAN

G141 German Vol. I: 10 cassettes (13 hours) and 647-page text, $135

G151 German Vol. II: 8 cassettes (8 hours) and 179-page text, $120

G160 Advanced German: 18 cassettes (17½ hours) and 375-page text, $195

FRENCH

F170 Basic French Part A: 12 cassettes (15 hours) and 194-page text, $135

F181 Basic French Part B: 18 cassettes (25 hours) and 290-page text, $159

F260 Advanced French Part A: 18 cassettes (27 hours) and 567-page text, $195

F290 Advanced French Part B: 18 cassettes (22 hours) and 567-page text, $195

F250 French Phonology: 8 cassettes (10 hours) 394-page text and manual, $105

Other languages available: Arabic, Bulgarian, Cambodian (Khmer), Chinese, Danish, Finnish, Greek, Hausa, Hebrew, Hungarian, Japanese, Korean, Polish, Russian, Serbo-Croatian, Swahili, Swedish, Tagalog, Thai, Turkish, Twi, Urdu, Vietnamese and Yoruba.

For additional information, contact any of our service representatives by calling B-O-T: **1-800-626-3333.**

THE GRANADOS SCHOOL OF LANGUAGES

The Granados School of Languages specializes in bilingual education in Spanish and English. Its innovative on-the-job language training programs teach both Spanish and English to the mutual benefit of labor and management. These programs have also served to increase the employability of non-English speaking persons. These language programs are used by individuals, companies and educational facilities throughout the United States and Latin America.

SPANISH IN THREE MONTHS

The Basic Spanish Course is a unique and non-traditional method for learning Spanish designed for the English speaking person who is interested in learning conversational Spanish quickly and thoroughly. This method is used in industry to teach management conversational Spanish for effective communication with Spanish-speaking employees. It is also used at the college level.

SPANISH IN THREE MONTHS: Basic Spanish I

GS1) $75—Sale Only
8 cassettes, 60 minutes each, and 60-page text.

The emphasis of this course is the *mastery* of the basic recurring structures of Spanish which allow the student to absorb vocabulary quickly. Exercises are programmed so that the student is *speaking and thinking in Spanish immediately*.

Lesson material includes the basic structures of Spanish in the present and the present progressive tenses, direct objects, the verbs "to be," special construction, nouns, pronouns, adjectives, adverbs, idioms and more. Emphasis is on the most commonly used Spanish verbs. The text contains drills, Spanish-English vocabulary lists and verb charts.

SPANISH IN THREE MONTHS: Basic Spanish II

(GS2) $75—Sale Only
8 cassettes, 60 minutes each, and 67-page text.

This course is designed for those who have completed Basic Spanish I, or students who have knowledge of Spanish. It is ideal for those who have had basic Spanish courses in high school or college.

Basic Spanish II covers more advanced structures, interrogatives, reflexes, past and future tenses of regular and irregular verbs, possessive adjectives and pronouns, special constructions, idioms and more. It also contains extensive conversational drills to develop fluency and pronunciation. During these drills the student practices with the cassette "teacher" in a series of conversations that cover all the material taught in Basic Spanish I and II. The text contains Spanish-English vocabulary lists, lesson drills, verb charts, and frequently used Spanish expressions.

INTERMEDIATE SPANISH

The Intermediate Spanish course from the Granados School of Languages is a unique and nontraditional method for learning Spanish. It is designed for the English speaking person who has already mastered Basic Spanish and is interested in perfecting his or her conversational skills quickly and thoroughly.

SPANISH IN THREE MONTHS: Intermediate Spanish I

(GSI1) $75.00—Sale Only
Eight cassettes, 60 minutes each, and 79-page text.

The emphasis of this course is the mastery of the more advanced tenses which gives our student a complete knowledge of simple as well as compound tenses, such as the Present, Past, Future and Conditional Perfects. This course also gives the student an indepth study of the usage of Prepositions, Conjunctions, as well as Special Verbs in their relationship to certain prepositions and prepositional phrases. The student is introduced to more advanced vocabulary. Also, throughout the whole course and especially in the review tapes, there is a constant review of all that has been learned from the beginning with Basic Spanish I.

Books on Tape™'s service is 100% guaranteed

LANGUAGE/30 BRIEF COURSES

These "crash courses" are an ideal way to pick up a working vocabulary in a foreign language in the shortest possible time. You may choose from any of the languages listed below.

These remarkable intensive courses were introduced by author and linguist Charles Berlitz. Each is a quick, highly condensed introduction to the words and phrases you'll need to communicate effectively in the country you're headed for. A course includes two cassettes and a phrase guide book in a vinyl album.

Programmed for fast learning, each course gives you 1½ hours of guided practice in the essentials of each language. You'll learn a host of short easy-to-remember words and phrases covering virtually every situation. Greetings and introductions, hotels, restaurants, the theater, the post office, the railroad station, the airport, shopping, driving—and many more. You'll be able to explain what you want, ask questions, and understand the answers.

As a bonus, there's a special section, prepared by Charles Berlitz, on the customs and idioms of each country. The words and expressions in this section will turn you overnight from a tourist into a traveler. "By using them you will be stamped as someone who understands and respects the social customs of the country," explains Mr. Berlitz. "In return, you will be thought of as polite and charming and made to feel comfortable and welcome."

"All courses, for purchase only, are $21.95 each:

#N1032 Arabic	#N1037 Norwegian
#N1033 Danish	#N1038 Persian
#N1034 Dutch	#N1050 Polish
#N1048 Finnish	#N1028 Portuguese
#N1022 French	#N1029 Russian
#N1023 German	#N1039 Serbo-Croatian
#N1024 Greek	#N1030 Spanish
#N1025 Hebrew	#N1040 Swahili
#N1045 Hindi	#N1046 Swedish
#N1035 Indonesian	#N1047 Tagalog
#N1026 Italian	#N1049 Thai
#N1027 Japanese	#N1041 Turkish
#N1036 Korean	#N1042 Vietnamese
#N1021 Mandarin Chinese	

"NO-TIME" LANGUAGE METHOD

This unusual method, which uses no text or other printed materials, offers you courses in many languages. These courses have been introduced by A.E. Van Vogt, a well-known writer, language expert and author of 46 books. The courses are introductory-level and help you master the basics of the language for business or travel; yet the grammar and sentences are comtemporary and not simplistic.

The courses start with one hour conversation, using sentences one would normally need in everyday communication. They are structured so that there is a sentence in the language followed immediately by a general English translation. After 15 or 20 sentences, they are repeated in the language in succession, without translation. At the end of the first hour of tape, numerals and the alphabet are introduced.

Without half trying, and before you know it you begin to acquire a vocabulary and comprhehend sentence structure by hearing it only—and it does work!

Courses available for purchase only are:
#N140 No-Time French I: 8 hours, $96
#N141 No-Time French II: 6 hours, $72
#N130 No-Time German I: 6 hours, $72
#N131 No-Time German II: 6 hours, $72
#N210 No-Time Greek: 6 hours, $72
#N200 No-Time Hungarian: 6 hours, $72
#N170 No-Time Italian: 8 hours, $96
#N160 No-Time Japanese: 6 hours, $72
#N220 No-Time Persian: 6 hours, $72
#N180 No-Time Russian: 8 hours, $96
#N150 No-Time Spanish I: 8 hours, $96
#N151 No-Time Spanish II: 6 hours, $72
#N230 No-Time Swahili: 6 hours, $72
#N260 No-Time Tagalog: 6 hours, $72
#N240 No-Time Turkish: 6 hours, $72

Allow 4 weeks for delivery.

Our association with G.K. Hall Audio Books allows Books on Tape to offer our customers a wide variety of titles for sale in categories of fiction, adventure/suspense, mystery, romance and science fiction. Best of all, these recordings are complete and unabridged enabling listeners to enjoy the entire book. Not a word of the original is missing.

G.K. Hall is proud to bring the narrative skills of well-known actors and actresses to their selection of top-notch books including such names as: Sir John Mills, Derek Jacobi, Susannah York and Claire Bloom.

Full-color, durable, book-like packages make Audio Books easy to shelve, and the rugged plastic cases are designed for years of use.

AFFAIRS AT THRUSH GREEN

By Miss Read
(9811X) $39.95—Sale only
Six cassettes
Read by Gwen Watford

Here is one of Miss Read's delightful chronicles of English village life, a life which has changed little for centuries. Thrush Green hums with the smaller and larger concerns of its inhabitants: What should be built on the site of the burnt-out-rectory? Would Jenny ever consider becoming Percy's third wife? Will the returned native, Kit Armitage, ever settle down?

BLOOD SPORT

By Dick Francis
(98225) $39.95—Sale only
Six cassettes
Read by Tony Britton

A quarter of a million dollars' worth of Derby-winning stallion vanishes into the bluegrass of Kentucky . . . and a young man and a girl spend a dangerous afternoon in a punt on the Thames. From these far-apart but related beginnings, Gene Hawkins finds himself trailing lost blood-horses over half of America, until he in turn becomes the prey.

THE BRIDGE ON
THE RIVER KWAI

By Pierre Boulle
(97555) $29.95—Sale only
Four cassettes
Read by Sir John Mills

The famous story of a British colonel and his men in a Japanese prisoner-of-war camp who are ordered by their captors to build a bridge.

THE CHRYSALIDS

By John Wyndham
(9775X) $$39.95—Sale only
Six cassettes
Read by Robert Powell

Imagine a world beset by genetic mutations in plant, animal and human life . . . it seems all too real in this frightening account. "Robert Powell reads the first-person narrative with grace and feeling . . . Fans will appreciate this complete text from the pen of an acknowledged master of the genre." *(Booklist)*

THE CINDER PATH

By Catherine Cookson
(97784) $39.95—Sale only
Six cassettes
Read by Susan Jameson

This powerful account takes Charlie from the rural Northumberland of Edwardian times to the Western Frontier of WW I.

CIRCUS

By Alistair MacLean
(97679) $39.95—Sale only
Six cassettes
Read by Simon Ward

"Marvelously read . . . One feels and is caught up in the constant danger of this masterful story in a recording sure to be quickly snapped up by suspense aficionados." *(Booklist)*

DEATH IN KENYA

By M.M. Kaye
(98276) $39.95—Sale only
Six cassettes
Read by Virginia McKenna

With her aunt, Lady Emily DeBrett, offers her a home at the family estate in Kenya, Victoria Caryll accepts—realizing that it will mean seeing her former fiance, Eden DeBrett. What Victoria does not realize is that she will arrive in a remote, dangerous region still recovering from the Mau-Mau revolt, and into a household thrown into grief and confusion by one murder—with the threat of more to come.

THE DIAMOND AS BIG
AS THE RITZ
AND OTHER STORIES

By F. Scott Fitzgerald
(98691) $39.95—Sale only
Six cassettes
Read by Vincent Marzell

A superb collection—replete with uncanny social dissections, dazzling descriptions, and wit—that epitomizes the Fitzgerald touch. In the title story, a blasé prep student reevaluates his ideas about wealth when confronted with a diamond that's literally bigger than the Ritz-Carlton Hotel. Other tales include "The Cut-Glass Bowl," "The Rich Boy" and "May Day."

ENQUIRY

By Dick Francis
(97717) $39.95—Sale only
Six cassettes
Read by Tony Britton

"Reading a good racing mystery by Dick Francis is always a delight. Hearing one read by Tony Britton may be even better . . . This sort of thing could bring back listening." *(Library Journal)*

EXOCET

By Jack Higgins
(97873) $39.95—Sale only
Six cassettes
Read by Martin Shaw

The Falkland Island conflict serves as the backdrop for this high-tension triangle of love, espionage and power.

FORFEIT

By Dick Francis
(97644) $39.95—Sale only
Six cassettes
Read by Tony Britton

"Dick Francis creates tough characters. Britton's narration gives them power and believability . . . *Forfeit* was heralded as a winner in 1969. This very British and professional narration serves it with distinction." *(Library Journal)*

THE GIRL OF THE
SEA OF CORTEZ

By Peter Benchley
(97768) $39.95—Sale only
Six cassettes
Read by Jenny Agutter

"With unwavering confidence, Benchley redirects the relationship between sea creatures and humans . . . Paloma's aquatic feats, her myth-like bond with the manta, and the fabulous texture are quite beguiling." *(Booklist)*

HIDE MY EYES

By Margery Allingham
(98748) $39.95—Sale only
Six cassettes
Read by Bernard Archard

A woman finds that she cannot hide her eyes from the sinister truth in this razor-sharp mystery. But with the aid of Allingham's Superintendent Luke and Mr. Campion, the blinders are lifted. The formidable sleuths investigate a grisly murder trail that leads from London's theater district, to a mysterious country couple, to a Museum of Oddities, and finally, to a blood-curtling dump in the East End.

THE INIMITABLE JEEVES

By P.G. Wodehouse
(98195) $39.95—Sale only
Six cassettes
Read by Jonathan Cecil

When Bingo Little falls in love at a Camberwell subscription dance and Bertie Wooster gets involved, there's work for a wet nurse. Who better than Jeeves?

JEEVES IN THE OFFING

By P.G. Wodehouse
(97849) $39.95—Sale only
Six cassettes
Read by Ian Carmichael

Bertie Wooster has an assortment of curious problems and eccentric characters to contend with, like the kleptomaniac Broadway Willie, French chef Anatole, and the beautiful Bobbie Wickham. The unflappable Jeeves sorts it all out with his usual aplomb.

JOURNEY INTO FEAR

By Eric Ambler
(98756) $39.95—Sale only
Six cassettes
Read by Edward Fox

The traveller is a British businessman returning home from Istanbul: a man comfortably secure who, like most of us, believes that some things could not possibly happen to him. Then, the chaotic world bursts in on his reverie and he discovers that a horrible death is at hand. Here is thought-provoking suspense at its best.

THE LITTLE SISTER

By Raymond Chandler
(97776) $39.95—Sale only
Six cassettes
Read by Ed Bishop

"Ed Bishop, known to BBC radio listeners, gives a wonderful reading of Chandler's Philip Marlowe and *The Little Sister* through voice changes that allow the listener to create their own visual images of the shady world of Marlowe." *(Library Journal)*

MADAM, WILL YOU TALK?

By Mary Stewart
(98284) $39.95—Sale only
Six cassettes
Read by Nyree Dawn Porter

Charity Selborne arrives at the enchanting walled city of Avignon anticipating with pleasure her summer holiday. But at that moment, most of the actors in the most frightening episode of her life are assembling in the unpretentious Provencal hotel. All but one—and her, with murder on his mind, is not very far away, moving in a dark circle of his own personal hell.

MISTRESS OF MELLYN

By Victoria Holt
(98101) $39.95—Sale only
Six cassettes
Read by Felicity Kendal

One of Victoria Holt's earliest and greatest successes. Mystery and romance surround Martha, a Victorian governess, when she arrives in Cornwall to take up her new post at Mount Mellyn.

MUCH OBLIGED, JEEVES

By P.G. Wodehouse
(97636) $29.95—Sale only
Four cassettes
Read by Dinsdale Landen

Pandemonium erupts when the Book—an infamous collection of secrets about the upper classes—disappears from the Junior Ganymede Club.

RAT RACE

By Dick Francis
(97547) $29.95—Sale only
Four cassettes
Read by Ian Ogilvy

Sheer coincidence prevents the death of the occupants of a charter plane on its way to the horse races. Who was the intended victim?

THE SPEAKER OF MANDARIN

By Ruth Rendell
(98713) $39.95—Sale only
Six cassettes
Read by Michael Bryant

The mysteries of the Orient have more to do with murder than mysticism in this top detective yarn. When the Chinese government asks for advice on crime prevention, Scotland Yard sends a team of expert sleuths. Among the conferees is Reg Wexford, who stays on for a vacation. Upon his return, a murder victim is coincidentally identified a as a woman he met in China. Before the case is solved, Wexford unearths some fatal, intriguing clues.

**TOLL FREE credit card
order line 1-800-626-3333**

MasterCard **VISA**

A SPLASH OF RED

By Antonia Fraser
(98233) $39.95—Sale only
Six cassettes
Read by Patricial Hodge

Everyone loved Chloe Fontaine—or did they? This Jemima Shore mystery centers around Chloe's sudden disappearance, which leaves Jemima in charge of her London flat. A sinister story of what happened in a modern penthouse in Bloomsbury, one hot summer.

THE THIRTY-NINE STEPS

By John Buchan
(97571) $29.95—Sale only
Four cassettes
Read by Robert Powell

This exciting adventure of peril, murder, conspiracy and espionage is read by Robert Powell, star of the film version. "Clearly it has achieved status both by its longevity and its literary quality." *(Library Journal)*

THREE MEN IN A BOAT

By Jerome K. Jerome
(97520) $29.95—Sale only
Four cassettes
Read by Ian Carmichael

The adventures of the immortal trio, George, Harris and "I" (not forgetting Montmorency the dog) and their disasterous boating holiday.

UNDER THE GREENWOOD TREE

By Thomas Hardy
(97598) $29.95—Sale only
Four cassettes
Read by Robert Hardy

Robert Hardy reads Thomas Hardy's timeless story of Wessex country life. Dick Dewy, a young peddlar, falls in love with Fance Day, the school mistress.

UNNATURAL CAUSES

By P.D. James
(98012) $39.95—Sale only
Six cassettes
Read by Michael Jayston

The death of a mystery writer seems to be due to natural causes, but Adam Dalgliesh has another theory. "Fine, firm plotting, well-drawn characters . . . a grand creation." *(The New York Times Book Review)*

AGES OF MAN

By William Shakespeare
(CP 200) $19.95—Sale Only
Two cassettes
Performed by Sir John Gielgud

This play is recorded in its entirety and includes a complete text.

ALL CREATURES GREAT AND SMALL

By James Herriot
(TC-LFP 7024) $14.95—Sale Only
Approx. 2 hrs. 30 mins.
Read by James Herriot

James Herriot's entertaining stories about his career as a veterinary surgeon in the rugged Yorkshire Dales are presented here in an abridgement. The account is memorable and the narrative rich in warmth and humor.

ALL THINGS BRIGHT AND BEAUTIFUL

By James Herriot
(TC-LFP 7050) $14.95—Sale Only
Approx. 2 hrs. 30 mins.
Read by James Herriot

The author tells us more of his adventures with a wide range of animal patients and their equally diverse owners. This recording continues in the same style that has made James Herriot universally popular.

ANIMAL FARM

By George Orwell
(NCC7046) $14.95—Sale Only
Two cassettes
Read by Alan Bennett

Orwell's classic political fable details the revolution mounted by the animals of Manor Farm—who prove to be only human after all.

ANNE OF GREEN GABLES

By L.M. Montgomery
(45091) $14.95—Sale Only
Two cassettes
Read by Megan Follows

For generations, this classic has captivated audiences young and old alike. Now the delightful, unpredictable adventures of Anne Shirley comes to life.

With a special reading by Megan Follows, star of the PBS production of *Anne of Green Gables,* this double cassette abridgement of L.M. Montgomery's timeless classic provides a unique experience.

THE BEST OF BENCHLEY

By Robert Benchley
(CP 1731) $9.95—Sale Only
One cassette
Complete stories
Performance by Bob Elliott

Robert Benchley is pure fun! Bob Elliott (of "Bob and Ray" fame) brings these words to life as he saunters through Benchley's humor with beatific innocence.

Pieces included in this collection are "The Treasurer's Report," "Uncle Edith's Ghost Story," "A Good Old-Fashioned Christmas," "The Social Life of the Newt" and "The Woolen Mitten Situation."

"THE BEST OF BOB & RAY—Vol. I

(RA02) $29.95—Sale Only
Four cassettes

After 38 years of partnership Bob Elliott and Ray Goulding are still the undisputed masters of comedy-as-conversation. "Using nothing but their resonant, elastic voices and some sound effects, Bob and Ray create a world of silly characters in satirical sketches that mimic the style of old-fashioned radio show," comments *The Wall Street Journal.*

The Best of Bob & Ray—Volume I is a collection of excerpts from the Bob & Ray Public Radio Show and is sure to delight Bob & Ray fans as well as become a favorite gift-giving item.

"THE BEST OF BOB & RAY—Vol. II

(RA03) $29.95—Sale Only
Four cassettes

The Best of Bob & Ray—Volume II is a collection of excerpts from the Bob & Ray Public Radio Show and is sure to delight Bob & Ray fans.

BEVERLY SILLS: ON MY OWN

With Beverly Sills
(45064) $7.95—Sale Only
One cassette

With the beauty of one of her own arias, opera star Beverly Sills speaks directly to her many fans. Based on an exclusive interview, this is a rare behind-the-scenes look at the life and career of an extraordinary woman.

Compelling and candid, Sills recounts the triumphs and disappointments of her professional life and the devastating traumas of her personal life. *Beverly Sills: On My Own* captures the essence of this remarkable woman.

THE BIG SLEEP

By Raymond Chandler
(TC-LFP 7009) $14.95—Sale Only
Approx. 2 hrs. 30 mins.
Read by Daniel Massey

An impertinent introduction to a beautiful client leads detective Philip Marlowe on the trail of drugs, guns and blackmail through the seamy recesses of the California underworld.

The Big Sleep is Raymond Chandler's first Philip Marlowe adventure, and is superbly read by Daniel Massey.

THE BLACK ROCK COFFIN MAKERS

NEW

By Louis L'Amour
(45051) $7.95—Sale Only
One cassette

Cattleman Jim Gatlin isn't the kind of man who goes looking for a fight. But he never turns away when one comes looking for him. And that is what happens when he finds himself mistaken for another man—a man who has some very dangerous enemies.

"[L'Amour is the] kind of storyteller that makes the wolves come out of the woods to listen." *(People Magazine)*

BOB & RAY: A NIGHT OF TWO STARS

(RA01) $24.95—Sale Only
Two cassettes

Recorded during sold-out concerts at Carnegie Hall, *Bob & Ray, A Night of Two Stars,* contains all of their classic routines—Slow Talkers of America, Wally Ballou in Times Square—plus other favorites such as Biff Burns in the Sports Room; Mary Backstayge, Noble Wife; Garish Summit with Agatha Murchfield; Neil Clummer, Editor of *Wasting Time* magazine; Mr. Trace, Keener than Most Persons and many others.

BRAIN

By Robin Cook
(88179) $14.95—Sale only
Two cassettes

"A chiller that will scare you—literally—out of your skull!

BREAKFAST OF CHAMPIONS

By Kurt Vonnegut, Jr.
(CP 1602) $9.95—Sale Only
One cassette
Read by Kurt Vonnegut, Jr.

Nothing is sacred to Kurt Vonnegut. He treats sex like plumbing and plumbing like sex. If there is a single sacred cow left untouched at the end of *Breakfast of Champions,* we do not know what it is. The book, read in Vonnegut's familiar laconic style, was a best seller as much for its humor as for its depth in probing the American psyche.

THE BROTHERS KARAMAZOV

By Fyodor Dostoyevsky
(88194) $14.95—Sale Only
Two cassettes

An obsessive, suspenseful tale of life and jealousy, murder and redemption.

CANTERBURY TALES

By Geoffrey Chaucer
(TC-LFP 7101) $14.95—Sale Only
Approx. 3 hrs.
Read by Martin Starkie
and Prunella Scales

Chaucer's *Canterbury Tales* is one of the great literary achievements of the Middle Ages. Begun about 1386, it is a collection of diverse tales told by a group of travellers on a pilgrimage to the shrine of Thomas à Becket at Canterbury. This recording presents in abridged form five of the 'Tales' linked together with parts of the Prologue and the lively episodes between the tales.

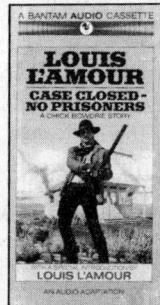

CASE CLOSED— NO PRISONERS

NEW

By Louis L'Amour
(45060) $7.95—Sale Only
One cassette

Ride with the legendary Texas Ranger Chick Bowdrie as he helps out a small town with a big problem. Someone has brutally killed a banker and made off with forty thousand dollars—and it seems to be the work of someone who knows their way around town.

Also features a personal introduction by America's favorite storyteller Louis L'Amour. You'll learn what the Texas Rangers were really like and discover some little-known facts about the dangerous outlaws they pursued.

CATCH 22

By Joseph Heller
(NCC 71257) $14.95—Sale Only
Two cassettes
Read by Alan Arkin

Discover how Yossarian acts crazy enough to get out of flying combat missions only to prove he is sane enough to know that flying is crazy—the perfect catch.

THE CHOSEN

By Chaim Potok
(88186) $14.95—Sale Only
Two cassettes
Read by Eli Wallach

A provocative story of fathers and sons, a bittersweet voyage from boyhood to manhood.

CHURCHILL IN HIS OWN VOICE

By Winston Churchill
(CDL 52018) $19.95—Sale Only
Two cassettes
Performance by Sir John Gielgud,
Lord Laurence Oliver, Winston Churchill,
Franklin D. Roosevelt, Harry S. Truman,
King of England George VI, Dwight D.
Eisenhower, Neville Chamberlain, Eleanor
Roosevelt, George Patton

Cemented by narration from Churchill's memoirs, the story of the great prime minister and his era is retold through quotations selected from speeches delivered in his own voice and from appropriate comments in the voices of his contemporaries, including Roosevelt, Eisenhower, Truman and others.

THE CRUEL SEA

By Nicholas Monsarrat
(TC-LFP 7036) $14.95—Sale Only
Approx. 2 hrs.
Read by Robert Powell

This is the story of how the men of the Royal Navy Volunteer Reserve on board the refitted escort ship *Compass Rose* fought the ravaging packs of German U-boats during WW II. Even more, it is the story of how they fought the strength and fury of the ocean—its violence, its power, its unremitting treachery.

THE DANGER

By Dick Francis
(NCC7107) $14.95—Sale Only
Two cassettes
Read by Tim Piggot-Smith

Known to American audiences as Captain Merrick of the Masterpiece Theatre series *The Jewel in the Crown,* Tim Piggot-Smith reads this adventure of kidnapping in international racing circles.

DEAD-END DRIFT

By Louis L'Amour
(45045) $7.95—Sale Only
One cassette

Louis L'Amour's life is as exciting as the fiction he writes. And in this audio presentation, one of America's favorite storytellers talks about his early experiences as a miner searching for gold and silver in the hard rock mines of the old West.

You'll also hear a reading of *Dead-End Drift*, one of L'Amour's famous *Yondering* tales. This harrowing story of a real-life mine cave-in is the fictionalized account of the last hours of four trapped miners and their courageous struggle to save themselves from certain death.

DEATH OF A SALESMAN

By Arthur Miller
(CDL 5310) $29.95—Sale Only
Two cassettes
Performed by Lee J. Cobb, Mildred Dunnock

There is no truer play then *Death of a Salesman*. It is the story of a failure who confronts himself and his family in a reality that knows no escape. Since its first opening, Arthur Miller's play has profoundly affected those who see in it something of themselves and the times in which we live.

DIARY OF ANNE FRANK

By Anne Frank
(CDL 51522) $9.95—Sale Only
One cassette
Performed by Claire Bloom

Perhaps the most remarkable thing about this most remarkable book is that it was written by a very young teenager who, in spite of her circumstances, was a very happy girl. There is never a trace of the maudlin or the sentimental. The saddest thing about the book is that Anne Frank's promise was lost to us forever when she disappeared into a German concentration camp and died on a date unknown.

DINNER AT THE HOMESICK RESTAURANT

By Anne Tyler
(55042-0) $14.95—Sale Only
Two cassettes

Anne Tyler's acclaimed best-selling novel of family life, *Dinner at the Homesick Restaurant* is superb entertainment.

Beautiful . . . funny, heart-warming, wise . . . it edges deep into truth." *(The New York Times Book Review)*

DOCTOR ZHIVAGO

By Boris Pasternak
(TC-LFP 7054) $14.95—Sale Only
Approx. 3 hrs.
Read by Paul Scofield

Episodes describe with great feeling the effect of the Russian Revolution on a variety of characters, but in particular on a sensitive young doctor. Zhivago's early optimism fades as his life is turned inside out by the events of the war and the post-revolutionary era.

DYLAN THOMAS READING A CHILD'S CHRISTMAS IN WALES

By Dylan Thomas
(CP 1002) $9.95—Sale Only
One cassette
Performed by Dylan Thomas

"A Child's Christmas in Wales" has become a classic among Christmas tales. It is included here with several selections of Thomas' best known poems. Cassette contains: "A Child's Christmas in Wales," "Fern Hill," "Do Not Go Gentle Into that Good Night," "In the White Giant's Thigh," "Ballad of the Long-Legged Bait" and "Ceremony After a Fire Raid."

THE EAGLE HAS LANDED

By Jack Higgins
(TC-LFP 7040) $14.95—Sale Only
Approx. 2 hrs. 30 mins.
Read by Edward Fox

The date—November 1943. The place—Studley Constable, a remote Norfolk village. German paratroopers posing as Polish commandos arrive with orders from Hitler to kidnap Churchill and bring him back to Germany! This exciting, well-plotted and entirely credible story recounts how the attempt almost succeeded.

EMILY DICKINSON: A SELF-PORTRAIT

By Emily Dickinson
(CDL 52026) $19.95—Sale Only
Two cassettes
Read by Julie Harris

This is a portrait of the gifted poet composed of selections from her letters and poems. In the letters one senses the tension between her retiring and reclusive persona and the passionate intelligence that churned below, a duality and conflict that produced some of the world's most beautiful poetry.

ERNEST HEMINGWAY READING

By Ernest Hemingway
(CP 1185) $9.95—Sale Only
One cassette
Read by Ernest Hemingway

This contains the Nobel acceptance speech and five recordings made by Hemingway during 1948-1961. In addition to the speech are: "Second Poem to Mary," "In Harry's Bar in Venice," "Work in Progress" and "Saturday Night at the Whorehouse in Billings, Montana."

FAREWELL, MY LOVELY

By Raymond Chandler
(55048-X) $14.95—Sale Only
Two cassettes

Farewell, My Lovely stands with *The Big Sleep* as one of Raymond Chandler's masterpieces—a novel remarkable for its suspense, speed and style, and above all for its detective-hero, Philip Marlowe. Marlowe tells the story of murder, mayhem and corruption as the American private eye incarnate.

THE FIRST DEADLY SIN

By Lawrence Sanders
(88178) $14.95—Sale Only
Two cassettes
Read by John Lithgow

"Powerful and haunting, with mounting, tautening suspense." *(Charleston Evening Post)*

FROM RUSSIA WITH LOVE

By Ian Fleming
(NC7137) $14.95—Sale Only
Two cassettes
Read by Ian Ogilivy

SMERSH unleashes a powerful weapon in its attempt to eliminate James Bond: the irresistible Tatiana, who offers to defect to the West, bearing an important cipher machine.

GLITZ

By Elmore Leonard
(88141) $14.95—Sale Only
Two cassettes

"Leonard is best at what he does and what he does is marvelous." —Robert Parker

GOLDFINGER

By Ian Fleming
(NCC71447) $14.95—Sale Only
Two cassettes
Read by Ian Ogilivy

James Bond is back to battle with the infamous killer with the Midas touch. How will Bond prevent Goldfinger from ripping off Fort Knox?

THE GOOD WAR

By Studs Terkel
(55044-7) $14.95—Sale Only
Two cassettes

The Good War, Studs Terkel's magnificent oral history, offers a moving account—in their own words—of the lives of ordinary Americans, at home and abroad, during WW II.

Here are men who in their youth were thrust into the inferno of war. Here, too, are those who stayed at home, women and men whose lives were shaken and redirected in a suddenly changed society.

The Good War was the winner of a 1984 Pulitzer Prize for non-fiction.

GOSPEL BIRDS AND OTHER STORIES OF LAKE WOBEGON

By Garrison Keillor
(NCC90501) $16.95—Sale Only
Two cassettes

A new selection of heartwarming stories from "the town that time forgot and the decades cannot improve." This satisfying program includes "Bruno, the Fishing Dog," "Babe Ruth Visits Lake Wobegon," and many other classic favorites.

THE GRAPES OF WRATH

By John Steinbeck
(CDL 51570) $9.95—Sale Only
One cassette
Read by Henry Fonda

Of those great books of social consciousness there is not one that strikes so painful a nerve as John Steinbeck's *The Grapes of Wrath.* From this epic volume, redolent of America's grittiest times, Henry Fonda reads excerpts dealing graphically with the condition of the Okies, their land and their travels.

THE GREAT ESCAPE

By Paul Brickhill
(TC-LFP 7028) $14.95—Sale Only
Two cassettes
Read by Richard Todd

Six hundred Allied POW's worked for a year to help two hundred men escape the German prison camp Stalag Luft III in this story of group determination, ingenuity and heroism.

HAMLET

By William Shakespeare
(TC-LFP 7021) $14.95—Sale Only
Approx. 3 hrs.
Read by Sir John Gielgud
and the Old Vic Company

Shakespeare's tragedy of Hamlet, Prince of Denmark, is one of the great classics—if not the greatest—of English drama. The legend of murder within a pre-Christian Danish royal family was probably written by Shakespeare between 1598 and 1602.

HERZOG

By Saul Bellow
(CDL 51584) $9.95—Sale Only
One cassette
Read by Saul Bellow

Nobel Prize winner Saul Bellow's *Herzog* was specifically mentioned in his award citation. The labors of Moses Herzog, his introspection, his self-contemplation and self-deceit loom large in the company of literary history's anti-heroes. And who best to life to the mix of gloom and cheer that is Moses Herzog than Saul Bellow himself, who tells us here of two of the man's satisfyingly unsatisfying romances.

HIGH STAKES

By Dick Francis
(TC-LFP 7005) $14.95—Sale Only
Approx. 2 hrs.
Read by James Bolan

Successful race horse owner Steven Scott discovers that his trainer, Jody Leeds, has been less than honest in his dealings, and understandably decides to take his horses away. Leeds, who has just bought a new training establishment, primarily to deal with Scott's horses, is bitter and resentful. The form his resentment takes gives the listener a gripping story, and in true Francis fashion informs as it entertains.

THE HOBBIT and THE FELLOWSHIP OF THE RING

By J.R.R. Tolkien
(CP 1477) $9.95—Sale Only
One cassette
Read by J.R.R.Tolkien

This recording contains poems and prose from the first volume of Tolkien's famous *Lord of the Rings*. Also included are one of his unpublished poems and a song sung to a tune of his own invention.

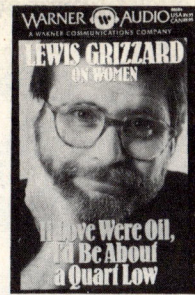

IF LOVE WERE OIL, I'D BE ABOUT A QUART LOW

By Lewis Grizzard
(88648) $9.95—Saley Only
One cassette—Abridged

"Imagine Andy Rooney with a Georgia accent . . . and a sense of humor." *(The Houston Post)*

If Love Were Oil, I'd Be About A Quart Low is the bittersweet account of Grizzard's three marriages and three divorces. Based on his bestselling book, this program features the inimitable talent of Lewis Grizzard and his very personal, humorous views on women.

ILLUSIONS:
The Adventure of a Reluctant Messiah

By Richard Bach
(CDL 51585) $9.95—Sale Only
One cassette
Read by Richard Bach

It is the story of two barnstorming vagabonds who meet in the fields of midwest America. Each is a free spirit doing the things he really wants to do, but one is a reluctant messiah, a messiah who knows the reality behind the illusions and is seeking a further truth.

THE IMPORTANCE OF BEING EARNEST

By Oscar Wilde
(TC-LFP 7001) $14.95—Sale Only
Approx. 1 hr. 40 min.
Ready by Sir John Gielgud,
Dame Edith Evans and Full Cast

Probably the wittiest comedy in the English language; it is certainly the least earnest. The subtitle 'A Trivial Comedy for Serious People' gives a clear indication of its nature; it is a play about the only subjects the Oscar Wilde would admit to taking seriously—wit, elegance and paradox.

JAMES JOYCE SOUNDBOOK

By James Joyce
(SBC 112) $29.95—Sale Only
Four cassettes
Read by James Joyce, Cyril Cusack,
Siobhan McKenna and E.G. Marshall

Excerpts from: *Ulysses, Finnegan's Wake, A Portrait of the Artist as a Young Man, Shem the Penman* and others.

KING LEAR

By William Shakespeare
(CP 233) $39.95—Sale Only
Four cassettes
Performed by Paul Scofield
and Rachel Roberts

This play is recorded in its entirety and includes a complete text.

LADY CHATTERLEY'S LOVER

By D.H. Lawrence
(TC-LFP 7061) $14.95—Sale Only
Approx. 2 hrs. 30 mins.
Read by Janet Suzman

This famous novel is about Constance Chatterley's love for Mellors, her husband's gamekeeper. It is an honest and powerful account of the love between two people who are isolated, lonely, incomplete and who find in each other the vitality and tenderness they so badly need.

LES MISÉRABLES

NEW

By Orson Welles (and Victor Hugo)
(3CMR-5) $24.95—Sale Only
Three cassettes

In the beginning was Orson Welles. It's hard to think of a time when there wasn't an Orson Welles on Broadway, in the movies or on the air. This presentation of *Les Misérables* is one of Welles' first appearances before network radio microphones in 1937.

Relying on Victor Hugo for little more than the plot, Welles seems to have spent considerable energy on the script, working and reworking the characterizations and dialogue for the ear. Welles' selection of literary properties has always borne his personal stamp . . . and social injustice was obviously a theme he could get his teeth into.

This is the complete 3.5 hour presentation, exactly as heard in seven installments, on the Mutual Broadcasting System, between July 23 and September 3, 1937.

LINCOLN

By Gore Vidal
(55043-9) $14.95—Sale Only
Two cassettes

Here is Abraham Lincoln, richly and vividly brought to life as Gore Vidal reads from his novel *Lincoln*—a great best seller, a critical triumph.

"Utterly convincing . . . lucid, intelligent, highly informative . . . extremely compelling." *(The New York Times Book Review)*

THE LITTLE DRUMMER GIRL

By John le Carré
(TC-LFP 7090) $21.95—Sale Only
Approx. 6 hrs.
Read by John le Carré

Charlie is a young English actress who is sometimes called "Charlie the Red" in deference to the color of her hair, and to her somewhat crazy radical stances. On a Greek beach she meets a man who will change her life in a way she could never have imagined—by giving her the leading role in a deadly true-life drama.

John le Carré, creator of the lugubrious master-spy George SMiley, reads his story, staged precariously amongst the irreconcilable conflicts of the Middle East.

THE LORD GOD MADE THEM ALL

By James Herriot
(TC-LFP 7102) $14.95—Sale Only
Approx. 2 hrs. 30 mins.
Read by Christopher Timothy

In this autobiography by noted author/veterinarian James Herriot we are reunited with some favorite old friends: Sigrid and Tristan, Helen and their two children. Herriot notes the progress of veterinary practice following the war and people's concepts of animal well-being. He also departs from his usual practice to accompany a shipload of sheep to Russia and a planeload of cattle to Turkey. Charming adventures for all lovers of animals, tenderly read by Christopher Timothy.

THE LORD OF THE RINGS

By J.R.R. Tolkien
(CP 1478) $9.95—Sale Only
One cassette
Read by J.R.R. Tolkien

On this recording J.R.R. Tolkien takes us through the last two books of his *The Lord of the Rings*. The selections include: *Poems in Elvish, The Introduction of the Small Hobbits to Treebeard, The Ent, The Lament for Boromir* and many, many marvels.

THE LOST WORLD

By Sir Arthur Conan Doyle
(TC-LFP 7070) $14.95—Sale Only
Approx. 2 hrs.
Read by James Mason

The Lost World concerns a group of English explorers who stumble across an elevated plateau in the heart of South America, where conditions have not changed since the Jurassic period. The explorers combat the iguanodon, the pterodactyl and varous dinosaurs before meeting a tribe of ferocious man-apes, called "the missing links."

THE LOVER

NEW

By Marguerite Duras
(64105) $14.95—Sale Only
Two cassettes—Abridged
Read by Leslie Caron

Set in the colonial era of pre-war Indo-China, Marguerite Duras' *The Lover* shimmers like the sun-baked paddies of the Mekong River Delta. A merciless portrait of the relationship between two outcasts—a 15-year-old girl shunned by her family, a man scorned by an autocratic father—*The Lover* glows with feverish eroticism, overwhelming joy and bittersweet tears.

"A rare find" says the *Washington Times Magazine* while the *Boston Herald* finds *The Lover* to be "as seamless and polished as a pearl."

MACBETH

By William Shakespeare
(NCC7053) $14.95—Sale Only
Two cassettes
Read by Sir Alec Guinness and
The Old Vic Company.

One of the best-loved tragedies from the pen of Shakespeare.

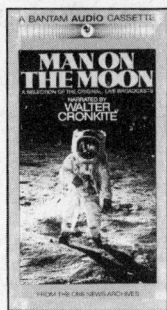

MAN ON THE MOON

With Walter Cronkite
(45050) $7.95—Sale Only
One cassette

Walter Cronkite is our guide through one of our nation's greatest dramas: the first manned landing on the lunar surface—and the stirring story that led up to it.

You'll hear the voices of the astronauts and Cronkite's commentary from the Houston Command Center, as the awe of the moment made poets of scientists and newsmen alike.

THE MAYOR OF CASTERBRIDGE

By Thomas Hardy
(TC-LFP 7077) $14.95—Sale Only
Approx. 3 hrs.
Read by Alan Bates

Michael Henchard, a tough and headstrong West Country hay trusser, rose to become the richest corn merchant and chief citizen of the town of Casterbridge. Yet despite his great wealth and power, Henchard cannot escape the consequences of that terrible day at the Weydon Prior Fair when as a young man, normally sober but then drunk, he sold his wife and child in an auction.

MEANS OF EVIL

By Ruth Rendell
(88140) $14.95—Sale Only
Two cassettes

Short stories from "undoubtedly one of the best writers of English mysteries and chiller-killer plots." *(The Los Angeles Times)*

A MIDSUMMER NIGHT'S DREAM

By William Shakespeare
(NCC7062) $14.95—Sale Only
Two cassettes
Read by Sir Alec Guinness and
The Old Vic Company.

THE MIST

By Stephen King
(62138-6) $9.95—Sale Only
One cassette

Stephen King's sinister imagination takes us to a sleepy New England town beset by a macabre menace. Listeners will be startled by the breath-taking realism as they experience a new dimension in sonic terror. This unforgettable performance will envelop the listener in its awesome mayhem.

THE MOON'S A BALLOON

By David Niven
(TC-LFP 7010) $14.95—Sale Only
Approx. 2 hrs. 10 mins.
Read by David Niven

Take a young Scotsman who, after doing a stint in the regular army, goes to America during Prohibition, becomes a bootlegger and then an indoor pony racing impressario. Point him toward Hollywood, introduce him to Errol Flynn and Humphrey Bogart—and of course a few girls—and make him a star. Call that young Scotsman David Niven and call his autobiography *The Moon's a Balloon.*

MURDER IN THE MEWS

By Agatha Christie
(TC-LFP 7020) $14.95—Sale Only
Two cassettes
Read by Nigel Hawthorne

The uproar of Guy Fawkes Night provides both backdrop and camouflage for a case of apparent suicide in Bardsley Gardens Mews; will Hercule Poirot discover that it was really murder?

NEWS FROM LAKE WOBEGON

By Garrison Keillor
(MPR 900) $34.95—Sale Only
Four cassettes

Fans of American Public Radio's *Prairie Home Companion*—who are legion—know and love Garrison Keillor's Lake Wobegon as the Middle-American community "where all the women are strong, the men are good-looking, and the children are all above average." This package features stories appropriate to each of the four seasons.

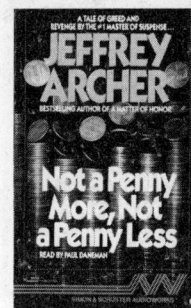

NOT A PENNY MORE, NOT A PENNY LESS

By Jeffrey Archer
(62702) $14.95—Sale Only
Two cassettes—Abridged

Four intelligent, basically upstanding and very different men have been lured into an enticing North Sea oil deal—then swindled out of one million dollars. Join Jeffrey Archer, master chronicler of human drama and passion, and his quartet of amateur swindlers as they set out to sting the King Bee of the Con Game.

THE OLD MAN AND THE SEA

By Ernest Hemingway
(CDL 52084) $19.95—Sale Only
Two cassettes
Read by Charlton Heston

Charlton Heston brings an immediacy and yet a timelessness to the story of the old Cuban fisherman whose idol was Joe DiMaggio, in a reading that places Hemingway's jewel in a golden setting.

OLD POSSUM'S BOOK OF PRACTICAL CATS

By T.S. Eliot
(CP 1713) $9.95—Sale Only
One cassette
Read by Sir John Gielgud
and Irene Worth

Eliot's merriest lines are feline. These verses, the basis for the Broadway musical *Cats*, are cat tales of "Mr. Mistoffolees," "Tug—TheTheatre Cat," "Macavity—The Mystery Cat," and others.

**For faster credit card
ordering call 1-800-626-3333**

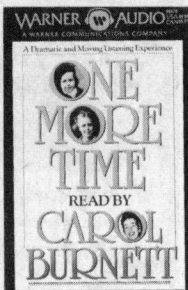

ONE MORE TIME

By Carol Burnett
(88478) $9.95—Sale Only
One cassette

Speaking straight from the heart, Carol Burnett tells her dramatic and poignant story. What began as a letter to her three daughters became a rich and powerful memoir—both inspirational and unforgettable.

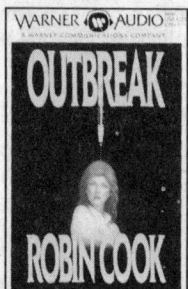

OUTBREAK

By Robin Cook
(88397) $12.95—Sale Only
Two cassettes

When Dr. Marissa Blumenthal is assigned by Atlanta's Center for Disease Control to investigate the source of an untreatable and contagious new virus, she soon becomes caught up in a web of intrigue. The ultimate nightmare occurs when she discovers that behind this medical crisis lurks the sinister possibility of man-made sabotage.

THE OX-BOW INCIDENT

By Walter Van Tilburg Clark
(CDL 51620) $9.95—Sale Only
One cassette
Read by Henry Fonda

Probably the most powerful anti-lynching story ever written. Of its genre it is a brief and violent masterpiece. Henry Fonda, who starred in the memorable film, performs with a brilliant reading.

POWERHOUSE and PETRIFIED MAN

By Eudora Welty
(CDL 51626) $9.95—Sale Only
One cassette
Read by Eudora Welty

Eudora Welty writes in *Powerhouse* of a pianist who is manifestly Fats Waller, giving a graphic portrait of that mighty musical personage and his milieu. In *Petrified Man* Welty writes of her Mississippi with a warmth and point to be expected of one of America's foremost authors. Add to this her voice and delivery which are just right for the material.

PROOF

By Dick Francis
(NCC7134) $14.95—Sale Only
Two cassettes
Read by Charles Dance

Accidental witness to a gruesome murder, Tony Beach, a noted wine connoisseur, must find the courage he feels he lacks. A complex, satisfying mystery set in the racing world that Francis portrays so well.

THE PROPHET

By Kahlil Gibran
(55049-8) $7.95—Sale Only
One cassette

Cherished by millions around the world, translated into more than twenty languages, the universally inspiring words of *The Prophet* are here magnificently read aloud.

THE RED PONY

By John Steinbeck
(CP 2047) $19.95—Sale Only
Two cassettes
Read by Eli Wallach

The Red Pony is the story of a boy on the threshold of adolescence, growing up and pushing out against the stress of parents and the demands of life. It is a book that is genuinely interesting to students and teachers alike.

ROMEO AND JULIET

By William Shakespeare
(TC-LFP 7068) $14.95—Sale Only
Approx. 2 hrs. 40 min.
Read by Alan Badel, Claire Bloom
and the Old Vic Company

One of the world's great love stories, *Romeo and Juliet* is perhaps the best loved of Shakespeare's plays. Excellent as it is on the stage, it is above all a reader's play. Shakespeare was at ease in his treatment of ideal love, and may have been the greatest poet of love in world literature.

A ROSE FOR EMILY and WASH

By William Faulkner
(CDL 51638) $9.95—Sale Only
One cassette
Read by Tammy Grimes

Faulkner is universally regarded as one of the great American authors of short stories. Perhaps "A Rose for Emily" is the best known. Set, as is "Wash," in Faulkner's Mississippi, it is a tale which requires a masterful reading to bring it to life and this Tammy Grimes provides in excelsus. "Wash" is another Mississippi story of a man gone wrong.

RUMPOLE OF THE BAILEY

By John Mortimer
(NCC7110) $14.95—Sale Only
Two cassettes
Read by Leo McKern

Come and meet Rumpole. The delightfully eccentric barrister brought to life by the actor who brought the role to the Thames Television series.

SHANE

By Jack Schaefer
(TC-LFP 7032) $14.95—Sale Only
Approx. 2 hrs.
Read by Peter Marinker

A mysterious stranger dressed in black rode into the Wyoming valley where Bob Starrett lived with his parents. Shane was powerful yet gentle, dangerous yet kind; and although they could discover nothing about his strange past, Shane touched the life and heart of each member of the Starrett family.

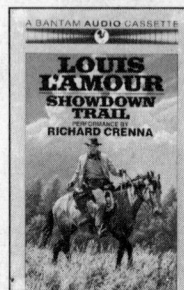

SHOWDOWN TRAIL

By Louis L'Amour
(45083) $14.95—Sale Only
Two cassettes
Read by Richard Crenna

Rock Bannon is a man bred to the Colt and the rugged law of frontier survival. But to a group of naive homesteaders, his reputation as a gunfighter marks him as an outcast among decent folk. So when a smooth-talking scoundrel comes to camp, no one is ready to listen to Bannon's warning.

SMILEY'S PEOPLE

By John le Carré
(TC-LFP 7106) $14.95—Sale Only
Approx. 2 hrs. 30 mins.
Read by John le Carré

When a Russian exile is found murdered, George Smiley is coaxed into performing the last rites on the case. Instead, he finds himself stalking the phantom that haunted him all his professional life—Karla.

SOMEDAY, THE RABBI WILL LEAVE

By Harry Kemelman
(88138) $14.95—Sale Only
Two cassettes

"Harry Kemelman combines the excitement of a detective story with interesting insight into contemporary Judaism . . ." —Madeleine L'Engle.

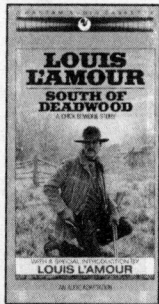

SOUTH OF DEADWOOD

By Louis L'Amour
(45021) $7.95—Sale Only
One cassette

Louis L'Amour brings you back to the real Deadwood, South Dakota as he describes life in the rough and wild town where even school kids packed guns and talks about some of Deadwood's most famous and infamous inhabitants—Wild Bill Hickock, Calamity Jane and Seth Bullock.

Take the stagecoach into Deadwood with Ranger Chick Bowdrie to bring a notorious killer back to Texas—and justice.

SPACE

By James Michener
(55041-2) $14.95—Sale Only
Two cassettes

Michener's best-selling novel.

THE SPY WHO CAME IN FROM THE COLD

By John le Carré
(NCC7121) $14.95—Sale Only
Two cassettes
Read by John le Carré

Le Carré's fourth novel established his reputation for chilling authenticity about Cold War espionage.

STORIES FROM THE HERRIOT COLLECTION

By James Herriot
(NCC7119) $14.95—Sale Only
Two cassettes
Read by Christopher Timothy

The star of the popular television series based on Herriot's books reads this selection of previously unrecorded stories.

STORIES FROM *NIGHT SHIFT*

By Stephen King
(88192) $14.95—Saley Only
Two cassettes

Just when you thought it was safe to turn out the lights. "A spellbinding journey through horror by a master of the craft." *(The Los Angeles Times)*

THE STORIES OF JOHN CHEEVER

By John Cheever
(55045-5) $7.95—Sale Only
One cassette

Selections from one of fiction's great writers.

STRANGE PURSUIT

By Louis L'Amour
(45001-8) $7.95—Sale Only
One cassette—Dramatization

Here is the story of Texas Ranger Chick Bowdrie's legendary search for the infamous killer Charlie Venk. Follow Bowdrie into the dusty cowtown of Chollo where rumor has it Venk hung the town sheriff with his own rope before disappearing into the sunbaked badlands.

Give a Books on Tape™ Gift Certificate Call 1-800-626-3333

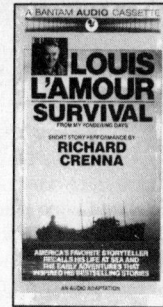

SURVIVAL

By Louis L'Amour
(45031) $7.95—Sale Only
One cassette

You'll hear Louis L'Amour's first-hand observations of life on the docks of San Pedro and the rough-hewn men whose simple courage on ship and shore have been the inspiration of many of his stories. You'll also hear a reading of *Survival* one of L'Amour's famous *Yondering* tales.

This is the harrowing adventure of shipwreck and survival based on the true story of merchant seaman Tex Worden and his efforts to save the passengers of the doomed *Raratonga*.

T.S. ELIOT READING *THE LOVE SONG OF J. ALFRED PRUFROCK*

By T.S. Eliot
(CDL 51045) $9.95—Sale Only
One cassette
Read by T.S.Eliot

T.S. Eliot's voice, precise and angular, is tailor-made for these verses. He reads many of his most famous poems, including "The Love Song of J. Alfred Prufrock" and a section from his play *Murder in the Cathedral.*

TALES OF HORROR

By Edgar Allan Poe
(TC-LFP 7039) $14.95—Sale Only
Approx. 2 hrs.
Read by Christopher Lee

Edgar Allan Poe's themes explore the bizarre; his images evoke the world of the dim and the sinister. Through his tales we are introduced to experiences on the borders of sanity. "The Fall of the House of Ushers," "The Pit and the Pendulum," "The Cask of Amontillado" and "The Black Cat" are included in this collection.

THINNER

Stephen King writing as Richard Bachman
(NC71277) $14.95—Sale Only
Two cassettes
Read by Paul Sorvino

Thinner spent more than 35 weeks on the best-seller lists, proving the market for Stephen King, even under a pseudonym.

THE THIRD MAN

By Graham Greene
(TC-LFP 7103) $14.95—Sale Only
Approx. 2 hrs.
Read by James Mason

Rollo Martins is invited to Vienna by his school friend hero Harry Lime, but he arrives just in time to attend Lime's funeral. Rollo is determined to find out the truth behind Harry's death, and in doing so he discovers that his hero was involved in one of the dirtiest rackets going in post-war Vienna. *The Third Man* was originally written as the screenplay for Carol Reed's 1939 thriller with Orson Welles, Joseph Cotton and Trevor Howard.

TINKER, TAILOR, SOLDIER, SPY

By John le Carré
(TC-LFP 7082) $14.95—Sale Only
Approx. 2 hrs. 30 mins.
Read by Michael Jayson

This is John le Carré's masterpiece of espionage and counter-espionage. "A mole is a Russian double-agent, so called because he burrows deep into the fabric of Western Imperialism." There is a mole in the Circus, at the highest level of British Intelligence. That was why Smiley left the service, and also why he came back. Smiley's unenviable task is to discover the identity of the double-agent who is pulling the Circus apart.

TOUCH THE DEVIL

By Jack Higgins
(NCC7117) $14.95—Sale Only
Two cassettes
Read by Ian Holm

The story from the author of *The Eagle has Landed* pits two seasoned IRA terrorists against a killer bent on delivering the latest NATO missile system to the Russians.

A TOWN LIKE ALICE

By Nevil Shute
(TC-LFP 7048) $14.95—Sale Only
Approx. 2 hrs.
Read by Leo McKern

"The Imperial Japanese Army do not make war on womans and childs." With this proclamation Jean Paget and 32 English women and children taken prisoner by the Japanese in 1941 began an ordeal far worse than prison camp. This book is Nevil Shute's celebration of one young woman's bravery, not only in the Malayan jungles, but also in the Australian Outback, where, with the same initiative and energy, she set about creating a town like Alice.

A TRAIL TO THE WEST

By Louis L'Amour
(45009-3) $7.95—Sale Only
One cassette—Dramatization

This time join famed Texas Ranger Chick Bowdrie as he tracks the notorious John Queen, wanted for murder and kidnapping. Riding under an alias, Bowdrie joins up with Queen's ruthless gang to rescue the pretty niece of a powerful Texas judge. But when Queen discovers the lawman's true identity, Bowdrie must do some fast thinking and even faster shooting to beat the odds—five guns to one.

THE TRIALS OF RUMPOLE

By John Mortimer
(NCC7118) $14.95—Sale Only
Two cassettes
Read by Leo McKern

Read by the actor who created Rumpole for the Thames Television series, these two stories showcase the irreverence and legal sublety of the delightfully eccentric barrister.

TROPIC OF CANCER

By Henry Miller
(NCC71247) $14.95—Sale Only
Two cassettes
Read by Martin Balsam

Characterized by the *Cambridge Guide to English Literature* as "mordantly funny and uncompromisingly bawdy" and banned in the U.S. for years after its publication in 1934, Miller's book now enjoys the recognition it deserves as a milestone of American literature.

2001: A SPACE ODYSSEY

By Arthur C. Clarke
(CP 1504) $9.95—Sale Only
One cassette
Read by Arthur C. Clarke

Arthur C. Clarke is one of the most widely known and respected authors of science fiction. On this recording he reads the final eleven chapters of *2001: A Space Odyssey*.

2010: ODYSSEY TWO

By Arthur C. Clarke
(CP 1709) $9.95—Sale Only
One cassette
Read by Arhtur C. Clarke

Stanley Kubrick made *2001: A Space Odyssey* into the most outstanding science fiction film. *2010* is Clark's long awaited and ambitious sequel exploring regions beyond our limiting layers of time and space.

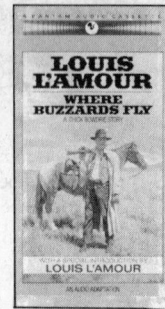

WHERE BUZZARDS FLY

By Louis L'Amour
(45015) $7.95—Sale Only
One cassette

Ride with the legendary Texas Ranger Chick Bowdrie as he tracks the killers of an infamous Mexican outlaw, Zaparo, and fourteen of his desperadoes. With scarcely a clue to the solution of this ruthless ambush, Bowdrie is led to the K-Bar ranch and the beautiful girlfriend of the last living member of Zaparo's gang—only to find his prime suspect is a "friend" of the Texas Rangers.

WHERE EAGLES DARE

By Alistair Maclean
(TC-LFP 7084) $14.95—Sale Only
Approx. 2 hrs.
Read by Martin Jarvis

Where Eagles Dare is the story of a handful of men led by Major Smith who get inside an 'impenetrable' Gestapo command post. Their mission is supposedly to rescue a high-ranking American general who is being held prisoner in the fortress, but Alistair Maclean's sudden twists of plot make *Where Eagles Dare* one of his most famous thrillers.

THE WIT AND WISDOM OF WILL ROGERS

By Will Rogers
(CDL 52046) $19.95—Sale Only
Two cassettes
Read by Will Rogers

Will Rogers was the political and social "common man" who regularly claimed, "All I know is what I read in the newspapers." Here, with charm and humor, he makes shrewd judgments on the American scene and with a gentle scalpel dissects the political corpus.

WOMEN COMING OF AGE

By Jane Fonda with Mignon McCarthy
(SS 1857) $7.95—Sale Only
One cassette

Jane Fonda inspires women to improve the quality of their lives in this dynamic audio version adapted from the #1 best seller *Women Coming of Age*. Narrated by the author, Jane directs all of her savvy, energy and honesty to the special needs of women 35 to 65 years of age.

WUTHERING HEIGHTS

By Emily Bronte
(TC-LFP 7017) $14.95—Sale Only
Approx. 3 hrs.
Read by Daniel Massey

Passion, hatred, love and revenge are stirred together in this remarkable novel written in 1847 by a refined and sheltered young woman with scant experience in the world. Emily Bronte created Heathcliff out of her private fantasies, gave him a prideful and noble will, started him in life as an urchin, reclaimed and refined him, dealt him a mortal insult, then let him work his vengeance on his enemies in a most cruel way. Heathcliff, and his love Kathy are unforgettable as is the novel which is as powerful today as when first written.

Books on Tape™'s service is 100% guaranteed

CHILDRENS

Allow 4-6 weeks for delivery.

ALICE IN WONDERLAND
Unabridged

By Lewis Carroll
(ABC 1) $19.95—Sale Only
2-1½ hour cassettes—Gift album
Read by Flo Gibson

Savor this great classic delightfully read in its entirety by Flo Gibson. Among the stories are: "Down the Rabbit-Hole," "The Cheshire Cat," "A Mad Tea-Party," "The Queen's Croquet Ground" and "A Caucus-Race and a Long Tale."

THE CALL OF THE WILD

By Jack London
(TC-LFP) $14.95—Sale Only
Approx. 2 hrs.
Read by Stewart Granger

Jack London's famous novel about the dog 'Buck' who inherited the looks and cunning of a Shepherd from his mother and the huge size and strength of his St. Bernard father. The story is set against the background of the wild and frozen frontiers of Alaska, where at the turn of the century thousands of men rushed in search of gold. These men wanted dogs, and the dogs they most valued were those that could pull the heavy sledges and survive the freezing winters of the Klondike.

CHRONICLES OF
NARNIA SOUNDBOOK

By C.S. Lewis
(SBC 123) $29.95—Sale Only
Four cassettes

Includes *The Lion, The Witch and the Wardrobe; Prince Caspian; The Silver Chair* and *The Voyage of the "Dawn Treader."*

DR. SEUSS: HAPPY BIRTHDAY
TO YOU!

By Dr. Seuss
(CP 1287) $9.95—Sale Only
One cassette
Read by Hans Conried

Dr. Seuss wears well: there is never too much of him; there is never even enough. Cassette includes: "Happy Birthday to You!," "The Big Brag," "Gertrude McFuzz," "Scrambled Eggs Super!" and "And To Think That I Saw It On Mulberry Street."

GREAT EXPECTATIONS

By Charles Dickens
(TC-LFP 7074) $14.95—Sale Only
Approx. 3 hrs.
Read by Anton Rodgers

Superb story told with typical Dickenson warmth and humor and woven around unforgettable characters—Miss Haversham, in her faded bride's dress; Magwitch, whose life becomes inextricably intertwined with Pip's: and Pip himself, who strives always to do better and learns the many lesson life teaches.

THE HOUND OF
THE BASKERVILLES

By Sir Arthur Conan Doyle
(TC-LFP 7007) $14.95—Sale Only
Approx. 2 hrs.
Read by Hugh Burden

Marvelous story of the ruthless exploitation of a family legend by an unscrupulous outsider, who is foiled by the quiet acuteness of Sherlock Holmes and the dogged persistence of Watson. After the horrible death of Sir Charles Baskerville what will happen to his heir, Sir Henry Baskerville, is a question that will keep the listener guessing until the last minute.

THE LITTLE PRINCE

By Antoine de Saint-Exupery
(CP 1695) $9.95—Sale Only
One cassette
Translated by Katherine Woods
Performance by Louis Jourdan
Music by Linda Danly

This is a poignant story with charming characters. An innocent exile, the little prince learns the true secret of the heart. One of the top ten best sellers in children's literature, this classic endears itself to all who never fully grow up, who, like the author, recall "the tender sympathies" of being young.

LITTLE WOMEN

By Louisa May Alcott
(TC-LFP 7080) $14.95—Sale Only
Approx. 3 hrs.
Read by Carol Drinkwater

Here is Louisa May Alcott's widely read story of Jo March, the tomboyish literary member of a family of four girls. She constantly disappears into the attic when "genius burns," and is usually in hot water the rest of the time. With Jo as central character, we follow the joys and tragedies of these four sisters and the decisions and paths they follow for the future.

MORE WELL-LOVED FAIRY STORIES

(TC-LFP 7056) $14.95—Sale Only
Approx. 2 hrs.

Four accomplished readers here present a collection of well-loved fairy stories for the delight of young listeners: "Snow White and the Seven Dwarfs," "Rumplestiltskin," "The Little Match Girl," "The Gentle Giant and The Horrid Little Mouse," "Rapunzel," "The Gingerbread Man," "Beauty and the Beast" and "Hansel and Gretel."

THE SECRET GARDEN

By Frances Hodgson Burnett
(CDL 51463) $9.95—Sale Only
One cassette
Read by Caire Bloom

The Secret Garden is an old-fashioned mystery about a plain little girl and her metamorphosis in a great English manor house. Recording includes "There's No One Left," "Mistress Mary Quite Contrary," "Across the Moor," "Martha," "The Cry in the Corridor," "The Key of the Garden," "The Robin Who Showed the Way," "The Strangest House," "Kickon," " The Nest of the Misel Thrush," "I Am Colin," "A Young Rajah," "Tha' Munnot Waste No Time," "It Has Come!," "I Shall Live Forever," "Ben Weatherstaff," "When the Sun Went Down," "Magic" and "In the Garden."

THE STORY OF SWAN LAKE

By Petipa/Tchaikovsky
(CP 1673) $14.95—Sale Only
One cassette
Read by Claire Bloom

This charming reading coupled with the romantic music is an astonishing production. Such a wedding of words and melody tells the story and adds to the appreciation of the great ballet. Music performed by Orchestre de la Suisse Romande.

THE STORY OF THE NUTCRACKER

By Ernst Theodore Amadeus Hoffman
(CP 1524) $9.95—Sale Only
One cassette
Read by Claire Bloom

The music of Tchaikovsky and the story of the little girl who receives a gift of a magical nutcracker from her grandfather has been a Christmas favorite for many years.

A TALE OF TWO CITIES

By Charles Dickens
(TC-LFP 7059) $14.95—Sale Only
Approx. 3 hrs.
Read by John Carson

Famous tale set against the background of the French Revolution. Doctor Manette, his devoted daughter Lucie and the young French aristocrat Charles Darnay are memorable characters etched by the skillful pen of Dickens, but above all the others rises the reckless Sidney Carton, whose selfless devotion makes him one of literature's great heroes.

THE TALES OF PETER RABBIT AND OTHER STORIES

By Beatrix Potter
(CP 1314) $9.95—Sale Only
One cassette
Read by Claire Bloom

It would be hard to imagine a childhood world, without Beatrix Potter, creator of Peter Rabbit, Benjamin Bunny, Mrs. Tiggy-Winkle and other such characters. The enduring charm of her stories is a result of her respect for the children to whom she is writing as well as her understanding of the animals which are her characters. This collection includes stories of the three unforgettables mentioned above plus "The Tale of Mrs. Jeremy Fisher" and "The Tale of Two Bad Mice."

THROUGH THE LOOKING GLASS

By Lewis Carroll
(ABC 4) $19.95—Sale Only
2-1½ hour cassettes—Gift album
Read by Flo Gibson

Read in its entirety, this continuation of *Alice in Wonderland* introduces new characters, including Jabberock, Tweedledee and Tweedledum, and the Walrus and the Carpenter.

TREASURE ISLAND

By Robert Louis Stevenson
(TC-LFP 7018) $14.95—Sale Only
Approx. 2 hrs.
Read by Anthony Bate

Classic adventure of the search for buried treasure. The expedition becomes increasingly dangerous for young Jim Hawkins and his companions as they discover that they are not the only fortune hunters. Ruthless pirates and the infamous Long John Silver are all determined to win the race for the treasure!

WINNIE THE POOH

By A.A. Milne
(TC-LFP 7052) $14.95—Sale Only
Approx. 2 hrs.
Read by Lionel Jeffries

This recording includes nine of the ten enchanting stories about honey-loving "Winnie the Pooh" and his many friends in the Hundred Acre Wood.

For quick ordering
1-800-626-3333

MasterCard   VISA

FULL-LENGTH SELECTIONS FROM BOOKCASSETTE™

Books on Tape is now able to offer for sale titles recorded by Brilliance Corporation and marketed under the name of BOOKCASSETTE.

What makes these recordings special is that they are unabridged, multi-voice presentations of some of the most popular current titles. They utilize a special recording technique that allows the entire book to be recorded on as few as four cassettes.

However, these cassettes can only be played on stereo tape players with balance controls (left/right adjustments). Bookcassette adaptors are needed for listening with headphones and are also available. Simple instructions for listening are on the package and can be heard on each tape. As with every item offered by Books on Tape, your satisfaction is guaranteed.

BOOKCASSETTE STEREO ADAPTER

This small in-line electronic device is only needed for listening to Bookcassettes on personal stereos with headphones. The adaptor allows the listener to select the proper channel as the cassette is played.

STEREO ADAPTER

(BR00) $8.99—Sale Only

THE BROTHERHOOD OF THE ROSE

By David Morell
(BR11) $17.95—Sale Only
Three cassettes

Saul and Chris are "brothers" through shared experiences: orphaned; childhoods spent in an institution; loneliness; and training by the "foster father" as world-class intelligence agents.

Experts in espionage at twenty-one, they are thirty-six when Saul learns that their "father", Edward Eliot, chief of counter-intelligence for the CIA, holds a secret so terrible it could alter the balance of world power.

DEADLOCK

By Sara Paretsky
(BR07) $17.95—Sale Only
Three cassettes

V.I. Warshawski, the feminist sleuth who specializes in corporate crime, returns in Deadlock, a topnotch mystery that critics say even surpasses Sara Paretsky's first novel, *Indemnity Only*.

The smart young detective becomes suspicious when her cousin Boom Boom, a former ice hockey star, drowns in a questionable dock accident. As she explores the cargo shipping world, Vic uncovers a murderous rivalry between shipping magnates.

THE FRATERNITY OF THE STONE

By David Morell
(BR12) $19.95—Sale Only
Four cassettes

David Morell, author of *First Blood* and *The Brotherhood of the Rose,* has written another thriller which will keep you listening until the very end!

For the past five years, Drew, a former secret agent, has been residing in a secluded monastery in Vermont. His time is spent in penance, having renounced all worldly pursuits in reconciliation for the inhumanities he has committed. Suddenly peace and tranquility are replaced by horror and intrigue when an unknown enemy tries to kill Drew. He is forced back into the outside world, fleeing for his life.

THE QUIET ASSASSIN

By Thomas Kirkwood
(BR13) $17.95—Sale Only
Three cassettes

The Quiet Assassin is an unusual and original thriller that occurs in East Berlin during the cold war. The heroine Kate Frassek, like Lucy in Ken Follett's *Eye of the Needle,* is an unparalleled and intriguing woman protagonist. Frassek, a respected scientist, leads a double life and, with pen in hand, becomes the quiet assassin. Her main goal is to begin a revolution which would ultimately free the German people from a police state. She intends to begin this revolt by killing the head of the East German secret police.

THE SICILIAN

By Mario Puzo
(BR02) $19.95—Sale Only
Four cassettes

Michael Corleone is returning to the U.S. after the two-year exile to Sicily where readers left him in *The Godfather*. Mario Puzo has created a sequel to *The Godfather* that is every bit as compelling and dramatic. But The Sicilian is a distinct literary achievement in its historical inspiration and its vivid portrait of Sicilian peasant life.

Stay on the fast track with these thought-provoking, action-oriented programs! From single cassette offerings to extensive management discussions, you will find programs that should be a part of your business library. Allow 4-6 weeks for delivery.

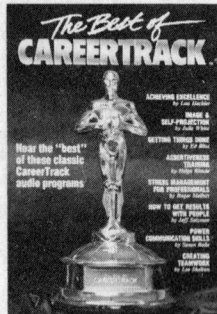

THE BEST OF CAREERTRACK™

(66255) $29.95—Sale Only
Two cassettes

Projecting a stronger image . . . getting more done in a day . . . building personal power and confidence . . . managing your stress . . . and much more.

The Best of CareerTrack is just that: three hours of the most powerful, most inspirational material from CareerTrack's best-selling programs, presented by eight of America's top trainers.

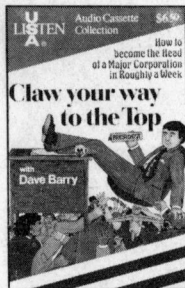

CLAW YOUR WAY TO THE TOP
How to Become the Head of a Major Corporation in Roughly a Week

With Dave Barry
(84103) $6.50—Sale Only
One cassette

You'll laugh all the way to the top and to the bank if you take the valuable and amusing advice of syndicated columnist, humorist, Dave Barry. You'll get the hilarious scoop on the basics . . . memos, telephone messages, business finance, making sales, handling subordinates, business lunches . . . so you'll be fully prepared for your next business encounter!

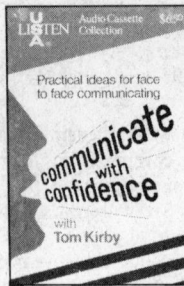

COMMUNICATE WITH CONFIDENCE

With Tom Kirby
(84010) $6.50—Sale Only
One cassette

In this lively engaging seminar by master speech coach of Fortune 500 executives, Tom Kirby, you'll witness the process of step-by-step communicating with confidence. Skills emphasized include the practical techniques for speaking to groups of 2 or 2000!

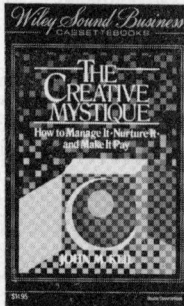

THE CREATIVE MYSTIQUE

By John M. Keil
(84701) $14.95—Sale Only
Two cassettes

No matter what side of the creative fence you're on *The Creative Mystique* can help you. If you're creative, it will help you succeed where most "creatives" fail—getting down to business. If you're management, it will help you get better results from your creative people. If you're in marketing or advertising, it will sharpen both your problem-solving skills and your ability to work with other creative people.

John M. Keil is Executive Vice President and Executive Creative Director at Dancer Fitzgerald Sample, one of the world's largest advertising agencies.

THE EXCELLENCE CHALLENGE

By Tom Peters
(142A) $52.50—Sale Only
Six cassettes

These six cassettes offer important new lessons, insights and dozens of practical examples you can use to make a difference in your professional career and personal life.

Twelve 15-minute sessions include:

Winners Win Big
Paying Attention—Symbols
Effective Wandering
Success by Small Wins
The Heart and Soul of Excellence
Accepting the Challenge
Strategic Edge #1: Customer Service
Strategic Edge #2: Quality
Strategic Edge #3: Innovation
People, People, People

For more than a decade, Tom Peters has analyzed American management in action. His research has centered on corporate revitalization, continuous innovation, customer satisfaction, productivity improvement and strategy implementation.

Besides co-authoring *In Search of Excellence*, Peters has also written for *The Wall Street Journal* and *The Harvard Business Review*.

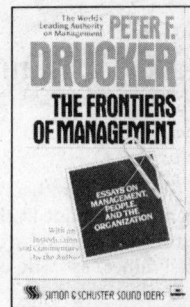

THE FRONTIERS OF MANAGEMENT

By Peter F. Drucker
(64110) $8.95—Sale Only
One cassette—Abridged

A bestselling author since 1939, Peter F. Drucker understands better than anyone the new economic and social forces and the global trends that are shaping the future of business and management.

The Frontiers of Management has been hailed as masterpiece of insight and innovation, and this audio version, featuring an introduction and commentary by the author, culls the most forward-looking ideas from the book to teach you how to master the "people" side of managing. From choosing and cultivating to organizing and evaluating staff this is an illuminating program.

HOW TO DEAL WITH DIFFICULT PEOPLE

NEW

With Dr. Rick Brinkman and Dr. Rick Kirschner
(66263) $49.95—Sale Only
Four cassettes

At last—the audio version of CareerTrack's popular seminar. If your know people who sulk, throw temper tantrums, always overstep their bounds, never deliver what they promise or constantly complain . . . then you need *How to Deal With Difficult People*.

Drs. Brinkman and Kirschner show you how to thwart the most frustrating types of behavior—quickly and confidently.

LETITIA BALDRIGE'S GUIDE TO EXECUTIVE MANNERS

(88426-7) $9.95—Sale Only
One cassette

Make your business encounters smoother, more professional—and more productive. From running a meeting to the art of business entertaining, learn the best way to handle all kinds of business situations.

Letitia Baldrige discusses corporate protocol and the subtleties of interpersonal relationships in the workplace that can make or break a career.

Give a Books on Tape™ Gift Certificate Call 1-800-626-3333

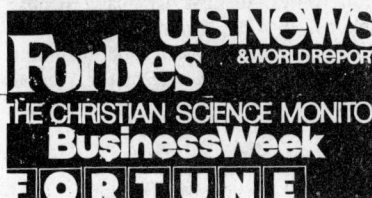

NEWSTRACK© EXECUTIVE TAPE SERVICE

With the ever increasing flow of business and market information many executives find it difficult to absorb 100 issues of the leading 30 to 40 business periodicals each month.

Newstrack Executive Tape Service simplifies this task by combining current vital business information, advice and trends from today's outstanding thinkers onto premium quality audio cassettes.

Twice each month you will receive a 909-minute tape containing articles from the latest issues of over 40 magazines including: *Fortune, Forbes, Institutional Investor, The Christian Science Monitor, Dun's Business Month, World Business Weekly, Industry Week, U.S. News and World Report* and many other important publications.

Enjoy and benefit from the Newstrack perspective of essential business news. Ideal for the commuter—Newstrack means business.

(NT1) $195/Annual Subscription
Published twice monthly
24 - 1½ hour cassettes per year

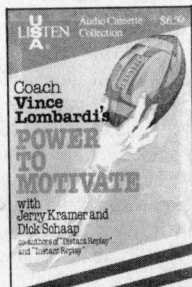

POWER TO MOTIVATE

NEW

With Jerry Kramer and Dick Schaap
(84105) $6.50—Sale Only
One cassette

This highly motivating program features former Green Bay Packer Jerry Kramer, and Dick Schaap, Emmy award-winning journalist/correspondent, discussing lessons in championship living. They detail how Coach Vince Lombardi's motivational methods have brought high degrees of success to others. Improve your position by following Coach Lombardi's winning ways.

THE WALL STREET JOURNAL ON MANAGEMENT

By the Editors
(00348) $9.95—Sale Only
One cassette

A selection of the most current (1986) and quotable *Journal* editorial page features from the "Managers Journal" column. Hear what these top CEO's, corporate presidents and VP's, management consultants and other business professionals working on topics such as: what it takes to be an effective leader, working with and learning from others, getting the most out of your employees and keeping in touch without wasting time.

WIN-WIN NEGOTIATING

By Fred E. Jandt with Paul Gillette
(84700) $14.95—Sale Only
Two cassettes

Conflict. It's an unavoidable fact of business life. Most people avoid dealing with conflict, hoping it will go away. When it doesn't, they explode—and both sides lose. But you can turn conflict into a positive force leading to communication, teamwork and agreement.

In this conversation with his co-author, Paul Gillette, Dr. Jandt will tell you how to use the same negotiating techniques and tactics used by people whose job is managing conflict—labor negotiators, diplomats and corporate managers.

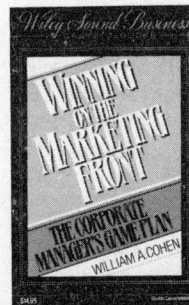

WINNING ON THE MARKETING FRONT

NEW

By William A. Cohen
(85662) $14.95—Sale Only
Two cassettes

Business isn't like war. It *is* war . . . and it's won on the marketing front. Let Bill Cohen help you become more effective and competitive by approaching your marketing problems strategically.

In his nationally known seminars, Bill Cohen advises managers to plan their marketing strategy the way a general plans a battle: concentrate your strength where it will achieve the greatest impact. *Winning on the Marketing Front* is a conversation with an expert who is one of the country's leading authorities on marketing and business management.

CLASSICAL

Vox Turnabout has captured magnificent performances of favorite classical music. Each set contains three cassettes and complete program notes packaged in a colorful book-like container. (Please allow 4 weeks for delivery).

BEETHOVEN

(CBX 577) $15.98—Sale Only
Three cassettes

Chamber Music for Flute—Serenade in D for Flute & Piano; Six Themes and Variations for Flute & Piano, Op. 105; Ten Themes and Variations, Op. 107; Allegro and Minuet in G for Two Flutes; Sonata in B-Flat for Flute & Piano; Trio Concertante in G for Flute, Bassoon and Piano; Trio in G for Three Flutes—Jean-Pierre Rampal, Alain Marion & Christian Larde, Flutes; Robert Veyron-Lacroix, Piano; Paul Hongne, Bassoon.

DEBUSSY

(CBX 5127) $15.98—Sale Only
Three cassettes

The Complete Orchestra Works, Vol. I—La Mer; Preludes a l'apres-midi d'un faune; Incidental Music to Le Martyre de Saint Sebastien; Le Triomphe de Bacchus; Le Roi Lear; March Eccossaise; La Boite a joujoux; Berceuse Heroique; Excerpts from L'Enfant Prodigue—Orchestra of Radio Luxembourg; Louis de Froment, Conductor.

GERSHWIN

(CBX 5132) $15.98—Sale Only
Three cassettes

The Complete Orchestral Music—Rhapsody in Blue; An American in Paris; Piano Concerto in F; Promenade; Cuban Overture; Variations on I Got Rhythm; 2nd Rhapsody; Lullaby; Catfish Row (Suite from Porgy and Bess)—Saint Louis Symphony Orchestra; Jeffrey Siegel, Piano; Leonard Slatkin, Conductor.

GREGORIAN CHANTS

(CBX 5206) $15.98—Sale Only
Three cassettes

Offertories, Alleluias, Graduals, Hymns, Antiphons, Introits, Communions for the *Christmas & Easter* Seasons, and important Liturgical Services—Choir of the Vienna Hofburgkapelle; Josef Schabasser, Conductor.

HANDEL

(CBX 5203) $15.98—Sale Only
Three cassettes

Messiah—Jennifer Vyvyan, Soprano; Norma Procter, Alto; George Maran, Tenor; Owen Brannigan, Bass; London Philharmonic Orchestra and Choir; Sir Adrian Boult, Conductor.

LISZT

(CBX 5452) $15.98—Sale Only
Three cassettes

Complete Hungarian Rhapsodies—Louis Kentner, Piano.

MOZART

(CBX 5153) $15.98—Sale Only
Three cassettes

Works for Solo Flute—Two Flute Concerti, K. 313 & 314; Andante in C, K. 315; Rondo in D, K. Anh. 184; Four Flute Quartets, K. 285, 285a, 285b & 298; Six Sonatas for Flute & Harpsichord, K. 10-15—Renee Siebert, Flute; Rodney Friend, Violin; Walter Trampler, Viola; George Neikrug, Cello; Judith Norell, Harpsichord; Wurttenberg Chamber Orchestra; Jorg Faerber, Conductor.

RACHMANINOFF

(CBX 5149) $15.98—Sale Only
Three cassettes

Complete Works for Piano and Orchestra—Piano Concerti Nos. 1-4; Rhapsody on a Theme of Paganini—Abbey Simon, Piano; Saint Louis Symphony Orchestra; Leonard Slatkin, Conductor.

RACHMANINOFF

(CBX 5152) $15.98—Sale Only
Three cassettes

The 3 Symphonies—Saint Louis Symphony Orchestra; Leonard Slatkin, Conductor.

RAVEL

(CBX 5133) $15.98—Sale Only
Three cassettes

The complete Orchestral Music—Boléro; La Valse; Rapsodie Espagnole; Menuet antique; Le Tombeau de Couperin; Alborada del gracioso; Valse nobles et sentimentales; Ma Mere L'Oye; Suites 1 & 2 from Daphnis et Chloe Un Barquesu l'océan; Fanfare; Pavane pour une infante défunte—Minnesota Orchestra; St. Olaf Choir; Stanislaw Skrowaczewski, Conductor.

SCHUBERT

(CBX 5487) $15.98—Sale Only
Three cassettes

Music for Solo Piano—Impromptus, Op. 9 & 142; Wanderer Fantasy, Op. 15; Moments Musicaus, Op. 94; Two Scherzi, D. 593; March in E, D. 606; Variation on a Waltz by Diabelli, D.718; Allegretto in C, D. 915; Three Piano Pieces, D. 946; Adagio in E, D. 612—Peter Frankl, Piano.

TOLL FREE credit card order line 1-800-626-3333

MasterCard VISA

Please allow 4 weeks for delivery

ALCOHOLISM

By Joseph A. Pursch, M.D.
(JP01) $29.95—Sale Only
Three cassettes

Dr. Joseph Pursch, the nationally recognized specialist on drug and alcohol abuse, has helped business executives, industry employees, politicians, military personnel, movie stars, adolescents and others with the problems of chemical addiction.

In his nationally syndicated column, Dr. Pursch helps people recognize chemical dependence and guides them on what they can do about it. He also provides concrete advice on how to get a victim into treatment.

The three cassettes included in this package are: How to Motivate the Alcoholic to Get Help, Alcoholism is a Family Disease and Different Types of Alcoholics.

ANXIETY

By Marvin R. Goldfried, Ph.D.
(T44B) $11.50—Sale Only
One cassette

The causes of anxiety—explained in language you can readily understand—and clear, lucid instructions in relaxation, as well as restructuring cognitive skills and applying this knowledge to anxiety-related situations. Includes self-instruction manual.

THE ART OF CREATIVE LISTENING

By Paul J. Meyer
(7180) $10.95—Sale Only
One cassete

Communication is a two-way street. Listening is just as important as telling. *Creative Listening* presents active strategies for developing your ability to listen and benefit from what you hear.

THE ART OF PUBLIC SPEAKING

By Mildred Bennett
(5181) $10.95—Sale Only
One cassette

Learn to stand in front of an audience and express your ideas confidently and persuasively and thus more influentially.

THE ART OF REMEMBERING

By William D. Hersey
(7169) $10.95—Sale Only
One cassette

Tapping your own memory power can increase your income, influence, prestige and your power with people.

BREATHING AND MEDITATIVE TECHNIQUES

By Judith Procter
(T12) $11.50—Sale Only
One cassette

Easily followed instructions in three basic breathing techniques promote physical relaxation and mental calm and provide an ideal introduction to the straightforward, non-mystical meditation procedures presented on side two of the cassette.

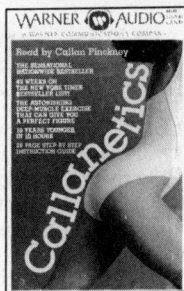

CALLANETICS

By Callan Pinckney
(88686) $9.95—Sale Only
One cassette

The secret of Callanetics goes straight to the foundations of a good figure. It is a series of unique exercises carefully designed to activate the body's deepest muscles. Simple and easy to follow, this program will help you melt fat, flatten the tummy, stretch the neck and slim inner thighs and legs. One hour twice a week will get you spectacular results. Includes 28 page instruction guide.

COMPOSITE RELAXATION TRAINING PROGRAM

By C.H. Hartman, Ph.D.
(T34) $11.50—Sale Only
One cassette

This exceptional exercise sequence has proven its value in several major hospitals and clinics. The cassette offers a unique combination of progressive relaxation, autogenic and autoinduction techniques in a compact, two-step procedure as well as specific instructions for incorporating relaxation skill into daily life.

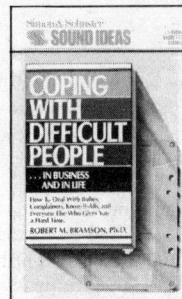

COPING WITH DIFFICULT PEOPLE

By Robert M. Bramson, Ph.D.
(61785) $8.95—Sale Only
One cassette

We've all encountered them: bullies, wet blankets, yea-sayers that never come through. More often than not, we're left fumbling for words, stumbling through the door . . . frustrated, enraged, or just plain depressed.

Dr. Robert M. Bramson, a psychologist and management consultant, will show you that it is possible to remain sane, dignified and optimistic when dealing with even the most difficult people.

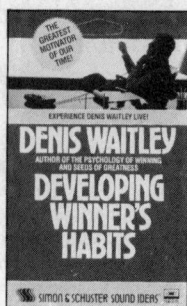

DEVELOPING WINNER'S HABITS

By Dennis Waitley
(64108) $8.95—Sale Only
One cassette

Best-selling author Denis Waitley presents an inspirational program that will allow you, quite literally, to *re-create* yourself and your outlook on living. Dr. Waitley not only shows you how attitude can trigger your success—he'll explain how to develop that attitude by enumerating and elaborating on the ten positive attitudes, and their matching actions, that will lead you directly to a winning style—and a winner's life.

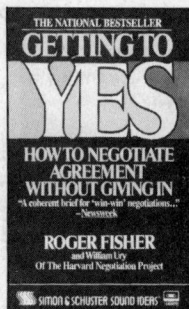

GETTING TO YES

By Roger Fisher
(63406) $8.95—Sale Only
One cassette

Most of us see the bargaining as a contest—with only winners and losers. Roger Fisher, Director of the Harvard Negotiation Project, will teach you instead how to "negotiate on the merits"—a proven method for getting what you are entitled to, without giving in and without straining your relationship with the other side. Based on the best-selling book by Roger Fisher and William Ury.

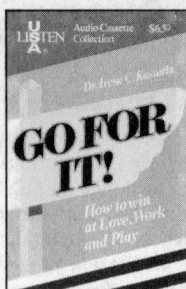

GO FOR IT!

By Dr. Irene C. Kassorla
(84028) $6.50—Sale Only
One cassette

In this exclusive tape interview, Irene C. Kassorla, Ph.D., internationally known psychologist and author who has helped people change losing to winning behaviors for over 20 years, shares her experience and research on how you can present yourself more positively by being that authentic original you.

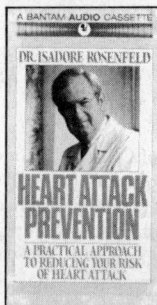

HEART ATTACK PREVENTION

By Dr. Isadore Rosenfeld
(45013) $7.95—Sale Only
One cassette

Now you can benefit from the expertise of one of the world's foremost cardiologists. In this exclusive audio consultation, Dr. Isadore Rosenfeld answers the most often asked questions about heart attack prevention.

Dr. Rosenfeld discusses the common conceptions—and misconceptions—of what a heart attack really is, who is most likely to have one and what those at risk can do to prevent them. He helps you identify risk factors in your life and tells what you can do to reduce them. His sound, personal and practical advice will help you overcome your fears and give you the facts you need to safeguard your health.

HOW TO DEVELOP THE POWER OF ENTHUSIASM

By Paul J. Meyer
(5139) $10.95—Sale Only
One cassette
(Abridged from the best seller)

Discover the limitless strength of your untapped potential—the dynamic power of your own achievement. Learn to feel and act more enthusiastically and influence others with this powerful personality tool.

HOW TO DISCIPLINE WITH LOVE

By Dr. Fitzhugh Dodson
(7173) $10.95—Sale Only
One cassette
(Abridged from the best seller)

When parents and children get along well, continuous, positive discipline is being exercised. Learn to use the positive discipline strategies presented: Rapport—the emotional foundation of all discipline; The Positive Reward System; The Law of the Soggy Potato Chip; The Time Out; The Parent/Child Contract; Expressing Feelings; Positive Feedback.

HOW TO GET YOUR POINT ACROSS IN 30 SECONDS— OR LESS

By Milo O. Frank
(60247) $8.95—Sale Only
One cassette

You can get your message across in 30 seconds. Media research proves it. Television commercials capitalize on it. People are only able to give their full, undivided attention in 30 second bites.

Milo Frank, former CBS-TV casting head, who teaches communications skills to top executives, shows you how easy it is to get your point across fast—and get what you want. Whether you're writing a memo, making a speech, asking for a raise, making a point or closing a sale.

**For Visa and MasterCard
order line 1-800-626-3333**

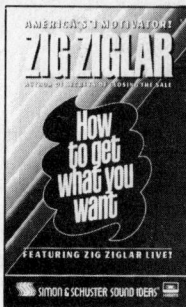

HOW TO GET WHAT YOU WANT

By Zig Ziglar
(63978) $8.95—Sale Only
One cassette

Irrepressible, enlightening—and extraordinarily successful—Zig Ziglar is presented live in one of his electrifying public seminars. The techniques that this master motivator has used to motivate his audiences in numerous multinational corporations are adapted here for everyone's use—and endless benefit.

Arguing that one of the biggest reasons that people don't set goals is they're not sold on the idea, Zig will sell you fast—on the conviction that goal-setting is the single most important step you can take on your new road to success.

HOW TO FEEL GREAT 24 HOURS A DAY

With George Sheehan, M.D.
(UT07) $6.95—Sale Only
One cassette

Aging is a myth when you learn to feel great!

HOW TO GET PEOPLE TO THINK AND ACT FAVORABLY WITH YOU

By Millard Bennett
(5167) $10.95—Sale Only
One cassette
(Abridged from the best seller)

One of America's foremost experts on communication tells you how to attract the attention of your superiors, the cooperation of your subordinates and the admiration of everyone.

HOW TO GET WHATEVER YOU WANT OUT OF LIFE

By Dr. Joyce Brothers
(60515-1) $7.95—Sale Only
One cassette

Money, power, prestige, love—success is many things to many people. Now Dr. Joyce Brothers, one of the ten most influential women in America, speaks directly to her vast audience, providing an invaluable resource: a clearly marked map that charts certain routes and proven short cuts to getting everything—whatever you want out of life!

HOW TO IMPROVE YOUR MEMORY

By Harry Lorayne
(67529) $7.95—Sale Only
One cassette

By applying the Loryane link and peg system of memory development, you'll be able to double your powers of retention, increase your concentration and remember almost everything that you want to remember.

HOW TO LIVE WITH ANOTHER PERSON

By David S. Viscott, M.D.
(7107) $10.95—Sale Only
One cassette
(Abridged from the best seller)

Whether you are an incurable romantic or a practical, action-oriented realist, Dr. Viscott offers you exciting, workable ideas for making life more satisfying, more rewarding, more romantic!

David Viscott is heard nationally on many ABC radio stations and syndications.

HOW TO MAKE WINNING YOUR LIFESTYLE

By David S. Viscott, M.D.
(7105) $10.95—Sale Only
One cassette
(Abridged from the best seller)

Everyone wins part of the time, but few of us win all the time. Listen and learn some new techniques to establish a whole life-style based on winning. You can achieve your goals. You can be a winner.

David Viscott is heard nationally on many ABC radio stations and syndications.

HOW TO MEET PEOPLE & MAKE FRIENDS

By Don Gabor
(67570) $7.95—Sale Only
One cassette

Everyone needs friends. This program will teach you where and how to meet your kind of people, how to develop and sustain friendships, and how to expand the right situation into a romantic involvement.

HOW TO SPEAK/HOW TO LISTEN

With Mortimer Adler
(UT17) $6.95—Sale Only
One cassette

Practicing this valuable advice can improve your speaking and listening skill.

HOW TO START A CONVERSATION

By Don Gabor
(67508) $7.95—Sale Only
One cassette

Tired of being tongue-tied? This program will teach you how to strike up a conversation with anyone in almost any situation. You'll be able to overcome your shyness, make new friends and be the winner you've wanted to be.

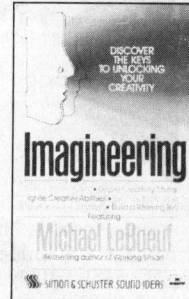

IMAGINEERING

By Michael LeBoeuf
(62491) $8.95—Sale Only
One cassette

Everyone is born with creative potential—and this program will show you how to unlock the incredible powers you already possess. Myths about creativity, and about our own limitations abound—Dr. Michael LeBoeuf will show you practical steps to clear away "idea traps" and promote innovative thinking.

Learn how successful innovators and inventors—Bell, Edison, Einstein and others—systematically produced creative, worthwhile ideas, and learn how you can gather support from friends, relatives and colleagues.

INSOMNIA

By Richard R. Bootzin, Ph.D.
(T43B) $11.50—Sale Only
One cassette

Most people have little difficulty in understanding insomnia once they have heard this cassette. More importantly, they also learn several easily mastered ways to minimize the difficulty in falling asleep . . . and remaining asleep. Includes self-instruction manual.

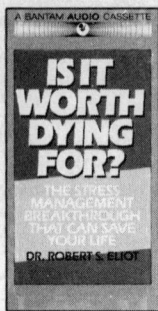

IS IT WORTH DYING FOR?

By Dr. Robert S. Eliot
(45032) $7.95—Sale Only
One cassette

Cardiologist Dr. Robert S. Eliot brings you the stress management techniques he developed and tested at his world-renowned Life Stress Simulation Lab and Clinic.

Dr. Eliot teaches you to recognize, reduce and reverse the harmful effects of stress in your life—to make stress work for you, not against you and your health.

JANE FONDA'S FITNESS WALKOUT

(25601) $18.95—Sale Only
Two cassettes and handbook

With Jane Fonda's *Walkout,* you're just steps away from a healthier body and mind. There's a good reason why most cardiac programs base their exercise programs on walking. By placing less stress on the body than other aerobic activities and allowing conditioning to take place gradually, walking is an ideal form of exercise.

You'll learn how to warm-up cool down and walk your way to health. *Walkout* contains two hours of music and narration for use on portable headset players. A special handbook details correct walking posture, what to wear and where to walk, and offers realistic fitness targets as well as diet and lifestyle pointers. *Walkout* progressively challenges you with a regular regime of brisk walking with three different levels to choose from. Let *Walkout* set the pace as you walk your way to fitness.

LISTEN AND LOSE

By Dr. Robert Parrish
(4561) $10.95—Sale Only
One cassette
(Abridged from the best seller)

Listen and learn how to lose weight and how to maintain your weight loss by changing some of your basic ideas about yourself and your eating habits. *Listen and Lose* gives you a new image of yourself and a system to help you achieve this image.

LISTEN AND STOP SMOKING

By Dr. Robert Parrish
(7111) $10.95—Sale Only
One cassette
(Abridged from the best seller)

Combine listening and relaxation techniques to feed yourself positive and realistic suggestions to stop smoking. Develop a new self-image—picture yourself as a non-smoker, one who breathes fresh, clean air with comfort and ease. Imagine the freedom that will be yours when you no longer want to smoke!

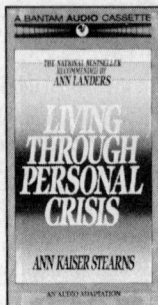

LIVING THROUGH PERSONAL CRISIS

By Ann Kaiser Stearns
(45100) $7.95—Sale Only
One cassette

All of us suffer times of personal crisis: the death of a loved one, the impact of divorce, the loss of a job, serious illness—painful experiences that force us to re-examine our lives.

In this audio adaptation of the national bestseller, psychologist Ann Kaiser Stearns speaks frankly, providing practical advice on understanding and coping with grief, both our own and that of loved ones. She draws on personal experience and case studies and presents comforting yet realistic assistance for those travelling over life's rockier roads.

MAINTAINING THE ROTATION DIET

By Martin Katahn, Ph.D.
(45043) $5.95—Sale Only
One cassette

Maintaining the Rotation Diet is your audio guide to the bestselling diet breakthrough of the 80's. In this exclusive audio complement to his bestselling book, Dr. Martin Katahn explains the basic principles behind the Rotation Diet and offers special advice that will help you stay on the diet until your reach your goal.

MEMORY NOW!

With Dan V. Mikels, Ph.D.
(WCS001) $19.95—Sale Only
Two cassettes plus booklet

Memory Now! is a memory improvement program based on the visualization well theory which can greatly improve your retention and comprehension skills. Simply stated, it is important when trying to remember something to go beyond the words and lock in the picture that the words represent. That is the secret behind *Memory Now!*

Dan V. Mikels, Ph.D. teaches memory improvement techniques for business corporations and at colleges throughout the United States.

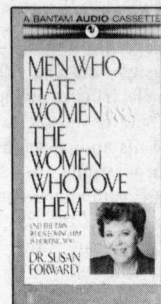

MEN WHO HATE WOMEN & THE WOMEN WHO LOVE THEM

By Dr. Susan Forward
(45080) $7.95—Sale Only
One cassette

Dr. Susan Forward talks to women trapped in relationships with angry, intimidating and controlling men. Using dramatized case histories and one-to-one counseling, Dr. Forward teaches you to recognize your man's destructive patterns, the part you play in it—and how to break free from these patterns to start living your own life again.

Her practical self-help exercises and behavioral techniques will enable you to regain your self-respect, heal the hurt and either rebuild your relationship or find the courage to love a truly loving man.

Books on Tape™'s service is 100% guaranteed

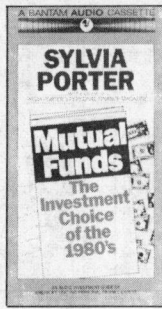

MUTUAL FUNDS: THE INVESTMENT CHOICE OF THE 1980'S

By Sylvia Porter
(45052) $7.95—Sale Only
One cassette

Safer than the stock market, as convenient to use as a checking account, mutual funds are clearly the investment choice of the 1980's. Now you can assemble a portfolio designed to meet the financial challenges of the new tax law and the years ahead.

In this audio program, financial expert Sylvia Porter shows you how to invest with confidence in the mutual funds market for steady income, capital growth or both.

ONE MINUTE FOR MYSELF

By Spencer Johnson, M.D.
(00354) $9.95—Sale Only
One cassette

How long has it been since you took a moment to take care of you? Surprisingly, many of us are unwilling to spend even one minute on ourselves, thinking about our goals, taking a moment for a quiet thought or an honest pat on our own backs.

Here is a modern parable that can help you gain a new perspective on your life. Taking a minute a few times a day to really listen to yourself can prevent stress from building up, increase your energy and clarity, improve your ability to communicate and bring greater harmony to your whole life.

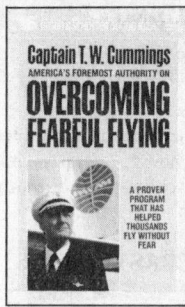

OVERCOMING FEARFUL FLYING

By Captain T.W. Cummings
(62844) $9.95—Sale Only
One cassette

If you are one of the estimated 25 million Americans who are afraid to fly, former Pan Am pilot T.W. Cummings may just change your life. In a little over a decade Cummings has helped thousands conquer their fear and take to the air with undreamed-of-calm. First, Cummings works on your irrational fears—those caused by an overly creative and unrealistic imagination. Next, you'll be taken on an imaginary flight where he'll address your rational fears, by explaining every noise and activity that you would encounter on a real flight. With Captain Cummings at the controls, new horizons will be yours to enjoy.

PASSAGES

By Gail Sheehy
(7183) $10.95—Sale Only
One cassette
(Abridged from the best seller)

Learn how your way of living undergoes subtle changes in four areas: your self-identity, your feelings of safety, your perception of time, and your sense of aliveness or stagnation. Adult life brings about "passages" in these areas—the better able you are to cope with the changes, the better off you are.

THE PRITIKIN PROMISE: 28 DAYS TO A LONGER, HEALTHIER LIFE

By Nathan Pritikin
(60517-8) $7.95—Sale Only
One cassette

The Pritikin Promise addresses millions of Americans who have embraced a vigorous lifestyle only to discover that it cannot ensure longer life and better health. In a fascinating documentary designed especially for audio, graduates of the Pritikin program explain the basics of this diet and exercise system that are crucial to preventing heart disease and other physical problems.

RISKING

By David S. Viscott, M.D.
(7163) $10.95—Sale Only
One cassette
(Abridged from the best seller)

How do you know when it it right to take a risk? You can learn to take advantage of "opportunities" for profit, for happiness and for personal growth. Learn the technique of asking the right questions so that you will know when to take a risk and when to play it safe!

Dr. Viscott is heard nationally on many ABC radio stations and syndications.

THE ROAD LESS TRAVELED: PART I DISCIPLINE

By M. Scott Peck, M.D.
(SS62137) $9.95—Sale Only
One cassette

Dr. Peck's compelling vision of human problems and humane solutions is a landmark achievement: never before have psychological and spiritual guidance come together so powerfully. This program focuses on discipline, the key to confronting problems and ultimately transcending them.

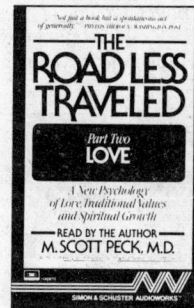

THE ROAD LESS TRAVELED: PART II LOVE

By M. Scott Peck, M.D.
(62701) $9.95—Sale Only
One cassette

In this, the second in a series of audio programs based on his landmark work, M. Scott Peck explores love, our key to personal growth and fulfillment. Dr. Peck offers both case histories and personal experiences in an attempt to define what it is we mean by love, and to clarify the confusions and misconceptions that arise in our search for love.

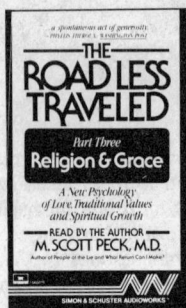

THE ROAD LESS TRAVELED: PART III RELIGION & GRACE

By M. Scott Peck, M.D.
(63468) $9.95—Sale Only
One cassette

NEW

Dr. M. Scott Peck has helped millions find their way with his compelling union of psychological and spiritual guidance. In *Religion & Grace*, the third and concluding audio program based on his bestseller, Dr. Peck shares his unique insights on religion and grace—two concepts that are relevant and crucial to enjoying life in our secular world.

Speaking with force, he demonstrates how everyone has a religion—a set of beliefs that defines an understanding of life—and the cultivation of one's own religion is the key to achieving spiritual and psychological self fulfillment.

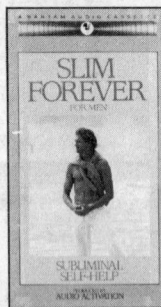

SLIM FOREVER

FOR WOMEN (45004) $7.95—Sale Only
FOR MEN (45005) $7.95—Sale Only
One cassette

It's a scientific fast: subliminal persuasion works. Now you can lose weight anywhere, anytime—without dieting. Play *Slim Forever* on your cassette player as you dress in the morning, travel to work, or when you want to unwind. Just listen to this gentle combination of soothing relaxation techniques, soft music and persuasive affirmations and let your subconscious do the rest. Soon you'll discover a new inner energy that will burn off pounds quicker and easier than you ever dreamed possible—and keep them off forever.

SPEED READING

By Richard Stack
(67527) $7.95—Sale Only
One cassette

Using these simple, effective techniques, you can learn how to increase your reading speed dramatically—without any loss of comprehension.

STOP PROCRASTINATING: DO IT!

By James R. Sherman
(9413) $10.95—Sale Only
One cassette
(Abridged from the best seller)

Killing the procrastination habit removes a major stumbling block to your success—both professionally and personally. Simply by listening to this tape, you will learn four fundamental steps: 1) Learn about procrastination and what can be done to break the habit. 2) Admit that you procrastinate and decide to stop. 3) Choose a definite Plan of Action. 4) Carry out your plan. Begin listening to the tape today and say "goodbye" to the big "P."

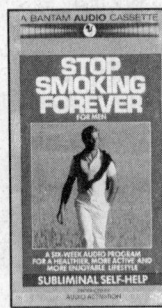

STOP SMOKING FOREVER

FOR WOMEN (45035) $7.95—Sale Only
FOR MEN (45036) $7.95—Sale Only
One cassette

Whether this is the first time you've tried to quit, or the hundred and first, *Stop Smoking Forever* works! Now you can stop smoking permanently without the cravings, weight gain and stress that so often lead to failure. Just listen to this smooth combination of soothing relaxation techniques, soft music and persuasive affirmation regularly for six weeks and let your subconscious supply you with the confidence, attitude and will power you need to kick the habit once and for all!

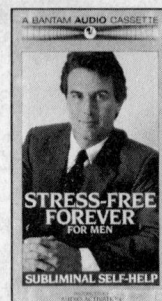

STRESS-FREE FOREVER

FOR WOMEN (45041) $7.95—Sale Only
FOR MEN (45042) $7.95—Sale Only
One cassette

Having it all can mean a fast-paced lifestyle that causes unhealthy stress. Now you can dissolve the tensions and anxieties of the day to naturally restore your lost energy and motivation. Just listen to this gentle combination of soothing relaxation techniques, soft music and persuasive affirmations and let your subconscious trigger your body's automatic relaxation response.

Each time you listen you will find the inner peace to overcome even the most stressful thoughts and feelings. At the same time, you will reinforce a new positive self-image that will enable you to maintain a healthy, successful stress-free lifestyle.

SUCCESS IS THE QUALITY OF YOUR JOURNEY

By Jennifer James, Ph.D.
(64106) $8.95—Sale Only
One cassette

NEW

National Public Radio personality and author, Jennifer James, has redefined the traditional barometer of success—and helped thousands lead happier, healthier, more rewarding lives.

In a society that worships wealth, appearance, and popularity Dr. James offers different yardsticks for defining self worth. Her new perspectives on life are refreshing alternatives to the beliefs we accept as fact and are truly helpful approaches to life's many trials and tribulations.

THINK AND GROW RICH

By Napoleon Hill
(5113) $10.95—Sale Only
One cassette
(Abridged from the best seller)

Are you looking for happiness, success and money? Then *Think and Grow Rich* is a must for you! Its ideas are vital, fresh and powerful and worth listening to repeatedly.

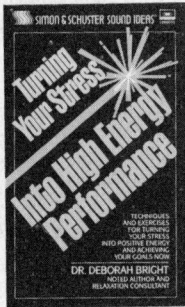

TURNING YOUR STRESS INTO HIGH ENERGY PERFORMANCE

By Dr. Deborah Bright
(62331) $8.95—Sale Only
One cassette

Whether you're nervous about a presentation, trying to put a business or personal crisis behind you, or simply coping with a hectic daily routine, Dr. Bright zeroes in on the various sources of stress and offers proven methods of dealing with each. You'll learn how to let go of paralyzing anger and fear and use "Quick Charges" to channel stress into a potent force for achievement. While we cannot possibly eliminate every stressful situation from our lives, we can remove ourselves temporarily with Dr. Bright's own "Creative Relaxation" technique—a set of relaxation and imaging exercises that you'll look forward to every day.

UNLIMITED POWER

By Anthony Robbins
(62146) $8.95—Sale Only
One cassette

Robbins is one of the foremost experts in Neuro Linguistic Programming—a system *Science Digest* says is "the most powerful vehicle for change in existence." Plug into *Unlimited Power* and you'll agree. Based on the simple fact that success stems from specific patterns of behavior which can be studied, then imitated, *Unlimited Power* explains the four criteria for achievement: defining your goal, taking focused action, gauging your results and adjusting your behavior until the goal is reached.

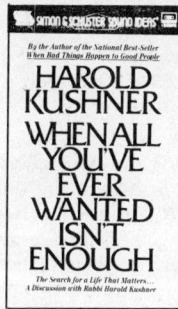

WHEN ALL YOU'VE EVER WANTED ISN'T ENOUGH

By Harold Kushner
(63402) $8.95—Sale Only
One cassette

The author of *When Bad Things Happen to Good People* examines the boredom and sense of futility that we feel after we've chased down the successes, the popularity or power we desired.

Based on his best seller, *When All You've Ever Wanted Isn't Enough* takes on life's most difficult questions—Is this all there is? Does my life matter at all?—and explores the many paths people take to discover the meaning in their lives.

WINNING THROUGH INTIMIDATION

By Robert J. Ringer
(5189) $10.95—Sale Only
One cassette
(Abridged from the best seller)

Transfer yourself from the position of the intimidated to that of the intimidator by maintaining a position of strength based on top-quality service, thorough knowledge of your field, and sound business-like procedures.

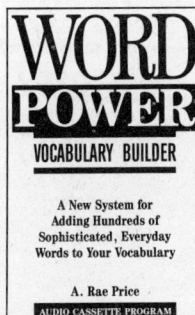

WORD POWER

With A. Rae Price
(66247) $49.95—Sale Only
Four cassettes

Here is your chance to build a vocabulary people notice, respond to and respect. *Word Power* is an easy, natural system, based on the latest knowledge of how adults learn. After *Word Power*, even sophisticated words will come easily. Add hundreds of words to your vocabulary—and retain them forever.

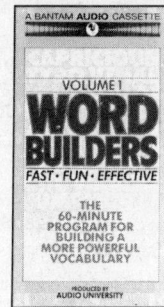

WORDBUILDERS

By Audio University
(45092) $7.95—Sale Only
One cassette

Wordbuilders is the easy way to build a more powerful vocabulary. The cassette features words you often hear in conversation or read in magazines, books and newspapers but which most people skip, finding them difficult to define or even pronounce.

Using proven mnemonic devices, entertaining dramatized vignettes and special exercises to aid retention, this program will teach you how to pronounce, define and use a new selection of common but hard-to-use words.

YOU ASK . . . BUCHWALD ANSWERS

With Art Buchwald
(UT29) $6.95—Sale Only
One cassette

Money, power, love, sex . . . Buchwald's famous humor is guaranteed to provide an alternative to traditional problem solving.

YOUR MARVELOUS MIND

By Larry Kettlekamp
(9405) $10.95—Sale Only
One cassette

A perfect gift for teenagers! Do you ever feel dumb? Do you think good grades are out of your reach? Think again! *Your Marvelous Mind* tells you about the wonderful computer inside your head that is just lying there, waiting for you to plug it in. Listen to this cassette and begin to play the games that will bring you better grades, more fun, and new ideas for success and enjoyment of life!

Allow 4 weeks for delivery.

WORLD POETRY

CARL SANDBURG READING *FOG* AND OTHER POEMS

By Carl Sandburg
(CDL 51253) $9.95—Sale Only
One cassette
Read by Carl Sandburg

Carl Sandburg found beauty in the ordinary language of the people, the "American lingo" as he called it, and turned it into poetry. His rhythms caught the pulse of America and his poems entered its bloodstream. There poems were recorded during 1951 and 1952 in the quiet of the home of a friend.

DYLAN THOMAS READING HIS POETRY

By Dylan Thomas
(CDL 52014) $19.95—Sale Only
Two cassettes
Read by Dylan Thomas

Author's Prologue, If I Were Tickled by the Rub of Love, Light Breaks Where No Sun Shines, The Hand That Signed the Paper, Should Lanterns Shine, After the Funeral plus others.

E.E. CUMMINGS READING HIS POETRY

By E.E. Cummings
(CDL 51017) $9.95—Sale Only
One cassette
Read by E.E. Cummings

A varied collection of some of his favorite works.

ENGLISH ROMANTIC POETRY

(CDL 53005) $29.95—Sale Only
Three cassettes
Read by Clair Bloom, Anthony Quayle, Frederick Worlock and Sir Ralph Richardson

Includes works by Samuel Taylor Coleridge, Walter Savage Landor, Thomas Moore, James Henry Leigh Hunt, Thomas Love Peacock, George Gordon Lord Byron, Percy Bysshe Shelley, William Blake, Robert Burns, William Wordsworth, Sir Walter Scott, John Clare, John Keats, Thomas Hood and Thomas Lovell Beddoes.

AN EVENING WITH DYLAN THOMAS

By Dylan Thomas
(CDL 51157) $9.95—Sale Only
One cassette
Read by Dylan Thomas

This evening of readings was given by Dylan Thomas in 1950 at the University of California. It includes selections from his own poetry as well as some of his favorite poems by other poets such as James Stephens and Thomas Hardy.

FOUR QUARTETS

By T.S. Eliot
(CDL 51403) $9.95—Sale Only
One cassette
Read by T.S. Eliot

Four Quartets, is a testament of faith even for those who profess no faith, a book of far-from-common prayer for many who reject prayers and prayer books and all religion in the formal sense.

OGDEN NASH READS OGDEN NASH

By Ogden Nash
(CDL 51015) $9.95—Sale Only
One cassette
Read by Ogden Nash

Kind of an Ode to Duty; Portrait of the Artist as a Prematurely Old Man; Good-bye, Old Year, You Oaf, or, Why Don't They Pay the Bonus?; Geddondillo; Watchman, What of the First First Lady? plus others.

THE POETRY OF KEATS

By John Keats
(CDL 51087) $9.95—Sale Only
One cassette
Read by Sir Ralph Richardson

Ode to a Nightingale, Ode on a Grecian Urn, To Autumn, Ode on Melancholy and more.

THE POETRY OF ROBERT W. SERVICE

By Robert W. Service
(CDL 51218) $9.95—Sale Only
One cassette
Read by Ed Begley

At the turn of the century, Robert Service was one of many who joined the Alaskan Gold Rush, hoping to make his fortune. His poetry, roistering lyrics, became popular in both America and Canada and has some of the flavor of Jack London's prose.

THE POETRY OF WILLIAM BUTLER YEATS

By William Butler Yeats
(CDL 51081) $9.95—Sale Only
One cassette
Read by Siobhan McKenna, Cyril Cusack

The Song of Wandering Aengus, No Second Troy, The Wild Swans at Coole, Broken Dreams, The Second Coming, Sailing to Byzantium, A Dialogue of Self and Soul plus many others.

ROBERT FROST IN RECITAL

By Robert Frost
(CDL 51523) $9.95—Sale Only
One cassette
Read by Robert Frost

This record was preserved for us by the foresight of The Poetry Center of the 92nd Street YM/YWCA, in New York city, which recorded Frost during three readings given at the Kaufman Auditorium in 1953 and 1954. It is scarcely necessary to say that Robert Frost was, is and will be likely to remain America's foremost and favorite poet.

ROBERT FROST READS *THE ROAD NOT TAKEN* AND OTHER POEMS

By Robert Frost
(CDL 51060) $9.95—Sale Only
One cassette
Read by Robert Frost

This recording was made in May of 1956 at Robert Frost's home in Cambridge, where ebullient spirits, rural quiet and a feeling that this was to be the definitive Frost recording influenced the fine vitality of this reading.

ROBERT PENN WARREN READS SELECTED POEMS 1923-1978

By Robert Penn Warren
(CDL 51654) $9.95—Sale Only
One cassette
Read by Robert Penn Warren

Novelist, teacher, winner of many honors—among them the Pulitzer and Bollingen as well as Chair of Poetry of the Library of Congress, Robert Penn Warren is a major American poet.

SYLVIA PLATH READING HER POETRY

By Sylvia Plath
(CDL 51544) $9.95—Sale Only
One cassette
Read by Sylvia Plath

Of the many American poets who reached their ascendency in the last decades, perhaps none looms so large as Sylvia Plath. Sylvia Plath died on February 11, 1963. Through the cooperation of the BBC and the Poetry Room of the Lamont Library of Harvard College we are able to bring you these recordings made at these two institutions.

T.S. ELIOT READING *THE WASTELAND* AND OTHER POEMS

By T.S. Eliot
(CDL 51326) $9.95—Sale Only
One cassette
Read by T.S. Eliot

Includes *The Ariel Poems: Journey of the Magi, Corioloan: Difficulties of a Statesman, Old Possum's Book of Practical Cats* plus others.

CHILDREN'S POETRY

A CHILD'S GARDEN OF VERSES

By Robert Louis Stevenson
(CDL 51077) $9.95—Sale Only
One cassette
Read by Dame Judith Anderson

Fashions have changed in grownup taste since Robert Louis Stevenson wrote his verses, but children of today will love them as much as ever. With man's craft and child's sense he created this perennial Garden.

CLASSICS OF AMERICAN POETRY FOR THE ELEMENTARY CURRICULUM

(CDL 52041) $19.95—Sale Only
Two cassettes
Read by Eddie Albert, Hal Holbrook
Basil Rathbone, Brock Peters and others

Poets include John Greenleaf Whittier, Oliver Wendell Holmes, Henry Wadsworth Longfellow, Walt Whitman, Emily Dickinson, Lawrence Thayer, Sam Walter Foss, Edwin Charles Markham, Carl Sandburg, Robert Frost, Langston Hughes, James Weldon Johnson, Edgar Allan Poe and John McCrae.

CLASSICS OF ENGLISH POETRY FOR THE ELEMENTARY CURRICULUM

(CDL 51301) $9.95—Sale Only
One cassette
Read by Boris Karloff, James Mason
Cryil Ritchard plus others

Poets include Samuel Taylor Coleridge, Sir Walter Scott, Robert Browning, Edward Lear, Elizabeth Browning, Alfred Lord Tennyson, Rudyard Kipling and Alfred Noyes.

GATHERING OF GREAT POETRY FOR CHILDREN, KINDERGARTEN AND UP

Edited by Richard Lewis
(CDL 51235) $9.95—Sale Only
One cassette
Read by Julie Harris, Cyril Ritchard, David Wayne, Robert Frost and Carl Sandburg

Includes works by A.A. Milne, Robert Frost, William Blake, Edna St. Vincent Millay, Carl Sandburg, Edward Lear and others.

A GATHERING OF GREAT POETRY FOR CHILDREN, SECOND GRADE AND UP

Edited by Richard Lewis
(CDL 51236) $9.95—Sale Only
One cassette
Read by Julie Harris, Cyril Ritchard, David Wayne, Robert Frost, Carl Sandburg, Robert Graves, E.E. Cummings and T.S. Eliot

Poets include Thomas Nashe, Emily Dickinson, Carl Sandburg, Robert Graves, Edna St. Vincent Millay, Padraic H. Pearse, E.E. Cummings, A.A. Milne, Robert Frost, T.S. Eliot plus others.

Traveling with an AUTO TAPE TOUR is like traveling with your own personal tour guide, but even the best guide could not duplicate the excitement of an Auto Tape Tour.

You'll hear the roar of cannons at Gettysburg—the crash of the surf at Big Sur—wagon wheels clattering over the Great Divide!

Learn the history, geography and local legends that help you actually experience a place so it becomes part of you. And experience it in the comfort and privacy of your own car—at your own pace.

Auto Tape Tours are the positive, informative way to travel. Why visit an area and miss some of the things that make it unique? You not only get a thorough, complete guided tour—you'll see the sights and learn about the manners, the mode of living, the folklore of the area through which you are passing—but you also get complete driving directions, including maps, so you just can't get lost and won't waste gas or precious time trying to find where you are.

Allow 4 weeks for delivery.

CANADIAN TOURS

BANFF NATIONAL PARK

(AT15) One cassette—$10.95—Sale Only

JASPER NATIONAL PARK

(AT16) One cassette—$10.95—Sale Only

(2 Canadian tours—each sold separately)

Here is some of the most spectacular scenery in Canada. Lake Louise is known the world over for its unsurpassed beauty. But there's more than scenery here. Sports enthusiasts will find everything from skating, sleighing, tobogganing, swimming and fishing to bathing in hot sulphur springs. Learn about the different kinds of bears and beavers that exist here, relive Indian legends, learn how to tell the age of a Rocky Mountain sheep, what a glacier is and what makes it move!

EUROPEAN TOURS

A new and exciting way to enjoy England, Wales and Ireland . . . tapes that take you on an expertly guided tour, providing background information on the history, folklore and other attractions of each region's towns, cities and countryside.

ENGLAND TAPE #1

(AT17) One cassette—$10.95—Sale Only

London to Glastonbury. Winchester, the capital of King Arthur's England . . . Salisbury, an exquisite 13th century city . . . Stonehenge, the most famous and mysterious prehistoric monument in Europe . . . Glastonbury, the center of medieval monastic life . . . and much more.

ENGLAND TAPE #2

(AT18) One cassette—$10.95—Sale Only

Glastonbury to Stratford. The Wye Valley, Wales' answer to the Garden of Eden . . . Warwick Castle, a seat of political power for nine centuries . . . Coventry Cathedral, a source of modern inspiration . . . Stratford-Upon-Avon, the birthplace of the greatest poet and dramatist of the English language . . . plus a fascinating discussion of the differences between the English and the Welsh . . . and much, much more.

ENGLAND TAPE #3

(AT19) One cassette—$10.95—Sale Only

Stratford to London. Blenheim Palace, the birthplace of Sir Winston Churchill . . . the Cotswold with its fairy-tale villages . . . Oxford, a magnificent city containing the magnificent University . . . Windsor Castle, the home of British kings for one thousand years . . . plus shopping tips, walking suggestions and fishing spots.

IRELAND TAPE #1

(AT20) One cassette—$10.95—Sale Only

Shannon to Sligo. The lakes of Fergus, famous for fishing . . . the cliffs of Moher with an unequalled view . . . well-known Limerick . . . romantic Galway . . . ancient abbeys and ruins . . . the center of William Butler Yeats country . . . plus prehistoric artifacts and remains.

IRELAND TAPE #2

(AT21) One cassette—$10.95—Sale Only

Sligo to Cork. Dublin, the capital of Ireland and a favorite of all lovers of romance through the ages . . . Waterford, home of exquisite glassware . . . Ennisberry, one of the most beautiful villages in Ireland . . . plus all sorts of helpful hints about Dublin.

IRELAND TAPE #3

(AT22) One casssette—$10.95—Sale Only

Cork to Shannon. Ireland's oldest church . . . tiny coastal villages perfect for fishing . . . the fabulous lakes of Kilarney . . . the roses of Tralee . . . the lace of Limerick. Plus suggestions for wonderful detours, fascinating history of the area and useful driving information.

UNITED STATES TOURS

GETTYSBURG CIRCLE TOUR

(AT23) One cassette—$10.95—Sale Only

Few episodes in U.S. history are as devastating and emotional as the Civil War. Listen to the historically accurate presentation of the fierce three-day battle that turned the tide of the Civil War. You can be certain of experiencing all the thrills, the sadness, the splendor and the majesty that have set Gettysburg aside as a National Park.

GLACIER NATIONAL PARK

(AT24) One cassette—$10.95—Sale Only

George Bird Grinnell is the man who almost single-handedly made Glacier into a National Park. Learn about Grinnell, the park's early settlers, 57 species of resident mammals and a fascinating Blackfoot Indian legend. Find out why it cost almost $80,000 a mile to build the road you drive upon through this "diamond of parks."

GRAND TETON NATIONAL PARK

(AT25) One cassette—$10.95—Sale Only

The park is located in one of the most awe-inspiring range of mountains in North America. Become familiar with glacial moraines, learn about the old beaver stove pipe hat and stop at Dunningham Homestead Cabin, where you'll hear about the bygone days of rustling, posses and shootings! More than 200 species of birds live within the protection of the park, matchless for magnificence and splendor!

LANCASTER CIRCLE TOUR

(AT27) One cassette—$10.95—Sale Only

Learn about the culture, customs and lifestyles of the Amish people as you drive past neat Amish homesteads, one-room schoolhouses, whitewashed tree trunks and fences. These quaint people live today in the heart of Lancaster County as they did in the 17th century. And, for a change of pace, return to the excitement of America's rip-roaring railroad days at the State Railroad Museum in Strasburg. There's much to see and learn about in Pennsylvania Dutch country.

MYSTIC/NEW LONDON/GROTON STONINGTON, CONNECTICUT

(AT28) One cassette—$10.95—Sale Only

New London and the drama of the great days of whaling. Groton—the touching story of farm boys who fought and died in the Revolution and the high excitement of ships that fight under the seas. Stonington—an architectural gem of a village almost forgotten by time. Mystic—the village and the seaport. The U.S. Coast Guard Academy, Nathan Hale, Benedict Arnold. This is your personal guide through the highways, byways and seaways of an area rich in history, a sweeping panorama of our nation's progress from sailing ships to nuclear submarines. Accurate history, local color and directions.

NEWPORT, RHODE ISLAND

(AT29) One cassette—$10.95—Sale Only

The splendor of the mansions of Newport's Gilded Age. Stories of the super-rich who lavished millions on their "summer cottages," why they built them and what they did in them. Newport's Golden Age as a colonial seaport, and the notorious triangle trade of molasses, rum and slaves. The Navy and Newport—an on-and-off love affair that made history. Your personal guide in and around "The City by the Sea." A peek into 350 years of history, full of surprises, and accurate in every detail.

WASHINGTON, D.C. Our Nation's Capital ARLINGTON, ALEXANDRIA & MT. VERNON CIRCLE TOUR

(AT31) One cassette—$10.95—Sale Only

Hear the fascinating story of the founding of our nation's capital and of the people with vision who built it. From the Mall . . . to the Capital . . . the White House . . . the monuments . . . Embassy Row . . . National Cathedral . . . Georgetown . . . Alexandria . . . Mt. Vernon and more. Easy to follow directions. Accurate in every historic detail. Map included.

YELLOWSTONE I

(AT32) One cassette—$10.95—Sale Only

Learn about the largest thermal area in the world and the wildlife found there. Hear about early visitors and unique Glass Mountain.

YELLOWSTONE II

(AT33) One cassette—$10.95—Sale Only

Visit Lake Yellowstone and the awesome Grand Canyon. See the largest fossil formations in the world and learn about the wildlife and botanical gardens.

For Visa and MasterCard order line 1-800-626-3333

A

Prices in this catalog supersede all prior prices and special offers.

Notes
Books to Order

RENTAL Order Form

For faster ordering call 1-800-626-3333.

Catalog Number

1.		
3.		
4.		
5.		
6.		
7.		
8.		
9.		
10.		
11.		

Rental Ordering

- Check to make sure you found your selections in the rental section.
- Call 1-800-626-3333 and place a VISA or MasterCard order.
  OR
  Fill in this *rental* order form. (Use other side for sales purchases.)
- Send order form with payment to:
  Books on Tape
  P.O. Box 7900
  Newport Beach, CA 92658

SUB-TOTAL . . . . $ _____

Less 10% for three (3) or more books . . . . —$ _____

SUB-TOTAL . . . . $ _____

California residents add 6% sales tax . . . . . . + $ _____

Shipping and handling charges
First class delivery (arrives in a week or less.)
$5.00 per book . . . . + $ _____

Fourth class delivery (arrives in 10-21 days.)
$3.50 per book . . . . + $ _____

TOTAL . . . . $ _____

Payment method

☐ **MasterCard**   ☐ **VISA**   ☐ **Check/Money Order**

Credit card number:

Expiration date: MasterCard interbank number:

mo.   yr.

Rental Agreement: I agree not to record any Books on Tape, not to play them before an audience or over the radio, and not to commercially exploit them in any manner. I will return them within one month following date of receipt to avoid a late penalty charge of 25¢ per day.

Signature _____ Date _____

Mailing address: (Please print, and show name exactly as on credit card.)

Name _____

c/o Company Name _____

Street or P.O. Box _____

City _____ State _____ Zip _____

Phone number (_____) _____

Delivery Instructions:

☐ Ship all books at once. ☐ Ship a book every _____ days.

Please indicate: ☐ Old account   ☐ New account

If you are a new account, please tell us how you heard about *Books on Tape?* _____

_____

☐ Please send me more order forms.

Books on Tape
P.O. Box 7900
Newport Beach, CA 92658
Call toll-free 1-800-626-3333

☐ **YES**, I want to share B-O-T with my friend.
(And get a FREE rental B-O-T if my friend orders.)

Friend's name _____

Street address or P.O. Box _____

City _____ State _____ Zip _____

SALES Order Form

	Title	Catalog Number	Price
1.			
2.			
3.			
4.			
5.			
6.			
7.			
8.			
9.			
10.			

Sub-Total . . . . $ _____

California residents
add 6% SALES tax . . . . $ _____

Shipping Total . . . . $ _____

TOTAL . . . . $ _____

Sales Ordering

- Call 1-800-626-3333 and place a VISA or MasterCard order.
  OR
  Fill in this *sales* order form. (Use other side for rental selections.)
- Send order form with payment to:
  Books on Tape
  P.O. Box 7900
  Newport Beach, CA 92658

Shipping and handling charges should be computed according to the grid below for all sales items.

AMOUNT OF ORDER	SHIPPING AND HANDLING
Up to $14.99	Add $1.50
$15.00-$39.99	Add $2.50
$40.00-$74.99	Add $4.00
$75.00-$149.00	Add $5.00
Over $150.00	Add $10.00

Payment method

☐ **MasterCard**   ☐ **VISA**   ☐ **Check/Money Order**

Credit card number:

Expiration date:
mo.   yr.

MasterCard interbank number:

Signature   Date

Mailing address: (Please print, and show name exactly as on credit card.)

Name _____

c/o Company Name _____

Street or P.O. Box _____

City _____ State _____ Zip _____

Phone number (_____) _____

Please indicate: ☐ Old account   ☐ New account

If you are a new account, please tell us how you heard about *Books on Tape?* _____

_____

☐ Please send me more order forms.

Books on Tape
P.O. Box 7900
Newport Beach, CA 92658
Call toll-free 1-800-626-3333

☐ **YES**, I want to share B-O-T with my friend.
(And get a FREE rental B-O-T if my friend orders.)

Friend's name _____

Street address or P.O. Box _____

City _____ State _____ Zip _____

RENTAL Order Form

For faster ordering call 1-800-626-3333.

Catalog Number

1.		
3.		
4.		
5.		
6.		
7.		
8.		
9.		
10.		
11.		

Rental Ordering

- Check to make sure you found your selections in the rental section.
- Call 1-800-626-3333 and place a VISA or MasterCard order. **OR** Fill in this *rental* order form. (Use other side for sales purchases.)
- Send order form with payment to:
  Books on Tape
  P.O. Box 7900
  Newport Beach, CA 92658

SUB-TOTAL . . . . $ _____
Less 10% for three (3) or more books . . . . —$ _____
SUB-TOTAL . . . . $ _____
California residents add 6% sales tax . . . . + $ _____
Shipping and handling charges
First class delivery (arrives in a week or less.)
$5.00 per book . . . . + $ _____
Fourth class delivery (arrives in 10-21 days.)
$3.50 per book . . . . + $ _____
TOTAL . . . . $ _____

Payment method

☐ **MasterCard**   ☐ **VISA**   ☐ **Check/Money Order**

Credit card number:

☐☐☐☐☐☐☐☐☐☐☐☐☐☐☐☐☐☐☐

Expiration date:

☐☐☐☐
mo.   yr.

MasterCard interbank number:

☐☐☐☐☐

Rental Agreement: I agree not to record any Books on Tape, not to play them before an audience or over the radio, and not to commercially exploit them in any manner. I will return them within one month following date of receipt to avoid a late penalty charge of 25¢ per day.

Signature   Date

Mailing address: (Please print, and show name exactly as on credit card.)

Name _____

c/o Company Name _____

Street or P.O. Box _____

City _____ State _____ Zip _____

Phone number (_____) _____

Delivery Instructions:
☐ Ship all books at once. ☐ Ship a book every _____ days.

Please indicate: ☐ Old account   ☐ New account

If you are a new account, please tell us how you heard about *Books on Tape?* _____

_____

☐ Please send me more order forms.

Books on Tape
P.O. Box 7900
Newport Beach, CA 92658
Call toll-free 1-800-626-3333

☐ **YES,** I want to share B-O-T with my friend.
(And get a FREE rental B-O-T if my friend orders.)

Friend's name _____

Street address or P.O. Box _____

City _____ State _____ Zip _____

SALES Order Form

	Title	Catalog Number	Price
1.			
2.			
3.			
4.			
5.			
6.			
7.			
8.			
9.			
10.			

Sales Ordering

- Call 1-800-626-3333 and place a VISA or MasterCard order.
  OR
  Fill in this *sales* order form. (Use other side for rental selections.)
- Send order form with payment to:
  Books on Tape
  P.O. Box 7900
  Newport Beach, CA 92658

Sub-Total . . . .$ _____

California residents
add 6% SALES tax . . . .$ _____

Shipping Total . . . .$ _____

TOTAL . . . .$ _____

Shipping and handling charges should be computed according to the grid below for all sales items.

AMOUNT OF ORDER	SHIPPING AND HANDLING
Up to $14.99	Add $1.50
$15.00-$39.99	Add $2.50
$40.00-$74.99	Add $4.00
$75.00-$149.00	Add $5.00
Over $150.00.	Add $10.00

Payment method

☐ **MasterCard**   ☐ **VISA**   ☐ **Check/Money Order**

Credit card number:

Expiration date: MasterCard interbank number:

mo.   yr.

Signature   Date

Mailing address: (Please print, and show name exactly as on credit card.)

Name _____

c/o Company Name _____

Street or P.O. Box _____

City _____ State _____ Zip _____

Phone number (_____) _____

Please indicate: ☐ Old account ☐ New account

If you are a new account, please tell us how you heard about *Books on Tape?* _____

☐ Please send me more order forms.

Books on Tape
P.O. Box 7900
Newport Beach, CA 92658
Call toll-free 1-800-626-3333

☐ **YES**, I want to share B-O-T with my friend.
(And get a FREE rental B-O-T if my friend orders.)

Friend's name _____

Street address or P.O. Box _____

City _____ State _____ Zip _____

RENTAL Order Form

Catalog Number

1.		
3.		
4.		
5.		
6.		
7.		
8.		
9.		
10.		
11.		

Rental Ordering

- Check to make sure you found your selections in the rental section.
- Call 1-800-626-3333 and place a VISA or MasterCard order.
  OR
  Fill in this *rental* order form. (Use other side for sales purchases.)
- Send order form with payment to:
  Books on Tape
  P.O. Box 7900
  Newport Beach, CA 92658

SUB-TOTAL	$ _____
Less 10% for three (3) or more books	—$ _____
SUB-TOTAL	$ _____
California residents add 6% sales tax	+ $ _____
Shipping and handling charges	
First class delivery (arrives in a week or less.)	
$5.00 per book	+ $ _____
Fourth class delivery (arrives in 10-21 days.)	
$3.50 per book	+ $ _____
TOTAL	$ _____

Payment method

☐ **MasterCard**   ☐ **VISA**   ☐ **Check/Money Order**

Credit card number:

Expiration date:
mo.   yr.

MasterCard interbank number:

Rental Agreement: I agree not to record any Books on Tape, not to play them before an audience or over the radio, and not to commercially exploit them in any manner. I will return them within one month following date of receipt to avoid a late penalty charge of 25¢ per day.

_____   _____
Signature   Date

Mailing address: (Please print, and show name exactly as on credit card.)

Name _____

c/o Company Name _____

Street or P.O. Box _____

City _____ State _____ Zip _____

Phone number (_____) _____

Delivery Instructions:

☐ Ship all books at once. ☐ Ship a book every _____ days.

Please indicate: ☐ Old account   ☐ New account

If you are a new account, please tell us how you heard about *Books on Tape?* _____

_____

☐ Please send me more order forms.

Books on Tape
P.O. Box 7900
Newport Beach, CA 92658
Call toll-free 1-800-626-3333

☐ **YES,** I want to share B-O-T with my friend.
(And get a FREE rental B-O-T if my friend orders.)

Friend's name _____

Street address or P.O. Box _____

City _____ State _____ Zip _____

	Title	Catalog Number	Price
1.			
2.			
3.			
4.			
5.			
6.			
7.			
8.			
9.			
10.			

Sales Ordering

- Call 1-800-626-3333 and place a VISA or MasterCard order.
  OR
  Fill in this *sales* order form. (Use other side for rental selections.)
- Send order form with payment to:
  Books on Tape
  P.O. Box 7900
  Newport Beach, CA 92658

Sub-Total . . . . $ _____

California residents
add 6% SALES tax . . . . $ _____

Shipping Total . . . . $ _____

TOTAL . . . . $ _____

Shipping and handling charges should be computed according to the grid below for all sales items.

AMOUNT OF ORDER	SHIPPING AND HANDLING
Up to $14.99	Add $1.50
$15.00-$39.99	Add $2.50
$40.00-$74.99	Add $4.00
$75.00-$149.00	Add $5.00
Over $150.00	Add $10.00

Payment method

☐ **MasterCard**   ☐ **VISA**   ☐ **Check/Money Order**

Credit card number:

Expiration date: MasterCard interbank number:

mo.   yr.

Signature   Date

Mailing address: (Please print, and show name exactly as on credit card.)

Name _____

c/o Company Name _____

Street or P.O. Box _____

City _____ State _____ Zip _____

Phone number (_____) _____

Please indicate: ☐ Old account   ☐ New account

If you are a new account, please tell us how you heard about *Books on Tape?* _____

☐ Please send me more order forms.

Books on Tape
P.O. Box 7900
Newport Beach, CA 92658
Call toll-free 1-800-626-3333

☐ **YES**, I want to share B-O-T with my friend.
(And get a FREE rental B-O-T if my friend orders.)

Friend's name _____

Street address or P.O. Box _____

City _____ State _____ Zip _____

RENTAL Order Form

Catalog Number

1.		$ _____
3.		
4.		
5.		
6.		
7.		
8.		
9.		
10.		
11.		

Rental Ordering

- Check to make sure you found your selections in the rental section.
- Call 1-800-626-3333 and place a VISA or MasterCard order.
  OR
  Fill in this *rental* order form. (Use other side for sales purchases.)
- Send order form with payment to:
  Books on Tape
  P.O. Box 7900
  Newport Beach, CA 92658

SUB-TOTAL . . . . $ _____
Less 10% for three (3) or more books . . . . —$ _____
SUB-TOTAL . . . . $ _____
California residents add 6% sales tax . . . . + $ _____
Shipping and handling charges
First class delivery (arrives in a week or less.)
$5.00 per book . . . . + $ _____
Fourth class delivery (arrives in 10-21 days.)
$3.50 per book . . . . + $ _____
TOTAL . . . . $ _____

Payment method

☐ **MasterCard**   VISA ☐ **VISA**   ☐ **Check/Money Order**

Credit card number: _____

Expiration date: ___ ___ ___ ___
mo.   yr.

MasterCard interbank number: ___ ___ ___ ___

Rental Agreement: I agree not to record any Books on Tape, not to play them before an audience or over the radio, and not to commercially exploit them in any manner. I will return them within one month following date of receipt to avoid a late penalty charge of 25¢ per day.

_____   _____
Signature   Date

Mailing address: (Please print, and show name exactly as on credit card.)

Name _____

c/o Company Name _____

Street or P.O. Box _____

City _____ State _____ Zip _____

Phone number (_____) _____

Delivery Instructions:

☐ Ship all books at once. ☐ Ship a book every _____ days.

Please indicate: ☐ Old account ☐ New account

If you are a new account, please tell us how you heard about *Books on Tape?* _____

_____

☐ Please send me more order forms.

Books on Tape
P.O. Box 7900
Newport Beach, CA 92658
Call toll-free 1-800-626-3333

☐ **YES,** I want to share B-O-T with my friend.
(And get a FREE rental B-O-T if my friend orders.)

Friend's name _____

Street address or P.O. Box _____

City _____ State _____ Zip _____

SALES Order Form

	Title	Catalog Number	Price
1.			
2.			
3.			
4.			
5.			
6.			
7.			
8.			
9.			
10.			

Sales Ordering

- Call 1-800-626-3333 and place a VISA or MasterCard order.
  OR
  Fill in this *sales* order form. (Use other side for rental selections.)
- Send order form with payment to:
  Books on Tape
  P.O. Box 7900
  Newport Beach, CA 92658

Sub-Total . . . . $ _____

California residents
add 6% SALES tax . . . . $ _____

Shipping Total . . . . $ _____

TOTAL . . . . $ _____

Shipping and handling charges should be computed according to the grid below for all sales items.

AMOUNT OF ORDER	SHIPPING AND HANDLING
Up to $14.99	Add $1.50
$15.00-$39.99	Add $2.50
$40.00-$74.99	Add $4.00
$75.00-$149.00	Add $5.00
Over $150.00	Add $10.00

Payment method

☐ **MasterCard**   ☐ **VISA**   ☐ **Check/Money Order**

Credit card number:

Expiration date: MasterCard interbank number:

mo.   yr.

Signature _____   Date _____

Mailing address: (Please print, and show name exactly as on credit card.)

Name _____

c/o Company Name _____

Street or P.O. Box _____

City _____ State _____ Zip _____

Phone number (_____) _____

Please indicate: ☐ Old account   ☐ New account

If you are a new account, please tell us how you heard about *Books on Tape?* _____

☐ Please send me more order forms.

Books on Tape
P.O. Box 7900
Newport Beach, CA 92658
Call toll-free 1-800-626-3333

☐ **YES,** I want to share B-O-T with my friend.
(And get a FREE rental B-O-T if my friend orders.)

Friend's name _____

Street address or P.O. Box _____

City _____ State _____ Zip _____

"Tell a Friend . . . About Books On Tape!"

If you have enjoyed your experience with Books on Tape, please help us pass the word. Just give us the name of a friend and we will send our handsome Introductory Newsletter with your compliments. When your name is mentioned with the first order, we notify you . . . and say "thanks!" with a complimentary rental book.

Please send your Introductory Newsletter
for **BOOKS ON TAPE** to:

Name

Company name or c/o

Street   Apt. or Suite #

City   State   Zip

Compliments of (please print) _____
Name

Please send your Introductory Newsletter
for **BOOKS ON TAPE** to:

Name

Company name or c/o

Street   Apt. or Suite #

City   State   Zip

Compliments of (please print) _____
Name

"Tell a Friend . . . About Books On Tape!"

If you have enjoyed your experience with Books on Tape, please help us pass the word. Just give us the name of a friend and we will send our handsome Introductory Newsletter with your compliments. When your name is mentioned with the first order, we notify you . . . and say "thanks!" with a complimentary rental book.